# I WILL

A DIARY OF

# BEAR

THE NAZI YEARS

# WITNESS

1942—1945

## VICTOR KLEMPERER

Translated by Martin Chalmers

THE MODERN LIBRARY

NEW YORK

2001 Modern Library Paperback Edition

Translation, preface, and notes copyright © 1999 by Martin Chalmers
Discussion Guide copyright © 2001 by Random House, Inc.

This translation was originally published in Great Britain
by Weidenfeld & Nicolson, London, and in the United States
by Random House, Inc., New York, in 1999.

First published in Germany under the title *Ich will Zeugnis ablegen bis zum
letzten: Tagebücher 1933–1945 von Victor Klemperer.*
Copyright ©Aufbau-Verlag GmbH, Berlin, 1995.

Library of Congress Cataloging-in-Publication Data

Klemperer, Victor.
[Ich will Zeugnis ablegen bis zum letzten. English]
I will bear witness: the diaries of Victor Klemperer.
p. cm.
Contents: [1]. 1933–1941.
ISBN 0-375-75697-3 ([1] : alk. paper)
1. Klemperer, Victor, 1881–1960—Diaries.
2. French teachers—Germany—Diaries. 3. Philologists—Germany—
Diaries. 4. Germany—History—1933–1945—Sources. I. Title.
PC2064.K5A3 1998
943.086'092—dc21
[B] 98-15429

Modern Library website address: www.modernlibrary.com

Printed in the United States of America

24689753

Design by Mercedes Everett

Frontispiece photograph of Victor Klemperer by Eva Kemlein, Berlin.
Photograph on p. vi ©Aufbau-Verlag GmbH.

# Critical acclaim for *I Will Bear Witness*

"Together and separately, the two volumes form a stunning, engrossing, and magnificently human document, created by a shrewd and honest man during an insane and cataclysmic time. . . . An eloquent and essential testament."
—*Chicago Tribune*

"Klemperer's personal history of how the Third Reich month by month, sometimes week by week, accelerated its crusade against the Jews gives us as accurate a picture of Nazi trickery and brutality as we are likely to have. . . . *I Will Bear Witness* is a report from the interior that tells the horrifying story of the evolving Nazi persecution with a concrete, vivid power that is, and I think will remain, unsurpassed. To read his almost day-by-day account is a hypnotic experience; the whole, hard to put down, is a true murder mystery—from the perspective of the victim."
—PETER GAY, *The New York Times Book Review*

"Riveting and invaluable."
—*Arizona Republic*

"There is no better record of what it felt like to live through the war in Germany as a German Jew. *I Will Bear Witness* will take its place with the great human records of our time."
—*Newsday*

"What has been called one of the most remarkable documents to come out of the Second World War turns out to be one of the most compulsively readable books of the year."
—*The San Diego Union Tribune*

"The diary is his obsession . . . the point is not to write history, but to provide evidence. That, of necessity, means confession. *I Will Bear Witness* is of great value to historians in their present debate as to how far ordinary Germans collaborated in the death of six million Jews. But it is even more precious as a story of love between two sixty-year-olds, both hypochondriacs who try each other's nerves almost to the breaking point but who know—this is the entry for March 18, 1945—'the main point after all is that for forty years we have so much loved one another.' "
—PENELOPE FITZGERALD, *The Wall Street Journal*

"Klemperer's writing has a mesmerizing quality that draws readers on."
—*Denver Post*

"Richer and more profoundly disturbing than Anne Frank's journals."
—*Time*

"This is color film of Nazi Germany after years of black and white. Klemperer's diary deserves to rank alongside that of Anne Frank. . . . It is certain to become not only the main primary source for historians of the Nazi period, but also an essential read for anyone who wishes to understand what it was like to be a Jew living in Germany in the 1930s."
—PHILIP KERR, *The Sunday Times* (London)

I shall go on writing. That is my heroism.
I will bear witness, precise witness!

—May 27, 1942

*Eva and Victor Klemperer, c. 1940.*

# PREFACE*

*. . . but I want to tell that he was a hero. He could not say three sentences without talking about his fear, but I want to tell of his courage.*

Jurek Becker,
Jakob the Liar

## I

On New Year's Eve 1941, Victor Klemperer gave a little speech to the remaining occupants of the Jews' House at 15b Caspar David Friedrich Strasse in Dresden. It had been, he said, "our most dreadful year, dreadful because of our own real experience, more dreadful because of the constant state of threat, most dreadful of all because of what we saw others suffering (deportation, murder)"—but, he concluded, there were grounds for optimism. The regime, he implied, was close to collapse, the guilty would receive just punishment.

As we now know, and the diarist Victor Klemperer was soon to discover, the worst was very far from over. The German advance after the surprise attack on the Soviet Union on June 22, 1941, had created the conditions for a "final solution of the Jewish question" by extermination. While the Jewish population of the newly occupied territories was massacred, the Jews of Germany and of the territories under German control were to be deported eastward and, together with the Jews of Poland, murdered immediately or starved and worked to death. The year 1942 would be, in Raul Hilberg's words, the "most lethal . . . in Jewish history."

At the end of 1941, Klemperer was still unaware of the massacres taking place behind the German front. The extent of his knowledge was summed up in a diary entry of October 25, 1941: "Ever more shocking reports about deportation of Jews to Poland. They have to leave almost literally naked and penniless. Thousands from Berlin to Lodz." Dependent on rumor and secondhand reports of foreign broadcasts, Klemperer was only dimly able to discern the scope and radicalism of the Nazis' plans and actions. The repercussions of the plan of genocide, however, were soon to be felt in Dresden.

---

*For an account of Victor Klemperer's life and work, see the Preface to *I Will Bear Witness: A Diary of the Nazi Years 1933–1941* (Random House, 1998).

On January 13, 1942, Paul Kreidl, a fellow resident of the Jews' House where Klemperer lives, passes on a rumor—"but it is very credible and comes from various sources—evacuated Jews were *shot* in Riga, in groups, as they left the train." On the fifteenth, the first "evacuation" from Dresden is announced. The Zeiss-Ikon plant, in which a large number of the remaining Jews in the city work as forced labor, manages to retain its Jewish workers. Nevertheless, on January 21, 224 Jews from Dresden and nearby towns, including Paul Kreidl, are transported to the Riga ghetto.[1]

After that, the blows come hard and fast: the brutalities of the Gestapo house searches, the step-by-step removal of elderly Jews to the Theresienstadt concentration camp, the suicides of those who prefer to snatch at least death from the Nazis.[2] All this was accompanied by the steady shortening of rations for Jews, the lack of privacy and overcrowding in the Jews' Houses, and the continuing military success of the Axis powers.

The Jews left in Dresden are uncertain of the fate of those deported to the East or even to nearby Theresienstadt. The arrest and murder of individuals, however, are a token of the deportees' likely fate. Yet even uncertainty can still give rise to hope of *something* better. On July 24, 1942, Klemperer notes: "The general mood among Jews is that they do not fear evacuation quite as much as before and now even regard Theresienstadt as a relatively humane place. . . . People say to one another, things are *so* bad here that anywhere else they can at most be equally bad, but perhaps also somewhat better."[3]

A few months earlier, on March 16, 1942, Klemperer had recorded another rumor. "In the last few days I heard Auschwitz (or something like it), near Königshütte in Upper Silesia, mentioned as the most dreadful concentration camp. Work in a mine, death within a few days." The planned, deliberate extermination of millions of Jews was still unimaginable to Klemperer (and most others). The realization that "deportation" was, in Nazi terms, equivalent to extermination only gradually established itself in his mind; for a long time he retained quiet hope that there would be news. On September 21, 1942, after visiting friends about to be deported, he writes, "They were really going into a beyond, from which as yet there had been no reliable news. Because what had been reported was no more than supposition."

## II

On November 23, 1942, 279 Jews, the overwhelming majority of those left in Dresden who were not in mixed marriages or otherwise "privileged," were forced to move to some newly erected barracks at Hellerberg, just outside the municipal boundary north of the city. The adults and adolescents of this group were largely employed at Zeiss-Ikon's Goehle plant, which manufactured fuses for the German navy. The company took responsibility for the construction and day-to-day running of the camp.

This was a step that had been planned for some time. Pressure to segregate the Jews working in armaments factories had come from both local Nazi Party organizations (there was a macabre competition between Nazi authorities to make their towns and districts *Judenrein*—free of Jews) and from the Nazi leadership. There was harsh criticism of the role of companies that, encouraged by the army and the armaments ministry, had argued for the maintenance of trained Jewish workforces.

Very unusually, there exists a film of this initial stage of deportation: "Assembling the Last Jews in Dresden in the Camp at Hellerberg on November 23–24, 1942."[4] This twenty-seven-minute silent film shows not only the building of the camp, the removal of the Jews from Jews' Houses in Dresden, and the initial humiliations, like "delousing," inflicted on them (as a kind of prelude to subsequent degradation), but also a number of identifiable persons, among them several mentioned in Victor Klemperer's diary.

For the Nazis, the camp was no more than an interim, local "solution," part of the preparations for the so-called Factory Action, which began on February 27, 1943. On the morning of that day, Jews throughout Germany were picked up at their workplaces without warning, so that they would have no chance to escape and go underground. The Factory Action was intended to eliminate those Jews working in the armaments industry. They were to be replaced by forced labor from the occupied countries.

In Dresden, the camp at Hellerberg was sealed off early on the morning of February 27, 1943. More Jews from Dresden and from nearby towns were also assembled there. On the evening of March 2, nearly all the inmates, including 293 Dresden Jews, were taken to Dresden-Neustadt station and loaded onto cattle trucks. They reached Auschwitz as part of a train that was by then carrying 1,500 people.

On learning that the Hellerberg camp inmates were to be deported, Victor Klemperer wrote in his diary: "We shall not see any of them again. Frau Voss, the Seliksohns, Reichenbachs, Frau Ziegler—I count them all among the dead."

In the calendar of events at Auschwitz–Birkenau compiled by Danuta Czech, the arrival of the train, on March 3, is recorded as follows: "Approximately 1,500 Jewish men, women and children, including Norwegian Jews, arrive from Berlin with a transport. . . . After the selection, 535 men, who are given the numbers 104,890 to 105,424, as well as 145 women, who are given the numbers 36,935 to 37,079, are admitted to the camp as prisoners. The remaining approximately 820 people are killed in the gas chambers."[5] Among those selected as fit for entry to the camp were about fifty of the 293 Dresden Jews. As far as is known, ten survived, seven men and three women.

Now the only Jews left in Dresden who were not "protected" by mixed marriage or "privileged" status were the two officials of the National Association of Jews in Germany. On June 10, 1943, it was wound up and the officials and their dependents were deported shortly after. On June 12,

Victor Klemperer noted: "The National Association of Jews in Germany has been dissolved. As yet nothing is known about the significance and consequences of this measure. Lewin thinks: They want to demonstrate that there are no Jews in Germany anymore. But there are still some nevertheless, and among them still a number conspicuous because of the Jew's star! In Dresden, out of 600,000 inhabitants there are 60 wearers of the star running around. What will happen to those with privileged status, what, above all, to us wearers of the star?"

## III

It is probable that the Nazi leadership decided to postpone "solving" the problem of the category of Jews in mixed marriages to avoid the risk of public disturbance and because of possible effects on morale.[6] Instead, individuals and small groups were picked off for infringements of the decrees concerning Jews. In the meantime, if they avoided drawing attention to themselves, Jews like Victor Klemperer, married to "Aryan" women (Jewish women married to "Aryan" men were classified as "privileged" and did not have to wear the star), inhabited a strange limbo. The threat and fact of death were ever-present, the dwindling number of Jews' Houses became increasingly overcrowded, most remaining Jewish men were forced into unhealthy and exhausting factory work.

Klemperer, who was compelled to carry out "labor duty" from April 19, 1943, until June 23, 1944, found his period of forced labor especially hard, since it was difficult for him to keep up his study of Nazi language. There were, however, factors that ameliorated the hardships and the sense of threat. It was clear, at the latest from the surrender of Stalingrad, that Germany was losing the war, even if for the Jews still alive in Germany and in territories under German control the pace of the Allied advance was numbingly slow. The feeling of isolation was not quite as complete as before: There were a greater number of sympathetic "Aryan" contacts, there were discussions and arguments both in the Jews' Houses and in the factory, and in the factory sometimes the radio was even switched on. (Though never absent: the fear of the Gestapo, of arbitrary arrest, torture, death, the misery of walking out on the street wearing the yellow star.)

In all this time, however, Klemperer never wavered in his commitment to keeping his diary—if discovered, it would have cost his life and possibly that of people mentioned in it, as well as of the "Aryan" friend who safeguarded the pages that Eva Klemperer regularly brought her. The diary was at once the everyday record of one Jew's experience, a way of staying sane for a scholar who had always lived by the pen, and finally a memorial, the material for a memorial. On September 2, 1942, on the eve of the move to a second Jews' House, he writes: "As far as it lies in my power, the Jews' House at 15b Caspar David Friedrich Strasse and its many victims will be famous." It is a wish he repeated several times, although one that was realized, quite unexpectedly, only decades after his own death.[7]

# IV

The most obvious portent of Germany's approaching defeat was the Allied air campaign against its cities. Growing ever bolder, more destructive, and larger in scale, it was viewed with ambivalence by Dresden's remaining Jews. It was evidence of Germany's weakness, for sure, but it also contributed to their sense of dread. Would the Gestapo put them up against the wall before the end, would they be transported after all—or would the bombs kill them, along with the "Aryans"?

Throughout 1943 and 1944, Klemperer, indeed the whole population of Dresden, puzzled over the absence of air raids on the city, while so many other places, from Cologne to Hamburg, Berlin, Königsberg, and nearby Leipzig, were being devastated. People speculate (the city has been allocated to the Czechs when peace comes) and tell jokes (Churchill's aunt is buried here). There are the regular air-raid warnings, the comedy of air-raid drills, the repeated trips down to the cellar; even, from the second half of 1944, a couple of minor raids.

Finally, on February 12, 1945, the waiting appears to be over. Most of the remaining Jews, whether in mixed marriages or "privileged," are to be ordered to report for labor duty on February 15. In all likelihood, they would have been deported to Theresienstadt; among those summoned for forced labor were children under the age of ten.[8] Victor Klemperer himself is not included in this transport, although on February 13 he has to deliver some of the orders. He fully expects to be included in the next batch. Now there is no one who does not believe that this summons means certain death.

Then, on the night of February 13, another long-anticipated event comes to pass: the Anglo-American air raid that reduces the historic center of Dresden to rubble. Almost all the Jews survive the attack, and during the raid or its aftermath they remove their yellow stars and destroy or hide the documents that identify them as Jews.

Many years later, in a television interview in February 1995, Henni Brenner, one of the Jewish survivors—she was still living near Dresden—recounted her feelings about that night: "In the morning my father received the order to report for the transport. He became very depressed and said: 'Henni, only a miracle, a bolt from the blue, can save us now.' We survived the air raid and then walked toward the city center."

"What did you feel?" asked the journalist.

"It was terrible, the bodies, the city burning. But my father wanted at all costs to see what had happened to the Gestapo building. We couldn't get that far, because everything was burning, but from a distance we saw that it [too] was ablaze. Well, then we felt some satisfaction."[9]

## V

Provided with temporary papers, but nevertheless afraid of being recognized, the Klemperers did not want to stay close to the city (or risk being sent back to it). And so they begin a long and still dangerous journey through Germany. The fear of denunciation and the Gestapo fades, though not the threat of sudden death. The end of the war finds the couple in a village in Upper Bavaria. The story of their weeks on the run is related in frequently quite lengthy diary entries, written in moments of rest. It is one of the most fascinating parts of the whole of Klemperer's diaries since 1933 for its record of ordinary Germans' views and fears in the closing days of the war. But the value and interest of even this section is overshadowed by the account of the long trek home in late May and early June of 1945.

Victor Klemperer's diaries, kept from the beginning to the end of Nazi rule, give an account of everyday life from below, from the perspective of a German Jew whose life for years on end is at risk at every moment of every day. As such they are unique. Klemperer's view of defeated Germany is equally unique. Now he is both "inside" and "outside," "below" and "above." He is exhilarated at being alive, at still being together with Eva, at the prospect of getting back to work, of contributing to rebuilding Germany. He has survived, he is among the victors. Yet he is still German; the Allies, the Americans, put obstacles in his way, his feelings are mixed.

"They [the Americans] drive quickly and nonchalantly, and the Germans run along humbly on foot, the victors spit out the abundance of their cigarette stubs everywhere, and the Germans pick up the stubs. The Germans? *We*, the liberated, creep along on foot, *we* stoop down for the cigarette ends, *we*, who only yesterday were the oppressed, and who today are called the liberated, are ultimately likewise imprisoned and humiliated. Curious conflict within me: I rejoice in God's vengeance on the henchmen of the 3rd Reich [ . . . ] and yet I find it dreadful now to see the victors and avengers racing through the city [Munich], which they have so hellishly wrecked" (May 22, 1945).

The ambivalence of his feelings, however, allows Klemperer to give a much more differentiated account of Germany in defeat than many of the famous journalists who entered the country with the Allied forces. The journey from Munich to Dresden takes more than two weeks. The Klemperers cover much of the distance on foot, sometimes get lifts on carts or tractors, are dependent on the kindness (or not) of villagers, priests, and innkeepers; only toward the end are they sometimes able to travel by train. The roads are lined with the debris of battle, the cities they pass through are in ruins, and the couple bear with them the memory of all those who have not survived. And yet, for all that, there is an aspect of idyll as well as melancholy to their odyssey.

It's summer, of course, the weather is warm, the landscapes endure, they are *going home*, it is a joy to be alive. But perhaps the sense of idyll that is evoked also has something to do with the absence of government—not least such a government as that of Nazi Germany. It has gone, and the Allies have not yet imposed anything in its place. There is often something rather cheerful about people they meet; the weight of war and dictatorship, the fear of death has been lifted from everyone's shoulders. It was an atmosphere that would change with the coming of autumn and winter, with food shortages, with the unending flow of Germans expelled and deported from their homes east of the Oder–Neisse line, with the enforcement of tighter controls. But for a while there was an air of anarchy, a sense of opportunities to be grasped. A curious description, a curious time—one catches no whiff of it in the reports of, say, Martha Gellhorn or Lee Miller. In Klemperer's account, the mood begins to cloud over only when the couple cross into Russian-occupied territory. An informal interrogation in a pub by a suspicious Russian officer reminds him of a Gestapo man ordering him off a tram for questioning.

The journey and this volume of diaries concludes on June 10, 1945. The entry for that day was made on the thirteenth, with the Klemperers installed once more in their house in the village of Dölzschen, just outside Dresden. The day of their return to the city, writes Klemperer, turned into a fairy tale. A policeman assures them they will have no difficulty in reclaiming their house, they find their friends, the Glasers, unharmed, and after eating with them, they triumphantly mount the hill back to their old home. "The travails of the mountains," as Brecht put it, lay behind them, "the travails of the plains" lay before them. But for the moment, the Klemperers were happy.

## VI

Finally, it remains for me to make good a serious omission in my introduction to the first volume of Klemperer's diaries, *I Will Bear Witness*. It was Dr. Hadwig Klemperer, Victor Klemperer's second wife and widow, who deciphered the handwritten text of the diaries, produced after his typewriter had been taken from him.[10] She then prepared a typescript. Hadwig Klemperer's continuing determination and advice were indispensable in the preparation of the German edition of the diaries.

Martin Chalmers
London, 1999

## Notes

1. Figure in "Chronologie zur nationalsozialistischen Judenverfolgung in Dresden 1933–1945" in Norbert Haase, Stefi Jersch-Wenzel, and Hermann Simon (eds.), *Die Erinnerung hat ein Gesicht. Fotografien und Dokumente zur nationalsozialistischen Judenverfolgung in Dresden 1933–1945,* prepared by Marcus Gryglewski (Leipzig, 1998), p. 167.

2. Konrad Kwiet writes that the Nazi terror had driven many Jews to commit suicide. Suicides and suicide attempts rose after the boycott of Jewish businesses in April 1933, after the incorporation of Austria into the German Reich, and during and after the November 1938 pogrom. By far the greatest number, however, occurred during the deportations that began in autumn 1941. There was a "suicide epidemic," with between 3,000 and 4,000 victims (134,000 Jews were deported from Germany during this period). See Konrad Kwiet, "Nach dem Pogrom: Stufen der Ausgrenzung" in Wolfgang Benz (ed.), *Die Juden in Deutschland 1933–1945. Leben unter nationalsozialistischer Herrschaft* (Munich, 1988), p. 651.

3. Theresienstadt (Terezin) concentration camp, in Bohemia but less than forty miles from Dresden, was set up in a former Austrian garrison town. Being sent there was supposed to be a privilege, and by comparison with the extermination camps in Poland, the chances of survival were certainly higher. But (a) by any other standards it was a death camp, and (b) it was used as a transit camp for Auschwitz. According to figures quoted in Marcus Gryglewski, "Zur Geschichte der nationalsozialistischen Judenverfolgung in Dresden 1933–1945" in Haase, Jersch-Wenzel, and Simon, *Die Erinnerung hat ein Gesicht,* footnote 147, p. 131, of 42,832 inmates taken there from the territory of the German Reich, 20,729 died in Theresienstadt, and 15,036 were deported to other destinations.

4. For details and bibliography relating to the Hellerberg camp and of the making of the film, see Marcus Gryglewski, "Zur Geschichte der nationalsozialistischen Judenverfolgung in Dresden 1933–1945," as above. *Die Erinnerung hat ein Gesicht* also contains stills from the film. For brief comments by a former inmate of the camp and survivor of Auschwitz, see the letter from Heinz Mayer to Rudolf Apt, printed as "Am Beispiel Dresdens" in Gerhard Schoenberner (ed.), *Wir haben es gesehen. Augenzeugenberichte über die Judenverfolgung im 3. Reich* (Wiesbaden, 1988), pp. 413–417. The original is in the Wiener Library, London.

5. Danuta Czech, *Kalendarium der Ereignisse im Konzentrationslager Auschwitz–Birkenau 1939–1945* (Reinbek b. Hamburg, 1989), p. 429. This is a German translation of the original Polish edition.

6. It was in the course of the "Factory Action" that the wives of Jewish men in mixed marriages who had been caught up in the sweep demonstrated in Berlin for their release. The regime relented in this instance, and the husbands were released—a few were even brought back from Auschwitz. The Nazis took no further general measures against Jews in mixed marriages until the closing months of the war. See, on this, Nathan Stoltzfus, *Resistance of the Heart. Inter-*

*marriage and the Rosenstrasse Protest in Nazi Germany* (New York and London, 1996). For a near-contemporary reference by an "Aryan," see Ruth Andreas-Friedrich, *Der Schattenmann. Tagebuchaufzeichnungen 1938–1945* (Frankfurt/Main, 1983, first published 1947), pp. 103–104.

7. He had made a good start, however, in *LTI—Lingua Tertii Imperii*—his book on Nazi language, which is based on material contained in the diaries. An English translation of *LTI* is forthcoming.

8. See Marcus Gryglewski, "Zur Geschichte der nationalsozialistischen Judenverfolgung in Dresden 1933–1945," as above, p. 144.

9. Quoted in Wojciech Pieciak, "Requiem für die Stadt Dresden" in Ewa Kobylinska and Andreas Lawaty, *erinnern, vergessen, verdrängen. Polnische und deutsche Ehrfahrungen* (Wiesbaden, 1998), p. 356. Dresden has, of course, become a symbol of the futility of war in general and of the alleged pointlessness of Allied area bombing of cities in particular, in a way that no other German city has. This is not because the air raid, or rather air raids, on Dresden were more destructive than elsewhere. The damage to Dresden, although severe (and unimaginable, inconceivable to those who lived through the bombing), was not as great as to many other cities. There is no certain figure for the number of dead, but 25,000—at most 35,000—is the figure accepted by serious historians. This is large but by no means exceptional when compared to the fate of other large cities, like Hamburg, or even of small ones, like Pforzheim. Likewise, although Dresden was regarded as a beautiful city with an irreplaceable character and architecture, the same can be said of a number of other German cities that were devastated. The late point in the war at which the raids took place was certainly a factor, as were the grossly inflated casualty figures announced by the Nazis. Such figures are still sometimes quoted today, and they helped fuel postwar German criticism of the air raids, particularly on the right of the political spectrum, as a "war crime." It is perhaps no surprise that the far-right English historian David Irving wrote a book about the destruction of Dresden (1963). More recently, Irving has made a career out of denying the genocide of the Jews.

The late date of the raids, however, also led Soviet and East German commentators to allege that the bombing of Dresden was an early move in the cold war, a lesson to the Soviets advancing toward the city as much as to the Germans, who were close to defeat, in the air superiority of the Western Allies. The bombing of Dresden was then used to help promote anti-Western attitudes in East Germany. In other words, the singling out of Dresden as "war victim" owed something to a convergence of interests of right-wing elements in the West and Communist governments in the East. None of this should obscure the legitimate sorrow felt by the inhabitants of Dresden at the loss of life there and at the destruction caused, or the regret of "outsiders" for whom the destruction caused by the Allied air raids represents a loss to Europe as a whole as much as to Germany. (For a summary of the issues, see Pieciak's article, as above.)

10. I am grateful to Dr. Derek F. Klemperer of Bristol, England, Victor Klemperer's great-nephew, for bringing this to my attention.

# CONTENTS

1942

## January 1, Thursday

[ ... ]

It is said children still have a sense of wonder, later one becomes blunted. — Nonsense. A child takes things for granted, and most people get no further; only an *old* person, who *thinks*, is aware of the wondrous.

## January 4, Sunday

[ ... ]

Situation obscure. The Neumanns did not know either, where the Eastern Front stands. — The lies outdo and contradict one another. First, the word was: into winter quarters, we are shortening our line, let the Russians claim that as a success, we are masters of the situation ("we have the initiative"). Then Ribbentrop explained: The Russians are attacking our rear. Now Hitler has issued two New Year messages. One to the nation: Should it become necessary, we, too, shall make the greatest sacrifices. One to the soldiers ("*My* soldiers") that talks frankly about the Russian offensive, which "must and will" fail.

The Neumanns in Kötzschenbroda: The Russians attack on horse-drawn sledges and with cavalry, tanks frozen up. Retreating Germans are losing immense quantities of equipment. — Hitler has dismissed not only Brauchitsch, but something like thirty generals altogether, or "Brauchitsch and something like thirty others have left of their own volition" or "have been shot." Reason: Brauchitsch had already considered winter quarters necessary in the autumn but when Smolensk was reached, Hitler ordered the advance to continue. — German tank divisions are massed on the Spanish frontier. Against Gibraltar? To protect the Portugese coast? Will Spain remain neutral? Which side will it join? Where does the German Eastern Front stand? Nothing but questions without answers, in Kötzschenbroda as here. —

Yesterday Trude Scherk wrote something very funny in a letter. Heinz Machol is exempted from Jew's star and social deduction (the 15 percent value-added tax), because he has children from his first marriage with an Aryan. But this first wife was a wildly active Austrian Communist, he got a divorce.

Finished reading *I, Claudius*. [ ... ]

**January 12, Monday**

(Latest "post office box": Folder V. Hugo Poetry)

It was such a shock, that only today am I capable of writing it down; so far I have tried to regain my balance working on the Curriculum.

At four o'clock on Thursday afternoon, January 8, I am returning from shopping at Chemnitzer Platz on the front platform of the no. 16 tram. At the county court, people crowding on as usual. Just before the station, a young man turns toward me, very clean-cut face, cold gray eyes, and says quietly: "Get off at the next stop." I, quite mechanically, since I change trams there: "Yes." Only as I get off does it strike me as curious. I'm waiting for the no. 14. Then he's standing beside me: "Where have you come from? Where are you going? Come with me." I did not even ask for any identification. As we are walking, he says: "State Police. Do you want to see my ID?" — "Not here." Opposite the station, on the Hohe Strasse side, where I used to park, a big office building between the hotels. So this is the Gestapo building, about which so many terrible stories are told. My dog-catcher says to a comrade coming toward him: "He's wandering around on the tram during rush hour; I want to frisk him." To me, incidentally without shouting: "You wait here, behind the stairway." I stood there for a few minutes. Very short of breath. All the time with the feeling: "When will they let you go?" Someone who was passing bawled at me: "Turn around!" (I had [ ... ] to face the wall.) My dogcatcher reappeared after a while and beckoned me to come up. Upstairs a very large office; one can look into another room, a kind of living room with the table laid. He looks through my pocketbook, my briefcase. "What are you doing?" — "I'm writing a book." — "But you will never be able to publish it. — From tomorrow you'll have work to do. The Goehle plant (Zeiss-Ikon). — Do you have problems with your heart?" — I was probably very pale and speaking laboriously, gasping for breath. Thus far the treatment had been almost decent. Now another policeman appeared, perhaps one rank higher, average height, brown, mocking eyes. He addresses me familiarly: "Take your filth (briefcase and hat) off the table. Put the hat on. Isn't that what you do? Where you stand, that's holy ground." — "I'm Protestant." — "What are you? Baptized? That's just a cover-up. As a professor you must know the book by . . . by somebody Levysohn, it's all in there. Are you circumcised? It's not true that it's a hygienic prescription. It's all in the book. — How old? — What, only sixty? Man, you must have been running riot with your health. — What were those paws of yours doing? You've stolen something, haven't you? Empty the briefcase." — I had to open everything once again. A loaf, a bottle with half a liter of milk. "Good milk." — "But no, skimmed milk." — "Good milk!" — "But it really is skimmed milk." — Three little pieces of cake. — "Looks good!" — Half a pound of blackberry tea. (For smoking!) — "Why so much at once, you can buy it every day." — "Who's going to win the war? You or us?" — "What do you mean?" — "Well, you pray for our defeat every day, don't you? — To Yahweh, or whatever it's called. It's the Jewish War, isn't it. Adolf Hitler said so—(shouting theatrically:) And what Adolf Hitler says is true. — Why do you shop at Chemnitzer Platz?" — "We used to live there." — "You shop there, because they give you more there. That's going to stop. Tomorrow you'll register your coupons at the nearest grocer's. You'd better not let yourself be seen on the tram here. You can walk. And if we see you here again, you're going. You know where to. Understood?" I simply said: "Yes." He left. The dogcatcher stood motionless and sullen in a corner. — "May I go now?" He came as far as the stairs with me, and his final words were: "And if you weren't so old and decrepit, you would be put to work." Only when I was outside did I notice how much my chest and left arm hurt. Still, I was free (as it is called here, I could also have disappeared for a long time—Ernst Kreidl has been inside for seven and a half weeks— forever with the help of an injection). I walked home very slowly. I have still not completely recovered. I registered my J-coupons at Wasaplatz; since then I have taken only a very few steps in the open air, have not left this area and shall not leave it again. The business of their fabulous tyranny, brutality, mocking humiliation has taken hold of me far too much. Since then, I have no longer been able to get rid of thoughts of death.

According to what I hear from the Kreidls and Kätchen Sara, similar cases occur here and there. The point of it all is supposed to be to lay hands on people for labor service. But that could be done through the Community. I think they want to intimidate people and drive them from the streets, perhaps also nose out shopkeepers who are friendly to Jews. — Only comfort: The reverse in Russia can no longer be disguised. Paul Kreidl read out a very serious article from *Das Reich*—all at once the Russians, who have only just been annihilated, are tremendous and quite inexhaustible opponents. Kätchen Sara tells us how a tram driver poured out his heart to her one morning. She should be brave, it would soon be all up for the bloodhounds, he knew the mood of the soldiers; there were so many men on leave riding on his platform in the mornings, they didn't want to go on fighting, etc., etc. —

But who can estimate how far the inner tension, the external defeat have progressed? *I* cannot wait much longer. And that is probably the prevailing mood of all wearers of the star.

It has turned very cold, and once again, as last winter, our heating makes no headway against the frost, and we are more badly fed, and our nerves are in a worse state than last winter.

### January 13, Tuesday

Paul Kreidl tells us—a rumor, but it is very credible and comes from various sources—evacuated Jews were *shot* in Riga, in groups, as they left the train. He fears for a married sister, living in Prague, marked down for transport. On the other hand, he is optimistic: In the center the Russian offensive is pushing toward Poland. I don't really believe it; today's military bulletin again mentions fighting near Leningrad and east of Kharkov, so the center cannot have been pushed so far back at all. —

A great deal is being made here of the success of the fur collection. The fur and woolen things were taken from the Jews, the Aryans had to surrender them "voluntarily" and handed over some 50 million items. That is equivalent to "a plebiscite," testifies to the unshakeable attachment of people and army, people and leader, etc., etc. —

[ . . . ]

## January 17, Saturday

Since midday of the day before yesterday (Thursday, January 15) great agitation or in fact apathy, mixed with "Hurrah, I'm still alive," which in turn alternates with [ . . . ] the question as to whose lot is the better. Evacuation of all the Jews here on the coming Wednesday, excepting anyone who is over sixty-five; who holds the Iron Cross, First Class; who is in a mixed marriage, including one without children. Point 3 protects me—for how long? (There are three or four holders of the Iron Cross, First Class, in Dresden.) One of the other women workers at the Goehle plant brought Kätchen the news. Since then terrible agitation in the house, Paul Kreidl downstairs, Kätchen here. With her a jumble of childishness, hysteria, serious heart problems, real dread. Early this morning I saw and heard through the glass door that she was being shaken by a fit of hysterics in her room. I went to her, she clung to me, gripped my hands, her head fell on my shoulder; I had to stroke her, speak words of comfort to her. "I shall be without a bed—you must all be with me on the last night, including mother, including Ludwig (the brother-in-law and heir, who has been telegraphed to come); otherwise I shall take my life—I am like Jesus on the cross—why must I suffer so . . ."

Half an hour later a calm coffee together. I believe that she is precisely the person whom it will not hit so terribly hard. They will not treat much-needed workers all that badly, she will continue to have company. — Still, the severe cold makes everything more difficult, and she leaves here stripped and naked. — Terrible scenes of despair are said to be taking place at the Community and in the factory, where very many Jews work. Married couples are allowed to stay together, but parents and children are separated without pity. Thus the fifteen-year-old daughter of a pharmacist remains behind here alone. — Different government departments appear to be at cross-purposes. The evacuation order appears to have originated from a Reich department and to have landed on Saxony without warning. The Zeiss-Ikon [ . . . ] factory is fighting for its Jewish section, which is working well. They must employ about 400 people there. First, all of them were to go. Then yesterday an initial reclaim succeeded in retaining 50%— Kätchen *not* included. Then the company no doubt called on a military commission for help, and it is possible that a further number will be retained today. — Paul Kreidl is on a different work detachment, as a laborer on railway construction. Here he recently expressed the fear that Jewish transports would be shot down on arrival. But there is obviously a tremendous shortage of labor, and what work can a dead Jew do? — What are the consequences for the two of us? 1) How long shall I remain in Dresden? 2) How long shall we remain in this apartment? (And how will Muschel survive another move?) 3) What are they going to do with Dresden's Jewish remnant anyway? It appears as if anti-Semitism is going to increase even further, partly because of the more than critical external situation, partly because the Jew's star did not meet with much approval on the part of the public. Cf. my arrest recently, even though traveling by tram is officially permitted. Many similar cases have meanwhile been reported.

The severe frost (about 27 degrees below freezing) for several days now makes everything more difficult and gloomy. — I hardly get out of the house anymore. (Always the fear of the dogcatchers.) All errands fall to Eva. But I think one is almost as cold in the poorly heated apartment as outside. My share of domestic work ever greater. To washing up and scrubbing pots there is now added in greater measure the *brushing* of potatoes. I cannot peel them—but well brushed they can be eaten in their jackets. Three hundredweight have been delivered for us, and to a great extent I live on them. Warm or cold, potatoes substitute for scarce bread, at dinner I stuff as many potatoes into me as I can. Diet gets ever worse, we both look really pitiful now.

The Curriculum creeps along. But I keep doggedly at it. And also I would far too much like to be the chronicler of the cultural history of the present catastrophe. Observing to the last, taking notes, without asking whether the utilization of the notes will lead to something worthwhile again. I have the impression that the external and internal position of the 3rd Reich is extremely strained. But perhaps I am deceiving myself, and everything will go on for another two years.

### January 18, Sunday morning

Yesterday dramatic reversal in the evacuation business. The first news reached the Jews' House in the afternoon. There had been a fierce argument between the Party on the one hand, the company and the army on the other; many hours of negotiations, a threat to close the factory, to appeal to Göring, should the Jewish section be touched—finally the plant won completely: Not only does the whole workforce remain, but it will probably take over all the other Jews working in Dresden factories, so that the transport will not take place at all. Very emotional scenes are said to have occurred in the factory. — Thus the usual Sunday evening here was very lively. The Kreidls in hopeful mood, Kätchen intoxicated. Naturally everyone tended to see the overall situation in a favorable light. Things seemed to be going very badly at the front, revolution seemed to be imminent at home. Forsechè sì, forsechè no . . . (In the newspaper only yesterday mockery of London papers, which "invented" and printed a map of Berlin with SS machine-gun positions marked on it.) A passionate debate between Paul Kreidl and myself: He was for a large degree of reconciliation *after* things change, for Christian renunciation of revenge; I on the other hand in favor of an eye for an eye, tooth for a tooth. — On the tear-off calendar and in the leading article, yesterday or the day before yesterday, the 1933 election for the parliament in Lippe was noted as a commemoration day. The sudden advance of the Party in the smallest German parliament, symptom and prelude of the *seizure of power.* Perhaps the fight over the Zeiss-Ikon Jews is also a final symptom. [ . . . ]

### January 19, Monday

The trial of strength: The Gestapo has struck twenty from the list of those reclaimed by Zeiss-Ikon, it has stopped transfers of workers from other companies to the plant. In total, 250 people will after all leave here on Wednesday. Among them Paul Kreidl, a very heavy blow for his mother. Among them is also said to be a mother with three small children, the youngest a baby two months old. A transport also left Berlin yesterday. Unspeakable misery, aggravated by the continuing very severe cold (between 27 and 36 degrees of frost). Boundless arbitrariness and uncertainty. For a moment Kätchen Sara believed herself to be one of the twenty and almost passed out. I for my part also no longer feel safe. —

My Curriculum has been at a standstill for several days. On top of the commotion about the transport, Eva caught a cold. Great amount of domestic work. I am reading Shmarya Levin's *Childhood in Exile*, 1935. A great work of art. Content tremendously interesting, very important for the last book of my Curriculum. The man, born in Russia at the end of the 1860s, in Swislowitz on the Beresina, grows up in the ghetto, becomes a pioneer of Zionism. For the first time it dawns on me that *Zionism is humanism*. The book was lent to me by the Seliksohns; Seliksohn, early forties, Russian Jew by birth, came to Germany as a boy, volunteered in 1914 at 17 years of age, frontline service and interpreter in the East, afterward Socialist and Zionist, ill-treated in a concentration camp, becoming diabetic, his wife at Zeiss-Ikon; both were on the transport list but were taken off it. We know them through Kätchen. I have already debated with him repeatedly—yesterday afternoon they were here for a long time. I must make more detailed notes on Levin.

### January 20, evening

Yesterday with the Kreidls downstairs until midnight. Eva helped sew straps for Paul Kreidl, so that he can carry his suitcase on his back. Then a feather bed was stuffed, which one has to hand over (and apparently one does not always see again). Today Paul Kreidl carted it to the prescribed forwarding agent on a little handcart.

## January 21, Wednesday morning

Before a deportee goes, the Gestapo seals up everything he leaves behind. Everything is forfeit. Yesterday evening Paul Kreidl brought me a pair of shoes that fit me exactly and are most welcome given the terrible condition of my own. Also a little tobacco, which Eva mixes with blackberry tea and rolls in cigarettes. I have already been on pure blackberry tea for many weeks. — This morning a kind of visit of condolence to his mother. — The transport now includes 240 persons; there are said to be people among them who are so old, weak, and sick that it is unlikely that everyone will still be alive on arrival. (Continuing severe cold.)

Eva racked by a bad cough, much weakened. She made an attempt to get up yesterday, but was too weak. — She *must* go out today; we are completely without food, and *I* do not have the confidence to go into town.

## January 26, Monday evening

Since Friday, four days now, Eva has been completely confined to bed with serious fits of coughing, only rising to oversee a primitive supper. Shopping limited to Wasaplatz and Jew's card, food even more wretched than usual. Everything made more difficult by the continuing frost (35 degrees of frost at night), and the fact that the rooms cannot be heated, and by my own heavy cold. Whatever time is left to me after domestic work, I use for reading aloud. Levin, volume 2, completely finished in very short time—I must at all costs make careful notes. Since Eva did not get to Paulig's [lending library], I looked through Frau Ida Kreidl's little bookcase yesterday and first of all took *Ben-Hur* from it. [ . . . ]

The war takes its unpredictable course. Every day there is said to be "heavy fighting" in the East. In Africa, the English offensive has been halted at Ajdabiyah. If it cannot get any farther, the outcome will be undecided, and Italy, too, can muddle on. —

## January 29

Today, after several weeks of severe cold, a thaw is setting in, beginning with snow. We have suffered greatly and are still suffering. Eva constantly coughing badly, has spent a lot of time in bed. I have bad influenza, the cold has punished my hands cruelly. — It was impossible to give a thought to the Curriculum. — A lot of *Ben-Hur*. — Even worse food than usual. —

[ . . . ]

All the things that are a problem: No one wants to do our washing. The Dippoldiswalder Laundry kicked out its more recent customers over a month ago, other laundries are not taking on any new customers. It is not *only* the Jews who suffer from such measures, but the Jews always first of all and most drastically. Reason: not only shortage of materials, but above all of staff. Everything for the army, the East eats it up. — No one wants to repair our vacuum cleaner. "Repairs are not accepted." A sign hanging in x shop windows. Applies also to watches, umbrellas, etc.

Letter from Martin. Some weeks ago I had to let one of his letters go back with "acceptance refused." Stamps had been included. The letter was held at the customs office here; to have it released, I would have had to make an application to a government office in Berlin. [But] the application of a Jew would have been rejected. Stamp collections are also included in confiscated Jewish property. — Now Martin writes—formal as always: Sender Arne Erik Johannsson, Stockholm 1, signed "Your Arne" and requests me to use this address. What is behind it? I suspect—impossible to ask—that he expects a German invasion. Whereupon he might then share the same fate as the Jews who emigrated from Germany to Holland and France. — And if there is something else behind it? And if the Gestapo should ever take an interest? Then I could end up like Ernst Kreidl. He has been inside for ten mortal weeks now. No one knows why, no one knows for how much longer.

[ ... ]

### January 31, Saturday

Since yesterday a new, extremely depressing difficulty: The house in Dölzschen appears, or is finally, lost. Notice of calling in the mortgage on July 1 was received a long time ago, but it would perhaps have been possible nevertheless to ward it off. Or: It's a long time to July 1, and so much can happen before then! But for now: Yesterday I am summoned "for questioning" to the police station here, where, by the way, they are very friendly and very evidently hostile to Gestapo, SS, Party, etc. A long communication from Dölzschen District to the Dresden county administration, first of all asking the police station for information about the "nationality of the Jew Klemperer." ("Because if you were a French citizen, Professor, things would be easier for you," says the inspector.) My plot of land is completely neglected, repairing the damage is likely to cost 2000M; since it cannot all be put into shape at once, a trustee will have to be appointed, who is to effect the "Aryanization" of the house. So not only will the house be taken away from me, a further 2000M for future repairs will be deducted from the fixed minimum price. We shall be beggars. What hits me hardest about this business is Eva's bitterness. (I now hear from her every day: "I am bored to death." Shopping, cleaning, cooking is now her hated daily routine. — My own does not look so very different.)

On the same January 30, Benghazi, in Africa, was recaptured by the Germans. That means a camphor injection for Italy, a new prolongation of the war. —

[ ... ]

## February 5, Thursday evening

Letter from Caroli Stern in response to our last epistle to Lissy Meyerhof. Lissy was evacuated on January 25, during the days when the frost was hardest. Admittedly, she was requisitioned by the Health Administration and departs as a nurse to practice her profession, and thus she may experience the deportation as good fortune. Nevertheless robbed and expelled within 48 hours.

[ . . . ]

Every day when she comes from the factory, Kätchen Sara tells us about house searches that are accompanied by the most brutal *beatings* and by indiscriminate theft.

A decree forbids Jews from using the rear carriage of the tram—on which the front platform is not partitioned off from the compartment— and from using the tram at all on Sundays. Since my arrest, I myself have not traveled by tram anymore, have not gone into town at all anymore. —

After almost two years, no doubt at Trude Scherk's instigation, a card from Grete. D'outre-tombe. At first I was surprised at the smooth hand and the clearly formulated sentences, including admittedly the words, "I wish I were dead." Then I saw the date, or rather Eva discovered it: May 5, '41. It was followed by a few lines of greeting of January 31, '42. The writing was shaky, and the two sentences were only suggested, contained disconnected words that did not make any sense as a whole. Complete decline.

[ . . . ]

In Africa, Rommel takes back Cyrenaica, in the East the Russians cannot advance any farther—the war can last for years.

Daily visits by the tearful Ida Kreidl. Ernst Kreidl has been in prison for eleven weeks now, there is no news, no one is allowed to talk to him, he is not allowed to write anything.

No longer severe, but nevertheless continuing, very bothersome frost, which is very much felt in the apartment itself. [ . . . ]

Curriculum making the most pitiful progress. [ . . . ] But I absolutely want to finish the second volume.


## February 6, Friday evening

In the new soap coupons issued today (always for four months) there is, for the first time, no shaving soap for Jews. Is there such a shortage—do they want to reintroduce the medieval Jew's beard by force? I still have a small hoarded reserve. I hope it will not be noticed during a house search. I hope being clean-shaven will not make one suspect.

[ . . . ]

**February 8, Sunday**

Always the same seesaw. The fear that my scribbling could get me put into a concentration camp. The feeling that it is my duty to write, that it is my life's task, my calling. The feeling of vanitas vanitatum, that my scribbling is worthless. In the end I go on writing anyway, the diary, the Curriculum. —

Especially depressed since yesterday. Eva exhausted by morning errand through frost, snow, and ice; so I was at the Neumanns' alone. The whole time they talked of nothing but the unspeakable house search they (and others likewise) had suffered. Eight-man squad. [ . . . ] vilest abuse, pushing, blows, Frau Neumann boxed on the ears five times. They rummaged through *everything*, stole indiscriminately: candles, soap, an electric fire, a suitcase, books, half a pound of margarine (legitimately bought with ration coupons), writing paper, all kinds of tobacco, umbrella, his military decorations ("You won't be needing them anymore"). — "Where do you have your laundry done?" — "It's done at home." — "Watch you don't have the cheek to have your laundry done outside!" — "Why do you all get so old? — Go on and string yourselves up, turn on the gas." Unfortunately also letters, addresses, written matter in general taken away. — Finally one signs a statement that one has voluntarily put everything at the disposal of the German Red Cross. — To get arrested, it's enough for them to ascertain contact with an Aryan. — A lady in her seventies arrested.

Nowhere a ray of hope. The English are losing all of Cyrenaica again. Rommel is said to have received material support from Tunis from the Pétain-Darlan government. Japanese making progress, the Russians stuck fast. Germany will nevertheless certainly lose the war, but when? And who will live to see it? The words of a Russian Zionist in Levin's memoirs, addressed to God during the time of the pogroms, constantly go through my head: "*You* can wait, for *you* a thousand years are as one day—but *we* cannot wait."

**February 9, Monday**

Again and again news of house searches, of theft of every kind, mistreatment . . . I cannot stop worrying about my manuscripts anymore. I cannot remove *everything*. Yesterday Kätchen brought this news from a visit to relations: a certain Stern, about sixty years of age, arrested some weeks ago, because of a *pastoral letter* found during a house search. Police prison— then concentration camp—now an urn has been returned. — I find it difficult to muster the composure for the Curriculum. Admittedly, kitchen chores for the greater part of the day. Recently also reading aloud in the early morning. I do not like it if Eva is lying awake, left to her own thoughts.

Kätchen gave me the documents to read that are handed out to those listed for transportation. Their property is confiscated, they have to make an inventory on printed forms. These forms go into the most wretched detail: "Ties . . . shirts . . . pajamas . . . blouses . . ."

**February 10**

Under pressure of impending house search Eva is going to Pirna again. — Curriculum manuscript gone. — Probably complete interruption.

**February 12, Thursday evening**

Father died 30 years ago today. His dying is in front of me all day, and all those who were present then and have meanwhile departed.

Tense and resigned. Work on the Curriculum. People at the beginning of May 1919. My articles for the *Leipziger NN.*

"The District President of Dresden-Bautzen" has appointed a lawyer, Heise, as Aryan trustee for my property.

The Japanese have taken Singapore, the Germans have had new successes in the East.

[ . . . ]

Didn't leave the house all day. I am burying myself more and more.

**February 13, Friday evening**

At six o'clock a messenger came from the Jewish Community; I had to report at eight o'clock tomorrow morning, in Räcknitz, *to shovel snow*. That is exactly *the* work at which my heart protests after five minutes. It is to last "until the early afternoon." I also lack boots with good soles. It was too late for any kind of objection or any attempt to procure boots. I have to accept it. I can do no more than die.

**February 15, Sunday morning**

Yesterday, February 14, the first day clearing snow, from eight till two, but this coming week it will probably last from eight or half past eight until five o'clock, plus a march of one hour there and one hour back. Yesterday left after seven o'clock in the gray of dawn, almost darkness, with Dr. Friedheim. Snow-covered streets unrecognizable. Toward Zschertnitz, past the old brickworks, then straight past the Moreau monument as far as the Elysium, a large inn just at the beginning of Langemarckstrasse, formerly Bergstrasse, in Räcknitz. On the way Dr. Friedheim fell twice, once very heavily; later he produced a certificate from Dr. Rostoski: gallbladder, liver, hernia, diabetes . . . went home. A pitiful group assembled in the house entry. One rupture without rupture belt, one cripple, one hunchback . . . Seventeen "older" men should have come, two had not turned up, three were sent away, of the remaining twelve *several* were over seventy, I at sixty literally the youngest. I considered whether I should go to the medical assessor immediately. A man in uniform (municipal street-cleaning department) arrived in a van with tools, took a kind of roll call. Very polite. He advised me: "Try it first, you could get into trouble otherwise." We shouldered shovel and other tools and first marched to the "Little Toll House." There a delivery van was struggling at the entry to the Südhöhe road. We got it free, widened the roadway. As I was shoveling here, I was aware of my heart. Then we marched along Innsbrucker Strasse almost as far as Nöthnitz Manor near Bannewitz [ . . . ], opposite it a shed, where we had our morning break, facing Dresden, and a few hundred yards from Kaitz [ . . . ]. How often have I gone driving there, at the wheel of my own car. Now . . . Widening of the roadway; a high wall of snow had already been piled up on the side away from Kaitz. It had to be pushed farther back, a passing place was being made. When throwing the snow up became too much of a strain, I lugged the full shovel to the free side of the road and let the contents roll down the slope. It was blowing terribly; at times there was a snowstorm. The pains had stopped very quickly; I held out remarkably well. We worked at a very moderate pace, we stood around a lot, chatted—it was very exhausting nevertheless. And it is very doubtful whether I shall last until five o'clock tomorrow. Standing around is unquestionably part of all such military-like collective tasks, standing around, tedium, boredom, and the hours creeping by. Up here a sociable, gray-haired foreman in civilian clothes was in charge. He addressed us as "Herr"! And to me he said: "You must not overexert yourself, the state does not require it." I became friendly with a doctor working beside me, Dr. Magnus, orthopedist and surgeon, 67, but much stronger and younger than I. Sportsman, horseman, well prepared. He had a supply of coarse mittens and gave me a pair. He asked about my health problems. "Pains from the chest down to my left wrist." — "Typical symptoms of angina." — It was a blow, nevertheless, to be told so bluntly what I had long known and did not want to know. Angina sounds different from "nervous heart." — But Dr. Katz, the medical assessor, was a "shit." Besides, with the heart one never knew how it would respond. Perhaps all the fresh air would actually do me good. I should only make sure to take regular breaks. Finally: "You look very well." I had little in common with the other workers. Businessmen, small-time dealers in this and that, one quite proletarian. — The breakfast room: a toolshed, separated off from it a tiny room with an iron stove, bench and table, meant for three workers. We used it in two groups of six, are supposed to divide into three groups for our midday break. — Very similar to fatigue duty in the army. But I am sixty after all. — The work is interrupted: "Look out!" and we press up against the wall of snow. I always find it frightening when the heavy long-distance buses with snow chains around their huge wheels roll past a few inches away; they could so easily slide to the side. One with a protruding metal triangle as a plow. — Then a proper snow plow, drawn by horses [ . . . ]. A couple of crude farmers' horse-drawn sleighs, carrying barrels with animal feed. Occasionally a delivery van or a military vehicle. Almost never a private car, of which there used to be so many here. A horse-drawn cart, the rear wheels placed on runners. — I constantly say to myself: It is a thousand times better than being in prison [ . . . ], time passes; but for all of that it is still a deadly boring waste of time. And with "angina symptoms" how much time is left to one?

The Sunday is gone—what have I achieved? Washed myself down, [ . . . ] brushed potatoes, this diary entry, read aloud a few lines of *Ben-Hur*, the end of which is very disappointing [ . . . ]; a so-far vain attempt to make notes on Levin. And now five quite merciless snow-clearing days lie before me. It keeps on snowing.

Curriculum completely put aside.

Today we were supposed to go to the Seliksohns for tea. Called off, the wife's father (Kornblum) has died in a concentration camp, ashes forwarded. Was informed without warning in the Zeiss factory. Kätchen tells us: Screaming and fainting and frequent nervous fits [in the factory]. It was now nothing out of the ordinary there for people to faint, have fits of weeping, etc. A (Jewish) personnel doctor was busy all the time. Three people had been arrested some time ago, because a hostile pastoral letter had been found in their homes, Kornblum senior one of them. A second died in a concentration camp a few days ago, a third (Matthias, director of a large brewery) hanged himself in prison right at the start. People always seem to be put in Dresden police prison for a while before being transferred to a concentration camp. It is said that heavy work is required there (carrying stones); anyone who does not stay the course is badly mistreated. —

"Friday the thirteenth"—should I be superstitious? It was not only the snow-clearing order that was a blow, but with the shock I forgot about the blackout of my room. Almost exactly a year since it happened to me the first time. Not until about nine o'clock in the evening did it occur to me. We immediately switched off the light and blacked out. Since no one has come to see us, the business has passed without any consequences. I would have spent many weeks in prison at least, or even gone to a concentration camp. So the thirteenth was merciful to me after all. —

A notice at the baker's: Cakes may no longer be dispensed to Jews and Poles. A general ban on cakes for Jews is already said to be in force in Berlin.

[ . . . ]

Yesterday Frau Ida Kreidl came to see us with her new tenant, Frau Pick, a lady (really a lady) of 76, formerly well-off (some kind of very large malt factory), now impoverished, family abroad. Uncommonly vigorous, full of the joys of life (very Austrian), yet her demeanor is at once hearty and dignified. She stroked my hand: "You could be my son; in my day girls married at 16."

## February 16, Monday evening

Clearing snow no. 2. Outside from half past seven in the morning until half past five. Pains on the snow-covered way there via Mockritz and Kaitz to Nöthnitz. I found the shoveling easy, the standing around was bearable—but now nevertheless very tired and my hand is trembling. A gray-haired man in uniform and with a goatee, roads inspector, not only very humane, but also very clearly and emphatically expressing his sympathy and his dissatisfaction. [ . . . ] Old Social Democrat [ . . . ]. At half past four we marched down to the Elysium, where we handed in our spades and where we must "report" tomorrow at 8:00 A.M. It keeps on snowing. — Eva came up with the Possendorf bus, chatted for a while with Magnus and myself. (She looked on as she had done when I was learning to be a gunner on the Oberwiesenfels.) I walked as far as Zschertnitz with Eisner, a shopowner from Löbau, and the roughest and most proletarian man in my squad. In the middle of the conversation, he began to weep. "My son! He is mentally retarded, by himself he is helpless, and they have taken him away and I'm left here!" Utter love for the thirty-two-year-old idiot [ . . . ]. I comforted him. Chatted a lot to the elderly traveling salesman of a big coal firm. One feels close to the whole group; not much work is done, the day passes. The breaks for food in the little shed. I was given half a cigarillo (broken in two) as a present, I inherited a sandwich, with liver sausage even. — Everything was bearable—but what will happen tomorrow?

It does disturb me after all, that Magnus talks so matter-of-factly about my angina. His favorite subject of conversation: equestrianism.

Steinitz, the traveling salesman, garrulous but warmhearted, is writing the history of his coal firm (Weinmann or something, one of the two biggest in Moravia) "in English" (as an exercise) "more anecdotal" than business history. So yet another curriculum vitae.

## February 17

Fear again after being told of house searches, in which private papers were torn up.

## February 18, Wednesday evening

Yesterday and today "mustered" at the "Elysium," marched off, Langemarckstrasse as far as the Toll House, continued along the main road in the direction of Kaitz. [ . . . ] Different foreman, different supervisor, again both were very humane and anti-Nazi. "Don't say that we treated you well, not at the Community either, rather say we were bad; otherwise we'll be in trouble." — "Don't knock yourself out." — "Look, I can't tell you, 'Work more slowly,' you have to know that yourself," etc., etc. The senior supervisor, a younger man, puts in a brief appearance only in the morning. The foreman always with us. Fifty-five, glassblower until 1930, then unemployed for a year, since then municipal worker. Social Democrat, trade unionist, house search in '33. Entirely for us. But timid. Lets us go at half past four, makes things easier as far as he can. Nevertheless I am astonished how well I keep up. [ . . . ] Yesterday a young woman or lady, stopping: "But that's too hard for you" (meaning all of us)—"You're too old, and one can see that you have other professions"—(with passionate emphasis:) *"That's* what Germany has come to!"

The foreman tells us: "The snow came too late, the ground is frozen to a depth of a yard or more, the potatoes have suffered. At Christmas I had to dig up potatoes near Magdeburg, they were damaged." — Such are today's consolations. — Low spirits yesterday because of unpleasant reports of new house searches in which papers were destroyed. As a result Eva off to Pirna today heavily laden. I shall place this page inside a book, inside the Lanson bibliography of Voltaire.

Today Frau Dr. Magnus brought her husband lunch. Eva's visit set an example. In the builders' hut, the doctor was greeted by a man in uniform, whom he had treated. Likewise, by someone on the street as we were working.

### February 19, Thursday evening

Work (toward Kaitzer Weg) and eating place as yesterday. Breaks prolonged by fifteen minutes each because of more severe frost [ . . . ], stopped at four, nevertheless more exhausted and chilled than previously. One fellow worker, Müller by name, without the star, "privileged marriage," has a small, formerly large leather factory in his wife's name—four workers instead of seventy, lack of material, everything rationed, [ . . . ], no real leather at all, only ersatz stuff. [ . . . ] Blum, the foreman: two sons on the Eastern front. Huge losses. Victory impossible. And America is coming. A quite ordinary man! Further: They won't destroy Bolshevism, that's impossible. — He and Steinitz told us all about the giant furnaces of the glassworks that swallow whole wagonloads of coal at a time and produce thousands upon thousands of bottles in a few hours. — But despite all that, the hours creep by, and it is a pointless waste of time, and how much time do I have left with my "angina symptoms"? I have been a laborer now for almost a week. It's an insult.

For the first time an anti-Semitic remark by a young passerby: "Just let them work! It's good to see them working for once." — Magnus is again and again addressed by passing workers, on whom he operated.

### February 22, Sunday morning

On Friday shoveled our way to the first houses in Kaitz before the morning break. Then to the barracks of the [municipal] works department on Zellscher Weg; shoveled snow for the never-ending remainder of the day down in the university quarter (Hempelstrasse, Zeunerstrasse, etc.: names of former colleagues). Shoveling snow with a view of the (new) university! Unfortunately, the clock tower of the Lukaskirche was also constantly in full view. The minutes crept by. — Yesterday, Saturday, 25 degrees of frost in the morning; back at Zellscher Weg again. Right next to our hut a pile of cinders. Sift it, break off the frozen top layer with a pickax, crush the larger pieces with a ram. In a group of four. The rest away with a hand-cart to put down the cinders. A prolonged morning break because of the cold and finished at a quarter past one instead of a quarter to two. Distri-bution of wage packets. Names without "Israel." (Roads inspector: "I've got too much tact for that.") Much standing around, but also a great deal of effort, cold and hunger. I had been very much looking forward to the half Saturday and the whole Sunday. Tiredness shatters plans and mood. [ . . . ] Hands chapped all over, feet and legs bruised.

[ . . . ]

*The group: Dr. Magnus-Alsleben,* 67, very youthful, orthopedist and sur-geon, horseman above all, son of a horse dealer, had been a bit of a rake. Married at 55, wife (brings him his food) twenty years younger, simple pleasant manner, Aryan; my guess is he married his receptionist. Only university-educated man apart from myself. Range of culture and inter-ests not very extensive.

*Steinitz,* the traveling salesman. Boasts that he knows every joke, of which 99 percent are sexual. (All of these old men like to tell and hear sex-ual jokes.) Is writing the memoirs of his forty years as traveler for Wein-mann's, the coal wholesaler, "in English," constantly quoting Shaw in English. Has had a cataract operation on one eye, is blind in the other. Face of a fat, old woman. Good natured, self-satisfied. Also 67.

*Müller.* The starless leather manufacturer, business in his wife's name. Quiet man, a gentleman. Well into his sixties. Always has a little bottle of schnapps; I get a swig. (And from Steinitz, a pipe of tobacco or a supple-ment to my blackberry tea.)

*Aufrichtig.* Imposing, very tall, white-haired. Works (like Müller) only half days. Seventy-two. Retired farmer. Was tenant of large Silesian es-tates. Retired to a house on the Weisser Hirsch. His daughter, a doctor, broke down, mentally ill—done away with. Father received notice of death.

*Eisner.* The loud, proletarian country Jew, like an old horse dealer. But had a fashion shop in Löbau. The man with the deported idiot son.

The others: Businessmen, mostly shopkeepers. Very unpleasant is a cer-tain *Schein,* clothing shop in a working-class quarter ("600,000M turnover a year in the good times"). Criticizes everything without grasping the sit-uation, a danger to the group. Blum, the foreman (something of a stage character [ . . . ], small, tough, resourceful, puckered-up roguish face, mane of light brown hair): "*We* are already under martial law and *must* work, and everything counts as sabotage—and that goes for *you* more than anyone!" I to him: "We are very happy to be with you; don't pay any attention to the *one* man who is putting the whole group at risk. *We* always stand with one foot in a concentration camp and the other in Poland."

A very hoary, old, little man, *Böhm* by name, very senile, with small, fixed blue eyes, fumbling feebly around.

In time the remainder may also turn into individuals for me.

In the barracks yard there is a coming and going of municipal workers. All very friendly to us wearers of the star. At the heap of cinders an older man came toward us, friendly and smiling: "That's the wrong way to do it; you have to do it like this; it's easier too." I: "It has to be learned. Also my body isn't used to it. In the war I carried ammunition. Afterward I stood at the lectern over there"—I pointed at the TU [Technical University]—"and now I'm shoveling snow here." —

Will I still have time to write my books? Every morning my fingers are numb when I wake up. The blood does not circulate properly anymore. I first became aware of the breakdown of Grete's mind in 1938 in Dölzschen, when she repeatedly told me with a spiteful, radiant smile: "Your fingernails are gray, too, that's a sign of a poor heart." Since then the symptoms have become more pressing.

[ . . . ]

Yesterday afternoon distribution of the *wage packets*. For the days from Saturday, February 14, to Sunday, February 21, I received a provisional payment of 30M, no tax deducted. I informed the pensions office of this secondary income for "snow removal" and wrote to the foreign currency office that I was paying the money into my blocked account, since the works department of the City of Dresden had handed it out to me, despite my declaration that I was not allowed to receive it in person. — The whole thing would be a comedy, if it were not an insult and took up so much of my much more limited time.

[ . . . ]

The hated Estreicher has met his doom. Sent to a concentration camp, which amounts to a death sentence. The man enriched himself at the expense of the defenseless Jews. He will have known too much for the Gestapo.


### February 24, Tuesday evening

While I did not leave the house on Sunday, a storm raged outside—without snow. The next day the whole stretch by the Toll House and down to Kaitz, the whole of the single lane which we had cleared was destroyed again, simply by snow blown from the fields. [ . . . ] All day yesterday we worked to clear a path once more. Likewise today until the morning break. Then Nöthnitzer Strasse had to be cleared; tomorrow we are to go up the hill again. We stood around in the afternoon; toward evening I come home exhausted. Then housework.

Every day the impression grows stronger that a crisis is drawing near.


### February 25, Wednesday, before six o'clock in the morning

In pitch darkness up an hour too early, before five. If I lie down again, I'll oversleep and have to go out unwashed and without breakfast as I did recently. Sometimes if I'm too early I read aloud to Eva—today she was still asleep. So a little time gained for the diary. (In the afternoons there is always so much to be done in the household and so much time is needed to eat one's fill.)

It does me good to be with people who are all older than I am. Most are clumsier, weaker, more sickly than I am, all are closer to death, and all leading quite *unintellectual* lives as a matter of course. All of them get less out of each day than I do, go to bed at nine. Admittedly: Which of them still has business he would like to bring to a conclusion? — Basically no difference between old and young. When the older ones are by themselves and they have no need to maintain an air of dignity, then 90 percent of the conversation is filled with jokes about sex. Apart from that, eating and drinking—just as in the last war. — The serious conversation is of course about one thing: How much longer? [ . . . ]

[ . . . ]

### February 26, Thursday evening

Yesterday spent the whole day a long way out. Cleared Kaitzgrundstrasse along Kaitzbach stream from Mockritz up toward Cunnersdorf. Mountains of snow. [ . . . ] Ate in a primitive barracks. At midday our good foreman, Blum, took his leave of us. Unexpectedly summoned for an examination, perhaps for labor service on the Eastern Front. An older worker took charge of us temporarily. One trembles at every change. I was very careless. Two French prisoners came past; I did not notice that they were preceded by a German, who was in charge of them, and chatted with them for a little while. It can mean concentration camp, if it's reported. How did they feel? — They would like to go back to France. Was I a prisoner too? — Not really, but I wasn't allowed to talk. — They understood. "Il faut que l'Allemagne perde la guerre." — "Faut pas parler!" — As they walked on, one of them said to me: "Bon courage!" (To his question as to why I could speak French, I had said I was a university professor.) —

Today I was *free*, so that I could fetch things from the clothes store and talk to Heise, the lawyer, our Aryan trustee, with whom only Estreicher has negotiated thus far. Then housework all afternoon, now dead tired, and tomorrow shoveling snow again. The lawyer not entirely unpleasant, evidently lives from the administration of Jewish houses, but appears to proceed in a straightforward manner, does not appear to want to squeeze anything out of me. I told him I would hold on to the house to the last, I was in ill health, and my widow Aryan. — At the clothes store I was lent a pair of lace-up boots with thick rubber soles, which were too large, and paid three marks for a secondhand pair of rough woolen work trousers, and four marks for two pairs of thick socks. — No possibility of getting off the snow clearing. For that, I am at the mercy of the Jewish practitioner, Dr. Katz (of whom everyone speaks very badly), who is too afraid to declare anyone unfit for work. —

Yesterday an article about agriculture in the East, which was very much of a damper. It will be a long time before it is capable of providing anything significant for us; the yield of the Ukraine is overestimated, the German difficulties are underestimated. — At the same time, a declaration by Hitler to his old guard, with whom he used to celebrate the Foundation Day of the NSDAP [February 24] in Munich. He could not leave the front, since the thaw was already beginning in the Crimea, and he was making preparations for the offensive. He will carry on the war until the Jews have been exterminated, who for their part had wanted to exterminate the Aryan peoples.

[ . . . ]

### March 1, Sunday

Great tiredness, muscle pains in my calves, sore feet, my hand incapable of guiding the pen. Incapable of intellectual work. Yet the shoveling is carried on very slowly. But constantly in the open air from half past seven until half past five, exerting oneself physically. Too little sleep. If on Sunday I wash myself down thoroughly, listen a little to Eva's playing, make a scanty diary entry, read a few pages aloud, then that is a great deal. I am constantly fighting the need to sleep. —

On Friday morning, to my joy, I met Blum at the Elysium. The group had been given permission to use the E bus; Blum waited for me. He had been released because of his teeth; otherwise he would immediately have had to go to the East to build roads. On the way we talked about the war, he thought as I do. Worked on the road along the Kaitzbach stream again. Big, beautiful winter landscape, stretching into the distance, high-lying fields, the snow glittering in the sunshine, the stream incised far below, bare trees beside it. A four-in-hand, powerful workhorses pulling their coal wagon from the road into the field: impressive image. [ . . . ] On Saturday to Zellscher Weg again, then finished clearing Langemarckstrasse and its continuation to Kaitz. (We had begun the job at the beginning of the week, after the storm last Sunday, then abandoned it again. Our orders are very muddled.) Saturday work ended at half past one. At home: housework. Ida Kreidl and Frau Pick were here in the evening. I could hardly keep my eyes open. —

About two weeks ago, we heard that Müller, cigarette manufacturer, 72 years of age, was taken to the concentration camp with Estreicher. Three days ago: The Community has been notified of his death. Concentration camp is now evidently identical with a death sentence. The death of the person transported is notified after a few days. — My friend Professor Wolff, Julius Ferdinand Wolff of the *Dresdener NN*, has committed suicide with his wife after several house searches. Admittedly, he is said to have been going blind.

Inquiry from the foreign currency department "for the purpose of reassessing your monthly allowance." Apparently there are going to be very considerable reductions. Constant fear of house searches. The Gestapo are said to be creating the most dreadful havoc.

In the East the Russians are attacking day after day.

## March 3, Tuesday evening

Yesterday a considerable thaw, morning and midday breaks in a little old house in Altzschertnitz; from there we cleared Münzmeisterstrasse as far as the Südhöhe road. Then a long walk down to Mockritz, to Gostritz, worked on a road running toward Nöthnitz–Bannewitz across a deeply cut stream. Hobbled home very painfully on damaged feet. The roads supervisor made a short speech: He had been very satisfied with us, he hoped that we would continue to be lucky, he had recommended us to his colleague; admittedly, there was someone there with one of those (circling movement on his lapel, indicating a Party badge). Apart from that, there should be only three more working days for our group, discharge would be on March 5. I can hardly believe it; it would be too good to be true. Taking leave of Blum turned out very brief and ill-humored. We stood around together for the last quarter of an hour and were very exhausted.

[ . . . ]

So today I had to be at Wölfnitz Inn at a quarter to eight. Torture getting there. Out of the house before seven. Black ice, darkness. The no. 9 at Wasaplatz so packed that I got on only after begging to be allowed to do so because I had to get to work, and I had to cling onto the edge of the platform. Changed to the no. 7 at Opernplatz.

## March 6, Friday

Yesterday, after twenty days duty (on one of which I was not present), the group was discharged. Slip in third "wage packet": 121 working hours at 70 pfennigs an hour = 84.70, of which 12.07 is income tax, leaving 72.63— but I think another 15 percent Jews' "social compensation" is deducted as well. The foreign currency office has already inquired, how much I earn "monthly" on labor duty. I should always pay my wages into my blocked account, I was not allowed, for example, to credit it to my allowance.

So on the last three days travel through the city to Wölfnitz. From there march to Altgorbitz. The usual road-workers' barracks in a corner of the village, Lesskestrasse. From there marched up the hill to the first houses of Pesterwitz. A very icy and snow-clogged road toward Gorbitz to be cleared. Usual work, usual view over a snowy landscape, not very different from before. Only this time the knowledge: Dölzschen and your house are close by! Then another repetition of earlier feelings: You used to drive your car here! Regnavi—sum sine regno. Everything else also repetition aside from very minor variations. The morning passes more quickly, the afternoon is hard, but we stop about an hour before five. The long march back together, now the long journey home as well. On the first day, the morning break came right at the beginning, before we climbed the hill to our place of work. Then the time until midday was endless and very exhausting. Tuesday and Wednesday were like early spring: thaw well under way, a greenish shimmer on the trees. Three hares were playing on the snow covered field. Unfortunately, the little Hitler Youths were playing in Gorbitz and followed us, jeering and shouting. Then yesterday morning, snow fell again; very pretty in the gray of dawn was the way the snow stuck to all the trees in the Great Garden, marking every contour. Increasingly cold as we worked, and a strong icy wind blew without letup. It made itself particularly felt when we changed our workplace after the morning break. There is a track across the fields from Kesselsdorfer Strasse to Nausslitz. Here the wind was terribly strong. Mittens and shovels iced up, the grip slipped in one's benumbed fingers, the icy snow stuck to my shovel blade, my face stung, my nose ran, my eyes hurt, I felt dizzy. Even the foreman found the situation unbearable. But we had to wait and stay where we had been working until the roads supervisor turned up with our payment. [ . . . ] The new people: It was not quite as sociable as when working around Kaitz, but the atmosphere still humane and courteous. The roads supervisor an elderly and rather phlegmatic man without the warmth of the supervisor over there. The foreman, a little humpbacked and bad-tempered-looking, but friendly in a comradely fashion, did his best to chase away the little Hitler Youths on skis who swarmed around our hut on the last day; himself not very fond of hard work, considerate toward us, using a pickax to break up the stuff that had been frozen together; in favor of finishing early—"but don't let anyone see you!" Unconcealed philo-Semite: Traveled all over Bavaria as a peddler for a Jewish textile company, Sommerfeld, in Chemnitz, taking the goods with him in a car, and remains very attached to the Jewish house. It seems as if very many people in the municipal street-cleaning department—the pen slipped, I had to lie down on the settee for a while, after all I have been up since five o'clock—were in other professions before '29, '30, and then, after unemployment, found refuge in municipal employment; Blum was a glassblower, the new foreman a peddler, his colleague a roofer. This roofer the most interesting man in all the three weeks. The Party member we had been warned about. Fifty years old, finely chiseled features, a little reminiscent of the Nazi Party's favorite types, enthusiastic worker, chopping up the snow into huge cubes. He soon became friendly and obliging to all of us, chatted, helped, didn't hound anyone. He spoke his mind to Magnus, in part also to me. Already a committed Party member before '33, Social Democratic workmates behaved badly toward him. We were being treated harshly, mistakes were certainly being made—but the Führer did not know about it, and National Socialism as a whole was the only Truth. Convinced of Germany's victory and England's destruction, convinced above all by what the newspapers report—however neither stupid nor brutal. He talked about air-raid drills. I said, Dresden wasn't worthwhile [as a target] for the English. He: Military targets were not what counted for "them." "Just look at Paris!" (Yesterday's attack on German armaments plants there.) "Six hundred dead, 1,000 wounded—and all French, *not a single German!*" But I think for every *one* believer like that there are by now fifty unbelievers. And the proportion of those who are pleased to see us working, or who shout abuse, to those who express sympathy, is probably the same. After we were dismissed, I quickly walked to the tram alone, taking a shortcut, Hofwiesenstrasse. An older man, probably a tradesman, came toward me. "You must be working out here?" — "Yes, clearing snow." — "You must be getting on a bit too." — "I'm sixty." — He, as he walked on, passionately to himself: "That rabble, that damned, godforsaken rabble." It was a consolation for the little Hitler Youths. — During the last few days the loquacious Steinitz, the coal traveling salesman retired, talked about himself and complained about his wife (Aryan, twenty years younger); she gets into a temper, shouts abuse at him, calls him her misfortune, but does not want to get a divorce, because otherwise her financial situation would be so bad, but looks after him touchingly, is hysterical. Schein, the clothing-shop man, got on my nerves with his grumbling and his utter laziness. There was a lot of gossip about the Seliksohns—everyone is on top of everyone else in the Jews' House in Strehlener Strasse. — I came home very exhausted with sore hands and feet; I feel very fatigued today.

According to Kätchen's information from Zeiss-Ikon, where they always know everything, and sometimes it's even true, the group is already going to be "deployed" again next week. Should I nevertheless be granted a longer break, then, after working up my reading notes, I should like to describe the three snow-clearing weeks in the form of a separate study, in the same way as I recorded my days in prison.

The worst thing recently is the constant anticipation of a house search. We are again and again told frightful things about the squads carrying out the raids. —

Today came the ban on using the tram "out of consideration of the repeated undisciplined behavior of Jews on the trams." In the last few months it was preceded by restriction to the front platform, ban on traveling in the rear carriage, ban on traveling by bus. When one hears what Kätchen Sara reports of drivers' remarks, then there seems to be fear behind the ban, a desire to isolate [us]. But journeys to work and from work to home are allowed. Yesterday a circular "for strictest compliance": no "unnecessary correspondence," "purchase and stockpiling of medicines . . . to be restricted to the utmost," "the use of electrical appliances is likewise to be restricted to the utmost," ban on buying or subscribing to illustrated or weekly periodicals. Ban on using food coupons not marked with a J.

In the newspaper: Dentists refuse "cosmetic treatment," because too many are needed in the army. — Annemarie said that there is a shortage of space and of doctors in the military hospitals. But Isakowitz is in London, and Magnus, orthopedist and surgeon, is shoveling snow.

[ . . . ]

The cold more severe again today, the same explicitly reported from Russia. [ ... ]

### March 7, Saturday evening

[ ... ]

The house searches have got as far as Wasastrasse. There Steinberg, the pharmacist, was told: "Why do you not all hang yourselves?" and they *showed him* how to make a noose. Ida Kreidl reported it this morning [ ... ]. The sickening feeling of anticipation. Eva says: "To me the very second when the earth shook in Naples was interesting, the second when our car crashed into the field—I find this interesting too."

### March 8, Sunday morning

The stiffness of my finger joints, my hands going to sleep when I lie down—angina—I must go to the doctor. To whom with this star? Katz, the Jew, is said to be impossible, an Aryan can refuse me or accept me out of pity. People speak highly of Fetscher, who was a young lecturer at the TU during my time as a dean. I must try to forestall another demand to be a laborer. Otherwise, marked thaw, the rooms cold, shortage of coal. —

Conversation at breakfast: Were the shortages in 1918 greater than now? How can one make a comparison? With *what awareness* does the present generation face the shortages, do they experience them more strongly or weakly? — There is as little a science of history (at most we know *what* happened, not *how* it came to pass) as there is a science of aesthetics. — [ ... ] One can always only *interpret* subjectively, not know objectively. [ ... ] Que sais-je? And que sais-*je*? I as a Jew [know] of the present frame of mind of Aryan Germans? ... With all that: Yesterday Ida Kreidl told us: " 'They' were at my brother-in-law's at half past ten on Sunday morning. He had a barber with him, and his ears were boxed because of it." — Hochgemuth slipped Eva ten cigarillos for me yesterday. "How many blows if they surprise me as I'm smoking?" Eva laughing: "How young one will feel if one is hit." — In my desk I found seven unused pencils. How many blows? — Now back to the Levin notes again and this diary page into the reference book.

### Evening

The whole day very happily at home. Read aloud a lot, made a lot of notes on Levin. "They" did not come. The waiting grinds one down. Eva took apart an electric fire, I divided a bundle of pencils among several drawers. Nothing is safe.

[ ... ]

For the two of us the currency office conceded, from April, an allowance of 190M, out of which 84M have to be paid for rent and storage.

Thus only a crippling 53M each for food, gas, laundry, repairs. The reserve at Annemarie's will probably last until the beginning of June. Why think any further? The future is completely dark, the end, *one way or another*, is close.

### March 9, Monday evening

By midday, two-thirds of notes on Levin, volume 2, completed. In the afternoon a time-consuming visit by Steinitz, who brought a couple of interesting books. As he was about to leave, a messenger from the Community brought the order to report for "snow removal" again tomorrow (March 10 to 14). I have not seen a doctor, I submit to everything fatalistically.

### March 15, Sunday

Paid yesterday for the working days Tuesday–Saturday, March 10–14, and absolutely exhausted today. In many respects it was an exact repetition of the first period of laboring. The same roads, across which the snow had been blown once again, on Tuesday, Wednesday, Thursday from the Toll House and over the Kaitzbach stream, the road to Cunnersdorf on Friday and Saturday, starting from Mockritz a) the route from Kaitz to Nöthnitz, b) the Altgostritz–Nöthnitz road. The same works-department huts for our breaks, often a considerable distance from where we were working, the same people in charge: Blum as foreman and a couple of others already familiar to me, as roads supervisor the same tall Guards cavalryman as recently. The same squandering of time with only short periods of work, the same great fatigue simply as a result of all the walking and standing around outside. The last two days were especially dreadful: We stood without shelter in an easterly gale, which swept across the fields without interruption. My hands, my nose, my feet. On the night of the twelfth to the thirteenth (Friday) there had been 20 degrees of frost in the city, up in the open countryside there had been 29 degrees. Around midday the sun brought a thaw—but only wetness, without warmth.

### March 16, Monday

Recovered a very little. — It was really only my workmates who were new. Only leather manufacturer Müller was there from the previous gang. Seventeen people reported; until Friday I was part of a group of 7, then I was together with the whole group. Most were lost in the crowd [ . . . ]. A few stood out: Johann Neumann, by now an old acquaintance, whose company I sought. He was very cheerful and optimistic, once in particular he was quite bumptious when he arrived. He had heard from an "absolutely reliable source" how catastrophic the situation in the East was: "Let's hope the English get here before the Russians, so that we have an

English occupation and not a Russian one." He looked after a Herr Perl, an ailing gentleman in his seventies, urging him to do nothing. The Community had sent Perl out with the best of intentions: As long as he is working, he does not have to "report" to the Gestapo. These demands to report are now a favorite method of torture. The man (or woman) summoned for half past seven. Has to wait, is thrown out, told to come again, and is chased all morning like that. In between he is struck, kicked, even spat on. Threat of prison, which is sometimes made good after eight or ten days. "Reason": with Perl it was a little pack of tobacco found during a house search; with a Frau Neumann, the mendacious assertion that she had walked *through* the Great Garden, whereas in truth she used the permitted road bordering it. (But a Gestapo driver saw her "coming out.") They asked Perl: "With whom does your son associate in England?"

With Neumann, many a conversation on Jewish things in connection with Levin, on which I had just finished making notes. — Schleimer, a (business) representative. Somewhat boastful, usually good-humored, at times quick-tempered man. The interesting thing about him was how he wallowed in wartime memories. — He played the role of the hero, whose services remain secret. Much talk about war service also with Neumann. Altogether: The Jews' favorite topic, immediately after the Gestapo and the current situation: their participation in the 1914–18 World War.

In the large group: Dr. Fried, tragic figure. Late sixties, south German army doctor, surgeon-major, then medical officer in the Pensions Office (assessor on invalid cases). Completely alone. Sons overseas, his wife sclerotic and mentally ill, a couple of weeks ago he took her to a Jewish hospital in Koblenz. She was "raving a little sometimes," "could not hold her urine and excrement, we had so few underclothes and had to wash each piece ourselves, the nurse was evacuated, I could no longer manage it all. On the way there she was as gentle as a lamb, she looked charming, with a film star's head, once we had untwisted her braids, I did not even know that she has such a fine head. An SS soldier said: 'You have to stand, Jew!' I showed my identification as surgeon-major and war veteran. 'I don't care! You stand!' Later a policeman in uniform said to me: 'Take my seat, sir, sit down!' " The man cooks, sews, looks after himself all alone. Does not make a desperate impression.

Dr. Glaser, the lawyer, long, snow-white hair, mid-sixties [ ... ]. Garrulous—half senile, half touched by genius. Is a "privileged" Jew (mixed marriage with Christian children), wears medal ribbons. Is not a member of any church and philosophically a monist. Was wealthy. Art collection ("degenerate art") [ ... ], plays the violin. We are to be invited.

Standing out from the crowd: a Hungarian Jew, blond, European-looking, with the Hungarian's broken-sounding German. Naturalized, his Aryan wife has a shop for baby clothes on Prager Strasse and is now requesting him as a worker. He tells us that in Hungary the Jewish laws have gone through *only to a very limited extent. No star,* doctors still practicing. Seliksohn, about whom there is so much gossip. Neumann was almost blunt in warning me about him, they shoveled coal together. I asked: "Is there anything definite against him?" — "I don't know of anything, but he's too forward and I find him very disagreeable." On the very first morning Seliksohn invited the two of us over. Eva was for accepting. To us he is interesting. He makes no bones of his Communism. [ . . . ]

On our way back on the last day: Gimpel; seemingly cheerful, harmless man, mid-fifties, Jew's star, spectacles, the left lens black. Tells me: artist, was chairman of the Dresden Association of Graphic Artists, well known for his advertisement designs. — Going blind, left eye completely blind, cataract, right eye badly affected, Berlin professor does not want to risk an operation. Because of high blood pressure, the still partially sighted eye must not be strained in any way. The local ophthalmologist, Aryan, says: "Working in the snow is very bad for you, I shall tell the Jewish medical assessor so." In this case, as always, Dr. Katz, the Jewish assessor, refuses a certificate—the man has to shovel snow. Alleviation: He pretends to shovel, Blum and the roads supervisor were even more patient this time than recently. During the morning break, Blum told Hitler jokes, the roads supervisor opened up to me in a private conversation: How the Nazis had harassed him because he was an SPD man, how the war was lost . . . On one occasion another gang was working close by, workers partly from Austria and Bohemia, partly from Freital. Their mood altogether anti-Nazi. A complete stranger as he walked past me: "Well, Professor, how's it going?" (Blum throws the title around.) — "Thanks, it has to go." — "It won't last much longer!" —

Cohn was at Frau Voss on some kind of errand. He said to Eva in private that he had told Dr. Fetscher, who is treating him, that I was anxious about my manuscripts. Consequently he was passing on a message from Fetscher: I could bring my papers to him, Fetscher. The first and only sign of decent feelings among my colleagues at the TU. —

Fräulein Ludwig sent a fish's head for Muschel—as an Aryan she had got the fish from friends. Fish is exceedingly rare and completely prohibited for the Jewish household. Instruction: Cook the head immediately, burn the bones! The fear of the Gestapo, 90 percent of all conversations among Jews revolve around the house searches. Everyone knows of new cruelties and robberies. — Friedmann, who was arrested recently—a large quantity of wine and bottled fruit is said to have been found in his rooms—is now in a concentration camp.

Friday is very important. At midday on Friday relatives bring underwear for the prisoners in the police cells. As long as the underwear is accepted and exchanged for used underwear, then the man is at least still there. If the underwear is refused, then he has been transported to a concentration camp. Elsa Kreidl comes home almost consoled: "He's still inside." (For four months now—no one knows why.) In the last few days I heard Auschwitz (or something like it), near Königshütte in Upper Silesia, mentioned as the most dreadful concentration camp. Work in a mine, death within a few days. Kornblum, the father of Frau Seliksohn, died there, likewise—not known to me—Stern and Müller, in whose homes the banned pastoral letter had been found. — Buchenwald, near Weimar, is said to be not necessarily and immediately fatal, but "worse than prison." "Twelve hours work [a day] under the SS," says Seliksohn. —

A comfort to Jews in general are the *death notices with a swastika*. Everyone counts: How many? Everyone counts how many still fall "for the Führer."

So, yesterday afternoon in the Jews' House in Strehlener Strasse. A notice on every door: "Here resided the Jew Weiler . . ." — "Here resided the Jewess . . ." These are the people who have been evacuated, whose household goods have been sealed up and are gradually being removed. So first of all to the reviled Seliksohns. Very friendly welcome with real tea and home-baked cake. The woman looks unhealthily puffed up and pale. *One* room. Two beds, good washing facilities, bookcase. The conversation produced nothing new. Except he got worked up about Karl May, "that criminal," and of course he was the Führer's favorite author. We: He could not do anything about it. After that with farmer Aufrichtig for a while, who lives opposite on the same hallway. The Reichenbachs are his subtenants. Aufrichtig's wife, bent by age, an estate manager's wife, almost a stage character, could not be more Aryan. Farming [ . . . ] and the usual weighing up of the possibilities and of when. During our laboring days, Aufrichtig had boasted about a contact and promised me potatoes; this was the ultimate reason for our visit. Now the potatoes had also given out here. However, Seliksohn, a diabetic (Aryan diabetics are allocated vegetables, but *not* Jewish ones), is going to give us a bag of potatoes in exchange for a packet of dehydrated vegetables.

The food shortage gets worse and worse. I nibble whatever the better-supplied Kätchen Sara (she eats less and receives a lot from her mother) leaves lying open or partly eaten. A spoonful of honey, a spoonful of jam, a little piece of sugar or bread. Yesterday a thick, already-cut sausage was lying on the table. I sliced off a minute scrap. Soon afterward I heard Eva chasing Muschel out of the kitchen: He, too, had wanted to steal from the sausage. —

In the newspaper a few days ago: The seven thousand (7,000) Dresden nursery gardens are switching over half of their acreage to vegetables: give them your flowerpots for rearing plants and buy fewer flowers! Now a *ban on Jews buying flowers* has come out. Not a day without a new decree against Jews.

We are in great need of bread, potatoes, and coal.

### March 17, Tuesday

Eva came home from her arduous shopping expedition with one foot completely failing her and had to lie down for a couple of hours. What will happen if the foot trouble gets worse? I am completely tied and am afraid of the street. One of the two women, who for days have been tormented with summons to the Gestapo, falsely accused of having been in the Great Garden, has now, as the ubiquitous expression puts it—"been kept there," i.e., is in prison.

[ . . . ]

I made notes on *Ben-Hur.* [ . . . ] I am slowly coming to grips with Arthur Rosenberg's *Origins of the German Republic.* All of it is intended one day to benefit the final volume of my Curriculum. I have no other choice except to work as if I were completely certain of tomorrow and the day after tomorrow. And yet from day to day I am reckoning on some catastrophe—arrest, disappearance into a concentration camp, etc. — It has been made impossible for me to continue writing, the manuscript [of the Curriculum] is out of the house, I don't have a typewriter. So I shall study whatever I can get hold of. Two things interest me: the rise of National Socialism and the history of Zionism. (I shall not even mention *LTI.* It's always there.)

### March 19, Thursday

[ . . . ]

Que sais-je? I know nothing about the past, because I wasn't there; and I know nothing about the present, because I was there. — That's what goes through my head while reading Arthur Rosenberg's *The Origins of the German Republic,* Berlin 1928.

Eva's foot is very bad once again. The never ending errands, the pavements, the carrying. She stays in bed for a couple of hours whenever possible, then I read aloud. As today *The Man in the Dark: The Life of Sir Basil Zaharoff, the Mysterious European* by Richard Levinsohn (Morus). I shall probably finish the whole of the little volume. Basically the same view of history as the one Hitler always emphasizes: The arms manufacturers bring about world war in order to make money out of it. Except Hitler says *the* Jew is behind the armaments people, and the whole thing is merely the "democracies" doing business and not Germany. Whereas Morus says Krupp is involved as well and clubs together with Patiloff.

### March 20, Friday evening

Today in the newspaper, reductions in the bread, meat, and fat rations (½ pound bread, 3½ ounces meat weekly, 9 ounces fat every four weeks). That, at the time of the greatest shortage of potatoes and vegetables! Also, after a couple of mild days, it is just beginning to snow again. We do not know whether we should be happy or despair. We are very short: no certainty of bread for the next ten days, potatoes for about another four meals, coal for less than a week. — But the impression on the people must be disastrous. — Eva is at an end with her nerves and with her feet.

I am slowly finishing off Rosenberg's *Origins of the Republic.* Tremendously interesting; nevertheless, often I can hardly keep my eyes open from hunger and fatigue. It is very rare now that I stand up after a meal having eaten my fill.

I no longer have the necessary peace of mind to read. I should so like to go on with the Curriculum. But I have had to place all my papers elsewhere. [ . . . ] Also every day I expect a new summons for labor service.

[ . . . ]

### March 22, Sunday

What does Eva always have in her handbag, out of fear of a house search? Soluble vitamin tablets, shaving stick, cigarette tobacco, sweetener.

Yesterday, because of our extremity, Eva went begging to Pirna. She came home with a heavy load: a basket of potatoes, about two pounds of bread, a can of French beans. Bread coupons are supposed to follow; if they don't come, we shall be literally starving as of Tuesday.

[ . . . ]

Yesterday evening with Ida Kreidl and Frau Pick. Treated to home baking. But one constantly has to comfort Ida Kreidl, who is on the verge of collapse, and this morning she was up here again weeping—she cannot bear it any more. Frau Pick, the seventy-seven-year-old, is much more able to cope. — Via Zeiss-Ikon, Kätchen Sara reports new house searches and suicides.

### March 24, Tuesday

So far Annemarie has let us down with bread coupons; Eva exchanged margarine coupons for a four-and-a-half-pound loaf, but how we shall get through the one and a half weeks till the next coupon issue is a mystery. On top of that the complete lack of potatoes. Today Eva taught me how to prepare turnips. I can do it quite well. I find mornings the hardest. Shivering (in the unheated room), feeling hungry and falling asleep with weariness at my desk is usual. Then I look in Kätchen Sara's kitchen to see if I can steal a spoonful of jam or a piece of bread, but that is only possible when there is so much there that she won't notice. And I always worry that she will nevertheless become suspicious. I also keep my miserable secret from Eva, who usually returns from shopping at about two o'clock with a sore foot, heavily laden but nevertheless unsuccessful.

Were at the Glasers on Sunday. The husband somewhat senile. The wife looking youthful at first sight, but then worn-out after all. One daughter, of about thirty years of age, has become mentally ill, one son abroad. "Privileged" marriage. He and Eva played violin sonatas by Mozart and Beethoven. That is, he imagined he was playing. In reality his violin produced only a quiet scratching and no real tone anymore. The Neumanns were there with us. From him I borrowed *History of the Jews in Germany* by Ismar Elbogen (the husband of cousin Regina Klemperer, the brother-in-law of the musician Otto Klemperer), and have already read three-quarters of it, as well as (for reading aloud) a German translation of Disraeli's *Tancred*.

Steinitz was here on Monday afternoon. Very happy when Eva played for him. I had borrowed a couple of books from him recently. Of these I have already worked through Rosenberg's *German Republic*, but cannot manage to finish the notes on it, also I want to keep the book in exchange for something. — After consulting Dr. Neumark, the Jewish "legal adviser," Steinitz had applied for his allowance to be raised, supporting his claim by reference to his wife's Aryan status and to her illness. It really worked. As a result I have made an appointment with Dr. Neumark for Thursday afternoon, to attempt something similar.

The attempt to take the house away from me is now at a very serious stage. Berger, who was so friendly and such an anti-Nazi, has betrayed me. Presumably he succumbed to temptation. He has now, as I have learned from my "Aryan trustee," Heise, the lawyer, become a "political officer"; he recently tried to acquire the house for 12,000M (the remaining 4400M would be needed for repairs!), he has now dug up a legal paragraph, according to which a Jewish house "being used for commercial purposes" can be expropriated. His application is supported by the local authority in Dölzschen. ("The man has the only grocer's shop in Dölzschen," says Eva, "of course he's on good terms with the local bosses!") Heise writes that the legal position will "cause headaches," since my house was only later converted to commercial use by the present tenant. At the same time, the tax office is demanding property tax for the time in which I myself was no longer living in the house. Heise has appealed against this. At the same time, to be on the safe side, he has had me pay him 200M in advance. How long shall I be able to keep up this struggle? My reserves still amount to 643M. Once they are finished, I shall have to pay all taxes from my pension alone. But we have too many worries to bother thinking about any others. We live from day to day for as long as we are allowed to live. One thing *must* happen in the course of the coming months: Either Hitler perishes or we do. At all events the end is near. We intend to await it calmly. Ida Kreidl's example is a warning, she comes to us weeping two or three times a day, or has to be comforted in the street. Again and again she declares that she is depressed, that she has to die, cannot go on anymore; again and again one has to give her new heart. —

At the Glasers, Frau Neumann told us that she spends a great deal of time in the morning and the evening taking essential things out of their hiding place and putting them back in their hiding place. And occasionally she cannot find something again. For example, her husband's briefcase. — The house searches are the nightmare weighing on all of Jewry. New cases all the time of beatings, abuse, thefts of every kind (recently also of money), arrests, summons to the Gestapo (especially feared). Every day I reckon on it being our turn next.

I feel it very badly, that I cannot continue working on the Curriculum (since all my papers have been brought to Annemarie). I read as much as

I can and take notes—but it is in some degree a waste of time after all, and of necessity I proceed unsystematically, always dependent on what I happen to be able to borrow. It is all supposed to be for the benefit of the last book of the Curriculum and of the *LTI*, but the years 1919–1933 remain to be written, and I had to stop writing a few pages before the end of the second volume. In the morning, when I wake up and my hands hurt and my feet are numb, when my throat hurts as I am walking and the pains shoot down my left arm to my hand—then I often think that neither my Dix-huitième nor my Curriculum will ever be concluded. In the morning I usually feel low; in the afternoon I pull myself together.

[ . . . ]

## March 25, Wednesday

Kreidl taken to a concentration camp. The women here in the house keep silent about it, the gossip headquarters at the Zeiss-Ikon factory knows all about it.

Yesterday an elevating Goebbels speech. On the whole, the unusually cold winter had turned out favorably for the Axis powers. The Russians were not "in the heart of Europe," the English were not in Tunis. Naturally, after two and a half years of war, things were a little harder for us as well. Food rations had been reduced, if necessary "radical measures would be taken." (Threats, not bread.) On the other hand, they would try to ease things wherever that was possible, thus, to general jubilation, the radio programs had been "relaxed." (Music, not bread.) A great deal would improve if, despite the tension, we would all treat one another with courtesy.

Almost every day Frau Voss reports the most vehement Communist remarks by the tram drivers. There appears to be a particular hotbed of dissatisfaction here.

*LTI.* Why is "liberalistic" pejorative, "socialist(ic)" neutral? In both cases the ending "istic" does indeed entail a narrowing and a partial undermining, an "as if." Liberal means generous. To be *liberal*, also in the party political sense, therefore, is to be generous or tolerant on every side. Someone who is liberalistic, on the other hand, is only pretending to be liberal. Likewise: *Social* entails a sociability that is to the benefit of society as a whole: Beneficium dare socialis res est—To be charitable is social behavior (Seneca). *Socialist(ic)* restricts the social to a single party or to the political relationship, limits it dogmatically. Comparisons; "pacific" (in "Pacific Ocean") = *peaceful* in general; pacifistic: narrowing it down to the political. [ . . . ]

## March 27, Friday, toward evening

With very great difficulty completed meager catchword notes on Rosenberg's *German Republic*. Very poor state of health. I suffer a great deal from the unheated room, my cold hands, the constant tiredness. —

Recently Seliksohn said in utter seriousness: "I cannot eat pork and black pudding. That's a five-thousand-year-old tradition in my blood." His wife put in: "But you eat ham." — How great an effect does tradition have? What shakes me in Elbogen's *History of the Jews in Germany,* which I have now plowed through to the end and will make notes on, is the precariousness of my position as a German. Equal rights for Jews not until 1848, restricted once again in the 1850s. Then in the 1870s anti-Semitism already stronger again and, in fact, all of Hitler's theory already developed. I knew very little of all of that—and perhaps did not want to know anything of it. Nevertheless: I *think* German, I *am* German—I did not give it to myself, I cannot tear it out of myself. What is tradition? Everything begins with *myself.* No, certainly with my parents. If in his youth Father had accepted the American rabbinate he was offered . . .

I am considering writing an appendix to the second Curriculum volume drawing on my current study reading: *Que sais-je?* Of the events that I witnessed, what did I really experience and how? That would be psychologically interesting and would allow a couple of facts of general importance to be introduced. —

Yesterday at Dr. Neumark's, the very Oriental-looking "legal adviser" (i.e., the lawyer authorized for Jews). On Steinitz's advice, to risk an appeal on the "allowance." Like Steinitz, I deployed an Aryan and ailing wife. A more important factor turned out to be that I am living not on assets, but on a state pension. Neumark's opinion was that the allowance of 190M would most likely be increased because of that. — Neumark's office is by the Kreuzkirche; I had to walk there and back. Neumark, in his early fifties, told me of great resentment in Austria, also expected a speedy end. —

Latest restriction: "It is to be emphasized that Jews are not allowed to store foodstuffs, but only to buy as much as they need for immediate consumption." I asked Neumark how much was one then allowed to have at home (e.g., the whole sugar ration for a four-week period?). He replied, that depended on the Gestapo whenever they searched a house. — Dread of this house search dogs me day after day. The most dangerous time appears to be eight o'clock in the evening.

I am reading Disraeli's *Tancred* with great pleasure. [ . . . ]

*LTI.* Death notices under the swastika: "Sunny," which flourished in the first two years, still appears, but more rarely. "Full of life" appears in at least four out of five notices, and just as frequently the news, by which one is deeply shocked, is "incomprehensible." All three expressions are life-affirming and in this context emphatically unchristian. Religious formulae ("as God wills" and the like) are *very rare,* but the rune signs (ᛉ ᛦ) are also the exception. Now infrequent, no, only less frequent, by no means unusual: "For Führer and Fatherland" and "in proud sorrow."

## March 31, Tuesday

*LTI.* The language brings it out into the open. Perhaps someone wants to conceal the truth by speaking. But the language does not lie. Perhaps someone wants to utter the truth. But the language is more true than he is. There is no remedy against the truth of language. Medical researchers can fight a disease as soon as they have recognized its essential properties. Philologists and poets recognize the essential properties of language, but they cannot prevent language from testifying to the truth.

[ . . . ]

We exchange margarine coupons for bread, we beg and get by. At Ida Kreidl's we made the acquaintance of Frau Fleischer, a gray-haired wearer of the star, godmother of Paul Kreidl. She has evidently transferred her house in Bernhardstrasse to her Aryan son-in-law. Eva went to see her and came back laden like a packhorse and with her foot giving out. At least 20 pounds of potatoes, a jar of French beans, as well as coupons for 4½ pounds of bread. Eva's foot gives out every day—I cannot spare her the errands and the carrying. —

An article by Goebbels in *Das Reich* appears to be disseminated everywhere. "We *had to* reduce the rations; the timing is unfortunate, but we *had to.* Every act of black marketeering will run the risk of a heavy sentence, of the *death sentence."* — Also in recent days: People who travel only for pleasure run the risk of *concentration camp.* At every point now the threat of senselessly harsh punishments. Altogether the senselessness of the very harsh punishments.

## April 2, Thursday evening

Neumark had given me grounds for hoping that my disposable allowance would be increased. The currency office has rejected my application. 190M, i.e., 106M for *everything* aside from rent. *Every* "Jewish household" is permitted the same 100M amount (excluding rent), no matter whether it contains a single person, a married couple, a married couple with a child. Indeed in one case the sum is said to have been allocated to a family of five. I have available reserves at Annemarie's, which will last eight to ten weeks. —

Jews prohibited from entering the railway station; Jews prohibited from engaging Aryan tradesmen "for personal needs." (But the cobbler in the Jewish clothes store is to be evacuated. So where to take one's torn shoes? There are more such question marks. Our dirty laundry has been piling up here since December. Our vacuum cleaner is broken in half.)

I finished reading Disraeli's *Tancred* aloud. [ . . . ]

Today for the first time doubts whether *LTI* really provides the material for a book. Actually it's only about a handful of phrases and expressions. But what should I do with my time now? First, the Dix-huitième was torn from me, then the Curriculum—now I am collecting reading matter that fits in with the *LTI* plan. [ . . . ] Today I borrowed Steinthal, *Über das Judentum* [About Judaism], from Elsa Kreidl, and Eva brought me the first volume of Houston Stewart Chamberlain from Paulig. I still have lying here (from Steinitz) a National Socialist propaganda pamphlet in French: Hans Keller, *La troisième Europe* [The third Europe]. Also I at last want to work through *Die sozialen Strömungen* [The social currents] by Th. Ziegler, the companion piece to R. M. Meyer's *Literatur des 19. Jahrhunderts* [Literature of the 19th century], which I inherited from Gerstle. Thus, for a couple of weeks, I am provided for. I also borrowed the novels *Sanin* by Archebashev and *Friedemann Bach* from Elsa Kreidl for reading aloud.

With all of that my main interest every day is: How shall I get enough to eat? My main desire, to be able once again to uninhibitedly eat as much bread as I need. —

The general situation unchanged. It can go on like this for *years* yet.

### April 5, Easter Sunday, evening

Springlike weather for the first time. — At the Neumanns' in the afternoon; Glaser also there with his soundless violin (Frau Glaser begged off; her mentally ill daughter needed care). [ . . . ] Balance sheet of the holiday: four suicides among the Jews so far. A married couple, summoned to the Gestapo after a house search, took Veronal. A tailor and a businessman hanged themselves in prison before transport to a concentration camp. — New evacuation transports have left Berlin and several other cities. — Against that: From April 15 all public officials will get a revolver. A symptom of the general mood. The tenseness of the situation and, correspondingly, the cruelty in judaeos increase daily. Latest decree: A Jew's star is to mark the front door of Jewish homes.

[ . . . ] I read my way into H. St. Chamberlain. I read a trifling amount of *Friedemann Bach* aloud. — Very difficult to eat one's fill.

A few weeks ago Ida Kreidl brought me a huge stack of writing paper, which she had found among Paul's things. It was hidden in the cellar. I am now using a small part of it—the rest went back to the sheltering dark. Nothing, really nothing at all is safe. Anything can be stolen, anything can be the cause of boundless cruelties. — We have not had toothpaste for weeks. Not to be found anywhere. Nor toilet paper. So far we have managed to buy very small quantities of paper table napkins. We have been unable to get our laundry done since December. I am almost down to my very last shirt and handkerchief. — Eva cut my hair—barbers don't do it (or only as an exception, for which one has to beg). — [ . . . ]

### April 7, Tuesday morning

Yesterday, Easter Monday, not out of the house; the rest of the Easter reckoning reached us nevertheless—via Kätchen: another *two* suicides in the

Turmeck [Jews' House], which was ravaged recently (the fifth and sixth there); dreadful house search in the Judenburg, the big, Jewish tenement block on Strehlener Strasse, where we have visited the Reichenbachs, the Seliksohns, the Aufrichtigs. The Gestapo turned up there, 15 strong, on Thursday or Saturday, at any rate at five o'clock on the day before a holiday, at a moment therefore when everyone had bought their provisions. They took away all the provisions (*ration-coupon provisions!*), fats, meat, vegetables, they found. There is said to be have been no lack of beatings.

I read a lot of Chamberlain and repeatedly fell asleep over the book, partly because of general exhaustion and, *literally*, pangs of hunger, partly because of my inability to understand philosophical writing. It is astonishing that I have made my career with such narrowly limited intellectual abilities. (Equally astonishing: with so little knowledge of my subject!)

The only cheerful impression at this time in which every day is more burdensome: that it already gets light so nice and early now. We still suffer from the cold—but at least the battle with darkness is over.

### April 11, Saturday morning

Each day brings a change for the worse in the general Jewish situation and in our particular situation, and each day I feel my heart failing more and more. I have to stop in the street, my throat hurts so badly. I tremble and feel faint before any excitement. — We are sure to lose the house now, and it is as good as certain that we shall not be paid a penny. The penultimate state of things was: Berger wanted to get the house in return for payment of the mortgage, the remaining sum (at least 4,600M) would be swallowed up by necessary repairs. Heise, impartial in his own way, refused, as I had not given my consent. Berger and Dölzschen authority declared: The house was now being used for "commercial purposes," so it could be expropriated immediately. Heise objected: But it was a private home when it was let, the case has to be clarified, and I had not given my consent to the sale. [ . . . ] Yesterday Kätchen told us from Jewish sources that Köhler, the Party representative at the Jewish Community, called "the Jews' Pope," that Köhler "was foaming at the mouth at the philo-Semitic Heise." — Early this morning a registered letter from the "President of Bautzen Administrative District": Heise is no longer trustee, his place is taken by a real estate company. That means, therefore, that the house will be wrung from me. All efforts, worry, everything that has been put into it, in vain. —

Nor will anything come of raising the allowance. The regulations change from day to day, from place to place, according to whim. "The pension remains disposable, it's earned income": at the beginning Neumark relied on that, that's how he had got Steinitz's application through.

Now they say: Pensions are savings, count as assets, are not disposable. Then Neumark wanted at least to extract another five marks a month for me, because my Aryan wife has problems with her foot, and when she goes shopping in town has to eat lunch there. A doctor's certificate is now being demanded for that, which I shall have difficulty supplying.

In connection with these efforts, I came into somewhat closer contact with the Glasers. He wrote to me that he knew what to do, I went to see him, but instead met with his wife and (for a moment) his daughter; the couple visited us the next day. The advice was trifling: Eva, as an Aryan, should approach the currency office herself. But there she is granted only, case by case, what she can prove she needs for herself alone (for a dress, for a journey). Glaser is a curious mixture of senility and eccentricity. He is a musician and does not notice, that he does not get a note out of his violin. He is an art collector (engravings, etc.), he had read the Zola section in my history of French literature and attacked me stubbornly, because I declare Zola's determinism and his optimistic hopes of education to be contradictory; he himself has written commentaries on tax law. He does not appear to concern himself excessively with his family. He lived in Berlin for two years, he roams around the streets and in his thoughts. (He is "privileged" and does not wear the star.) Worries seem to be left to his likeable wife, who must be in her fifties. She grumbled a little to me recently. The daughter, a quite good-looking little blonde of thirty, is mentally ill, is afraid of people, of her own relatives, suffers from feelings of inferiority—sanatorium and psychoanalysis have not helped at all, there is a risk of suicide. She is a master dressmaker, she used to have a flourishing business, now survives only with difficulty. She declares she "is unable to cut out anymore." Her mother helps her. There is supposed to be a son as well—doing land-labor service somewhere. The whole atmosphere very depressed. "My husband doesn't notice it so much . . ."

What we heard from the Turmeck, about the dismissal of the "philo-Semitic" Dr. Heise, is true. Detectives came to make inquiries because of the seven suicides. They were thrown out by the Gestapo.

New decree in judaeos: [ . . . ] Even on the way to work Jews are permitted to use the tram (in Dresden) only when the distance from home to place of work is more than five kilometers [three miles], in Berlin more than seven kilometers [four and a half miles].

We are now facing complete starvation. Today even turnips were only "for registered customers." Our potatoes are finished, our bread coupons will last for perhaps two weeks, not four.

### April 12, Sunday

What have we been talking about every Saturday *for months* with Ida Kreidl and Frau Pick? (Yesterday, by the way, downstairs again, instead of up here: downstairs there's heating, and downstairs there are still cakes sometimes—we are the beggars of the house, and Kätchen has to do labor service.) About the most recent house searches and suicides. When and how will the house search take place here? About the evacuees. Are they still alive? No news for months now. Shall we have to go? How much longer? Will they murder us first? — Yesterday something unheard of. After five months a sign of life from Ernst Kreidl: *A card from Buchenwald*. The joy at it was shattering. He is alive, he is not in Auschwitz, he is permitted to write every two weeks and receive post, he is permitted 15M a month—one can hope that he will survive!

What Kätchen reported today about a colleague at work is both characteristic and consoling. He was held in the Dresden police cells for three weeks, because he had signed a letter without "Israel." He had an easy time of it. Work together with Aryans, *good warders,* tolerable food. The warder told him not to lose heart, it would not last much longer. On leaving: If they bother you too much, or if you don't have enough to eat, "then just sign your name without Israel again"! You'll be all right with us!

### April 18, Saturday toward evening

Put aside the diary for a whole week, took notes on Chamberlain, in order to give back the first 500 pages (a volume in itself) to Paulig. Afterward Eva's foot, which gets worse every day, was so bad, that I could not expect her to tackle the winding staircase there. Shopping in town is becoming ever more troublesome and unrewarding (one follows on the other!). Add to that begging trips for potatoes (to Pirna and to Frau Fleischer, whose house on Bernhardstrasse is a long way out).

This morning a card from Frau Neumann: I had comforted her husband so well once before, he was very depressed, could I visit him, without revealing that it was at her suggestion. I went there. Just outside our house, a young man, blond and brutal-looking, shouted from his car: "You wretch, why are you still alive?" Perhaps a Gestapo creature. I found Neumann alone at home; he looked thin and pale. To begin with I asked him about a source of potatoes—at the start of the winter, the Neumanns had said they were getting regular supplies and were not suffering from a shortage. I also received a bagful from them as a present. Neumann told me: Nine Gestapo men had been there—not a house search, merely an inspection of the apartment with a view to taking it over. The men beat him without cause, hit him in the face and spat at him; they broke a hanukkiah; it was since then that he had been so downcast. I heartened him, it helped. His wife came—delighted, he was already looking better, my paternal inheritance was making itself felt! A pity only, that the rabbi has no effect in his own home and on himself!

### April 19, Sunday

From the week before last: Glaser wrote that he knew what to do in the case of our disposable allowance business. I went to see him and found him alone with his accordion. At my urging, he picked it up and played for a while. He said: "I play the violin quite tolerably—I can't play the accordion." Self-criticism! Perhaps my "quite tolerable writing ability" is no different from Glaser's violin playing, which produces only a faint scratching sound. As regards the allowance, Glaser was no help at all. Another Jewish lawyer here had helped Dr. Simon, I should ask this other lawyer what to do. But Dr. Simon is licensed to treat Jewish teeth, therefore has an earned income, which means that his case is different from mine. With Glaser, for all his intellectual activity, I always get a definite impression of senility. —

Three men turned up here, I really thought it was the Gestapo to carry out a house search. But it was only "Customs Investigation Department." It concerned Kätchen Sara (who happened to be out); a matter pending for some time. She has spent my share of rent in addition to her allowance, a foolish deception, since it was bound to come out sooner or later; she will certainly have to pay a fairly high fine, perhaps go to prison and will then have a "criminal record." But now I have been embroiled in the affair: I should have known that I was not allowed to give any cash to a "safeguarded Jewess." I defended myself: As far as I had known, she had always immediately paid the money into the house owner's blocked account, stating that her own rent made up only half the amount. — I had to go to the Investigation Department, which occupies a floor of a tenement block in Moczinskystrasse, corner of Lindengasse. Chief Customs Inspector Otto, who questioned me and then dictated the statement to a typist, was uncommonly nice and at pains to allow me to display myself to the all-important currency department in all my innocence. [ . . . ] Interesting to me was the man's complete *cluelessness* with respect to the miseries of the Jews. "It isn't far for you to come, Professor, you take the tram from Wasaplatz to Georgsplatz . . . Oh, *you are not allowed to take the tram?*" — During the questioning: "First name?" — "Victor Israel." — "By which name are you known?" — "Victor." — "Fräulein, underline 'Victor.' " What Neumark recently told the Neumanns is of a piece with this civil servant's cluelessness. (He has a furnished room with the Neumanns in Winckelmannstrasse and regularly receives permission from the police to visit his family on the weekends. His wife (Aryan), with his son from a first marriage (Aryan), lives in Werderstrasse. His stepson has taken over the parents' apartment there in his name.) So an Aryan, who was not a Nazi, not anti-Semitic, said to Neumark: "America's entry into the war must really have given the Jews a great lift; I now see many more Jews on the streets than before, they have the confidence to go out again." Neumark retorted that the Jews were more frequently to be seen on the streets because they were forbidden to take the tram. The man was completely unaware of this. —

To Steinitz on Friday afternoon. I had to go there once, so as not to offend him; I did so reluctantly, because he always complains about his sick and hostile wife. She is Aryan and believes that he has brought disaster upon her, but does not want to get a divorce—presumably for financial reasons. Apartment—they still have a whole apartment—in Reichenbachstrasse—has a direct view of the Lukaskirche. At the front door the Jew's star above the bell and "Steinitz" nameplate, in the middle of the door the Aryan wife's visiting card. (Things are similar, but worse, on the floor above us: Ernst Kreidl—at present in Buchenwald—with the Jew's star; in the middle of the door on a very large piece of cardboard: "Frau Elsa Kreidl, Aryan.") Steinitz, who does not look his 66 years (nor does one notice the cataract on one eye), proudly showed me all kinds of books and pictures he has collected. Also the manuscript, written "in English," of the anecdotal history, as he says himself, of the Weinmann coal company in Aussig (Bohemia), whose traveling salesman he was for forty years. He wants to send this history to his boss in the USA and hopes that it will be printed and he will be paid for it; through writing this book he wants to learn enough English so that he can later work as an interpreter and teacher. This time I borrowed the following books: *Jewish History* by Joachim Prinz and H. G. Wells's *The Outline of History*. — His wife arrived, perhaps 15 years younger, behaved quite well, but there is something unpleasant about her face. — At the tram stop Eva was greeted by Lange, the carpenter (in the uniform of a corporal). She went to a pub with him, and he had a beer and talked. He had been in Russia for several months during the winter (until Christmas) as a driver for the military police. Ghastly mass murders of Jews in Kiev. The heads of small children smashed against walls, thousands of men, women, adolescents shot down in a great heap, a hillock blown up, and the mass of bodies buried under the exploding earth. — Typhus raging—vehicles blown up in hurried retreat. — He had also passed through Holland: hostility of the population, closed doors, could not even get a glass of water.

Kätchen Sara wanted to consult Professor Fetscher (my former colleague, who offered, through Cohn, to look after manuscripts and who is said to be very philo-Semitic). At first the nurse at the telephone refused to consider Kätchen's request, after all there were not so many Jews left in Dresden, Dr. Katz, who "treated the sick," would manage. Kätchen mentioned her late husband, the insurance company director, whom Fetscher had known, and now she was told the professor would be pleased to see her in the afternoon. She went there and was received by the nurse, who was in a very depressed state: The professor had just been given a heavy fine for being too friendly to Jews; Frau Voss would have to excuse him, he could not now risk treating her after all. —

A very Austrian-sounding, talkative, elderly man, Steiniger by name, was just up here, wanted to talk to Frau Dr. Klemperer. Reason: He is an Aryan friend of Frau Pick. If he is surprised by the Gestapo during a visit, he wants to come up here and pass as a friend of my Aryan wife. Otherwise he and Frau Pick will go to prison.

The day before yesterday Eva received a mysterious letter, signed "Your Bertel." From the style and the spelling we concluded that it was perhaps from a former maid, but found it quite impossible to put a name and circumstances to it. — The letter was intended for Frau Voss and came from Frau Paul (with the many men), whom I had credited with more education. — The Aryans' justified fear of associating with Jews! The Gestapo rages against every relationship. —

[ . . . ]

The inherited carpet in the dining room, which I have always hated, is thick with dirt; the heavy vacuum cleaner has been broken for weeks. Before Easter I dragged it to a repair shop near Wasaplatz for Eva, but had to take the heavy thing all the way back again because the workshop was too full. "After Easter perhaps." Meanwhile there was the prohibition on employing tradesmen "for private use." I discussed the case with the Steinitzes. Analogy: They have just taken an electric lamp for repair. Justification if need be: 1) The household may be Jewish, but the piece belongs to the Aryan wife. 2) The Jew is obliged to treat his furniture (which he is not allowed to sell!) "with care," and our vacuum cleaner is absolutely necessary for that.

All my shoes are more or less in shreds. The Jewish cobbler at the clothes store has been evacuated. But there is still a Jewish cobbler on Holbeinstrasse; I must walk over to him in the next few days. — Our laundry has not been washed since December. Eva washes a few of the most essential pieces in the bathroom.

English bombers over Germany every day (no longer only at night). But Dresden has been left in peace all winter. Berlin is also quiet. In recent days I felt sad for the beauty of Lübeck. [ . . . ] It appeared to be an English act of revenge—nothing but destruction of art. Yesterday I heard from the Neumanns that there is a big blast furnace plant in Lübeck to process Swedish iron ore. Lange told Eva, he had heard from a comrade, there were still hundreds or even thousands under the ruins, there were 40,000 homeless in Lübeck. Very little of all that may be true, but *something* of it is true, and one [ . . . ] gives much more credence to rumor or grapevine than to the newspaper, which lies and withholds information. — Every couple of days lists of death or prison sentences for black marketeers and food profiteers.

### April 23, Thursday

Numbers. From Berlin, evidently in *all* newspapers, big news. Our submarines have so far sunk two million tons of American shipping. The USA's total tonnage is eight to nine million tons, ergo a quarter has been sunk—ergo an American offensive in Europe is impossible. — On this: 1) How are the two millions calculated? 2) According to Knaur's encyclopedia, in 1925 USA shipping already amounted to 14½ million tons. If one adds to that a) the growth of 17 normal years, b) exceptional growth, as, since 1939, the USA has been participating in the economic war at least, c) everything that the South American states have placed at the disposal of the USA, d) America's enormous expenditure since entering the war—can one not assume four to five times the "eight to nine million tons"?

House searches go especially badly for Jews if tobacco goods are found.

Eva now frequently eats at Steuer, a small restaurant by the market hall and the general post office [ . . . ]. She often sits at the same table with post-women. Two were having a conversation about a theft by another woman (which is punishable with prison or the death sentence). "She so much likes a smoke, she only pinched packets of cigarettes." — "How did she know what was inside?" — "Everything's so poorly wrapped nowadays, half open. Recently at the Henriettenstift, at the Jews' House, I handed over an empty box and the cigarettes, which should have been inside it, one by one out of my pocket . . ." If this conversation is overheard by an extreme Nazi or a member of the Gestapo, then there will be a frightful house search in the overcrowded Henriettenstift with beatings and prison sentences for everyone. —

The Seliksohns were here yesterday afternoon. He is diabetic, and we exchanged dried vegetables for potatoes. Yesterday they brought us 11 pounds, we are to get 55 pounds from them in the next few days. (Our, especially my, principal nourishment, morning, noon, and evening, cold or warm, in their jackets, I am quite bloated as a result.) Seliksohn profoundly pessimistic: It could still take years before the regime here collapses, but if it fell tomorrow, that wouldn't help us either, we would be murdered at the last minute, only a miracle could save us from certain death, our chances of survival stood at one percent at most. — After months of peace there was a very violent dispute with Kätchen about potatoes. She has a big tub full of them in the cellar, they are already sprouting profusely and quite rotting away. She does not want to let us, who are going short, have any. She makes impertinent and tactless remarks, that is her speciality. — I really believed that I had learned to be stoical in my relations with her, the last serious clash took place months ago. But yesterday I lost all patience again. Afterward I always feel ill and reproach myself.

### April 26, Sunday afternoon

Eva's Sunday recreation: "Just to go for lunch, without carrying anything, and walk part of the way into town." It is very important that she gets something to eat there, then more bread is left for me here. — Today she returned with news: at three o'clock "government declaration in the Reichstag." We shall not be able to find out anything about it before tomorrow: Has Sweden been occupied, or Turkey, or Spain? It will be some act of force, for sure, "to forestall the English by a few hours." — Downstairs at Ida Kreidl's yesterday evening, Frau Pick told us an "Aryan" witticism: "Optimists say it will last another six weeks, pessimists, it will last another six months." I am always afraid that it could last for years yet.

Shortages are certainly increasing. But for Aryans to the same extent as for us? We really are hungry. Eva begged a lot during the last few days. Bread coupons from Frau Fleischer. Potatoes from Seliksohn in exchange for a meager amount of dried vegetables. A blocked strip of our potato card was partly unblocked; I pushed a handcart to Jentsch, who stops on Wasaplatz with his barrow, loaded 48 pounds for us, 36 for Frau Kreidl, and she let us have another 11 pounds for doing the fetching. Eva carried two heavy bags from the Seliksohns' supplier in town; I waited for her at the tram stop and carried the bags home. From the market hall, Eva brought the only turnip she could find, 6 pounds. When I cut the thing open, it was completely rotten and stank. I am constantly bloated and full of gas; I stuff a bowl of potatoes into myself two to three times a day; bread, dry, forever in short supply, is an extra delicacy, there is no fat, there is no meat. A large part of our double ration [of meat], which now amounts to 1⅓ pounds a week, is given to the tomcat. We both freeze a lot, I am always tired, Eva (*much* thinner than I) handicapped by her foot, very depressed. — And always the fear of a house search. Yesterday an eighty-year-old aunt of Kätchen's was beaten in the house in Altenzeller Strasse. The recent interrogation at the Customs Investigation Department is not the end of the matter. I have been summoned to the currency office on Thursday; for all my innocence I shall end up with a fine.

*Latest decree:* Jews are not allowed to stand in queues. — Jews must surrender: "Hair clippers—unused hair scissors, combs." Jews are reminded *on pain of severe punishment* to wear the star firmly sewn on, because stars that are pinned or held in place by snaps could be temporarily removed. The combs are a consolation, they reveal extreme shortage—nothing is too wretched for them.

Just as much a consolation, almost, is the visit I pay to the new house trustee; the name of the company is Schrapel, that of the owner is Richter, in Victoriastrasse. I had no reason to expect anything but a bloodhound, because as such he has been imposed on me; instead I encountered a secret ally—*that* is how much the Party can now rely on its chosen people! That is a comfort, even if it does not help me in the end. Richter, a man in his thirties, shook my hand, carefully closed the door on the secretary next door, said Heise had been forced to resign, because he was too friendly to Jews. If he, Richter, did not accommodate those people a little, I would have a third trustee in a couple of months, which would be no good to me, but he would like to help me; he was aware of our inhuman situation. (I spoke my mind when I realized what his views were.) He reported: He had already offered a new mortgage, but conversion of the loan required permission from the Party (that is, from district headquarters, that is, from Köhler, the brutal "pope of the Jews"), which would not be forthcoming since the local Party official in Dölzschen was in league with my tenant and prospective purchaser. (I spoke my mind again.) However, he, Richter, had another plan and some hope of success. Dölzschen district had cash available, he would offer it the mortgage. It was permitted to take a higher percentage from a Jew than from an Aryan. Köhler in turn would believe that if the village took over the mortgage, then the house was half lost to me anyway. Which was not in fact the case. I said it was most important to me to keep the house, again pleaded my heart problem and the interests of my Aryan wife, but said as I left: "It cannot last so very long anymore." We assured each other of the utmost mutual discretion; there is to be no written communication. — I do not believe that the house will be saved, but the man's attitude did me good. —

[ . . . ]

### April 28, Tuesday

Hitler's Reichstag speech on Sunday, April 26. Going by that, it is no longer five minutes to twelve, but 11:59. He talks about how close catastrophe was last winter. He says he is better prepared for the next one. So when will it end? He says the outcome will be decided in the *East*. But what about England? But what about the USA? Incomparably more important: He says he has only rarely had to resort to "harsh" measures, where obedience broke down. (So it has broken down!) Most important of all: He demands the right to be allowed to get rid of officers, civil servants, *judges*, instantaneously, without due process. Very important here the expressions: "sentenced to be cashiered" or "remove from office and position" "without regard for 'duly acquired rights' " (three times, afterward once again used by Goering). Cashiering > officers, "duly acquired rights" are very old terms from the civil service code. — It's mad, it's tyranny outdoing itself, it reflects the utmost insecurity, if someone already long-invested with all dictatorial powers once again demands what he already possesses; if a sultan expressly declares that he himself will directly intervene in the justice dispensed by his judges, if they practice merely "formal law." Linguistically amusing once again the relationship to numbers. "Napoleon had to cope with 19 degrees of frost, I had to cope with minus 50 degrees and once with 60 degrees. Even my winters are twice as grand as other people's winters! And yet I am still victorious." Still on numbers: the worst winter for 140 years. — The concentration of hate has this time turned into utter madness. Not England or the USA or Russia—*only*, in everything nothing but *the Jew*. — Pay attention to the mixture of hide-and-seek and open threat. 11:59, but shall we live to see the end of the day? It has by now become a firm rule: On the day after a house search there are suicides. We heard of the new case at the same time as the Hitler speech. A couple called Feuerstein, living in Altenzeller Strasse, had been pillaged, then summoned to the Gestapo and beaten and kicked there; during the night the people were found dead in their gas-filled kitchen. — From day to day I wait for the house search to take place here. The apprehension is always worst in the evening between seven and nine. No doubt wrongly, for the squads are said to appear at any time of day. They are said to steal *everything*: even food that has been bought on coupons, writing paper, postage stamps, leather briefcases. They are said to drink up skimmed milk, etc.

I am reading Arthur Eloesser, *Vom Ghetto nach Europa* [From the ghetto to Europe]. The effect of LTI on the Jews is worth a chapter on its own. But to what extent will my language history be only "camouflaged" intellectual history? No, I must always hold on to this: in lingua veritas. Veritas is part of intellectual history; lingua provides a general confirmation of the relevant facts.

[ ... ]

### Toward evening

Do Hitler's speeches still have an effect after all? An older worker (*older* and *worker* in all probability!) called to me from his bicycle: *"You damned Jew!"* Something like that makes me unsure that it really is 11:59.

A German Jew, no matter of which profession, can write nothing today without placing German-Jewish relations at the center. But must he, for that reason, capitulate before National Socialist views, and must he adopt the language of the National Socialists? Arthur Eloesser, once the open-minded and German theater critic of the *Vossische Zeitung*, does both without reservation.

### April 29, Wednesday morning

Another house search, another suicide. A physician, a Dr. Korn, Catholic-Jew, wife Aryan. Pillnitzer Strasse. The Aryan wife was beaten; the husband was supposed to report to the Gestapo next morning. Suicide during the night. The usual. Kätchen brings the news home from the factory. In addition the squad's pronouncement: "We'll make sure that none of you gets out alive." In the newspaper, summing up the Reichstag session, it was stated once again, that the Führer henceforth has the right, approved by the Reichstag and therefore by the people, not to adhere to articles of law and prescribed procedures, [and the right to] intervene directly in everything. From that and from the Jewish aria a path leads straight to the methods of the Gestapo.

### May 3, Sunday afternoon

The uninterrupted hauling, brushing, and eating of potatoes is slowly getting on my nerves. I have to be grateful that a few coupons are released, that acquaintances give us their share, because otherwise we would starve. But in the long run eating nothing but potatoes is terrible. Eva is not quite so badly off, because at lunchtime she manages to find a "meal of the day" somewhere, even if a pitiful one, and because she needs smaller amounts than I. —

Last Thursday morning at nine I was questioned at the currency office, Amalienstrasse. Much more brusquely than recently at the customs investigation department. "You were an accessory—you have already admitted knowing of the existence of a blocked account." It took a long time, before I was able to explain what I had already explained the first time. It will not help me much: I had not personally satisfied myself, that Voss really was passing on the money immediately. I am required to attend again on Wednesday. — From the currency office I went to my new trustee, Richter. He said that there was an "80% likelihood" that Dölzschen village would take over the mortgage on my house. But will that help me? As principal creditor the local authority will harass me more than ever. Everything depends on how long the government holds out. "It is very solidly organized," said Richter.

We spent an afternoon with the ill-famed and very interesting Seliksohns, from whom we took 55 pounds of potatoes in exchange for a small amount of dried vegetables. Seliksohn again and again attacks the "comedy" of my baptism, tries to win me back for national Jewry. He lent me Holitscher's *Reise durch das jüdische Palästina* [A journey through Jewish Palestine]. I have just finished taking careful notes on it. Quite unconverted. The Zionist Bolshevists are pure National Socialists! But I found the book uncommonly interesting. My studies are very curious now. Chance—books I find in acquaintances' apartments. Directed chance—I grab everything that is suitable for my plan. It must be of help either to the *LTI* or to the Curriculum or both. I have to address these things. But there's always the thought in my mind: probably *nothing* will be finished, neither *LTI,* nor Curriculum, nor Dix-huitième. I shall fall victim either to angina or to the Gestapo. I am never free of fear of a house search, I am never free of extreme tiredness—I fall asleep as I am reading and writing, walking gives me pains in my heart. I confidently preach to others that it is "11:59," but I am far from believing it myself.

[ . . . ]

At Zeiss-Ikon there is a "kindergarten" in the Jews' section. Jobs that have to be done with a magnifying glass by very young eyes. Girls of 15 and 16 work there. Protection of young people has been expressly annulled for Jews. Last week these children had to work day and night shifts so that they were working 24 hours out of 48; they are paid 27 pfennigs an hour.


### May 7, Thursday lunchtime

At last a little warmer and more springlike, but the coldness in my hands, the tingling of the frost in my numb fingertips persists.

Currency office again yesterday morning. 150M fine for "knowingly abetting." I objected to the "knowingly." "I am not in a position to argue with you; if you do not comply, I shall pass the matter on to the State Prosecutor—you're getting off lightly, I could have called in the sum total paid to Frau Voss, that is 1175M." I signed. Financially I am no worse off. Kätchen had the rent reduced, had the difference of 5M deducted, backdated for 13 months; she is also contributing 100M toward the fine from what she keeps under the mattress. But it's depressing enough: I now have a "conviction" (my blackout sentence was a summary punishment, this business, on the other hand, goes onto my "police record"), also for three months the department is at liberty to express its dissatisfaction at my "compliance" and to reopen the case. All I need now is for the Gestapo to sit up and take notice of it . . . I feel much closer to a house search, evacuation, etc., than before the affair. — Kätchen has had the stuffing knocked out of her and is contrite, but what good is that?

From the currency office I went to the only Jewish cobbler, in Sporergasse. The man has to work for *all* star-wearers and is overwhelmed. He refused to accept more than one pair, as an act of charity it will be ready in four weeks time; in general he requires eight weeks, and in the next few days he will have to stop taking on new work altogether. In Holitscher's *Palestine Journey*, there's a verse from a Yiddish folk song: "Ich bin a armer Chaluz, /a Chaluzl aus Poilen;/ich lauf auf Stiefelach,/Stiefelach ohn' Soilen" [I'm a poor lad,/a poor lad from Poland;/the boots I walk in/are boots without soles]. I recite it all the time now.

It is by now a standing arrangement that Steinitz comes here on Monday afternoons. He brings a little tobacco. Sometimes (rarely) he gets a cup of tea. He recovers from his wife, who is very Aryan and very hysterical, he reports what he has heard of vox populi; Eva plays the piano. He spoke with some pleasure of the Aryan vox populi. But how long will it be before there's an explosion, and will we live to see it?

Yesterday afternoon Seliksohns here. Similar conversations, similar mood.

[ . . . ]


## May 8, Friday midday

"Jew sow, you only have young so you can bring them up to be rabble-rousers!" Gestapo pronouncement to seventy-year-old Frau Kronheim, who had been "summoned," as her daughter told us yesterday. (To be "summoned"—to be sent off on hour-long walks, to report for repeated abuse and blows, that is the usual torture following a house search.)

But yesterday also this. On Wasaplatz two gray-haired ladies, teachers of about sixty years of age, such as often came to my lectures and talks. They stop, one comes toward me, holding out her hand, I think: a former auditor, and raise my hat. But I do not know her after all, nor does she introduce herself. She only smiles and shakes my hand, says: "You know why!" and goes off before I can say a word. Such demonstrations (dangerous for both parties!) are said to happen frequently. The opposite of the recent: "Why are you still alive, you rogue?!" And both of these in Germany, and in the middle of the twentieth century. —

I was just coming back from the Marckwalds'; Frau Pick had told me I should pay them a visit; I would be doing a good turn. Villa in Wiener Strasse, close to Strehlen railway station. Divided up among a number of Jews, internal staircase, one reaches the various parties by way of a common room. Marckwald, whom I did not know, a paralyzed gentleman of

seventy years of age, mentally altogether intact, but legs completely paralyzed by some mysterious illness, sits—as he has done for years—in an
armchair, his sixty-year-old wife nurses him, tall crutches are close to his
chair. Cut off from the world. He was a farmer, an official at the Saxon
Chamber of Agriculture [ . . . ]. He and his wife are congenial, educated
people. He was pleased to hear about other things, for once, apart from
house searches. He has already had one that was as bad as can be (his wife
was beaten). The couple were baptized decades ago—she dare not call on
her Aryan friends anymore, their children are abroad. The husband—they
were driven out of their own apartment of course, sits at the table, has solitaire cards in front of him, reads. ("My favorite authors, to whom I turn
again and again: Reuter and Fontane.") [ . . . ]

The house in which the Jewish cobbler lives belongs to the Jewish community. It wants to install a Jewish barber there as well; to this end the circular recently requested scissors for cutting hair, and unused combs.

For months a very frequently repeated version of the war-death notices
reads: "Deeply shocked . . . still incomprehensible [to us] . . . we received
the painful news . . ." "His greatest wish, to see his loved ones again, remained unfulfilled." Then, the day before yesterday, a letter from an officer serving "at the most exposed part of the front": This "greatest wish"
distorted and degraded the sacrifice of the soldier, out in the field he
thought above all of his heroic duty. The home front should likewise act
heroically and pull itself together — The letter is without question written
to order, is without question printed in all the German newspapers and
will without question have its effect. From now on the version that goes:
"For Führer and Fatherland" — "in proud sorrow" will dominate. —

I fight constant tiredness; I regularly fall asleep at my desk, especially in
the mornings (as today).

What kind of wishes go through my head? Not to be afraid every time
the doorbell rings! A typewriter. To have my manuscripts and diaries by
me in the house. Use of a library. Food! Cinema. Car. —

The last war was such a decent business.

## May 11, Monday

On May 10 there was a commemorative article in the newspaper: The offensive in the West began on May 10, 1940. For me the time is divided up
like this. In spring 1940, we were just moving into the Jews' House. I was
very depressed: driven out of our house and Hitler seemingly the ultimate
victor. Then the summer turned out a tiny bit better than I had feared: England held out, and Eva's foot improved. Summer 1940 is the time of our
beautiful, long walks. There was also plenty to eat, bread was easy to get
without coupons, fish was available in abundance. — The summer of 1941
saw the end of our beautiful long walks. If one was not in a restaurant by
six, the acceptable dishes were sold out. But after dinner we took the bus
to the Toll House, drank our apple juice, walked home, and had plenty of

tea and bread there. At home we also often feasted on fish. Now here are the first fine days of spring, the prelude to the summer of 1942. Since September 19, 1941, I am no longer allowed to go into a restaurant, I go out on the street only if it is absolutely necessary, and as it is getting warm now, I shall restrict going out even further—because I do not want to have the loathsome star sewn on my jacket, where I would constantly have to look at it, and so I am forced to wear a coat. And eating: sheer hunger. In the last few days the quality of the bread has also grown worse and become more like that in the last war: It has a bitter taste, a gray color, is said to contain turnip (the turnip that is nowhere on sale). Perhaps there is some comfort in all of that: the prospect of an end before the next winter. But perhaps it is only a false prospect after all? Here and there one hears people say now that the Americans will probably attack by way of Murmansk.

The tyranny grows worse with every day—probably also a comfort, just as the deteriorating bread is. House search in the Güntzstrasse old people's home. Women between 70 and 85 years of age spat on, placed face to the wall, cold water poured over them from behind, their food, which they had bought on coupons as their weekly ration, taken from them, the filthiest words of abuse. — Eva wanted to buy black silk thread. It is given out only for mourning clothes, if proof of death is authenticated. — An article in the newspaper, "Successful swoop on Jews in Magdeburg-Anhalt district." It brings a blush to the cheeks of the suffering national comrade: The Jews were found to have whole chests full of foodstuffs, and on top of that the criminal Jews had been insolent to the police. Why do they lie so shamelessly? So many Aryans know how cruelly the Jews are being treated. Do they want to justify themselves, do they want to prepare the way for new "measures of atonement"? — Frau Pick has an Aryan friend, gray-haired man, boisterous Austrian. He, Steiniger, comes upstairs to introduce himself to us; if the Gestapo surprise him, he's visiting Eva, who now has her own calling card on the front door, to the side of the Jew's star and without a "Sara"—(but not like Frau Kreidl upstairs, whose husband is in a concentration camp, who has the word "Aryan!" in big letters and with an exclamation mark). Yesterday, as a Sunday treat, Steiniger brought me 1 cigarillo and 4 pounds of bread coupons: He works as a bookkeeper in a small bread factory—which, furthermore, is threatened by closure, because it has no gasoline to make deliveries. —

We shall be unable to increase our 190M limit inclusive of rent. Eva was supposed to provide a doctor's certificate about the disablement of her foot. That would have been possible only through Hugo Krüger, who x-rayed and treated her torn tendon in 1927. She called on the man, who is no longer practicing. He had aged to the point of being senile, and at his clinic, which has been handed on, the records for that year had already been destroyed. If Eva wanted to turn to another doctor now, then lengthy examination and observation would be necessary—and the outcome would be doubtful, since the intimidated doctors are all too sparing with certificates, and especially so when it comes to cases that are directly or indirectly Jewish, and since Eva's foot is good for days at a time and swells up and fails her only when she overtaxes it. [ . . . ] Money? The reserves in Pirna will last two, three months, as they have now been topped up by Kätchen Sara—and how will things stand in two, three months, what is the point in thinking that far ahead?

I am plowing laboriously through Ziegler's *Geistige und soziale Strömungen des 19. Jahrhunderts* [Intellectual and social currents of the 19th century], repeatedly falling asleep and failing to grasp everything philosophical, but it is not unprofitable. It is perhaps quite good that I am being forced to do something to improve my general education. General? In the background there is always the thought of the Curriculum and *LTI*. How these two books should eventually be set apart from one another, whether both will come to pass or only one or neither—no matter: I read and take notes as if I were certain of both and of the next ten years. And thus I get through the day in halfway-decent fashion. (Insofar as it is not taken up with kitchen chores.)

I am reading aloud, with the greatest interest, something that John Neumann lent me: Sammy Gronemann, *Tohuwabohu*. I am fighting the hardest battle for my Germanness now. I must hold on to this: I am German, the others are un-German. I must hold on to this: The spirit is decisive, not blood. I must hold on to this: On my part Zionism would be a comedy—my baptism was *not* a comedy.

Dr. Friedheim presented me with a bouquet from the little almond tree in the garden. Last year it was Ernst Kreidl, now in a concentration camp, who did so. Embarrassingly odd business: For Elsa Kreidl, Friedheim is in a way substitute and soul mate. He keeps her company every evening, looks after her garden, etc. The pair of them live a somewhat secluded life. The ladies downstairs dislike him for being bad tempered, and Elsa Kreidl (Aryan!) is not on good terms with her sister-in-law either. We ourselves are caught between the two parties; Elsa Kreidl lends me books—but we are only truly friends with the Kreidls on the ground floor.

### May 14, Thursday (Ascension, not a holiday)

Two boys, perhaps twelve and six, not working class, come toward me on a narrow pavement. Tussling as they pass me, the older one catapults his brother at me and shouts out: "Jew!" — It is ever more difficult to endure all this humiliation. And always the fear of the Gestapo, hiding and getting rid of the manuscripts and of paper that has not been written on, the swift destruction of all correspondence . . . My powers of resistance grow weaker every day, my heart problems increase every day. —

Because I am paying *five marks* less in rent from now on, my allowance has been reduced by *ten marks*.

The worst thing is the impossibility of working systematically. Mere "improvement." Exhaustion on top of that. I repeatedly fall asleep in the mornings. I continue with Ziegler, slowly and with little gain. In addition a little bit of *Wilhelm Meister's Travels*—quite unfamiliar to me.

Surprisingly good and enthralling is Sammy Gronemann, *Tohuwabohu*.

## May 15, Friday toward evening

Yesterday afternoon to lawyer Neumark, the Jewish "legal adviser" behind Kreuzkirche. At Georgsplatz some packers from Thamm were working. One immediately came toward me holding out his hand. "It is very kind of you to shake my hand" (it is more than kind, it is a dangerous demonstration). "How are you doing?" — "Badly, very badly." — "Sometime you'll have to tell me more about it." He went back to his van. — Neumark advised that we should discuss Eva's case with Dr. Magnus, perhaps a certificate could somehow be obtained after all. — I met Friedheim there, who does not want to submit in the Voss business. Neumark regretted that I had submitted. He was very concerned about the consequences of having a criminal record. The threat of evacuation is even more serious than before. — Finally Neumark warned me against Richter, the new trustee of my house, he was a "false Saxon" and, if it came to it, would leave me in the lurch. — Both yesterday and of course today depressing because of the German victory at Kerch. The war, and that was also Neumark's opinion, can last a very long time; it is unquestionable that the German side has lost, but probably equally unquestionable that it can hold out for a long time. And we meanwhile—since a couple of hours ago all the insults of yesterday seem trivial and far away. Frau Ida Kreidl, whom I met while I was shopping, reported the latest decree, she then showed it to us in the *Jewish Community Newspaper:* Jews with the star and anyone who lives with them are, with immediate effect, forbidden to keep pets (dogs, cats, birds), it is also forbidden to give the animals away to be looked after. This is the death sentence for Muschel, whom we have had for more than eleven years and to whom Eva is very attached. He is to be taken to the vet tomorrow, so that he is spared the fright of being fetched and put down together with others. I feel very bitter for Eva's sake. We have so often said to each other: The tomcat's raised tail is our flag, we shall not strike it, we'll keep our heads above water, we'll pull the animal through, and at the victory celebrations Muschel will get a "schnitzel from Kamm's" (the fanciest butcher here). It makes me almost superstitious that the flag is being lowered now. Recently the animal, more than eleven years old now, had been particularly lively and youthful. He was always a support and a comfort to Eva. Her powers of resistance will now be less than before.

## May 18, Monday morning

Muschel's imminent end weighs heavily—I wish it were behind us . . . [ . . . ] And the tomcat's end is only one especially bad shock amid a multitude of afflictions that grow worse with every day. —

**Afternoon**

The Neumanns were here on Saturday; on Sunday we were at the Seliksohns'; while we were there Katz, the Jewish medical assessor, came on a
professional call: We heard bad news from all three; the intention is evidently to wear us down, as many individuals as possible are to be driven
to suicide. Dr. Magnus, the orthopedist with whom I shoveled snow, was
stopped on Stübelplatz. A man jumped out of a Gestapo car: "You wretch,
why are you walking around here, why aren't you at work? This is the second time we've seen you." And spat in his face. Magnus is working at the
Jewish cemetery now—I don't know whether as a gravedigger. — An
eighty-five-year-old man had been walking along outside the Great Garden. The general perimeter road, but on the park side—I learned yesterday
that the park side of the road is part of the area of the park from which Jews
are banned. Summoned to the Gestapo and so badly beaten that he had to
be brought home and put to bed. He was supposed to go to the Gestapo the
next morning—Dr. Katz stated that he was incapable of doing so. "Why is
someone like that taking our bread away from us?" says the Gestapo. Calling to see another patient on this same Sunday, Katz was caught up in a
house search. He was detained in a side room; he heard the beating going
on next door. In this squad there is supposed to be one man in particular,
who, as it were, holds the office of beater. He punches in the face, kicks
with his boot, women as well. Above all, they're trying to drive old people
to their death. At the moment they're looking for medicines and repeat prescriptions with particular zeal. All of it is taken away to the accompaniment of many blows and summons to the Gestapo. — Dr. Katz, sometimes
addressed as "Herr Doktor," sometimes as "Katz," is allowed to make a
call only when a patient is in a critical condition. — Katz is obviously in a
very difficult position between Gestapo supervision and Jewry. "People always see me as a Jew, and only then, last of all, as a doctor." He has a very
bad reputation among those dependent on him. "He shits himself," Magnus had already told me, "he doesn't put anyone on the sick list for fear of
the Gestapo." — "In his waiting room there's a picture of him in uniform,
on horseback, with the Iron Cross, First Class, and wearing a monocle"—
said Seliksohn. — Although, as I said, I understand his difficulty, the man
makes a bad impression on both of us. "Affected," said Eva summarily of
his manner of speaking and expression. There is something deceitful in his
pale blue eyes in a narrow, scrubbed face! Apart from that, graceful, elegant, of indeterminate age. — The general mood at the Seliksohns' was
very depressed. *He* emphasized again and again we would not escape with
our lives. — Dr. Katz advised us always to walk on the street in such a way
that the star was facing away from the road, then one was not exposed to
the Gestapo patrol cars. — We brought the Seliksohns, from whom we
were hoping for potatoes—this time in vain—6 ounces of asparagus. Eva
carried it, because it is a pure Aryan vegetable and would see a Jewish
bearer to the Gestapo and into prison. — At the moment there are little Ital-

ian artichokes unrationed, which are not bought much, first of all because they are unfamiliar and second because they are a mere delicacy. Eva and Kätchen eat them reverentially—they would only make *me* even hungrier. — Recently Eva has got a fish card for herself, but whereas the Jews believe that Aryan hunger is stopped with fish, here, too, it's a matter of tiny amounts at lengthy intervals. Eva received 7 ounces of cod, 3 miniature rollmops, and a few ounces of chopped herring, which used to be unrationed, and that appears to be all for a week. On the whole it really does look as if general starvation is imminent.

It also looks as if Kerch is only a partial German success, and it is the Russians who are still really on the offensive. But since the catastrophe with the cat befell us, Eva's powers of resistance and consequently mine also have declined very greatly.

All of Sunday morning Eva lay in bed very depressed, and I read out the last hundred pages of *Tohuwabohu* in one go. I must make notes on it. A surprisingly good book. But it cannot convert me. I cannot escape my Germanness. But I am quite beyond nationalism. And I no longer take the Germans to be a chosen people.

This morning—very oppressive heat, and because of the star I'm wearing my coat—to the Community because of a tax matter (mistakenly assessed for property tax). An elderly gentleman chatted to me. "I think we're about the same age—I'm 74." It was the same thing at the Gestapo in autumn—how old and wretched I must look. But yesterday there was a pair of scales at the Seliksohns'. We used them and weighed exactly as much and as little as on September 18, 1941, the last evening on which, starless, I was allowed to enter a restaurant: Eva 122 pounds, myself 145 pounds. — I then went to the adjoining house, where the Jewish community kitchen and an old people's home are located. Steinitz had written to me that Herr Hammer, who is in charge of the Community library, lives there and would no doubt have books by Herzl. As far as the books are concerned, the trip was fruitless. Also depressing. A room like a prison cell, luggage in the anteroom. Hammer, a small, elderly man, lay in bed fully clothed, leaped up courteously, when I entered after knocking, roared angrily at people who wanted to speak to him after me, and, at once flattered and vain, began to talk about attending Walzel's lectures and his interest in theater and literature [ . . . ]. I was happy when I could escape, But I did not really escape. "I shall make an effort to obtain books for you—may I bring them to you in person?" And of course I had to agree. —

If only the cat business were over and done with. Someone else may find it absurd or even immoral, when so many are suffering because of the fate of their relatives. But I see how it pulls Eva down. Muschel is pampered, for his last meal he got veal, as in peacetime—am I hard-hearted if I secretly note: 1 pound—when a pound and a quarter are the weekly ration for *two* people? Am I hard-hearted if I wish the moriturus days were over? Today Eva said: "The little animal plays, is happy and does not

know it will die tomorrow." — Is there anyone among us who knows: Tomorrow you will die? I constantly have to repeat myself: muddled feelings about the cat. I feel sorry primo loco for Eva, secundo loco for myself,
tertio loco for Muschel. Sometimes primo loco for myself. But Eva's, "You
still have your work, your production," is justified after all. And would I
be better served if I had a submissive woman for whom cooking and playing bridge were enough? And do I have the right to be jealous of this great
love of an animal? And is it a pleasant thought for *me* that we must have
the animal, which is healthy and full of life, poisoned? —

### May 19, Tuesday toward evening

Muschel †. Eva had already made inquiries last week. Someone has taken
over the practice of good Dr. Gross (in Grunaer Strasse), who castrated our
tomcat and put down Nickelchen, and last year died of a heart attack,
aged fifty at most. We hesitated for days. Today news came that a hand-
over order was on its way from the Community, after reception of which I
would no longer have the right to dispose of the animal as I saw fit. We
hesitated until four o'clock—the man's surgery hours ended at five. Unless the regime collapsed by the very next morning, we would expose the
cat to an even crueler death or put me in even greater danger. (Even having him killed today is a little dangerous for me.) I left the decision to Eva.
She took the animal away in the familiar cardboard cat box, she was
present when he was put to sleep by an anesthetic that took effect very
rapidly—the animal did not suffer. But *she* suffers.

   With bad pains in my throat I lugged up 30 pounds of potatoes from
our van trader on Wasaplatz. There the man already had my card in his
hand, when a young female, dyed-blond hair, dangerously narrow-
minded-looking face, perhaps a shopkeeper's wife, stepped up from behind: "I was here first—the Jew has to wait." Jentsch served her
obediently, and the Jew waited. Now it is almost seven o'clock, and for the
next two hours the Jew is again waiting for the house search (which usually takes place in the evening).

   I am making an effort to get into the second volume of Chamberlain.
Basically semper idem.

### May 22, Friday morning

Eva's distress about Muschel is not passing, and I, too, am haunted by the
poor beast. I read aloud a great deal, to help Eva, during the night, in the
early morning, at any time. [ . . . ] An hour ago reading was interrupted:
weeping and shouting above or below us. Immediate assumption: Elsa
Kreidl will have received news of the death of her husband in the concentration camp. Whether this is so or not: the fact that we and Kätchen immediately assumed it and consider it to be almost certain is the most
characteristic thing about our situation.

Today a letter arrived from "Arne Erik Johansson." He had "definitely made up his mind," he writes in encyclopedic style, "to come to the spring or autumn trade fair in Leipzig next year (because this year a trip to Germany was not yet feasible, even for us Swedes)." I do not know whether we shall pull through, whether we shall be allowed to pull through, if things continue like this for another whole year (and with the torture getting worse every day).

### Midday

Our first assumption was correct: Telegram from an SS Obersturmbann-führer to Elsa Kreidl: "Ernst Kreidl deceased this morning May 22, letter follows." — We shall probably never learn why and how the poor devil met his death. He was summoned to the Gestapo six months ago and did not come back. He was in the Dresden police cells for five months. His wife was allowed no contact with him. Neumark, the lawyer, was told it was a trivial matter, he would soon be released. He was awaited here first at Christmas, then at New Year. Later I suspected he was somehow in-criminated in the Czech business. His wife vehemently denied it. A month ago the laundry she brought for him every week was no longer taken. Two weeks later she received a postcard from Ernst Kreidl in Buchenwald: Things were not too bad, he was allowed to write and receive post every two weeks, he was allowed to receive 15M a month. Then nothing more and today the telegram. — Such a fate also hangs over me all the time. Everyone thinks of himself. Eva said: "Muschel died three days too early; today he could officially belong to the Aryan widow Elsa Kreidl." I thought of the danger I was in, and Eva's thoughts wounded me. After the first shock, Eva Kreidl will console herself with her bosom friend Fried-heim and even more with the feeling, as an Aryan widow, of now being out of all this misery. Ida Kreidl mourns her son Paul, deported and pre-sumed dead. And she mourns her two condemned canaries a little. [ . . . ]

Yesterday afternoon I visited the crippled Marckwald again. [ . . . ] Ter-rible, how the man made his way on crutches from his armchair to the sideboard, a distance of perhaps six feet, how he pulled himself up, how he then let himself fall back. He showed me family pictures, gave me a type-written copy of a history of his family ("500 Years of Family History by Ludwig Herz"), to which I must return, as symptomatic of the Third Reich. [ . . . ] Marckwald told me that there had been *two thousand Jewish suicides in Berlin* since the beginning of the evacuations last autumn. The Marck-walds also have to hand over a bird. They considered it terribly risky that we had had our pet killed. "If the Gestapo found out about that!"

### May 23, Saturday afternoon

Yesterday morning the news of the death of Ernst Kreidl, in the afternoon the long expected house search. Essentially I was once again the innocent.

I left at quarter to five (very reluctantly) to visit Steinitz once again—the usual conversations, [ . . . ] the dreaded wife behaved tolerably—I came back at half past seven. The raiding squad had appeared here at five and departed shortly before my return. First of all, I saw the chaos on the ground floor through the open front door. Friedheim showed me the side of his neck and chin, black and blue from blows, he complained of a kick to his body which struck a hernia scar. Frau Kreidl and Frau Pick had also been beaten. In our rooms I found Eva, who was completely calm. Everything had gone according to the familiar pattern. "You're Aryan?—You Jew's whore, why did you marry the Jew? In the Talmud it says: 'To us every non-Jewish woman is a whore' . . ." She was sent downstairs, where she got a couple of slaps—"stage slaps rather than anything serious," she said, whereas Ida Kreidl, for her part, complained of ringing in her ears. But they repeatedly spat in Eva's face and on her head. In our apartment— and likewise in that of Frau Voss, who like myself arrived after the event, I found exactly the same chaos, the bestial devastation by cruel, drunken apes, which I have often heard described, but the reality of which nevertheless appeared monstrous. Even now we are still sitting in this chaos, which has hardly been cleared at all. Contents of cupboards, drawers, shelves, of the desk, all over the floor. Torn playing cards, powder, pieces of sugar, individual pills, contents of a sewing box strewn among them and stamped on: needles, buttons, shards of smashed Christmas decorations, pastilles, tablets, cigarette papers, Eva's clothes, clean linen, hats, shreds of paper—all mixed up. In the bedroom, the space between beds and wardrobes, the beds themselves were strewn with things. It is impossible to ascertain what has been stolen, what destroyed, what arbitrarily hidden, what overlooked. Of the drugs and medicinal preparations, Pyramidin is completely gone and most of the sweetener, brown tannin powder and some kind of pink throat pastilles are scattered everywhere. Every bit of food that had been bought on ration coupons has been taken, butter, bacon, sugar (insofar as it is not crunching underfoot on the carpet—yes, my blackberry smoking tea is down there as well)—also what meager reserves of gravy powder we still possessed—against that a couple of eggs were spared—against that fermented blackberry tea had been lifted. My writing paper was in part left here, was in part not found, d'altra parte all envelopes have disappeared, all my visiting cards, of which I still had a hundred [ . . . ]. Eva's calling cards were lying in the bedroom. [ . . . ] The bottle of sparkling wine, given by Frau Schaps for the housewarming in '34, saved up for the day of salvation, was lifted. My Service Cross is missing, some foreign coins (e.g., a gulden) are missing. Of my books, none appear to be missing, although reference books are said to be popular. My manuscripts were hardly out of their folders, only the wartime letters jumbled up. A couple of books had been taken off the shelves, lay on the desk. But the Greek dictionary with the last diary pages was untouched, Eva's music cabinet with a few of my manuscripts and with a large packet of paper untouched. The diary manuscript would unquestionably have cost me my life. A Mendelssohn music book lay open on Eva's music cabinet. The title page was torn from top to bottom. — Apart from the blackberry tea, the sugar, the cigarette papers, a whole quantity of little pieces of gummed paper is lying on and in the carpet; I always collected these gummed edges of stamp sheets in a cigar box and used them to append notes and corrections to galley proofs. It's fortunate that our vacuum cleaner has been repaired and is in working order. — So all in all we have got away not too badly this time and have again vowed to one another to keep our heads. But what an unthinkable disgrace for Germany.

The most difficult part of the business for me did not occur until today. Ida Kreidl appeared after nine o'clock yesterday evening, very upset; she had been appointed to present the Gestapo's booty at Bismarckplatz at eight o'clock this morning. First the order had been given to Friedheim, who had excused himself with his hernia, then to her. There were five suitcases downstairs, four traveling cases of medium weight, a very heavy full-sized trunk. What on earth is in them, remains a mystery. We shall only gradually discover what has been lost, since of course no one is allowed to watch while the looting is going on. So a handcart had to be found for these cases, and we wearers of the star are not allowed to go out after 9:00 P.M. So Eva off to the shopkeeper on Wasaplatz. Without success. Friedheim said, the gardener opposite opens at six and would definitely give his cart. He and I will set out together with Frau Kreidl at half past six. — I was not able to go to bed until one; I had to climb over the chaos on a sheet of packing paper and a woolen blanket, I read aloud for a while [ . . . ] (unwind!), and at six Frau Kreidl was already ringing the doorbell. Went downstairs unwashed. The gardener shut. Friedheim unable to move. (But later he was noticeably better.) Kätchen Sara's tiny handcart took only half the cases. Thus Frau Kreidl and I—and essentially I—had to trek to the station twice. The first time I dragged the very heavy trunk from the station diagonally across to the Gestapo entrance. The second time, on Eva's urgent advice, I took the now somewhat lighter handcart only as far as the station, where I entrusted it to Ida Kreidl. I did not want to enter the thieves' den again. I had very great trouble with my heart, was very exhausted and very much the worse for wear. On Strehlener Strasse a passerby shouted at me: "What are you Jews doing with those cases?" At the entrance to the building a couple of Gestapo officers (truly officers) shouted: "You Moishe rascals!" The second load did not get there until nine, the first admittedly at half past seven. Still: I feared the worst for having failed to meet the time limit. At that moment I would have been unable to help Frau Kreidl: one is so used to the greatest unpleasantness. I feared they would keep Frau Kreidl there, they would also take further reprisals against the rest of the Jews in the house. But they were merciful: They merely reviled Frau Kreidl with the usual obscenities, had her drag the cases up three flights of stairs and then let her go. — Downstairs yesterday these people found, among other things, a bowl of spinach; the contents were thrown in the ladies' faces and smeared over their dresses;

they also painted it on the bathroom door. Up here everything stank of garlic: A couple of bulbs, which had been lying on the balcony, had been cut into small pieces and distributed in the various rooms and could not be discovered at once. — Apart from all foodstuffs and a pair of boots, Frau Voss is missing two rolls of toilet paper and an electric cushion. Less appears to have been stolen from us than from the others. —

New decrees today: *Ban on going to Aryan barbers' shops.* (Some people still had "connections.") "It is the duty of a Jew to see to the care and cleanliness of his own hair." — Replacement of spectacle lenses, repairs of household objects must first be reported to the Jewish Community; "there must be no cosmetic repairs whatsoever." (Recently cycling on Sundays for the purpose of making visits was forbidden.)

## May 24, Sunday morning, Whitsun

The dining room nine-tenths cleared up, the bedroom still not, the mood gloomy. Whitsun! Yesterday evening—for the first time in ages, there was no Sunday tea at the Kreidls'—I was downstairs for a few minutes. The people downstairs were after all treated more brutally than Eva knows; she was able to return to our apartment after a while. Friedheim, in whom they evidently hated the money Jew, banker and capitalist, suffered worst. The man is completely changed; usually arrogant and unsociable, he now draws one into blathering conversation. He pulled me away from Ida Kreidl, forced me into his bedroom, opened his trousers, displayed the protruding hernia, showed the bruised half of his face for the umpteenth time, told again and again how he had been kicked. And Frau Pick related how these people had put a top hat on him, with his blue house jacket, then pressed a chamber pot into his hand and sent him down to the cellar. To Frau Pick, to the accompaniment of slaps: "Do you have any children?—And apart from putting these bastards in the world, you've never worked?" And she was spat upon and besmirched again and again. A tube of toothpaste was squeezed out all over her bedding, ersatz honey over her bedside rug. —

This morning we heard the fit of weeping again. The letter with particulars of the death has no doubt arrived now. Admittedly the spasm of mourning does not prevent Elsa Kreidl maintaining the most intense friendship with Friedheim. The two are inseparable. —

## Evening

Ernst Kreidl was "shot while attempting to escape," at 2:55 P.M., that is, in broad daylight. Eva saw the printed form, completed in typescript. "Cremation at Weimar-Buchenwald Crematorium," the urn is at your disposal. It is impossible to lie more shamelessly. The man certainly did not have the faintest thought of attempting an absolutely impossible escape. Sixty-three years old, weakened, prison clothing, without money ... And in broad daylight . . . Undisguised murder. One of thousands upon thousands.

## May 25, Whitmonday afternoon

Since yesterday morning Eva has been working at clearing up the chaos. This morning I myself have been picking up the scattered halma pieces here, and in the bedroom countless nails and needles out of the rough, deeply furrowed runner, a labor of hours. The bedroom still looks terrible. Yesterday evening, when it was half tidied up, Eva said, "Now it looks almost as it did two years ago." It occurred to me that we had moved into the Jews' House on May 24, 1940. The length of the imprisonment weighs heavily on Eva. —

I read aloud a great deal, to help her get over her depression. This morning from four until half past five. [ . . . ]

Downstairs, those who had been more badly affected, still very agitated yesterday. At the Gestapo Frau Kreidl had to drag the heavy cases one at a time up three flights of stairs. She was harassed as she did so: "Faster, you pig!" Then she had to go to the Gestapo once again: "There are another couple of envelopes on the desk." They had found a linen cupboard in Friedheim's rooms. Two cases were emptied and sent back, had to be filled with linen once more and taken [to the Gestapo] by Fräulein Ludwig, his housekeeper ("Jews' whore!").

## May 26, Tuesday morning

I did not leave the house over Whitsun. Only when it is absolutely necessary do I venture onto the street. — Toward midday Dr. Glaser came for a short visit. In the afternoon Steinitz. On Saturday he and his wife had innocently found themselves caught up in a house search while visiting acquaintances: punches to the back of the head. —

I often heard of a Jewish pharmacist called Magen. The man was arrested several times. His seventeen-year-old son fled, as he was about to be evacuated, and evidently escaped. That was in January. As a result, the father, a fifty-year-old, was arrested again, he was put in the familiar solitary confinement of the police cells. — Yesterday Kätchen tells us: "Magen has died." — "One murder more!" — Kätchen almost indignant: "But no! They don't do things like that at the Police Presidium, they behave properly there. He simply had bad heart trouble and won't have got any care there." So this is no longer considered a murder but a normal end. —

[ . . . ]

## May 27, Wednesday midday

Eva's nerves are in a very bad state. Repercussion on me: I am reading aloud at improbable hours of the night and early morning and am *even* more tired during the day than otherwise. — Thus I turned the pages of the second part of Chamberlain in a tormented semi-trance. But perhaps if I had been completely fresh I would have gone through it in the same semi-trance. Philosophy stupefies me. I shall now make only a few notes on it. — It is not only the death of the cat and the distress of the house search that is to blame for the exhaustion (Eva's and my own), but also sheer hunger. Bread and potatoes—otherwise nothing, and the potatoes are running out. — Steiniger was upstairs just now and once again gave me 6½ pounds of bread coupons as a present. —

This afternoon Eva is going to Pirna to fetch some money. I shall give her the diary pages of the last few weeks to take with her. After the house search I found several books, which had been taken off the shelf, lying on the desk. If one of them had been the Greek dictionary, if the manuscript pages had fallen out and had thus aroused suspicion, it would undoubt-edly have meant my death. One is murdered for lesser misdemeanors. [ . . . ] So these parts will go today. But I shall go on writing. That is *my* heroism. I will bear witness, precise witness!

### May 28, Thursday morning

[ . . . ] (Recently I asked Marckwald whether he had anything by Herzl in his library. *Neither he nor his wife had ever heard the name Herzl.* I was so as-tonished that I asked again: "Herzl?" — "No. People talked about Zion-ism, but we don't know the name.") [ . . . ]

### May 29, Friday morning

I find it difficult to report everything in chronological order.

Yesterday at midday I went in oppressive heat (wearing my starred coat) to Victoriastrasse to see Richter, the house trustee, who had re-quested me to visit him. He said, the new mortgage on the house in Dölzschen was almost certain ("95 percent"), but it would not be provided out of local authority funds but by a private individual in Dölzschen. He said further, that the extravagant bills which the previous trustee, the lawyer Heise, had sent Frau Voss and myself, could be contested. Köhler, the all-powerful Jews' pope, did not like me, but he hated Heise, who had not been willing to comply with his wishes; furthermore Köhler was vain; if I went to see him therefore and enlisted his help against Heise, he would proceed against the man and help me retrieve the extra money I had paid. I retorted that I would not go to Köhler. — "Why not?" — "If you give me your word of honor that you will remain silent, I shall tell you everything, but if you blab it out, it means certain death for me." He gave his word of honor [ . . . ]. I trusted him, although Neumark had declared Richter was a "false Saxon." I think it is in the man's favor that he openly acknowledges his situation: "I have to look after myself, I have to get along with these people, I want to help *you, as far* as I can . . ." I gave vent to my feelings, related every detail of the house search, said that Köhler looks on with satisfaction smoking a cigar, also talked about Ernst Kreidl's death, of the pets being taken away . . . Richter was horrified. Again and again: "such bestiality," "such sadism!," again and again: There was deep dissatisfaction everywhere, and people were hardly aware of the cruelty inflicted on the Jews. He wanted to give me envelopes, since I had mentioned that mine had been stolen; I took *one* "to show you that I am touched by your goodwill." I had told him how hard it was for me to come into town and what dangers it involved. From now on he intends to inform me about everything in writing. ("But I must be sharp when I write to you!") —

After tea at home I was busy with the potatoes, when I saw a very large and very elegant car outside the house. Immediately afraid. About an hour later, violent ringing of our bell. I opened the door and was immediately smacked about the ears, because I had opened up too slowly. Two young men. It was, just as Eva said recently, a stage slap, and likewise the kick in the pants on the stairs afterward was only suggested, but my heart missed a beat, I suffered badly from shortage of breath and pains, I again had the feeling of being close to death. I saw how one of the two fellows spat at Eva in the living room, and how she remained quite calm. "We need a small suitcase." — "In the cellar—I'll go down with you." [ . . . ] I wanted to spare her that, but downstairs it occurred to me that she had put things in *one* of the cases to keep them safe, and I did not know in which. So I had to call her down after all. After a while she returned with a small wicker case, the man had not done anything else to her. The beasts disappeared, we had scarcely been touched. Aside from the case, this time they had merely—but for the second time within a few days!—stolen the open butter on the plate. (We shall not have a single gram of fat until Monday.) After a while Elsa and Ida Kreidl and Fräulein Ludwig came up. Dr. Friedheim had been the target of the raid. Ida Kreidl and Frau Pick had been less badly treated this time (still Frau Pick had been forced to stand for two hours and had fainted, a couple of marks had been stolen from Ida Kreidl's purse, all reserves of butter and bread—bread!—taken, milk poured away). These people, again with Köhler's assistance, had shut themselves in with Friedheim, in his rooms, for two hours; no one knows what went on there. They had then arrested him, taken away documents, sealed the rooms. — All of us in the house are convinced that Dr. Friedheim is a dead man. He still has a large fortune, so he will die in a concentration camp in a few weeks. — My particular worry: that they will find the Voss-Klemperer currency business among his papers. —

From Monday, the beginning of the next ration-card period, Jews will no longer receive any milk. — The bread is so damp and sour (turnips? potatoes?) that I can hardly swallow it. But we have destroyed three Russian armies at Kharkov and "so far" taken 165,000 prisoners.

Everything here is stuffed full of soiled linen. No possibility of getting to a laundry, no appliances here to wash them ourselves, fear of Gestapo confiscation if we take something out of storage. Eva attempted to draw

Annemarie's attention to our plight; it was embarrassing for her to beg openly. She came home having achieved nothing, hinting had been no use—the others simply cannot put themselves in our position, they have no notion of everything that is being taken from us, that we are forbidden to do, that is prescribed for us. —

Today Frau Ida Kreidl must hand over her canary in a pet shop, way, way out on Bautzener Strasse, on foot. Good, that our Muschel rests in peace.

In the evening I managed to rouse myself to make some notes [ . . . ], later and then today at five o'clock in the morning I read aloud [ . . . ]. And now I want to conclude my notes on the second volume of Chamberlain, which I skimmed through. To the very last moment I want to live and *to work*, as if I were certain of surviving. Je n'en ai qu'un très faible espoir.

## May 30, Saturday morning

Eva is just now returning the second volume of Chamberlain, which I have only partly read. I believe, however, that I have taken everything important from it, and I have just completed the very thorough notes. These really are the "foundations," but not of the nineteenth century, rather of the 3rd Reich. Strange that the funeral of Eva Chamberlain-Wagner was in the newspaper only yesterday. They were indeed right to celebrate the man as "seer of the 3rd Reich." Will my notes on its perfidious style ever be used? In the LTI? In the Curriculum? I doubt whether my heart will last out—the most recent shock was particularly violent.

Today over breakfast we talked about the extraordinary capacity of human beings to bear and become accustomed to things. The fantastic hideousness of our existence: fear of every ring at the door, of ill-treatment, insults, fear for one's life, of hunger (real hunger), ever new bans, ever more cruel enslavement, deadly danger coming closer every day, every day new victims all around us, absolute helplessness—and yet still hours of pleasure, while reading aloud, while working, while eating our less than meager food, and so we go on eking out a bare existence and go on hoping. —

Yesterday afternoon to see Marckwald. The great distress of the paralyzed invalid. While we were chatting, he was given a morphine injection. He related that his father, a farmer, had had himself baptized in 1873, "his profession required it"; he himself had been baptized at birth; at the outbreak of war had been a first lieutenant in the reserves (but already ailing and no longer fit for frontline service). [ . . . ] The man is now in his mid-seventies. Mutatis mutandis Arthur Eloesser's problem is also my problem. The return of the assimilated generation—return to what? One cannot go back, one cannot go to Zion. Perhaps it is not at all up to us *to go, but rather to wait: I* am German and am waiting for the Germans to come back; they have gone to ground somewhere.

A great deal of reading aloud all too early in the morning. [ . . . ]

Friedheim's fate is ghastly: He is facing certain death; every time the cell door opens he will expect removal to a concentration camp, and there he will expect the end at every moment. But do I feel pity for *him*? I only think: When will it be *my* turn? After all I now have a "previous conviction." And if there is no fortune to be got out of me, then nevertheless a pension can be saved. And what else do I think with respect to the Friedheim case? Perhaps his housekeeper can let us have some potatoes—he is or was supplied from his own piece of land.

### May 31, Sunday morning

During the day I pull myself together, suppress, forget my fear. In the morning it shakes me. It is now literally fear of death. Particular worry: the Gestapo could bring up the currency business once again. — I often tell myself that I was also in mortal danger in 1915. But here death threatens me in a more awful form. How must Dr. Friedheim be feeling now? —

### June 2, Tuesday toward evening

Two hours ago saw dispatch printed in bold letters in the *Dresdener NN:* Germany has just given Turkey a credit of 100 million rei to buy arms in Germany. And that means: Turkey is on Germany's side, or at least: She will give Germany passage (and has *more* confidence in the latter's victory than in that of its opponents!); that means an offensive against Syria, Palestine, Egypt; it means the endless prolongation of the war. Very, very depressed, and since my heart rebels more and more and since our position is becoming ever more precarious, so my hope of seeing the end of this calamity sinks ever lower.

On Sunday evening, after I had sat at home for 48 hours, short walk to Südhöhe, Toll House. Everything in bloom. The last time I was there, had to fight my way uphill in the cold, against a biting wind, to shovel snow. *Then* we still had enough to eat, *then* we had not yet been beaten and spat upon by the Gestapo. And even then we already believed that things were going very badly for us. Perhaps in three months we shall say: In June we could still almost live in comfort. There is a big blue patch on Eva's arm from the recent ill-treatment. "I thought you got only 'stage slaps'?" — "That was only where one of them grabbed me and pushed me aside." Eva is still cleaning up. She has learned from the experience. Things that can "cause a nuisance" are safely packed away: Nails, needles, Christmas-tree decorations were put in the cellar, many things are pushed under cabinets ("They are too lazy to bend down"); even the butter is now in a safer place. The surviving solitaire cards (it was days before they were all found) are carried around in Eva's handbag.

Yesterday toward evening to Steinitz for half an hour. He had written to me that he would no longer be able to call on me on Mondays. The in-

terruption of this tiresome regularity is at least one agreeable consequence of the Gestapo terror. When Steinitz was recently caught up in a
house search at friends' and was punched on the neck, he was immediately asked: "Where are you working?" Someone who is "working" is
supposed to be treated a little more leniently. Steinitz thereupon registered with the Jewish Community and is now, like Dr. Magnus, employed
in an "honorary" capacity at the Jewish cemetery. I met him after his first
day at work, in shirtsleeves and barefoot. His wife, who is not very nice
to him, brought him his food and scolded him, because in his blindness
he was dribbling on his trousers. He told me that there were a couple of
old men under a gardener out there. Each person gets allocated a grave to
clean. A whole day is spent killing time like that, but one had an answer
to "Where are you working?" and perhaps even some cover against the
next evacuation. At the moment factory work is no longer given to people
over sixty. — For my part I shall keep away from such tedium for as long
as I possibly can. One is in danger everywhere, with and without "work."
My days at home are not very fruitful either—the terrible tiredness!—but
yet not completely sterile. I am now working my way into *The Myth of the
Twentieth Century*. I am also reading aloud a great deal, usually very early
in the morning, at four or five, and for a while following afternoon tea.
[ . . . ] New decrees in judaeos. The choker is being pulled ever tighter;
they are wearing us down with ever new tricks. All the things, great and
small, that have accumulated in the last few years! And a pinprick is
sometimes more agonizing than a blow with a club. I shall list the decrees
once and for all: 1) To be home after eight or nine in the evening. Inspection! 2) Expelled from one's own house. 3) Ban on radio, ban on telephone.
4) Ban on theaters, cinemas, concerts, museums. 5) Ban on subscribing to
or purchasing periodicals. 6) Ban on using public transport: three phases:
a) buses banned, only front platform of tram permitted, b) all use banned,
except to work, c) to work on foot, unless one lives 2½ miles away or is
sick (but it is a hard fight to get a doctor's certificate). Also ban on taxi-
cabs, of course. 7) Ban on purchasing "goods in short supply." 8) Ban on
purchasing cigars or any kind of smoking materials. 9) Ban on purchasing
flowers. 10) Withdrawal of *milk* ration card. 11) Ban on going to the barber. 12) Any kind of tradesman can be called only after application to the
Community. 13) Compulsory surrender of typewriters, 14) of furs and
woolen blankets, 15) of bicycles—it is permissible to cycle to work (Sunday outings and visits by bicycle are forbidden), 16) of deck chairs, 17) of
dogs, cats, birds. 18) Ban on leaving the city of Dresden, 19) on entering
the railway station, 20) on setting foot on the Ministry embankment, in
parks, 21) on using Bürgerwiese [street] and the roads bordering the
Great Garden (Parkstrasse, Lennéstrasse, and Karcherallee). This most recent restriction since only yesterday. Also, since the day before yesterday,
a ban on entering the market halls. 22) Since September 19 [last year] the
*Jew's star*. 23) Ban on having reserves of foodstuffs at home. (Gestapo also
takes away what has been bought on food coupons.) 24) Ban on use of

lending libraries. 25) Because of the star all restaurants are closed to us. And in the restaurants one can still get something to eat, some "dish of the day," if one has nothing at all left at home. Eva says the restaurants are packed. 26) No clothing card. 27) No fish card. 28) No special rations such as coffee, chocolate, fruit, condensed milk. 29) The special taxes. 30) The constantly contracting disposable allowance. Mine at first 600, then 320, now 185 marks. 31) Shopping restricted to *one* hour (three till four, Saturday twelve till one). I think these 31 points are everything. But all together they are nothing as against the constant threat of house searches, of ill-treatment, of prison, concentration camp, and violent death. —

We are now literally living off charity. Yesterday Ida Kreidl gave us two pounds of potatoes; today she brought me a plate of boiled potatoes and a bagful of potatoes donated by Fräulein Ludwig. Eva returns from her shopping trips fairly or completely empty-handed. There's only spinach—and even that only in tiny amounts—and that is something *she* cannot eat, and to prepare it we also lack a chopping knife. (And in any case, I find it repugnant to eat anything that is cooked *only* for me.) I eat at least five-sixths of the bread and potatoes here at home; the plate of vegetables that Eva gulps down in some restaurant during her shopping trips is only a small counterbalance. Also, she has lost much more weight than I. —

### June 4, Thursday midday

Yesterday afternoon the Seliksohns were here. Seliksohn originally in various commercial jobs, for a while in the Vorwärts bookshop, past somewhat opaque, but certainly of an intellectualist nature and with some education; during the war a very young volunteer; finally a cavalry sergeant, and thanks to his knowledge of Russian—eastern Jew from the district of Kharkov—used as a messenger in southern Russia; now most emphatically Jewish and Zionist. — Seliksohn is now training as a hairdresser, in particular a ladies' hairdresser. A Jewish coiffeuse is teaching him, the Community is giving him instruments and allocating him a room for his trade. He will pay home visits to favored clients, or they can also be attended to in his own home. *We* are among the favored clients. [ . . . ] Seliksohn also said that very many Aryans, soldiers and civilians, were being shot "one after the other," in Torgau, in the court building on Münchner Platz, on the rifle ranges on the heath. There was talk of blood pouring into the drains.

*LTI.* While reading the *Myth* it occurs to me that perhaps one has to trace the blood theory—"myth of blood," etc., is something different again from the old expressions blood relation, my flesh and blood, prince of the blood, etc.—that perhaps one has to trace National Socialist theory back to the literal *blood lust* with which these people became intoxicated during the world war—because all of them are somehow drunk, obsessed, dangerously delirious, have lost their equilibrium. — [ . . . ]

## June 5, Friday morning

Yesterday afternoon, all of the night completely disrupted, because *the house appeared to be finally lost*. Eva clings to it with the utmost ardor; she also always says *I* should have secured it in good time (by transferring it to her), *I* acted negligently, *I* had always been reluctant with respect to the house. (She is right in that; I have never felt equal to the business.) The last few days were also particularly hard, the Gestapo twice, the dead cat, now the house. It was very painful. — Frau Ida Kreidl called me in: Her brother-in-law, Arndt, had been to see her, he and several other Jews had been summoned to the Gestapo and had to "sign" that their assets and house were *confiscated*. So I should at least not be too alarmed, if I received a summons to the Gestapo. The people had not been ill-treated there, nor had they been arrested. Only, coal was just being unloaded, and they had to help out—without shovels, with their bare hands!—Until this morning we had given up our house as finally lost. Today we are wondering, whether these are not isolated measures against a couple of rich people and whether Frau Kreidl was not in part confused and mistaken in what she reported: Because so far there have been frequent repetitions of the insistence that Jewish real estate will be expropriated only *after* the war, so that those who had served in the war could participate in the bidding. And why should expropriation require our signature at the Gestapo? — We are weighed down by so many troubles and something new is added every day, that there is no point in anticipating any others.

I read aloud [ . . . ].

Work: *The Myth of the Twentieth Century*.

[ . . . ]

## June 6, Saturday toward evening

Yesterday we inherited a potato-ration card from Ida Kreidl. Eva brought 44 pounds in two bags from town on the tram; I waited for her at Wasaplatz, and then hauled the bags up here from the tram. Now we shall again have enough to eat for a few days. We, c'est à dire, I. Quantitatively Eva eats much less, and at lunchtime she eats a bowl of something or other in town. Lately I have found it hard to do without saccharin; the last 500 pills fell victim to the house search. — Toward evening yesterday an hour with the Marckwalds. Much misery there. He long-windedly told me the history of a family related to him; once—landed property—they disposed of over six and a half million marks, and now, completely destitute, they are scattered across every continent.

New Gestapo cruelties all the time. Especially against elderly people. Now a group has been summoned to appear wearing *winter coats* (with a temperature of 79°F). Then they have to walk around town for hours, at intervals report again to Bismarckplatz, where they are beaten. — But also no day passes now on which someone does not report: "An Aryan told me:

'Bear up—it's all falling apart, here and at the front—it'll be over before the winter.' " — Downstairs Frau Ida Kreidl and Frau Pick are completely distraught with all their fears; Frau Pick is more in control of herself, but unburdens her heart to us every day; Ida Kreidl is often in tears. — Of the five men in the house: Ernst Kreidl, Paul Kreidl, Dr. Friedheim, Richard Katz, myself—I am now the only one left: Katz dead of cancer, Ernst Kreidl shot, Paul Kreidl deported, Friedheim imprisoned without hope.

This wretched hunger: How often do I steal a slice of bread from Kätchen's bread tin, a couple of potatoes from her bucket, a spoonful of honey or jam. I do it with a good conscience, because she needs little, allows much to go to waste, is given many things by her aged mother—but I feel so demeaned.

Tomorrow afternoon we have been invited to the Neumanns, who are being forced to leave their apartment. [ . . . ]

### June 7, Sunday midday

The most dismal Sunday evening downstairs yesterday. No tea, no hospitality, for fear *they* would come. The room blacked out early, so that *they* do not simply break in through the veranda door. (The garden gate cannot be locked; we keep the front entrance permanently locked.) Apart from ourselves Elsa Kreidl and Fräulein Ludwig were at table. It is quite unbelievable how terribly thin the two women have become since our days of catastrophe. Very tiny, pale pointed faces. With Elsa Kreidl the withering away only emphasized by the black clothes. The conversation revolved only around "them" and our helplessness. Fräulein Ludwig is the most terrified. Her devout Catholicism does not appear to give her any special strength. —

The bathroom here is served by a gas boiler. (Which we put on secretly, to avoid Kätchen grumbling.) One lights a tiny flame. If one then turns on the water, in a moment a whole row of flames lights up explosively and very quickly heats up the water flowing through. — The image has been going through my head all day today. *Every* idea is present in almost every age as a tiny individual flame. The racial idea, anti-Semitism, the Communist idea, the National Socialist one, faith, atheism—every idea. How does it come about, that suddenly *one* of these ideas grips a whole generation and becomes dominant? — If I had read Rosenberg's *Myth* in 1930, when it appeared, I would certainly have judged it to be a tiny flame, the crazy product of an individual, of a small unbalanced group. I would never have believed that the little flame could set anything alight—set anything alight in Germany!

### June 8, early on Monday

Yesterday afternoon at the Neumanns'. He reports as *absolutely authentic*, unanimously vouched for by various sources (including an "official"

source): Last week there had been a small fire in the "Soviet Paradise" exhibition. It was declared to be "Jewish arson," 500 men were arrested.
Thirty of them were released, 220 were put in concentration camps, 250
were *shot*, and the families of all 470 who had been removed were "evacuated." He told us as likewise vouched for: In Prague, after the attempt on
Heydrich (died a few days ago), there were house searches of the Czech
population. Wherever weapons were found, the whole family, man,
woman and children were exterminated. — The *Myth of the Twentieth Century:* blood lust. D'altra parte: we also heard the same old song at the Neumanns': "The Aryans say: 'Hold out! It's coming to an end!' " We were
agreed that our existence is now a race with death. [ . . . ] The Neumanns
must now leave their apartment, which they had occupied for twelve
years, although they now shared it with several Jews. (Neumark had a
room there.) *Renting storage* was forbidden some months ago, no married
couple gets more than *one* room, all surplus furniture and objects fall to
National Socialist Welfare in return for an arbitrarily fixed, completely
sham compensation in worthless money, which is placed in a blocked account. (Just as I received 40M for my typewriter.) Under these circumstances Neumann gave me a few volumes from his small library. He said,
if he lived to see the change come, he would immediately go to the USA
and could take only very little with him. I accepted the things "in trust."
[They included:] a three-volume popular edition of Grätz's *Geschichte der
Juden* [History of the Jews] (I can still see the eleven-volume edition in its
yellowish marbled boards in Father's bookcase, I slept under it; when
Father died I simply had it sold as "Jewish literature—of no interest to
me!"). [ . . . ]

Eva cut Frau Neumann's hair yesterday. Now she is going downstairs
to Frau Pick and Ida Kreidl with our vacuum cleaner, to do some cleaning
there. (Charwomen are forbidden—the old ladies do not know how to use
our appliance, Frau Pick cannot bend down.) In return potatoes and bread
coupons are cadged, and she also exchanges one white-bread coupon for
two rye coupons, Frau Pick also occasionally receives cigarettes from her
in-laws and gives them to Eva. — Elsa Kreidl still has a store of tobacco;
Eva wants to exchange dress fabric for it (as she has already done once
with Vogel on Chemnitzer Platz). Eva still clings to nicotine much more
desperately than I do, and there is ever less to be had on the female
smoker's card. I have for months been quite resigned to blackberry tea.
Eva rolls a mixture in cigarette papers, a big item of trade, which is now
also becoming scarce.

I intend to finish reading the *Myth* today; the notes will take up several
days. After that I shall recover with the Dubnow memoirs.

### June 9, Tuesday morning

Eva was vacuum cleaning in Ida Kreidl's rooms at about ten o'clock. Then
she came running upstairs out of breath with the vacuum cleaner.

"They're here again, they must not steal the vacuum cleaner." After a while the doorbell rang, I opened, four men. This time no box on the ears, got off lightly. One even addressed me formally. They wanted to see the apartment, a hundred questions, we will have to leave. In between, the most tyrannical inquisition again. "What kind of stuff have you been smoking here?" — "I have been smoking blackberry tea, my wife a cigarette." — "Does the book belong to you, did you buy it?" (*Myth of the 20th Century*) — "Lending library, borrowed by my wife." — "Which library still issues that?" — "How old are you? Why are you not working at Zeiss-Ikon?" — "Zeiss-Ikon is not taking anyone on at the moment." — It all passed off not too badly; they left without any stealing, beating, insults. But how crushed all of us were afterward, how bitter! All of us, because everyone came up to this room, Ida and Elsa Kreidl, Fräulein Ludwig, who was weeping in despair, Kätchen who did not stop her blathering. And the threat remains, weighs more heavily. We shall be packed into a single room somewhere, we shall be deprived of the lending library; I shall have to do some kind of mindless work or other. —

In the morning a pitiful letter from Trude Scherk about Grete's condition. She will have to be put in a home for the incurable. Because 1) she soils her linen, and who can wash it all, 2) the landlady behaves very inconsiderately to her and two feeble-minded girls, who are likewise quartered there, and 3) there were many evacuations taking place in Berlin again, and Grete's landlady was also threatened. Grete feels "that she is mad," and weeps a lot, when things she does not understand are discussed in her presence. She had taken greetings from us amiss, we had "offended" her. — How much in this letter really reflects Grete's subjective distress? How much of it is Trude's infantilism? Our last meeting with Grete (on her seventieth birthday) was a friendly one—she always got on *very* well with Eva. Trude Scherk also wrote, Änny Klemperer very rarely came to see Grete, she was avoiding the Jews' House. — As far as I know, Änny has cared loyally for Grete, but she always disliked her, and does not have a clue about her illness. In one of her last letters to me, she wrote that it was necessary to deal "strictly" with Grete's soiling of her laundry. She believed Grete's illness to be partly simulated, also believed it to some extent to be acquired out of egoism. I broke off my correspondence with Änny many months ago, when she was jubilant at German culture saved from the Russians. As a widow she will have come under the influence of her Aryan uniform-wearing relations; her sons do not suffer too greatly. While I was thinking about this a special chapter occurred to me—once I would have been hurt by the fact that I am not a writer, now I constantly think about the Curriculum, about "bearing witness": the Aryan wife, the mixed marriage. Types, cases observed: Änny Klemperer—Frau Feder—Elsa Kreidl—Frau Steinitz, who holds her husband answerable as it were. D'altra parte: Frau Glaser—he floats romantically above things; she takes care of everything. [ . . . ]

The newspaper regularly prints an "NSDAP text of the week," some quote from the Führer accompanied by a little sermon. Yesterday, and this was the most comforting aspect of recent days, the following Hitler sentence, a nation proves itself not so much in victory as in holding out through apparent failures. The accompanying text went: thus we had held out through the terrible winter at the front and at home, and thus we were now victorious again. Of course the sermon mitigated the ominousness of the text, but nevertheless, the text tells its own tale.

Elsa Kreidl gave us her little-used potato-ration card, and yesterday we went to Kaden, the greengrocer. Eva bought, I waited and afterward hauled back the 30 pounds. This waiting in front of shops, which is often my lot, is particularly horrible. There are prams; children and dogs are playing, blathering females are coming and going (all kinds of shops are close together there, butcher, greengrocer, baker, dairy, etc., etc.), and the whole world eyes my star. Torture—I can resolve a hundred times to pay no attention, it remains torture. Also I never know whether someone walking or driving past is not in the Gestapo, whether he will not insult me, spit on me, arrest me.

I must now go at my notes on the *Myth*. Much of it I did not understand, and the little bit is always the same. As mere LTI the work I have in mind would contain little more than two dozen words and expressions. I must expand it—but in which direction? Perhaps everything, the language, what I have studied and experienced, will flow into the *one* fourth volume of my Curriculum. [ . . . ] For the time being I can do nothing but read and make excerpts from whatever I can get hold of, and keep my diary with the greatest precision. Which, moreover, is a courageous act and which again and again makes me afraid. —

Talking to Eva, Frau Pick excellently summed up Kätchen Sara's very difficult character and mental state as: "Infantile, kind, with a strong sense of self-importance." Good, but not sufficient. Petit bourgeois in all her judgments. Very materialistic. Her intellect in a most curious state. As if from time to time firm lumps bob up in a dissolved mass of brain. Occasionally a pertinent remark about a person, a book, occasionally a touch of peasant cunning, then again and very, very often, absolute stupidity, aimless blathering, the same sentence is repeated a thousand times, the same expression, the same fragment of an idea. [ . . . ]

### June 10, Wednesday morning

Yesterday evening I went to see Steinitz for a while. At first only his wife was there, with whom he lives in a state of conflict, whom he fears, but who behaves reasonably to me. *He* came back from the cemetery only toward seven. He is afraid of house searches, deliberately comes home late (Magnus does likewise). He held a position in Bohemia for many years, both of the Steinitzes had spoken to a Czech, who had been in

Prague immediately after the assassination attempt. Heydrich had always taken a well-known route, in a car with police in front, between the castle and his villa. The police had been hit by submachine-gun fire, the Protector's car by a bomb. The newspaper had then published the names of the many who had been put in front of a firing squad with their families, almost without exception intellectuals, very many professors of the Technical University and doctors. —[ . . . ]

Eva bargained with Ernst Kreidl's widow to exchange her tobacco inheritance for peacetime clothing fabric. (She did a similar deal in the winter with Vogel, the grocer.)

### June 11, Thursday afternoon

After an absolutely terrible day a permanent worsening of the situation. Yesterday lunchtime at about half past one—I had the potatoes on the stove—the Gestapo again, the fourth time in two weeks. Upstairs everything seemed at first to be vented on Kätchen, who was sitting in the bath [ . . . ] and appeared in her bathrobe. In the morning she had received a long, typewritten report from her brother-in-law about the air raid on Cologne and about the great destruction. In itself nothing punishable, since the raid had been described in all the newspapers and since Ludwig Voss's letters are patriotic. But to a Jewess! "That makes you Jews happy! You use it to make mischief!" The envelope lay on Kätchen's table beside a postcard from her mother, who promised her cooking oil from her ration card (that, too, a crime). The letter was found crumpled up in a leather armchair ("hidden"!). Everything ransacked, Kätchen had to roll up the carpet, was kicked as she did so, wailed, was threatened, had to write down her brother-in-law's address. Her rooms were in as great a chaos as on the first attack. The range of nasty words of abuse was rather narrow. Again and again "pig," "Jewish pig," "sow," "piece of dung"—nothing else occurs to them. I was forced onto a chair in the lobby, was forced to see and hear everything, all the time trembling because of my diary. I had to help take down the heavy paintings. So far nothing very bad had happened to me. "Why has your old dear got so much wool and fabric lying around? Doesn't she know there's a fabric collection?" — "But yes, she's just looking for things for the collection." I thought I was out of danger, when *The Myth of the Twentieth Century* and my sheet of notes beside it led to catastrophe. The time before, with an officer who was evidently more senior, book and notes had hardly aroused any objection. Now *this* reading matter was held against me as a terrible crime. The book was thumped down on my skull, my ears were boxed, a ridiculous straw hat of Kätchen's was pressed onto my head: "You look pretty!" When I replied to questioning, that I had held my post until 1935, two fellows, with whom I was already acquainted, spat between my eyes. At the same time Eva returned from shopping. Her bag was immediately taken from her, they also shouted at her because of the book. I wanted to come to her aid, was

JUNE 1942 73

slapped and pushed and kicked into the kitchen. (This time, too, slaps and kicks were bearable—but my poor heart and my fear of further developments!) Eva defended herself very calmly. "*I* borrowed the book; I'm interested in your approach, I'm writing about it to my cousin, the mayor of Potsdam, Arno Rauscher." — One of the fellows roared: "You're trying to threaten us, you'll suffer for that!" ([But . . . ] this time they didn't hit her and "only once spat" at her "a little.") She said very calmly that there was no question of a threat, she did not even know whether her cousin was still in office, she had had to approach him a little while before, because of her proof of ancestry, she had mentioned him just now to account for an interest in a book of the Third Reich. — "If I had a relative who was involved with a Jew, I would despise her utterly, you traitor to your race!" So it went on for a little while longer, but there were no further assaults on Eva. Only, to the accompaniment of the most violent threats, we were pressed to return the book and not to dare make further use of a lending library. (Afterward I told Eva, that her defense had been risky and could have unpleasant consequences. She responded: "These beasts are cowards." — A few years ago she found the name and picture of this cousin, with whom she had spent a great deal of time as a girl, in an illustrated magazine. Today she discovered from the Potsdam Directory that he has meanwhile retired, but lives in Schloss Sans Souci, Potsdam. Perhaps really a very last hope.) The balance sheet of yesterday's house search for us: All bread was gone, an untouched two-pound loaf, a packet of matches, all the soap in the bathroom, almost all the sugar, a five-mark note from my wallet. Terrible! *But the really irreparable harm is the stopping of the lending library.* Now my possibilities of study have been even further restricted than before. I shall plead and beg from all the Jewish families and from Annemarie, but I am undoubtedly even more checkmated, as it were, than before. In addition there is the fear, the ever-greater fear of having manuscripts in the house. The 18ième, the Curriculum, the *LTI*—everything has come to a standstill. I can no longer work, only keep myself busy. And the uncertainty, which has become even more intense. — The real catastrophe, however, did not take place upstairs with Kätchen and myself. — (I forgot, on the floor things looked as they did when we first cleared up, only not quite so bad. Nevertheless, the sheet of notes on the *Myth,* two days' work, was torn to shreds, and Eva's cigarette papers were scattered and trampled on, likewise again her solitaire cards.) — The catastrophe befell seventy-seven-year-old Frau Pick. She has again been terribly beaten and knocked about. "Your husband had the malt factory. The bloodsucker! Your *litter* is abroad and inciting hatred against us, but we've got you, and you won't get away from us. — You will be at the Gestapo at seven o'clock tomorrow morning — you'll go alone—anyone accompanying you goes straight to a concentration camp." Frau Pick told us that, when we went downstairs afterward. She added something noteworthy. Three fellows had tormented her, a fourth, alone with her for a moment, had whispered to her in the most friendly manner: "Take some good advice, don't go there tomorrow morning." (We recently heard of a similar case from Kätchen: a woman she works with came home, the driver of a Gestapo car at the front door called out to her: "Fräulein, go and take a walk for a while, they're upstairs!" So there are "traitors" even among these people.) Frau Pick said she was physically incapable of going all that way to be ill-treated again, she had had a good life, and now it was over. Frau Pick, in contrast to Ida Kreidl, is not at all sentimental and sloppy, she had previously always emphasized her joy in life and her will to live. We were seriously concerned about her. At nine she came upstairs to see us, brought 55M, some jewelry, and a couple of little things, we should have them if she were to be arrested tomorrow. Just before ten I went down to her again; she was sitting quietly in her leather armchair, a blanket pulled over her, very calm, but very pale, and there was a constant twitch between her eyes. I told her: "We won't pretend; you intend to kill yourself. Think about your children, think that where there's life, there's hope, that the Nazis' cause is hope*less*, stay brave . . . ," etc., etc. I tried to give her strength in every way possible, to appeal to her. I said: "Give me your word, that you will not do anything to yourself." — "I cannot promise that, I will consider things once again." — "Why don't you give me your Veronal?" (Where do all these people get the Veronal from?) — "That would not make any difference, Professor, I have other remedies besides that one. I am so tired now, and I feel so unwell." — I went upstairs, we were all convinced that she would kill herself. — At six, we were still in bed, Kätchen—she then fled to work—opened our bedroom door, behind her, looking upset, stood Frau Ida Kreidl. Frau Pick was sleeping very deeply, her breathing was very weak, we should take a look at her. The woman appeared to be sleeping calmly, but her breathing was very quiet, very flat and fast, and she was not moving, even though we were talking beside her bed and opening and closing the door. We hesitated until almost eight o'clock, then I went across the road to the nursery garden—very friendly, sympathetic people, anti-Nazi people—and telephoned Dr. Katz. I was not a doctor, but I suspected Veronal poisoning. He said he had little freedom of movement—he was allowed a car *only at night* for the most serious cases—he would send a nurse *immediately* and come in the course of the morning. When the nurse, a calm, mature woman, came, Frau Pick was still unconscious, but her breathing was better, she was also moving occasionally. It did not appear to be a serious poisoning. We had reckoned on the Gestapo appearing at eight, but they had been notified by Dr. Katz. We repeatedly went downstairs to Frau Pick's; we chatted and listened anxiously to every car. (The heightened fear and uncertainty are the worst things.) Katz arrived toward midday and was somewhat aghast to find a case that was not a serious one. [ . . . ] According to her own statement, Frau Pick had taken *only* Adalin; the Gestapo regarded such acts as "deception" and "sabotage"; these people merely wanted to avoid the summons. He, Katz, would present the case in a more serious light, not least to protect both of us. But Frau Pick will have recovered in two days, and after three or four days will again receive an order from the Gestapo, where she will now be ill-treated with a vengeance. — Thus I foresee further calamity. The suicide attempt will be repeated, this household will continue to attract the Gestapo's attention. [ . . . ] I saw and heard something of Frau Pick gradually coming to. Distressing. She is a refined, good-looking, slim old lady, a real lady. How, helpless and stupefied, she was placed on a chamber pot, how the naked thighs were yellow bones with a little covering, how through some clumsiness the pot broke . . . Afterward, she began to say a few words: usually a vigorous, spirited voice, now a plaintive, unintelligible singsong. And I felt horror rather than pity. — Yesterday, and for most of today, I was shattered, the growing fear for one's life, the tightening stranglehold, the remorseless uncertainty weighed very heavily. Now, toward evening, I am calmer again. Things must go on even under these circumstances. Some kind of worthwhile reading will after all be found, and I shall risk continuing with the diary. I shall bear witness to the very end. — [ . . . ]

## June 12, Friday morning

I have such a strong feeling of being cast down into the next circle of hell by being cut off from borrowing books. Unmetaphorical: The day before yesterday, on June 10, 1942, a new, worse phase began. A great deal is still blocked out by restlessness, worrying about downstairs, piles of washing up, the day passes quickly. But when our everyday life gets back to normal again—with what shall I fill the emptiness? — Meanwhile we are constantly in suspense. Everything is hidden as quickly as possible after use—really everything: solitaire cards, pens, envelopes, every crumb of food [ . . . ]. Before I fill my pipe, I look out of the window, in case there is anything suspicious . . . No animal can be so hounded, so timid.
     [ . . . ]

## June 13, Saturday morning

*LTI.* The limited number of insults, the small register; any Spaniard surpasses it. A couple of stereotyped phrases: "The Talmud says that for you every woman who is not a Jewess is a whore." The question: "Do you have children?" If yes: "Of course, your brood is stirring up hatred against us abroad." If no: "Of course—you pigs abort them!" Frau Pick has a niece, whom I met on the catastrophic afternoon and who asked me to give her news by telephone of the developments of the next morning. Married to an Aryan, whom I do not know, a Professor Gaehde. The Gestapo people asked me: "Do you know Professor Gaehde? He is married to a Jewish sow. — You must know him." I denied it quite truthfully. I then discovered that the man had been a teacher (with the title of professor) until 1920 [ . . . ], after that joined the management of the Picks' malt factory. Thus, changing his profession, he had enjoyed the wealth of the Pick family. —

After the suicide attempt, of which she was informed, the niece did not show her face for one and a half days. Yesterday afternoon she came to the garden gate, rang the second-floor bell, so that the *Aryan* Elsa Kreidl appeared, and said her husband had forbidden her to enter the house (he was waiting a few yards away)—could the inhabitants of the house take care of her aunt. Then she fled with her husband. — I must remember these people. Perhaps one day I shall after all have standing and influence again. —

Frau Pick is markedly better, almost too much so, and now her fear of what is impending is growing all the time. Ida Kreidl cannot cope with the nursing and the anxiety, her in-law Elsa makes herself as scarce as possible, Fräulein Ludwig has fled. Yesterday morning Eva scrubbed the kitchen downstairs, I pulled clothes poles out of the garden, poured out what water was left in a laundry boiler . . . The nurse was there for a couple of hours, intends to come once again today. An able, calm, hardworking woman, who also lends a hand with the housework. Frau Lampen relates that this very morning she had been addressed on two different streets by two different gentlemen, both wearing medal ribbons, in almost the same words: "Head up—there'll be good weather again," and "Bear up—the sun's coming." (Since the weather was indeed changing from rain to sunshine, the expression suggested itself.) A while ago Frau Lampen was in custody for four months but was then acquitted, because the witness for the prosecution had begun to waver. On a winter's morning Frau Lampen had shivered in the bath and said "brrr!" at the very moment the witness had said "Heil Hitler!" According to the denunciation, Frau Lampen had shivered loudly and contemptuously when she heard the German greeting. This happened two or three years ago—last winter Frau Lampen would no longer have been acquitted.

Late in the afternoon we were both (Eva for the first time) at the Marckwalds'. Frau Marckwald had been here shortly before that, had seen to Frau Pick, had given us two pounds of bread coupons as a present. [ . . . ]

The Gestapo recently took exception to Eva's woolen things, which were lying around. "Does your old dear not know about the fabric collection?" I said, she was just looking out for suitable things. Today the order came from the Jewish Community: For wearers of the star and their spouses compulsory surrender of linen, clothes, etc. Eva has just "voluntarily" taken a big bundle of her things to the Aryan collecting station. I myself have little to give away to the Community. Perhaps some of Eva's things can be got to Pirna and saved. If she goes over there this afternoon, then she will take manuscript pages with her again. But since Eva's clash with the Gestapo, I am almost more concerned about her than about myself. — Today I have not yet had fifteen minutes' peace. To the window again and again, in case a car had driven up. Again and again I hid sheets of paper, and playing cards, tobacco, pipe were stuffed into pockets. — Once when I rang the bell downstairs, Frau Ida Kreidl in the bathroom did not hear that it was the peaceful house sign and came rushing out, her blouse unbuttoned and her hands wet. An unutterably ghastly condition. —

*LTI.* The couple of pages of notes I had made on the *Myth* were torn up. I shall attempt to outline in a few words what sticks in my mind as important. As a student I made fun of the author of the Shakespeare monograph (Sieper?), who counts the drums, trumpet blasts and pipes; now I had prepared a sheet of paper to record the use of *blood,* in all its substantive, adjectival, verbal combinations, ditto of *species* and *race. Earthbound* should be checked for use as praise and rebuke. When Phoenicians, Etruscans, etc., it is a rebuke = materialistic. — The ironical quotation marks (the Jewish "nation") should be counted. The use of foreign words to give oneself a scholarly air [ . . . ].

Three parts: I. The conceptual and historical foundation. II. The art of Nordic man. III. Program of the National Socialist state. (The work was first published in 1930 [ . . . ], my edition dates from 1934. When the program was already beginning to be realized.) Much of what Rosenberg demands has by now long been taken for granted. In some respects he is more aristocratic than the present line (but in no way less brutal), in foreign policy he arranges the pieces in a pattern different from the current one. (He still places hopes in England, he is no friend of the yellow race.) He frequently repeats himself, for he knows only *one* sentence: The Nordic race, Nordic blood are the bearers of *all* culture, of *all* that is good—every mixing of blood produces something inferior. — Close relationship to Chamberlain, whom he often paraphrases and greatly admires. But goes far beyond him. Race research is more differentiated and self-confident now. And everything is incomparably more politicized, topical and fanatical than in Chamberlain. — Extensive discussion of matriarchy ("earthbound," Phoenician, etc.) and patriarchy, the Nordic sun-worshipping mentality (cf. *sunny!*). [ . . . ] Polemic against Spengler's cultural crisis. — The Jews even more despised than in Chamberlain: not a people, but—the phrase is a quotation, but from whom?—a parasitic "antirace," which must be extirpated, at least driven out of Europe. But the main thrust of the opus, repeated over and over, is against the Roman Church, against Pope and Jesuits. "Jesuits," "humanity," "Pope" are red rags to Rosenberg. The figure of the Nordic Jesus (No brown Jew boy with flat feet and a hooked nose! I think that's literally what it says) is venerated, everything Pauline, Jewish is forbidden. Protestantism also comes off badly, also Luther. Religion should build on Meister Ekkehard (viewed through Kant), have no dogma [ . . . ]. It should hark back to Odin, press forward as far as Emperor Frederick II. Its inmost essence, its "supreme value": honor. In contrast to Christian *love.* Love is not "character building." Love is often weakness, and in church policy it stands for universalism, just like "humanity," and equals hypocrisy! — Religion, including the Christian religion, is to be free—*but:* the "so-called Old Testament" [ . . . ] will be forbidden, Pauline doctrine (i.e., "Jewish" doctrine) will be rewritten, promi-

nence given to a blond, blue-eyed Christ—*blond* is a favorite word, once
*blond blood!* Ban on the Catholic bishops' oath to combat heretics. —*Two*
positions with regard to the family: 1) paterfamilias prevails over matriar-
chal sexuality. 2) The family is not the basis of the state, only male bonds
(classical antiquity, officers, SA). — Only Nordic man has true religion,
true artistic genius, true science, is truly able to observe nature. Inner freedom of the soul. (Jews without religion; materialistic. Jehovah's arbitrary
power—magic.)

Jotted down in haste before Eva left. — June 13, afternoon.

### June 14, Sunday, toward evening

Potatoes, morning, noon and evening [ . . . ], which I eat in their jackets,
cold or warm. Yesterday afternoon—while Eva went off to the fabric collection station and further afield (heavily laden)—removed the sprouts on
a basin of potatoes, which Elsa Kreidl had offered us from her plentiful
supply. — At lunchtime today at the Glasers, where Eva later joined us.
We were kept there and stayed for coffee. Classical gramophone records, I
leafed through a book *Conductors of the Twentieth Century*, which had pictures and essays. Otto Klemperer, "a man possessed," was very prominent. Perhaps he will be the only one of all the Klemperers to survive.
Vanitatum vanitas. Distraught talk about our experiences of recent days.
— Back at around four, soaked by a thunderstorm; had no sooner drunk
tea than Steinitz came to visit. The same themes. He thinks I should register "voluntarily" for work, a big paper factory in Niedersedlitz was still
hiring Jews. I would be safer because of it. With the great restlessness of
recent days and the ever-decreasing possibility of seriously carrying on
any of my own work, I am almost tempted. But I would think of it as desertion. I can still do a little bit (at the moment Dubnow's memoirs)—also
I don't like to leave Eva alone and quite without support. I shall go on
being a fatalist, wait and see what turns up, and intellectually get out of
these days whatever I can. In the factory the nine to ten working hours
will mean nine to ten hours of semiconsciousness, while at home there are
always intellectual oases. I am provided with study reading for a while. In
the worst case I've got *Wilhelm Meister* waiting for me. — After dinner we
must go down to Pick-Kreidl's for a couple of minutes.

### June 16, Tuesday afternoon

At lunchtime yesterday I registered with Dr. Simon, the dentist. His first
question: "Is Friedheim really dead?" — "I don't know, the rumor has
been going around since yesterday." — Toward evening Hirschel, the superintendent of the Jewish Community, was downstairs with the ladies
Pick and Kreidl. He had already received a telephone call from the police
presidium on Friday evening at half past ten, the corpse of Dr. Friedheim
should be fetched immediately. He has not yet received the death certifi-

cate, from which we shall learn the cause of death. A shudder ran through every one of us, every one of us is very close to death. (Frau Pick, Ida Kreidl, Elsa Kreidl, myself were present.) The atmosphere was made even gloomier by Hirschel's further reports. Three Berlin transports in a desperate condition have already passed through the city and been given coffee. They go to the Theresienstadt assembly camp, from where dispersal to Poland follows. Principally the widows and children of the men recently shot in Berlin or sent to concentration camps. Finally Hirschel told us of another Dresden case. A family by the name of Jadlowski (or something like it), elderly married couple, the woman 68, blood pressure 220. House search a few weeks ago. "Open the refrigerator!" The key not to hand, the officer lets the matter rest. Afterward the woman shouted with joy: "What good luck, I had half a pound of fish in it, which the kind sales assistant . . ." Someone hears it and denounces her. Investigation by the Gestapo, the couple interrogated separately. He confesses, she denies. He is released after a beating, she is sent to the police cells, and from there, a few days ago, to a concentration camp. Which she will certainly not survive. For half a pound of fish. —

This morning to Dr. Simon for treatment. The man both doctor and dentist, almost fifty, a little of the temper and manner of Dr. Isakowitz, but more boastful and garrulous, yet not without an intellect. He still has a fine peacetime apartment on the first floor of 15 Reichsstrasse, a large house beside the Orthodox church, but no longer has any staff. He opens the door himself, carries out the treatment alone, in complicated cases is assisted by his wife. She is Aryan and is *not* allowed to accompany him when he is called out to a Jewish patient. Among the Jews everything now spreads with fairy-tale-like speed: Did I want to speak to Frau Gaehde, who would be waiting for me after the treatment. (Who had told her that I would be at Dr. Simon's?!) I hesitated at first, said how angry I was at the couple's behavior. Dr. Simon said, "Fine, then you've simply canceled today's appointment," but then added, one should not condemn anyone too hastily, the woman was in a nasty predicament, she might put herself and her nearest and dearest at risk, without helping her aunt. At that I agreed to the conversation. Afterward I found Frau Gaehde in the waiting room, she looked very worn-out. She wanted to know how her aunt had reacted. I responded: "If you appeal to me to be frank—I am not going to pass judgment on your morals, but I was unable to make up my mind to talk to your aunt about you, because I cannot understand why you have stayed away, and I cannot understand how one could demand such a thing from you, and how you, madam, could agree to it." She said she knew that in our house we condemned her, she was in the most agonizing position and in constant distress, but she risked arrest if she came, and that would immediately result in the most serious threat to her husband and her son. She had been forced to make a choice. She was very attached to her aunt, she was suffering greatly, she begged me "to be her advocate." I finally promised her that, and we shook hands on parting. I shall go downstairs to Frau Pick later. — [ . . . ] Dr. Simon worked deftly and talked uninterruptedly about his surgical skill, his great deeds, his former "international practice," the incapacity of his German colleagues, the excellence of American dentistry, the political situation, reported as vouched for from Aryan sources [that] in Berlin not only had a couple of hundred Jews been shot, but 1,500 Aryans as well; [ . . . ] altogether there was a great deal of desertion and many shootings [ . . . ]. But he did not expect an end before a) the Americans had landed and b) the Italians had dropped out. We agreed that today the whole world and not only "*the* Jew" had at least one foot in the grave. —

New circular: Jews must hand over all electrical appliances, vacuum cleaners, gramophones and gramophone records. After the recently compiled special regulations for Jews I here begin a new list of the individual tortures: 1) Surrender of fabrics, 2) Surrender of electrical appliances. But Aryan wives appear to be excused number 2. Later I shall go over to Hirschel [ . . . ] and ask his opinion. He is a small man, who looks as un-Jewish as can be: pale blue eyes, blond hair. (His fat, bespectacled wife with her two little boys talked to me in Hähne's shop a few days ago. The few Jews who are still left here are forced together more and more.) Hirschel, said to have been the hardworking and well-to-do manager of the fur department at Hirsch's, a big store here, is now living off his savings and carries out his harrowing, distressing, and dangerous duties without the least compensation. Heroism without consolation. —

[ . . . ] The curious vitality and the curious force of habit: There are moments, particularly in the morning, when I am constantly running to the window, in case there is a car, when fear and dread make me incapable of anything, and then things get moving after all, reading and reading aloud is a pleasure, food tastes good, the day slips by, not even unpleasantly, lastly I even risk a page of my diary, which can cost me my life. [ . . . ]

### June 19, Friday morning

Wednesday, at about seven o'clock in the evening, furious ringing of the doorbell (the bell push remained stuck). Gestapo car. I opened up, Frau Kreidl was there also. Two of our tormentors, as well as an officer in army uniform with the Iron Cross, First Class. I was courteously asked a number of questions. I could go, Frau Ida Kreidl was also treated courteously and not molested, they merely unsealed Friedheim's rooms and rummaged around in them for a while, before sealing them again. — Later I said to Frau Kreidl: Only the lower ranks are really bad, when an officer is present, one has a degree of protection. She responded very emphatically: "No!" Immediately after these people, Hirschel came for a moment and announced that the funeral service for Friedheim would take place the next day, Thursday afternoon, at five o'clock. He said the officer was Major Schindhelm, head of the Gestapo here, familiar with all their methods and in agreement with them, occasionally also present at beatings.

After supper we now always sit for a while with Frau Pick, who is still very weak (and who gets on badly with Ida Kreidl—both complain about the other to us). The question arose of who would go to Friedheim's funeral service—a long walk, since we are banned from tram and Great Garden and the cemetery is at the end of Fürstenstrasse. Frau Pick is afraid of being alone. ("If *they* come . . ."). We promised to help, and so yesterday morning, after endless discussions with Frau Pick and Ida Kreidl and Kätchen Sara had already taken place over breakfast, I walked over to the Hirschels'. Wiener Strasse 85, very close to the Marckwalds. A very elegant property, owner Frau Hirschel, née Glauber, a very solid, elegant drawing room with two well-filled bookcases. Frau Hirschel, in her mid-thirties, two small boys, received me, it turned out there were curious connections. She had been an assistant to Walzel, with whom she still corresponded [ . . . ]. Julius Wahle, with whom I edited the Walzel festschrift, was her uncle, and died in this house a year ago at a very great age. Frau Pick was living with the Hirschels before she moved into our Jews' House. Frau Hirschel's attitude: German, emphatically non-Zionist, emphatically aesthetic, Goethe-German—"*we* shall save Goethe!"—but also, no doubt become so under the pressure of the times, emphatically religious, orthodox Jewish. Pleasantly discreet to me. I asked for books. Once she had "neither loaned nor borrowed" books, now she was happy if "there was a bit of life in her library" as a result. She gave me one volume of *Zionist Writings* by Herzl and lent me three volumes of Dubnow's *Jewish History*. — She organized help for Frau Pick for the afternoon. First she herself would come, then be relieved by a tenant. — She was unambiguous on the cause of Friedheim's death: It was, of course, possible that he had really died of heart failure, but . . . [ . . . ] There had been an old business pending against Friedheim, which they had probably taken up again. (He was the owner of the Bassenge banking house—God knows what he had tried to save.)

In the afternoon to the Jewish cemetery with Ida Kreidl, who complained incessantly. One and a half hours: Strehlener Kirche, Reicker Strasse, Rayskistrasse, Grunaer Weg, Grüne Wiese (Gusti Wieghardt's district!), Haenel Claus Strasse, Borsbergstrasse. Dresden is lovely: the dark hills, the abundance of nursery gardens, the magnificent flowers and aromas, the piece of open countryside with the gas works like a stopper in the middle of it. But Ida Kreidl complained incessantly about the excessive length of the way there and how we were being hounded and had to avoid the Great Garden . . . And on the way back (alone and, on Eva's advice, somewhat shorter, by way of Giesingstrasse—exactly one and a quarter hours) I was also very tired, so that yesterday I did not manage a diary entry. — I had first seen the bare cemetery hall two years ago. This time everything seemed even sadder. A dozen old women, a dozen men, some wearing top hats, Reichenbach looked like a plucked bird, the hat kept slipping over his eyes. Seven corpses were being dispatched. I found myself in an orthodox ceremony, the man wearing a gown read a long Hebrew prayer; afterward, after the coffin had been carried out, he recited a second Hebrew prayer while making curious Catholic obeisances to the altar wall. I then went outside for a while, Eva arrived, and we went back in together. The clergyman came up to me: He was a grammar-school teacher whom I had once met at the Breits as their tenant. For Sally Friedheim he read two psalms in German, while the covered black box stood in front of him. Of man's mortality, and that God, the Eternal, protects us. It was all very dreary and quite lacking in solemnity. Two people wept: Fräulein Ludwig and Elsa Kreidl (who was thinking of her husband who was shot). There were no relatives of the deceased. His sister had just died in Hildesheim, his brother was deported and has not been heard of. —

At midday on Thursday I had only a very small Gestapo fright: A man who identified himself as being "from the Geheime Staatspolizei" was courteous apart from that and wanted only to go into Friedheim's rooms. He seemed familiar, and he also asked Ida Kreidl about me: He was one of the group who had gone through my books in Dölzschen and relieved me of some, he was also looking for books in Friedheim's room.

In Shaw's *Saint Joan* there is a wild hunter of heretics, who breaks down in despair when he sees Joan burning. "I did not know . . . !" He was unable to imagine the horror. Until now I had found our situation *just as literally unimaginable:* I had always been told about being beaten and spat upon, of trembling at the sound of a car, at every ring at the door, of disappearing and not coming back again—I had not known it. Now I know it, now the dread is always inside me, deadened for a couple of hours or become habitual or paralyzed by "So far things have always turned out well in the end" and then alive and at one's throat again. It's a point of difference between Eva and myself. *She* says to her it was nothing new or surprising, she had heard it all a hundred times before. I: But only now am I experiencing it; my imagination or my altruism were not strong enough to experience it only through others. — I compare this dread of death with that in the field. This here is a thousand times more horrible. There it was at worst "the field of honor," there I was certain of every assistance were I to be wounded. Now—these horrible disappearances. What became of Friedheim? What happened to him, when he was dragged out of here? What happened in prison? How did he die? Snuffed out; drowned in the dirt after agonies. It is a thousand, a thousand times more horrible than all my fear in 1915. — And always being afraid, always running to the window, in case a car . . . Program for the rest of the morning: first some Dubnow notes for a little while, then remove sprouts from our scant remaining potatoes in the cellar. Our shortage of food is getting worse. [ . . . ] we have only one loaf due, and we shall have no new bread coupons for a week. I get pangs of conscience for eating too much.

### June 21, Sunday morning

Now they say that Friedheim committed suicide by hanging himself. No one will find out for certain. Fräulein Ludwig requested to be allowed to see the body. *Refused.* Fräulein Ludwig must now register for work. She was immediately referred to the political section of the Party; since she was in service with a Jew, she remains suspect.

Yesterday at the dentist, Dr. Simon, again. His spell completely broken: He works cursorily for two minutes, chatters for 58 minutes, praising himself, disparaging all his colleagues Aryan and non-Aryan.

For the first time with respect to food there is not merely shortage but real lack and hunger. Bread almost finished, the potatoes ancient and tasting disgusting, especially when cold.

*On the situation and LTI.* It appears as if they absolutely want to have Sevastopol by tomorrow—the war against Russia began on June 22, 1941. Yesterday there were "decisive successes." A catchword, which still flourished last summer, but is now never mentioned: "Blitzkrieg." [ . . . ]

Very intermittent enjoyment of life. In the evening after ten o'clock. "*They* won't come today at least." A couple of minutes reading aloud in bed—Eva falls asleep—I get the sentences mixed-up, the next morning I literally remember nothing of the pages I last read (or rather stuttered). But going to bed and falling asleep is also a pleasure and security. Then we are usually already up at five, and now I frequently—as today—read aloud for an hour. It's a good and stimulating hour. After that, while getting dressed, washing dishes, making breakfast, the misery closes in on me: uncertainty, loathing. And then I hear Eva sigh despairingly in the bathroom. —

[ . . . ]

Painful to me is the empty garden bench below my window. All last summer Ernst Kreidl and Dr. Friedheim sat there engaged in a hundred conversations. Now Kreidl has been shot and Friedheim has "died" in prison.

Very cool weather, but it is supposed to be beneficial to the harvest. The Jews say "*unfortunately* beneficial." But a *good* harvest is hardly possible after the damage of the winter, and a merely moderate one will hardly help. [ . . . ]

### June 22, Monday, before six o'clock in the morning

Reading aloud since quarter to five, and now Kätchen has to use the bathroom at an unwonted time. —

[ . . . ] Fabrics are due to be handed in by today, and Eva literally has to risk her head for something like Frau Pick's costume and woolen drawers—because getting them out of the house can cost prison-concentration-camp-death. Eva gave her own things, ten dresses, five jackets, three blouses, thirteen pounds of "other items" (serviceable linen), to an Aryan collecting station. After three years of being thrifty with a stock of clothes that was never plentiful, I do not have much left for the Community: a tattered suit, an even more tattered pair of trousers, two pairs of briefs, full of holes; eleven ancient ties. Povera e nuda vai . . .

[ . . . ]

I am always dogged by the thought: Will anything come of my present reading, and what? *LTI*? Curriculum? A third thing? [ . . . ]

## June 23, early on Tuesday

Tobruk captured by Rommel yesterday, Sevastopol about to fall. Very powerful impression. After weakness on the German side, it does not look as if there will be an end before winter. And the misery of fear and shortages goes on. — To see Steinitz for a moment in the evening. He is afraid to come back from the cemetery before seven; his wife bickers with him even in my presence; furthermore she does not tire in expressing her contempt for the English and her conviction of Hitler's final victory. Very unpleasant minutes.

Read Herzl's *Jewish State* with mixed feelings.

I can no longer believe in the completely un-German character of National Socialism; it is homegrown, a malignant growth out of *German* flesh, a strain of cancer, just as there is a *Spanish influenza*.

## Toward midday

When Eva goes out now, our leave-taking is always very affectionate; she does not know whether she will still find me here. Fear from one hour to the next, forever running to the window when a car rolls up. It is hardly an exaggeration anymore: Fear and hunger fill the day. Hunger alternates with nausea: When they are cold, I can only manage to eat the old, bad potatoes in spite of myself, and they agree neither with my stomach nor with my bowels. But more than that I am tormented by fear. Our coupons are so much at an end that Eva is completely dependent on the unrationed "dish of the day" at the restaurant. She has to go to Pirna again tomorrow. She'll take another couple of pages with her again.

## Afternoon

[ . . . ]

News of the day: Almost six weeks ago I gave my shoes to the only Jewish cobbler, a "Russian bear," as Eva always says, in Sporergasse—the house belongs to the Community and is inhabited by Jewish proletarians. I am waiting desperately for these shoes; only when they are fetched can I give the overworked man another pair, and there are almost no heels left on my much-patched boots. Eva, who has frequently inquired about them, was at last supposed to be able to collect them tomorrow. Now there was a house search at 3 Sporergasse, and the cobbler has been arrested (supposedly because cigarettes were found). So I shall have to go on walking in shoes without heels. [ . . . ]

Latest decree: Jewish schools will be shut from June 30, nor are children allowed to receive private tuition. An intellectual death sentence, enforced illiteracy. They will not succeed. A lorry, piled high with trunks and bundles, drove up: general collection of confiscated fabrics. (The Aryans give some things voluntarily; *everything* is wrung from the Jews. Whatever is necessary for "modest use" may be kept back. How will the Gestapo interpret that?) The entirely Jewish marriages also have to surrender all electrical appliances and gramophones. We—for the time being—are excused that. —

Study of Herzl's Zionist writings. Very great affinity with Hitlerism. Except that Herzl dodges the blood definition. To him a nation is a "historical group, which recognizably belongs together and has a common enemy." (Very weak-kneed definition.)

The schools' closure is number 3 in a second series of Jewish measures.

## June 24, Wednesday morning

We talked about our worsening situation. How inconsequential the house searches were in Dölzschen. And now . . . Eva said: "*These* are no longer house searches. They're *pogroms*." She's completely right in that.

[ . . . ]

There was an official statement in the newspaper: The Heydrich murderers were shot in a Prague church; they had landed by parachute from English airplanes in a village near Pilsen in December 1941. Benes Czechs, whose full names and dates of birth are printed. — Thus far the official report. What we *hear* is that the village in which the people stayed no longer exists. The menfolk shot, their families in concentration camps, the houses destroyed—nothing but farmland, plowed land now.

Letter from Sussmann (Arne Erik Johansson) heartfelt and clueless. Asks after my Curriculum. Shall I tell him, that I cannot keep a manuscript in the house? Wants to send me money from Georg. That is "permitted by the state." But he does not know what my allowance is. Asks after my health. Shall I describe the upsets, the hunger? Has hopes for the spring trade fair next year, or at least of the autumn one, "because business is going so well, after all." Shall I tell him, that we can no longer wait *that* long? — As last year, he is in the country for the summer and is clearing a plot of woodland belonging to his son-in-law. What one can envy a man for, all the things one can believe to be freedom. And yet: I do not know whether I would like to change places with him.

This afternoon, therefore, these pages go to Pirna. My latest fear is that they are not absolutely safe there either. Annemarie is notorious after all. If these manuscripts (and the rest) were discovered there, they would destroy Annemarie, Eva, and myself. It is as if the ghosts of Ernst Kreidl and Dr. Friedheim are always around me now. But the danger is so great and so omnipresent that it makes a fatalist of me. This manuscript is my duty and my last fulfillment.

Arne Erik also asks me whether "we are regularly going for walks." But Eva is chasing through the market hall, and I wear the star.

[ . . . ]

## June 25, Thursday morning

The mornings are so dreadful. Everything closes in upon me all at once. Shall I be beaten and spat upon today? "Summoned"? Arrested? Arrested now means certain death. Further: What is there to eat? The shortages have become so great: We still have two potato coupons, but no one can supply anything on them (in Chemnitz munitions workers are *said* to have rioted, whereupon the vegetables, etc., intended for Dresden were sent there, there is *said* to be absolute lack in Berlin and Thuringia—but I noted the same thing in 1916), we have no bread at all anymore, and the new ration cards are still outstanding. Annemarie says she herself is going short, her new, very much reduced staff is stealing from her. Steiniger, Frau Pick's friend, who occasionally helps me, evidently does not dare come to the house. — Pirna was also a disappointment: Eva took a small bundle of laundry with her and brought it back again. No possibility of having things washed there either. Since Christmas an ever-larger bundle has been lying under the bedroom table. We cannot wash at home because there are no appliances. In addition to the immediate emergency with the laundry—the weather is warm now as well—there is the fear of a house search. These people use anything as an excuse for their vindictiveness. — Eva brought me a cigar from Pirna. I smoked it right away, because storing it up is literally to risk one's life. The unaccustomed and overhasty indulgence, the anxiety and the painfulness of the resulting thoughts, the very bad tobacco made me feel very unwell. Sweat, hot hands, shortness of breath. [ . . . ]

Herzl's *Zionist Writings*. This is Hitler's reasoning, sometimes precisely his words, his fanaticism. [ . . . ]

The relief at having manuscript pages out of the house always lasts exactly twelve hours. Then an inner sense of duty (or vanity or a feeling of emptiness) conquers the fear of death. (Hiding place of the moment: Delteil—*Joan of Arc* notes, a manuscript file from the '20s.)

I find Herzl obnoxious but interesting. Buber's *Hasidism*, his introduction to Jewish mysticism, makes me downright ill. The most obscure pomposities.

[ . . . ]

I am racking my brains over my reply to Sussmann. *I* cannot answer any of his questions, and *he* cannot understand why I leave the apparently most harmless things unanswered. [ . . . ]

## June 26, Friday morning

Until now Jews on labor service were allowed to keep their bicycles. Latest decree (4): Bicycles can be kept only if the worker has to travel more than 4½ miles. Simultaneously: Those still allowed to use the tram (workers beyond the 4½-mile limit) are no longer allowed to buy twelve-journey tickets or transfer tickets, but only the expensive single-journey tickets. —

Since Elsa Kreidl has been detached from the Jewish context, I have been assigned the task of being the intermediary between the house and the Community (in particular fetching the food ration cards every fourth Thursday), and Eva will take it over for me, since she can use the tram. That will result in more lively contact with the Community.

[ ... ]

## Toward evening

Chronicle of the day, as I heard it at Simon's, then at Seliksohn's (source of potatoes!), finally from Kätchen. The cobbler has committed suicide in the cells at the Dresden Police Presidium. I doubt that, he did not look like someone who would lose his nerve so quickly—they will have given him a hand. — The old people's home in the Community House, where I recently called on Herr Hammer, who talked about his contacts with Walzel, is going to be evacuated. A number of other elderly people, named by the Gestapo, must also go. Among them Perl, the frail old man with whom I shoveled snow in the winter, and who enjoyed a kind of temporary protection while doing this work—he did not need to go to the Gestapo, who otherwise summoned him every day for beatings and marches through the town. The transport will consist of 50 old people. Since further evacuations from Berlin are going on all the time, a continuation of the operation can be expected here also. It is not quite clear how the selection is made. According to age, wealth, the degree of individual disfavor? At the moment the elderly are particularly vulnerable. In the house I often heard talk of a distinguished Aryan singer called Zottmayr, who was married to a Jew. He died of a cancer a few months ago. The wife (early seventies, good financial circumstances), until then not persecuted at all, immediately had to sew on the star. Now she is among the evacuees.

Today Kätchen was within a hairsbreadth of surprising me as I stole her butter and was about to steal her sugar. What would have been the result? It is truly naked hunger that drives me to these thefts of food. [ ... ] It is a dreadful humiliation for me that I pilfer these things.

## June 27, Saturday morning

The first dominant impressions of the day: 1) I crawl pitifully around on the floor to get at the shelves behind the piano; the bread is hidden right at the bottom. 2) I shiver at the open window—heat is a rare exception so far, a single day was almost hot—and as I shiver immediately think: "Good, because it harms the harvest, good, because I can go out in my coat and do not have to put the star on my suit."

[ ... ]

This morning as I woke up the thought went through my head: I must formulate an essay: Pro Germania, contra Zion from the contemporary standpoint of the German Jew. I shall get down to it, once I am through

Herzl's *Zionist Writings*, tomorrow, therefore. Insofar as I am still capable of that tomorrow—always afraid of the next fifteen minutes.

## June 28, Sunday evening

In the morning Herzl notes. In the afternoon at Seliksohn's. Discussion conducted with passion on his side, with uncertainty on mine. "You should be a Jew, you should teach Jews, you would be welcomed in Jerusalem, that would be your place." — I was only a German, I could not act in any other way; the National Socialists are not the German nation, the German nation of today is not all of Germany. — He: He hates all of Germany, everything German as forever cruel and barbarous, he would rather live in the greatest privation outside Germany than live in tolerable conditions here, etc., etc. — "And even if I hated Germany, I would not thereby become un-German, I could not tear what was German out of me. And I would like to help rebuild things here. — Besides: In Jerusalem I would only be the latecomer, opportunist, traitor." He himself had once told me: "I would vote against, if you were called to Jerusalem, and if I had any say in the matter." He: "Only if you didn't throw away your baptismal certificate first. But no one is demanding piety, going to the synagogue from you." Eva and I talked about it on the way back. Neither of us was completely against Jerusalem, completely for Germany. I quoted Jule Sebba: "If I have to support a nationalism, then I'll choose Jewish nationalism, which doesn't persecute me." — But even in today's debate Seliksohn said, "Now the German Jews come running." In a different context, Seliksohn related as a childhood memory, what impressive ceremonies had been held in Russian Jewish communities in 1904 on Theodor Herzl's death. There he must really have been regarded as savior [ . . . ].

Here in the house there is now a constant debate as to whether the present food situation is better or worse than that in 1918. The Kreidl group maintains: better, we: worse. — Yesterday Steinitz said: "The field of oats beside the teachers' training college is very high." Whereupon Eva: "Don't be such a defeatist!"

## June 29, Monday morning

A year ago on our wedding anniversary I was in the cells at Dresden police presidium. Very desperate and embittered. But how much better than today things still were for us then. The men of Caspar David Friedrich Strasse were all still here, without the star I could still walk, travel, go to restaurants with Eva, there was as yet no food shortage at home, the Gestapo was not yet carrying out any pogroms, I still had typewriter and manuscripts at home, still had the possibility of producing work, as yet I had no inkling of the later degree of slavery and impoverishment. — Nevertheless I can present a different reckoning: Hitler had not yet been stopped and was not so close to certain destruction as today. — We cannot celebrate at all. Eva will try to haul up another twenty pounds of potatoes from town, which Mother Kreidl is leaving to us on expiring coupons. That is Eva's present to me. I have nothing at all for her.

On Wednesday [the people from] the old people's home will be sent to Theresienstadt in an automobile. Dr. Katz will accompany the transport. We were told his characteristic remark: "I hope I'll come back." —

For the two weeks from June 29 to July 12 there are ten pounds of potatoes per head of the population. Of those every fourth potato is rotten. There are no vegetables, no radishes. Bread is bad and in short supply. For how long can fear make up for enthusiasm and goodwill?

The massive English air raids on Cologne and Bremen are supposed to be the prelude to an air offensive: "1,000 aircraft over north and central Germany!" Dresden is supposed to be among the marked cities. The flak positions here are being reinforced. (At Zeiss-Ikon and on the Town Hall.)

### July 1, Wednesday morning

Yesterday morning, as I was going to the letter box, Frau Ida Kreidl told me: "Now I have lost everything. My children in Prague are also being evacuated." She has a married daughter there, her grandson is ten years old. The family is being sent to Theresienstadt, from there into the unknown. Her son Paul has been gone since January. I comforted her: There were so many shootings in Prague that any other place would be safer. Ida Kreidl was astonishingly composed or blunted or stunned. — In the evening as we sat apathetically together in Frau Pick's room, Elsa Kreidl appeared: Her husband's urn and nine other urns have arrived for interment. Friedheim and Ernst Kreidl will be interred at half past nine on Sunday. Now, that is grotesquely awful. Eva and I had the same thought: Just as the two of them liked to sit together on the garden bench, so now their urns stand side by side. Kreidl's path to death began six months earlier, Friedheim caught up with him. The Jewish layer-out told Frau Voss that Friedheim had hanged himself. — But how far is the "self" in this report true, and if it is true, it does not express any voluntary act. (It was said that a rope is placed in the prisoners' cells.) I cannot rid myself of the fear of death anymore. It is worse than in 1915. One can be hauled off at any moment.

Eva is worn down by ever more errands. — She literally risks her head, no, our heads, for Frau Pick. ("For your manuscripts too," she says in response to a reproach.) Today—hours of work—I wrote out six money transfers. Huge amount of income tax from last year, from Georg's gift, second installment of the currency fine, tax on Jews, etc. In all 466M. Our reserves shrink to about 500M. But by now I am quite apathetic with respect to the money. As long as they don't come to "fetch" me, as long as I have halfway enough to eat. But things look ever worse with respect to this halfway. Steiniger, Frau Pick's friend, who gave me bread coupons, dares not come to the Jews' House again. I boiled the last six potatoes for this morning's breakfast; the biggest was completely spoiled, inedible even to me. Now Eva is in town again hunting potatoes. For days she has been reporting: Most of the market hall stalls are closed and the covers are down. A note pinned up: "No merchandise has come in today." Queues outside the shops. Very tiny turnip heads, one or two only, are distributed to those with ration cards. The Jew and the Jewish household do not have these cards. —

Notes on Herzl's *Zionist Writings*. Today I still want to add the summary of the Herzl-Hitler comparison. Today I began the *Denkwürdigkeiten der* [Memoirs of] *Glückel von Hameln.* [ . . . ]

## July 2, Thursday morning

If I should survive, I shall soon no longer be able to feel the apathetic wretchedness of the situation. Hunger exacerbated by what Eva denies and yet is probably true: The mass of others are better off, so they can wait. (They are better off: limited number of cards, but greater freedom to buy, to move around, to barter and trade illicitly, in addition canteen and restaurant and no house search, or almost none.) Hunger, which in the last few days has ceased to be in any way metaphorical. (Not a single potato in the house, no prospect of additional bread, not the tiniest amount of vegetables.) The fear of every ring at the door, every passing car. Terror, against all, but a hundred times over against the Jews. The fearful patience (or truly contentment and confidence in victory?) of the nation. The victories in Africa and Russia, which at the very least prolong the war, our absolute isolation. [ . . . ] The evenings, when we sit downstairs with the three women, are especially dismal. The first: both her children have now been evacuated; the second: her husband shot; the third: constantly threatened by the Gestapo. Conversation: Evacuations, cruelties, fear of the doorbell and passing cars, Eva's reports of the outside world [ . . . ].

## Forenoon

Kätchen Sara comes home from the factory late at night (on foot), gets up late and then tells us the latest news. Radio yesterday evening: Sevastopol fallen.

The removal of the old people's home to Theresienstadt brutal. Truck with benches, crowded together, only the tiniest bundle could be taken, cuffs and blows.

Kätchen has alternate morning and afternoon shifts. She has not been given permission to use transport, it takes her almost two hours to walk. Constant trouble with her feet, frequently unfit for work.

## July 3, Friday morning

Eva frequently helps out downstairs with vacuum cleaning and scrubbing. Then some potatoes can still be found for us. So yesterday a few "left behind by Fräulein Ludwig" turned up. Really the situation now is that Eva acts the charwoman, in order thus to acquire a bowl of potatoes for me. That is not the way it's put, but is in fact the cause and effect. I stuff 99 percent of the potatoes into me. Yesterday I wolfed down a bowl. Sometimes I think it balances out with Eva, because I leave her the butter, the sugar and by far the greater proportion of meat (that and the bread)—but she is losing weight even more quickly than I am. —

Yesterday I accompanied Eva (as I do frequently now) to Wasaplatz. There (after distressing—the star!—waiting) I take the purchases from her, and she goes in città. As we were on our way yesterday we met the newspaper woman as she was collecting the monthly payments. Eva went up to her: "I'll also pay for Kreidl downstairs." We both immediately had the same thought: "Avoid the doorbell being rung, otherwise they'll get an awful fright!"

A notice in the newspaper greatly limits all female domestic service for Aryans as well. One has to prove that no family member is available to do housework. This and the increasing shortage of foodstuffs points to the Germans being unable to hold out through next winter. But the big offensive in the East has arrived after all, and in Egypt it appears that the English are going to lose Alexandria.

Yesterday usual afternoon visit to Marckwald. Appalling, what an effort it is for the man to drag himself from the balcony to the living room on his crutches, how he regularly gets his morphine injection during the conversation, how he is always shivering. (Yesterday during the day it was properly warm for once; now I am wearing the cardigan again, and my hands are cold.) Every little bit of heat leads immediately to a thunderstorm and more cool weather.

### Toward evening

If the Gestapo discover Jews with ration coupons without a J, the coupons are torn up, and if the Jew is lucky he is beaten and spat upon, if he is not so lucky, he is "summoned," probably also "detained." But when buying rolls with bigger J coupons one often gets smaller ones, without a J, back. When that happened to Frau Ida Kreidl yesterday, she tore open the lining of her handbag and put the forbidden coupons on the inside, until she could exchange them with Eva. —

In the newspaper the reports of advances in Russia and Egypt were counteracted a little by a warning article from Berlin: Inflammatory news was being spread in a south German armaments factory. One principal offender had been listening to foreign broadcasting stations, half a dozen workers had passed on the "lies." The principal offender was sentenced to death and has already been executed, the others have been given hard labor sentences of between ten and one and a half years. News about broadcasting crimes was frequent in an earlier phase of the war. A selection of verdicts was published from time to time, always with long prison sentences. Then there was nothing more for many months. What is new about today's case is a) the death sentence, b) that it explicitly concerns an armaments factory. So they no longer feel certain of the workers; they are proceeding against a particular class, and against the decisive class, they are reaching out for the very last resort, the death sentence.

Today I shall finish reading the fairly disagreeable *Glückel von Hameln* and shall make notes on it tomorrow. My working material is getting ever more scanty. It's just like the potatoes: I do not know what the next day will bring and whether it will bring anything at all. [ . . . ]

Trude Scherk writes that Grete is in the Jewish Hospital after a "light stroke." She herself is expecting evacuation to Theresienstadt. Since she is almost seventy, they will probably leave her in Theresienstadt (here, too, they say that old people remain there permanently, only the younger ones are sent on elsewhere), and things are supposed to be not so bad at all. In Berlin they appear to know nothing of our sufferings here. On the other hand, there appears to have been mass shootings there, whereas here they are content with individual killings and otherwise merely ill-treat people.

### July 4, Saturday morning

Estreicher † in a concentration camp. — The Jewish Community is noti-fied of Jewish deaths in concentration camps and in prison, the corpses and urns handed over to the Jewish cemetery (sometimes also, [as in] the Friedheim case, the corpse is removed for incineration after the funeral, and the urn interred later). In all these cases the news always spreads quickly, there are x connections between the six or seven hundred Jews still to be found here. So yesterday news came of the death of the much-hated, extremely corrupt Estreicher. He endured long weeks in prison, then perhaps a whole year in the concentration camp. Cause of death is now given as "inflammation of the colon," and according to his wife, that could be true, he had already suffered from it once before. Likewise, with another recent concentration camp death the cause was said to be a "varicose ulcer." Do these people die a more "natural" death than those who have been shot? Hardly. They live under the greatest, most unbear-able pressure, they fall ill, no one looks after them, after all there are no doctors or medicines, perhaps things are also helped along with an in-jection. — I feel little pity for Estreicher, but dread makes me shudder as in all the other cases. One man is finished off in three days, another only after a year—but no one comes back, literally no one. Estreicher was two or three years older than I, looked a picture of health, as if he were fifty, did not wear the star, was "privileged," was a confederate of the Gestapo, beneficiary of the regime. Until, evidently, he was light-fingered on his own account. He has paid for it very dearly. What upsets me, however, is only common fear. Cras mihi—no one comes back. Under these circumstances is it at least a courageous act that I keep this

diary? I am not sure, nor of my inner justification in also exposing Eva.
— For myself I am ever more frequently in despair; I spend so much time
reassuring the people in the house, I end up believing my own words.

### July 5, Sunday toward evening

Sunday afternoon is the only time that is reckoned to be Gestapo-free. So
far, at least, no house searches have taken place on Sunday afternoon (in
the morning certainly!), so then one does not need to be so nervous, does
not need to put foodstuffs back in their hiding place. Foodstuffs—an almost euphemistic description. I am very greatly tormented by hunger. —
   The whole morning occupied with the cemetery. In considerable heat,
the walk, in my coat, was even more of an effort (there and back three
hours) than recently. But the summer view on Grunaer Weg (blooming
nursery gardens, fields of grain, the chain of hills beyond) again very
beautiful. At the cemetery everything even more wretched than before.
Some twenty women, some thirty men. All of them look miserable and
hungry. Particularly dreadful is how the top hats slide down into the
men's emaciated faces, how the top hats underline the threadbare shabbiness of the suits. The advanced emaciation was especially evident in
two people I had not seen for some time: Dr. Magnus now has a very narrow, shrunken face, Frau Kronheim has literally become a small-boned
skeleton, the tininess of the very pointed chin, nothing but skin on it, is
shocking. —
   In front of the lectern, where the coffin usually stood, there was a
heaped-up black cloth. Afterward, when it is lifted up and carried out,
one discovers the little urn. With Friedheim, for whom there had recently
been a service, there were only the words: "We lay him to rest." Outside,
between full-grown graves, a row of little holes had been dug, in each one
was stuck a post with a sign: Ernst Kreidl † on, Feldmann (the cobbler),
Dr. Friedheim . . . All in their sixties (including the giant cobbler). A
prayer was said, we filed past and threw earth three times onto the urn in
the miniature grave. In the hall the same psalm was read over Ernst
Kreidl's urn as recently over Friedheim's coffin. I found the text very misplaced, doubly misplaced: "A thousand shall fall at thy side, a thousand
at thy right hand—but evil shall not befall thee"—how can one say that
next to a coffin? "He shall deliver thee from the noisome pestilence"—
how can one say that when a victim of the pestilence is lying in his coffin?
And all eleven corpses, which were to be dealt with in the course of this
morning, were murdered by this same rampant pestilence, literally murdered.
   Again I was childish, cowardly, and egoistical: I remembered the giant
cobbler and saw the very, very small urn. Then the thought of extinction
came even closer and made me shudder even more than standing opposite a coffin. — In the afternoon, after I had slept for a long time, I studied

Grätz's lexicon for a while. From dates of birth and death I repeatedly observed how few people get past their mid-sixties, and I was shaken repeatedly by a feeling of annihilation. Even if I survive Hitler, how much will still be left to me? It is so stupid: I fear non-existence, nothing else. —

Yesterday afternoon, just as Steinitz had come to see us, Dr. Katz rang the doorbell. He had wanted to see how Frau Pick was, and no one opened the door for him downstairs. I invited him to have a rest with us for a minute, he accepted, talked, came out of his shell, and then stayed two hours. The man is disliked by everyone, until now we did not care for him very much either; but yesterday we felt much closer to him, and he half (not entirely) won us over. [ . . . ] The army is the central experience of his life. He relates with pride that although a Jew he became a reserve officer in 1905, that during the war he was a surgeon-major when wounded, he relates also—and here we part company—that in '39 he endeavored to be accepted into the army medical service. (He wears the Iron Cross, First Class; his patients take it amiss that on his waiting-room wall he is in uniform and on horseback.) He is very melancholy when he talks about his shattered view of life; he considers assimilation, without which he does not exist, to be definitively impossible. He attributes much of the blame—and here we are in agreement—to Zionism; much blame also to the unchecked influx of the money-hungry eastern Jews. (I said I would make an educational examination the condition of immigration.) He said he had known Theodor Herzl personally, maintained the man had become the founder of political Zionism out of injured pride, because he had once been insulted and not been given satisfaction. — For all his Germanness and evident lack of faith, Katz considers baptism a betrayal. — It appeared to give him considerable pleasure to have an intellectual discussion for once. I think it possible that we shall become closer. —

I do not quite know what reading I should undertake for my work. "Self-improvement" sounds very nice—but I so much want to produce things once again and am checked on every side. And always the little urns before me. — In the next few days I want to become a little more familiar with the popular edition of the Grätz lexicon and then borrow the Dubnow from Frau Hirschel.

I would now like to express the motto of the Curriculum as follows: We know nothing of the distant past, because we were not there, we know nothing of the present, because we were there. Only from the past that we have experienced ourselves can we gain a little—very little that's certain—knowledge through later recollection.

### July 6, Monday morning

Dr. Katz said recently, *the* Jew can neither obey nor give orders. He is too much of an individualist. I agreed—but for me the inability to give orders was due to inborn skepticism and acquired lack of self-confidence. Eva argued against, after all the Jews kept the strictest discipline in matters of religion. Eva's, Katz's, and my own statements are all quite obviously true. So what does it mean to talk about *the* Jew, *the* German, etc.? And yet there are group characteristics.

### July 7, Tuesday morning

Yesterday evening, eleven o'clock. Eva is lying in bed, I am reading from Oldenburg-Januschau. Kätchen, who came back in the afternoon with bleeding feet (because of the blood-soaked dressings she received permission to use transport *once*), is asleep. Furious ringing of the bell. Kätchen staggers out of her room looking distraught, my heart thumping I tear open the blackout in the kitchen. "Hello?" Woman's voice in the distance: "In the letter box." It turns out that Frau Paul has dropped in a rendezvous note for Kätchen; she does not dare appear in front of the house in the daytime—her never-ending divorce case, in which her husband accuses her of friendship with Jews. In her agitation, her signal of four short rings became one long alarm bell. And probably she cannot imagine what distress such ringing causes us.

Spent all day yesterday reading Grätz. [ ... ] — Today Elsa Kreidl gave me the *Französische Tagebuch 1939/40* [French diary 1939–40] by Alfred Fabre-Luce. I am putting the Jews aside to work through this borrowed volume. [ ... ]

### Evening

Kätchen reports: The Henriettenstift home, about fifty old women, is being evacuated. So her mother, the indestructible eighty-year-old, must go to Theresienstadt, too; Kätchen's brother has been arrested and is thus a dead man. This man, Joachimsthal, is a nasty fellow, with whom she has quarreled a lot and who extorted money from her—but why should he be murdered? He is supposed "to have concealed the star" or been out and about after nine. Death for that. — I am so afraid, I constantly see the little holes for the urns in front of me. Cras mihi. —

### July 8, Wednesday morning

Dr. Katz said recently, that they had "changed tack" with respect to the evacuations. First people *up to* 65, now those over 65 (unless they are working). It is nothing to do with organization and overorganization. They shift about, different departments work against one another, the wind changes as during a thunderstorm, several thunderstorms are roaming around, opposing and getting in one another's way. I see from Oldenburg's memoirs that it was already like that in 1914–18, but now everything seems to be carried to extremes.

New decree in judaeos (II, 4?), *table-tennis games* to be handed over. Presumably for military hospitals. Everything that is solicited from Aryans is taken from Jews by force under threat of punishment ("by order of the state"). The punishment is now invariably death. No one comes back.

Eva suffers especially from the ever more complete lack of tobacco. It is worse than during the last war, even though we have all of the Balkans under our control. [ . . . ]

I have learned to read reports, which in the last war I naively accepted. Yesterday a summary of the Crimean campaign just ended. The big talk of the amount of booty and of enemy losses and of the insignificance of our losses has as little effect now as the words "battle of extermination." But it concludes: This is the great German victory, which the lies of enemy propaganda present as a German defeat. From this one can say with certainty—and one does not need to commit a broadcasting crime to know—that the opponents are writing: Germany has lost an irreplaceable amount of time and men before Sevastopol. Now it is certain that the enemy figures of German losses will be greatly exaggerated (I assume that England and Russia exaggerate by 100 percent, Goebbels and Co. by 200 percent); but they are nevertheless basically right. Yesterday I read in Fabre-Luce: If France and Germany were each to lose a million men, then Germany would be the victor. One can say exactly the same about Germany and Russia now. At the moment I am gripped less by the Russian than by the Egyptian front. In Russia Hitler's victories are killing him; in Egypt he really could win. But since the day before yesterday Rommel appears to have been brought up short outside Alexandria. — [ . . . ]

What is happening to our house? Since July 1 a decision must have been made as to whether the new mortgage has been accepted or a compulsory auction has been ordered, and there's not a word from the "Aryan trustee." Basically it makes no difference what I hear from him: The moment I am evacuated, everything goes to the state anyway. If I die, one way or another, then Eva inherits as an Aryan. But would she be able or want to keep it? There is no point in thinking further than the next minute and the next potato. [ . . . ]

### July 9, Thursday morning

Sultriness and sudden thunderstorms. The heat ties me to the house—a matter of clothing, the star. —

When did I first hear the name Theresienstadt? (The existence of the place, which is supposed to be near Leitmeritz, formerly a small fortress, tiny little town, was completely unknown to me.) It must have been last winter, that the Kreidls talked about evacuations from Prague and Vienna to Theresienstadt. It must be less than two months ago that there was also talk of German transports to the place. Now Trude Scherk (about a week ago) uses the word as if it were completely familiar, an all-German institution not requiring any further explanation: One gets sent to Theresienstadt and that's that, and if one is over seventy, one also stays there. And

Kätchen mentions figures with five zeros: Room has been made for that number of Jews in Theresienstadt.

[ . . . ]

### July 10, Friday morning

[ . . . ]

The Marckwalds state as true and certainly not exaggerated that since the beginning of the deportations 2,000 (two thousand) Jews in Berlin had taken their own lives. — Yesterday, in addition to the transport of old people for Theresienstadt, a new evacuation of those capable of working was announced: seventeen people in their forties and fifties, including Lampen, the nurse, who came to look after Frau Pick, and whose father was recently sent to Theresienstadt, will be transported to Poland on Monday night. Literally every day now brings a new piece of terrible news. — Fear grows ever greater. Kätchen's brother-in-law has sent letters for her to Frau Paul. Eva brought these letters back in her shoe; she had stuck them there, because when she came back our entrance hall appeared "suspiciously lively."

Yesterday was our first day of complete catastrophe with respect to food. In both morning and afternoon Eva chased in vain through the city to shops, to friends, to the market hall. All for nothing: no potato, no vegetable, nothing. And nothing at all in the house anymore. She herself ate most inadequately in restaurants; morning, noon, and evening I drank ersatz coffee and stuffed bread into myself, a very few slices with the tiniest amounts of dripping. The bread, too, is almost finished—two weeks before the card runs out, but perhaps an exchange for margarine coupons can be arranged. — Now Eva is on the go again. I get attacks of despair.

Kätchen, whose feet are sore from walking, has recently been treated by a dermatologist. Eczema. He told her eczema of the feet was tremendously widespread at the moment. Infections and malnutrition. Variation on the previous war: sycosis—barber's itch!

Kätchen reports from our common house trustee that my mortgage business has been settled. The Wengler woman has been paid off, a new mortgage has been paid in. I myself have not heard anything at all about it—as a Jew I am quite irrelevant, everything is conducted over my head. Anyhow I may for the moment still continue to regard myself as a house owner. I think for Eva that is a comfort, a hope. —

This morning I read out the last pages of Oldenburg and the first pages of Werner von Siemens's memoirs. (Borrowed from the Marckwalds.)

Sultriness and tendency to thunderstorms. Bad conjunctivitis.

### July 11, Saturday lunchtime

Eva's nerves sometimes give way now. As yesterday in particular. The fruitless chasing after foodstuffs almost destroys her. On top of that sheer hunger for a number of days now. The restaurants serve only a limited amount, there is friction between "those in work and servicemen on leave"—a decree gives them precedence for the "dish of the day" from twelve until one, and it is served to them alone from six until seven—and families or ineligible individual customers. Now Eva also lacks coupons for fat, since she is not allowed to exchange the J coupons. And at home I subsist almost entirely on bread. — For a few days now nursery gardens have been allowed to sell a portion of their vegetables freely to the public. Eva queues for over an hour and gets very little or nothing at all. — If yesterday evening Elsa Kreidl had not at the last moment given us a few ancient potatoes, we would have been even worse off than we are. A soup made of our very last reserves of rice, semolina, and millet. Now Eva has been out and on the go for a long time again. —

Yesterday in her hunt for potatoes she went (in vain) to the Seliksohns. The woman, who gets such a bad press, has lost her father and now her first husband as well in a concentration camp. Her stepmother goes to Poland with the next transport. She lives in a constant state of discord with this woman. They still have all kinds of assets—the family (Kornblum) were the owners of Bach, the big clothing store—which now falls entirely to the state. Some things could have been saved for Lilly Seliksohn. The stepmother hates the stepdaughter to such a degree that she preferred the state to get everything. To that Frau Seliksohn said to Eva word for word: "I told her, 'You'll die in the street of spotted fever, and then they'll cover you in newspaper, so that the birds don't peck your body to pieces!' " Note: Now, that is a curse, the Gestapo people could learn something from that. [ . . . ]

### July 12, Sunday morning

Eva sixty years old. None of her birthdays, not even during the last war, celebrated under such terrible conditions. Hands completely empty, hungry and one's life in constant danger. I cannot even say: We'll make up for it, because how much of a chance do we have of living to see the moment when we can make up for it?

Kätchen, for whom birthday parties are an obligatory ritual, brought a little pot of primroses—a heroic deed, which can put one in a concentration camp and so cost one's life. Typical petit bourgeois heroism. She also brought, as inheritance from her mother, a little handbag. Around midday we are going to visit her mother in the Henriettenstift home. I am curious to take a look at this old people's home twenty-four hours before its evacuation. More curiosity and a kind of sense of duty as a chronicler than pity. —

[ . . . ]

It [the Jews' House] is coming to an end. The men are gone, and now the exodus of women is beginning: The Party has informed Elsa Kreidl

that from September 1 the ground floor has been rented to a head forester, the Jewish occupants will receive further instructions from the Israelite Community. (Presumably our first floor will also be made Jew-free then.)
[ ... ]

Program for the morning: from the old people's home to the Glasers, because Eva has the prospect of a "good" cigarette there, i.e., not mixed with anything. At the moment she is suffering even more from the lack of cigarette papers than of tobacco. Papers, too, are a dwindling scarce commodity. (When the Gestapo visits they are torn up one at a time and scattered.)

### July 13, Monday morning

If it was the most woeful birthday, it was also the most peculiar one. Kätchen and I went on foot, Eva took the tram to the Henriettenstift, at about eleven o'clock. For a couple of minutes on the way we thought we were being followed by a young man (Gestapo?), he had overtaken us in a suspicious manner and looked at us, he had taken up position in front of a shop window—only when he finally turned a corner were we reassured. Kätchen was the pilot on the forbidden Bürgerwiese: only the crossing Lüttichaustrasse/Zinzendorfstrasse is permitted for wearers of the star. The Henriettenstift is in Eliasstrasse, now Güntzstrasse by the Johanniskirche—I had never been there. Beautiful Dresden—handsome squares, gardens, the Henriettenstift, an imposing building, also has a large garden. In a fairly gloomy entrance hall: a melee, no space to move, chaos. Tied-up mattresses, trunks, evacuation luggage [ ... ] piled up everywhere, in between them the to-ing and fro-ing of star-wearing helpers, half the Community seemed to be helping the old ladies. I would have liked to walk through the house, but Frau Joachimsthal, even smaller and more inconspicuous than usual, was standing in the hallway and her room was just to the left. A tiny, narrow room, almost a prison cell; against one of the long walls a kitchen stove and a bed, against the other a table and a few chairs. The intermediate state of a half-completed move made the room even bleaker. We had exchanged only a few words—Kätchen by turns tender and rude to her mother—when Kätchen came back horrified from the hallway: "The Gestapo committee's outside, Köhler's with them, the 'Spitter's' with them—make yourselves scarce, they're just going up to the first floor with Hirschel." Eva was in particular danger (Aryans were not allowed to be here), so after two minutes we left. Kätchen accompanied us: "They're standing at the window, keep close to the garden wall." So we slipped away under cover, and Eva got a tram right away. (Then in the evening Kätchen told us it had been a false alarm, the supposed "Spitter" had been wearing a Jew's star, nor had it been Köhler, the Jews' pope. A polite official had merely inspected the rooms with Hirschel.) It now took me almost an hour to get to the Glasers'; back through the dangerous bottleneck at Bürgerwiese, in very low spirits, avoiding the area of the railway station and Gestapo headquarters by a detour along Werderstrasse, like a hunted animal. The Glasers live in an eccentric-looking house (a little colonial in style) at 23 Bergstrasse, close to Schnorrstrasse. There at one, and received by Frau Glaser who was extremely friendly. *He* was expected in the next half hour, but did not come until three. She had been used to his complete unpredictability for decades, she said with resigned admiration. Eva appeared soon after me, she had been able to eat lunch in town. We spent the next five, almost six hours with the Glasers. They were obviously pleased that we had come, they went out of their way to be hospitable. There were coffee and cakes, there was a crème, which substituted for whipped cream, there were cigarettes and cigars, truly in the plural, two. When we wanted to leave, at about five, Eva said, that now she had celebrated her birthday after all. At that we certainly had to stay. A bottle of heavy red wine was found, Glaser played his beautiful accordion [ . . . ] and then put on a number of recently acquired gramophone records, a long tone painting by Hindemith, which I grasped only in part, but was at no point repugnant to me, a mixture of *Egmont* declamation [ . . . ] and splendid *Egmont* music by Beethoven, lieder sung by Lehmann [ . . . ], etc. When we left, toward seven, in a very animated mood, we also carried home a bag of potatoes we had been given, a radish, a couple of pea pods, a couple of tomatoes, and from Glaser's library I had borrowed the *Geschichte der Vereinigten Staaten* [History of the United States] by Firmin Roz and *Eine Zeit stirbt* [An epoch dies] by Georg Hermann. — But what was most important and characteristic of the times about this agreeably idle afternoon were two revelations, which simultaneously illuminated for me the unconventional character and the fears of this old man (for he gives an impression of great age, although only in his mid-sixties). At Eva's recommendation the Glasers had been in the Huttig, as she calls the Restaurant Steuer by the market hall, a couple of times, and met her there once. "But we don't want to eat out anymore," said Frau Glaser, "it makes my husband anxious." Sometime later, he wasn't back yet, I asked her in some other context, whether he had always specialized in tax law. (He published on it.) No, she said, he had also conducted divorce cases, and above all he had defended the Communists in all their court cases in Dresden. Which was also why he had been the first to go in 1933. [ . . . ] After that there was talk of what had upset Glaser last week. He is the owner of the house and of another one, he has had to share his apartment with a star family, but is still living in his own property. He has invested his fortune in an art collection, which he keeps in a hiding place in his house. It is all banned, Expressionist, "degenerate art." It is not quite clear, whether he, as a Jew, is allowed to sell at all, at any rate no art dealer is allowed to disseminate *degenerate* art. But now an art lover, willing to pay good prices, has secretly been found and Glaser wants to pay off a mortgage with the anticipated money (whose origins could be concealed). The conversation led to a scene that really could have been in a film. In an adjoining, fairly empty room there were curtains, behind which one might have expected shelves, for example for kitchen appliances. Frau Glaser drew back the curtains, there on the floor were a couple of wooden sculptures, which at first glance I found stomach-turningly unpleasant and still find unpleasant when I think of them. [ . . . ] At the moment I find something else important, namely 1) Glaser as a characteristic figure, the Jewish lawyer with strong interests in the arts (music, painting and sculpture), the tendency toward extreme modernism, the tendency toward Communism (with a fortune of his own and a good income), a committed nonconformist, in some association of freethinkers, in music as in the visual arts—"My husband took an interest in Hindemith very early on." The son, whom I do not know, is a doctor, but a specialist in breathing technique—so likewise something of a Left extremist. In addition to all of that, the eccentric floating above everyday troubles and household rules. 2) The tragicomical concealment of the "degenerate" art treasures. 3) Glaser's now explicable fear, his now comprehensible pessimism. He believes in Hitler's lasting victory; he saw the collapse of the Left at close quarters—"there is no organization there anymore," he repeats again and again and trembles before the omnipotence of the tyranny.

### July 14, Tuesday toward evening

Kätchen had been given police permission to spend the last night with her mother. Yesterday afternoon the old ladies were taken from the Henriettenstift to the Community house, which is fairly close, and passed the night on deck chairs in a room there. At five o'clock they were then put in a truck (benches, canvas stretched over them), a trailer carried their baggage. Kätchen says a number of people, Aryans, had watched and expressed their considerable displeasure. "So that's how *they* treat the Jews! Load them up like cattle." Dr. Katz had accompanied the transport once again. He is altogether disliked. By contrast everyone speaks of Hirschel, the (unpaid) Community leader with the greatest affection and admiration. The man is wearing himself out. This morning he had said good-bye to the Poland transport at three, had then come over to see the old ladies, had gone back to his office immediately after their departure. All the work and all the suffering are loaded onto him. —

The whole day on notes on Fabre-Luce.

### July 16, Thursday morning

[ . . . ] Hunger and the sense of threat grow daily. Now it appears that we shall have to change our apartment in a few weeks—move into something even more crowded and worse. (Here there is greenery and a bathroom and a small number of people. But in our next living quarters?).

Letter from Sussmann. He does not understand why I decline monetary help, why I do not answer such "harmless" questions as those about my Curriculum—he understands absolutely nothing of my situation here, is "nervous and depressed," also no doubt a little offended, insists that I *must* let money be sent to me—"food prices here have risen by 100%, it must be just the same for you, you do need money"; he does not know that here the prices are not higher, but also that there is no food. How should I answer him? The censors suppress any elucidation or pass it on to the Gestapo.

Seliksohn here yesterday afternoon. He now appears to live in large part from his work as a hairdresser and he goes about it with great eagerness. He did the hair of the whole of the Henriettenstift before they were transported, this coming Monday afternoon he will deal with all the inhabitants of our house.

[ ... ]

### July 17, Friday morning

We are eating our last bread, and there are no new coupons until Thursday; the potatoes are at an end, and nothing is being supplied on the outstanding sections [of the card]. I don't know what is going to happen. [ ... ]

Notification of a money transfer from Sweden. I already wrote to Sussmann yesterday, that he would be doing me the worst possible service; today I declined to accept the gift.

In conversation the Marckwalds said: Dr. Glaser was "not an agreeable gentleman." I contradicted them and asked "Why?" — "He was such a Communist." Now I understand why Kätchen always talks so sneeringly about him.

Yesterday evening invited to Ida Kreidl's for a belated birthday party for Eva. We were properly entertained, as on that still almost peaceful Saturday before the Gestapo broke in: tea and homemade poppy seed crescents. But all conversation revolves around the wretchedness of the situation. Ida Kreidl and Frau Pick are certainly reckoning on Theresienstadt, the Marckwalds also. Marckwald says it would be a death sentence for him. He receives a state pension as I do, he believes it will not be paid to him in Theresienstadt. He needs 80M a month for morphine and other medicines.

### July 18, Saturday toward evening

Yesterday Eva had a bout of influenza with a slight temperature. She lay down in the afternoon, remained in bed during breakfast today. Then she had to go into town, there was nothing for her to eat here. Instead of feeling sympathy I was yesterday tormented by one question only: would she be capable of getting up today? She had no temperature, was only washed-out—going out was not bad for her, and that is the only good thing I can report today. The shortage of food cannot get worse, we no longer know whom to beg from, we do not know how we shall get through the next week. Eva is also very poorly provided for, she has no fat or bread coupons, and from twelve until one the "dish of the day" is reserved for "those in employment." We are both very hungry.

A card from Trude Scherk: Grete's condition had worsened, she would not leave the hospital anymore; that at least is what Änny Klemperer (who no longer writes to me) reported, because Trude herself no longer manages the distance to the hospital, two and a half hours on foot! One can wish Grete nothing better than a speedy deliverance.

Last Thursday the Marckwalds gave me a bag of potatoes—but they said they would hardly still be edible. Indeed, they stank and were falling disgustingly apart. Nevertheless today I brushed and boiled about half of what I had lugged over here, the ones that were still just about holding together. And truly a few pieces of some were edible. Disgusting. — The whole day today on domestic chores, also, to relieve Eva, scrubbed the stairs.

[ . . . ]

Steinitz was here in the afternoon. Suddenly much aged, very depressed. He again warned against Seliksohn; everyone has a very negative opinion of him. (But no one says what he has really done, or is supposed to have done wrong.)

## July 19, Sunday evening

The first day of truly remorseless hunger. A tiny remnant of potatoes, so black and stinking, that it turns the stomach, a tiny remnant of bread. Nothing to be had for Eva either, since she has no coupons. Tomorrow she will *have to* beg from Frau Fleischer. — In the afternoon to the Kronheims, who now live in Altenzeller Strasse, and whom we recently, after a long time, saw at Friedheim's burial. They wrote on Eva's sixtieth birthday and urged us to visit them. The woman has shrunk away to nothing after serious ill-treatment and, threatened with Theresienstadt, is now contemplating suicide (I said, Veronal should now be called "Jewish drops"). The very hysterical daughter, working at Zeiss-Ikon, would like to marry her elderly mother to an older fellow worker. (If one partner of a married couple works in an armaments factory, then supposedly they are not evacuated.) Gloomy atmosphere. But there were a couple of tiny little cakes with sweetened ersatz coffee, and that helped pass a couple of hours. — The house in Altenzeller Strasse is diagonally opposite the Pension Blancke, in which we stayed twenty-two years ago. The pension sign is still there, although the proprietors have changed [ . . . ]. For reasons that no one knows, the house in which the Kronheims are accommodated is repeatedly visited by the Gestapo, they have already brutally wreaked havoc there half a dozen times. A once-magnificent villa surrounded by very thick vegetation. High rooms, frescoes above the doors—but everything is said to be in a state of decay. —[ . . . ]

Latest imposition on Jews (II. 5?): Ban on subscribing to or buying newspapers; also, if the husband wears the star, the Aryan wife is not allowed to take or buy a newspaper in her name.

### July 20, Monday after dinner

Eva's nerves gave way yesterday; she laid the blame on me, but it's only the situation and the terrible hunger that are to blame. The first outburst was at lunchtime, when I told her to eat a little crust of bread with her soup. The afternoon was calm, we were at the Kronheims. I then told her, since it was late, to pick up something edible in town, going by tram she would be home hardly any later than I would. She did not come home until half past eight, had been to eight restaurants in vain, had got a plate of soup in the ninth, and was completely exhausted. I had prepared a remnant of black potatoes, Eva made a tiny bit of sauce to go with them and then got a spasm of the hiccups and a very bad cough that, despite codeine, has not cleared up even today. It was her opinion that I had chased her into town. —

Today again no possibility of buying anything and a continuation of the terrible hunger. Elsa Kreidl is going to let us have a bowl of old potatoes for the evening. Bread is finished—yesterday Elsa Kreidl gave us a little bit as a present. I have never experienced anything like it, not even in the last war. For the first time hunger is literally hurting me. I steal individual little pieces of sugar from Kätchen's drawer. Eva brought candy, had herself had only a little to eat in a restaurant. —

[ . . . ]

### July 21, Tuesday midday

After truly piercing hunger yesterday afternoon a momentary turn for the better: Elsa Kreidl gave us a little basket of old potatoes, from Jentsch, the trader, we got ten pounds of new potatoes (a long wait by an open van during a thundery downpour), and Kätchen lent us a one-pound-bread coupon. In the evening we ate our fill with mashed potatoes. But this morning again there was no more eating one's fill: The potatoes have to last too long, we still have very long to go before we get bread coupons, and there are no vegetables or anything else to be bought. (Eva eats sugar, I steal a little sugar from Kätchen, yesterday I was also helped by a little paper bag of candy, which Eva had got on her card—the first candy since Christmas. — The worst thing is not hunger, which produces only a dull unease. Much worse is the inadequate food. It's only after the first mouthfuls that I realize how hungry I am and what pleasure there is in even the most wretched muck; and after just these mouthfuls I have to stop.

Yesterday afternoon Seliksohn was here in his capacity as a hairdresser and dealt with everyone in the house. Eva and I were shorn, Kätchen got an elaborate permanent wave, Ida Kreidl had her hair washed. Seliksohn then departed feeling very satisfied, all in all he had earned about 4.50M to 4.75M.

[ ... ]

## Toward evening

Ida Kreidl, who owns the house, showed me the letter from the NSDAP, in which our floor, "the Voss Jews' apartment," is also disposed of from September 1. Eva is quite indifferent to this new move: Ever since our little tomcat met his fate, it makes no difference where we end up. Only one thing weighs on my mind: When we moved in here in May 1940, we told ourselves that it was a temporary arrangement. And now, after two and a quarter years, a new "temporary arrangement" is about to begin, and under conditions that are so much worse. The summers alone! In summer 1940 the long excursions, in summer 1941 still long walks and enough to eat, in the summer of 1942 Eva is forced to undertake long shopping expeditions in town, and I live like a prisoner, and we both starve. And every day I ask myself whether I shall live to see the summer of 1943. The other men of the Jews' House are all dead. [ ... ]

## July 24, Friday morning

Downpours, thunderstorms, wind, more rain, cool weather—we have put on thicker blankets—everyone who's Jewish says: If only the weather keeps up like *this* for another couple of weeks . . ."

The day before yesterday a letter from Trude Scherk: Grete appears to be moribund and quite abandoned; Trude cannot manage the two and a half hours on foot to the hospital, Änny Klemperer was "in urgent need of rest" and has gone to Lake Constance. Trude herself believes she will be sent to Theresienstadt in the course of the next week. She has already been inoculated against typhus and cholera, she has declared herself available for work, "in order to be able to buy medicines with the money she earns." The general mood among Jews is that they do not fear evacuation quite as much as before and now even regard Theresienstadt as a relatively humane place. In general people say to one another, things are *so* bad here that anywhere else they can at most be equally bad, but perhaps also somewhat better. I observe this mood every evening in Ida Kreidl, who is now much more calm and brave than in past months. [ ... ] When Eva (who distributes the ration cards, now that Elsa Kreidl has been completely Aryanized) was at the Community yesterday, she learned that today another fifty people are going to be called for evacuation. Everyone who is over sixty-five believes that he is among these fifty.

I feel it is especially shameless that in this distribution the egg-ration card has been taken from Jews (and likewise the vegetable card!). The

Aryan population is no better provided for as a result: Among 600,000 Aryans there are at most still 900 Jews living here, probably only 600 to 800. But they want to drive us to hunger and despair. —

Eva was at the Glasers a few days ago and brought them a potted plant. (Very difficult to find; wearers of the star are forbidden to buy any flowers whatsoever.) Late in the afternoon of the very same day Frau Glaser appeared here with three kohlrabi heads, about a pound of potatoes and a tiny quantity of red currants in return. But how afraid she was of entering our house! "Will the Gestapo not come?" Only when I told her, that handing over a packet at the garden gate in full public view was much more dangerous, did she come inside for a couple of minutes.

[ . . . ]

### Afternoon

It is three o'clock and Eva is still not back from town. Later she comes home without having eaten—there is hardly anything in the restaurants, especially given the lack of coupons at the end of the four-week period— exhausted, out of humor, with empty hands. That's how it is now, like that or something like it, day after day. And hunger is a daily visitor, every slice of bread, every potato is counted. — I was over at Frau Hirschel's at 85 Wiener Strasse, gave her back Herzl's *Zionist Writings*, fetched new things from her good library: Sombart, *The Jews and Economic Life*; Ricarda Huch, *Michael Bakunin und die Anarchie* [Mikhail Bakunin and Anarchism]; Dubnow, *Jüdische Geschichte, ein geschichtsphilosophischer Versuch* [Jewish history, an essay in the philosophy of history]. Thus I am once again provided with study material for a week, if I have the time for it. — I recently had the most conclusive evidence of the tremendous harm that Herzl caused us. An acquaintance of Kätchen's brought a copy of the *Deutsche Ukrainezeitung* [German Ukraine newspaper], of about July 11, with her. In it there was a remarkably undirty article, almost calm in tone, about the "Jewish nation." The author quoted a memorandum to Lord Lansdowne found among Herzl's literary remains. (I do not think that it is a forgery, because tone and expression corresponded very precisely with similar outpourings in the Zionist writings.) I cannot quote word for word, but the meaning was something like this: If England espouses the establishment of a Zionist state, then it [England] will gain many thousands of Jews in every country as admirers, supporters, propagandists and agents. From that, National Socialist Germany naturally concludes that there is a Jewish nation, which in its totality is an enemy and whose German parts are now betraying it. And on this precisely it bases its legal claim to treat us, at best, as prisoners of war, but preferably as traitors. With the increasing shortages the general terror is increasing, too, and with it especially that practiced against the Jews. A few days ago Kätchen told us of a Jewish foreman at the Goehle plant who ran into the arms of a Gestapo squad as he came home; he had thrown a fit and shouted for help, had been shut up with kicks in the face and loaded into the waiting car. Today Frau Hirschel named him as the latest dead man. Presumably "suicide by hanging" again. I: "I've told my wife, if she hears of my 'suicide,' then I've been murdered." — "My husband said the same thing to me. Because of his position he is much more vulnerable than you." Frau Hirschel, too, complained of hunger, above all, that she never has enough to give her children. She too found the canceling of the eggs particularly shameless. — The names of the fifty to be evacuated in the next few days are to be made known at the Community this afternoon. But each of those concerned has already received the news by first post this morning. So *this time* Ida Kreidl and Julia Pick are not yet on the list.

[ . . . ]

### July 25, Saturday toward evening

Yesterday—to ward off his all-too-long Saturday visit—to Steinitz for a few minutes in the evening. (It was an effort going, even more of an effort coming back: bout of influenza, stomach pains, temperature of 101, knocked out today, often falling asleep, but better.) I used the just-announced evacuation as an excuse for putting him off, saying I had to keep the afternoon free for possible visits of consolation. It has meanwhile transpired that the Marckwalds and Frau Kronheim are not on the list. This time, curiously, most of those concerned are people from the Zeiss-Ikon plant, which was thought to be safe, and, what is more, disabled veterans. The principle according to which they proceed is completely opaque, no doubt there is a wild, chaotic competition between various authorities. Mood of despair at the Steinitzes'; they have also been given notice for September 1, which has particularly affected the hysterical wife. In addition, the murder of the foreman, Goldmann, had made a deep impression. Working at the cemetery, Steinitz had heard the description by the people who had brought the dead man from the Police Presidium: The corpse lay naked in a pool of blood. —

The next murder can already be recorded. The doorbell rang half an hour ago, I opened the door downstairs to a woman, whom I did not recognize, who wanted to see "Frau Voss" and rushed upstairs. Then we heard a loud duet of weeping and screaming from Kätchen's room. Her sister-in-law had brought the news of the death of [Kätchen's brother] Joachimsthal, who had been arrested two weeks before. — Being arrested, no matter for what trifle—according to one story Joachimsthal had "covered up the star," according to another had been sitting in the restaurant, where his wife works, beyond the curfew hour—being arrested is now identical with being killed, right here and now, they don't even bother with the concentration camps anymore.

[ . . . ]

**July 26, Sunday morning**

As a couple of weeks ago Katz had come to see to Frau Pick, found no one at home, and sat chatting with us for an hour. Largely a variation on the first visit. [ . . . ] To the doctor the world war is the central experience, one that comes up again and again, his love of the German army is ineradicable, a disposition that was inherited and inculcated: Dr. Katz's father was in the Guards Hussars and forged his father's signature to serve as a sixteen-year-old volunteer in the war of 1870. (In 1933–34 he was, no doubt, a supporter of the Schoeps tendency: "To wait, full of enthusiasm, until German National Socialism needs us!") But Dr. Katz is nevertheless emphatically Jewish. — Even so, certain things in yesterday's conversation were new and valuable to me. Katz said, he had reckoned that today there were 1,500 calories for a Jew and 1,800 calories for an Aryan. A worker doing moderately hard work needed 2,800 calories. The "plutocrats" would be able to obtain some additional calories on the black market, which was starting up again. Katz expected "real blockade illness" ("blockade illness" was his own term) by about Christmas. I asked him whether there was any serious hunger yet. — "Yes, but for the time being only the first signs of fatigue are appearing. First, the body fats are broken down, then the muscles, including the heart muscle, are affected. That then gives rise to serious insomnia, starvation edema, inability to work. That affects the performance of the armaments industry." —

*On the LTI.* [ . . . ] Something completely new, a whole chapter of the *LTI* presented itself to me with Katz's immediately plausible (presumably based on remarks in *Mein Kampf*) assertion: Hitler had started from specifically Austrian politics, from Schönerer and Lueger. — I mentioned the Herzl-Lansdowne article in the *Deutsche Ukrainezeitung*. Katz said, Herzl had had a truly fascinating character. He, Katz, had been in Vienna for one and a half years as assistant to some big shot (Eyselsberg probably). As a German from the Reich he had been respected by his Christian colleagues *despite* his Jewishness and so was able to go between and observe both parties. He talked about Schnitzler, whose brother Julius Schnitzler was a distinguished surgeon. Arthur Schnitzler rushes into the operating theater in his inverness cape, just as an appendix is being taken out, waves a newspaper: "You must read the review, Julius!" and tries to push the paper into his hands. "Later, Arthur, you can see we're operating," and as soon as his brother has gone: "We shall sterilize ourselves once again." —

[ . . . ] Yesterday evening—we are alone downstairs—Elsa Kreidl talks in a halfway-reassured tone about her new tenants; the forestry official, a very pleasant man, will now take the first floor after all, and the Gestapo detective superintendent, the ground floor, because he has children and also wants to do some gardening . . . It sounds as if Frau Kreidl feels safer now. Then in the middle of the calm conversation Eva launched into a fierce attack on her: "They murdered your husband, they murdered your friend Friedheim, they called you 'whore' and now they are going to live peacefully in the same house as you and be in the garden, and the car in which they put the bodies of the murdered may drive up to the door here!" Elsa Kreidl replied very shamefacedly, probably a little conscience stricken: "But I cannot choose my tenants." ("Then why doesn't she move out herself?" Eva said to me later.)

From the altruistic point of view all these events and scenes leave me ice cold, vilely cold. My only concern is always to avoid shuddering with the fear of death. It shakes me again and again: They will come for me, too. It is no longer about property—anyone can be murdered. This man Joachimsthal was in a mixed marriage, had no fortune, had served in the war, was a worker in an armaments factory, was on the list (why?) of the latest transport (going on Monday) and was killed before that. (Why?) If they kill me, they save a civil servant's pension. Every time I go to the letter box, I think there might be a card summoning me to the Gestapo. [ . . . ] I would so very much like to live another couple of years, I have such a dread of just this death, of perhaps waiting for days in the certainty of dying, of perhaps being tortured, of being extinguished in absolute loneliness. Again and again I save myself by turning to what is now my work, these notes, my reading. I am not only cold in the face of all the ghastliness, I also always take a certain delight in curiosity and its satisfaction: "So you can also bear personal witness to that, you have also experienced that, yet another addition to the Curriculum or the *LTI*!" And then I feel brave, because I dare to make a note of everything. Very deep down inside me, of course, there lurks the feeling: I have got away so often—why should I not manage it this time, too? But the long moments of dreadful fear occur increasingly often. —

There is an aspect of awful comedy lurking behind the tragedy of this most recent murder. A few months ago Kätchen made a scene, because in her absence I allowed her brother to wait in her room. This criminal, who wanted to squeeze money out of her, must not be allowed to rummage through her things. She had even worse things to say about her sister-in-law. Now there is a mutual affection between the two women, and the brother is lamented like the most beloved relative. Eva says there is a great deal of convention in Kätchen's pain: *One* mourns a brother. Then again she really does mourn: The tears are genuine, as is the grayness of her face, as is her distress. And she really does have a heart problem, a doctor has once again put her on the sick list because of angina and dilation of the heart. Then again: Her mind always seems to me to be like a slate: nothing written on it stays, the next second the sponge of a new impression passes over it. Then again: During those minutes, in which the bad inscription appears, she really does suffer. —

### July 27, Monday morning

Yesterday afternoon at the Seliksohns'. Truly touchingly received: a cake, they had been given rhubarb; a cigar was forced upon me: "A seventy-

year-old, whose hair I had to dye, gave it to me as a present." Behind it
there is always: Just take it, who knows if I'll still have it in an hour's time!
Seliksohn always looks thin and poorly, but yesterday his face was more
deeply sunken than ever before. He himself says: fear. The Goldmann
case, the Joachimsthal case, yet another similar case looming up, arrest of
a man working at Zeiss-Ikon, Juliusburger, because he had "covered up
the star." — Murder is everywhere, reaching out for everyone, in ever
more of a hurry. And where do the people die? No one is with them and
there are signs of torture. Seliksohn's conversation revolves around the
two focal points: "If only I would be evacuated!" and "If only I had
Veronal!" He repeats a hundred times over, that we shall all be murdered.
And I think he is right. He: already in a concentration camp once, former
employee of the Social Democrats ("Vorwärts" bookshop). And I: After
doing away with me they will save a pension. I am too young for Theresienstadt (under 65), probably too old for work in Poland. Recently also
they seem to want to put an end to mixed marriages through murder of
the Jewish party (Ernst Kreidl, Joachimsthal . . . [ . . . ]).

At home we were again welcomed by the unrestrained weeping and
wailing of the utterly distraught Kätchen: "I saw him—don't ask—I saw
him!" She had gone to Tolkewitz with her sister-in-law and the latter's
parents and had in fact set eyes on the corpse. This morning (breakfast together) the whole thing continued. For me there is only one way of ward-
ing off the horror and shock of this business—when I was young I often
had a nightmare in which I was going to be executed, and now the nightmare is very likely to come true, I can see a room with gallows and chair
before me—only one way, and that is to concentrate on the ghastly comedy of the Joachimsthal case, to stick doggedly to my observations, to the
literary material, and thus to pretend courage to myself. [ . . . ]

[ . . . ] But the supporters of the regime must be somewhere, National
Socialist propaganda must have an effect somewhere. Yesterday evening
again a graybeard worker shouted at me from his bike, "You Jewish
scoundrel!" When Goldmann was fighting the Gestapo on the street, on-
lookers are said to have joined in to help the Gestapo.

Religion or trust in God is a dirty business. Every prayer of thanks
means only: "Hurrah, *I* am still alive!" How puerile Kätchen is, has been
demonstrated in the last few days by her frequent and serious repetition
of the question "Where is God?" But millions are just as puerile. Only
when (and because) things are going badly for them, do they doubt the existence of a benevolent God.

### Toward evening

One day I can work, the next I repeatedly fall asleep with exhaustion at
my desk or on the settee. Today is a "next." I would like to make a few
notes on the just finished *History of America* — I can't do it.

Yesterday Seliksohn spoke with gratitude of helpful Aryans, very ordinary people. A laundry employee had given the rhubarb for the cake, someone had given him cigarettes, etc. Immediately afterward he demanded, with utter hatred, that the whole German people must be exterminated. I said, he himself acknowledged that the atrocities were by no means supported by everyone. He responded: One could not allow the criminal whole to exist for the sake of the few who were good. —

A new law, of which we learned at lunchtime: absolute ban on institutions of higher learning for those fifty percent Jewish. (Those who are twenty-five percent may attend, "if there are places"—but there are no places!) My first emotion was a very nasty one, but I could not and cannot suppress it, nor consider it entirely unjust: this affects Berthold's second son and my sister-in-law Änny. Last year Änny expressed her joy to me at the deliverance of German culture from the threat of Bolshevism, she is now recuperating on Lake Constance (what from?), while we . . . etc. Perhaps now it will dawn on her what this delivered German culture is all about.

*LTI.* Among today's birth notices in the *Dresdener Anzeiger:* Y Volker, 21.7.42. In Germany's greatest time a little brother was born for our Thorsten. With proud joy: Else Hohmann . . . Hans Georg Hohmann, SS Untersturmführer, Dresden A20, General Wewer Strasse . . ."

At the beginning of the week the newspapers regularly print an "NSDAP text of the week" under a special heading. A quotation, usually one of Hitler's pronouncements, is presented, followed by a brief sermonizing commentary. Today the headline is PITILESS AND HARD, the Hitler quote itself: "Just as we were pitiless and hard in the struggle for power, we shall be pitiless and hard in the struggle for the survival of our nation." The sermon, which belabors the word "hard" says: Because our external and internal enemies were so "hard and implacable" toward us, then "we had to be and still have to be even harder, always, today, and in future. Every stirring of pity, no matter how small, would be interpreted as weakness on our part . . ." I do not know if Seliksohn is so very far wrong.

As I was waiting for Eva at Wasaplatz today [ . . . ] I noticed again, as so often, how many pregnant women there were, and how emphatically they stuck out their full stomachs. Once pregnancy was concealed, now it is affirmed. I read that certain Australasian Negroes, when they want to display themselves as men of fashion, flirtatiously hold out their penises between two fingers. These females are now similarly flirtatious with their pregnancies. They bear their stomachs like a Party badge. Like the runes and the SS lightning flashes it, too, is part of the LTI. All Germany is a meat factory and butcher shop.

### July 29, Wednesday afternoon

At about two I went to Wasaplatz to meet Eva, I knew she was there buying potatoes at Jentsch's handcart and wanted to carry the net for her. She had got there before one, and I had to wait more than an hour before I was able to haul the precious ten pounds of potatoes and a couple of cabbages home. Dead tired and out of humor. The fact that one can be annoyed at this trifling bit of wretchedness is a sign of the fading of the greater dread. But from time to time this greater dread of the gallows in prison rises up again nevertheless. — I am unable to feel pity for Kätchen for very long. [ . . . ] In floods of tears uttering meaningless phrases: "The poor martyr—like Jesus for his faith! — Eva, how much did the potato salad cost, is it good? — *I* make it myself—the poor, poor martyr . . ."

I make my observations everywhere, as yesterday at Steinitz's—he asked me to come, he wanted some writing paper from me (legacy of Paul Kreidl), had a book for me—there they were not especially dismayed by the Joachimsthal case, because 1) the man had been a nasty piece of work and 2) he had "really done something," that is, sat in a restaurant after nine o'clock with the star covered—after all the Gestapo don't do things for no reason at all. So they forget, that the star law is a tyranny in itself, they forget, that a violation of the tyrannical measure could "justifiably" at most be considered a misdemenor and punished with a fine, and, only as the height of tyranny, punished with a couple of days in prison. People are so humbled and dulled, that they regard the death sentence—effectively uncontrolled murder in the prison cells—as virtually an appropriate atonement . . . I have already heard this "he really did something" from Kätchen about similar cases; she repeats what others have said.

On Monday evening—we were downstairs with Ida Kreidl—there was the monthly police inspection. I opened the front door, the big uniformed man remained standing in the hallway. "Your name, sir?" (*Sir*—where the Gestapo shouts, spits, beats.) "Who else lives in this house, please? Are they all present? Yes? Thank you, good evening!" The police are always courteous, always emphatically different from the Gestapo—but we have never yet had such an almost disloyal gentlemanly inspection. I could almost believe that the man knows of the frightfulness of the present terror and consciously opposes it. —

At the pharmacy they told me that I would save almost half the cost if I bought my Uromed dietary supplement in a packet of 500 instead of 60. It was all the more preferable to me, since I could pay by *bank* transfer, because pharmacy bills are not "deducted from the allowance." But now the big jar with 500 shoe buttons is here, and I do not know where I should hide it from the Gestapo. Until now "under the wardrobe" was considered safe—now they are said to poke around with sticks. (Hunger makes them more ingenious.) —

Steinitz weighs only 105 pounds now and he really looks his almost 68 years; he's still writing, in English, the history of the Bohemian coal company, which employed him for forty years, an "anecdotal history" he says. He wants to send the manuscript to his boss in America and hopes to be remunerated for it. At the same time the thing is language practice for him. But in good weather he passes the day as a voluntary cemetery worker. He feels safer outdoors. Just like Dr. Magnus. [ . . . ]

With the appearance of more plentiful cabbage, unrationed, a very bad moment of hunger seems to have been surmounted. I cannot really be glad about it: People have enough to eat for two days and they forget the privation they have put behind them and the privation that lies before them. — The war drags on. German successes, but nothing decisive. [ . . . ]

### July 31, Friday, toward evening

Aufrichtig, the old farmer, and his little farmer's wife—I wrote about them when I was shoveling snow—there was no return visit following our visit (even then it was for the sake of potatoes!) and we lost touch with them. Just recently they were named as being part of the latest Theresienstadt transport. This morning the Joachimsthal widow (great friends with Kätchen) brought the news that the couple had gassed themselves, the wife saved, the husband dead. They had been only in reserve for the transport—a couple of people always have to be ready to travel, in case the numbers have to be made up; if they are not needed, then it's their turn the next time and they're sent back to their room, which has meanwhile already been sealed. Usual context: House search, the man summoned to the Gestapo for the next morning (at five o'clock his wife had said he was out shopping, but shopping is allowed only till four o'clock; also, despite the surrender order, some bits of fabric are said to have been found)—fear and the result as with Frau Pick recently. Later Eva brought the news from town—she had invited the Neumanns for Sunday—that both the Aufrichtigs are alive. Suicide, attempted suicide: nothing more commonplace. Tomorrow the case will be supplanted by another case. In my memory too. But I shall try to look the people up before their departure.

The most hated man in Dresden is undoubtedly Governor Mutschmann, also hated by the Aryans, by the Nazis. (The kind, of whom there are many, who always maintain the Führer does not know what bad things are happening, others are to blame for everything wicked.) Now there's a rumor going around, his villa has had to have special protection, he himself has kept out of sight for a while. He has had animals illegally slaughtered on a large scale for his own use; when it got out, the butcher involved had to commit suicide, but once again nothing has happened to him, Mutschmann, the Führer protects him. (Version 1, Mutschmann helped Hitler as he was starting out, version 2, Mutschmann "knows too much.")

[ . . . ]

Familiar present-day destinies: Yesterday the Marckwalds showed me pictures, film stills taken by their son Wilhelm. He had started in business, had become a (café) musician, then turned to acting, more precisely directing, had held posts in Germany, had to go in '33 or '34, became a film director in Barcelona, married an actress, fled from the Franco troops, fled to Stockholm, was deported back to France as a Communist, is now living with the woman in England or Ireland, she as a maid, he as a farmworker—

the parents do not know their daughter-in-law. Such a curriculum vitae (y en a tant) seems to me now just as much a matter of course as suicide or attempted suicide. Habituation, deadening. Just as I have become used to the woeful sights at the Marckwalds. He, ever thinner, motionless at the table, the lower part of his body wrapped in a blanket, and always shivering. After a quarter of an hour: "Give me an injection," and while his wife gives him the morphine injection, we go on talking. —

Tomorrow August 1, the outbreak of war in 1914. We are now sixty years old, and of these sixty we have lived through seven as wartime, more than ten percent. Europe in the twentieth century! But what a decent business the last war was, how little it horrified me in comparison to this one. Whatever I do or think, the image of the gallows in a prison cell is always with me.

### August 2, Sunday evening

The Neumanns came at half past four—*he* has become a skeleton, compared to him I am fat and rosy, and even Eva does not look as thin. Both Neumanns in low spirits. They are reckoning on Theresienstadt.

[ . . . ] I said to the Neumanns: I am working to get over the dread of murder in a prison cell. I direct the course of my studies as I would a balloon. It cannot be steered, but one can nevertheless tack a little. [ . . . ]

On Friday we received the newspaper for the last time. Now we can glance at the Aryan Elsa Kreidl's paper every day. Until August 31. —

[ . . . ]

### August 4, Tuesday afternoon

Eva has taken laundry to Bühlau, her report of the little excursion is almost animated, and I was even more conscious of my imprisonment than usual.

Trude Scherk writes: On August 10 she will be evacuated to Theresienstadt. —

Grete, in the Jewish Hospital in Berlin, seems to be slowly fading away. She is said not to recognize visitors, too weak to sit up, she sleeps, eats, soils the bed. So goes the report of a sister of Änny Klemperer, who had been to see her. Subjectively, therefore, Grete already seems to have crossed over. Objectively: dreadful. — We shall not be able to see Trude when she passes through, it will also be impossible for Eva. We have written to her, that in Theresienstadt she should stick to people from Dresden. She would find out about our fate from them. Perhaps then there will also be a possibility of communication; at least Steinitz maintains there's a connection Theresienstadt-Prague-Dresden. —

In two days of concentrated work I have read and made notes on the Dubnow pamphlet *Jewish History*. My objections are also on the same sheet. [ . . . ]

## August 6, Thursday morning

My hands are freezing. Cold and rain predominate this summer. The harvest *cannot* be good, it has had no chance to come up, to catch up after the long winter. But are the many Aryans hungry like the few Jews? J'en doute. For two weeks there has been plentiful cabbage—who is still thinking of the previous weeks of hunger? And meanwhile the German offensive is pushing ever closer to the Caucasus, and the English and the Americans look on without doing anything. I no longer believe the end of the war is near. I even consider that German final victory—perhaps in the form of a favorable compromise—is not completely out of the question. To be sure: The Hitler business will certainly not last "1,000 years"—but even 1,000 days would be an eternity for me.

Habituation: A couple of weeks have passed since the murder of Joachimsthal, a couple of months since the house searches here. And already I am living in a state of dull-witted placidity. Habituation: On Tuesday another transport leaves Dresden for Theresienstadt; and already it appears to me, appears to Jewry here as a matter of course. —

Kätchen has been on the sick list for some weeks now and has not gone to Zeiss-Ikon. Her zeal has been cooled twice over, since she has been forbidden to take the tram and since it has become clear that even Zeiss-Ikon is no security against deportation. But she is in constant communication with her people there and hears what is going on. A batch of very young Russian women, still half children, has been put to work and kept away from the Jewish women. But they've forgotten that many of the Jews speak Russian and so there is contact. The girls have been pressed into service and feel themselves to be abducted prisoners. They are starving in their camp, morning and evening one pot of coffee with *one* slice of bread, at midday a thin soup. They are so hungry that their Jewish workmates help them. It's forbidden; but people drop a slice of bread under the table, after a while the Russian woman bends down and disappears into the toilet with it. (The Jews get dinner in the canteen.) — Zeiss-Ikon is said to employ "a patchwork of nations": Polish, French, Danish women.

## August 7, Friday morning

On Tuesday and Wednesday evening, after sitting down all day, I walked to the Südhöhe. View of Borsberg and the Saxon Switzerland, view of the towers of the city, laden fruit trees, on one a scarecrow in the shape of a giant bird of prey, fields—it was like a little excursion, it was a complete rarity and exception. Eva said almost enviously: "*You* can go for a walk"; I said almost enviously: "*You* can *travel* into town and eat in a restaurant there." —

Kätchen Sara relates with the greatest bitterness: People who are being evacuated on Tuesday were subjected to a house search; even from these they took all the foodstuffs (provisions bought on *coupons*!), bread, and butter they could find.

My visit yesterday to the Marckwalds—the man grows ever thinner and grayer in the face, he says the impending evacuation will mean certain and agonizing death for him—was very interesting in several respects. — At the very beginning of the Hitler business I was invited to join an "Association of Non-Aryan Christians." I did not do so, because I would have seen such an act as an acknowledgment of the National Socialist principle. As we were talking yesterday—I don't know what led up to it—Frau Marckwald said that *she* had sent me this invitation nine years ago; she was the secretary, her husband the head of the local branch of the association, which was started in Berlin (Pastor Grüber) and soon came to nothing because the government banned it. Frau Marckwald is going to look for pamphlets of the movement or tell me more about it. — He, Marckwald, said that at the time he had felt great "anguish" and looked for contact with others. Even before he learned of the Berlin foundation he had turned to Duesterberg (the Stahlhelm chairman and [national] presidential candidate in 1933). He describes himself [ . . . in a letter] to Duesterberg: His parents, Jews, converted to Protestantism after their marriage. His father was a farmer, Erdeborn Manor near Eisleben was his property, worked by him until his death in 1900. He himself was born there in 1871, brought up "like every German boy," he grew into adulthood "full of enthusiasm about Sedan and for the new Germany." Member of a student fraternity ("recently, with an aching heart, I voluntarily returned my sash"), farmer, worked Erdeborn until 1914, first lieutenant in the reserve artillery. Already ill at the beginning of the war, estate sold, did not serve in the field, official in the Chamber of Agriculture in Dresden; due to progressive paralysis retired in 1930 as Senior Agricultural Councillor with Service Medal of Thanks. Now he was in the position of "thousands of other Germans, young and old." Where did he belong? To the Jews he was a "renegade," to the Germans not a German. What should his sons do? They could emigrate, if one were *allowed* to give them the means to start their lives anew. It would be necessary to emigrate as a group, found a colony. [ . . . ] Marckwald said, that it was odd what was passed on. He himself had not been an anti-Semite—but not at all philo-Semitic. His children had loved him and been very attached to him. But only one son had shared his viewpoint in semiticis. The other, the film director, and the daughter had been emphatically Jewish. [ . . . ] What one finds easy, what one finds hard. I talked about Sombart. I said, so far the only thing I had certain difficulties with was details relating to banking. E.g., the difference between a share and a bond; according to Sombart's definition I did not see any difference, a bond was also a share in a company. Marckwald, very surprised at my lack of understanding, immediately said: "But a bond yields a fixed rate of interest," and Frau Marckwald added matter-of-factly: "And of course a shareholder receives dividends."

## August 8, Saturday midday

[ . . . ] I went to see Aufrichtig: In the winter a very strong, well-preserved, animated man, now [sitting] in a leather armchair, apathetic, broken, hollow-cheeked. His wife, completely recovered from the suicide attempt, fresh complexioned, as nimble as before, whispered to me, his memory had suffered, he knew nothing about his suicide attempt, he was weak, not interested in anything, would repeatedly lie down on the bed and sleep. But then in conversation he was quite alert, interested, not even unhappy. I spoke words of comfort to him, in a few weeks he would be restored to health, Theresienstadt was a privilege, etc. I asked Frau Aufrichtig to give our greetings to Trude Scherk. With Aufrichtig I could perhaps attribute the emaciation to the gas poisoning. But then Eisner, the robust proletarian, who had been so attached to me when we were shoveling snow, and likewise transplanted to this Jews' fort, came into the room. He, too, no more than an old, shrunken little man, wrinkled skin over bones. Then a younger man, unfamiliar to me—always this coming and going—he likewise emaciated. — From here to "no. 41" [Altenzeller Strasse], where we were the Kronheims' guests a few weeks ago. A hallway, like a room on stage, a very untidy one [ . . . ]. An elderly man opened the door for me, it turned out that Frau Kronheim was not home. Through the open door I could look into the man's room. A huge space, two beds, a white-haired woman lay on one of them. The man drew me into conversation, I had to sit in the hallway with him as pitiful figures came and went. His name is Rosengart, he had an important post as district head of an insurance company, talks and talks. His wife is in bed because of a light stroke, the result of a severe Gestapo beating. "She was 74 yesterday. She's recovering. And when we get to Theresienstadt—I hope with the next transport!—she will be healthy again. She'll meet relatives there, she will be nursed, and I, I know the man in charge there (Where from? There are only rumors about Theresienstadt, nothing is certain!); he's called Stahl, he's an insurance man, as I am, together we'll publish an address book of all the evacuees there! . . ." —

When I came home, Kätchen Sara reported an experience of her friend Aronade, whom we also know. The day before yesterday she went into a shop during the permitted time, to buy a watch strap, a cheap strap for one mark. There two of the familiar Gestapo men, one of them the Spitter, turn up behind her, shout at her. "In twenty-five minutes you'll be at the Gestapo." At Bismarckplatz they swear at her and beat her; she was not allowed to buy anything for which she did not have ration coupons. "A rope is good enough for your watch—buying things to take them away from us!" And blows. The woman was ill for two days. — They became brutal to Aufrichtig, when questioned as to his profession he replied "farmer." "You swine, laying hands on our land?!" Just as I was spat at: "You taught our boys?!" —

[ . . . ] Sombart is no vulgar anti-Semite. But he is an anti-Semite, and his work gives credence to the most vicious sort of anti-Semitism. His own anti-Semitism betrays itself very clearly in certain passages. I shall probably finish this tremendously interesting book on Monday and then develop my objections as I make notes. In general I hold against him: Why is intellectualism "flat" and "without deep roots"? Reverential adoration is easier. — I also want very carefully to draw out Sombart's internal contradictions.

### August 10, Monday morning

On Saturday an elderly gentleman, who appeared familiar to me, came to look at the apartment. Not discourteous, greeted us with a "good day." Elsa Kreidl said this was Head Forester Fritzsche, and Eva, who exchanged a few words with him, recognized him as a brother of the Ministerial Councillor Fritzsche with whom we had exchanged the apartment in Holbeinstrasse for the one in Hohe Strasse. I called the head forester our enemy, Eva defended him, he could be retired, have no connection with the "movement," have been quite innocently referred to this apartment. In the evening Elsa Kreidl talked very enthusiastically about this new tenant, who had taken the place of the first-mentioned Gestapo officer: The head forester had told her he had been promoted and transferred to Dresden, in his new position he had to work directly with Governor Mutschmann, not such an easy task—all the same, the Governor "concealed quite a kind heart beneath the rough shell." Now it is quite out of the question that today anyone is promoted to a senior position without the Party being absolutely certain of him, and it is even more out of the question that anyone in Saxony could not know how much blood stains the hand belonging to this kind heart. — The head forester does not want to see what might be embarrassing for him, that is what makes him complicit, and in that he is typical and representative of a huge stratum (in which I also include, e.g., Dressel, Annemarie's colleague). This stratum is also guilty and must also be punished. Otherwise, to put it with some pathos, Germany's soul is lost forever and ever.

I once again had an opportunity to see the boundless misery, for which our rulers are knowingly to blame. Yesterday at the Jewish cemetery for the third time: funeral for Joachimsthal. There was a fairly large number of mourners: such shocking emaciation, difficulty in recognizing a person whom I have not seen for a couple of months. Kätchen's relative, Falkenstein, has changed from a strong man into a shriveled little figure with a pale, very sunken face, tall, broad-shouldered Cohn, who used to collect the "little Winter Aid" from us, has become a walking skeleton, etc., etc.— Magnus's mind has deteriorated more than his body. (Does he think the same of me?) I had promised Dr. Magnus that I would chat with him for a little while after the ceremony, and while I was waiting for him, Eva and I walked through the not-very-large cemetery. The ceremonies take place

close to the small urn holes of those murdered outright. By the wall we discovered quite fresh full-sized graves. Numerous double graves, married
couples who died on the same day. These are the recent suicides. Is the man
with the kind heart not equally responsible for these? (People maintain that
house-search pogroms of the Dresden kind are unknown in Berlin.) — The
ceremony this time somewhat more elaborate than usual. Harmonium and
violin, played by two very young brothers (Meyer), whom I have repeatedly heard mentioned as exceptionally talented, a flower on the urn, two
wreaths with big ribbons by the little grave. (I cannot get rid of the foolish
extra shudder before the miniature grave, before the utter destruction of
outward form.) For the third time I heard Pinkowitz—the retired mathe-
matics teacher at a Berlin secondary school, who performs in robe and
yarmulke, reads psalms, says a Hebrew prayer, but does not give a sermon—read a psalm, which seems utterly inappropriate to me. I must inquire whether it has any special ritual significance. The psalm seems in
itself immoral to me, in its naked egoism, in its Hurrah, *I'm* still alive tone.
"The Lord is my refuge, a thousand fall at my right, ten thousand at my left,
thou hast delivered me from the pestilence," etc., etc. That by a grave? But
the dead man is among the thousand and the ten thousand. And precisely
*this* man saved from the plague? I do not understand it at all. Kätchen again
showed her completely infantile character. It had all been so beautiful, so
comforting. The psalm was so right for the poor boy. (She can, therefore,
have understood nothing of it except a few pathos-laden vocal notes. Cf.
Church Latin, magic spells, etc.) Also it was so nice for poor Kurt to be lying
here "among the martyrs." The whole day and this morning, too, she again
displayed this unbelievable mixture of genuine sorrow, childish consolation, flickering interest in this and that, the most confused flights of ideas
and impressions. Impression is a word that I should not apply to her.
Nothing im-"presses" itself, everything slides easily and smoothly across
the slate. — The long detour around the forbidden Great Garden. I walked
for almost three hours, found myself in midday sultriness on the way back,
came home completely washed out, could not rouse myself to read Sombart until the late afternoon. — This morning a few lines of thanks from
Frau Kronheim, whom I had not found at home recently. The woman, the
most delicate, composed of the thinnest little bones, most anemic corpse
among all the walking cadavers here, and really only a fleeting acquaintance of ours, writes in the exalted tone of someone about to die and taking
leave of her closest relatives. She reckons on Theresienstadt (rightly) every
day, trembles at separation from her daughter. "Do not forget us . . . I entrust my Grete to you, should fate soon overtake me . . . ," she appears to
hint at an intention to commit suicide, sends "most sincere" greetings "in
loyal friendship." This letter, too, is a *j'accuse.* —

Eva says to me: *You* look in your mid-sixties, I look over seventy,
comme une vieille édentée (truly the gap in her lower set of teeth makes
her look particularly old—but there have been no dentures for months, all
supplies go to the army). —

Despite it all everyday life goes on: I read Sombart, I steal from Kätchen, etc.

## Afternoon

[ . . . ] Having finished Sombart—in the late afternoon—I want to go to the Marckwalds' (though it's not the usual time), look through their library (before it's sealed to the evacuees), talk to them about Duesterberg, etc.

### August 11, Tuesday toward evening

Dr. Katz may be good at the mechanics of being a doctor—he is certainly a bad doctor. I met him at the Marckwalds' yesterday afternoon; Marckwald is trembling at his imminent evacuation. The transport, which had just left, was still fresh in Katz's mind; shuddering, he talked of the Gestapo inspector's "cynical sadism," of the old and the sick crowded together on deck chairs in the Community House, of the fact that medicines were "scarce commodities," and that they were allowed to take only very small amounts with them, that Marckwalds had little prospect of bringing his wheelchair, still less his nightstool, that he would certainly be allowed only *one* principal medicine . . . When Katz was gone, Marckwald told me how much he would like to take his life. I brazenly consoled him and gave cheer. Afterward I said to Frau Marckwald, who complained about Katz: "A doctor must be able to lie." — I learned nothing new [ . . . ] about the non-Aryan Christians. And in the Marckwalds' library I found only a medley of novels and some editions of the classics, but nothing that was of use to my work. On the other hand I was offered 14 pounds of potatoes; I fetched them today, in very sultry weather, from the trader in Lockwitzer Strasse, i.e., I waited there for Frau Marckwald. How bent, scraggy, and worn-out the poor woman is. Perhaps she is to be pitied even more than her paralyzed husband. —
     [ . . . ]

### August 14, Friday morning

A certain Juliusburger, in his fifties, at Zeiss-Ikon, was arrested a while ago for "concealing the star" and was thought to be a dead man. He has now been released after three weeks in custody at the Police Presidium and is supposed to have been treated decently there by the police—without further contact with the Gestapo—much as I was last year, except he was in solitary confinement for three weeks without anything to read. It is almost comforting, that at last someone has come back alive again. I told myself that I therefore did not absolutely have to regard arrest as certain death. [ . . . ] Kätchen, who brought the news, has now begun to wonder whether her brother was hanged or only driven to commit suicide with the rope (*only!*).

Steinitz wrote and told me to visit him the day before yesterday, he could exchange tobacco for sugar; he himself could not come on Sunday because of the imminent move. The dangerous letter was destroyed immediately. I went there in the evening. His wife is very disagreeable, constantly squabbling with her husband, constantly painting the new (still unallocated) accommodation in the blackest colors. "You leave the house in the morning, come back in the evening, and I have to carry everything and do everything alone, and you would like to just move into rooms, which have already been put into shape . . ." so it goes on endlessly. But it did not suit her either, that he had canceled me for Sunday, he should leave the cemetery on other days and help her. So he will come on Sunday after all. [ . . . ]

Since April we have been trying in vain to find out Caroli Stern-Hirschberg's missing address—every letter is immediately destroyed—we believed her to have been evacuated long ago. Yesterday she wrote to us from Berlin, still unharmed [ . . . ]. She has heard nothing more from Lissy since deportation. —

Yesterday at the Marckwalds' with Eva. There we met Bernstein: a scraggy man, in his fifties, corn merchant, ended up as a medical orderly in the war, now male nurse of the Jewish Community. The man spoke even more despairingly to Marckwald about the last transport than Katz had recently done. The most crippled sick crowded together on benches on the truck like herrings, violently tossed around during the drive, even as injections are given, lack of medicines, no ambulance allowed to fetch the people from their homes, no possibility of taking wheelchairs etc. . . . We left together and I asked him why he had painted things so brutally. Reply: In private he would without equivocation advise Marckwald to commit suicide, he would only avoid needless torments. He, Bernstein, considered it quite certain, that in Theresienstadt the sick, who are incapable of working, are disposed of by injections, there was a lack of morphine, insulin, etc. — I asked, why not here? — Because there it takes place more secretly, Theresienstadt is completely isolated—not even Katz as accompanying doctor gets farther than Leitmeritz. Bernstein called the brutality of the transport indescribable. There was not the least regard for anyone's age, for paralysis, no matter how complete, for any pain whatsoever. — What I find so much more abominable in all of this than similar things with the Russians: There is nothing spontaneous about it, everything is methodically organized and regulated, it is "cultivated" cruelty, and it happens hypocritically and mendaciously in the name of culture. No one is murdered here.

[ . . . ]

The external situation is darker than ever. We are unceasingly victorious in southern Russia. We have "taken more than a million prisoners since May" (the civilian inhabitants of the cities are included)—but farther north the Russians have been attacking for weeks (naturally always without success). And the rumor is going around, that Germany has sent troops into unoccupied France, partly because of disturbances, partly because of the "second front." The "second front" is the catchphrase of the summer. It is treated as enemy bluff; at the same time it is constantly asserted, that we are in readiness everywhere. *Everywhere*—there's something monstrous about that. And in the beginning they emphasized how advantageously short our front line was (in comparison to the World War). —

[ . . . ]

### Evening

Afternoon post from Berlin. Frau Maria Schott, "on behalf of her sister Änny Klemperer, who is away," informs me, as she promised Trude Scherk to do, that Grete died on the evening of August 11. She had for some time no longer been of clear mind, she had not suffered, and she was now spared "evacuation." I am entirely apathetic and cold. I wrote a note of thanks for the news. I could not come to the funeral, since I am not allowed to leave the environs of Dresden. So: Grete ϒ 6.10.68, † 11.8.42. But in the last two years I felt she was already dead to me and indeed she probably was. Now there only remain Georg, Marta and myself. —

The Seliksohns were here, the afternoon dragged on.

### August 16, Sunday afternoon

About twenty years ago, when Walter Jelski was living with us, Eva saw a young dancer, Harald Kreutzberg, perform, whom Walter found interesting. Now the man was announced here again, for this afternoon in the "Theater des Volkes" [Theater of the People] (once Alberttheater, where we saw the English Players). Eva mentioned it, I persuaded her to go, and so she has just left, "on an Aryan pass," as she put it. Truly an event that weighs heavily on me, on us. It took me a long time to persuade her. Completely cut off from all public performances, theater, cinema, etc. The infinite poverty of our condition! Eva must keep her excursion secret, otherwise she will excite acute envy. Am *I* envious? Definitely not. I would have felt depressed, if she had not gone. Eppure . . . All the things that I lack and perhaps shall never have again come to mind. *Abstinence makes one dirty.* Whether it applies to sugar or cinema, tobacco or women, bread or cars. One is always obsessed by dirty greed for what one lacks. —

Today Frau Schott informs us that Grete will be buried at Weissensee cemetery on Wednesday. I have already written to Frau Schott on Friday that I am forbidden to leave the environs of Dresden. Eva would undoubtedly not receive permission to travel either. — When Grete visited us for the last time, probably in '38, she once said to me, gladness lurking silently in her eyes: "You have discolored fingernails too—do you know that's a sign of heart disease?" Behind the sentence I clearly sensed her satisfaction at not having to be afraid alone, at not having to face death alone, and I told myself that she was no longer mentally normal. There were other signs of it during the visit, at times she was downright childish. But the real collapse came only in spring '40. From then on her life was that of an imbecile and madwoman . . . To think, that I, too, could end like that! — From very early in my life, I have regarded the claptrap about "benevolent nature" with the greatest distaste. —

It has been ordained that we move out of here on September 1. Where to remains uncertain—certain is only the further crowding together and pauperization of the Jews' quarters. Now Superintendent Hirschel has informed Kätchen by telephone that we do not have to be out until the first of October. That is not disagreeable. At the moment the house faces the sun in such a way, that Eva can sit on the balcony, at least here we are living amidst greenery, we are used to Kätchen Sara—and now she is even supposed to be getting permission to use public transport, which would take her back to Zeiss-Ikon and allow us to live alone for more than half the day. And to gain deferment for a whole month—who knows how much that means. —

At the cemetery recently the decent and emaciated Cohn told us he intended to visit on Sunday (today) with his (Aryan) wife. Instead a card came yesterday, he is ill in bed with sciatica. So I felt obliged to go and see him. 9 Zinzendorfstrasse—I had to traverse the dangerous, permitted passage of Bürgerwiese. A huge, old apartment building; first I went in vain up to the top floor at the front—Jews' apartments only there, but no Cohn. He lives in the back house. Once again up three flights of stairs, here a quite execrable winding stair—but with a view of green parklike gardens. Again for nothing, no one opened. Then, as I was departing hesitatingly, met a lady in the passageway downstairs. "For whom was I looking?" It was Frau Cohn, a pleasant woman in her fifties. Up three flights for the third time. The apartment more spacious than expected. Cohn was on his back, suffering considerably, we sat by his bed. Conversation, of course, about the horror of the situation. Another suicide had occurred: an elderly woman; one of her two daughters had recently been evacuated, the other arrested in the last few days. We had met the evacuee at the Feders' two or three years ago—a Fräulein Taussig, a Hungarian. —

[ . . . ]

The joyful emotion with which Kätchen informed us of our continued cohabitation was exceedingly comical. She shook my hand, Eva got a kiss. When I consider what scenes there have been between us. And how shamelessly I have been thieving from her lately. And how she drives both of us to despair. But on the whole she is "the devil we know" and afterward we always get on relatively cozily again.


### August 17, Monday evening

I have wiped the hallway floor, in the morning I was at Frau Hirschel's in sultry heat (wearing my coat!) and in the afternoon fetched 4 pfennigs worth of milk on Wasaplatz: so the pen does not obey my hand. —

[ . . . ] — Frau Hirschel (Walzel's assistant until 1920) said that like her husband she was liberal Jewish (not orthodox) and *fanatically* German. I enlightened her about the word fanatically. "Fanatically German" a contradictio in adjecto, "fanatical" one of Hitler's favorite words. She: "I mean 'passionately,' I shall not use fanatical anymore." She gave me a volume translated from the English: Claude J. Montefiore, *Outlines of Liberal Judaism.* This was her viewpoint. — I spoke of my hatred of Romanticism, or Teutonic Romanticism. It is becoming ever more clear to me that, at bottom, National Socialism is a German growth, no matter how much it adopts that is foreign. Literal originality probably does not exist. Every idea has already been thought, is thought simultaneously in various heads and places and times. All demonstrable originality consists in adaptation. National Socialism adapts Fascism, Bolshevism, Americanism, works it all into Teutonic Romanticism. "Les extrêmes se touchent." Nation of dreamers and pedants, of cranky overconsistency, of nebulousness and the most precise organization. Even cruelty, even murder are organized here. Here spontaneous anti-Semitism is turned into an *Institute for the Jewish Problem.* At the same time (les extrêmes), all intellectualism is rejected as Jewish and shallow. The German feels and has depth. —

Frau Fleischer, shriveled up and the same age as Ida Kreidl, and her good friend, left her house (villa on Daheimstrasse) to her Aryan son-in-law in good time, on condition that she would be allowed to lodge with him. Lives there on the best of terms, so far undisturbed. We got to know her during the winter, she offered us help with potatoes, etc. Eva went out to see her several times and always came home showered with presents. Today Frau Fleischer was visiting Ida Kreidl, brought us a jar of jam and a couple of soup cubes and told us many things she picks up from Aryan circles. Her son-in-law has something like a paper factory and had relatives and friends in the field, etc. — The mood in Berlin is said to be catastrophic, the harvest very poor. Huge losses in Russia, troops continuously to France. Seventeen-year-olds are being conscripted, in the armaments factories declining output by undernourished workers. —

**August 18, Tuesday morning**

Today is a crisis day of the first order: a new list of those to be evacuated is to be made known. At risk in our closest circle: Ida Kreidl, Frau Pick, Frau Kronheim, the Marckwalds, the Neumanns. As had been arranged, a Frau Schlesinger, who had been in the next room to Trude Scherk in Berlin, has sent me a postcard from a friend of Trude's in Stockholm: He had made inquiries of the Red Cross, there was hope that "in the foreseeable future" the Geneva Red Cross would be able to make contact with the people in Theresienstadt. (I don't believe it, there will be too much to hide there.) I shall try to get the news to Trude by word of mouth.

Everything has to be kept secret now, at least from the Gestapo. The card from Stockholm passed the German censors, but God have mercy on me if the Gestapo found these lines here. — Kätchen brings me a page of yesterday's *Dresdener Anzeiger*—"but destroy it right away!" We are no longer allowed to have a newspaper; of course, every evening we see the headlines of the *Dresdener Neueste Nachrichten*, to which the Aryan Elsa Kreidl subscribes. In any case, the *Anzeiger* prints an article about the harvest, which beneath the surface gloss reveals a state of extreme crisis. "The worst fears" have *not* been realized; nevertheless, we must be very economical. If at all possible, something must also be done for pig breeding, which had been much reduced. *I* as a censor would not have passed the article—ominous headline "Our daily bread."

No doubt things are bad for *everyone;* but no one knows how bad things are for the Jews, not even those who are in contact with them and sympathize with them. Eva needs money from Pirna; Annemarie replies to the announcement of a visit: busy this week—next week on holiday: "if you need something, write what I should send." She has no idea how tremendously dangerous such an act would be, both for us and for herself.

There has been a curious case at Zeiss-Ikon: It turned out that a woman wearer of the star was seventy-five percent Aryan. (Just as once it was discovered from time to time that a woman was male.) Whereupon no more star, and the freed woman was placed in an Aryan work group. Kätchen asked the girl what she was doing now. Answer: The work group was treated more harshly than the Jews' room. *But* she immediately went to a restaurant and immediately went to a cinema, and she was doing that every day now. This seventy-five-percenter has a brother, who is also seventy-five percent, and who has been deported to a Polish ghetto. What will happen to him? He will certainly not be allowed back to Germany—he could tell tales. Probably (Eva's opinion, with which I agree) he will be packed off to a training depot and from there to the front. (Did I note that fifty percent mischlingen are being sent to the front again now? That Erich Meyerhof's son is fighting with Rommel in Africa?)

### August 19, Wednesday morning

Les faits nouveaux: Ida Kreidl, Frau Pick, Frau Kronheim are included in the new transport to Theresienstadt. — We have to leave the apartment by September 1 after all, the postponement to October 1 has been overturned. — Eva has reestablished contact with Natscheff, which broke off a few years ago. — After countless examinations and applications Kätchen Sara has received permission to travel to work. She has not been to work for weeks and was driving us to despair with her constant presence and blathering. But now the house community will come to an end anyway, and so this travel permit is no longer of importance to us.

I saw Ida Kreidl coming home tired at midday yesterday. She had been to the Community—no one there knew anything. An hour later one of the Hirschel children brought the (already customary) typed summons for Ida Kreidl and Julia Pick to appear at the Community "without fail" at a quarter to four. Frau Pick sent apologies because of her feet—consequently did not dare take her usual Tuesday walk to the Marckwalds' either. I had to deputize for her. There they already knew everything—the deputy superintendent lives in the same house. The Marckwalds themselves were spared this time, therefore safe for two to three weeks. He was afraid again because of the morphine, I gave him new heart, supported by his wife, and did not myself believe what I was saying. Frau Marckwald supported me and afterward said to me outside: "He will *not* get it, of course." — On my way home, I bumped into the Hirschels (their villa: 85 Wiener Strasse, the Marckwalds' lodgings: 95 Wiener Strasse). He came with me, he wanted to call on Frau Pick, his former tenant. He talked about the indescribable brutality of the Gestapo. In particular, the "Spitter" and the "Boxer," whom we had also encountered, were devils. They are not, as I had thought, quite junior officers. The Spitter with the mad dark eyes is an inspector, the other (small, pale blue, hard eyes, prominent nose, little hat on his blond head) has, as SS Sturmbannführer, a captain's rank; they are called Weser and Clemens. Hirschel and Kahlenberg (Pionkowski's youthful and not very agreeable successor) had been summoned to the Gestapo to receive the list of the new transport. "What are you rogues doing here? What have you been up to—you're always up to something." (Hirschel added: He had also been beaten there; in the presence of the two main beasts, the otherwise more moderate people felt they had to be brutal, too.) This time the Spitter and the Boxer were also present as the announcement was read in front of the old people in the Community House. They interrupted with abuse and threats (you'll regret it if the suitcases are too large, you Jew pigs!), they ordered the pictures of earlier superintendents and rabbis to be removed from the walls. Among those affected there are again said to be many who are ill or crippled. The decision as to fitness for transport is made by the Gestapo, not by the doctor. Today we received a scribbled card from Frau Kronheim: She was not well, trouble with her gallbladder, must go to the "doctor" on Monday. That's what had been agreed. —

Ever since Rosenberg was brought down on my head, we had not dared borrow anything from the lending library. But now I have run short of material. So Eva has resorted to Natscheff. She told him her foot was much better now and so she could come into town again. She brought me *Mussolini* by Görlitz and a modern French author in the original. I [ . . . ] immersed myself in the very solid Italy book. Studying, as if I were completely certain of tomorrow! It is the only way to keep one's chin up.

### August 20, Thursday midday

Frau Pick attempted suicide a second time, and this time successfully. Veronal. Fear of ill-treatment by the Gestapo during the transport, perhaps also fear of unknown Theresienstadt. In recent days she was extremely lively, in the evenings allowed hardly anyone else to get a word in, fre-

quently said one has to "think further than that," "disregard it." The fact
that she was giving away keepsakes—her husband's moonstone dress-
shirt buttons for her niece Gaehde, a little black outdoor jacket for Eva
(who had borrowed it for Joachimsthal's funeral and will now wear it for
Frau Pick)—did not attract any notice because of the evacuation. — Once
again Ida Kreidl came up in the morning. Eva was first to go downstairs,
at seven o'clock, and then told me, this time it was more serious, she was
groaning loudly. I was downstairs a quarter of an hour later, by which
time there was no sound anymore, mouth open, one eye open, obviously
dead. Again I went to Mickley's nursery garden to telephone; I told him
the whole miserable story. I told Katz, Frau Pick was clearly dead; he said
he would come at about eleven o'clock. Afterward I had pangs of conscience: *I* could not establish death with certainty, perhaps recovery was
still possible—fortunately for Frau Pick? So I telephoned once again: Katz
responded, if nature could not do it, then *he* could not do it either, it was
certainly too late to pump out her stomach. When he did come, rigor mortis had already set in. — Again I registered my own complete coldness of
heart and apathy. My first thought: We shall inherit potatoes. [ . . . ] We
had known Frau Pick since February. She was, in the best sense of the
word, a great lady [ . . . ] a person of intellect and a stoic character. She was
uncommonly vigorous. She neither showed nor acted her 78 years. —
Substitutes are listed in advance for every transport: The Gestapo takes it
as certain that a number of suicides will occur. German organization. —

During these last few months I have learned again and again: Jewish religion, the "law," the many hundreds of prescriptions that bind a Jew at
every hour of the day, even when carrying out the least act, to his religion
and remind him of God, has existed since the prophet Ezra. The Gestapo is
like Ezra. I should like, for once, to lay down the timetable of an ordinary
day (without anything exceptional like a murder or a suicide or a house
search). On waking up: Will "they" come today? (There are days that are
dangerous and days that are not—e.g., Friday is very dangerous, then
"they" presume purchases have already been made for Sunday.) While
washing, showering, shaving: Where to put the soap if "they" come now.
Then breakfast: taking everything out of its hiding place, carrying it back
to its hiding place. Then doing without a cigar; fear while smoking a pipe
[filled with blackberry tea leaves], for which one doesn't go to prison but
does earn blows. Doing without a newspaper. Then the postwoman ringing the bell. Is it the postwoman, or is it "them"? And *what* will the postwoman bring? Then my hours of work. A diary can be fatal; book from the
lending library earns blows, manuscripts are torn up. Every few minutes a
car goes past. Is it "them"? To the window every time, the kitchen window
is at the front, the workroom at the back. Someone or other will certainly
ring the doorbell at least once in the morning, at least once in the afternoon.
Is it "them"? Then shopping. One suspects "them" in every car, on every
bicycle, in every pedestrian. (I have been abused often enough.) It occurs
to me that I have just now been carrying my briefcase under my left arm—

perhaps the star was concealed, perhaps someone has denounced me. As the husband of an Aryan I do, nevertheless, not have quite as much to fear as the others when I am shopping. If Frau Kreidl gets back a couple of small coupons without a J, when she has handed over a big Jewish coupon (which cannot be avoided), then she sticks the "Aryan" ones inside the lining of her handbag, because it is forbidden to have Aryan coupons. Also Frau Kreidl is always carrying some scarce commodity that someone has slipped her. In these respects, too, I am a little safer. Then I have to call on someone. Question on the way there: Will I be caught up in a house search when I get there? Question on the way home: Have "they" been to our house meanwhile, or are "they" there even now? Agony, when a car stops close by. Is it "them"? Then the hiding place business again, as at morning and midday. (On my visit, talk was of course only and exclusively of the most recent distressing cases.) A little calmer toward nine o'clock in the evening. Now there is at most the policeman making his inspection. He is courteous, he is not Gestapo. Last thought on going to sleep: I usually sleep without dreaming, now I shall have peace until tomorrow morning. But recently I dreamed, nevertheless: I was to be hanged in a prison cell. I had execution dreams as a very young person. Not since then. In those days it was probably puberty; now it is the Gestapo. —

Frau Pick must have been completely calm when she committed suicide. A farewell note on her table is written in a very deliberate hand—quite different from my shaky one—and carefully composed: "I thank all, *all*, who by their heartfelt courtesy have made my two and a half years in Strehlen (she means the Hirschels, us here, and the Marckwalds) so pleasant." Heartfelt courtesy—how carefully considered!

### Evening

Everything went very quickly. At about twelve Katz confirmed rigor mortis, death about five hours earlier, and arranged everything else: The police were here half an hour later, half an hour after that the hearse with the people familiar to me from the cemetery and the equally familiar transport and ceremonial coffin, of which there is evidently only one specimen. God knows where the corpses that are not burned and stuffed into a little urn end up. In the late afternoon I brought the news to the Marckwalds, who were very shocked.

### August 21, Friday morning

Yesterday morning Eva settled the essentials of our apartment business and at the [suggestion] of Reichenbach (Estreicher's successor) decided on two rooms on Lothringer Weg in Blasewitz, which are supposed to have all kinds of advantages and disadvantages. After our evening meal Eva went to see Gaehde, Frau Pick's niece. We were prejudiced to some extent against the wife and very much against her Aryan husband. Eva says Frau

Gaehde made a favorable impression on her, and even the Aryan coward a not quite unfavorable one. The people were grief struck, depressed, angry. They evidently had too much to fear from intercourse with Jews, Frau Gaehde had repeatedly emphasized "the fates of seven people depend on me." Nevertheless: German courage, German morality. The man owes his wealth, his free existence to the dead Jew Pick. —

German morality: During the brutal roll-call scene at the Community House, I mean the reading of the list of names for the transport to Theresienstadt, a couple of Hitler Youths were present, evidently young blood getting their training as Spitter and Boxer successors.

*LTI.* Two new "orders" in judaeos are interesting for their style. Previously things were "forbidden," and there was the threat of "State Police measures." This time "*it is undesirable*," a) that, in written correspondence with the authorities, Jews mention their title or former profession (e.g., Assistant mistress, retired, Hilde Sara Heim), b) that Jews "continue to employ such maids of German blood," as they are permitted by the Nürnberg Laws of September 1935 (i.e., ones over 45 years of age). In both cases one "*can expect consequences in the event of nonobservance.*" Why the milder form of expression, which certainly does not mean milder treatment? Consider. Case 1: The state pensions office pays my pension to Prof., retired, the revenue office demands taxes from Prof., retired—and the Gestapo puts me away, if I call myself Prof., retired (just as they recently spat on me and beat me because I held my post until 1935). And case 2: The Nürnberg Laws are held to be important foundation stones of the National Socialist structure, and the Gestapo puts me away if I act in accordance with this basic law. That is a flagrant divergence, so things are obscured and kept secret. *Undesirable* and *consequences* are wonderfully elastic words. —

On a quarter-page of newspaper in the smallest room I found the article headline: MANKIND COMMANDS! Curious that it's allowed; it's "ideological" after all, a mockery of the formula "*the Führer commands.*" At the same time it dawned on me how important this latter formula is to the whole of National Socialist thought, and how in it one sees laid bare perhaps the strongest root of National Socialism and Fascism. (Less so of Communism.) The weariness of a generation. It wants to be free of the necessity of leading its own life. [ . . . ]

**August 22, Saturday morning**

We had—a solitary exception this summer—two, three oppressively hot days, then a thunderstorm yesterday brought cooler weather. Toward evening I was caught in the downpour and was soaked through. First I was with the Kronheims at 41 Altenzeller Strasse for a few minutes. This time they were both at home, packing. The mother, who must go to Theresienstadt on Tuesday, even more pinched, paler, tinier, hunched than the last time, a bent little matchstick skeleton, the daughter even more hyster-

ical, tearful, despairing than the last time. Helping them was their neighbor from the next room, Frau Aronade. We know her as Kätchen's fat,
easygoing, broad-faced bridge partner. She, too, with nothing on her
bones, utterly scrawny. Yet courageous and optimistic. In the house they
had thought we would rent Frau Kronheim's big room, especially as
Kätchen is moving in, and were somewhat disappointed at our choice.
(Now when a house is appraised among Jews, the first question is, how
often "they" have been there.) Altenzeller Strasse has a very bad reputation, especially, however, number 32. It is said to hold the Gestapo record
with 19 house searches. When, at the Community, Reichenbach offered
Eva Altenzeller Strasse, she replied: "I want to get my husband out alive."
But it was not just fear of the Gestapo; the thought of sharing with Kätchen
again, after that the fact that the Steinitzes are also moving to 41, made us
hesitate. We are more isolated in Blasewitz. Admittedly Kätchen says
"they" have already been to Lothringer Weg nine times, and in Altenzeller
Strasse it's really only number 32 that attracts them. — I said we would
both pay a farewell visit on Sunday at three o'clock and then went to the
nearby Glasers, where I was received with genuine pleasure. I came upon
Frau Glaser downstairs, she was just scrubbing (in her green trousers) the
lowest stair. We arranged to visit late on Sunday afternoon. That will
allow us to recover. They asked me to read to them from the Naples chapter of the Curriculum; but I shall probably tell them one is less threatened
in Blasewitz than here, so they can visit us and I can read it then. That
would have the advantage that Eva would not have to hear the same old
tune for the umpteenth time. —

Reading aloud: Georg Hermann. I feel so at home with him. A generation has more in common, after all, than a nation, than a profession.

Study reading: Mussolini. If only I could read something Italian (in Italian).

This afternoon the diary will at last be got out of the house again. I am
not calm until Eva is back.

### August 23, Sunday morning

The Mussolini book by Walter Görlitz is like a cake that has partly fallen
flat, in which good bits alternate with doughy ones. [ . . . ]

We have both been swept into the turbulence of the evacuation and of
our own move. Eva has been performing great feats. Yesterday she came
to an agreement with and through Thomas, the moving company, that we
would move to Lothringer Weg on September 3; she is working for Ida
Kreidl on the sewing machine, helping her in every way; yesterday she
was in Pirna. — I began the day by heaving furniture from Ida to Elsa
Kreidl, from the ground floor to the second floor. Eva is fetched downstairs every second now; the Community has sent a packer, who is quite
helpless. The problem: Every Jew pig is allowed to take only a small suitcase and a small handbag—everything else, furniture, linen, everything is

forfeit in the sealed room. And of course all assets are forfeit. (But everyone clings to the Roosevelt-Churchill promise of compensation on the conclusion of peace.) And all pull on, one on top of the other, as many clothes, pieces of underwear and socks as they possibly can.

Annemarie was a friend of Feder's doctor brother, who is now in England, and is still friendly with the wife, who has remained here. By this route we learned that the eighty-year-old mother of the brothers is included in tomorrow's transport. "Our" Feders have meanwhile been forced to move out of their apartment and into the Community House. With what revulsion did the narrow-minded Aryan Frau Feder once tell me: "No, I wouldn't want to go to a Jews' House!" I cannot suppress a base feeling of malicious pleasure. —

Annemarie sent me three cigars, I smoked them quickly, because they are so very much forbidden. [ . . . ]

At Woolworth's one can buy a toothbrush if one hands in a used one in return. — Toilet paper, tissue paper, paper napkins nowhere to be had. The day before yesterday our grocer at Wasaplatz was dispensing single rolls—but only against household cards, which we don't have. Of the new (the *new*) potatoes, which are now being supplied more plentifully (seven pounds per head per week—it should be ten pounds soon), we have to throw a large proportion away, because they are completely rotten. The old potatoes, try as one will, are no longer edible. A small inheritance of new ones from Ida Kreidl will be a help for a little while. —

On the German side much has been made of the attempted landing by the English, which was repelled at Dieppe (two thousand prisoners; it can hardly have been a major undertaking). Invulnerability of the European coast, new Dunkirk, etc., etc. [ . . . ]

I dream so rarely. And early this morning I woke up afraid. It was so hot, at a tramcar stop I had rolled up my coat and put it on the ground (the coat *with* the star) and stood there in my jacket without the star. Two gentlemen addressed me: "We have seen you so often with the Jew's star. Why . . . ?" At that I woke up with a dreadful sense of fear. Recently hanged in a dream, today without a star, it amounts to the same thing.

### August 24, Monday afternoon

Yesterday's farewell visit to the Kronheims very depressing. The daughter with her hysterical sobbing worse than the mother, who finally embraced and kissed me. Baggage and underwear in the room, a secret packet of sweetener sewed into a pink corset, between times mother and daughter shouted at each other in their agitation. — Glaser, who has known the people for a long time, came over; it was a deliverance when we left with him. Then a couple of hours recovering at the Glasers'; we heard a wonderful violin concerto by Bruch on his beautiful electric gramophone. It's a pity that he is convinced the war will last a long time and end in German victory. He told me that as a defense lawyer in Communist trials, he had been chased out of his job in 1933, but had always refused to join the KPD, so that in the end the Party had preferred their young Party member, the lawyer Helm. I once talked to this man Helm: He came to see me in Dölzschen as salesman for a car lubricating oil company. At the time that seemed quite like martyrdom. —

At home in the evening we were once again caught up in the evacuation. But Ida Kreidl was very calm, almost cheerfully excited: In Theresienstadt she will meet a sister from Prague, she is traveling with a sister-in-law. Her good mood (of course, accompanied by great agitation) also held up this morning. She repeatedly came upstairs to us from the early morning on. We "inherited" many more things: potatoes, flour, tools, etc. Then at about eleven a Gestapo inspector appeared; I opened the door to him, he addressed me politely, so almost a human one. Subsequently I saw Frau Kreidl weeping after all. "Now I am like a dog on the street," she said. Across the keyhole of the ground-floor flat there is now a row of four red Gestapo paper seals: Everything inside now belongs to the state, the owner is absolutely stripped naked. (I.e., she is wearing five dresses one on top of the other, likewise, she says, six drawers and six pairs of socks. And then she still owns what could be fitted into a suitcase and a handbag. When the inspector rang at the door—protracted ringing of every bell—she, interrupted in what she was doing, was wearing one brown and one gray sock.) Then she was upstairs with her sister-in-law for an hour. She was still brave when she took her leave of us—I was again embraced and kissed. The fifty people have to be at the Community House at two. They spend the night on deck chairs, evacuation early in the morning—next group two weeks after. — Late yesterday evening Superintendent Hirschel also came up to see us for a while, after he had been with Ida Kreidl, and invited us for tea on Saturday.

New orders (—how many now?): a) "Jews are forbidden to buy ice cream." (In general I see only little bands of children licking outside Baker Kramer. But recently the harassed Frau Marckwald said to me: now she was going to buy ice cream at Baker Kramer. Henceforth she is no longer allowed to do so.) b) All dispensable keys, "in particular trunk keys," are to be surrendered immediately.

[ . . . ]

### August 25, Tuesday evening

The sealed ground floor, the solitude in the house—we were never especially intimate with Elsa Kreidl—the ending of our evening visits downstairs: la maison juive morte. (Kätchen Sara is now working half days again. When she is at the factory, we live in complete isolation; when she is here, she irritates us with her blathering, usually tactless blathering.) One more week of this agony, then it's the turn of the second Jews' House. —

In our neighborhood there lives a doctor, Dr. Strüver, whose yellow setter bitch was the affectionate friend [ . . . ] of our whole Jews' House—the man is now in the field, and Nora, the dog, is no longer to be seen. This morning a young, blond, very pleasant-looking lady appeared. She wanted to visit Ida Kreidl, had heard . . . was appalled by the seals. Frau Dr. Strüver—she had sometimes exchanged a few words with Ida Kreidl. I brought Frau Strüver up to our apartment, we told her about the conditions and events of recent months. She: It cannot go on like this for much longer. "Everything is like an overheated boiler." She offered us help, if there was anything she could usefully do (she had wanted to help Frau Kreidl out with a suitcase); she then asked me to forgive her, if she did not greet me on the street. I told her, and they were not just words, it always made me happy when I met with Germans who made it possible for me to preserve my feeling for Germany. —

[ . . . ]

## August 29, Saturday morning

[ . . . ]

It has been very hot for almost a week now, the first time this summer; it's a torment, given my terrible lack of clothes and hampers me greatly. Thus I arrived at the Marckwalds' on Thursday and said I was like Monna Vanna, I could not remove my coat, I was wearing only shirt and trousers below it. So then I had to try on and inherit a light-colored linen jacket; *he* doesn't wear it, and why should it go to *them* after evacuation?! The item is of such quality that it is heavier than my black jacket, but it is light-colored and loose and will deliver me from the coat. Eva is altering it; perhaps I shall even wear it this afternoon. These times! Frau Marckwald encouraged me: She, too, was wearing "nothing but things passed on to her." — Question, is there really a boundary between civilization and culture? As little as there is one between body and mind. If I accept other people's cast-off clothes as a present, if I use newspaper instead of toilet paper, tooth powder instead of the more convenient toothpaste, if I am not allowed to use the tram—does all of that not also make me spiritually shabby and *unfree*?

Since the evenings at Ida Kreidl's have ceased, I only rarely, irregularly, and surreptitiously see the newspaper. I miss it. What Kätchen brings home is only the most unreliable fragment, and Eva sometimes catches only a snatch of the radio broadcasts. —

Thierack, the former Saxon justice minister—well known as a bloodhound—was announced as Reich Minister of Justice on August 20. The decree says his task is to "establish a National Socialist administration of justice": "*In doing so he can deviate from existing law.*" I read it one day after Steinitz had passed on to me a rumor, from an Aryan source, that he described as "wild talk." According to it, mixed marriages are to be forcibly dissolved. Eva and I consider it *very* possible; the will to extermination is growing all the time. In the same measure as the chances of victory are declining. —

[ . . . ]

In Lothringer Weg we are to share the kitchen with Community nurse Ziegler. The woman was here yesterday and made an agreeable impression. She said fear of the Gestapo had become a general Jewish psychosis. The owner of the house—she is over eighty—spends the whole afternoon by the window, waiting "in case 'they' come." However, this old lady will probably be deported to Theresienstadt with the next transport, and it is impossible to foresee into whose hands the house will fall and how soon we shall have to get out again. But *what* can one foresee now? Another case of psychosis: Dr. Magnus, likewise forced to move, had chosen the most cramped, proletarian rooms in the most proletarian city house in Schulgutstrasse: He thought he would perhaps be safer there than in a better district. Whereupon the Steinitzes began to waver and perhaps instead of moving to Altenzeller Strasse will also move to Schulgutstrasse. The trustee of our house, Frau Ziegler told us, had been summoned to the Gestapo for being too friendly to Jews. At his declaration that the people were decent, he was told there were no decent Jews and the "whole race was going to be exterminated."

On the night from Wednesday to Thursday, at 1:00 A.M. on the twenty-seventh, we had the first air-raid warning for almost a year. There was heavy shooting, but no bomb fell, and the all clear came after three-quarters of an hour. When a piece of shrapnel whistled uncomfortably close, we got up for a while.

A couple of days ago, on the tear-off calendar, I found: "Avoid waste": Strict care should be taken that schoolchildren do not let their breakfast sandwiches go dry and hence uneaten, they should be taught respect for the soil and for the sacredness of bread. There are two things to be said to that 1) How quickly such a calendar goes out of date! I should like to see the child and the adult who today let a sandwich go stale! Everyone is hungry. 2) *LTI*. Sacredness of bread. Compare the harvest festival to the Italian "Festival of the forest," to *ruralizzazione*. Again the question of relative originality.

Every morning I observe in myself: My face is more pinched, but my stomach is a tightly stretched (gas-filled) drum. Eva says she sees this figure everywhere in the restaurants, on the street. Especially with women. Skirts have become too long at the sides, because hips are thinner. But the stomach, the "typical hunger stomach," is a plump protrusion in contrast to the thin face.

### August 30, Sunday toward evening

At about one o'clock at night we had another air-raid warning (no. 2). There was no shooting, and we fell asleep.

Yesterday afternoon in my inherited jacket—Eva had shortened the sleeves and sewn the star onto the breast pocket—first to the Hirschels' for tea, then for a while to the Marckwalds' as well. The Hirschels live in their

own villa (partly rented out, it is true)—very elegant rooms, a beautiful veranda, a certain largesse in the hospitality (real tea, home baking—where
from?), very solid people. The husband, formerly head clerk of a large
fashion house here. Now as Community superintendent he has quite the
reputation of a martyr, of self-sacrificing devotion to duty. The Pinkowitzes, who are their tenants, were also there. Berlin secondary-school
teacher, exactly my age, looking much more emaciated, without a pension—the city of Berlin is not paying. He was previously Frau Breit's tenant, and is now the deputy cleric at burials. I asked him about the
"Hurrah, I'm alive" psalm. It was indeed ritual prescription—to comfort
the bereaved. (It is perhaps understandable that one leaves the corpse and
marches to the inn to the accompaniment of cheerful music—but this
psalm is already playing the tune for the march to the inn within sight of
the corpse.) — There had been a house search at Wiener Strasse the previous evening. The Hirschels got off quite lightly (Spitter and Boxer were absent, no one was struck, only books were stolen), at the Marckwalds' they
boxed a few ears, particularly of the old ladies, but here, too, the thing
passed without the complete ghastliness of other operations. Modest good
fortune. Gloomy at the Marckwalds', since they had been told he would be
allowed to take his armchair when transported. Which means that the
medical application to declare the man unfit for transport has been refused and that he will presumably be on this Tuesday's list. We already
heard it at the Hirschels', and at the Marckwalds' it had been confirmed by
Dr. Katz. For Marckwald this is more or less a death sentence—because
who will procure the necessary huge amounts of morphine for him there?
At the Hirschels we debated for a long time the old question, whether in
this case the wife could or perhaps should inject her husband with a sufficient final dose. Naturally we did not come to any conclusion. What was
curious about our conversation was the way we took the subject for
granted, the general numbness. The general mood is simply: We have
come to a terrible end. Each one of us may fall, each one of us may survive.
At all events: An end is within sight. Hirschel said the English broadcasts
had announced Russian victory on the central front, the Germans hardly
denied it. (Rzhev taken by the Russians, 45,000 Germans captured.) — At
the Marckwalds' we found him *very* composed, her reasonably so—but
that may be playacting. Again I held forth to *her* not to anticipate anything—one can never know what the next day will bring, one cannot
know what possibilities Theresienstadt offers. But I held forth without any
great confidence. — At the Hirschels' the conversation was still about suicide in general. Frau Hirschel argued: "*We*, in our situation, *must not*, it's
desertion." She condemned Frau Pick. Conversation over tea and cakes!

Half past eight. — Eva has just come back from Lothringer Weg—I have
not been there yet, much too far for a Jew—she has settled all kinds of
things, made preparations, cleared up. The confiscated furniture has been
removed. [ . . . ]

## September 1, Tuesday evening

Today was again a Polyphemus day, the new evacuation list must have appeared. We do not yet know who has been affected.

The troubles and tribulations of the move—Thursday morning seven o'clock!—have begun. The burden is entirely on Eva's shoulders and tugs at her undernourished nerves. She sleeps badly, and I read aloud during the night or very early in the morning. Yesterday, to spare her a trip into town, I went to the Community; one has to make an application and have written permission in order to call a tradesman (electrician to take down or attach lamps) to a Jewish apartment! I took advantage of the errand to look in on the Seliksohns, who are very wretchedly accommodated in a single room—kitchen stove and double bed in it—next door to the Community. It is the house that was formerly occupied by Fleischhauer, the lawyer, and where we once went to a *Schlachtfest*—but now Herr Fleischhauer has put quite a distance between himself and his alien friends—and between himself and the house, which later served as an old people's home. Seliksohn handed me the two volumes of Shmarya Levin, which I read two months ago. There was a dedication from their owner, the coarse Eisner, with whom I shoveled snow, who had attached himself to me and whom I recently saw again at Aufrichtig's. Had I known that Eisner was in the last transport, I should certainly have called on him. The man is said to have been in tears as he left. [ . . . ]

Very early this morning I finished reading out Hermann's *Eine Zeit stirbt* [The end of an age], and during the day managed *Les enfants gatés* as well. Hermann *very* important and to be treated here from the perspective of LTI: I find Hériat downright repellent.

## September 2, half past eleven on Wednesday evening. On a cleared desk

The chaos of the move. Ninety-nine percent of the work load was on Eva's shoulders, I had to share the disruption. [ . . . ] Toward evening at the Marckwalds' for a while, who really are among the next fifty. They appear composed. He hopes to find his sister in Theresienstadt, but trembles for his morphine. —

As far as it lies in my power, the Jews' House at 15b Caspar David Friedrich Strasse and its many victims will be famous.

## The Second Jews' House: Dresden-Blasewitz

## 2 Lothringer Weg

## September 3

## September 4, Friday toward evening

Doubly different from the house in Strehlen: There, an emphatically modern and petit bourgeois garden suburb, sham, cheap elegance with modern fittings and architecture. Here style and taste throughout, [ . . . ] the Spielhagen period (between the sixties and the eighties) [ . . . ]. Heavy, solid elegance of the grands bourgeois, in our decline, declining elegance. A huge box of confused and restless form: No line is left in peace, no part without special decoration, nothing is simple. Half gray, half redbrick, ornamental features, reminiscent of the Marienburg, of Northern Gothic, Baroque curves, a turret with a cupola, beside it a separate little house with a pointed roof set on top of the roof proper, tin embellishments added on everywhere (globes and points), reminiscent of pagodas, [ . . . ] scattered seeds of chinoiserie, bay windows, a huge veranda, a tiny balcony; everything at odds, and the trees of the big villa garden, half concealing the house, make everything even more restless. Opulence and restlessness inside also. A vast, square central hall reaching to the roof. Two floors. The ground floor very high, the second floor lower, and it feels *even* lower because of the heavy, dark brown wooden ceiling with its exposed beams. A wide gallery with heavy, carved wooden banisters runs around the second floor. From top to bottom every free piece of wall is crowded with paintings in heavy frames, mostly copies of famous Renaissance works. Downstairs, on heavy carpets, heavy easy chairs around a heavy table, wherever any ledge offers the opportunity, there are small works of art. Only a few rooms go directly onto the hall. [ . . . ] Here and there the line of the hall is broken by a couple of steps; they lead up to a corridor, and the inner rooms are off this corridor. We have two such corridor-isolated rooms on the second floor. They are a little gloomy, the dark beams of the ceiling are oppressive, the dark wooden paneling leaves only a narrow strip of white wall. The windows, too, are somewhat low and squat, and the door to the tiny balcony [ . . . ] is of course kept from providing proper light by a great deal of lead frame and a small glass painting, a pikeman and a coat of arms. But we look out onto open spaces and the greenery of the other bank of the Elbe and the Albrecht Palaces. The cellars are a subterranean town, high and extensive, storerooms, washhouse, space for the mangle, space for two gigantic boilers, porter's apartment, a second kitchen for domestics. The owner's name is mentioned with respect: the Jacoby Villa. The man was court jeweler, Elimaier's shop on Neumarkt, very wealthy, had everything executed according to his taste and desire. Nurse Ziegler has the former smoking room downstairs; there—in the smoking room!—the ceiling is covered with portraits, all copies of Old Masters, a famous head in each ceiling panel. Widow Jacoby, in her eighties, with a cane, bent, but intellectually alert, is among those to be evacuated next Monday. Her trunk, with "Jenny Sara Jacoby" in big letters, is already in the hall. That is all that is left to her of the grand villa. Beside it is another suitcase: "Rosa Sara Eger." She is the old mother of [Robert] Eger, who is married to an Aryan; they own the big clothing store. Halfway up the stairs, between ground floor and second floor, there is a big curtain. We supposed there was a window behind it. Why not let the light in? But behind the curtain is a door, which the Gestapo don't have to know about. A former employee lives there; because she is Aryan, she is not allowed to communicate with the Jews. Likewise, the porter's wife is forbidden to enter the Jews' House, because she is under forty-five. And I and the other Jewish parties were strongly advised to go out onto the big terrace as seldom as possible. This terrace can be seen from a neighboring house in which an influential Party member, I think even an SS man, lives. [ . . . ] The last time we were in this part of town was when we visited Frau Breit—1940? 1941?—before she left the country. — A serious disadvantage for us is the kitchen in the cellar, which actually is no proper kitchen at all: Water has to be fetched from the washroom. But Eva takes so much pleasure in this spacious cellar layout that the disadvantage appears slight to her. However, she has not yet had to cook anything down there; she has been out since eleven o'clock today and is unlikely to be back before nine. —

I myself experienced the last two days as a true misfortune; we have never had a more wretched move. Nothing went right.

### September 5, Saturday

The people from Thamm (only *one* familiar face among them), usually so friendly and cheerful, were from the start surly and bad-tempered—but not that it was directed against us. They were four and should have been six because of the grand piano. They were not a team; argued and shouted at one another about every movement. Every piece was too heavy for them. "But the wardrobe was just as full of things the last time." — "Yes, then! But now. — Where should we get the strength, we've got nothing inside us!" Again and again this: "We don't get enough to eat . . . only a laborer's allowance, but not a heavy laborer's allowance . . . but we work all the time . . . *they* do as little for the workers as *the previous lot* . . ." [ . . . ]

### September 6, Sunday midday

The chaos hardly altered, the same despair. Still unpacked. Not washed, not possible to cook or clean dishes. . . . Eva chases around all day—errands, cleaning the old apartment, bank, . . . and I am helpless here; cannot arrange the furniture, laboriously rinse the cups and plates in the washhouse, always the same few, boil a pot of potatoes on the one gas jet, see how Eva comes home ever more pinched and wretched, how she eats ever less, hear that now she had no time, now no coupons for the restaurant; try to get over the empty hours, the hopeless depression by reading. (Eva brought a new French author from Natscheff.)

The widespread and greater misery plays its part in our own misery. Tomorrow the next transport to Theresienstadt. This morning a band of young people wearing the star invaded the house. During the week they work in the factory, on Sunday they have to help out at the Community.

Apart from the grand hall, this house has sixteen rooms, the finest of which are still inhabited by the old owner. These rooms and the hall were to be emptied, their contents assembled for confiscation by the state. There was hauling, clearing, dismantling until midday. Now at half past one everything is quiet. The walls of the hall are empty, the niches are yawning, all the paintings—Eva says there were many originals among them—the art works have disappeared, the huge parquet floor downstairs is bare, the table in the middle, the heavy chairs, the carpet have disappeared. Left to Frau Jacoby are one of the three rolled-up quilts and one suitcase. — *Three* old women are leaving the house: in addition to the owner and old Frau Eger, there is also Frau Imbach, a friendly, very vigorous (albeit with a bad limp) seventy-year-old. Her daughter, more sickly than Jewish in appearance, told us at breakfast in the kitchen this morning: It was so hard for her, she was remaining behind alone (worker at Zeiss-Ikon); her only sister was arrested in the spring, because she walked across the street without a star and into the arms of the Gestapo, and was then taken from prison to the women's concentration camp of Ravensberg in Mecklenburg. — Our neighbor in the next room, a Frau Fränkel, told me earlier: "Don't be afraid tomorrow morning, the Gestapo is coming at nine to seal the rooms . . . A big squad came the last time and played havoc—in the other rooms as well . . . I want only to prepare you for it." — Was she herself afraid. — "Nothing makes any difference at all to me anymore. My son was deported to Poland, I have heard nothing from him." — Perhaps I should tell myself, that in the face of such great misery on all sides, I should be less gloomy about my own discomfort. But how do I know that tomorrow I will not be among those utterly lost? At any rate, tomorrow we are once again most cruelly threatened. —

I expect Eva back at two o'clock. Immediately after tea we must pay our farewell visit to the Marckwalds'. For me a long walk through the thundery, oppressive air. — The plundered hall outside—yesterday there was still a bit of life in it, today it's dead. Nurse Ziegler says: "Frau Jacoby is sitting on the veranda weeping."

### September 7, Monday morning

So I shall probably see Marckwald for the last time: Even thinner and grayer in the face than before, he sits in the doorway of the bedroom [ . . . ]; the big table in the middle of the living room is covered with porcelain; helpers, among them Superintendent Hirschel, carrying large pieces of furniture in and out; a changing group of people by Marckwald's easy chair, talking to him, but also chatting among themselves; two or three are at the open bookcase and choosing "mementos"—"Go on, take it, why should *they* have it?" I already came upon the Hirschels as I was ascending the stairs. "Marckwald is terribly unwell—how are they going to transport him? He'll probably be put in the hospital right away, and then it won't take long." But Marckwald sat quite calmly in his chair; he had been lying in bed in recent days, and everyone spoke to him as if he were only going away for a short time. Probably each person there was also partly blunted, partly busy with their own fate. (The old: "In two weeks we'll be in the next transport!," the young: "Where are they going to put us?" or "Will we be murdered here?") — The Hirschels were preoccupied with a private resentment. The Gestapo urge them—politely, but with veiled threats and open cynicism: "You'll end up in Poland *after all* and won't be able to take anything!"—to hand over *their* whole library, with the bookcases "voluntarily." ("Why?" — "Evidently an inspector wants to do a favor for some Party boss who needs a nice-looking library for a study.") [ . . . ] "So far we have resisted. Should we give in?" — "It's a matter of sheer survival now; I wouldn't provoke these people." — "Can you guarantee, that *after* handing over the books we shall be *safe*? I always used to say, I am devoted to three things: my husband, my children and my books." — "It's the sequence that counts." — "Go on, take something!" I took Fontane's poems. Frau Hirschel handed me a volume: "That'll be something for you." Paul Ernst, *Tagebuch eines Dichters* [Diary of a poet]. [ . . . ] Eva came over: "You can't spend the whole time at the bookcase." I went up to Marckwald again—what to talk to him about. He: "You have given me many pleasant hours; I am grateful for that." I: "I am certainly not going to bid you a tearful farewell. It will be our pleasure to meet again before Christmas." Frau Marckwald: "Would you do me a favor: Write—anonymously—to the Kutzbachs (her friends, my Catholic senate colleague centuries ago): 'Wilhelm's mother sends greetings before departure' " (Wilhelm is their artist son, the director). Afterward, in the Paul Ernst volume, I found an "Afterword by the editor Karl August Kutzbach" and a letter from the same Karl August to Wilhelm Marckwald. The generation before me and already two generations from today. — I was glad when this leavetaking was behind me. [ . . . ]

Also to be noted: *He* said, with a glance at the porcelain in front of him: There was a memory attached to every piece. Hirschel told me: Recently an evacuee had opened the door to him with an ax in his hand. "Do you want to kill me?" — "No, but I have just chopped up a wardrobe, which I don't want *them* to have." —

### Toward evening

The sealing of the rooms took place without any trouble.

Over lunchtime Eva paid Frau Fleischer a farewell visit. Ida Kreidl's friend, who lived with her Aryan son-in-law at the far end of Bernhardstrasse—she had transferred the house to him in good time—and who so kindly helped us and who, until a few weeks ago, had felt protected by her son-in-law's connections. Eva said that it had made a great impression on her to find a normally functioning household that does not know fear of the Gestapo and was unaware of its atrocities. But she also said, that it would be especially hard for Frau Fleischer, who had until now been free of all Jewish fears, to bear her exile, and she would experience oppression, where our people even felt relief. My only thought was: If there are still normally functioning households—how long will the war and the regime last? —

## September 8, Tuesday morning

New figures and parties are still turning up in the haunted house. Friendly contact with everyone, so far no intimacy with anyone, not even with Frau Ziegler, who is rarely here after all, nevertheless very helpful and not at all intrusive or bothersome. —

Yesterday a conversation in the hall with a middle-aged couple called Eisenmann. She is Aryan; however, two of her children are Jewish and the youngest (about four or five) is not registered with any confession—ergo *not* a privileged marriage. He is very pale, slim, beetle-browed, dark, very intelligent Jewish eyes, very calm manner. From the Protectorate; was in business, probably something technical, during the World War; saw two years active service in the Austrian army, is now foreman at Zeiss-Ikon. He expressed this opinion: *It* will hold on for another year, *it* will then fall from the inside—nothing Communist, military dictatorship. And then the front will be held until Germany gets an acceptable peace. It will not be defeated, and another Versailles or even a dismemberment would inevitably lead to a third world war after an interval of twenty years. — I asked him, on what did he base his view of such powers of resistance. Externally on the military incapacity of the Allies, internally on the tremendous organization. Was it really so tremendously good, were not countless things being organized to death? He: One year ago Zeiss-Ikon had still employed 7,000 *German* workers; now only 500 Germans remained, the rest, the 6,500, had been replaced by foreigners, Russian, Polish, French, Dutch, and yet everything was going like clockwork—"The new people take two days to get used to the work." But they work unwillingly after all. "They have to work, hunger forces them to, and everything"—this was his constant refrain—"the organization and organized violence, runs like clockwork." I: 6,500 foreigners, enemies, who are forced to work, as against 500 Germans, that surely was a state of utmost morbidity and a symbol of Germany's present condition. The country was like a man with serious heart disease. He does his work, walks around "quite healthily," and suddenly drops down dead. He: "But things haven't got that far yet." — He depressed me very greatly.

This morning Frau Ziegler came back from the Community, where she had spent the night looking after the flock to be transported. She said, the worst thing was the moment when the tarpaulins on the truck were let down on all four sides of those packed inside and then fastened. "Like cattle in the dark." She related how a letter was delivered to an old lady, just as a Gestapo inspector approached. The letter was harmless. From a daughter. But the enclosed picture of her grandchild was torn up: "You are not allowed to take any pictures with you." And one sentence went: "Perhaps, Mommy, we shall see each other again after all, miracles do happen." The inspector, who read it out, commented: "No miracles will happen for you, don't delude yourselves."

On the board of the Community there is a lawyer, Dr. Winskowitz, whom I once fleetingly met at Simon's. The same age as myself, kept from Poland because he holds the Iron Cross, First Class. He was informed yesterday that he will go to Theresienstadt with the next (and last) transport of the elderly, "as a privilege," like the war wounded, because of the Iron Cross, First Class. — What will happen to *us*?

The naked hall outside intrigues me again and again. The columns of the gallery, the huge, lightly tinted, leaded windows, the huge chandelier—a tall shoot, a wreath with candles, all dipped in bronze leafage— now that it has been stripped of pictorial decoration, it is almost more imposing than before. —

Chaos in our rooms, the difficulties downstairs in the kitchen and the washhouse, my unwashed body still hardly any different today than Thursday. I can shave, but I sleep without a nightshirt, tout nu. Eva is tired out to the point of collapse, hardly gets around to unpacking, arranging. I find little time to read, to write, the little bit of washing up, the little bit of washing myself, an occasional errand eat away the day. In the evening, when reading aloud, we fall asleep after 20 lines. —

### September 9, Wednesday early morning

Suddenly autumn since the day before yesterday, penetrating cool dampness—proximity to the Elbe. Hardly any change in the chaos, Eva very exhausted, I, resigned. — Yesterday tiring long walk into town (Emser Allee, Pfotenhauerstrasse with the hospitals, beginning of the city center—I am gradually getting to know the geography of our new accommodation; I am now, after twenty-two years, gradually getting to know Dresden), to the bank and to the Neumanns, who are now living with Neumark, the lawyer, and will probably have to go to Theresienstadt in two weeks. I could not console them as usual, was more depressed than they. I no longer believe in an imminent débâcle.

### Afternoon

We were sitting at breakfast when a large group of Gestapo people turned up to make an inspection of the house. They came in wearing their hats. "Stand up!" I obediently stood beside my chair. (The star was on my white jacket.) Eva remained seated, without looking up from her plate. The horde passed on. After a long inspection of the house, I heard them talking in the garden for a long time. In our room only a fat periodicals volume, which Frau Ziegler had lent us, was out of place. *Modern Art.*

Evidently they scented forbidden "degenerate art" behind the title. But it is a harmless volume, probably before 1911. — It is now very possible that in a few days, we shall be forced to change apartments again; there are already numerous precedents of this kind. Older residents are expecting to be thrown out. At any rate, we shall not be in a hurry to unpack. —

Eva feels so poorly (fatigue and upset stomach), that she lay on the sofa in the morning and is now in bed. I am reading aloud [ . . . ].

### September 11, Friday morning

New decree for Jews: Ban on using Aryan laundries. — The washhouse downstairs is a huge room; there is nothing intimidating about it for Eva; it's not cramped. — Perhaps the two of us together will do a big wash there. Like the Milke couple. He is a Party cell leader and is not allowed to make conversation with us, but he greets us politely, is no bother. [ . . . ] And then there's "Fräulein Hulda," for years Frau Jacoby's housekeeper, employed by Ralph von Klemperer before that, very philo-Semitic, continued to look after Frau Jacoby, long after she was forbidden to do so; will now possibly help us out with washing appliances. — Curious feature of the haunted castle! — The stairway, which leads from the vast cellar rooms into the depths of a second cellar. I have called it the Piazza di Spagna. A store of vegetables lies spread out on the steps, a cauliflower, tomatoes, baskets of potatoes, also sausages and meat. Because 1) it is cooler and less damp here than in the washing and cooking rooms, and 2) the Gestapo has not yet discovered this cellar (and tomatoes and cauliflower are forbidden scarce commodities—Frau Ziegler had a terrible shock yesterday, as she was carrying a half cauliflower, which she had been given, in her handbag and the "Spitter" turned up at the Community. She was just supervising a couple of children; she left the children in the lurch and fled.) —

My very wearying errands in town yesterday, 1) I was supposed to get a pair of slippers at the clothes store yesterday: slippers would be available again only in two weeks. Auerbach, the white-bearded manager of the place, was hardly recognizable compared to the last time, such hollow cheeks, such listlessness, his voice so weak. I asked him how he felt. — "I am just so tired." The man is 59; it was cold comfort that he looked much older than I. 2) Sidonienstrasse tax office. 148M income tax was due no later than yesterday. I showed the made-out Deutsche Bank check. It was no good. "If you cannot bring it here in cash . . ." — "I am not allowed to do that." — "I'm sorry, then the money will be here one day late: the penalty is 2.80M." I went to the bank, had the 2.80M transferred at the same time. At least they did not raise any difficulties, about it being "outside the disposable allowance limit." If they had been very pedantic, they could first of all have asked for written advice from the tax office—with the penalty increasing all the time. And I did not have a single penny left "within the allowance limit." 3) Richter, my Aryan house trustee. He had not written to me all this time; I knew only through Kätchen Sara that the

mortgage had come out right. He informed me yesterday, that he inten-
tionally writes as little as possible to me; I should get the statement on the
first of October. A master builder called Linke has assumed the mortgage,
happy about the six percent, which he can now get only from a Jew; costs
and rent receipts more or less balance; if there is no new law, the house remains ours. Only: The house is deteriorating because Berger is using it for
his grocer's shop, and he is not taking care of it—on the other hand, repairs
are impossible at the moment, men and materials are lacking. Actually,
more important to me than this information was what Richter said about
the general situation. "Ninety percent of all Germans know that victory is
impossible, that no peace will be made with this government . . . Who is
still content? Not even the little Party bosses, the block leaders . . . The
people will sweep the government away, hunger impels it . . . But when?
The SS has been greatly strengthened, the SS is really a force for a civil
war." He was appalled—"The swine! The dirty dogs!"—when I told him
about our fate; he wanted—I refused—to give me a piece of shaving
soap . . . "And yet I must strictly keep my distance from you!" — "Of
course, Herr Richter, you have a wife and child, you are quite innocent."
— "No one in Germany is innocent. Why have we tolerated this regime for
so long?" — I told him that I was as certain of a collapse in the not too distant future as he was, only I feared a general pogrom before the debacle.
He did not contradict me; he bade me farewell with a kind of emotional
solemnity, as if I were departing for the Russian front. (Here something
else occurs to me: He said that in Russia not many prisoners were being
taken anymore; a recent divisional order had "requested prisoners.") —
      [ . . . ]


### September 12, Saturday afternoon

Yesterday afternoon at the cemetery with Eva, less than half an hour from
here, to visit Steinitz and Magnus, who are gardening there. They were on
the brink of leaving, early closing because of Jewish New Year, beginning
of the Jewish high holy days. We had heard that an hour earlier from Frau
Ziegler also, that in Berlin and all other towns any kind of religious ceremony had been banned. (That goes far beyond the Middle Ages.) Jacobi,
the cemetery administrator, was with Steinitz and Magnus. All three in the
same mood: convinced that the regime is close to collapse, almost equally
convinced that we shall succumb to a pogrom and act of revenge beforehand. — Magnus and Steinitz have already been working together for
months, and for a week now they have been living in the same apartment,
sharing the same kitchen in wretched Schulgutstrasse. They get on badly,
and their wives do not get on at all. Magnus told me with great matter-of-
factness: "My wife has declared that she is prepared for suicide at any moment, if that is what I wish. But I shall wait and see and not give up hope
completely." [ . . . ]

Steinitz proudly showed us the grave of his great-grandmother, a Frau Abrahamson, who died in 1900 at the age of one hundred and four, who still went to the opera at the age of a hundred. He has cleaned the grave and planted new flowers. For Magnus and Steinitz the cemetery is a refuge; they are always inviting me to come with a book. The cemetery administrator has his house out there; he says he does not need to fear a house search; the Gestapo is afraid of the dead (of *their* dead!).

### September 13, Sunday afternoon

The Kreidl family was related by marriage to a family called Arndt (jewelry shop). I got to know the old man, who is about seventy, in the winter when shoveling snow; I saw and spoke to the son (in his thirties—his wife is in England, he himself was surprised here by the war) a couple of times at Ida and Elsa Kreidl's. The father was a reserve for the last transport to Theresienstadt and is therefore a certain candidate for the next and final one. The son has been arrested during the past few days. The Gestapo found a letter in which he asks a woman friend, employed at the Reka department store, to obtain a table service for him. Even if they don't make a case of race defilement out of it, this relationship and this request are enough for a concentration camp or an even earlier demise. The Aryan woman will also be ruined. — We used to hear such pieces of news through Kätchen Sara (who has already had her first house search in her new apartment—which made me feel almost cheerful, because Kätchen maintained that Lothringer Weg was "even more exposed" than 41 Altenzeller, such are our quarrels over precedence)—now we get the news from Frau Ziegler, in whom we discover a number of good features: She is helpful, friendly, unobtrusive and not loud, blathering and flighty . . . Also Eva was at the Seliksohns' today (potatoes in exchange for dried vegetables inherited from Ida). Her *nouvelles:* After deportation of the old people has been completed, the Jewish section of Zeiss-Ikon will be evacuated. — Just now interrupted by Steinitz's visit. [ . . . ] Seliksohn has got hold of Theodor Herzl's diaries for me, unfortunately only volume I of three volumes.

We showed Steinitz the Maginot Line of the two-story cellar. The house possesses a certain film romanticism, especially now—this naked hall, these Jew's stars on the doors, these destinies, the fear, which has settled on everything—and in addition the luxuriance of the garden, the wonderful view of the nearby Elbe hills and of the Albrecht Palaces.

[ . . . ]

### September 15, Tuesday midday

[ . . . ]

Frau Ziegler told us something of the lives of the inhabitants of this house. Frau Jacoby, who has now been evacuated, had two sons here, both in their fifties, and a daughter, a doctor, in her sixties, in Berlin. Both sons lived on income; one had managed the shop, the other had been a painter. Both bachelors. The painter cooked and took care of the house. It was already occupied by various Jewish parties. In the course of the last year one son died of pneumonia, the other was deported to Poland. The daughter came from Berlin for her brother's funeral, was ill-treated here by the Gestapo and immediately afterward deported from Berlin to a Polish ghetto as a physician. It was left to Fräulein Hulda, who lives behind the hidden door on the mezzanine, to care for the very bent (but mentally very alert) old lady. Fräulein Hulda is a most loyal Aryan housekeeper, who has long been forbidden to help out here, who has been sent to do labor service at Zeiss-Ikon—she is well into her fifties—and who now stands by the Jewish tenants, just as she looked after Frau Jacoby until the last moment. [ . . . ]

Today is Marta's birthday, 67 or 68. Is she still alive? Basically Hitler was a stroke of luck for her: He saved her from a life of stagnation and brought her to an exotic land. — How the fantastic comes to be taken for granted: my sister in South America, my brother in the USA, my other brothers and sisters dead, no contact whatsoever with these two. My brother-in-law in Stockholm writing to me under a foreign name. On his last card he has a new pseudonym. Why? It is an airmail card and announces that a letter is on its way. Perhaps it will contain an explanation.

### September 16, Wednesday toward evening

The John Neumanns are on the list of the last twenty-five "old people" to go to Theresienstadt. Further the Pinkowitzes; he is the teacher and undertaker. Only my age, but "privileged" because war disabled. The others are destined for forced labor in Poland. My fate also? —

[ . . . ]

Shortage of potatoes and Eva's unsuccessful chasing after provisions. But in the paper they triumphantly announce an "Increase in the bread and meat ration" for October. A bluff? A desperate measure? Nevertheless: Even if it is the latter, it stops mouths for a while; the war goes on, and time is won, which is needed for our extermination.

### September 18, Friday morning

Yesterday morning a long walk to the clothes store; a suit in fairly good condition, which almost fit me, was found. It is to cost 35M—impossible to pay within my allowance. I shall declare the amount as Winter Aid or some other charitable contribution—which is permitted outside the limit. I wanted to sort it out immediately at the Community; there was a car in front of it, ergo Gestapo, ergo flight. (I write all that down as if it were trifling and self-evident; one could produce endless commentary on these bagatelles for future students: how much slavery and humiliation and impoverishment behind them, how much effort! Walked from eleven till one, where in a few minutes a tram . . . ). I discussed payment for the suit with Hirschel at the cemetery in the afternoon, after the urn with Julia Pick's remains was laid to rest in the family tomb. Pinkowitz officiated in the usual way for the last time—it was the most wretched funeral that we had attended so far. Exactly twelve people, including the two of us. The men apart from myself only there out of duty or by chance. Jacobi, the cemetery administrator and urn bearer, the cemetery gardener; Steinitz and Magnus, who pass the day out there as "workers"; Superintendent Hirschel. On the women's side Elsa Kreidl—a brave deed, because she is forbidden to attend; it endangers her, and she was not duty bound to do so; that was a contrast to the behavior of Prof. Gaehde, who as a relative would *not* have been forbidden to attend, whose duty it was [ . . . ] and who was absent out of cowardice, just as out of cowardice he had left the living Frau Pick in the lurch and prevented communication between her and his wife. I intend to pillory him in my Curriculum. — Frau Gaehde, her body rigid, her face set, wrenched into a smile for greeting and condolence. She appeared to suffer from the absence of her husband; she knows how it is judged. The other three women were unknown to me; one, the only one weeping bitterly, is said to have been a former housekeeper of the once-wealthy house. [ . . . ] I then [ . . . ] sat with Steinitz and Magnus for a little while in the greenhouse of the nursery garden, which occupies the rear part of the Jewish cemetery. Steinitz stuffed his pockets with the tomatoes harvested here. That is his wage, so to speak. The remaining vegetable harvest of the garden, including the tomato harvest, goes to the "communal kitchen" at the Community. Tomatoes are to be had only on a ration card, therefore forbidden for us. If the Gestapo finds any, the consequence is blows at least.

[ . . . ]

### September 19, Saturday afternoon

The Jew's star was fastened on one year ago. What indescribable misery has descended upon us during this year. Everything that preceded it appears petty by comparison. — And Stalingrad is about to fall, and in October there will be more bread: So the regime will last out the winter; so it has time for the complete annihilation of the Jews. I am deeply depressed. — In addition the constant tiredness. Now off for a long walk over to Wiener Strasse. Farewell visit to Pinkowitz, cadging potatoes from the Hirschels. — Herzl's diary.

[ . . . ]

### September 21, Monday toward evening

Today is Yom Kippur, and this very day the last 26 "old people" are sitting in the Community House, from where they will be transported early tomorrow. So on Saturday afternoon we made our farewell visit to the Pinkowitzes, who lived in two rooms in Hirschel's villa. They were very composed and optimistic. Small comfort: It turned out that Pinkowitz, who looks like a scrawny seventy-year-old, is nine months younger than I. — Dr. Katz was there. Very depressed. The mixed marriage will not protect us. He thought it improbable that Marckwald was still alive. He would perish for lack of morphine. — The round of calls continued yesterday. Eva had already been to the Neumanns in the morning. [ . . . ] Things for "safekeeping." [ . . . ] I myself inherited a jacket and vest. Some things go to a reliable Aryan friend in the Neumanns' former apartment house. So we went to see them in the afternoon. Frau Arendt, the Aryan friend, also appeared, brought cakes; there was real tea. "Funeral meal," I said. Whereupon the Neumanns, who were defiantly merry: "Yes and no." On the one hand the corpses themselves were there. On the other they were really going into a beyond, from which as yet there had been no reliable news. Because what had been reported was no more than supposition. He gave me a prayer book with Hebrew *and German* text. I: How was it possible to forgive one's enemies on the Day of Atonement? He: "The Jewish religion does not require it. The relevant prayer says: Atonement for all Israelites and 'for the stranger in our midst,' that is, only for the peaceful guest among us." Judaism nowhere requires love of one's enemy. I: "Love of one's enemy is moral softening of the brain." From the Neumanns' (by the Kreuzkirche in the same apartment as Neumark, the lawyer) I had to continue my tramp to 42 Altenzeller Strasse, where Kätchen Sara had invited us. She now resides in two magnificent huge rooms with Frau Aronade, in the same house as Grete Kronheim, the hysterical daughter of our old friend, who was evacuated. The Leipzigers—the boastful health-board official and his likeable, much younger Aryan wife—also live there now. We saw all these people. Kätchen outdid herself in warmheartedness [ . . . ], put money at our disposal whenever we should need it. Enjoyed occasionally like this she is very tolerable. The mood of all Jewry here is without exception the same: The terrible end is imminent. *They* will perish, but perhaps, probably, they will have time to annihilate us first. People are apathetic about evacuation. (Things are much too dreadful here in Dresden.) All they want to do is survive.

Today letter from Sussmann. He always asks questions, and I cannot answer. [ . . . ]

### September 24, Thursday afternoon

[ . . . ]

Frau Ziegler related: Arnold Zweig was a relative. Family from Kattowitz. Father a saddler and dealer in leather. Grandfather had his sons learn a trade; they got on. Another son, a plumber, became a manufacturer. Zweig's sister a singer, his cousin a pediatrician. Rise of a Jewish family! Further—natural development!—Arnold Zweig was a thorough-going Zionist. He was not yet that in Kowno or Wilna in 1918. Where he is now, whether he is still alive, Frau Ziegler did not know.

She reported from the Hirschels: a) New tenants were moving in; mixed marriage. The sisters of the Aryan wife were visiting and having a conversation with the Jewess Kalter in the latter's room, when the Gestapo, the Spitter and the Boxer, unexpectedly appeared. The Aryan girls were shown the door—strictly forbidden to show themselves there again—Frau Kalter "thoroughly thrashed." b) One morning in the last few days the Gestapo rang the doorbell of the Community very early, and no one opened up. As punishment Hirschel was ordered henceforth to be present from seven every morning. —

As we were sitting at breakfast this morning, a couple of tradesmen came to look at the condition of the house. (If it is repaired and taken over by the Gestapo, then we shall have to get out.) They knocked, they did *not* keep their hats on, they apologized and "did not want to disturb us," and all that despite the fact that the Jew's star is on the door of our laundry room and kitchen parlor. What uncommon, what demonstrative courtesy—and literally dangerous for those practicing it! [ . . . ]

Eva falls asleep immediately at ten in the evening, but then she lies awake at night or toward morning, and I read aloud.

[ . . . ]


### September 25, Friday toward evening

Yesterday at about nine a young blond lady appeared here in the kitchen. Whispered report. Daughter of Frau Arendt, the friend and neighbor of the Neumanns in Winckelmannstrasse, who had come to take leave of the Neumanns last Sunday armed with cake, who is storing some of their things, and to whom Eva, it had been agreed, should convey a number of further pieces today. — Her mother asks, begs Eva not to come for a couple of weeks. She is being watched. She has attracted attention. A friend, of whom inquiries had been made as to what relationship Frau Arendt had had with the Neumanns, had warned her: "We are expecting a house search, we have been clearing things out all night, all the dangerous things are already out of the house." The daughter's evening errand to see us was in itself a dangerous expedition. —

[ . . . ]


### September 28, Monday morning

All in all, our new lodgings, which are now largely habitable, are preferable to the previous ones. Inconvenience of running up and down stairs and of excusing oneself, as it were—but the peace and quiet, no Kätchen Sara. The big house is almost uncannily quiet, although it has all of twenty inhabitants, including several children. A large part is always working shifts. Communication between us and the others is always friendly, but contact is rare. Often, usually, not a single word more than a greeting is exchanged for days. Frau Ziegler is the only person we see every day and often for lengthy conversations. But she, too, is absent for three-quarters of the day. And the common kitchen is so large, that no one disturbs anyone else. And Frau Ziegler is not Kätchen. And then one more thing: No one in the house is mockingly disapproving if I share in our housework. That is normal here and it is taken for granted, that each person does every kind of work. Every day I experience anew the feeling of relief, that I am spared the accompaniment of Kätchen's blathering while I am washing up. — Admittedly, however, I would not have acquired such a precise knowledge of Jewish fates in Jews' House II. —

### October 2, Friday afternoon

Very tired because of scrubbing the kitchen and because of deep depression. — Hitler's speech at the beginning of the Winter Aid campaign. The same old song mercilessly exaggerated: The stupendous German successes, German morality, German certainty of victory—things are going ever better for us; we can hold out for many years yet . . . Also mercilessly exaggerated is the abuse of enemies, the ministers are "numbskulls," "zeros, who cannot be distinguished from one another," a lunatic rules in the White House, a criminal in London. Merciless threats against England, against the Jews in all the world, who wanted to exterminate the Aryan nations of Europe and whom he is exterminating . . . The shocking thing is not that a crazy man raves in ever greater frenzy, but that Germany accepts it, for the tenth year now and in the fourth year of war, and that it continues to allow itself to be bled. And nowhere an end in sight. The forces of the Entente are not sufficient for a decisive blow—and inside the country all remains calm. Another winter, and then another summer . . . In a week I shall be sixty-one—what is left to me at best? [ . . . ]

### October 4, Sunday morning

[ . . . ]

From one until two, for the first time in weeks, a short walk with Eva in calm, warm autumn weather; we had planned it for a long time. [ . . . ] Then, after coffee, Steinitz and the Cohns came here. Cohn told us two very depressing pieces of news. A family called Bein, living in the Community house, the woman Aryan, the man, Jew in his fifties, their son eighteen years of age, mixed race but raised as Jewish. Father and son arrested a couple of weeks ago, supposedly because they had handed over too little for the fabric collection; a couple of days ago transported to Mauthausen concentration camp on the Austrian border; yesterday both father and son "shot while attempting to escape." — That is the security of a mixed marriage. I am shaken by the most wretched fear of death. The Enterlein box factory in Niedersedlitz, where Cohn works, is taking on new Jewish workers. That may cost me the remainder of my freedom. I dread that also. — But I cannot do anything about it: Make the most of every hour!

### October 5, Monday afternoon

[ . . . ]

Recently in Emser Allee! Two big Hitler Youths overtake from behind on their bicycles; they are joking with one another, laughing loudly, shouting something—I don't even think that I am intended; they could have seen the star only by looking around. Immediately afterward cycling in the opposite direction, a worker aged about twenty; he leans over to me with a friendly smile: "You mustn't take any notice of that!" I nodded to him.

### October 7, Wednesday toward evening

Frau Ziegler, mutatis mutandis, now taking over Kätchen Sara's role as bearer of news, related the day before yesterday: 1) Barracks for Russian prisoners occupy the space of the burned-down synagogue. They rummage in the Community's rubbish bins, pick out leftovers, and wolf them down. As starved as that. 2) Philippsohn, the well-to-do master tailor, elegant circle of customers, was doing labor service at Tempo, a laundry, which now works for the army, and was arrested. Supposedly because he "concealed the star" and had been talking to the company's Czech driver. Transported to a concentration camp and, like the Beins, father and son, "shot while trying to escape." To continue here with the chronicle of murder: Neumark (see below) reports: A cousin, the same age and close to him; in a privileged marriage; "for business reasons" lives separately from wife and son (eighteen years of age, brought up as Aryan) because his wife runs a company. Writes to the boy from his Berlin pension, "no doubt somewhat incautiously." The letter falls into the hands of the Gestapo; no one knows how. Father arrested, "news of death after only three days."

Today in beautiful, mild autumn weather went to see Neumark a second time because of the hat left me by Neumann, this time successfully: I met Neumark at one o'clock, and we chatted for a whole hour. The beautiful heirloom was hanging in the hall, on the room to the side the familiar seal, more precisely two red fiscal stamps holding a strip of brown paper stretched across door and doorframe and the familiar "here lived the Jew . . . and the Jewess. . . ." When I arrived, Neumark was just finishing dictating his letters and appeared about to take his lunch break. Apart from the case of murder, he told me: A law to separate mixed marriages had already been drafted, but withdrawn again. At the moment, therefore, the position of the mixed marriage was "a little more favorable." But it was impossible to say for how long. — An Aryan coming from Munich had told him, that Munich had been battered by English aircraft. There was nothing about it in the newspapers, but I had also heard it from someone else. — I talked about my *LTI*, and Neumark gave me a copy of *Deutsches Recht* [German law], the principal mouthpiece of the National-sozialistische Rechtswahrerbundes [National Socialist Bar Association]. He wanted to give me several copies, but one can more easily be hidden. —

[ . . . ]

### October 8, Thursday morning and later

Fränkel, the electrician, who lives in the room next to ours, passed me [in the street], looking like a worker, without a coat and with a knapsack over his jacket, I did not recognize him until he was past me, and I apologized for not greeting him. He: "No greeting, at most a wink. Just don't be conspicuous. Better, too, if you don't walk beside your wife. Aryans and non-Aryans shouldn't be seen together . . ."

[ . . . ]

### October 9, Friday toward evening

Gloomy birthday, even gloomier than last year. Then I was not yet acquainted with house searches, also there was not the constant threat of murder. Hope of survival has become very faint. Also material things count: Last year cigars, sweetener had not quite disappeared, the potato did not dominate so unconditionally. — And Eva had not yet grown thin as a skeleton. — In the morning I scrubbed the kitchen. In the afternoon I went to the Jewish cemetery—ominous route—to invite Steinitz for Saturday instead of Sunday. [ . . . ] Birthday letter from Sussmann. "Arne Egebring." Some censor's marks on it, diagonal blue lines over the whole page. It makes me anxious. With his change of name, with his naive questions, he can cost me my all-too-loosely-attached head: He writes that in my last letter to him, seven lines had been blacked out and made illegible. I suspect it was the figures of our weights, the sentence "It's modern to be slim; I'm still 132 pounds on the scales, Eva only 110 pounds . . ." [ . . . ]

Then touchingly there also came birthday greetings from Caroli Stern, whom we have neglected for so long. She writes that without further information being obtainable, news has come of the sudden death of Erich Meyerhof. He was in a camp in Australia, and he appeared to be in good health. I have made notes about him, his wife, his sons, subsequent to Lissy's visits. Mischlingen were pulled out of the army for a while. Now the oldest boy is on the North African front. — Erich Meyerhof was about three years younger than I, his coarse love of adventure and erotic energy were always somewhat alien to me. He was the *first* to tell me about Eva; he is closely bound up with my memories of 1904. I would never have thought that I would outlive him. I am so dulled that I can summon up no emotion. Nothing but: "So many fall around me, and *I* am still alive. Perhaps it is after all granted me to survive and bear witness."

Thomas Mann is supposed to have made a fierce plea for the German Jews in an American broadcast.

In response to the military bulletins of recent weeks I "coined" the saying: "In Stalingrad, after hard fighting at close quarters, we captured another three-room apartment with bath." —

### October 10, Saturday

New order to all Jews, who are obliged to wear the mark of identification: Surrender of metals, much more stringent than in the last war, including: ornamental alloys, nickel, tin, lead, *also every kind of lamp*. The question for us is whether the Aryan wife is also affected. The Community must decide.

Months ago Kätchen Sara told us of a particularly tragic case: A couple called Gelert, he a doctor, put in prison and then concentration camp for some trifle. Both deceased. Twin girls, sixteen years of age, working at Zeiss-Ikon, are left orphaned, poor and alone. Yesterday Frau Ziegler reported new house searches; butter and margarine just bought on ration coupons were taken away from these same two girls. Always the same and ever more repellent.

Since yesterday great activity in the hall downstairs: Workers from the tax office are removing a vast amount of confiscated furniture, books, etc., from the rooms that have been unsealed.

These were the impressions and the news on my birthday.

[ ... ]

### October 14, Wednesday afternoon

Yesterday, October 13 (it's enough to make one superstitious—my fingers are stiff with autumn cold ... ), yesterday we heard an unbelievable rumor, which today proved to be true: All meat and white-bread coupons are to be withdrawn from Jews. A few weeks ago there was an announcement: Increase in the bread and meat ration, because Germany's food supply situation is getting better all the time; a few days ago Goering explained: The German people will *not* starve; if need be, he will leave the occupied territories to starve. And so now the Jews can rummage through the rubbish bins like the Russian prisoners. I am in very low spirits.

The decree on handing over metal is so unclear that it will afterward be an easy job for the Gestapo if they want to pin sabotage on anyone. Especially unclear, the position of mixed marriages. Property of the Aryan wife remains unaffected—but what is her "demonstrable" property? I turned to Superintendent Hirschel for information and wrote: "After forty years of marriage, how is one supposed to provide documentary proof as to the wife's property in a household?" He replied in writing: "The property of the Aryan wife remains unaffected, insofar as it is proven to be her property." Fränkel, our neighbor in the house, determined with a magnet which of the metal lamps are made of iron (and therefore exempt). Now we can only hope that the Gestapo respects this conclusion. Finally we handed over: a small lead box for postage stamps, a nickel letter clip and a brass ashtray.

When we moved in here, Frau Jacoby was just being evacuated and her household effects collected in the rooms placed under seal. Now two employees of the tax office and an art expert have been at work for days making an inventory of it all, valuing, and removing it. The things are brought into the hall, also onto the gallery up here. The quantities of leather chairs, cabinets, tables, kerosene lamps, which have emerged, are unbelievable. All of it old, handicraft, precious. (The paintings are either already gone or are still to follow.) And all of it is being stolen.

Sunday afternoon at the Seliksohns was gloomy. The man had had an argument with the Aryan air-raid warden in the house, had thrashed him, and a complaint had been made to the police. It would undoubtedly have cost him his life. At his wife's entreaty the complaint was withdrawn. But now Seliksohn is in the most somber mood, and there is also tension between the couple. Seliksohn raged against the German people in its totality; he became abusive to me, for "running after" the Germans—it was not nice, and had it not been for the extra potatoes, I would probably have been less patient.

[ . . . ]

## October 16, Friday evening

Yesterday at half past five [ . . . ] I went for a walk and took Steinitz some writing paper. When I left the house, I saw a police car in the street and thought: Good thing that I'm going out and that Eva is in città. — On my return here consternation. Frau Eger was gone—she had been seen weeping as she came home; after the police disappeared, she had disappeared too; there was bread lying on the gallery balustrade and pots with food; her rooms were locked. Arrested therefore, and one must assume that when she came home she already knew something of her husband's fate. He works in Reick, is building a "potato bunker" for Zeiss-Ikon. (N.B. Follow up the expansion of the term *bunker*! *LTI*.)

During the day our Jews' House is completely quiet. In the evening the Zeiss-Ikon people and Frau Ziegler come back from work and bring news. So we were expecting elucidation. But no one, not at the factory, not at the Community, has a clue about the case. The two of them have been arrested, everything else is a mystery. — Supposition: The Aryan wife may have taken something to her parents for safekeeping, and a house search could have been carried out there. If that is so, then he is a dead man; she perhaps has a chance of surviving concentration camp. — The terrible thing is the uncertainty, murder sneaking up. No one knows anything, everyone's life is in constant danger, the flimsiest thing is good enough as a pretext for being done away with. Even today we do not know why Ernst Kreidl was killed. We shall also learn nothing about Eger. And always the feeling: perhaps *I* am next. — Keep working despite it all. [ . . . ] *Now* I must place in the foreground everything that, in the widest sense, has to do with the *LTI* as a whole, that is, which relates to the present and to its formation. Thus I have immersed myself in Rathenau's *Zur Kritik der Zeit* [A critique of the age]. Reading Sombart has proved useful here.

### October 17, Saturday late afternoon

Nothing can be learned about the Egers. They have simply been arrested, and *his* life at least is not worth tuppence. Her life, too, is in great danger. Today for the first time news from a concentration camp of the death of two women. Until now only the men died there. Of these two women, one had had a forbidden fish in her refrigerator, the other had taken the tram on her way to the doctor, when she should have used it only to go to her place of work. Both were transported from the women's camp in Mecklenburg to Auschwitz, which appears to be a swift-working slaughterhouse. Cause of death: "Age and heart failure." Both were about sixty, one of them especially robust. Report by Frau Ziegler.

[ . . . ] — Listlessly reading the Germanomaniac Rathenau. His inflated language irritates me greatly, his closeness to H. St. Chamberlain is repellent to me; I have no difficulty understanding his political economy.

[ . . . ]

### October 23, Friday evening

Very wet and—at least in the unheated north rooms—cold weather. We suffer greatly. I sit in my coat and am still (for weeks) without slippers.

[ . . . ]

From Kätchen Voss (Zeiss-Ikon), from Frau Ziegler (Community), from Steinitz, whom I looked up yesterday for a sugar-tobacco exchange (wife's Aryan relatives), from Frau Reichenbach, whom Eva looked after today (Community once again [ . . . ]) come the following rumors: 1) The commander of the southern front, Field Marshal Bock, is said to have been recalled. (Because he had got his teeth into Stalingrad, whereas Goering wanted the main emphasis to be on the Caucasus offensive.) 2) It is even supposed to have been in the German newspapers, but certainly reported in foreign broadcasts, that the USA "no longer regards Italian civilian internees as enemy aliens" and has released them. This would be a sure sign of separate negotiations by the Italians and a break with the Axis. Too good to be true. 3) In the course of this last week alone, literally eight Jewish women who were in concentration camps have "died." Related as the most cruel case among these: A woman surprised by the Gestapo as she goes to the garbage pit of her house. She is not wearing the star, but she is not on the street. Beaten till she is bloody and collapses. She is supposed to sign that she injured herself in a fall. Refuses, and is put in a concentration camp, where she dies. Kätchen Sara reports that to me, saying I should "write it down," and it is only for this case, which, anyway, I believe to be very likely, that I describe point 3 as rumor. The eight cases of death are fact. 4) Frau Steinitz's Aryan relatives report: In Dresden 25 people are killed without trial every day for dealing in food on the black market [ . . . ]. (This estimate is no doubt far too high, but a fraction may be true, and the important thing is that the whole figure is believed, that government and people are believed capable of it.)

From all four points one can conclude how bad things look for the National Socialist cause. But all conversations among Jews again and again lead to the same reflection: "If they have the time, they'll kill us first." One said to Frau Ziegler yesterday: He felt like a calf at the slaughterhouse, looking on, as the other calves are slaughtered, and waiting his turn. The man is right.

[ . . . ]

Eva intends to go to Pirna again tomorrow. Money must be fetched (it's running low), some things must be brought to safety—(Elsa Kreidl helped recently with metal things)—above all, of course, my manuscripts. Is it right to saddle Eva with them? If discovered it would cost her life as much as mine. One dies for the sake of more trivial matters now. I ask myself repeatedly if I am doing the right thing. I also ask myself ever more frequently whether the things are really safe with Annemarie. She has often made herself conspicuous as being anti-Nazi. If her house is searched, then all three of us will die. — But in the end I always tell myself, one has to be a fatalist; I am doing my duty. But is it really my duty, and should I expose Eva in this way?

### October 24, Saturday morning

The visit has been pending for some time, but the Hirschels will be here tomorrow afternoon. (Big to-do—only he is allowed to take transport on this long journey; his wife and the one small boy, who wants to visit the Eisenmanns' little girl here, have to walk the whole way.) Yesterday Eva met Hirschel on the street; they exchanged a few words. Later he passed on an apology by way of Frau Ziegler: He had felt himself being watched and followed. (Wearers of the star and Aryans must not be seen together; contravention puts the Jew, at least, in a concentration camp, if he gets that far.) — Today Eva will get a connection to Finkenfangstrasse and only there get on the bus to Pirna. The departure point at the station is too close to the Gestapo building. I continue to have the most serious doubts about endangering her like this, and do it nevertheless. I place the diary pages between the pages of notes. Should Eva be detained, *then she knows nothing* of the diary, this passage attests to that. She believes she is taking away only notes, because the Gestapo once tore up four pages of Rosenberg notes. [ . . . ] This is the state in which we live from morning to night, from night to morning.

And yet—the removal of this section, it could be the last, gives rise to a desire to sum things up—and yet I am downright happy for many hours of the day. I study, I prepare future work; in years to come I do not need to have any new creative ideas, only the opportunity to work out in detail what I have planned and sketched now.

Yes, when I think of the time when Hitlerism will have come to an end, then I am often in the position of the "my chaseirim [pigs]" Jew. (Blumenfeld once told me the joke. During the trade fair a wealthy European has to share a room with a poor eastern Jew. The Galician is wailing: "My chaseirim!" — "I really want to sleep—what's the matter with your chaseirim?" — "Will I be able to get rid of them?" — "Right, I'll buy them, here's the check." — After an hour again: "Veh, my chaseirim!" — "?" — "Where will I get some new chaseirim?") Thus I often ask myself what I shall undertake after Hitler's fall. With what shall I start? I very certainly do not have so much more time. The 18ième has slipped into the background for me, it would also first of all have to be brought up to date. — Tackle a supplement to my Modern Prose? — Continue with the Curriculum? — Leap forward to the section, no., volume on the Third Reich? — The *LTI?* — Or is that too narrow? Should I turn it into studies on the intellectual history of the Third Reich? Or revert to the plan of a Dictionnaire philosophique (du Hitlérisme)? Or do I stake everything on returning to my post, and remove the rust from my knowledge? Or should I now attempt to go to the USA, and so learn English? And will my health, my vigor, my strength of purpose be sufficient to carry on with any one of these tasks, or shall I hesitate between all of them and allow the remainder of my life to trickle away? — In short: Have I merely been indulging in fantasies for a couple of years? I am truly afraid of the moment when I shall have to realize them.

However, I often believe I shall not live to see it.

[ . . . ]

### October 27, Tuesday morning

Eva came back safely on Saturday—I had begun to feel very uneasy in the last quarter of an hour before half past seven. She had wanted to get off at the station. The conductor had said to her: "Finkenfangstrasse again, as on the journey out?" Since he recognized her, she thought it best to get out and change there after all. — [ . . . ] And everyone is getting more fearful in every respect. Recently people have been saying: Don't go to the garbage pit without the star! and today: always wear the star at home—the forth-coming auction will bring Aryans here, and then, if the Gestapo want to in-terpret it that way, one is accused of displaying oneself in a "public place" without the star. Hence Eva has just sewn a star onto my house jacket.

Eva reported of Annemarie that she (who always used to be so lively) was becoming ever more listless, "like someone who knows she has only a short time left to her and is no longer interested in what is going to hap-pen later on." She looked very ill and had a terrible cough. She had once explained this cough to us as a symptom of a heart problem. She is twelve years younger than we are and has often insisted that she had not been granted a long life. Coldheartedly, egoistically, I ask myself what will be-come of our things, if anything should happen to her. But there is no safety anywhere. Besides I believe Annemarie's altered character is above all re-lated to her disappointment with respect to Dressel. — [ . . . ]

On Sunday Frau Ziegler brought confused rumors of hope from the Community. Peace negotiations are said to be underway between the USA and Italy; the Russians have asked for an armistice . . . [ . . . ] The Hirschels were our guests in the afternoon, and they, too, knew about the Italian business and placed hopes on it. But the earlier distinction between opti-mistic and pessimistic Jews can no longer be maintained. Everyone, but everyone, says the same thing, usually formulated in exactly the same way: "They are lost in the foreseeable future, utterly lost, but if things don't happen quickly—and it does not look as if they will—they will fin-ish us off first." Truly murder is horribly at our heels as never before. *Eight* women in one week, eight Jewish women, out of the small Jewish com-munity in Dresden, "deceased" [ . . . ]. The number is from Hirschel. Worse, almost, than this killing is the starving of the children. Frau Hirschel gave us precise figures on the reduction of Jewish children's ra-tions, appalling reductions in meat, bread, sugar, cocoa, fruit . . . She says the constant complaints of hunger by her two small boys were the worst thing for her. " 'Mummy, look, that boy has a sausage and is biting into it! — Mummy, I'm just as hungry—Mummy, why have we got only two slices of bread? . . .' And so on, and so on all day long!"

The Hirschels had to surrender their library, "voluntarily"—"we could lock you up . . ." They were allowed to keep only books with Jewish au-thors and editors. Thus some editions of the classics could be saved. —

At the Community yesterday afternoon because of a tax declaration, then to Seliksohn for a couple of minutes; his face looks grayish-green and very pinched. For him, a diabetic, the new food regulation is nothing less than a death sentence. [ . . . ]

At the Community I met the nurse (Bernstein), whom I had got to know at Marckwald's. He said he had heard from a reliable source that many deaths had already occurred in Theresienstadt. He also believes Marck-wald is dead. (But where does he get the information from?) — Frau

Ziegler reports big new evacuations from Berlin. Those capable of work to Poland. [ ... ]

## October 29, Thursday toward evening

[ ... ]

The real tribulation of yesterday and the one that filled the day was the hauling up of four hundredweight of potatoes. At lunchtime I went to see if our trader at the tram depot on Emser Allee had a promising stock. Yes— so I was back there just after three. Could they reserve a couple of sacks for me, I would see if I could get hold of a handcart before four o'clock, possibly I would not come back until the next day. — Reservation, even against payment, was strictly forbidden; if, in the late afternoon, "working people" wanted to make purchases, then all stock had to be available to them. I should try my luck. So I hurried—heart trouble—to the Jewish cemetery on Fiedlerstrasse. The Community's little handcart was there and free; I took it, trotted back to the greengrocer with the squeaking thing; the woman there helped me load two hundredweight. I arrived here with the load, very drained and exhausted, was helped by Eva, the caretaker, and above all by the tall Jew, Eisenmann, who swung a hundredweight sack over his shoulder and carried it down to the lower cellar. Then I set out again, this time with Eva, as an Aryan she was allowed to make purchases even after four o'clock, and carted another two hundredweight here. I was very exhausted by this work and very woefully reminded of my age and my heart. — Today it was the long morning that knocked me out physically. I took the cart back to the cemetery. Then there was the long walk to the clothes store in the Pirnaische Strasse. My slippers, of which I am in desperate need, still not ready. At the Community I then made an application for three shirts, since mine are literally worn through and hanging in tatters. I called on Reichenbach in his office and on Frau Reichenbach in her sickroom. I walked back along Gerokstrasse and Fiedlerstrasse, again by way of the cemetery, in order to tell Steinitz that we were keeping Saturday afternoon free for him. (We have arranged to see the Reichenbachs on Sunday a week, the Seliksohns this Sunday, Kätchen and her room companion Frau Aronade tomorrow.) There is something grotesque about my contacts with the Jewish cemetery. Magnus, Steinitz, and Schein (the least likeable of the three, cf. my snow-shoveling memories) have an idyllic refuge there in the gardeners' shed behind the rows of graves, right beside all those who have been murdered and have committed suicide. They smoke, they fritter their time away, they play cards, they are happy to see visitors, as long as the visitors don't interrupt a game of cards.

[ ... ] And I myself am no longer in awe of the graves. One soon becomes hardened. — Reichenbach showed me a letter that he had just received from a relative in Berlin: Very extensive evacuations to Poland were once again in full swing there, married couples had been torn apart. What happens in Berlin today, will happen in Dresden tomorrow. — With Frau

Reichenbach there was a cleaner, a full Jewess in a privileged marriage, who does not have to wear the star. She maintains, says Frau Reichenbach, [ . . . ] that she has seen the pay book of a man on leave with the entry: "In case of an armistice with Russia" the man should report to his garrison. The rumor of an armistice has been circulating among Aryans for days. In yesterday's military bulletin it was denied as being a lie typical of English broadcasts. — After that I could almost assume that the Russians have been offered a cheap separate peace (perhaps: only the Ukraine for Germany, and a bit of Poland for Russia), so as to have a free hand against England and the USA. General opinion among Jewry: It looks very bad for "them," and consequently *we* are in greater danger than ever.

Early this morning I had a long conversation with Frau Eisenmann; she was washing in the washhouse, and I was rinsing our crockery. The woman is five foot eight, used to weigh 168 pounds and now weighs less than 126 pounds. Catholic from Bohemia, her eldest (eighteen years old) looks like a Hitler Youth, then there is also a little girl of ten, and Schorschl [Georgie], the very pretty three-year-old. The two older children have been brought up as Jewish, Schorschl is judged to be a "fix" [i.e., registered as Catholic], so the marriage is not privileged. The husband was a respected and well-to-do coal merchant, at first in Aussig [in Bohemia], since 1933 in Dresden. He is now a foreman at Zeiss-Ikon. His wife does all the housework for the big family alone, gets up at four o'clock in the morning (her eldest is also already at Zeiss-Ikon), has to slave away till late at night. And is constantly worrying about husband and son. What happened to the Egers, and so many others, is at every moment hanging over her family. — Whoever I listen to, wherever I look, it's the same everywhere. "Two years ago, when I saw my husband as a worker for the first time, crawling around under machines, smeared with oil, worn out, I cried so much . . ." — "I'm always dreaming about the Egers . . ." — "If it were only the two of us—but the children, the poor little things . . ." — The cleaner with Frau Reichenbach: "Now meat is to be taken away from our children as well. We describe to each other 'their' limbs being chopped off one at a time, beginning with the fingers, and then going on very slowly . . ." (A good-natured-looking young blonde, not yet starved . . . ) — Frau Ziegler [ . . . ]: "We'll all be in Poland before Christmas, and then 'they' will let us starve and shoot us. They'll certainly have enough time for that—we'll die before they do."

## October 30, Friday morning

Yesterday evening, expected and yet shattering, another blow striking so very close to us; news of the Imbach death. Fräulein Imbach, small, swarthy, in her forties, is the loneliest figure in the house. Walking past the sliding window of what is really the ground-floor kitchen, I see her busying herself in the huge room; there she appears especially small and lonely and careworn. Her mother was evacuated recently, one of her sisters was in Ravensbrück women's camp in Mecklenburg for months, because she had rashly stepped across the road without the star and run into the arms of the Gestapo. (Kätchen had already told us about the case; the Imbachs—there is also a brother here, who is married—are part of the Zeiss-Ikon workforce.) The sister in the concentration camp was described as determined and energetic; she was allowed to write once every two weeks [ . . . ]. The last expected letter did not arrive, and now news of her death has come. From Auschwitz, cause of death "stroke." She is the ninth Dresden woman, to be taken from Ravensbrück to Auschwitz.

With that news we went to sleep. This morning—I always meet Frau Ziegler in our kitchen, she goes off to work before Eva even comes downstairs—this morning Frau Ziegler told me, she had to inform me, because after all the people were our friends, but I must not, in Heaven's name, give her away, officially he was "sick"—anyway, yesterday Superintendent Hirschel and young Kahlenberg, the successor of Pionkowski and Steuermann, had been summoned to the Gestapo, and only Kahlenberg had come back. Once again the reason for the arrest is not known. — When the Hirschels visited us on Sunday, they told us about the mysterious arrest of a certain Kronthal, who had taught English in the Community and was now teaching their son Alfred privately. The man is in a privileged marriage, has no assets—so why? Perhaps he had "said something incautious." Frau Ziegler seems to suspect some connection between this arrest and that of the overanxious and overscrupulous Hirschel. But one is always tapping in the dark. — Only on Sunday the Hirschels were talking about how happy they had been before and how they now felt themselves to be in constant danger. — It is possible, of course, that Hirschel will be released very soon—but in all probability he is lost. And even *if* he is released: What torments must he be going through in the cell, must his wife be going through at home? He must expect death every time he hears a footstep outside, she must expect news of death every time the doorbell rings. — With all of that, I myself have only the feeling, the sensation, of increasing tension and, more strongly, the apprehension of mortal fear. I cannot help imagining that tomorrow—today—I shall be arrested, and Eva and I shall be in the Hirschels' situation—it is unimaginably dreadful, not to be compared with any memory of Flanders, or any mortal fear I have ever experienced. And yet I am unable to abstain from these notes: Courage? Vanity? Fatalism? Right or wrong? — The strangest thing: It always shakes me for only a few minutes: then I enjoy food, reading, work again; everything goes on comme si de rien n'était. But the weight on one's soul is always there. [ . . . ]

### November 2, Monday midday

[ . . . ]

The Arndt family. I got to know the old boy when shoveling snow, then saw him again a couple of weeks ago on the day before his evacuation to Theresienstadt. His son had just been arrested; I met the son at Elsa

Kreidl's. Old Arndt, jeweler, is brother-in-law to Ida Kreidl, young Arndt married at about the same time as his cousin Paul Kreidl; the young women got out to England; the young husbands were surprised by the war. Paul Kreidl is—perhaps still alive—in Poland. The Gestapo found a letter in the possession of young Arndt, in which he approached a sales-clerk at the Reka department store about a table service. The secret intent to buy was a misdemeanor; the connection with the Aryan salesgirl could be interpreted as race defilement. Young Arndt is now in a concentration camp. That always becomes known on Friday. On Friday underwear is brought for relatives in the police prison. If the underwear is refused, then the person concerned has been deported. And now usually already shot en route "while attempting escape." The Community is informed a little later. The Arndts and the Kreidls, therefore, make up one family. Ernst Kreidl, Ida Kreidl, Paul Kreidl, the Arndts, father and son—exterminated! And only *one* case among so many. And in me always only the curiosity of the chronicler and fear about my own fate. —

Frau Ziegler very bitter. Until now she was the officially appointed Community nurse. She has been given notice—compulsorily because of the reduced numbers—"with immediate effect." She has been left with no more than a "rachmoness position." Now she can be sent to an armaments factory at any moment, be evacuated at any moment. But strangely, what most wounds the woman is something different. The sudden dismissal of-fends her professional pride, the Community did not show her sufficient respect, Superintendent Hirschel treated her unfairly! That is the tenor of her complaint. Then beneath that: She would be sent to Poland, and in Poland Jews were being shot by the hundreds every day; she hears it most definitely confirmed; men on leave describe it with horror.

### November 4, Wednesday midday

For three months we have not been allowed to subscribe to or buy a news-paper. Nor Eva—"Jewish household." In Caspar David Friedrich Strasse Elsa Kreidl helped out. Here the Aryan Hulda, Frau Jacoby's householder, has done so. The newspaper subscription in her name was paid for by Fränkel and Frau Ziegler, who slipped it to me. Always taking precau-tions, secret places, fear, delay. Now Hulda is afraid, Frau Ziegler is afraid, Hulda has backed out. Now Fränkel wants to go on subscribing through the porter's wife; I have offered to share the cost—but the porter's views are said to be unreliable. Uncertainty, danger everywhere—a newspaper discovered is enough for Auschwitz. — I do not know how this business will develop. So far I have always managed to see the army bulletin. [ . . . ]

Dreadful misery, proletarianization all around. The Eisenmann family. A little boy of three, a little girl of eight, a son of seventeen years of age. Blond, huge, like a strong Hitler Youth, but "brought up as Jewish," wears the star, at Zeiss-Ikon. Frau Ziegler tells me that all five sleep in *one* room, are on top of one another in their kitchen-parlor. Father and son get on badly. I had a conversation with the lad; we were both busy with potatoes. He did not make a bad or unintelligent impression. Frau Ziegler says Herbert attended a good school, but only until he was fifteen [ . . . ]; then he was supposed to learn a trade, probably plumber; before he had finished his apprenticeship, he was put in the "kindergarten" at Zeiss-Ikon. Mechanical tasks are carried out there, which can be done only with very young eyes. Thus the young man is condemned to illiteracy. His father, formerly a well-to-do businessman, now factory worker, does have some education. The father irritable, the boy embittered and strong as a bull. Between them the mother with never-ending housework, with the two little children. And all in such a cramped space and in constant fear every time the doorbell rings.

[ . . . ]

Not out of the house since Sunday. I must rouse myself to go for a walk.

### November 6, Friday toward evening

On Wednesday I undertook the very long walk to Glaser. An hour and twenty minutes and the same back. Bad heart problems on the way there, especially when I passed the station and the Gestapo building; on the way home my foot tortured me—for the third time my fingers and the balls of my feet were numb with cold—also hampered by the profound darkness; nevertheless I had once again forced myself to go for a walk. Glaser, grown very thin after a bilious attack, received me alone. I got peppermint tea with sugar and yeast cake (he fetched it from the bakery, he's privileged after all—he was also sitting at his typewriter, when I arrived), so yeast cake with jam, and I reveled in a sweetness that I had long done without. He told me about a speech, which a legal big gun, Rothenberger or something, had given in Vienna: At a time when so many of our best were falling in the field every day, we could not "go on keeping the asocial elements in the prisons" here at home. That is: we would murder whomever didn't suit us, Jews above all, but also plenty of Aryans. I borrowed a couple of volumes by Maximilian Harden from his library. — I find it increasingly difficult to obtain books.

On Wednesday evening Frau Eger came back quite unexpectedly. She was inside for eighteen or nineteen days, interrogated once; she says she does not know what it is about, but they seem to have revived an old action on assets. She had not had a clue what would happen to her, she does not know what has happened to her husband. She was alone during the day, without reading matter, added up the miles as she paced. "At night there were two or three of us, once there were five. But what could I talk about to these people? One was from the country, had three illegitimate children by three different fathers. Will I ever see my husband again? Will he be able to bear prison and uncertainty? His powers of resistance are less then mine . . ." I consider the man lost. —

[ . . . ]

Today I did not get down to work at all. In the morning I scrubbed the whole kitchen, then to the Community's clothes store in Pirnaische Strasse. There I got three very beautiful, secondhand of course, shirts, originally belonging to some evacuee, for 1.50M each. On the other hand, the cobbler had returned my slippers unrepaired after five—five!—weeks; he does not have the machine needed to repair them. What is involved is nothing more than the fastening on of a pair of rubber soles. Now there is supposed to be a second cobbler there; perhaps he can do it. I went to the Community as well: Could they call in my debts as "Winter Aid" and then transfer the money? In that way I can pay outside my allowance limit. — Consequently I also saw yesterday's military bulletin: further large-scale attacks by the English in Egypt, orderly withdrawal to second positions. Passionate hope. Perhaps we shall be saved after all. I went back by way of the cemetery to invite Steinitz for tomorrow afternoon. Again the three of them were sitting over their grotesque game of skat in the gardeners' shed behind the graves. Steinitz was full of hope, Magnus was vacillating between hope and fear, Schein could no longer believe in anything good happening: The SS had been increased so tremendously, it was a match for any internal assault; our fate was inescapable.

### November 13, Friday toward evening

A letter from Caroli Stern-Hirschberg yesterday. She was marked down for evacuation on October 16 and taken to a synagogue with suitcase and knapsack. She was supposed to remain there with others for three days before being deported into the unknown—to Poland. After three nights and two and a half days she was suddenly and unexpectedly released, retained by her armaments factory (presumably as a skilled worker?). She is delighted at the freedom, as she really calls it, which has been returned to her. (Everything is relative.) —

In the afternoon Fränkel and Frau Ziegler brought home as certain fact what had already been circulating as rumor for a while: the Jewish workers at Zeiss-Ikon, about three hundred of the six hundred Jews still to be found in Dresden, are to be put in barracks. That amounts, in fact, to evacuation, because they, too, will have everything confiscated apart from hand luggage, and they will be held like prisoners: in a camp together, eating together, taken to work in groups—otherwise detained in the camp; no books, no newspapers, no communication with the world outside. — What will now happen to the remainder of the Jews here, to the mixed marriages, to *us*? Since strictest isolation of Jews is the aim, we shall not be allowed to live in freedom. It is said that all the mixed marriages are to be herded together in the Community House and the Henriettenstift home. I am very anxious. — Yesterday afternoon Eva went to see Kätchen Sara, who also has to move into the barracks. The doorbell rang, and the two of them sat in the dark for a long time with the door locked; it could have been the Gestapo, and Aryan visitors are forbidden. Eva says Kätchen

Sara had been completely demented with fear. But the barracks, which for so long had appeared to her as a nightmare, now left her almost cold. One does simply become blunted and worn down; one wants to save one's skin, that's all.

[ ... ]

## November 15, Sunday morning

An hour at the Steinitzes yesterday afternoon was especially unpleasant. His wife was once again in hysterical despair. Her Aryan lawyer told her on good authority: The law on mixed marriages would be published on January 30, 1943. After that the Aryan wife will have a choice between divorce and putting on the star, followed by evacuation. I left in very low spirits. What should, what shall *we* decide? There is so much to be said for and against, simply wanting to stay together is not enough, too much is at stake, one way and another. —

Eva had meanwhile heard the catastrophic Italian military bulletin on the radio: "Tobruk abandoned, enemy advancing on a wide front." That produced another spark of hope.

Eva does her utmost. Through the Seliksohns—he has some secret sources—we receive ample extra potatoes. The potatoes, cabbage, etc., that Eva hauls up here in bags and nets often weigh a total of fifty pounds. — Then in the evening she falls asleep early with exhaustion—then lying awake, reading aloud at night and toward morning. "Ne hibsh." —

[ ... ]

## November 16, Monday morning

The Seliksohns' room was very well heated yesterday afternoon—the weather, by the way, continues wet, nasty, but *unfortunately* no severe winter yet—there was real tea with sugar, together with home baking by the Seliksohns and cake we had brought, but despite these very rare pleasures it was ghastly. First of all the news of the death of the Arndt son, about whose case I have reported several times—of course, "attempting to escape," as with his uncle Kreidl. (Frau Ziegler said that another son of the family had already died in a concentration camp two years ago.) Even worse, almost, than this news was the Seliksohns' mood. He had been forced to spend all morning in the new barracks, with many other Jews, stuffing bedding with wood shavings under mocking Gestapo supervision. ("They chain-smoke cigars, they make the most vulgar remarks.") The wood shavings for the beds had been wet, the beds had been pushed close together in a dormitory ... "We were busy making our own grave ... we shall all be murdered ... I would prefer a better death ..." She interrupted him tearfully: "He wants to kill us with gas; I'm not going along with it; I want to see my child (from her first marriage) again," etc., etc. It was *even* worse than the day before with Steinitz. We both tried to give them new heart. I tried to give him a jolt, he was a "smart" fellow after all, he had the necessary energy, he would surely get through and he, he of all people, with his Soviet skills, must spare himself for the coming hour. That always helped for a little while, then the litany started from the beginning again. [ . . . ]

### November 17, Tuesday toward evening

[ . . . ]

The barracks business is terrible. Frau Ziegler is talking about wanting to commit suicide. Eva visited the Reichenbachs today: They, too, have to go to the barracks. Frau Reichenbach, both feet in plaster, was declared fit to travel. But it is a long walk across a yard, which is sandy at best, and often muddy, to reach the barracks latrines. — The herding together of all the mixed marriages in the Community House is said to be imminent. — Yesterday afternoon rather suddenly (appointment made by Eva) a long walk to see Simon, who filled a bad back tooth. I met Steinitz there, who had just had four front teeth taken out, afterward he walked home, his arm through mine. [ . . . ]

### November 19, Thursday morning

Here those condemned to the barracks (the Fränkels, Nurse Ziegler, Fräulein Imbach) scurry around, pack, complain, cannot sleep, and are worn-out. This morning, amid all the misery, Frau Fränkel told me, with an expression of hope in her face: "It is five minutes to twelve!" — I: Whence this hope, after all no one in the house is more skeptical and pessimistic than your husband. — Letter from a well-informed friend in Merano in Italy, which contained just those words. And then, "General mobilization in Spain to preserve neutrality—but they seem to be leaning more toward England/America than to Germany." — I left the washing up and ran upstairs to Eva, who was still only half-dressed. We embraced and had tears in our eyes. Afterward it occurred to me: How great, beyond all consciousness, must be our latent despair, if something so trivial—for what is of value in Frau Fränkel's report, offers any degree of certainty?—affects us so deeply!

How could it be any different? The misery is far too great. Yesterday Eva fetched a suitcase for the Reichenbachs from some Aryan friends; when she was not home at half past seven, I already imagined her arrested. Yesterday and today she removed names and ex libris from all the books that evacuees have given me for safekeeping or as presents. Otherwise even the thinnest booklet would be "anti-social" theft, sabotage, sufficient grounds for a death sentence. — I myself visited the Reichenbachs yesterday afternoon (was also in the Community rooms for a moment, where there was great activity). I found Frau Reichenbach out of bed, hobbling on shapeless, plaster-cast feet; packing had begun. She was more optimistic than I had feared. Zeiss-Ikon was in charge of the barracks, so things would be halfway human; also communication with the outside world would not be completely cut off. It did not really amount to evacuation: Assets would not be confiscated, even furniture would not be entirely forfeit, would only be auctioned, the proceeds going into the blocked account. One was allowed to receive and reply to mail, the Community was providing a camp library; Zeiss-Ikon was a guarantee of tolerable food—thus there remained only the lack of space, the primitiveness of communal living, the three-quarters imprisonment. Only! — Moreover, the barracks had been built for 700 inmates, hence for *all* Dresden's Jews, the mixed marriages and the privileged y compris. —

**Afternoon**

At lunchtime today to Schlageterplatz again, this time for a haircut at the Seliksohns'. I was welcomed with the greatest warmth. The Seliksohns clutch at us. Inmates of the house likewise clutched at us the day before yesterday. Fräulein Imbach came upstairs in the afternoon; she was feeling so lonely; over supper and afterward till eleven o'clock Frau Eger sat up here shivering. We had to assure her again and again that we believed in her husband's return. And yet we are firmly convinced that he, too, will meet his end "attempting to escape." —

[ . . . ]

**November 21, Saturday afternoon**

Frau Ziegler gave me a wonderful, almost new nightshirt belonging to her deceased husband. The first nightshirt of my life. In principle, the floppy, senile, philistine piece of clothing is repugnant to me. But when I read aloud early today from half past four until six o'clock [ . . . ] it did marvelous service and endeared itself to me, probably endeared itself permanently. It is quite usual now to accept such presents. For what the expellees cannot give away is stolen by the Gestapo (even if, perhaps, they receive a nominal equivalent paid into their blocked account, just as I received 40M for my typewriter). And to wear "inherited," secondhand things is now a general fate. How many of these heirlooms I am wearing now! A hat from John Neumann (still being saved for better weather), a house jacket of the same origin, a pair of shoes from Paul Kreidl, socks from Ernst Kreidl and likewise Herr Ziegler, trousers from unknown from the clothes store, three shirts from the same source, a shirt from the fallen Haeselbarth in Dölzschen. — Today Eva hauled up a tremendously heavy showpiece volume given her by Frau Aronade for safekeeping. *Napoleon 1812–1912*, text by Segur, some fifty reproductions of works of art. The library of books inherited and possibly for safekeeping grows ever more motley and abundant. Every evacuee tries to leave something behind. But the inheritor of today is the evacuee or murder victim of tomorrow. —

Today, again, there is a rumor that the mixed marriages will also be put in the barracks—a milder form of evacuation, at least, or so it seems. Today it's also said that Swiss broadcasts are talking about 75,000 Italian/German prisoners in Africa. — We do not see any newspapers for days on end and know even less about the true situation than the Aryans. Since they started preparing their departure for the barracks, our fellow-sufferers have lost all taste for political events. — They are preoccupied with themselves and are resigned. Nor did I learn anything from Steinitz, whom I went to see yesterday toward evening. —

[ . . . ]

Today I told myself: if I do not succeed, if I do not think I have enough time to work up *LTI* as a separate book, then I shall publish (polished, of course, and ordered) the totality of my diaries since '33. The anticipated fourth volume of my Curriculum, in fact (I is completely finished, II can be finished in a few weeks, III, Dresden professorship 1920–1933, would have to wait). This thought has already come to me often; what was *new* today was that I could give this fourth volume of the Curriculum the title "The Language of the Third Reich" summo jure. Because 1) It would contain my philological *LTI* material and 2) all the facts presented would speak the language of the 3rd Reich, e.g., the inventory of my inherited wardrobe I have just made! — and 3) the whole reversal or brittleness of my fundamental ideas since 1933, or my skepticism toward them, would speak of the shattering effect of the 3rd Reich.

[ . . . ]

Eva is constantly on the go, today again in the morning *and* the afternoon. In addition to the errands, she is helping the barracks people in all kinds of ways. She sews bedding for them, conveys (import and export) this and that for them. Yet she has a cold and is overtired. I ask myself quite selfishly what will happen to us if she has to stay in bed. *I* am allowed to go shopping for only an hour, I am not allowed to use the tram, and our kitchen is in the cellar. — I ask myself a hundred times a day which of the two of us has to bear a heavier burden. There is perhaps a balance. Should it be possible for Eva to avoid Poland or the barracks by a divorce, then she should unreservedly choose divorce, which could afterward be challenged as having been forced on us. Then 1) she could thereby probably retain some assets, 2) immediately come to my aid once I have lived to see a turn for the better—whereas imprisoned with me she could be no help at all, and 3) I do not like the burning of widows. If I am shot in Poland or "attempting to escape," she should take care of my manuscripts and go on living to the joy of a few cats. But things have not got to that point yet.

## November 24, Tuesday morning

(*First frosty day, firm snow on roof and streets*) "Jews' Camp Hellerberg." Eva said this new kind of evacuation is so shameless because everything happens so openly. What is undoubtedly new is that this time we have a view of the inferno and remain in contact with it. Is it a moderate hell? That remains to be seen. Young Eisenmann, who helped stuff the bedding, etc., said: "Catastrophic!" Unimaginably crowded and barbarically primitive, especially the latrines (in a row without dividing walls and far, far too few), but also the narrow beds, etc. The carpenters had said they had worked on barracks for Russian and Polish prisoners—luxury hotels compared to this Jews' camp in the sand and mud! On the other hand, one hears of privileges such as sending and receiving mail, leave to go to Dresden, a camp library, permission for the children to have toys . . . One will have to wait and see. Sunday and Monday [ . . . ] completely taken up with Hellerberg. On Sunday afternoon, my heart playing up, I carted a heavy load along Hindenburgufer to the Community for Frau Ziegler, who has left us a great deal. There we first took our leave of the Seliksohns—chaos and despairing depression, above all on his part; then the Reichenbachs. Frau Reichenbach was suffering greatly because of her feet and complained about Katz, who had declared her fit to travel out of fear of the Gestapo; for a few seconds Frau Reichenbach was also feverishly excited: "Do you *really* believe, Professor, do you *really* believe that it cannot last much longer, or are you only saying it to cheer me up?" — "To cheer myself up too" would have been the true answer [ . . . ]. But of course I "really" believed it, it was not a matter of faith, it was cold, sober certainty; Italy was going to break away in the next few weeks, and then everything would come to an end very quickly. But aside from such feverish moments, Frau Reichenbach's mood was optimistic, and *his* was consistently so. [ . . . ] Reichenbach has to sleep in the camp, but will travel daily to his work in the Community House. Thus we shall remain in contact. As a farewell present Eva received a beautifully hand-embroidered cushion. [ . . . ]

### November 26, Thursday toward evening

News is slowly coming out of the Jews' camp. First young Eisenmann reported of Frau Ziegler: she was relatively well off, she had her own, much-envied room. Then I talked to Reichenbach at the Community yesterday. I noticed that this always slight little man has become quite bent recently. It is not just that he walks with a stoop as I do—a real hump has grown under his left shoulder. But he was in good spirits. "It's not so bad—if nothing worse happens to us, then we can bear it." But I soon noticed how abject his satisfaction was. He had imagined it would be even *more* dreadful, he was happy simply because no one beat him. The room shared by nine married couples—"one gets used to it." The latrines: "only open at the front—but with dividing walls, and lids, no urinals—no toilets, of course." The washroom—"across the yard and very cold, but there are big washbowls there." The food—"it wasn't right yet yesterday, but it will be sorted out." Pitiful! — And today Eva spoke to Frau Ziegler at Simon's and brought her some things there. Simon is turning out to be the communications center. Frau Ziegler, as already mentioned, has a little room of her own and so is personally in a better position than all the others. Nevertheless she was *very* depressed. [ . . . ] Leave in town *only* to visit the doctor, strictest ban on going anywhere else. One inmate had wanted to go from Simon over to the Glasers (ten steps!)—but had not dared do so. (Eva later inherited the lunch prepared for this poor person.) All in all, therefore, imprisonment and a vegetating, full of anxiety. It could also be our fate any day.

It has become very quiet here since the departure of the camp people. And press news reaches us even more sparingly than before. Nevertheless: Yesterday I read a paper at the Community: Darlan, first the Americans had taken him prisoner, then they forged his signature under decrees. Now Darlan is the "traitorous admiral" who has subordinated himself to French West Africa, and Pétain is broadcasting calls for resistance to him, and the situation in France is "problematic." And in the East a "breakthrough" by the Russians south of Stalingrad is noted. Perhaps it's coming to an end after all.

[ . . . ]


## November 28, Saturday morning

Yesterday Frau Eger said to Eva, her husband had now been in the police prison for six weeks—Friday! delivery of underwear, critical day—he was lost if the change did not come soon. She now spends more time with Aryans than with Jews; she has a brother in the SS—so I would like to draw from these words perhaps a tiny bit of hope. But hope has been disappointed so often. — On the other hand: The Russians are on the offensive everywhere, and "there is fighting in Tunis." — Since half Jewry is in the camp, we are even more isolated, see newspapers even less than before. [ . . . ]

Yesterday afternoon to Steinitz and then home [ . . . ]. Steinitz gave me a razor blade (they disappeared from the shops days ago; for a long time one could only buy them individually). And then something grotesque: a cigarette packet full of teeth. Teeth are a scarce commodity; Eichler ran out long ago, so that for many months Eva has been running around with a huge gap in her mouth; he was going to write to Eva as soon as he had the materials, and never wrote. A dental technician, who had worked with the cemetery gardener, deposited this packet there—now Eichler is to pick out what can be used and pay the going price for it. But he must not know where the goods come from. Secret teeth from the Jewish cemetery; it sounds as gruesome as a fairy tale—but it is crazy enough even in reality, and how easily it can lead to catastrophe. Sufficient cause for prison and "attempted escape." [ . . . ]

## November 29, Sunday toward evening

My parents married on November 29, probably 1863. I have been thinking about them today, and the thought of disappearing does not become any more tolerable to me. [ . . . ]

This morning Frau Eger came to see us; could we help her out with a Jew's star. To sew on one of her husband's jackets, which she wanted to pass on to him as something warm. She had learned (a brother is in the SS) that he will be transported to a concentration camp tomorrow. It was the last thing she could do for him; she would also include a cap, into the lining of which she had sewn farewell greetings. But will he find the letter? She has lost hope of seeing her husband again. The transport takes up to eight days. People were picked up in various cities (Leipzig, Chemnitz, etc.), they spent the night in local prisons, larger groups arrived in the camps all at once. At the end of this journey death awaits the Jewish participants. — I comforted Frau Eger; perhaps the change will come overnight, perhaps it will occur with her husband still alive—but I do not believe at all that her husband will be saved in this way. Frau Eger was distraught with fear; she has been waiting for six weeks now. And her husband, too, has been waiting for six weeks now, and for six weeks (presumably in solitary confinement) looking death in the face for hour after hour. It is so horrible that I feel no pity for the man, only fear of having to experience his fate myself. And I think Eva is also haunted by it.

Go on working, get drunk on work!

## December 1, Tuesday morning

Saw the newspaper again yesterday after several days. It is displayed at the Community; I shall go there more often, now that I have a goal, otherwise I get too little exercise. There is always something to be dealt with or learned at the Community. Yesterday because of the gas hot plate and the enamel pot, which the "furniture store" (managed by Reichenbach) is going to lend us; today I want to hand in a couple of things, for which Frau Ziegler had asked. One communicates with the internees through the Community (and through Simon). The people in the Community [ . . . ] appear to have agreed to present life in the camp in a gentle light: It is tolerable, some adjusted more quickly, others more slowly. They make it sound as if the dissatisfied were spoiled and ungrateful creatures. Reichenbach speaks in this way, as does the secretary, Judenkirsch, who, it is true, lives in the Community house and goes to the camp only on official errands; also, Rubin, the other secretary, who does live in the camp, but at least comes to work at the Community during the day. But the bulk of the camp inmates are strictly imprisoned, are only very sparingly permitted leave in town, are always crowded together, etc., etc. It is quite deplorable that this imprisonment is already considered to be halfway good fortune.

It is not Poland, it is not a concentration camp! One does not quite eat one's fill, but one does not starve. One has not yet been beaten. Etc., etc. [ . . . ]

### December 3, Thursday morning

[ . . . ]

Eva continues to communicate with the people in the barracks, to help them in various ways, which are not without risk, since the Gestapo use everything as a pretext. E.g.: Frau Ziegler asks for a couple of plates and pots—then they can say that's smuggling confiscated property. Or: Fräulein Hulda sends two old rolls to the camp—by way of Eva/Simon; then they can say, where do these Aryan rolls come from, Jews don't have any white-flour coupons. Such trifling matters and trifling dangers (no, the *danger* is literally deadly, perhaps Eva, as Aryan go-between, would get away with prison, but how could she endure it, given her weakness, and without fresh air, a bath, cigarettes?). — [ . . . ] Eva is at Simon's right now, taking some things for Frau Ziegler; yesterday she met Frau Selik-sohn in a bank. As it turned out, she had not received the hoped-for "leave" to go to the bank—one is simply and solely allowed to go to the doctor—and had gone "AWOL" from the Goehle plant and come that far with the star covered. A foolish risk, since concentration camp and death would be the certain consequence of discovery, [ . . . ] since the town is crawling with Gestapo people, who have long been familiar with individual Jews. And what would Eva's fate have been if they had caught her with Frau Seliksohn? — According to several reports the worst thing about the camp business so far is said to have been the delousing of the women. While they ran around naked in the place from one station of the cross to the next, they were photographed by the Gestapo; in cold rainy weather they had to stand in the yard for a long time with wet hair; their baggage, which was open and had been rummaged through, was also left exposed to the rain. — A particular danger in the camp appears to be the envy of those crowded together there. If something is slipped to one person, he has to beware of all the rest. —

Letter from Sussmann, warmhearted, but disconcerting because of his cluelessness. Write to me about the (insignificant) details of your daily life, how you "do your shopping, go for a walk, etc." If I write that to him— what would the censors and what would the Gestapo make of it? Going for a walk—on which I am never without fear, of arrest, of insults, at least from children (which has occurred with greater frequency recently)—and on top of that the subject of "shopping!"

### December 7, Monday evening

[ . . . ]

The Eger affair is horrible. Today Frau Eger was with us for a while in the afternoon—at the moment she visits us only rarely. The last time, almost two weeks ago, she was almost certain that her husband was going to be taken away to a concentration camp. At that time she was mistaken. Today she told us he still appears to be here—although she had been unable to carry out the test of delivering underwear last Friday, since she had handed over things on the occasion of the false alarm. We had to listen to it all and were unable to tell her that transportation has now taken place and the Community has been informed.

[ . . . ]

### December 11, Friday morning

Since yesterday—in the morning a card from Richter, "urgent property matter," in the afternoon my visit to infinitely remote Victoriastrasse—upset because of the house. This time probably the final robbery, which I can no longer ward off. A double game, as Richter said. He himself was helpless, would be suspected of friendliness to Jews; I had no legal remedy. The Party had forced the present lender, a master builder by the name of Linke, to foreclose the mortgage and to warn anyone inclined to be his successor. Thus a new mortgage is out of the question; the present one expires on April 1; compulsory auction could be anticipated for May or June. ("That is a long time." — "Do you entertain hopes?" — "Yes." — "Things will not happen that quickly, there's an informer behind everybody, and the terror is too great.") More urgent and probably directly fatal is the other side of it, the actual deceit. Originating with the mayor, who is on army leave. Repairs to the amount of 3,000–4,000M are needed on my house—already stated once before, but treated as ninety-nine percent invention by Richter—including "moving earth" for 800M, because earth is sliding down toward the roadway. The mayor has applied to the Surveyor's Office for an order to secure this sum. If I cannot pay it, then compulsory auction is immediate, and I do not get a penny. If the house goes to compulsory auction, Berger loses his first right of purchase and since no repairs would be demanded of him, he is prepared to take over the house immediately for 16,500M. In that case I would at least get a little money paid into my blocked account. He, Richter, advises me to take this course as the lesser evil. — I have reserved my decision. Eva has now had the bottom completely knocked out of her. I do not need to repeat how passionately and desperately she clings to this house. — I read aloud a great deal during the night and then again toward morning. [ . . . ]

Yesterday's harsh experience has drowned out the lesser occurrences of recent days. On the seventh and the ninth and again today this house has been disrupted by the auction of the Jacoby possessions. We have to keep our rooms locked because the place is crowded with people inspecting the goods. On the first day the auction was held in the hall—I looked on (from the gallery), never having seen one. Involved were small household effects, and the bidders were menu peuple. After that more expensive objects and a somewhat better-off crowd—but now the proper thing is taking place in one of the big rooms downstairs. The house is ever emptier. Eisenmann believes we shall have to get out as early as January.

Solamen miserum, miserrimum: Because even in a single room, even in the proletarianized and bug-ridden city house in Sporergasse, we would still be better off than the people in the Jews' camp. On the eighth I went to see Seliksohn in Dr. Katz's diathermy room, at the same time Eva spoke to Frau Voss at Simon's. Their complaints are the same; Seliksohn looked wretched and ill, Kätchen Sara is also said to have shrunk greatly. The following day I was at the Community, saw Frau Ziegler—same complaints—wanted to talk to Reichenbach, read the newspaper, expedite our application for coal so as to do washing. (Unable to do a wash since September!) Suddenly I was whispered to: "Leave immediately and quietly! Inspector Schmidt has just arrived." Schmidt, still unfamiliar to me personally, has recently been mentioned as one of the worst in the Gestapo's Jewish Department. So I slunk away without having achieved what I wanted. — I saw the newspaper only at Richter's. According to the military bulletin, the "large-scale operations" of the Russians are stalling, and our "counterattack" in the middle section [of the front] is pressing ahead vigorously. In Africa the enemy had come to a standstill, and we were inflicting heavy losses on his naval transport. How much of it is true? Richter said: Two German armies were surrounded at Stalingrad, there were even larger German forces in the Caucasus, and they, too, were threatened. Italy was close to collapse. — But despite all that (and "although many people were already saying to themselves: 'It's better if we lose the war!' ") it can still last for years.

Frau Eger was here again late one afternoon, still knowing nothing of the fate of her husband. She gave me five razor blades as a present—a treasure! [ . . . ] In relation to the razor blades Frau Eger told us two things: 1) At police headquarters Jewish prisoners are no longer being shaved (they go to their deaths unshaven). 2) In the shop, where she bought the blades, a soldier on leave, wearing an "Africa" armlet, talked loudly and at length about the retreat from El Alamein. They had run for their lives; they had thrown away everything, literally everything, just to be able to run, kit bags, rifles, coats—except caps and uniforms, literally nothing else had been saved. —

[ . . . ]

### Toward evening

The auction today was dreadful; it raged through the house and emptied it; the big pieces went. I was crossing the yard with the rubbish bin, as a carpet lay spread out there for brushing like a piece of booty. A tall, rough fellow, who was busy with it, shouted mockingly at me: "Go on in, Jew!" Later he came into the kitchen and in a rude tone asked for thread and a broom. I said, I didn't have anything. "And these things here?" (He pointed at Frau Ziegler's stack of things.) "None of that is my property, it has been confiscated." With that he went off. The whole business made me feel sick. — Eva also came home in very low spirits from her shopping errands. With empty hands, also with an empty stomach. — Frau Eger has just brought up the new food-ration cards. Seven for Eva, four for me— but the Aryan seven are not much good for anything either. Frau Eger related as a rumor, that martial law had been imposed in Italy and, as vouched for, that very many German troops were going to Italy. —

[ . . . ]

### December 18, Friday evening

At the cemetery Jacobi said that yesterday he had had to go to the police presidium to fetch the body of a non-Dresden Jew, "deceased" en route to a concentration camp. He was hard-boiled, thanks to his job, but he had almost fainted at what he saw. [ . . . ]

Eva brought the latest news: She had tried in vain to borrow a new book from Natscheff. He is allowed to take back only those that have been borrowed; he is not allowed to carry on any further business. He is Bulgarian, his wife American, he has always had contacts abroad, with Dresden's Jewish intelligentsia, was evidently suspect. Eva says he seemed very distracted and embittered . . . We shall now go back to Paulig and thereby gain more than we lose: Natscheff was always somewhat snobbishly restricted to the very modern things. Eva had given up going to Paulig some months ago, when the Gestapo thumped me on the head with Rosenberg. [ . . . ]

### December 19, Saturday morning

Eva sometimes teaches Herbert Eisenmann now, and he is often—as just now—up here to practice. And he talks then. He and his father work at Zeiss-Ikon. His father, as foreman, gets a fixed hourly rate, which comes to about 150M a month. Herbert does piecework in the "kindergarten," the department employing young people (16–24 years of age). Precision work on tiny components, which are properly visible only under a magnifying glass, demanding very clear eyesight. Tiny pieces of measuring instruments for naval antiaircraft guns. On piecework for eight hours a day, Herbert Eisenmann has already managed to make as much as 320M a month. Now an upper limit has been placed on Jewish piecework. They are being forced to achieve maximum output—if they don't prove their worth, there's the threat of Poland—and are paid less than the Aryans. "It adds up to 320M, but then it's reduced according to some formula and I'm paid 220." What multiple immorality in the whole situation! — The people in the Jews' camp have now been forbidden to buy anything at all in the shops. By another hellish degree they are more completely prisoners and more badly fed than before.

[ . . . ]

## December 20, Sunday morning

"Messina," says Eva of our nighttime reading aloud, which has now almost become the rule. On our long sea cruises, we asked to be awakened
if the ship passed an interesting spot during the night. The strait between
Messina and Reggio di Calabria was the most interesting. But there is, of
course, a difference between the interruption to our sleep then and today.
How good things were for us then, how free we were, how sure of our
lives, of our human dignity. — Messina as the scene of the catastrophic
earthquake: In the same way I could call Hitlerism the "prise de pouvoir,"
our Messina.

[ . . . ]


## December 21, Monday midday

A good month ago—I can't check it in the diary, of course—Hirschel disappeared mysteriously; Frau Ziegler reported he had been "arrested," officially he was "sick"; his signatures were in circulation, he would return
to his duties soon, and after about two weeks he did reappear. Yesterday
he told us his story; I shall try to put it down exactly. Kronthal, a language
teacher, had been arrested because of some incautious remarks—he has
meanwhile been sent to a concentration camp; news of his death is expected. The man had a license to teach languages privately. A schedule
was found in his home, according to which he had *also* given the Hirschel
children lessons in geography and drawing. Hirschel, who is in Inspector
Müller's good books, was summoned to Bismarckstrasse. "*You* are the one
who should be put in a concentration camp for contravening the ban on instruction; I stood up for you, you will *only* be imprisoned and not for long;
Kahlenberg, the tax secretary, will bring you the documents that have to be
signed every day; your Community will be told that you have been taken
ill." — Hirschel then waited in another room to be taken away; in this
room he met Eger, who had been arrested the same day. After a while Inspector Weser came in—the animal, who also struck us and spat on us. At
first he was only taunting: "I hear you said I was the worst—well, you
won't see your Community again." At that point a long hospital train went
past. "Weser suddenly went into a frenzy, raining blows on both of us.
'You people are to blame for that . . . Normally I can't harm a soul, but I
want to murder every Jew. I want to kill your two boys as well . . . You
won't come back.' " This attack of madness fits with what Eva experienced
with these people (fear of the evil eye). Then Weser took Hirschel to the police prison. Mocking: "Look, I've brought the Jewish mayor . . ."

*Cell 47.—Polish rations.* A note on the door outside: "Polish rations." Cell
47, said Hirschel, is the notorious half-dark "suicide" cell, in which Friedheim and several others have been "suicided." Polish rations means half
the normal prison rations. For twenty-four hours Hirschel was uncertain
whether he would escape with his life. Then Inspector Müller arrived to

see him, was astonished at Weser's instructions, gave him encouragement; nothing would happen to him, he would get a different cell and normal food, not be inside for long, be able to attend to business every day with Kahlenberg. — Nevertheless Hirschel remained in the murder cell for another twenty-four hours; then he was given better accommodation; he was also slipped a newspaper occasionally—but the "Polish rations" remained. When he was released after ten days he weighed less than 98 pounds; before prison he (a slim little man) had weighed in at 105 pounds. During his imprisonment Frau Hirschel happened to encounter Weser in the street, and he accosted her: "Your husband has just died." She knew his ways and responded, no, he's alive. "Not at all," he said, laughing, "he's dead, just go home, you'll find the news has arrived . . ." Is the man *only* mentally ill, or is he a criminal? I talked about his and Clemens's thefts (butter, *money*, etc.). Hirschel thereupon related this incident [ . . . ]: A Jewish lady is stopped by Weser as she is coming back from shopping. In the entrance hall he takes her big bag from her, pulls everything out (just as he did with Eva) and strikes her hard in the face with the empty bag. At the same moment, as she stands there blinded, he tugs at her handbag and pulls something out. Later the lady finds her purse missing. — The man is a civil servant, a police inspector, a first lieutenant in the SS. He has the power of life and death; his colleagues, least of all those in the police, cannot go against him.

[ . . . ]

### December 22, Tuesday evening

[ . . . ]

It was not very easy for me to concentrate on my notes this afternoon. At the bank [ . . . ] Eva had copied out the military bulletin of yesterday, December 21. For the first time: the Russians have broken through at the bend of the Don. German divisions arriving at the front had occupied "prepared rear positions." A military bulletin from Russia has *never* sounded so pitiful, not even last winter. It must have been forced on them by terrible foreign reports. It can mean the beginning of the catastrophe. It *can,* but it *does not have to.* Why should the new positions not hold, why should Germany not be able to go on fighting for another year? Nevertheless: For a few hours our hopes were raised. Now, of course, I am depressed again. [ . . . ]

### December 26, Saturday morning

Second day of the holiday, light frost, a little above freezing in fact.

In truth I was mostly afraid of Christmas. But this time, for all the bleakness and oppressiveness, it is turning out to be halfway tolerable. Eva had obtained a very pretty little tree, decorated it beautifully, and put it up on the piano. Presents, good food, alcohol, sweets were completely absent, it was all even plainer than last year—and how much misery had we gone through and seen since then. Our thoughts circled constantly around these two things: "This will be our last Christmas in the Third Reich." — "But we already thought that last year, and were mistaken." Then again: "This time it's different." — "But we have so often underestimated National Socialism's powers of resistance." Etc., back and forth. Then, at about ten, when we wanted to go to bed, Herbert Eisenmann came up, and we chatted fruitlessly about the war for a little while. —

On the morning of the twenty-fourth I was at the Community. I took a pitiful little packet there for Frau Ziegler; a couple of grams of cod roe, a slice of cake—what an effort to get hold of a piece of wrapping paper, the paper shortage is ever more bothersome; where would I be without an old telephone book, which I lighted upon here and which is now also nearly used up! . . . —a couple of lines for the Seliksohns, a couple for Kätchen Voss. [ . . . ]

The morning mail of the twenty-fifth brought a letter from Caroli Stern-Hirschberg, who is daily expecting evacuation. In her last letter she had informed us of Erich Meyerhof's death, in this one she reports the death of her sister Hanna Christiani. She reached the age of only 57, ailing since October, a few weeks ago an inoperable tumor was discovered in her bronchial tubes (presumably cancer?). Heart failure on December 4. Shocked me very greatly. Naturally again only in an egoistical sense. Everyone around me is dying. Why am *I* still alive, what claim to longevity can I make with my 61 years? And yet I would so much like to go on. Hanna's death has shaken us both with particular force, because we knew her only in the bloom of youth. Later we saw her in Frankfurt for an afternoon or an evening, probably on our way from Paris, in 1925. Even then she was only forty. [ . . . ]

This afternoon Eva will go to a tango concert and dance in the trades house; little Lewinsky (Siegfried) will probably pay me a visit in the meantime; I ran into him the day before yesterday. It required a great deal of deliberation, also persuasion on my part, to get Eva to go to this entertainment. Because we have only—the disposable allowance limit!—six marks in the house, and Eva cannot visit our friend Brigitte in Quedlinburg until Tuesday. (That is Kätchen's contribution to encyclopedic style, to always begin names with the next letter of the alphabet.) Moreover, there is no more of our own money at Brigitte's: She will have to lend us money. Not a large sum, about thirty marks a month is a help. Nevertheless: All the counting and economizing is now on Eva's shoulders; I don't have a single pfennig on me anymore, have long (since I lost the last one) not even had a wallet.

[ . . . ]

## December 28, Monday morning

The odious days of self-contemplation, this time made even longer by the Sunday, are almost over. There remains only the New Year.

Lewinsky came on Saturday afternoon; he was here from a quarter to three until a quarter past six, and I had to endure him all alone, since Eva was at a tango concert. (My Christmas present—three marks out of six, which constitute our total expendable assets until January 1, or perhaps only until tomorrow, when Annemarie will have to help us [ . . . ].) I found Lewinsky very boring. [ . . . ]

Afterward the evening provided something interesting, though depressing on the whole, a vox populi, to which I attach great value as evidence. Without money and yet obliged to give a present, we had given the caretaker's wife one of Eva's scarves, and the caretaker himself a gray tie I inherited from Ernst Kreidl. The man came to express his thanks, got talking, and for something like an hour there flowed from him views that overheard by an informer would have consigned him to a concentration camp. He must be about forty, is a smith, a milling cutter in an armaments factory, veteran of 1914, quite clearly an old Social Democrat, close to the Communists. (Apart from that his eyes are inexpressive, and he has a way of looking at the floor while he is talking that I do not quite trust; *I* would not have spoken to him with such openness—also, I did not try to draw him out with questions, but just let him talk.) He said: So many troops were being sent to the West, "to Spain"(!), to Africa. Everything that could stand up to the tropics was being sent there—"we are building so many big transport planes—there's going to be a big offensive, something involving parachutes, soon." Did we have enough gasoline? — Yes, because the vehicles had been converted to liquefied gas, and there was no shortage of all kinds of war matériel; after all for a long time we had used captured Czech and French matériel (huge quantities!). Nor was there a shortage of men yet; the losses were not so great. The situation in Russia was not good, of course; the Russians broke through sometimes, but our superior generalship always contained them. — Only: The war was going on too long; "ordinary people" had had enough of it. Admittedly "nothing" will happen at home, but the army, "the ordinary man" in the army, did not want to go on. There had already been many executions. And they were asking themselves: "what for?"—always just "for the Party nonsense." "The young officers are all for it, say 'Heil Hitler,' and stretch out their arms; but the old ones put two fingers to their caps and say 'Good morning' . . . And then there's the hostility between the army and the SS. If it hadn't been for 'Adolf,' things would already have gone wrong last winter. But Adolf suddenly turned up at an outpost right at the front, asked the men about their coats, their rations, and Adolf personally took off the officers' furs; that helped for a while. But now they've all had enough." — "And the workers? Are they not afraid of unemployment after a lost war?" — "No, there'll certainly be work, because everything's needed; *there aren't even pots any more.* But they have small savings, they can't spend anything after all, and they are afraid for themselves. And we're not short of labor either; the Russian prisoners work very well, the French, too. No, nothing will happen inside the country (although there are still Communist Party people—but they laugh and say: 'You've still got it far too good, just wait a while!') But the soldiers will do it. Both sides carry on propaganda; when our boys arrive, the officers show them how the Bolsheviks were living, and the Russians tell us every night through loudspeakers to come over to their side. There were also people [i.e., Russians] who came to the outposts, brought them cigarettes and vodka, and a couple of our men went over with them . . . The English and the Americans are dropping leaflets on Hamburg, but people remember 1918 and don't believe their promises . . ." The chorus was always: "Nothing will happen inside the country . . . but the war is lasting too long, and everyone has had enough of the Party nonsense, and the soldiers at the front don't want to go on." However, the main thing that I took from all of this was only that a new offensive is imminent in Africa, that militarily there is not yet any talk of real defeat, that the government has a firm hold of the reins of power and that "Adolf" as a person has not lost his aura. For sure there are also signs of discontent and war-weariness, even of collapse, but that in the distant future. And how shall *we* live to see this future?

[ . . . ]

### December 29, Tuesday morning

Yesterday afternoon the enormous walk to Simon's, who is treating Eva *secretly*. I did not see him, the surgery hours had ended earlier; no one opened up. I took the few steps farther to the Glasers, to show my face and to rest. A younger sister of Glaser's wife, Aryan and married to an Aryan, resident in Vienna, was visiting. She said: Schirach in Vienna was perpetrating far greater brutalities against the Jews than Mutschmann against us here. The city is now being completely rid of Jews. (Berlin was now also being evacuated en masse, Glaser added, and that tallied with the remark in Caroli's recent letter, she was *still* in Berlin.) She talked about ghastly atrocities against Romanian Jews. (Had to dig their own mass grave, strip naked, and were then shot. Just as Eva reported of Kiev long ago.) She talked about her husband, who has now been sent to a Naples hospital as a junior army surgeon. Italy was crowded, stuffed full of German troops. It was public knowledge that the country, including the army, was split into two parties. One around Mussolini, who was now no more than Hitler's slave, the other around Crown Prince Umberto, the army commander in upper Italy. What would happen was completely obscure. Glaser, always pessimistic, was again very skeptical about when the war would end, and this time I had to agree with him. In Russia, according to announcements, a German counterattack in the bend of the Don is making progress—so once again there has been no decisive Russian breakthrough; in Africa the Americans' Tunis offensive is at a standstill, so the Germans have time to prepare their own attack. — Glaser was in very low spirits, and I came home in very low spirits.

[ . . . ]

Now I shall wrap up the little manuscript package for Brigitte in Quedlinburg. I asked Eva to ask Brigitte for bread coupons. — "Begging is so unpleasant; she has already declined twice, she seems to need the coupons for her brothers and sisters!" —

## December 30, Wednesday afternoon

[ . . . ]

When I was a child there was once a case of the plague in Berlin. A laboratory attendant (at the Charité Hospital, I think) had placed his cigar butt on a plague culture and then continued smoking it. In 1915, at the front, I was astonished that in the dugout baskets full of shells were stored right next to glowing hot iron stoves, but a couple of days later I no longer paid any attention. Analogous to both cases: Yesterday Eva brought back the packet of manuscripts from Quedlinburg. What with money matters— 100M for Kätchen put in a spectacles case, and contrary to expectations there were still 50M, which belonged to us—and with talking she completely forgot about the manuscripts. This forgetfulness corresponds exactly to the behavior of the plague attendant: Danger has become so much a matter of course to us. And our subsequent composure corresponds to the mood in the dugout: If I am careful with our shells, I can still be hit by an enemy one—being cautious is no help at all—so what is the point of being cautious in the first place?! — Annemarie sent me three cigars, which I got rid of by smoking immediately, since they are more dangerous than manuscripts. After long abstention little pleasure and some nausea. Annemarie, formerly very well rounded, now weighs 103 pounds. The doctors are all overworked, but do not get workers' supplementary rations; also no doctor is allowed to prescribe any kind of tonic or whole milk to a sick colleague.

[ . . . ]

## December 31, Thursday evening

In the morning a very tiring walk to the bank (rent), Community (New Year's greetings to the camp, newspaper completely without content), Steinitz. Shortly beforehand, coming from the dentist, he had been stopped on Prager Strasse by a Gestapo man: "You've no business being here; clear off onto the side streets!" — In the afternoon laid low by severe stomach pains—cabbage and potatoes, potatoes and cabbage. — Very bitter mood. Everyone with whom we spent last New Year's Eve has been blotted out by murder, suicide, and evacuation. Of the ten Nazi years thus far, this year, 1942, was the worst: We have suffered ever new humiliation, persecution, ill-treatment, slander, murder splashed all around us, and every day we felt ourselves in mortal danger. And yet I can only say: Thus far the worst year, for there is every prospect that the terror will grow more intense, and there is no telling how long the war and this government will last.

I was unable to produce anything all year—everything has been knocked out of my hand. I merely attempted, with whatever reading I could lay my hands on, to go on increasing my knowledge, very generally with respect to *LTI* (including the Jewish chapter); most recently also with respect to the latest French literature, but that has already come to an end, because Natscheff's library was shut down.

On September 3 we moved here, into the second Jews' House.

Of the friends of our youth, Erich Meyerhof and Hanna Stern-Cristiani died. Of my family, my sister Grete died in August.

# 1943

## January 1, Friday evening

The paper shortage is so great that I was unable to come by a block calendar anywhere.

[ . . . ] Herbert Eisenmann reported a proclamation by Hitler to the soldiers at the front and to the people: In this year of 1943 he will achieve a "clear final victory." Eisenmann senior again expressed the opinion that the regime will collapse in March. — Frau Eger, who stays aloof, always wears a mask of smiling equanimity, and never even hints that she knows her husband is in a concentration camp, paid us a New Year's visit. To her and Lewinsky I maintained categorically that the regime is close to breaking down—so categorically that I almost talked myself into it. But in my heart of hearts I am quite without hope. I am no longer capable of imagining how I could ever live without the star as a free man again and in tolerable financial circumstances.

[ . . . ]


## January 3, Sunday toward evening

[ . . . ]

I spent the morning at the Jewish cemetery, where the urn of Arndt, who "had been shot while attempting to escape," was interred. Jacobi, the cemetery custodian, read a proper little sermon in an unctuous monotone from a sheet of paper. Ghastly. "He was so well liked." — "He was very happily married for two years; his wife went to England, he was unable to follow." (But everyone knows that he consoled himself here with a close friend.) — "For my ways are not your ways" . . . "We shall trust in God, the Father" . . . Jacobi then said the Kaddish; I was embarrassed when someone had to whisper to me: "Turn to the east!" The funeral took place in a rather small room—the Gestapo has had furniture stored in the large hall. — It had snowed during the night and was still snowing; it was an effort walking to the cemetery, and I was worried all the time about [being ordered] to shovel snow once again. Eva, who is suffering badly from pain in her lower jaw—probably neurosis; the dentist cannot find anything— remained at home. —

[ . . . ]

I miss the block calendar more than I can say. Time stands still.

### January 6, Wednesday midday

Yesterday Eva spent all day in bed, got up of necessity only toward seven o'clock to make our main meal. Today, although snow is on the ground and she is only half recovered, she has gone into town and to the dentist. I am worried whether it will do her any good; my conscience is suffering because her getting up and going out—which she has not done since midday on Saturday—takes much of the burden off my shoulders. I myself am extremely handicapped if I do the shopping. In a bakery I was refused bread, even though the ban refers *only* to wheat products—obviously because of the salesgirl's fear and stupidity, not because of malice—but it was nevertheless painful for me. I was completely unable to come by any matches; once Reichenbach gave me a dozen loose as a present, once Frau Eisenmann gave me a box. Here I gave an onion in return. On the other hand I was very touched when, in a Paschky shop on Blumenstrasse, I found Krone, the same salesclerk who had been my friend at Plauen station near Dölzschen. A theatrical figure, young face, hair brushed stiffly upward, slim; he greeted me with a handshake (a deed, a profession not without risk) and immediately let me have a pound of minced fish and meat with real fish tails. It remains to be seen whether today's trip did Eva's nerves good or makes them worse again. I always reproach myself for not showing her enough sympathy. Things are wretched for both of us—but so much worse for the people in the camp, which is a solamen miserrimum however. — My hands, my feet, too, are covered in small cuts because of the frost; exhaustion makes me fall asleep without fail for ten to thirty minutes every morning and afternoon. Certainly I am already reading aloud in the very early morning; but then I am also asleep early, by eleven o'clock at the latest. —

[ . . . ]

### January 7, Thursday afternoon

Quite a few weeks ago, when I first called to see Seliksohn at Katz's place, Katz, noticeably tired and preoccupied, came into the diathermy room for a moment, evidently from his office; we shook hands, he disappeared right away; hardly a word was exchanged. Then Katz appeared here yesterday evening; he had been unable to stop thinking about the fact that he had recently behaved "coldly" to me, so despite his lack of time he wanted to pay us a private visit. We were genuinely moved. He thinks highly of us, clings to us a little. He is in the most agonizing position, in constant contact with the Gestapo, slavishly dependent on them, always threatened, hardly less hated by the Jews than Estreicher once was, since they make him solely responsible for all alleviations (medical certificates and the like) they are refused. Thus it is supposed to be thanks to his pulling strings that his receptionist was not put in the camp. (But it was the Aryan medical assessor who insisted on that, he said. — And Seliksohn said she was the avowed girlfriend of Kahlenberg, the Gestapo favorite.) Katz, much aged, who has just turned sixty, talked about the difficulties in the camp. One woman is expecting a child. What a struggle it had been to get a midwife approved for her. What a struggle had preceded the granting of two bathtubs. How he was still fighting to improve the latrines . . . [ . . . ]

### January 8, Friday morning

The tax people are working in the house again; many large chests are being removed now, the art objects presumably. When I came down the stairs recently, two huge fellows roared "Good morning, Professor" and shook my hand. Old removal men from Thamm renewing an old friendship (old SPD men at least, probably old KPD men). It did me good, but it helped as little as the war news. At the Community, where I fetched the new ration cards late yesterday afternoon and glanced at the newspaper, Hirschel informed me of Eger's death. In his fiftieth year. Myocardial insufficiency. Auschwitz camp. The ashes are not being sent. The widow is to be notified. Hirschel asked me to undertake this notification. I hesitated without refusing. "I cannot say to her: 'God will comfort you, etc.' " — "Nor can I anymore . . . I shall ask her to come here; in the office she'll pull herself together, and that will help both of us." As he was dictating the letter, she herself was announced. (Probably because of ration cards.) So she found out about it there, and we are left to offer condolences. (And feel horror.) —

A new push from Dölzschen. Christmann, the mayor, has summoned me for 10:00 A.M. tomorrow. [ . . . ] But I need permission to travel. I have written to Richter, whether he can act as intermediary. Eva has just taken the letter to Richter. She herself intends to go to Dölzschen tomorrow in my place, if Richter considers that at all possible. I am very skeptical, however. What can rational argument and legal objections do against blackmail and a will to murder? Also Eva is constantly ailing, lies in bed a lot, complains about pains as soon as she is out of bed. Also there is a lot of snow, and it is snowing again today, and getting to Dölzschen town hall is a matter of mountain climbing and winter sports. The business makes us even more depressed than we already are. But I now feel a certain degree of apathy. Our general situation is so very hopeless. —

[ . . . ]

### January 13, Wednesday morning

Continuous frost (up to eighteen degrees at night), snow-covered icy streets. Eva still quite ill. I take over errands from her, read aloud in the very early morning—the days pass quickly and monotonously. Food absorbs much thought—lack of potatoes and hunger and tiredness. The war stagnates.

The still unresolved *Dölzschen business* required a couple of trips to Richter and to the Community. This is how matters stand: The mortgage has *not* been foreclosed—Master Builder Linke has evidently not let himself be intimidated by the threat from the Party; perhaps he sees a ray of hope on the horizon. Nor has anything been heard from the Public Surveyor's office yet. By summoning me, the mayor probably wanted to put pressure on me in person. Against the summons for last Saturday I objected that I required a travel permit from the Gestapo and had to obtain it through the Community. Thereupon the summons was deferred to today, January 13 (through the intervention of the trustee by telephone). Now the Community (consultation with Reichenbach and Hirschel) helped to carry on a little further obstruction: My application for an exit permit to Dölzschen can be passed on to the Gestapo only if proof is provided that the matter can be dealt with neither by the trustee nor in writing. Richter has now conveyed this to Dölzschen. It is truly a painful tragicomedy.

[ . . . ]

### January 14, Thursday afternoon

Yesterday afternoon we were sitting over afternoon coffee. Then Steinitz appeared, the Community had telephoned the cemetery, to get a message to me immediately because of the "Journey to Dölzschen." Since then I have not had a moment's peace. At the Community at four, was right away chased over to the Police Presidium; after losing my way [in the building] I got the relevant officer as he was about to leave and received, with a growl, a form, which permitted "the Jew Klemperer" to leave the area of the city on January 14 between 8:00 A.M. and 4:00 P.M. to go to Dölzschen. I should collect the requisite public transport permit from the traffic police at Sachsenplatz (on foot, of course) the next morning. Back to the Community, where I received the following information from young Kahlenberg. Mayor Christmann had gone directly to the Gestapo, and "we had got it in the neck from them." In Dölzschen they would now certainly demand my consent, in writing, to the sale of the house. From his experience, he, Kahlenberg, would advise me not to refuse. Refusal brought the risk of concentration camp and death. I: Then my Aryan widow will inherit the house, as happened in the Ernst Kreidl case. He: That was not certain, there were also cases in which property was confiscated—if, e.g., it accorded with "sound popular sentiment" or the "interest of the state" (with these two formulas they can do anything) to make the parish of Dölzschen, in which my house was the only Jewish property, free of Jews. — In contrast, Eva argued vehemently that it would be more convenient for them to get our house while I was still alive than after my death, that it would be more convenient (cheaper) to murder me after I had surrendered the house, that I must not allow myself to be intimidated. She also said meaningfully that Kahlenberg was Estreicher's successor, that he wanted to coax Kätchen's house out of her, at the very least to make himself popular with the Gestapo, perhaps even to make some money out of it as well. There was an extremely unpleasant argument. ("With your income as a widow, you won't be able to keep the house." — "To follow *your* argument: Then it would be my fault if you were put in a concentration camp? As if they needed a pretext for murder and this one of all things." Etc., etc. Of course implicitly and explicitly the whole, old story of the house business unfolded again from the beginning.)

Today I left the house just after seven. Very close to a thaw, but the south wind very strong, the ground smooth—heart problems. At Sachsenplatz, where I had expected to wait a long time, I received the public transport permit very quickly. (As I was waiting, I overheard a series of telephone calls of the same kind. "Name? — How many persons? — 85 years of age? — Yes, you are allowed to go. Call the taxi switchboard in ten minutes." So each time an Aryan orders a taxicab—Jews are completely forbidden to do so—it has to be done via the traffic police, a reason has to be given, and the police officer enters the trip in a notebook!) At half past eight, I was already standing on the front platform of a number 16, was at Planettastrasse by nine, and did not have to be at the district office until ten. To pass the time, I walked very slowly, step-by-step, up the familiar route. Struggle with wind and smooth snow-covered ground; the magnificent view. Then I waited on a bench in the accounts room from half past nine until half past ten. Christmann, the mayor, was very courteous to me once before and then—at least according to Estreicher, but what is his word worth?—very venomous about me behind my back. The man has meanwhile got graying hair and made an even more favorable impression on me than before (in civilian clothes with medal ribbons). He said "Good morning" very clearly to me, in front of other people; he offered me a seat. He said, he wanted to talk to me in friendly fashion. At present there were about 3,000M worth of repairs outstanding, and Berger was offering to take over all this repair work and to pay the full purchase price of 16,000M. I: I was ill, my wife, an Aryan, should inherit the house. He: "Don't you trust our money? It's solid . . . And your widow will not be able to move in right away either—the tenant has rights! What's the point of maintaining such a luxury?" I: "Emotional value. I feel obliged to do so. If you want to put me under pressure, then I cannot refuse. I am under Gestapo supervision, and they are not pleasant customers. But if I can do so without risk, then I would prefer not to comply with Berger's suggestion. I can pay for the essential digging job, which will cost a couple of hundred marks, right away, and if my circumstances improve after the war, I can borrow from friends and relations." — He: There was no risk to me. "I am a soldier and have no interest in the matter; I shall not report you to the Gestapo. I wanted to settle things amicably, the offer is a very favorable one. But your attitude is to some degree very comprehensible from a human point of view. Let us know in writing through your trustee—so that I am covered, as having attended to the matter—that you are not willing to sell your property." With that I was dismissed and arrived back here quite exhausted and bitter. If the man betrays me, the Gestapo has a handle against me ("antisocial behavior"). At best the slow torture of tapping money from me will continue. My statement, which has already been sent off—via Richter, since I am not allowed to communicate with any government body in person—went as follows: "... that for the moment I cannot make up my mind to accept Herr Berger's proposed offer." So no general and definitive refusal to sell. — Mentally I am knocked out. The humiliation of the "travel permit," the issue of the house between Eva and myself, the constant dreadful fear of Auschwitz. Last night I dreamed in great detail that I had gone into a café without the star and was now sitting there afraid of being recognized.

[ ... ]

### January 17, Sunday midday

[ ... ]

At the Zeiss-Ikon plant large numbers of Jews are being given notice. Half the (Jewish) workforce has already been given the sack. Previously the company resisted the Gestapo: The Jewish section was particularly familiar with the work and must be maintained. In the course of last January's evacuation there was a dramatic about-face: First the Gestapo gave the order, then the company fetched back its Jews, who were ready to be transported. Now there is supposed to be a new Reich decree: No Jew can be employed in an armaments plant anymore. (Fear and terror run parallel with the worsening of the external situation.) For the present, those dismissed are being employed elsewhere in Dresden. Kätchen Voss cleaning carriages for the railways. But Poland looms.

A language teacher called Kronthal was arrested at about the same time as Eger. Mixed marriage. No property—but is said to have made incautious remarks and given private lessons beyond what he was permitted. (To Hirschel's children, for example, and Hirschel was inside as a result.) Now news of death from Auschwitz—the urn will not be sent. Jacobi, the cemetery custodian, told me that yesterday. [ ... ]

When I go home along Fiedlerstrasse, I pass a large school [ ... ]. Often the schoolboys are pouring out, and then I always have the same experience. The older boys walk past me and are well behaved, the little ones, on the other hand, laugh, shout "Jew," and so on at me. So it has been drummed into the little ones—it no longer works on the older ones. Eva says she notices how unhealthy the schoolchildren look. By contrast the very little ones and the infants are blooming. Children's food and, above all, full-cream milk are provided only up to the age of six. —

### January 18, Monday afternoon

On Saturday, 8:30 P.M.—we were about to sit down at table—the sound of the all clear. We were still wondering about it, when the air-raid siren followed. There had been no air-raid warning here for so many months, that the wrong siren button had evidently been pressed. Once again Dresden was spared. [ . . . ] A little antiaircraft fire in the distance, and after a quiet one and a half hours the all clear. [ . . . ] Yesterday, at exactly the same time, another warning, again lasting one and a half hours; again no attack on Dresden. Frau Eger was just here—she asked for a cigarette, and we offered our condolences—and told us the aircraft had been to Berlin again and caused a very great deal of mischief.

On Sunday afternoon, as is usual now, Lewinsky was here. Recited Schiller's *Das verschleierte Bild zu Sais* and Uhland's *Des Sängers Fluch,* and once again the comical *Totentanz* by Goethe, and in a nicely unpretentious fashion recited the wonderful and, to me, unfamiliar *Unverhoffte Wiedersehen* (with the dead bridegroom, the miner, preserved in iron sulfate after fifty years) from Hebel's *Schatzkästlein* [Treasure Chest]. [ . . . ] Talked about Buchenwald, near Weimar, where he was imprisoned during the Grünspan business. At that time I was not yet directly affected by the calamity; I had heard the name Buchenwald mentioned for the first time by Marta in Berlin only a short time before. Buchenwald will be described by others; *I* shall stick to my experiences.

This morning saw Richter (the trustee). For a "brief discussion" of my visit to Mayor Christmann and how the repairs could be supervised. The "brief discussion" turned into a conversation of one and a quarter hours, and I went home almost in high spirits. Richter told me that he had been a passionate Nazi before the "seizure of power" and had had a good post in Propaganda, but had resigned his Party membership in April '33, because even then he had already clearly seen the deterioration. *Now* they had reached the end. If only it would come quickly. In the propaganda lectures the talk was now only of "holding out," no longer of victory, in which no one believed anymore. The losses were immense, the tyranny, *even* against Aryans, was unbearable. The question, what "will become of the nation," was now secondary; everyone was asking himself, whether he would survive. Perhaps the revolution would come very quickly. The Waffen SS was certainly being doubled in size, but "volunteers" were being *pressed* into it. The situation on the fronts was very bad everywhere, with very heavy losses. The Russians were not only aiming at the Ukraine in the south, but at the Baltic lands in the north, and they were already not very far from Riga. He said his son was in the seventh grade at Kreuzgymnasium. He now had a history reader that goes backward from the present and dissolves history into individual stories. Titles of the pieces in this order—"it turns one's stomach"! (Hitler, Goering, Horst Wessel, Herbert Norkus, Bismarck, Frederick the Great.) I took Richter as vox populi just as I did Rasch, the smith and caretaker, recently. A different class and equally disgusted. The phrase, which I have heard frequently now: "If only it happens quickly. That alone would be deliverance." Richter added: " 'They' will try to flee but not escape with their lives. But, is the mere fact of their death expiation enough for the millions of people who have died because of them?" I said he would have a better chance of surviving than we who wore the star. He: "A few percent for sure," but perhaps it will happen so quickly that they have no time to murder us. Just like Rasch recently, he thought a change must come "through the army."

[ . . . ]

### January 24, Sunday midday

[ . . . ]

Hirschel told me recently: Clemens and Weser came to him unexpectedly, looking for an apartment for an SA official. They behaved like animals; struck Frau Hirschel and himself without warning, took away a couple of boxes of matches and a couple of paper napkins as forbidden, scarce commodities. Clemens, the big blond fellow, who also hit me, said, "I hate you so much; rely on it, I'll finish you off." Hirschel, who often has to negotiate with him, responded: "Why do you hate me so much?" Clemens: "I can tell you exactly. Because you're a Jew. I'll kill you for sure." Hirschel also thought: Only quick change can save us. — It looks as if the decision must come soon now. The military bulletins are catastrophic for Germany. In Africa, in the Caucasus "we are disengaging from the enemy"; Stalingrad appears to be lost.

[ . . . ]

We had a long conversation with Eisenmann senior, who repaired a faulty electric cord for us. He believes the collapse of the Hitler regime to be imminent, gives Easter as the date, but believes Germany will go on fighting under a military dictatorship. He says a dismembered Germany, a repetition or even exaggeration of Versailles, would be the worst mistake its enemies could make, and would mean eternal war. — But how can its enemies trust an undismembered Germany again?

[ . . . ]

### January 27, Wednesday, toward evening

Yesterday afternoon at the Community met Feder, whom I had not seen for perhaps a year. (Broke with him because of the anti-Semitism of his narrow-minded wife.) "Have you heard about Natscheff?" — "Yes, they've closed down his lending library." — "And he's been inside since January 5. He's supposed to have made an incautious remark; he's been sentenced to twelve or eighteen months in prison." — I've just told Frau Eger, who came to listen as Eva was playing. She, enviously: As an Aryan and Bulgarian it won't be bad for him in prison, and he'll escape with his life—and the prisons will be opened immediately when the change comes; it'll be less than a year. "I wish it had been as easy as that for my husband!" . . . The people one can envy! . . . I too used to envy Natscheff because he could move freely. Apart from that, the man is part of Dresden's cultural history in these past years and so belongs in my Curriculum. Well-groomed, slightly graying, graceful fellow with large gray eyes;

small and quick and elegant. Graduate engineer of Dresden TU, on the committee of the Bulgarian Association here in the city, almost an official figure. Tacking before the National Socialists at association meetings and in formal speeches, very anti-Fascist in private conversation and an Anglophile. Married to an American. He had exchanged the profession of engineer for the lending library out of choice. He called it "rental library," was a little snobbish and so had an intellectual and also a considerable Jewish clientele. He had the latest French and English authors in the original—he himself spoke fluent English and French and supplied information about the books in accordance with the most modern criticism—in fact (it was his weakness and led me to Paulig's old-fashioned family business) he had only the most up-to-date literature. As soon as a book was no longer in demand here, he shuffled it off to his two (I think) branches in Czechoslovakia. The Third Reich robbed him of his best customers, banned his most popular books—he did not hate it out of completely altruistic love of freedom alone. He certainly long ago became suspect to the Party; he was no longer allowed to let me have anything (or at any rate no longer dared to) at a time when I was still unhesitatingly served at Paulig. (Where I likewise found modern literature, but also plentiful older and sometimes even old literature—only contemporary foreign authors were absent ... Until the Gestapo people thumped me on the head with Rosenberg. But we shall now strike up a relationship with Paulig again.) —

At the Community, people were in high spirits: The news from the front is truly catastrophic. (As again today.) It has been admitted that a whole army, the Sixth, together with Romanian and Croatian armies, have been lost at Stalingrad; we are falling back along the whole Eastern front; in Africa there is no Italian colony any more, only Tunis is holding out and is caught in a pincer movement. Admittedly the Jewish elation is mixed with great anxiety. We all fear a pogrom, and those in the barracks camp feel most threatened. "They've got us all in one place; we can be finished off with a couple of hand grenades." I hear that again and again.

On the way back went to Schulgutstrasse to see Steinitz and Magnus. Bad for me that they live next door to one another. Thanks to my influence they are once again reconciled as card players, but the jealous tension has of course remained, and I have to maneuver between the two. I cadged a couple of potatoes from Magnus ... Is it not characteristic that in our small Jewish circle here I have met the same type three times: For all three the First World War represents the biggest and best experience one they always hark back to—as an adventure and as a time of completely shared interests with the Germans; yet all three are proud—as of a Kantian fulfillment of duty!—of the fact that they have remained Jews. For Magnus the tie to the wider German world was expressed not only in the war and in the uniform but also very strongly and continuously in the social side of equestrianism. He is as proud of riding in tournaments and of his relationship with diverse aristocratic Amazons and gentlemen riders as the late lamented Katz was of his relationship with aristocratic officers. But the war experience—he had "so many horses" at his disposal in the Russian military hospital position!—is also the very best one Magnus ever had. He showed me an album with many wartime and equestrian photographs. — At Steinitz's there was literally a feast for me. I arrived chilled to the bone and with bad "angina" pains and got a cup of coffee with real sugar and a real buttered roll—a pleasure, which I have not had for a very long time. (That I leave sugar and butter to Eva is a very small appeasement of my conscience, given my excessive consumption of bread and potatoes. God knows with what we shall fill ourselves in the next few weeks, especially as we are both tormented by hunger from day to day . . .) Steinitz, who is quite possessed by Shaw—I gave him, as a present, the small copy of *Back to Methuselah*, which my English teacher sent to me from England shortly before the outbreak of war—said he could see nothing heroic in what the military bulletin—another obituary notice!—praised as the immense heroism of the Sixth Army; these people could, after all, do nothing else but what they were forced to do. He would call someone heroic who took a stand against Hitler or against the war . . . He gave me a copy of an emigrant's letter from among his circle of friends. Typical. Parents write here from Buenos Aires. They hint at their concern that [the son] could be evacuated. "We know what has been happening at home." They are sad still to have to accept assistance from friends. But "Daddy has been lucky and people envy him: He's already earning quite nicely as a cake seller in a restaurant. Mummy unfortunately is still looking for employment . . ." [ . . . ]

### January 28, Thursday morning

Ideas come to me very early in the morning, when I wake up. They are not very original, they are drawn from recent reading, but these morning thoughts are simply the best that my head comes up with at the moment. Yet my reading and I are often at cross-purposes. The book and I do not listen to each other with any understanding. Everything that is mystical or philosophical, I do not understand. But the trains of thought I do not understand stimulate thoughts of my own or ones that are half or a quarter my own. Thus at the moment I am absorbed with that fatal compilation *Juden in der deutschen Literatur* [Jews in German literature], also Armin Wegner. Lines of thought, which can be utilized in Curriculum IV or III or in *LTI:* I have thus far placed Taine above Gobineau because the determination of man by race, milieu, and time is more intellectual and allows more freedom than that by blood alone; but I have always mechanically repeated the received accusations, 1) that he neglects the particular, the *unique,* 2) that he uses "race" imprecisely. I now withdraw both accusations. a) The decisive modifying factor, the personal quality of an individual remains excluded or is a condition, just as for Boileau's *Art poétique,* innate genius is the self-evident condition. To the nation belongs whoever is average and not personality, or rather each person with all those parts of his being, which are average and lacking a personal stamp. b) Race is a relation, a flexible, elastic, onion concept. Race: the whole of mankind as opposed to flora and fauna; race: the nation, the tribe, the family as opposed to specific other groups. And even parts of the individual—atom splitting, irrecoverable self!—are detached as racial (also as time and milieu-bound elements!). There remains as core of the self, as personality proper, the faculté maîtresse.

Which is the Jewish faculté maîtresse? Originally probably the orientation to the purely spiritual, the abstractly spiritual. It expresses itself in monotheism as in mystical raptures, but its main line of development must lead to thinking, because going into raptures brings feeling, sensuality, materialization into play. Chamberlain, the Romantic, says the Jews are without religion, because they lack the imagination for polytheism, for the deification of nature; Buber, the Romantic, places the emphasis on Jewish mysticism, because it is dominated by rapturous materialization. — Out of the striving for the purely spiritual there emerge advantages and weaknesses, fanaticisms and tolerances, which the Jews share, more or less, with the civilized nations, because all culture consists in arriving at an intellectual domination of matter, of coming "to reason." In modern times, therefore, or in Europe (to which America belongs), the notion of an original faculté maîtresse no longer expresses anything absolutely distinctive.

The truly distinguishing characteristic and literally the faculté maîtresse of the modern Jew is his insecurity—enemies and the poetical say *the Wandering Jew*. Insecurity drives him into the segregation of the ghetto and of the Talmud, drives him into overemphasis of Germanness, Frenchness, etc., drives him into internationalism and political Zionism; drives him into certain professions (money making, cf. Sombart and a thousand others, empathetic literary and acting trades [ . . . ]). The moment he is given security, he will be a different man. Wegner's striking remark, that the colonists in Palestine were quite different people from the eastern ghetto dwellers, has to be expanded. It is not simply a matter of physical regeneration. Jews, without the pressure of anti-Semitism, or and above all without the fear of this pressure, will be different people in all their thinking and feeling—they will have ceased to be Jews, they will belong completely to the nations in the midst of which they live.

Belonging to a nation depends less on blood than on language. (In parenthesis: The *state* or the Reich [empire or realm] can consist of nations—should consist of them—ideal progression: Switzerland, Austrian Switzerland, Europe, League of Nations—consists everywhere of tribes, that is, of small or subordinate races). Language belongs both to the physical and the intellectual, but the intellectual factor is the more powerful (and human) one; the physical nestles against it. It is not being born into it that is decisive, but immersion as an infant, as "one who does not yet speak." Given the pliability of a child's organism, a black or a yellow child

growing up in purely German surroundings will speak just as pure German, or rather with as pure a Berlin or Munich accent, as one whose fore-
fathers are without exception from Berlin or Munich. But all the elements
of culture, which one absorbs consciously or unconsciously, are carried
along by the river of language. Music, painting, architecture provide individual aspects—language contains the totality of the intellectual. And the
totality of the intellectual cannot be separated from language. λογοσ
[Logos] is the word, and λογοσ [logos] is thinking, and thinking is the
willed deed. For God, speaking, thinking, doing are one: "In the beginning was the word" and: "I call thee by thine name." The magician, who
believes he has divine powers, conjures them through words. If I have
grown up in a language, then I am under its spell forever; I can in no way,
through no act of my will, withdraw from the nation whose spirit lives in
it, and no stranger's command can detach me from it. — [ . . . ] That is why
in Zion they are trying to introduce and enforce new Hebrew. But it can be
effective only for the coming generation. And it is of necessity new Hebrew, i.e., an artificial mixture of European and American elements with
ancient Jewish ones.

### January 30, Saturday late afternoon

[ . . . ]

For me, today, the anniversary of the "seizure of power" was wholly a
potato day. The weather is mild, and there are again whole hundred-
weights; we can have another three hundredweight until the end of July
(till the end of July!), and with a lot of effort I got two hundredweight here.
Two journeys with the handcart from the stall at the beginning of Emser
Allee. The sack was not tied; after two steps the potatoes rolled onto the
ground. I picked them up and knotted the sack with my handkerchief. Another two steps and the potatoes rolled out again. I bent down in despair,
and my scarf fluttered to the ground. Signum coeli! I tied up the sack of
potatoes with the scarf. For the second trip, in the afternoon, Eva armed
me with string. I got home more easily with that, but I had bad heart trouble [ . . . ]. Eva for her part had come back from town very depressed: For
some days there has been nothing to buy, food is getting ever more problematic. In addition Eva is greatly tormented by her dental prosthesis. We
call the wobbly thing "the rocking horse" [ . . . ].

I borrowed the handcart at the Jewish cemetery from the custodian, Jacobi; he is very well disposed to me, ever since I described his oraison
funèbre for the murdered Arndt as "very dignified." He gives me a little
tobacco and makes refined conversation, when I visit his apartment at the
cemetery. He told me there will be seven funerals next Wednesday, of
which six have to be kept secret. The bodies of Jews from the Protectorate,
who were condemned to death. They were brought to Dresden for execution. In the county court building on Münchner Platz, there is an electrically powered guillotine, a head every two minutes; not just Jewish ones;

the main killing time is 6:00 P.M., often as many as twenty-five heads fall one after the other. I unhesitatingly assume that "often" and the number are exaggerations, but even if only half of it is true . . . Jacobi also maintains that a kind of state of siege has been declared and announced on the radio, and sentence of death by shooting has been placed on every act of insubordination and every act of sabotage of the new labor law. — Strange, and to me inexplicable, how the government's measures combine public intimidating terror with secret brutality. Jew-baiting knows no bounds—but the worst measures against them are concealed from the Aryans. Even people who are close to the Jews are not aware of the petty bullying or the brutal murders. Annemarie does not know that we are not allowed to sell any furniture, that everything has been confiscated—she wanted to buy a bookcase from us. The mayor in Dölzschen did not know that I am restricted to the city limits and am forbidden to use public transport. Recently Frau Eger said: "The most terrible thing for me is that people always say: 'But your husband *must* have done something; they don't just kill someone for no reason!' " (I know something even more terrible, that in such a case even Jews say: "He must surely have done something, covered the star or been on the street after eight.") [ . . . ] The same inner submission.

[ . . . ]

### February 5, Friday afternoon

Long, friendly, and clueless chatty letter from Stockholm. Again and again the question about my "daily routine." As if I were allowed to report on the daily routine of someone who wears the star. The question: "When do you go for a walk?" sounds like mockery. Lately Jews have been stopped on the street, their shopping bags inspected. — Lotte Sussmann has become an ardent Catholic. Going to early mass!

At the Jewish cemetery yesterday—I am now almost at home there—to fetch the two-burner gas hot plate borrowed from the "Community." Reichenbach had sent it that far for me from the "furniture store" [ . . . ]. Chatted to the three "volunteer workers"; they were putting compost on the vegetable beds behind the rows of graves. The never-ending guessing game: How much longer? Defeat or debacle? Will we survive? — Lately Jacobi, the custodian, has received me very warmly in his apartment, next to the dead house. He always has a little tobacco or a cigarillo for me. Yesterday I burst in on his family's midday meal for the second time. As he opened the door, Jacobi whispered to me: "Not a word today. My youngest sister-in-law is here. She can't help it; her father is dead, her mother weak. Influence of her surroundings, her own mother is afraid of her: She is a BDM leader." — A pale, shy girl of perhaps fifteen or sixteen, undernourished, very big, stupid pale eyes; she timidly gave me her hand; she ate with lowered head; her National Socialism was compatible with the Jewish cemetery, the Jewish brother-in-law, the Jewish meal.

Yesterday evening a small political disagreement with Herbert Eisenmann: The boy said a dismemberment of Germany would lead to new wars and "all the Jews in Germany would be shot down." I told him very forcefully that Germany must start from the beginning, in modest circumstances, and with the ABC of morality, without the power to cause harm. Beyond that, what happened to the Jews was not so very important. With respect to this conversation, Frau Eisenmann remarked this morning that the boy was probably influenced by her husband, who, as a Bohemian Jew, had experienced the injustices inflicted on the Germans of Bohemia by the Czechs as injustices that also affected him. (Thus a similar attitude as Sebi Sebba in Danzig had to the Poles!) What madness it was and is for the National Socialists to force the Jews out of their German patriotism. The only comparison is the Spanish expulsion of the Jews. [ . . . ]

### Evening

Eva has come from Simon with good news. The débâcle in Russia is said to be a real and decisive one; England is said to be putting out peace feelers; in the Simon household they are hoping for a rapid end. It would mean inexpressible happiness, ten thousand times greater than in 1918—but I cannot believe it. There is too much against it. What kind of peace should it be, with whom should it be concluded? Still, the mere hope of peace is rousing. And since Simon also swears that Eva will become accustomed to the rocking horse, our mood is better for the moment. For how long? — [ . . . ]

### February 6, Saturday afternoon

At the beginning of the war Natscheff told me: "Hitler's high point and real triumph was Munich. *He walked on air*, is how the English put it." [ . . . ] We are expecting the Hirschels for coffee (and Lewinsky—laborious preparation and pitiful hospitality; coupons in very short supply!) [ . . . ]

### February 7, Sunday evening

[ . . . ] On the whole we did not talk politics much yesterday, if only because Lewinsky is completely apolitical. We talked a lot about Jewish things. Frau Hirschel emphasized that they were *liberal*, they were equally opposed to Orthodoxy and to Reform Judaism, which was no Judaism at all anymore. She said she saw no conflict between being German and being Jewish. I: Insofar as one was Jewish and religious, I could understand that. But if a relation to dogmatic Judaism, to Yahweh, was just as absent as one to Christian dogma, to the risen Christ, then the *free* Protestant outlook, the Christianity without dogma of Lessing was the only thing for me. (I was no longer quite able to believe what I was saying.) —
[ . . . ]

### February 11, Thursday morning

*LTI.* [ . . . ] Stalingrad report (*Frankfurter Zeitung*, February 5, 1943): "On January 9 as the enemy made yet another attempt to start negotiations, speaking choruses at the very front of the German lines replied they did not want negotiations, they wanted victory." The speaking chorus is a propaganda tool of the Nazi struggle for power in Germany, the speaking chorus is extreme theatricality. It denotes most clearly the Nazi element in the language of the army. — I also regard abuse of the enemy as a Nazi element. Again and again Russian *hordes*. [ . . . ]

### February 12, Friday evening

[ . . . ]

Herbert Eisenmann reported: The day before yesterday a certain Heilbutt, an utterly decent man, had been arrested at Zeiss-Ikon during work. Reason unknown; he had been a Social Democratic editor before '33—but before '33 and nothing against him since. Herbert Eisenmann said: "They seem to get a bounty for every Jew now."

### February 14, Sunday midday

I must single out yesterday, the second Saturday of February 1943, as especially important. It brought the first sign, and almost certainty, that the revolution I had believed impossible is brewing inside Germany. I was at Richter's, nominally because of the tax declaration; in fact, because I wanted to hear what Richter had to say about the mood and the situation, the "Aryan view," as it were. He opened the door to me himself; we talked for more than an hour (from about twelve till after one) in his private office, he was even more friendly, urgent in his friendliness than at previous meetings. How could he help me—I should tell him everything. He pressed me to take razor blades—new, improbably thin ones, a blessing!—he telephoned his wife, how large was her surplus of potatoes, we agreed to meet again next Saturday, when I shall get from him money, potatoes, bread coupons, probably also "the dirty book, which made him a millionaire and which they let him write in prison; I've seen the 'cell,' a room as large and as comfortably furnished as this one and a garden with it, in which to go walking, and that for high treason!—democracy was too weak, that was its mistake, which must not be repeated . . ."—so I shall probably also get Hitler's *Mein Kampf* from him. But much more important than all of this was something else. Richter came back to it again and again: "Where will you go if disturbances break out? You must *remove* yourself immediately to the country . . . there could be massacres here." I told him that was impossible for me to leave Dresden. Then I must go into hiding here. He could provide an empty room, an emergency place. I asked him bluntly what he was expecting. In the course of the next twelve months—by which he did

not mean to say in only twelve months—there would definitely be a revolution. "From the right?" — "No, from the left." — But the bourgeoisie is
afraid of Communism! — "From the old Social Democrats," he knew it for
certain. — But something could be achieved only through the army. — Certainly, but it was coming, only he could not say more. And if it didn't come
quickly, then of course the Jews were in great danger; I absolutely had to
"remove" myself; I could come to his office, he would find an empty room
for me somewhere. He could not help everyone, he had obligations to his
family; if need be he would have to disavow me—in between there was a
telephone call with someone, whom he addressed a dozen times as "Comrade Captain" and greeted with "Heil Hitler"—but after all he had got to
know me over the months, and he would so much like to help me . . . I said
in my state of isolation I could not find out anything; at some point I would
be attacked and my throat cut. "Of course that may be your fate—but perhaps you will find out in time that something is imminent, and then you
must remove yourself, and then I shall certainly find a room for you."
[ . . . ] That was repeated again and again as our conversation went back
and forth over tax declaration, our needs, military situation, etc., etc. — Before the war, during the early years of the 3rd Reich, I sometimes heard,
from the butter seller, from the greengrocer, from one person or another:
"Next spring the Stahlhelm, or the Communists, or the army will . . ." At
that time the whole world was still playing with such dreams of an overthrow of the regime. The word was always: "next spring . . ." And the National Socialists consolidated their position ever more firmly, destroyed
opposing groups ever more thoroughly. Thus the idea of their invincibility
establishes itself ever more deeply inside one. Only a military dictatorship,
it was said, could remedy matters. Then there was not a word about military dictatorship either. The army command *must* put up with the Party as
long as the war lasts. — And now this very definite statement by a very
calm, circumspect man, who is at the center of "Aryan" life and has considerable contact—officially!—with the Party. (Curious, left the Party at
Easter '33 and is nevertheless appointed as trustee of Jewish houses!) The
man's whole behavior yesterday made it obvious to me that he knew *more*
than just a rumor, that something *must* be under way involving the moderate working class, the bourgeoisie, and the army. — He in turn was struck
by what I said about the future role of the Zentrum. [ . . . ] On the military
situation: He believes, on the one hand, that there will be a German summer offensive—(on the eleventh or twelfth the *Dresdener NN* had a disagreeable editorial, in which they referred to the winter of 1917; then, too,
"the front had been shortened," and yet there had been a powerful German
offensive in 1918!)—on the other hand, he told me that the civilian population had already been evacuated from Riga. — I said that recently I had
often been harassed by children on the street. He: His oldest, eleven, was
now with the "Jungvolk"; while they were marching, they would suddenly
be ordered "Eyes right." And then: "There you saw a Jew; do you know
what you need to remember about the Jew?" Whereupon the appropriate

instruction followed . . . I mentioned the six executed Jews from the Protectorate whose corpses had recently been handed over to the Jewish cemetery. He: An acquaintance had been transferred to the county court at Münchner Platz and had the job of seizing the valuables of those condemned to death; Richter knows from this man [ . . . ] how busy the guillotine here is: Recently 21 (twenty-one) heads had fallen on *one* day, by no means only Jewish ones. —

[ . . . ]

Eva must take the diary to Annemarie again soon. The guillotine at Münchner Platz goes to work for less cause. —

[ . . . ]

### February 18, Thursday late afternoon

Downstairs for hours: made coffee, cleared up, helped with the big washing. Now Eva, worn out, is in town on a desperate attempt to shop. If tiredness permits I can work up here from six until seven. After that, red cabbage has to be chopped: The history of the red cabbage has to be added. We live almost exclusively from our shrinking store of potatoes; vegetables not classified as "scarce commodity" are hardly to be found. So, yesterday in a shop in Gerokstrasse, the shopkeeper, woman in her forties, is already known to me as accommodating. In the shop a couple of women customers, one of them a gray-haired woman of the people, perhaps the mother of a married tram conductor. She is very fond of her big brown boxer dog, relates how he flees to granny, when he should get a thrashing, and she strokes him, etc. I probably win her heart when I say a few friendly words about boxers in general. The shopkeeper, when it's my turn: "Sauerkraut, I'm afraid, only with a customer card; matches—no, salt—no." To win favor I began with a turnip—no one likes them; the turnip winter of 1917 is still on everyone's mind. In any case, I am doing her an injustice. The woman compassionate, hesitant: I could have a red cabbage, however. Weighs it, puts it beside the turnip, also fetches a bag of salt (extremely obliging!). "75 pfennigs." As I am pulling out my wallet, the granny beside me says: "Put it away—I'll pay it for you." I felt hot all over. I thanked her and handed the mark note over the counter. She: "But let me pay." I: "It is really very kind of you, I am very grateful—but it's not the money, it's the card." Now the shopkeeper: "Come back toward evening, I'll give you more. During the day—I supply the SA here, I have to be careful." — I said: I am allowed to shop only between three and four. — She: She was not so very bothered about that. I: "You are not—but if someone else sees me and reports me, it will cost me my life." The shopkeeper: "Then drop by during your time—I'll make a sign if the coast is clear." I went out almost shocked. Later I was afraid, because I had said, in the presence of the customers, it would cost my life, if . . . etc. Atrocity stories! Enough for concentration camp and attempted escape.

[ . . . ]

**February 20, Saturday afternoon**

[ ... ]

Yesterday Eva was Frau Ahrens's guest, was fed cake, even brought cake and a very heavy bag of potatoes home, but unfortunately also the woman's opinion that there will certainly be a German summer offensive, and collapse will not occur until autumn. — My spirits were raised again only by Richter, whom I visited this morning as arranged—very exhausting, especially hauling things home. Result: Thirty pounds of potatoes, of which I took half away with me this time, four pounds' worth of bread coupons, a little packet of tobacco, resolution of our money shortage—I transfer to him the 360M (in installments of 50M) to which he is entitled for liquidating the 12,000M mortgage, and which I am allowed to transfer over and above the allowance, and which he will only nominally claim. Above all, however, Richter talked about the anticipated disturbances again and in greater detail this time. They could definitely be expected to begin in Berlin and on the coast. Whether sooner or later, he could not say. If I received a postcard from him: "Call me about your property," then I should get in contact with him immediately. He set forth a plan to save us, which was already well advanced. I mentioned the arrests of people on the Left. He had also heard of them. But the offensive could not be held up anyway. I said, *without* army units nothing could be achieved. He: Of course not, but there would be no shortage of army units. And he impressed the address on me once again. — I feel as if I were in a wild adventure and revolution film. But when I think of Goebbels's speech of February 18 in the Berlin Sportpalast, then I take Richter's opinion and warning completely seriously. Richter gave me the *Dresdener Anzeiger* of the nineteenth with the text of the speech, and I want to pick it over immediately for the *LTI*. They were already very depressed about it at the cemetery yesterday, because the speech contains a threat to proceed against the Jews, who are guilty of everything, with the "most draconian and radical measures" if the foreign powers do not stop threatening the Hitler government because of the Jews. Moreover, the government also threatens and terrorizes the "comrades of the people." "Total war—the shortest war" was the legend "of the only banner at the front of the hall," and whoever resists the necessity of *"total war"* will lose his head, declared Goebbels. (Closure of luxury hotels and bars, ban on riding in the Tiergarten, universal labor service, heavier burdens placed on civil servants, no right to holiday.) [ ... ]

**February 24, Wednesday morning**

This afternoon Eva intends to go to Pirna, to take manuscripts, the recently forgotten ones and the new ones, to safety—I wish she were already back. — She need not borrow money: Today I transferred "360M brokerage for conversion of mortgage" to Richter. "Outside allowance limit."

Why did the man *not* demand the money from me before? Sympathy from the beginning? — Everyone is afraid of everyone else now. Richter has a friendly young secretary. The other day, when he let me leave the potatoes in a side room: "Please leave directly by the corridor; the young woman in the office is very reliable—but she does not need to know everything." — The guillotine at Münchner Platz [ . . . ] threatens me; it also threatens Richter. Is what he hints at true? [ . . . ] The Eastern Front is falling back, but there has been no breakthrough; in Italy all is calm, and in Tunisia there have even been successes announced. And yesterday was an exhaustingly warm spring day, and a thaw has already been mentioned once in the military bulletins of recent days. But if there is one, then the Russian offensive will come to a halt, and the German army will have time to lick its wounds and prepare a summer offensive. — On the other hand: How will they continue, if the hope of grain from the Ukraine is gone? [ . . . ] Eva has tried, so far in vain, to find out the exact location of the Pötzschen-Wahla address. A detached house by the railway station, said Richter, I could reach it on foot. (Some twelve and a half miles from here.) A long walk, one on which there is the risk of death—but I would certainly face the same risk with a vengeance if I stayed here. [ . . . ] A hat manufacturer, a democrat, has lost his seventeen-year-old only son in the field, knows Inspector Clemens personally. That was the reason I was given for his willingness to help . . . The thought of the guillotine haunts me. —

Lewinsky was here for a few minutes, very weary and depressed; brought me the *Frankfurter Zeitung*.

[ . . . ]


## February 27, Saturday afternoon

[ . . . ]

I had three reasons for considerable pessimism. 1) The proclamation, which was read on Hitler's behalf at some Party anniversary in Munich [ . . . ] two or three days ago. I learned of it on the evening of the day before yesterday, when I visited Steinitz and met Katz there. No one had actually read it, but it was said that it threatened the murder of all Jews even more nakedly than the last speech by Goebbels. Then the next day Eva, who had read it at lunchtime, told me that it was bad, but not really any worse than what Hitler had already said a dozen times on the subject of the "Jew." 2) The shock this morning was more severe: A week ago Caroli Stern-Hirschberg wrote us an innocuous and fairly calm letter—I probably noted at the time, that a couple of months ago she was successfully recalled by her company, at the last moment, from an evacuation group—I replied to her on the twenty-fifth, and the card came back today. Blue stamp on it "returned," note in pencil "emigrated." Note on *LTI*: "Emigrated" for *been* emigrated. Innocuous word for "robbery," "expulsion," "sent to one's death." Now, of all times, one can no longer assume that any Jews will return from Poland alive. They will be killed before the retreat.

Besides, people have long been saying, that many of the evacuees don't even arrive in Poland alive. They were being gassed in cattle trucks during the journey, and the truck then stopped on the line by an already-dug mass grave. I am very bad, I have less pity for Caroli than fear of a similar fate. Eva was also very shaken. 3) But the hardest blow came as I was on my way to Richter. Curious that it did not affect my blunted mind, I felt it only as heart trouble and as a dull burden. I had had the intention of going to the Community, either on the way there or the way back, as I had done last week. It grew too late to do so on the way there. As I passed the Community toward eleven, Lewinsky rushed up to me, pale and agitated. "We are all being ordered to appear and immediately detained—the privileged people as well—I have only permission to inform my wife—messengers from the Community are on their way to everyone—certainly to you as well—don't go in—you will be detained immediately . . ." I: What was it about? — That was uncertain; perhaps the camp inmates were being deported to Poland, and *we* would now be transported to the camp . . . I said: "You haven't seen me, I know nothing, I have to take care of an errand now, and if I find the order at home in the afternoon, I still have time to present myself." All the time I kept thinking: Perhaps he is exaggerating, but if it isn't the camp or Theresienstadt, it will be "labor duty" and with it the end of any possibility of studying. — I talked to Richter about the threatened new sanctions. He: He believed the mixed marriages were still safe. Clemens (his tenant) had recently been expressing his hatred of the Jews to him and had remarked: "If only we could get at the mixed marriages!" I: "They don't know anything either. They get their orders from Berlin." — I got back at one very preoccupied. In the garden I met Eisenmann père, who since dismissal from Zeiss-Ikon is still unemployed: No messenger had been here, and Lewinsky was always overexcited. Probably, almost certainly, it will have been a matter of urgent labor duty (such as is often demanded on Saturday afternoons and Sundays, e.g., unloading goods), and the Community had drummed up whoever could be reached most quickly, and held onto everyone within reach. — It is now seven o'clock in the evening; I appear to have been spared. (I am always exceptionally friendly to young Kahlenberg, who gives out the work; I have learned a lesson—had I cultivated the late Estreicher as devotedly, I would still have my typewriter.) —

The day before yesterday, the widowed Frau Eger moved out of here and to her parents'. The only Jews living in the big house now are ourselves on the upper floor and the Eisenmanns downstairs. We have seen the house gradually spew out its people, its pictures, its furniture. How long shall we be left in peace here? Because there really is a certain peace here. On the third of March we shall have been here for six months. In all this time no house search, not even a police check. Only the fear of it every day.

[ . . . ]

## February 28, Sunday morning

Letter in pencil from Lewinsky [ . . . ]. I should not worry, the current action did *not* concern the mixed marriages. Jews from elsewhere had been brought to the camp, and the camp completely sealed off; evacuation was imminent. I went down to the Eisenmanns, Eisenmann senior was still in bed; it was about eleven o'clock. Herbert Eisenmann told me: The isolation of the camp has been in force since yesterday morning. All those not in mixed marriages, who until now lived outside the camp [ . . . ] literally all are in the camp since yesterday. Only Hirschel and Kahlenberg have been left at liberty, to wind things up. All the rest will be evacuated. — We shall not see any of them again. Frau Voss, the Seliksohns, Reichenbachs, Frau Ziegler—I count them all among the dead. How long will they let us live here? And how shall we live? — Eva has just left to go to the Simons'. They usually know something there via wife and Kötzschenbroda, and a fraction of it could be true. At any rate one finds out there what the mood is. — I intend to force myself to work until the last moment. Recently in a restaurant Eva heard a woman say that her son had sent a card from the Eastern Front; on it was only, "I'm still alive, I'm still alive, I'm still alive!" That is also how far my feelings go; depending on my mood, and changing from hour to hour, the emphasis is now on "alive," now on "still."
  [ . . . ]


## March 2, Tuesday afternoon

[ . . . ] I read aloud in the evening, and for longer and with greater receptiveness in the very early morning [ . . . ]. And yet the dreadful event and the terrible personal danger is always weighing on us. The transport leaves tomorrow, the Jewish camp together with the addition of others from Halle and Erfurt. It cannot be assumed that we shall see a single one of these masses again. Left behind are only those protected by mixed marriage. Protected for how long? Odysseus in Polyphemus's cave: "You will I eat last." Except that none of us can play Odysseus. Help must come from outside. One clings to any hope. The Russian offensive has slowed down, at the very least; the winter, which was never severe, appears to be finally over; mud and thawing snow give the army a rest from fighting. — Ribbentrop was with the Duce. New hope—perhaps Italy really is ready to defect. — Eva is in town a lot, shopping, making inquiries. She heard from Simon that there is something brewing in the army. That alone would be deliverance. But all these hopes last only for minutes at a time. — Eva also brought news from the Community. Hirschel is almost the only one working there. They are leaving him here for the time being, and this for the time being seems to encourage him in a cheerful mood of "Hurrah, I'm still alive!" Lewinsky, at first satisfied with his post there as an assistant, has already reported back to the factory. It was too dreadful.

He had to help unload the transport of Jews from Erfurt. A blind eighty-year-old man was carried over to a car waiting at the Gestapo building. A couple of old women clung to the compartment and had to be pulled out by force. A Gestapo man snapped at Lewinsky, why was he not wearing the star. — "I am privileged." — The man spat in his face. — Eva had at last got back a pair of rubber gloves that she gave away to be repaired for Frau Voss a long time ago—the repair was carried out after *months* had passed—[ . . . ]—and wanted to get them to Kätchen Sara. Meanwhile a new order has been issued: Anyone who passes something on to Jews awaiting evacuation will be "shot by the police." Frau Glaser reported this to me in despair; she still had something she had wanted to give her friend Frau Reichenbach. After she had gone to the Community yesterday, Eva also visited the Glasers and Simon. The same mood everywhere: desperation and bitterness, fear for one's own life, flickering hope and—above all—"I'm still alive, I'm still alive, I'm still alive!" (With the emphasis changing). — [ . . . ]

### March 4, Thursday evening

Need to talk to people about the desperate situation. At the cemetery yesterday. These three: Magnus, Steinitz, Schein at their usual tragicomic game of skat in the gardeners' shed behind the graves. Very depressed; they assume separation of mixed marriages is imminent. I.e., either the wife divorces her husband, or is declared Jewish and is evacuated with him. All three share the same point of view, which is ours also: The women stay here and save what can be saved. [ . . . ] It was doubted whether those evacuated the day before yesterday were still alive; more likely that they had been gassed in their cattle trucks—two pails as latrines in each truck. — I inquired about Jacobi. He had been suffering from inflammation of the middle ear for some time; there was no place for a Jew in the hospitals here; he was supposed to travel to Berlin and be operated on in the Jewish Hospital there. Yesterday I learned, that at the last moment the Gestapo had refused him permission to travel; instead he was operated on in the Friedrichstädter Hospital and taken home in an ambulance immediately after the operation. He is said to be doing well. I merely sent greetings and shall visit him on Saturday morning. — At the Community today, fetched food-ration cards and talked to Hirschel. He is almost isolated there now. He and Kahlenberg (with mother) are left here as almost the only Jews not protected by mixed marriages. Exact figures: 290 Jews were evacuated; there are now altogether 300 Jews still in Dresden, of whom 130 wear the star. Hirschel, too, was in a somber mood. He had just been informed by the Gestapo that his house had been "bought," that he must leave it within ten days. He gets rooms in the Community house. Only a small portion of his furniture will fit in there; he is not allowed to rent storage space. He will try to stow away as much as he can in the cellars of the Community house. — The next dangers, which hang over us are a) the crowding together of the mixed marriages in the proletarian (and probably bug-ridden) tenement in Sporergasse, in which months ago I once called on the meanwhile suicided Jewish cobbler; b) labor service for me, ten hours of daily tedium engaged in the most mechanical employment. A further, ever more urgent worry is food. We are ever more exclusively dependent on potatoes and even with everything we have managed to beg and haul up here, we shall not get past April 1. But who knows what will have become of us by April 1? The good thing about the excess of worries is that one becomes astonishingly indifferent to all except the immediately urgent ones. —

With reference to food, I long ago wanted to report [the following]. Richter, this modest, almost petit bourgeois, certainly not wealthy man, father of three children, told me recently: "Do you know what a pound of coffee costs now on the black market? 200M. I cannot manage without coffee, I'm a night worker; I bought two pounds today." From which can be concluded, that as far as money goes, things are the same for Aryans as in the last war: They no longer believe in its postwar value, they have it at the moment, are turning it into foodstuffs and are ready to pay any black-market price. And everything is traded on the black market—despite the guillotine.

[ . . . ]

### March 6, Saturday morning

The extreme depression of Jewry (myself included) continues. Yesterday, as I was scrubbing the kitchen, Glaser was suddenly standing in front of me. Had Reichenbach still received his spectacles via Glaser-Eva. Yes—through Hirschel. Unfortunately I had also meanwhile heard that Reichenbach had been badly beaten as he was being put in the cattle truck . . . Glaser, very *down*, asked me whether I believed that one died more easily in the company of many fellow sufferers than alone. I was very skeptical about that. — In the evening at Steinitz-Magnus, where I fetched something to read aloud, the same depression. — Dropped off to sleep again just now (one can see it in the previous sentence). I now want to pay the invalid Jacobi a visit; perhaps I shall be fresher in the afternoon. Admittedly I began the day at six with a good wash and went to bed after midnight yesterday. Eva fell asleep during the first few lines, even though I had brought something very interesting [ . . . ].

### Afternoon

[ . . . ]

I spent only a few minutes with Jacobi; he is still in bed, very much the worse for wear and very bandaged. It seems that only his wife's determination saved his life. He *had* to be operated on, it was high time. The Gestapo refused to let him travel to Berlin. Here he was told: There is no

single room available, and a Jew is not allowed to lie in a general ward—so the operation is refused. Then Frau Jacobi, the Aryan, insisted on seeing the head surgeon of the Friedrichstädter Hospital and said angrily to him: So you're going to let my husband die, because he's a Jew. That must have roused the surgeon's conscience; he himself argued with the Gestapo on the phone. Result: The operation was permitted, but Jacobi had to be sent home in an ambulance immediately afterward. The doctors and nurses were very friendly to him; before the operation he was told: difficult, and this is the last, the very last possible moment. Immediately after the skull had been trephined, he was put in the ambulance, a rattling old thing, in which the stretcher was not on springs—it was already considered a favor that motor transport was permitted at all. Jacobi is out of danger now; Dr. Katz is responsible for aftercare. "Today a Jew must not fall ill," Jacobi told me. [ . . . ] As already mentioned, he talked about the doctors and nurses with considerable gratitude. Except that the omnipotent Gestapo weighs on everyone.
[ . . . ]

### March 10, Wednesday morning

For all the variations, grinding stagnation and monotony. Continuing battles in the East, withdrawals in one place, successful counteroffensives in another, continuing calm in the West, continuing talk of increasing internal tension, continuing calm and terror—the calm of the population, the terror of the regime. Continuing extreme optimism and extreme pessimism among the Jews. I see the few people with whom we still have contact very frequently—on Sunday afternoon Steinitz and our Lewinsky were here, in the evening Eisenmann senior sat down with us in the kitchen—every forty-eight hours or so I pull myself together and go to the cemetery or to Steinitz's rooms or to the Community and on the way attempt to buy some cabbage—usually in vain.

Eisenmann senior is an optimist, thinks the collapse will come as early as Easter; Eisenmann junior is utterly depressed since he witnessed the deportation. Among those evacuated, says his father, was a girl who was his first love. [ . . . ]

### March 14, Sunday morning

[ . . . ]

My usual errands, which tire me out more and more. Once I got as far as Neumark's apartment near the Kreuzkirche. Today in quest of books on political economy [ . . . ]. No luck. After that to the Community. There was talk of the beating that Reichenbach got during the deportation. Via Glaser, Eva, Hirschel, the shortsighted man's repaired spectacles had been passed to him at the last moment. After that he probably roused the anger of a Gestapo man by carrying his trunk too slowly. Hirschel: "Here are the spectacles, I picked them up later; they knocked them off and stamped on them." One earpiece was missing, one lens was smashed. — At the cemetery Steinitz pointed out a woman to me. She came here every day, decorated an urn grave with fresh flowers and printed texts. A Frau Bein, an Aryan. Her Jewish husband and her son, who had been declared to be a "Jewish mischling," were arrested for unknown reasons and shot a couple of weeks later "attempting to escape." — [ . . . ]

### March 15, Monday evening

Although the nights are frosty, spring is here with snowdrops and first leaves, and at sunset I went for a little walk up the Elbe opposite the three castles. When shall I ever be able to go walking with Eva again? I have not dared go for a walk with her for a long time.

The German lines in Russia appear to be consolidating again; Kharkov has been recaptured; now things can go on for another summer. Meanwhile my energies are diminishing all the time; today I slept for hours at my desk again. Admittedly I find the Buber book particularly objectionable.

A very long letter from Arne Egebring with the brown and blue zebra stripes of the censors. Medical advice. In an earlier letter he had written, my symptoms did not seem to suggest real angina; now he thinks I was describing the usual symptoms exactly, and advises this and that, to prevent it getting worse. It is something of a shock; after all it means certain death in the very foreseeable future. [ . . . ] I find it difficult to continue working as if I still had the time to finish something. But working is the best way to forget. Except that I repeatedly fall asleep with exhaustion. And that I give out so completely in the face of so many styles and subjects. — Sussmann then goes on to write at length but obscurely about himself. There appears to be some kind of quarrel with his son-in-law; Sussmann appears to be living quite by himself on the tiny remnants of his wealth—I do not even know if in his daughter's house. He has to economize greatly, he looks after himself, cooks (spirit burner), washes up, patches, darns, sews. Apart from that "his grandson Bertil spends hours with him, and he makes toys for him and takes him for walks." The boy is between three and four, and so will not yet be able to cross the street alone. Perhaps Sussmann has a room in the same house? The situation is quite unclear. In the last letter Sussmann still wrote about a Christmas celebration together with a big dinner. And now: he has been cooking for himself "for over a year" . . .

### March 17, Wednesday evening

Provisionally concluded the Buber notes with a profound feeling of incomprehension. — Very depressed since the reconquest of Kharkov and the certainty of my angina. "Paper soldiers" stand at the beginning and at the end of my life. The 18ième, the Curriculum, the *LTI*—they will always remain *paper soldiers* and disappear just like the real paper soldiers of my childhood.

[ . . . ]

### March 20, Saturday afternoon

Eva is suffering considerably—her foot is failing her once more, and the nervous inflammation in her arm is appearing again; I am not feeling very well—exhaustion at home and angina complaints while walking; the German counteroffensive in southern Russia is making progress, the débâcle of the autumn appears to have been overcome, and all hopes of a breakdown in spring, the spring that begins tomorrow, have been disappointed. So I and we escape into *Buddenbrooks*, and I read aloud a great deal during the day. That I only now really appreciate the brilliance of the work! That I did not get to know it soon after its publication, but only after the World War, when my horizons were most limited by my discipline. Very curious. —

*LTI.* The language of boxing is indispensable to Goebbels. In the *Reich* of March 14 [ . . . ] an optimistic note is already being struck again, in fact Goebbels defends himself; the previous issues had not cultivated any "calculated pessimism" [ . . . ], things really had been going very badly for us, and now the utmost effort was required, if another relapse was to be avoided. In this context there is the boxing sentence: "In the deciding round one must still dispose of enough strength that one can easily take an opponent's every blow and reply with a harder blow." [ . . . ]

### March 23, Tuesday toward evening

[ . . . ]

Despite Eva lying down we had a lot of visitors on Sunday. People sat by her bed. First Glaser turned up unexpectedly around midday, then, expected and unrelenting, for the afternoon, Lewinsky, and finally after dinner, the Eisenmann couple. [ . . . ]

Glaser brought me an article from the *Frankfurter Zeitung* [ . . . ]; he collects words for me, but mechanically, superficially, without bothering about their inner meaning. Lewinsky also donated copies of the *Frankfurter* again.

Hitler spoke on Sunday (the twenty-first)—it is supposed to have been the usual extermination and victory stuff—and afterward he inspected something or other. So he let himself be heard and even seen and thus contradicted the rumors of his illness and even of his death. On the other hand optimism judges: His speech for "Heroes Remembrance Day" was postponed from the fourteenth to the twenty-first of March and lasted only twenty minutes and not the usual two hours; so he must have been ill and still be sickly. He himself is said to have given a reason for the post-ponement: He had waited until the front stabilized. —

### March 29, Monday midday

[ ... ]

I continue to be very exhausted—heart trouble, constant tiredness—and very depressed. I share the depression with the whole of Jewry. Also with Richter, from whom I fetched money and bread coupons on Satur-day. He said this about the situation: He saw the position more gloomily than the last time. If Germany were to capitulate unconditionally today, it would save ninety percent of its fabric. Instead it was continuing to bleed to death, and every day meant worse peace conditions. Because defeat was absolutely certain. But it was equally certain, that there would first be another summer offensive in the East, which would then raise morale and keep it going through the next winter. He, Richter, was dismayed at the apathetic patience and stupidity of the people. It had accepted the ex-traordinary brutalities of "total mobilization" without a murmur, it ac-cepts the tremendous losses at the front, the unceasing work of the "gulyotine"—Richter is in other respects a not uneducated man, but no one does French anymore—it accepts everything and allows itself to be butchered. There were large numbers of discontented, also local organiza-tions—but he simply did not know whether there was an umbrella orga-nization. [ ... ]

The things one can be envious of! Frau Eisenmann, worn-out by work, said to me: "Frau Eger has got it easy. She has been granted a stay of sev-eral weeks in a sanatorium." They killed Frau Eger's husband, kept her in prison for three weeks, and now "she's got it easy."

Today's correspondence. Gertrud Schmidt writes to Eva, she should visit her with her big shopping bag, so that Gertrud can relieve her of the cutting. That means: Frau Ahrens is letting us know that there are potatoes ready for us.

[ ... ]

### April 5, Monday morning

[ ... ] Yesterday "Wehrmacht Day." There was constant banging at the rifle range near here. "Storming a Russian village," for an entrance fee until 2:50 P.M. Is that not shameful, while there is real storming and dying going on? Eva says that in town the posters of this Russian village alternated with pictures of the animal acts of the Sarrasani Circus that is playing here at the moment. Other units tempted the public with the offer of unrationed sausage. These aspects of the army day also belong to the LTI. —

[ ... ]

On Saturday Lewinsky was here and read [ ... ] to us, also brought the

*Frankfurter Zeitung* and a little volume by Johst. On Sunday di nuovo Lewinsky and Steinitz.

I am so cautious that I put away every sheet of paper, even if I am only interrupting my work for a couple of minutes. I pay attention to every noise outside. Yet earlier I was taken by surprise while writing. There is a knock, and uniformed policemen are already at the door, making an inspection of the house. They did not come in; they were harmless—nevertheless. This scribbling, this manuscript in the house is undoubtedly a constant risk to my life—and also to some mentioned in it. And yet I cannot stop writing. And despite all depressions and all the symbolism of the "paper soldiers," I cannot give up hope.

### April 8, Thursday toward evening

[ . . . ]

Last year, when I was shoveling snow, I wrote a lot about the "privileged" Johannes Müller, whose wife was running his leather factory. A decent man, he sometimes helped me out with bread coupons, occasionally passed me a piece of candy—I envied him a little, because after all he enjoyed certain freedoms. I then heard nothing more from him. He was arrested last week—reason unknown; it is said, but it is not certain, that a new order compels those privileged Jews whose Aryan children are abroad to wear the star, and he had not learned of it in time—two days later he hanged himself (or was strangled) in the police presidium. The corpse was handed over to Jacobi naked, apart from the marks of strangulation it showed no sign of injury. The case once again shook me terribly.

[ . . . ]

### April 13, Tuesday morning

Basically monotony. Eva lies down a lot, I am very fatigued because of reading aloud and domestic chores. [ . . . ] Potato chow three times a day; peeling potatoes, hunting for potatoes, carrying potatoes. The Hirschels help out with a hundredweight, Gertrud Schmidt with two hundredweight, Frau Steinitz occasionally. —

And yet not really monotony, but growing tension. Continuing defeat in Tunisia, corresponding intensification of terror. In the last week four arrests here of men in mixed marriages, among them is said to be Leipziger, the medical officer. Hirschel gave me the latest statistics (in round figures) from the "National Association": On March 1 there were still 43,000 Jews in the whole of Germany, on April 1 only 31,000. Of the 12,000 deported during the last month, 8,500 were transported from Berlin. Hirschel was very gloomy about our future. His wife was recently summoned to the Gestapo—summons alone is torture, because no one knows whether he will come back—treated badly there, but nevertheless still released. During the last house search a note had been found on her desk in which she listed all the foodstuffs that were supplied to Aryans but *not* to us. After a bullying interrogation the inspector said to her: "Unfortunately we have failed to prove that you used the note for propaganda purposes." — Dr. Katz calls the somewhat precious Frau Hirschel—who is always ready with pearls of wisdom—"Madame Privy Councillor," and that is not so far wrong, but she is very friendly to me and genuinely helpful. Her library and her knowledge are of excellent service to me, because she is familiar with Jewish and modern German literature. [ . . . ]

### April 16, Friday midday and later

It's a beautiful spring day outside, with fruit blossoms, and the birches turning green. I feel my imprisonment all the more keenly. It has become more and more constraining from year to year. My pipe dreams always end up with the car. I got so much pleasure from it, there were such great hopes of travel attached to it. Today I am not even allowed to use the tram, I am not allowed to step outside the city boundary, I am not allowed to be seen with Eva; since the latest wave of arrests it is best not to be seen on the street at all. (At the very least I avoid the elegant city center, like all wearers of the star.) — I have spent all morning scrubbing the kitchen and am about to go downstairs again to make tea and wash up; of course I feel very depressed. Nevertheless: I have *still* not been arrested, we have still to be given the threatened notice to leave, I have still to receive the threatened call-up for labor service. I can still read aloud for hours, still sit at my desk. And in Tunisia things look very bad for the Axis.

Two small pieces of comfort voce populi, they just don't last very long, they have too often been deceptive. The first: Yesterday, as several times already, things were being removed from the house. I.e., the furniture of the evacuees is taken, as required, by the NSV (People's Welfare) or by some hospital or other. A Nazi supervisor, a few workers. Yesterday, therefore, inter alia, Frau Ziegler's remaining things, some of which were still in the common kitchen. When I came downstairs at about lunchtime, a gas hot plate had disappeared along with the Ziegler stuff. The Community's furniture store had loaned it to me about two months ago; that was still in Reichenbach's time. A two-burner to replace the two one-burners here, one of which treacherously fails again and again. The borrowed hot plate was no use either. Eisenmann senior strove in vain to make it work; it stood there uselessly—nevertheless I was liable to the Community for it. I had the caretaker's wife, a decent woman, ask the swastika man to have the erroneously removed piece returned. Reply: No mistake, the Gestapo wanted it, and I only needed to tell the Community that. — Well and good, then let the new owner enjoy the useless thing. But an hour later I also found the potato pot was missing, and that is our most important and at present irreplaceable utensil—it is impossible to buy pots. We had to use a pot that was much too small, and felt exasperated. This time Frau Rasch spoke to the workers—presumably the supervisor was no longer there. Reply: They had another day's work here and would bring the pot back. Contrary to expectation they, two men in their forties, really did arrive with it yesterday. I thanked them warmly. "Don't mention it—why didn't you say right away that it was yours?" [ . . . ] "Well, it didn't help with the hot plate—why should it have this time?" They said nothing and left. Immediately afterward one of them put his head through the half-open door and said in a low voice: "Chin up!" I look at him in surprise. Whereupon he: "These damned swine—the things they're doing—in Poland—they drive me into a rage, too. Chin up, it won't last . . . they can't last another winter in Russia. — Chin up, things'll get better . . ." At which point his mate came back, and he stopped and left. His mate was certainly no friend of the Nazis either, otherwise I would never have seen the pot [ . . . ] again—but who trusts his workmate today? At Münchner Strasse there's a guillotine. — The second piece of comfort, also a potato story, naturally. We are to get a whole two hundredweight from "Gertrud Schmidt." Since it must remain secret, and since no one is permitted to work for a Jew, and since I cannot allow myself to be seen at Gertrud Schmidt's, it was to be expected that Eva would have to haul these two hundredweight here peu à peu, just as I am slowly fetching the one hundredweight from the Hirschels'. (Still, Eva can go by tram; on the other hand she has more shopping to do, and the nervous inflammation.) Then "Gertrud" said to her yesterday there was a porter in the neighborhood, who was a friend of hers, snowed under with work, but very well-disposed to Jews. "Mention my name and say, it's for a Jew!" (Frau Ahrens is completely Aryan, but an ardent partisan of our side.) Eva went to the man, he immediately smiled knowingly before she offered any explanation, and so will transport the two hundredweight here—which is not at all without risk to him. — I took these two occurrences as symptoms, and they warmed my heart. But soon I was telling myself again: What good are a million and more such workers and porters? Nothing at all against the prodigious organization and unscrupulousness and power of the government. —

[ . . . ]

### April 18, Sunday morning

Yesterday with the morning post the order to report for labor service from Monday, April 19. I had to go to the Community, where I was told the name of the company: Willy Schlüter, 30c Wormser Strasse, working hours from 2:00–10:00 P.M. daily; it was very light work, weighing and packing teas. I do not care about light or heavy, only about the irretrievable loss of time and the deadly dullness of these eight hours. When I was ordered to shovel snow, there was the hope of being released in the spring, now I am irredeemably cheated of my days for the duration of the war. It will not be possible to seriously continue with anything. This new blow, however much it was expected, depresses me greatly. My life grows ever more miserable. And this may not at all be the final blow. — I have just come from Johannes Müller's funeral. (When will my urn be buried like that?) It was especially dreadful. The widow, a fat, big, old woman, completely veiled, shook with sobbing, wailed without stopping. While shaking hands at the miniature grave constantly: "The poor soul, the poor soul!" Jacobi, who once told me that he "doesn't believe in all this nonsense," once again cobbled together meaningless bits of prayers and formulas from sermons. Of course, nothing at all was said about the man's true fate and end. This time there were floral decorations and Aryan mourners, as well as a couple of Jews, who filled the little side room. The Jews composed and indifferent. Also quite accustomed to servitude. The man's death seemed almost just to them: He should have known that privileged Jews whose children are abroad now have to wear the star. So he was guilty! I hear similar opinions so often now. —

[ . . . ]

### April 25, Easter Sunday morning

The Catholic phrase "le leurre éternel du printemps," from some famous French novel (which?), has always stuck in my mind. I have said it to myself so often, but it has never haunted me as much as now. This spring is as beautiful, early and complete as in 1920, when we passed into Dresden through fruit blossom. And the luxuriant splendor on the opposite bank— when I walk to the factory, there are flowers in all the front gardens, on a plot of land below street level on Wormser Strasse, blossoming fruit-tree crowns at eye level, at the edge of the park here at Lothringer Weg a glowing red and delicate cedonia bush—the threat of death ever closer and more suffocating: Juliusburger, a bit superior (Lewinsky says "oberchochem"), but nevertheless full of life and a good fellow, my coworker at Schlüter for two days, arrested on Wednesday, dead on Friday; Meinhard, whom I only caught sight of fleetingly, arrested and dead—and yesterday evening news of Conradi's arrest. With that falls the last remaining barrier in my imagination between myself and death. Conradi is also a professor, pensioned-off civil servant, war veteran (surgeon-major), politically more right than left, in a mixed marriage, respected as a scholar, cautious and calm—I got to know him only on Monday, was biased against him, because I had always heard only bad things about him, and yet I found I really liked him. — It can happen to me at any moment. And then to sit in the cell and wait minute by minute for the executioner, perhaps for a day, perhaps for weeks, and perhaps no one strangles me here [ . . . ], but I die only on the way to the concentration camp ("shot while attempting to escape") or in Auschwitz itself (of "heart failure"). It is so awful to think through all the details with regard to myself, with regard to Eva. I repress it again and again, want to make the best of every day, every hour. Perhaps I shall survive after all.

[ . . . ]

According to its doorplate the Willy Schlüter company produces medicinal baths and herbal teas. [Situated] in a back house something between
apartment, office, and factory rooms. At ground level essentially two long
rooms with stone floors side by side. Tables at right angles to the windows, on the inside of the room a wide passage running its whole length
from outer to inner door; against the long inside wall and in the adjoining
smaller back room cartons with merchandise. Along the passageway, on
top of empty chests, boxes of tea; we stand beside them filling the contents
into 3½ oz. paper bags with a tin scoop. On the tables, scales: Here the bags
are made to weigh the exact amount. One place farther along the bags are
folded. At other places they are packed into cartons. [ . . . ] During this first
week I stood filling paper bags most of the time; I also did a little bit of
sticking down bags and of weighing. In between, I am part of a chain passing cartons in and out. (Sealing and sticking down the full cartons is the
job of a women's section on the upper floor, which I have not seen.) For
me, of course, the strain, the deadly wearying aspect of the work consists
in its dreadful monotony and dullness, a ten-year-old child could perform
it more quickly and better. Aside from that, the time passes more quickly
than I had feared—only there is always a dull regret inside me at the irretrievably lost time; I am incapable of thinking anything through, I fall into
a semi-trance. My fellow workers don't find it half as bad. "Should I sit at
home and catch flies?" a robust seventy-year-old, a certain Witkowsky, a
former businessman, tells me. He has something to pass the time, has
never done work that was much more mentally demanding, earns a little
money. Hourly rate 60 pfennigs. Whoever is "privileged" and consequently is not in tax group one and does not have to pay "social contributions," is paid probably about 50 of that; for me it will be between 35 and
40 pfennigs. There is a five-minute break at four; we get a mug of thin ersatz coffee. The workers supply the coffee; it is made at the factory. The big
meal break is from half past five until six. I have an aluminum box with
cold potatoes and a jar of sauerkraut with me. Coffee is provided again;
one can also have one's food heated up. Moreover, canteen food—from an
NSV [National Socialist Peoples' Welfare] catering center—is "also"
planned for Jews, but so far only applied for and "planned." At eight, a
five-minute break once again, this time with peppermint tea, which the
company supplies. Clearing up begins at half past nine; we leave very
punctually at ten. The long room next to our packing hall is more factory-
like. The different herbs, which are to be mixed, are in a row of large barrels; opposite them the mixing drum, hardly any different from a cement
mixer. During the day an almost entirely female Aryan shift works here,
supervised by an Aryan fitter (these are presumably the same women who
make coffee and tea for us in a hallway cum kitchen), at night a Jewish
group. Whether one should volunteer for night shift or not is an inexhaustible subject of discussion. One camp: We should leap at the chance:
longer breaks, 80 pfennigs an hour, long-hours bonus (bread and meat)

"also planned" for Jews and applied for; the other camp: on no account: terribly dusty, terribly exhausting. I have volunteered for it, so as to find out what it is like, and because it seems a little romantic to me and so will perhaps pass more quickly than the day shift, and because it will perhaps leave me a little more time than the day shift. — Because in the morning Aryan women work in "our" room from 6:00 A.M. until 2:00 P.M. and because the mixing room is also served by it (and because they treat us very decently), so the radio is on, sometimes all afternoon, sometimes only in the evening, sometimes too quiet and drowned out by the noise of work, sometimes ignored as a never-ending noise, sometimes objected to by half the shift and then switched off by the foreman—on the whole, however, a help in passing the time. Much music from Vienna, from Berlin, from here and there. A couple of Italian songs, a bit of *Fledermaus*, a bit of *Cavalleria* gave me pleasure. The military bulletin; Goebbels' speech on the Führer's birthday (very low-spirited, nothing but the trust in the Führer, which will ensure final victory), a couple of fragments of a speech by the "Reich Health Leader" (will to carry on, nation, etc.—then it was switched off, partly because it was boring, partly because people are afraid of listening to anything National Socialist—the Gestapo can come in at any moment after all). All in all, however quickly I become indifferent and deaf to it, the time does pass a little more quickly with the radio than in silence, and sometimes I do pick up a few things as substitute for the newspaper. — The people: There are supposed to be about twenty Jews employed, their number changes, now one turns up after an illness, another is arrested, a third is only occasionally—God knows according to what rule—on my shift for an hour here and an hour there, a fourth is to be seen as a guest for the few minutes of the break or when the shifts are changing over. Among these fleeting figures was a strong younger man called Meinhard. It was said of him that he had had a fierce quarrel with an Aryan worker; he was very quick-tempered, as a result of a skull wound from the last war (silver skull plate). He is on the latest suicide list. Another of the guests is such a startling likeness to Goebbels in bearing, figure, face, that he could easily be his understudy. Sometimes joining us for an hour in the evening, always there for the night shift: Feder, in an apron as are most of the others, and with a scarf and cap. But his cap—the others have white ones, such as bakers wear, or "lumiche," peaked cyclists' caps—his is unmistakably and only very little knocked out of shape, an original judge's black biretta. He, Professor Conradi, the half-blind painter Gimpel, whose acquaintance I had already made while shoveling snow, and who now takes my arm on the way home—he lives on Deutsche Kaiserallee—lastly a humpbacked and bad-tempered pharmacist called Bergmann, represent the professions; the other people had shops or were company employees. — On arriving for work on Monday I was shown up to the offices on the first floor, and the boss, a gentleman in his forties, looked at my papers. "A pity that we don't have the time; we could have such fine lectures, every faculty is represented here now!" It sounded good-natured—nor have I encountered a flicker of anti-Semitism anywhere in the factory. But who protects us? When the Aryan fitter heard that Juliusburger was missing, he merely said: "For heaven's sake!" He knew what there was to know. The subjects of conversation usually quite unpolitical. The men talk about their former businesses; they compare the work at Schlüter with that at Zeiss-Ikon; they are not dissatisfied, insofar as they are not startled and frightened by a new shock. When I arrived, they had already almost got over the wave of arrests of recent days. Then came the new blow. The two most interesting men for me are (or were) Conradi and Jacubowski. At the beginning of my professorship, I heard a great deal of talk about disciplinary proceedings against Conradi. Then nothing about him for many years. After that Kätchen Sara talked about her "cousin" Conradi, who was working at Zeiss-Ikon—a famous man, but so anti-English, so anti-Semitic, almost Nazi. Thus I was all the more surprised to find Conradi an obliging, natural, pleasant person, with whom, it turned out, I had a number of points of contact. A calm, elderly-looking man of sixty-six. His post at the TU was secondary; he was, first of all, an official of the Saxon Board of health; he was in the chemistry department, which is why I never met him. [ . . . ] I had high hopes of conversations with Conradi—he sat far away from me, we met only during the breaks. On Thursday he reported that he had been shouted at, as he left a shop: "Watch that you don't cover your star; you know where you'll end up otherwise!"

He had protested immediately; he was not covering it; it had probably been only a warning and intimidation; the man, whom he already knew as a Gestapo officer, had not taken his name. — Frau Hirschel [later] took up the story: The Gestapo had telephoned the Community to identify the man, who had bought radishes at Antonplatz today and subsequently had an argument. Radishes, says Eva, are a scarce commodity and therefore forbidden to Jews. Conradi is likely to die for them. The lesson of sufficient cause. — I talked more frequently and, I hope, shall still talk to Jacubowski. He is a man of sixty-two years, born in Kalisz, in Dresden since 1912, stateless, formerly Russian, [exiled] to Tomsk for three years as politically suspect—"my best years!" He explains Russian phrases to me [ . . . ], talks about Russia before the First World War without hatred (about the people's universities, about the natural common sense of the people, of the tolerable life—not of the political and other criminals, but of those sent to Siberia for fixed terms as suspects). —
   [ . . . ]

### April 26, Easter Monday morning

On Thursday I said to Conradi, he could still laugh at it: "We're in a cholera ward without an inoculation." I can no longer rid myself of fear, only deaden it. — Similar mood at Hirschels' yesterday. [ . . . ]

**Midday**

[ . . . ]

A special postage stamp has been issued for the Führer's birthday, I think in the Protectorate, of all places, and some post offices have stamped it: "We are defending Europe against Bolshevism." (I do not know if those are the precise words. I first saw it a week ago in the newspaper.) The theme of *anti-Bolshevism* dominates with a monstrous degree of hypocrisy. [ . . . ] I shall try to come back to it. I no longer dare to store newspapers up here. Today I took a pile down to the cellar. I shall ask Lewinsky *not* to bring me the *Frankfurter Zeitung* anymore. My time has become so infinitely limited now, that I can read and analyze only very little. But I have managed to make good use of the Easter holidays. A good bit of Dwinger read aloud, and all these notes. Now I have to prepare for Steinitz's visit; tomorrow morning there are errands to be run again, and tomorrow evening I begin the night shift, of which I am now a little afraid after all. I must try it out.

**Evening**

Steinitz brought the news that Conradi is already dead—Jacobi was ordered to the police prison to take delivery of the corpse. It could strike me at any moment; I cannot get rid of the feeling of dread anymore.

**April 27, Tuesday morning before seven o'clock**

Up since half past four, [ . . . ] read aloud for an hour; then Eva slept, and I got ready until now. Unusually I had already been lying awake for a long time at half past four, before that I dreamed—the dread is so very great. I was walking through Berlin, down Courbièrestrasse, past Wally's first apartment in Berlin. (Dream link: presumably conversation about cancer on Sunday.) I thought: at that time she was happy and young. I came into a room in which there was a friendly meeting of colleagues; we sat at a long table; new colleagues were constantly coming in. I do not remember a single one. I was intrigued by my Jew's star; first it was half hanging off, then it consisted of two layers stuck together, and the upper layer of the Mogen David was coming off, and my neighbor wanted to pin it with a needle and could not find the right place; then I remembered: "it must not be pinned, must be sewn on"; then I heard noise in the neighboring room, and someone said: "an arrest"; after that I awoke—with no particularly acute feeling of fear, in exactly the same state of mind as yesterday evening: dread filled (and fills) me: dull, loathsome and always there, all my thinking and doing has no effect at all.

In this connection I have been tormented by a particular fear since yesterday evening: if the censors object to my postcard to Martin and pass it on to the Gestapo, if the latter do not believe my "angina complaints" and

read my sentences as "atrocity propaganda" . . . I tell myself again and
again, being strangled is also no more than dying and a more agreeable
way of dying than death by cancer. But the dread remains. Luckily it does
not prevent me from making intensive use of my time.

As far as the night shift is concerned, I have slowly taken fright at my
own courage. How shall I endure it; how, when and for how long shall I
sleep during the day? And above all: Shall I still be able to support Eva
with the domestic chores, shall I not be lying around like a clod, getting in
the way of her daily routine? I must try it; at worst I can give it up at the
end of the week—assuming I am still alive.

Frau Steinitz told us yesterday: One of her relations—petit bourgeois
Aryan—an in-law presumably, is doing service on the railways. In the last
few days a truck with 80 fettered soldiers had arrived, "deserters." The
prisons were stuffed full of soldiers, there were many shootings. Torgau,
in particular, was mentioned as a place of punishment for the army.
[ . . . ]

### April 29, Thursday afternoon half past five

A long room with a cement floor. Against the long window wall, a row of
tubs with the various herbs; opposite, a larger and a smaller mixing drum;
beside them, another couple of tubs. One man stands on a wooden platform and fills the drum, through a rectangular funnel, with the herbs,
which are handed to him in cardboard boxes. Light, white savory, like
wood shavings; dark, very heavy heather, like peaty soil; some parts of
hay, like fine cigarette tobacco; brightly colored, granular heather flowers,
like the poppy seeds on chocolate biscuits; all kinds of brown and greenish-
yellow dried, crumbled, crackling leaves: hazel, peppermint, etc., etc.
Seven cartons into the smaller mixer, nine into the larger one [ . . . ]. The
filler man removes the funnel, tightens the screws of the mixer itself and
of the metal lid of the cover, switches on the motor, the drum turns. The
worker who hands up the cartons empties the dust box under the machine, pushes away the chest into which the tea pours when it has been
mixed. As one drum is turning, the other is emptied and refilled. When
emptying [ . . . ] as when filling [the worker] swallows an unspeakable
amount of dust, which immediately gets into his eyes, congests nose and
mouth. There may be dust everywhere else in the room—but to some extent it is removed by the ventilation at the window; the filler, however, in-
hales the dust directly and irremediably. I am the filler; after a few minutes
I am so hoarse that I can no longer speak loudly over the whirring of the
drive belts and the noise of the ventilator; when I blow my nose there's a
black mass of stuff in my handkerchief. Mouth, nose, throat, eyes itch and
burn; my head, when I remove the chafing cycling cap, is as gray with
dust as my hands. Apart from the two people at the machine, there are another two men working: One shovels the herbs from the tubs into the cartons, the other is the "transport man," who wheels up more supplies in

sacks on a heavy iron barrow, dumps them in front of the tubs, and empties the tea from the open chests into large paper sacks, elaborate objects
consisting of five loosely joined layers, which hold 66 pounds each. The
other three help the transport man whenever a chest has to be placed on a
tall stand, so that the tea can flow from above into the new sack, or when
the contents of a heavy sack of herbs have to be poured into a tub. The
sacks of tea are rolled through the kitchen into a storeroom, where they are
first of all weighed.

We work from ten until twelve, then there's a coffee break of about ten
minutes in the kitchen; work from twelve until two. Then the big meal
break; the others have heated up a supper on the gas range; there is coffee
again, too. After my evening meal at home, I have only a bite to eat. We sit
in the big room of my day shift. Then work from half past two until four,
and another short break in the kitchen, this time with peppermint tea. In
the last quarter of the night the actual work stops at five, and the arduous
and to some extent illusory sweeping up begins. The new shift appears
toward six; an Aryan foreman, a couple of women, young star-wearing
Aris, who in coat, neckerchief, and cap looks like a Parisian apache. —
Toward four o'clock in the morning I am racked by extreme tiredness,
which soon passes, however; by the second night I was already less sensitive to the dust than on the first night. And on both, the time passed more
quickly than on the day shift. God knows why—because the work is
hardly less monotonous and dull than during the day—but the time really
did pass more quickly. Nevertheless, I shall give up the night shift; the experiment [ . . . ] leads conclusively to this: I get too little sleep during the
day, I disrupt Eva's daytime life too greatly, I do not manage a single
minute more of my own work than if I go on the day shift. [ . . . ]

My workmates on the night shift: on the machine, Joachimsthal, mid-
fifties, cousin of Kätchen Sara, half educated, formerly in bookselling and
journalism, a genuine psychopath, distrustful, overwrought, constantly
sighing and railing against everything; always believes he is being attacked and disregarded. He trusts me—so far—he argues with the others,
recklessly goes so far as to appeal to the Aryan foreman. (Question: how
far does he have to sweep, how far the others. Whether one should leave
the building at six or quarter past six in the morning. Etc., etc.) Carton
filler is Bergmann, the humpbacked, hard-of-hearing, bad-tempered pharmacist; rather proletarianized. I get on tolerably with him. Transport man
is the scrawny, somewhat theatrically affected, but very likeable Stern, 63;
in the textile business; was in South Africa for a long time, interpreter for
English during the First World War (but repeatedly says: "pathalogical"—
what is education?), night shift specialist; has been on it for three weeks
without interruption. —

Catching up now on yesterday's musical afternoon: Glaser and Eva
played a suite of old dances for piano and violin, which she had written
twenty years ago. — Frau Kreisler related how she recently found an addressed postal package in the street; there was something red coming out

of it—meat! After a struggle with her conscience she handed the package in. A petit bourgeois man had lost it from his bicycle; his despair turned to rejoicing. Contained a huge rabbit. As a finder's reward Frau Kreisler got a leg and piece of liver. She said to the man: "I am non-Aryan—you see, a non-Aryan can be honest, too." He: "What on earth does 'non-Aryan' mean?" (After 10 years of Nazi propaganda!) After the explanation: "I don't care in the least about that!"

### May 1, Saturday morning

The night shift experiment has ended, I hope forever, certainly for a fairly long time; it wreaks havoc with my eyes, destroys my day. The third night was essentially the same as the two others. The atmosphere was somewhat friendlier, since everyone truly mourned a new deceased, without any unpleasant gossip and without any immediate fear for their own person. Everyone liked Gimpel, the painter, and he is not quite a victim of the Gestapo; he was close to losing his sight, he was probably no longer holding on tightly to life, and as he was now supposed to give up his apartment and was affected by the murder of people close to him—Conradi sat beside him at Schlüter, they chatted all day—he opened the gas tap when his Aryan wife was not at home. I had fleetingly made Gimpel's acquaintance while shoveling snow last year, met him again at Schlüter. He asked me to give him my arm in the darkness on the way home—he lived in Deutsche Kaiserallee. So we walked there together twice. He invited Eva and myself to look at his paintings. Even more than a landscape painter he was a scene painter. Afterward I found out that he had designed church windows, that he had produced the wall decorations for the Rostock crematorium, that he had been president of the Association of Graphic Artists (of Germany or Saxony?). He himself told me that until the ban on school instruction for Jewish children, he had taught them drawing. He showed no sign of great depression, still less of despair. Perhaps the news of Conradi's death was "suddenly" the last straw for him. He was only in his late fifties.

[ . . . ]

Since I am so short of time and errands in town are so risky for me, Eva went to see Richter this time instead of me. He was fairly optimistic. Tunisia was almost over, the English were little more than twenty miles from Tunis itself. Rommel had long ago fallen out of favor and been replaced by a General Arnim. He had heard from two reliable and informed sources that a military coup was anticipated as early as mid-May; the war simply could not outlast the year. There was a great shortage of means of transport (rolling stock). There had been a conspiracy trial in Berlin: a dozen death sentences, many sentences of hard labor, even for virtual adolescents who had handed out leaflets . . . The man in Wehlen will perhaps even hide me, if I should be summoned to the Gestapo [ . . . ]: Eva will get information about that (and bread coupons at the same time) on

Wednesday. — For a moment all of that raised my spirits. But only for a moment.

On *LTI*. [ . . . ] In the *Reich* of April 4, '43, an illustrated article: "Soviet People. Fates in the East by Willy Beer." Examples are supposed to prove how Bolshevism destroys the intellect, castrates the individual, reduces the scholar and the philosopher to mechanical specialists with functional goals; like everyone else "not only their clothes and homes, but also their minds and actions . . . have long ago taken on the gray color of mass society." The manager of an agricultural district is "employee of a dogma." "He had become a specialist in agronomy—he did not know what a farmer was."

— The character of a professor of philosophy reveals "the boundless contempt for the individual will that the Soviet dictatorship had produced." Her father was sentenced to twenty years hard labor by the Bolshevists, but she has joined them. Her philosophy goes "straight from Aristotle to Hegel, Marx, and Lenin and means automation of the spirit." It is a philosophy that places "the dogma of mass terror above the values of individual personalities" . . . "Here the intellect itself has become a machine. It does not function of its own volition, but because the regime wills it." The ultimate in "slavery"! — "There is no demand for knowledge, skill, hard work, creativity beyond what is of use to the success of the Soviet dictatorship at home and abroad. Soviet man is truly the annulment of what constitutes human right and human dignity." All of this is exactly what can be said of man under National Socialism. It *feigns* individualism, which Bolshevism honestly disavows. [ . . . ]

## May 3, Monday morning

Now I want to make it a point of pride that, despite everything, I make good use of my time and persevere with my studies—and my paper soldiers. The normal six-day week begins today. I absolutely must try to permanently avoid the night shift, because the resulting inflammation of my eyes has only now come to a climax. — I am fairly satisfied with the achievement of the two days of holiday; the loss of time and the boredom of Lewinsky's visit yesterday afternoon was very much counterbalanced by his reading from Perez. He left the little volume here, I immediately read on a little, and my enthusiasm increased. I suspect that it will add a great deal to my *"LTI. The Sketchbook of a Philologist"*—as it probably will be in the end; in it I shall be able to summarize all the ideas that have emerged from my studies.

We talked about Juliusburger, who was buried yesterday with a certain degree of opulence—half a dozen wreaths, most with lilac blooms, two dozen people, a large amount of quotation and prayer from Jacobi (all in marked contrast to the scantiness of the following ceremony for Meinhard). I knew the man for only a few days; one gesture has imprinted itself on my mind as typical of his somewhat cocky and self-confident character.

He was working beside me in his blue overalls and smoking a cigarette. "Do you dare do that here? If you're surprised—is it worth risking your life?" — "*You* shouldn't take the risk, *I've* got practice." At that moment the door opened; an Aryan fitter came in. At the very same moment, Juliusburger's cigarette had disappeared. Afterward he asked me triumphantly: "Did you see where it went? With cigarettes I'm Rastelli." Before the ceremony itself Lewinsky told me something curiously touching, which I—I was leaning against the wall some distance away—had missed. The deeply veiled widow, constantly shaken by violent sobbing, had repeatedly stroked the urn. (Here, too, a contrast to the Meinhard ceremony: The widow, a young blonde woman, sat completely immobile, without tears, without a veil; instead of a hat only a broad black band, like that of a tennis player, over forehead and hair.)

[ . . . ]

### May 4, Tuesday morning

The first full week of the day shift with no holiday has begun. Every hour has six hundred minutes. The room has become emptier—two people dead, one detailed elsewhere [ . . . ], otherwise everything is the same as before the night shift week. Yet not quite. The radio is not switched on—a plant inspection by the Gestapo is expected, and radio in the Jews' room would be a mortal sin. The Aryan foreman switches it on only after nine o'clock. He is allowed to. Depressed atmosphere. Kornblum, an elderly war invalid and pensioner, was stopped in Tittmannstrasse by a Gestapo officer. "What are you doing walking around here? By which tram did you come? . . ." Otherwise nothing happened to him. But that's the way it started with others. Who knows what happens next — "If they summon me—I just won't bother going . . ." And even if nothing at all happens this time—they are constantly watching out for us. — Sometimes—rarely—I listen to the others' conversation during these eight hours. All those that remain are business people, most had shops, ready-made clothes, lingerie, etc. They know about one another, where they bought, who "made money." They are all without hope for the future. "Germany will never be good for us again; there was always anti-Semitism, now it's gone too deep." One says: "Meinhard was a worker; I am always pleased when I hear that a Jew was a worker." Another: "That doesn't impress me. An unskilled worker, not even a saddler or a locksmith by trade." — "I wish," says the emaciated and bent Lewin beside me, furniture dealer from Baden-Baden, later an employee here following bankruptcy because of anti-Semitism, "I wish my parents had let me learn a trade." — Vehement objection all round. "The Jews in Poland are tradesmen, and they were in a wretched state." — "You can't earn anything with a trade. Highest wage is 80 pfennigs an hour." — "And no Jew became a master." [ . . . ]

Mostly the work is carried out doggedly and in silence. The women upstairs manage twice as much; what will happen to us if we are accused of sabotage? — The hours at home are a comfort. But in the evening we sat a long time over coffee; this morning I read aloud a little. Then I fell asleep over the diary entry, and now it is already twenty to one, and I have to leave at half past.

## May 5, Wednesday morning

Yesterday's drudgery passed a tiny bit more quickly, but the feeling of being dead, of an irretrievable loss of one's life continues to weigh heavily. At four, we were sitting down for coffee, the foreman appeared: "You had better put the coffee away—the inspection!" Then an officer in uniform, one in plainclothes. The one in plainclothes (Müller) to me: "What's your name?" I gave my name. Both walked through the room. The one in uniform (Schmidt or Schmitz): "You're all asleep—you have to work faster." With that they disappeared. Once this had passed—with the tremendous danger it involved—we heaved a sigh of relief and put on the radio, which had been silent the day before. Aside from music and a military bulletin— the Germans are on the retreat in Tunisia, and so hope rises again— nothing but quite extravagant, incessantly repeated Jew-baiting. A talk: From ancient times Jews had been permitted, indeed encouraged to mur- der; "thou shalt not kill" applied only among Jews; a discussion arose over this talk; people wanted to turn it off, I was in favor of listening to it, but was outvoted. Later a talk about the Jewish will to destruction, which was behind both the Bolshevists and the plutocrats. Because: The Russians have shot 10,000 Polish officers—mass graves discovered at Katyn—"at Judah's command." Etc., hour after hour. In the factory they say: However the war ends, the Jews would never be at ease here, anti-Semitism goes too deep. I: It has overreached itself, it has unmasked itself, it will have bank- rupted itself.

[ ... ]

For a few coupons and 50 pfennigs the Jews are now to receive the food delivered by the National Socialist Welfare. What a relief that would be for me! But 3½ ounces of meat coupons are required, *Jewish* meat coupons in my name. I do not have them, and so the nonprivileged go empty- handed.

How deep does anti-Semitism go in the population? I am carrying a heavy tea chest with Konrad, the chargeman [at Schlüter's]. An Aryan worker to me: "You shouldn't be doing that, let me!" — "It's really all right; I'm not that shaky yet." — "Come on, give it to me, you don't get enough meat." —

## May 6, early on Thursday before seven o'clock

Result of the Gestapo inspection the day before yesterday: yellow arm- bands, so that those without the star are also marked out; the wearers of the star also wear the armband in all factories, moreover. Particular instruction: to be worn at full width! To make it smaller would be a crime equivalent to covering the star. — Uninterrupted Jew-baiting on the radio. Utterly insane and undignified. Especial indignation yesterday because the Americans want to occupy (or have occupied?) the island of Martinique. [ . . . ] And again and again in every report, every talk, every context, the word Jewish. Jewish Bolshevism, Jewish plutocracy, Jewish murder (e.g., political murder in Sofia, the perpetrator escaped without being recognized, is to be looked for in Jewish circles), Jewish influence in the White House, etc., etc., etc. I always hear only fragments. The Aryan foreman turns the radio on; the chargeman, Konrad, turns it off when there are talks, out of fear of the Gestapo. What that leaves is the news service with the military bulletin at eight o'clock, together with music in the late afternoon and evening. [ . . . ]

Konrad, the foreman, gave me some information about the Schlüter company, which has evidently expanded from a very small business ("Willy Schlüter Chem.-pharm. Laboratory") in the course of the war: Five tons of tea are produced daily; the annual turnover has risen to four million marks. The supplies for the army are dispatched in 66-pound sacks, those for the civilian population in cartons, each containing 13 pounds, that is fifty packets. Hundreds of such cartons go to the post every day (I am often part of the chain that loads them); the Jewish section produces about seventy packages a day. [ . . . ]

## May 9, Sunday midday

At the cemetery more terrible news: a) three arrests at the Enterlein factory, among them two Jews with privileged status. The Community was instructed to call the people to Zeughausstrasse at half past seven this morning for "Sunday duty." Gestapo officers were waiting for them. Thus people disappear in utter secrecy. b) Kornblum, our hussar with the spine problem [ . . . ] has been summoned for tomorrow morning. There's a story to that. About a week ago a Gestapo man stopped him in Tittmannstrasse, close to Schlüter. "What are you running around here for?" He supplied the information and was allowed to go on his way without abuse. He arrived at the factory upset. We reassured him that it was of no consequence. Only yesterday evening, as he limped off as usual at seven o'clock, I told him: "You see, there was no need for you to be alarmed." — "So far," he replied. — Hirschel tells us: he was at Kornblum's, presumably to deliver the summons. Kornblum really wanted to commit suicide. Hirschel made an effort to talk him out of it, using two arguments. 1) "In the past few months, three of those summoned have got out again, without being arrested—one of them Frau Hirschel—why should you, Kornblum, not be the fourth?" 2) "If *you* commit suicide today, there will be twenty new arrests tomorrow, to achieve six more suicides." We shall learn tomorrow, whether Kornblum is still alive, whether he went, whether he came back. The whole business is unspeakably horrible. Whose will be the next urn grave?

The two funerals took the usual course. For both there were many flowers, for both there were so many mourners, that people were standing in the hallway; both times there was the usual meaningless stringing together of Bible quotations, worn-out German verses, formulas—both, Conradi, the sixty-six-year-old; Gimpel, the fifty-eight-year-old, were "taken too soon,"—false pathos. [ . . . ]

Eisenmann senior is here at the moment, repairing a wall socket in the bedroom. He has been warning us so insistently that I should not go out on Sunday, that I should neither pay nor receive visits—the Gestapo watches everything, uses anything as a pretext! So far we have deliberately disregarded these warnings; we told ourselves that the plague bacilli were swirling around invisibly everywhere and fear did no good either. But now we have become apprehensive after all. Especially because Eisenmann said people were already talking about Steinitz's lack of caution. [ . . . ]

### May 10, Monday morning before seven o'clock

I remained at home yesterday and took notes on Dwinger. At the Steinitzes they took my staying away more calmly than we had feared. He, too, had apparently already been warned. For the next little while communication will be maintained by Eva alone, and even then only with circumspection. We shall likewise call off Lewinsky. Perhaps all of it is no different than the precautionary measures taken against cholera before the disease had been identified, the vinegar-soaked cloths in front of one's mouth and the smoke fires. [ . . . ]

The Elsa Kreidl problem. While her husband was still alive, we thought she was cold, anti-Semitic, Nazistic. Then, after Kreidl's death, we began to like her more, she behaved well to Ida Kreidl, to ourselves, something like a friendship arose, she did us all kinds of favors. She did not dare venture here (for which she cannot be blamed), but Eva went to have tea with her a couple of times, the two of them usually meet in town for Saturday lunch, Elsa Kreidl lends books, gives us potato and coffee coupons, the relationship is a good one. Now—they had not met for three weeks—Eva tells me: Elsa Kreidl is praising the virtues of her tenant, a senior Gestapo officer. The man was really a good person, but was just now dealing with the Jewish cases; he did not allow his subordinates to take liberties! — Does Frau Kreidl really not know that only someone tried and trusted reaches such a post? Does she not know what cruel acts are taking place? Does she not know that she is consorting directly with her husband's murderers? Eva says the woman is living in cozy widowhood; she evidently does not need to economize very much. Has the woman, in her pitiful little bit of comfort, forgotten everything? Is she unthinking, stupid, bad?

Eva says: She is as pleasant and obliging as before, and she herself, Eva, had become very undemanding with respect to "people" and had got out of the habit of being surprised. And I have become quite hardened: If this association brings us potatoes and coffee . . . But the affair is contemptible nevertheless. And problematic.

### May 11, early Tuesday morning

Yesterday a whole day without any radio, with minimal conversation. The crippling fear. The new arrests are said to have begun with a worker at the Enterlein factory called Michaelis, very loud and incautious in his conversation. Thus the arrests are attributed to "politically suspect conversations," which have somehow been overheard, denounced, perhaps inadvertently betrayed. One man is interrogated, pulls down the others with him—out of weakness, out of stupidity, unintentionally. What is a politically suspect conversation? Everything and anything. Ergo: *We* don't turn the radio on; if Rössler, the Aryan foreman does so, tant mieux. Rössler, however, was not to be seen all day. [ . . . ]

Kornblum did not go to the Gestapo yesterday; he has had a nervous collapse, which Katz reported to Bismarckplatz. How will matters now unfold for the unfortunate man? Last year I observed the similar torment of Frau Pick, who was then driven to suicide.

Fear is also crippling in other respects. The Hirschels have recently been sending their boys here, to play with the Eisenmann children, and to get some fresh air. (The children were used to the garden of their villa and are now shut up in the cramped Community house.) The unaffectedly good-natured children of the caretaker innocently joined in the loud games. Sometimes passing children looked through the gate. Now one is afraid: children with the star and Aryan children together! It can cost the Jewish parents their heads. Frau Eisenmann saw (or thought she saw) a man repeatedly observing the Jacoby property for a long time—"so we are being 'watched.' " The Hirschel children have been sent away. The only place left for them to play is now the Jewish cemetery; the vegetable patch behind the graves.

[ . . . ]

At the factory "long-hours bonuses" were introduced for the night workers yesterday. That means that one gets seven ounces of meat for *one* week as well as the coupons required for *four* weeks of canteen food. What a dilemma for me! Should I sacrifice my nights? It is a wretched alternative. But what does it all mean in the face of the perpetual fear of lurking murder. *This* feeling, the sheer dread of being strangled in the dark; I must put *that* down in the Curriculum; it is also what is particular to this last year: One no longer reckons on prison or a beating, but straightaway with death for everything and anything. —

Eva wants to get the manuscript pages to Pirna today. Since we have been receiving money from Richter, she goes out there only very rarely. Each time I experience an especial fear and especial qualms of conscience. For what do I expose Eva to danger? Vanitas!

[ . . . ]

## May 12, Wednesday morning

Eva says Annemarie was friendly and apathetic, had been to some degree not there as always in recent months. [ . . . ]

New arrests at the Enterlein factory: three mixed-race brothers from the Protectorate, only recently forced to wear the star by a new interpretation of the law. People suspect that political conversations are continuing to claim victims and have become even more fearful. Each person warns the next; at every loud word no matter how harmless the content, someone says: In the courtyard one can hear everything through the open window. The radio is taboo. But after eight o'clock, a woman worker, cigarette in hand, came in and fiddled around with it, until Strelzyn, the engraver, helped her tune it. So then there was music for the rest of the time. [ . . . ] The radio played something classical I didn't know. Freymann, the ruin of a man beside me, with a quarter sight and half a lung and a quarter hearing, whispered: "Beethoven really is the most beautiful." I agreed with him. After a couple of minutes there came a familiar theme of the symphony, and it gave me real pleasure. [ . . . ]

## May 14, Friday morning

[ . . . ] Yesterday news came that the summons to Kornblum (who then had a breakdown) has been canceled, but that Kahane, a new man at Enterlein, has been arrested. The viewpoints, according to which the Gestapo is proceeding, become ever more puzzling. Death hangs over everyone at every moment. [ . . . ]

At home in the evening, Eva reported what Eisenmann senior had meanwhile told her. Eight of them had been working at one table at Enterlein. He, Eisenmann, was the only one left. Kahane was the sixth to be arrested, the seventh man was Imbach, the remnants of whose family we got to know as our fellow lodgers—the mother was sent to Theresienstadt, one daughter lived here alone, until she was deported to Poland, another daughter died in Auschwitz during our time; we occasionally met the married brother; he lived on Emser Allee—so this seventh man, in a mixed marriage, was summoned to the Gestapo for yesterday, he did *not* go and has disappeared. Perhaps suicide, perhaps in a hiding place. Eva related a few characteristic phrases. Eisenmann said: "If he didn't go, then from now on the Gestapo will no longer 'summon,' but directly 'fetch.'" He implored Eva not to say anything in the meantime to his terrified wife. Frau Eisenmann in turn afterward said that she had been so afraid when her

Herbert came home late. Word for word to Eva: "I feel least anxious at night, when I can hear them all breathing around me." [ . . . ]

## May 20, Thursday morning

Vox populi: "Fräulein Hulda," our good-natured, scrawny Aryan fellow lodger, formerly Frau Jacoby's mainstay, now bottle washer in a factory, said: "The war cannot last much longer; we don't have anything any-more—Africa lost and the meat ration reduced by a quarter pound a week." That is a characteristic juxtaposition. In which the quarter pound counts for more than Africa. [ . . . ]

In the night of October 15–16 a very brief air-raid warning, the second in recent days. In ever-spared Dresden there is complete indifference.

Lewin, the good-natured South German, told me a "better class of gen-tleman," well dressed, had spat at his feet that morning and then ostenta-tiously given him a wide berth. For myself, children often shout after me. In the factory constant discussion, to what extent are the people anti-Semitic. Lazarus and Jacobowicz [sic] assert the absolute anti-Semitism of *all* classes in Germany, inborn, universal, ineradicable; I deny it, my argu-ments more resolute than what I believe, and find support here and there. Konrad: "If the people really were so hostile to the Jews, then with all this propaganda not one of us would still be alive." Frank: It's not the work-ers—only the people with university educations. —

Among our arrested, Medical Officer Leipziger and a Fräulein Schweiger, of mixed race and with two illegitimate Aryan children—she must be a good and likeable person; everyone speaks well of her, without any personal remarks—are already in a concentration camp, therefore doomed and beyond help. Of those who "bolted," Imbach is the only one still missing; a certain Schwarzbaum has been washed up as a corpse at Meissen. Lazarus said: So many Jews had been able to remain in hiding in Berlin, because the Gestapo could be bribed. The corruption had got to such a point that recently the whole of the Berlin Gestapo had been ex-changed for the stricter Vienna Gestapo.

## May 21, Friday morning

Konrad, the chargeman, has "officially" ascertained at the Community that Jews are forbidden *only* to own a radio, not to listen to it. Thus the Schlüter set is now going at full blast again, often no more than a drowned-out noise; on the whole, a help nevertheless. During the news hour at 5:00 P.M. everything is quiet.

The last few days have been dominated by the river dam business. First: The English have "criminally" bombed two dams (location not stated); very many civilian casualties. Then: It has been proved, proved by an English newspaper article, that this criminal plan was hatched by a

Jew; it therefore belongs on the list of Jewish "misdeeds" and will, like the other Jewish crimes, be atoned for. The same thing was printed in the newspapers, and since then the rope around Jewish necks has been drawn *even* tighter. The river dam business—it has superseded the 10,000 officers' corpses at Katyn—is reinforced by the American child murder in Italy: There the Americans dropped toys filled with explosives (also similarly prepared ladies' gloves). A "Serbian newspaper" writes, this murder of children is a Jewish invention. No news hour without such reports. [ . . . ]

The day before yesterday (May 19), it was already a whole month since my packing phase began. To a small degree I have become accustomed to it, to a small degree the radio helps. But the eight hours are still infinitely long and kill the whole day for me, and I never get rid of the feeling that my life is being wasted. Are my workmates more modest than I am or merely less sensitive? Or are insensitivity and modesty synonyms? In a way it does me good to be among people who are of the same age, or older, and are suffering more. I often tell myself: If all of these accept life, without staring at the death before them, or at youth behind them, why should I not manage that too?

A blond little girl runs through the room, winningly gives each person her hand; everyone knows her: the five-year-old illegitimate daughter of a young woman upstairs in the office. Where is the instinctive race hatred? There is not a trace of anti-Semitism among the male and female office and factory workers of the company.

[ . . . ]

## May 22, Saturday morning

[ . . . ]

*Men at the Schlüter factory*

1) *Konrad,* the chargeman. He does not show his 63 years. Looks 50 at most. Fresh, healthy-looking face, small bald patch, vigorous manner, very strong and agile. Maintaining his authority with skillful use of humor. [ . . . ] Had a wholesale pig-slaughtering business [ . . . ]. Had a master butcher and two journeymen. Bought from the livestock market and sold to the butchers. "If, for example, the Bärenschenke pub needed pork knuckle with sauerkraut for two companies of SA . . ." Was forced out of the meat trade as a Jew, turned to supplying bakeries. "If they needed preserves, for example." Then sent to Zeiss-Ikon. No children, one of the 60 or 70 people in Dresden still wearing the star.

2) *Lazarus.* Early sixties, big, strong. Proud of his physician son, who as a mischling is not allowed to practice, but has found work in a chemical factory. Had something like a poster factory. Is proud of his knowledge of painting and art history. Strongly inclined to Zionism. Is an advocate of the idea of the absolute anti-Semitism of the Germans. Despite his Aryan wife, his son, the pro-Jewish atmosphere at Schlüter.

3) *Witkowsky,* the robust seventy-year-old. [ . . . ] Especially rich stock of Hebrew expressions, revels in memories of his native province of Posen, very attached to his Jewishness, but without any hostility to Germany, hardly interested in politics. Wears the star. But of course—as *everyone* there—living in a mixed marriage. Had a draper's shop; was probably a traveling salesman for a long time.

4) *Lewin.* Quite the same age as me. With his crooked shoulder looks considerably older. Had a heart attack five years ago. Easygoing South German, good-natured. Had a furniture business in Baden, was forced into bankruptcy by National Socialist boycott, was a manager somewhere here in Dresden for a couple of years, has a small invalid's pension. Talks with great affection of his wife, who works as a clerk in a vinegar company for an hourly wage of 55 pfennigs to avoid claiming relief. Has a hobby horse, about which he gets very passionate. "Why did my parents not let me learn a trade? Why is the Jew in Western Europe not a farmer, not a worker, *only* a 'dealer'?" He does not say "businessman," he says "dealer" contemptuously. Quite the same tone and reasoning as H. St. Chamberlain and Sombart. With whom he agrees "on this point." Conflicts with the others. Discussions with me. (About "productive" work.)

5) *Bergmann,* small, humpbacked, hard of hearing, ill-humored. Late fifties. So much proletarianized that it is hard to believe he is Jewish or has a university education. Is a pharmacist, was Scherner's predecessor at the Börsen pharmacy in Leipzig. Is Protestant without any connection with Judaism. Is bitter at the powerlessness of the Grüber and Loeben group, bitter at Germany. Which at all events he wants to leave after our deliverance. Childish in character, the least all-around education.

6) *Frank,* in his sixties, the chemist with the old head wound, whose wife is a matron, whose son wants to go back into the army, who stutters; has a rough, loud, quite cheerful disposition, deals out paternal thumps on the back and advice on my posture.

7) *Jacobowicz,* early sixties, the tailor from Kalisz, who enthuses about Siberia, about his adult children, of whom he is proud [ . . . ], has a rough, loud, cheerful manner, has translated Russian and Hebrew expressions for me.

8) *Berghausen,* the unskilled worker, market porter.

Thus far, at the moment, the permanent figures of my changing group.

9) *Kornblum,* the hussar and semi-cripple, who, since he was "summoned," has probably dropped out permanently due to illness. Formerly manager in Bach's clothing store, in his sixties.

10) *Juliusburger,* already buried. Lives on in the group; people repeatedly talk of his inexhaustible fund of Jewish jokes; again and again I hear: "I just cannot believe that Juliusburger is dead." Was in the ready-to-wear clothing trade, shop owner. Mid-fifties.

11) *Prof. Conradi.* I have written about him repeatedly. He, too, lives on. His anti-Semitism is held against him. "He didn't appreciate Jewish jokes—he didn't want to understand them."

12) *Freymann,* the sensitive ruin of a man with scholarly interests, formerly branch manager of Messow & Waldschmidt in Chemnitz, in his fifties, dying miserably, has dropped out permanently as unfit for service.

13) *Feder.* Who has adapted so astonishingly well to life as a worker. His headgear, which I took to be a judge's biretta and which I *want* to take as such; but it is a summer hat belonging to his wife, and her I cannot forgive him.

14) *Stern,* the Don Quixote whom everyone ribs because of his flowery greetings, who has now been working on the night shift for six weeks or longer, but always works an extra hour with the preceding shift. About 63, very strong, lean.

15) *Neufels,* often turns up in our room, but constantly employed on laboring work in the basement. Forty-two years of age, looks much younger, is astonishingly strong. Goebbels' double. Small and slight, yet very powerful and agile. Always wearing a sackcloth smock, he looks like a worker, except that several gold fillings flash in his cared-for teeth. Was in business in the film trade, but has technical knowledge and skills. Has a Germanic wife as blond as a pig, a blond boy, a black Scottish terrier, who often meet him from work.

16) *Aris,* who with his coat, red neckerchief, and cap looks like a Parisian apache, and who recently impressed me with his Hebrew literary knowledge. Mid-thirties—he and Neufels represent youth among us. Was in business in the metal trade. Was foreman at Zeiss-Ikon (as was Frank); says it was useful for his line of business. Since our recent conversation he treats me with respectful friendliness. Lewinsky says he behaved brutally to the group in his charge (the "kindergarten," young people with especially good eyes) and was a wild and quick-tempered man.

17) *Edelmann,* whom I have seen only for a moment, not yet spoken to, and who is employed as a new laborer in the cellar. A blond giant, not at all Jewish-looking. About fifty, turning gray, very handsome with pale eyes. Was a tobacco worker.

18) *Levy,* [ ... ] brawny fellow in his fifties, formerly window dresser; weak, short-sighted little eyes, pale blue behind spectacles, blinking; the back of his head slopes, all neck really; loud, childish, inexpressive voice. Teased by everyone. Recently I heard him talk quite sensibly a couple of times. I keep my distance from him and from the teasing. In part I feel sorry for him, in part he gives me the creeps.

19) *Joachimsthal,* eternally dissatisfied [ ... ] transferred some weeks ago to the Mackensenstrasse department.

20) *Gimpel the painter* †.

Once again: *All* these people, the core of businessmen, the academic and the proletarian wings, are separated from orthodox Jewry by mixed marriage. In some, the inclination to Germany, expressed in various ways, is dominant (Feder, Frank, Lazarus), in others Judaism has retained or gained a hold (Lazarus, Witkowsky).

**May 29, Saturday morning**

[ . . . ] Konrad brought a newspaper clipping of a talk or article from the *Freiheitskampf,* "The Jew is to blame" by Prof. Dr. Johann von Leers [ . . . ]. Argument: The Jews prepared the First World War; from the beginning of the century, as Socialists, they pursued the aim of making Germany defenseless, of destroying it. Enumeration of all the Jewish names and only the Jewish names in the Socialist Party, among the pacifists, etc. [ . . . ] Conclusion: "If the Jews had not been granted citizenship, but had been left in the ghetto, they would have been unable to hatch the revolt (pejorative for revolution!) of 1918 and to lay us low." Thus *only* the Jew is to blame for everything; we must *exterminate* him in Europe. That may be terrible, but is retribution and self-defense "in the face of his thirst for blood." "If the Jews are victorious, our whole nation will be slaughtered like the Polish officers in the forest of Katyn . . . The Jewish question became the core and central question of our nation, once it had let the Jews loose." — The most absurd sentence, perhaps, on the defeatism of the First World War: "There were non-Jewish criminals also, unquestionably (pretense of objectivity)—the worst was certainly Matthias Erzberger, a non-Jew, but from the old Jewish livestock dealers' lair of Buttenhausen" (so contaminated after all!). — Every sentence, every expression of this lecture is important. The feigned objectivity, the obsessiveness, the populism, the reduction of everything to one denominator, the emphasis: *The Jewish question is alpha and omega.* [ . . . ]

**June 1, early Tuesday morning**

On Sunday Lewinsky related as an entirely vouched for and widespread rumor (originating with soldiers): there had been a bloodbath in Warsaw, revolt by Poles and Jews, German tanks had been destroyed by mines at the entrance to the Jewish town, whereupon the Germans had shot the whole ghetto to pieces—fires burning for days and many thousands of dead. Yesterday I asked several people at Schlüter about it. Whispered reply: Yes, they, too, had heard the same or similar, but not dared pass it on. Eva, coming from the dentist, reported that Simon stated with certainty, 3,000 German deserters had also taken part in this revolt, and that battles lasting weeks(!) had taken place before the Germans had mastered the situation. Simon's credibility is limited. Nevertheless: *that* such rumors are in circulation is symptomatic. Simon had added: There was also unrest in the other occupied countries.

Just at the right moment, Eva told me, that there is a new poster in town—two people whispering to each other—with the caption: "Anyone who whispers, is lying." [ . . . ]

Rössler, the Aryan foreman, formerly a confectionery dealer with his own business: "You want to join us on nights again?" — "Yes, because of the coupons." — "It certainly does make a difference. I recently exchanged half a loaf (2 lbs) for 12 'fags.' We don't cook at home at all. My wife works for the army, in the officers' mess. The food there's great. And there's so much of it. Because there are always officers who eat in the hotel. She regularly brings home food for both of us. Only once a week is there no meat. In what my wife brings me, there's often a quarter pound of meat!" — Bergmann, the pharmacist, had been listening. Afterward he said to me: "He's doing well. And the workers too. They have so much to eat and more money than ever. They won't make a revolution; they don't care about the end of the war." — Where is the truth, here or with the Warsaw rumor? And if both are true—which is decisive?

[ ... ]

## June 4, Friday morning

[ ... ]

Again and again I observe the comradely, easygoing, often really warm behavior of the male and female workers toward the Jews; there will always be an informer or traitor somewhere among them. But that does nothing to alter the fact that, as a whole, they are certainly not Jew-haters. Despite that, some of us cling to the idea that *all* Germans, including the workers, are, without exception, anti-Semites. An all the more nonsensical thesis, as its advocates are all in mixed marriages. Yesterday our people had an especially jolly carrying-on with the (mostly older) women in the neighboring room. What would have happened if at the moment people were fooling around, yelling, and cheerfully touching, gestures that could also have been interpreted as demonstrations of affection, Gestapo or an informer had opened the door. Tonerti, a woman worker, bangs a pile of cartons. "They're all empty. Bluff, gentlemen, bluff!" A second woman: "What isn't bluff today? There's a dress in a shopwindow. Go into the shop and ask for a dress. Or anything else! There's nothing there, bluff, all bluff!" A Jew, gleefully: "Bleating forbidden!" First worker: "Is there a goat here? I don't see one." Second worker: "And what if you're the old goat?" The two women grapple cheerfully. Frank, the chemist, waves his little tea shovel like a dagger and throws himself between the two wrestlers ... How little imagination it takes to turn the scene into catastrophe.

[ ... ]

## June 5, Saturday morning

On the radio on Friday evening, Goebbels's leading article from *Das Reich*. On the dissolution of the Comintern. The Jewish *race* always master of camouflage. They adopt every political position that can benefit them. According to country and circumstance. Bolshevism, plutocracy—behind Roosevelt, behind Stalin there are Jews, their goal, the goal of this war is Jewish world dominion. But our propaganda is gradually having an effect, even in the enemy camp. The victory of our ideas is certain . . . Hardly has half the article been read out, than the majority of our group demands it be switched off. "Rot"—"Rubbish"—"We know"—"Turn that muck off!" etc., etc. Only Frank, Konrad, myself wanted to go on listening. The radio is switched off. [ . . . ] But the general question arises: What effect does broadcasting have? Are not the Aryans as a whole similarly irritated or indifferent? . . . And does the listener, who has a radio at home, not prefer to turn the dial to England or Moscow or Switzerland? — Intimidation through prison sentences for listening to foreign stations? One also becomes indifferent to fear—how quickly, I see once again from our group. For two weeks now there has been no new arrest, no new case of death—and Leipziger is said to have been taken "only" to the Auschwitz labor camp and not to Auschwitz concentration camp—and already the great fear has been forgotten. "Just because Eisenmann sees pink elephants, I'm not supposed to visit you!" Steinitz recently said to me at the cemetery, and yesterday it was arranged via Eva, that Steinitz will come here on Sunday (tomorrow), and we shall be their guests on the second day of the Whitsun holiday. [ . . . ]

### June 7, Monday morning

[ . . . ]

Troubles of this time: [ . . . ] The Hirschel children had been sent to play in the Jewish cemetery [see above]. There they were noisy and romped around in an unseemly way, also got on badly with Jacobi's naughty little daughter. That made things even noisier, and now the cemetery is also to be closed to them. Frau Hirschel thereupon turned to Eva as mediator: Surely the Hirschel children could play here with the little Eisenmanns again—during their visits the Aryan children of the caretakers can be confined to another garden. But that is a quite impossible demand. In normal times the Rasch children would have the same rights as the Eisenmann children, to say nothing of the Hirschels', who don't live here, and even in normal times it would hardly be possible and at any rate unpleasant and tactless, to segregate the caretakers' children. But today, when the Eisenmanns are dependent on the goodwill of the caretakers' family, when the latter are acting courageously if they allow their children to play with wearers of the star . . . Also Schorschi Eisenmann follows Frau Rasch around like a chick behind a hen, and the good-natured woman really mothers him.

[ . . . ]

### June 9, Wednesday, 6:30 P.M.

[ . . . ] — Rössler, the Aryan foreman, appeared toward six for the early shift. An intelligent, by no means National Socialist man, favorably disposed to the Jews [ . . . ], well into his forties. "Two-thirds of the war is behind us," he said in a conversation over cigars, "I reckon on another two years." — I: "Not as long as that." (I immediately regretted saying it, became anxious.) He: "Yes, two years, unless there's a miracle. If we don't manage to deal with Russia now . . . America can't do much to harm us, the English can't invade, and we can't invade them—but whether we can deal with Russia now . . ." I smiled at him and said nothing more. But I remained depressed all day. If *that* is the true vox populi, if the majority of the people are confident that Germany will still win after all, and accept another two years of war—then the war really will last another two years. — The exhausting night was again followed by a ruined day. I slept from quarter past ten until half past two, then lurched out of bed for afternoon coffee; I read aloud for an hour or less, slept on the sofa for less than half an hour, woke up shivering and have only managed this entry, before I begin to make ready for the evening. I am deeply depressed and disgusted. —

[ . . . ]

### June 10, Thursday afternoon

[ . . . ] At seven Eva came back from town, where she had wanted to fetch potatoes from the Hirschels. The Community has been sealed. No one answered the door of the Hirschels' private apartment. — Have the last Jews not in mixed marriages been deported? What will happen to us? If I go onto the night shift today, will I ever come back? —

[ . . . ]

### June 12, Saturday afternoon

Particularity of the fourth night, Thursday to Friday: We were all of us depressed by the news about Hirschel. The work went haltingly, and strangely the machines also broke down: Once the small mixing drum knocked so violently that we had to take out a load, clean the slide tray, and then refill it, so that a lot of time was lost; immediately afterward the drive belt of the larger drum heated up so much that a piece of the belt got charred, which caused another halt. Thus we remained far below our target.

[ . . . ]

So Eva brought the first news on Thursday afternoon. At Schlüter in the evening, people already knew, that Strelzyn, the goldsmith, who lives at the Kahlenbergs, had been given time off to help with the packing, because Kahlenberg and the Hirschels would be evacuated "tomorrow." On Friday morning, Eva received a very friendly farewell letter from Frau Hirschel, in which potatoes were even made over to us. Eva thereupon ventured to go to the Hirschels' apartment and learned the following: Hirschel and the Kahlenbergs, mother and son, have already been in the police cells since Thursday. Frau Hirschel has been left in the apartment with the children. These last Jews *not* in a mixed marriage will be deported to Theresienstadt immediately after Whitsun. Theresienstadt is considered a privilege and probably is one, compared to Poland; nevertheless this deportation, too, means slavery and complete loss of property. What the truth is about Theresienstadt, whether people starve and die there, or whether they exist in a halfway human state, no one really knows. The scanty news that leaks out—who is allowed to correspond with whom, and how much truth there is in the news that arrives here or there, is also quite unclear. The Hirschels, at any rate, appear to have expected something *even worse*. Eva says, Frau Hirschel had been very composed and that this composure had probably not been simply pretense. I sent word— because I know what gives her pleasure—that I owed her thanks for many stimulating suggestions, that her name would have a part in my opus if I ever published it. [ . . . ] Then on Friday at Schlüter I learned: The National Association of Jews in Germany has been dissolved. As yet nothing is known about the significance and consequences of this measure. Lewin thinks: They want to demonstrate that there are no Jews in Germany anymore. But there are still some nevertheless, and among them still a number conspicuous because of the Jew's star! In Dresden, out of 600,000 inhabitants there are 60 wearers of the star running around. What will happen to those with privileged status, what, above all, to us wearers of the star? Again and again the two contradictory rumors: We shall be exempted from the star—our marriages will be separated by force. They probably correspond to two conflicting currents within the Party. From hour to hour, my mood constantly shifts between fear, hope, indifference.

[ . . . ]

### June 13, Whitsunday midday

While I was talking to Herbert Eisenmann in the garden, Eva joined us as well; little Lisel Eisenmann (9 years of age) and the caretakers' son and daughter were exercising on the horizontal bar, and Schorschi, the three-year-old youngest child of the Eisenmanns, was romping about between the older children. It is unbelievable, and in a sense an image of new times and of the new female generation, that little Lisel exercises with such skill, strength, and asexual naturalness in the display of her body, swinging by her knees and doing all kinds of turns. The Rasch and Eisenmann children are always to be seen playing together; Schorschi (the "fix," the child raised ad hoc as Christian after the two star-wearing siblings, who were brought up as Jewish, and who brought his father release from the fifteen percent social charge but not from wearing the star—incidentally one is only "privileged" through a living child, and the privilege expires as soon as the child dies or goes abroad [ . . . ])—so Schorschi is always behind Frau Rasch like a chicken behind the hen, and yesterday afternoon, the Rasches took him with them on a long walk on the heath and in the evening carried him home asleep on their backs. But on Saturday, as we were chatting beside the horizontal bar, Herbert Eisenmann told me: Both Herr and Frau Rasch and the boy were good, dependable people (as was Milke, the somewhat gruff "block leader" on the top floor, who is often to be seen in his SA uniform—"inside he looks quite different!")—however, the Rasches' daughter, a blond eleven-year-old [ . . . ] was quick to utter the phrase: "I'll report that to the Gestapo." Late in the evening, Frau Eisenmann confirmed all these particulars. Que faire? The others of the Rasch family are so very nice. Lisel has no other playmates, and one absolutely must keep the friendship of the Rasches.

We are not mere indifferent bystanders in this whole business. The Rasches also do us some small favors; thus we now obtain milk from their source, and as a result have much more in the house than Eva could previously carry from town (and by the time she had got her ration here, it had usually spoiled, *her* ration, because, of course, *I* don't have a milk card). And now, at the Rasches' request, Eva has promised to give the girl some piano lessons. I warned her: We cannot allow the Aryan girl into our room; if, out of boastfulness or malice, she tells that . . . it can cost me my life. But the girl said to Eva: "It's quite safe for me to come to you; mother will certainly warn us when the Secret [*sic*] comes." This whole business must go into the Curriculum; it is tremendously characteristic of the Third Reich.

[ . . . ]

### June 17, Thursday toward evening

[ . . . ] Just now, as I was reading some Dwinger aloud, Frau Gaehde, who has taken a great fancy to Eva, turned up on a brief visit. She, too, has to do labor service now: Jewish women, even those married to Aryans, are deployed up to the age of sixty (Aryan women only up to forty-five), and she is in her fifties. —

To be appended: The work passes issued by the company, which stated our special shopping hours, have recently been reclaimed. The special times have been canceled; the Aryan wives should do the shopping, the Jewish men be even more isolated than before. When the passes were replaced, the chargemen at the various companies were summoned to the Community, which is now open again with an extremely reduced staff. There, Köhler, the "Jews' Pope," i.e., the NSDAP's agent for Jewish affairs, delivered this speech: Every political conversation was strictly forbidden; the chargemen had to report any transgressor immediately. Should it emerge that they had failed to make such a report, then they would receive the same punishment as the guilty man; should the Gestapo learn of any political conversations, and the guilty party could not be discovered, then the whole group would be imprisoned.

[ . . . ]

**June 21, Monday midday**

[ . . . ]

All this week on night shift I was cosseted by Stern: I always had to take a little bit of his food, from time to time he had a cigarillo for me, and always demonstrations of affection. He had spoken of his longing for music, and so I had invited him to visit us yesterday morning. He came and brought his son, a good-looking, well-behaved eighteen-year-old, who has just completed his school-leaving certificate, and is now apprenticed as a car mechanic, in the hope of studying engineering later on. Eisenmann senior, who knows Stern from Zeiss-Ikon, and is very fond of him, also came up, and Eva played Schubert and Chopin.

**June 22, Tuesday morning**

Wretched dreariness of the day shift, not mitigated by the radio. A new man has been added: Jacobi, the cemetery custodian.

[ . . . ] Aris said he is teaching his two children, the eldest is nine, himself, so that "afterward" they would immediately be able to enter a secondary school. Likewise Eisenmann senior told me, that he teaches his nine-year-old Lisel himself. The ban on schooling is a dreadful disgrace. The Jews are simply supposed to sink down into a state of illiteracy. But the Nazis will not achieve that. — I stood at the front door with Herbert Eisenmann, watching the caretakers' children and the Eisenmann children exercising on the horizontal bar—Lisel like an Olympic champion. We talked about the situation and the impossibility of making any predictions. [ . . . ] We asked him why he did not come to play music with us anymore. He could not anymore, since the last evacuation. (His first love appears to have been among those deported.) I sermonized and told him that asceticism does not help anyone else and makes us unfree. [ . . . ]

Our people at Schlüter are incautious in their dealings with the mostly older, friendly women workers. There are jokes, laughter, an arm is perhaps put around a waist. All completely harmless. — But if the Gestapo finds out . . .

[ . . . ]

The Hirschels and the Kahlenbergs were taken to Theresienstadt yesterday. The Kahlenbergs, mother and son, and Herr Hirschel were probably in prison here for two weeks. — [ . . . ]

**June 23, Wednesday midday**

[ . . . ] Eva has begun to teach Lisel Eisenmann and Hildegard Rasch, the caretakers' daughter, the rudiments of playing the piano. If the Aryan girl boasts about it, if the story leaks out, it will cost Eva and the caretaker people prison, and me, by way of concentration camp, my life. Provided that there's no talk of procuring and corruption of minors: Then Eva would end in the concentration camp, and I would end under the guillotine. These are no wild fantasies, but very real possibilities. [ . . . ] Another danger: Eva has taken over Frau Hirschel's potato-ration card; the supplier is in the picture and obliging. It's a matter of 150 pounds.

Yesterday evening in Wormser Strasse an older worker—as far as I could discern in the twilight—cycles right up to me from behind, and says in a kind, fatherly voice: "Things will turn out differently in the end, won't they, comrade? . . . Let's hope very soon"—at which he circles back and into a side street . . . The day before yesterday, on the other hand, a family comes toward me, father, mother, little boy, evidently the "better class of people." The father says instructively (and loudly) to the little boy, presumably responding to his question: "So that you know what a Jew looks like!" Now what is the true vox populi? In the Schlüter factory I can always assume it's the friendly one. The day before yesterday a slight, wretched-looking woman worker picked up a box that I was about to lift. "Let me, sir. I can do it more easily, I've got the knack of it." —

[ . . . ]

## June 24, Thursday midday

Vox populi: At ten o'clock in the evening on Wormser Strasse, a group of boys on bicycles, fourteen to fifteen years of age. They overtake me, shout, wait, let me pass. "He'll get a shot in the back of the head . . . I'll pull the trigger . . . He'll be hanged on the gallows—stock exchange racketeer . . ." and some other muttering. It soured me much more profoundly and lastingly than the words of the old worker had cheered me the previous evening. —

[ . . . ]

## June 27, Sunday afternoon

On Friday, as is now usual, Eva, after announcing her call in writing, was going to pick up 50M and the promised four pounds of bread coupons from Richter, as well as hear his opinion of the situation. His secretary explained: Richter had already been in prison for four weeks; it was not known why, and who had denounced him. He was at Münchner Platz, since the Gestapo cells at police headquarters were crowded. His case would be tried in about three weeks; he was allowed a lawyer. — My very first reaction was to be almost quietly pleased or amused that my protector and guardian was now worse off than myself, that Aryans, too, were personally experiencing the hand of tyranny, that indeed it was a sign of weakness, that this tyranny was ever increasing. But then I was tormented by what this arrest meant for us. Loss of bread coupons, loss of extra money (I still had 200M reserves with Richter, which would have helped us through four months)—the house in great danger, for who will be the next trustee? On top of that the overlapping anxiety: If they were to arrest

Annemarie and carry out a house search! — I do not need to note that in addition to all that, there is pity for Richter, and that this pity is odiously blunted. Yet Richter's life is undoubtedly at stake. If he is involved in an affair of high treason, then, as he himself knows, the guillotine is waiting for him in a courtyard of Münchner Platz. If it is merely that some rebellious remark has been picked up, he will still get a long prison sentence, which will ruin him financially and, since he is an ailing man, also ruin his health.

[ . . . ]

### July 4, Sunday midday

The night shift week passed in the usual manner: The nights went quickly, the days, despite or because of the lack of sleep—a maximum of four hours—were destroyed. What I could squeeze out in the way of work was no more than notes on reading [ . . . ] and a little reading aloud. [ . . . ]

I was depressed by the stagnation of the military situation, by what Goebbels recently called the "twilight war." For the last two or three days considerable Jew-baiting again. It had diminished for a while, and the Jews reveled in hopes of the disappearance of the star. Now documents on Jewish war guilt have been published, and already Jewish hope is turning into new fear of deportation and worse. [ . . . ]

### July 5, Monday morning

[ . . . ]

*Voces populi:* On Saturday conversation with Rasch in front of the rabbit hutch, which the family has constructed, and which so far is filled only with a single very lively animal with huge white-pink ears. "We are producing so much . . . I have been in the arms factory since '35 . . . New models all the time, quantity production, improvements . . . Everything was tested in Spain . . . (How well that fits with Goering's: We got up earlier, our warehouses and barrels are *full to bursting*, how badly with the just proclaimed war preparations and war guilt of the Jews!) We are now producing whole series of 'Tiger' tanks; and all of it, arms and men, is going east on a massive scale, a train every fifteen minutes! Our offensive is sure to start in the next few weeks . . ." [ . . . ]

### July 8, early on Thursday

[ . . . ]

Eva overheard two ladies talking in a restaurant. The older one reported a letter from her daughter, who had fled Düsseldorf. The frightfulness of the destruction. In one street, which had 91 houses, three are still standing. Three thousand dead. "They make such a fuss about Cologne Cathedral, about dead stones—they don't care about the dead people ... They should stop at long last ... Everything has turned bitter ... And then the profiteering on foodstuffs! ... In the last war the Jews are *supposed* to have been profiteering—but now there aren't any more Jews!" — Consoling, to hear something like that; there are many Düsseldorfers after all. But I no longer believe in such voces populi. They can be used as proof for *every* mood. One knows only afterward which one is decisive. [ ... ]

### July 11, Sunday toward evening

Low point of our mood on Friday: Germany announces great successes at Kursk; high point on Saturday: Allied landing in Sicily. New low this morning: Eisenmann senior said: "It'll be a second Dieppe, it's dead certain." Balancing out in the afternoon: Stern said, things must be going very badly in Sicily, because the newspaper is monosyllabic, and in Russia they are locked in battle without a decision. —
    [ ... ]
On Thursday afternoon—Eva was in town—a lady I did not know turned up; delicate Mongol-looking face, very thin, in mourning, perhaps in her late forties. Frau Winde, Eva had made her acquaintance at Frau Kreisler's. Her husband, a wood sculptor, was professor at the Academy; had to go "because of a study trip to Russia," is otherwise untouched, has state commissions. Frau Winde knew of our difficulties and brought a carton of vegetables. (Now Eva is also receiving vegetables from the Eisenmanns and the Rasches—instead of the piano fee, which she refused. On the other hand, a potato shortage is beginning. *New* potatoes are supplied only to Aryans; starred Jews have been allocated four pounds each—*four!*—for the next two weeks. We are also supposed to receive 150 pounds that Frau Hirschel left for us with her dealer; we are *supposed* to receive them, but it is doubtful whether the dealer can get hold of another 150 pounds of *old* potatoes.) Frau Winde, very anti-Nazi, her eldest son fell in the east, aged twenty; another son is serving in Smolensk, a third has just been enrolled in the army reserve; Frau Winde says it cannot last much longer; the classes being mustered now were far too young. She said further the Allies will not repeat the mistake of 1918; they will break Germany up, but not let it starve. "They will break us up into small states—I don't care. On the contrary—I have always admired little Switzerland, which doesn't need to conduct any wars." That, too, a vox populi; the penalty is being paid for the surfeit of great power politics. — [ ... ]
On Saturday afternoon I went to the Jewish cemetery, and Eva went there, too. It had been arranged: Steinitz was on duty alone, his workmates and enemies had the day off. We sat in the little glass (and skat) house behind the graves with the Steinitzes, with Jacobi and Bär, the gardener, and chatted a long time and with excited optimism about the military situation. [ ... ] Steinitz told me about two new Jewish laws that had just appeared: 1) Jewish property of men in mixed marriages falls to the

state on the husband's death; the Aryan wife "may" receive "compensation." 2) German law does not apply to Jews; their offenses are punished by the Gestapo! (In fact, this has long been so, but that they expressly present it as a new law!) — Glaser, who has privileged status, who always wears his ribbons, as well as always carrying in his pocketbook the decree that explicitly permits the privileged, unlike the star wearers, to wear ribbons, was stopped in the street by a Gestapo man. "Come here, Glaser! You're wearing a ribbon; off with it!" He appealed to the law. — "Off with it immediately!" He removed it. "And now clear off!" —

[ . . . ]

Frau Steinitz gave me the *Reich* of July 4. Goebbels's leading article: "The monument of national solidarity." The heroic attitude of the air-raid-damaged western area. How on his journeys to bring aid and encouragement he encounters only bravery and silent patriotism and hatred ("spit on them"). (Yet from various sources we hear quite the opposite: Goebbels travels with an escort, stones had been thrown at him in Essen, the "grumblers" in the West were being shot, etc., [ . . . ]) The heroic (also *humorous!* Rhineland) attitude of those affected is reproachfully held up to those who complain about their "little aches and pains," those "contemporaries, who think that their own interests come before the interests of the war, and also behave accordingly." [ . . . ] new: The *terror aircraft*. [ . . . ]

### July 12, Monday midday

Eva's birthday. I have no present for her. But in the morning I scrubbed the kitchen, so that now my hands are shaking, and she gets the 6 ounces of meat coupons that I earn with the night shift, four ounces in coupons, the rest in kind.

[ . . . ]

### July 13, Tuesday afternoon

The war situation wears one's nerves terribly, especially nerves badly affected by the night shift. A "planned counterattack—the enemy was yesterday unable to enlarge the strip [in Sicily] he has occupied." German military bulletin yesterday. Will it be a second Dieppe, or will the Allies succeed this time—and how long will it take them? . . . [ . . . ] A question one asks oneself all the more bitterly, the more heavily the slavery of the factory work weighs on one. [ . . . ]

### Later

From town Eva brought favorable news about Sicily, not unfavorable news about Russia. — Among other places, she had been to Richter's office. Our house continues to be administered there; the secretary, who is informed about everything, gave Eva the news that Richter had been indicted for a *political* offense, date of trial not yet fixed. We have the impression that it's a matter of life and death. His wife is meanwhile in the Südklinik hospital, expecting her fourth child. Very touching that the secretary handed over 50M. That in his desperate situation the man has thought of us! [ . . . ]

## July 17, Saturday afternoon

[ . . . ] I am unable to do any of my own work. All that I have managed this week is to read aloud a good handful of pages of Dwinger. If, apart from that, I managed to contribute the little I can to the domestic chores, then I was doing a lot. At the same time never fresh, always depressed. The opacity and the bloody stagnation of the war situation weighed on me. The thought of living for a long time to come, perhaps for years in this slavery, drives me to despair. I could be a little fresher if I gave up the night shift. But the few ounces of extra coupons, which would then be lost, have become completely indispensable since the new potato shortage began and since, with Richter's arrest, the extra bread stopped. Thus it is now literally the case that I am ruining myself physically and mentally for this ration card, which allows me two and a half pounds of bread a month, five canteen meals every fortnight. [ . . . ]

## July 19, Monday morning

The Saturday duty passed quietly: a mere six hours, Sunday to look forward to; in addition such a tortuous military bulletin that one could read the critical situation between the lines—all of it had an effect on the general mood. — Sunday morning at the cemetery; there Frau Jacobi, acting as the Community secretary, gave out slips for four and a half pounds of *old* potatoes—most dealers, however, would give *new* potatoes for them. [ . . . ]

On Sunday afternoon as I was coming from the cemetery, an elderly gentleman—white goatee, about seventy, retired senior civil servant—crossed Lothringer Strasse toward me, held out his hand, and said with a certain solemnity: "I saw your star and I greet you; I condemn this outlawing of a race, as do many others." I: "Very kind—but you must not talk to me, it can cost me my life and put you in prison." — Yes, but he wanted to say it and he had to say it to me. — The chorus of voices of the people. Which voice dominates and will be decisive? —

[ . . . ]

## July 21, Wednesday midday

[ . . . ]

The military situation—I am listening to the radio again now—appears very depressing for Germany, and so the Jew-baiting is on the increase again. Feder came to work very *down*. A new poster has been stuck up on Wiener Strasse: A Stürmer caricature of a Jew wearing the star; legend: "Who is to blame for the war? — He is!" Abuse had been shouted at him twice on his way to Schlüter. Reporting the "terror attack on Rome," the radio said the attack had been ordered by the Jews, it represented the war of Judaism against Christianity! — Frau Winde was here this morning with excellent gifts of food [ . . . ], literally begged me to keep no manuscript in the house, to put nothing in writing. — During breakfast little Lisel Eisenmann came to the cellar window: "Don't be scared, Frau Professor! There's a boy at the Rasches', he's ringing the garden gate bell just for fun!" — Everyone expects that the Jews will not be spared.

Signs of shortages: There are no razor blades to be bought; shops will now hone ten blades for 50 pfennigs — A questionnaire of several pages has to be answered for the register of a new Jewish administration. It came to the factory yesterday, but there were no envelopes to post it in. (We still have a couple at home.) A number of people agreed to send off their forms together in a *single* envelope. — In the hat shops: will buy old hats; one new hat in exchange for two old ones. — Likewise to be recorded under "signs of shortages" is Schlüter's fear of inspection by a committee of the farmers' organization, which is in store between now and Friday. We Jews have been informed orally, the Aryan workers by a pinned-up notice, and all literally begged to be models of diligence on the threatened days, not to take off our work clothes before the next shift has arrived, to keep the room clean, etc. Because if objections were made, the factory would be closed. It appears to be the case that the committee is bent on closure to gain hands for farmwork.

[ . . . ]

### July 23, Friday midday

The feared committee came yesterday; as expected it came during the change of shifts to see as many people as possible. So we Judeans sat around the table in the cramped changing room, and waited for the Aryan women's shift to finish. There were flowers on the table, with cards for an Aryan woman worker, whose birthday it was, leaning against [the vase]. (Flowers are forbidden to Jews.) The door opened, a young civilian, mid-thirties, dark, not blond, but very SS military-like, stepped into the room with raised arm and a loud "Heil Hitler!" Then he saw the stars, no doubt regretted his greeting and said, mockingly: "Ah, so it's *that* fraternity. What are they doing here? Has their sabbath already begun then? And flowers, what are the flowers for?" We had meekly stood up; Schlüter, the boss, standing behind the committee man, gave the necessary explanations; the little upstart muttered something else about "sabbath," looked at one of the cards, and went. — I felt bitter; Jacobowicz, the tailor, said consolingly: "I'd like to see his face in a year's time!" Later we heard that the woman worker concerned had been literally interrogated, whether it was really her birthday today, whether the flowers had been a present for her . . . So the boss is not trusted. Now the question on people's minds is whether the factory will be closed down. For *us* things can only be worse.

[ . . . ]

### July 24, Saturday midday

For weeks Eva has been complaining about pains in the area of her diaphragm, and recently these pains, which at first we thought to be nervous, have become agonizing. We rack our brains about it and are anxious. Eva thinks it is some kind of rupture, I, that it is something even worse, although she does *not* have any of the other complaints that should then appear. And now for days the distress of looking in vain for a doctor. At which point private misery and general misery become one. Katz is *not* allowed to treat Eva, but from among the Aryan doctors we would like to have a non-Nazi one, because Eva has to give my name. There is a tremendous shortage of doctors in general, made worse at the moment because it's holiday time. Fetscher, my former colleague, great friend of the Jews, who has been prevented from treating Jews; Fetscher is on holiday until the beginning of August. Dr. von Wegmarn, who once made a home visit to Eva in Hohe Strasse, is no longer at the place listed in the address book, and as a Baltic German his views are doubtful. Professor Grote of the Johannstädter Hospital "is not taking any new patients before the middle of August." Our first thought was, of course, Annemarie. But two things told against her: 1) In our experience she never risks giving us proper examination or treatment. And 2) she did not send congratulations on Eva's birthday and has not replied to our congratulations on her own birthday on July 20. Is she ill? Or on holiday? Or arrested? Eva says if the last were the case, we would already know about it. But why would they have subjected her to a house search? She could be imprisoned for some remark or other. 3) We find her relationship with Dr. Dressel, who is, at the very least, politically spineless, awkward. Despite all that, this afternoon Eva intends to go out to Pirna to see what can be done, whether Annemarie can carry out an examination herself or can recommend someone else; perhaps she will simply approach Dr. Dressel directly; as a doctor he is reliable, and there has never been any friction between him and us. — One very great worry on top of all the others.

[ . . . ]

### Toward evening

Happy end to a depressing day. Eva found Annemarie at home—not writing excused with excessive work—and was thoroughly examined. Result: It can be only a nervous stomach. Eva also brought the military bulletin back with her, which I had already heard about via Eisenmann: Palermo fallen—the Italian report candid, the German one so obscure that one can draw conclusions about the reliability of German reports from the Eastern front—the Russian offensive in the East is continuing.

For a week now I have again been dependent on what I am told, since I have no access to newspapers. But have I got much from the radio in recent days apart from the military bulletins? Nothing but boundless Jew-baiting. So boundless and heavy-handed, repeated so endlessly and stupidly, that surely it cannot continue to have an effect. The Basilica di San Lorenzo in Rome struck by bombs—Jewish pilots, Jewish declaration of war on Christendom. The suggestion of a Chicago newspaper that England should become one of the United States: Jewish plan to finally achieve world domination, the Jews in the White House would then be rulers of the world. *And so on.* — Yesterday the usual reading of the latest Goebbels article: *Conditions of victory.* We shall win if our morale remains firm; because we hold the greater sureties, and the enemy has had only insignificant marginal successes.

[ ... ]

Today I hurriedly gave Eva some sheets of my diary to take to Pirna; I lack all sense of the continuity of my notes, and for that reason there can be no question of real work.

Sussmann included a number of clippings of newspaper articles with his recent letters. I simply do not get around to reading them all.

### July 26, Monday afternoon

Stern appeared at about ten o'clock; he must let us know immediately: Early this morning German radio broadcast news of Mussolini's resignation and the order to men on leave returning to Italy, to go immediately to their garrisons. Strange how, after a few moments, the tremendous news left me so very cold. It really is tremendous and probably decisive—but, beginning with Röhm, how many pieces of news have there been in these years of torment that we took to be decisive, to be the beginning of the end, and we have been disappointed again and again. And now? Why should Germany not hold on for a year and a day even without Italy? And what if there is a pogrom now? And what if . . . there are so many possible ways of being disappointed, and I am so blunted. We spent a long time with Stern weighing everything up, and when he had gone, Herbert Eisenmann came with the same news, and we chewed over the same thoughts again, and I was unable to feel real happiness and optimism. —

Then despite the great heat, I had to go into town, order a stomach powder prescribed for Eva and hand in the airmail letter for Sussmann. The stomach powder caused difficulties in the very philo-Semitic Stephanien pharmacy. Six ounces? Impossible! They would prepare a smaller amount by the afternoon, the product was in very short supply. Also, they could not provide a box, only a paper bag. I thanked them for the great favor—because to what is a star-wearer entitled?!—and must now go there once again. On the way back, I dropped by at the Jewish cemetery for a moment. There, too, they already knew what I knew, but no more; there, too, they wanted to be happy but no one dared feel happy because the possibility of renewed disappointment, and the possibility of a final pogrom weighs on everyone. In addition there was the usual atmosphere of bickering between Steinitz on the one hand and Magnus and Schein on the other. [ . . . ]

### July 27, Tuesday toward evening

On night shift the four of us were in a happy, excited mood: The end is now in sight—perhaps another six to eight weeks! We put our money on a military dictatorship. Yesterday and today press (and presumably also broadcasting) were helpless and clumsy. On the one hand they are quite shameless in covering things up or passing over them in silence. By the way, in small print, the reader is informed that "Prime Minister Benito Mussolini, presumably for health reasons" has tendered his resignation, which has been accepted by the King, and that Marshal Badoglio is his successor, as if it were a normal and inconsequential "change of government"—thus the heading, not a headline—in a parliamentary state; then again they print Badoglio's decrees, which unconditionally point to revolution, military dictatorship, absolute reversal; they even print the proclamations of the King and of the Marshal, in which the words final victory, allies, Axis, Germany are entirely absent, and which sound completely defeatist (that of the King like a funeral speech), in semi-bold, and there is not a word of sympathy for the Duce. — Absolute opacity of the situation. Emphasis on the seat of government being transferred to the Quirinal, that "in a solemn ceremony"—why solemn?—the king is assuming supreme command of the army. Badoglio's words: "The war goes on." But nothing about victory, about common cause with Germany. Only: "We remain true to our word." To which one? Who is fighting whom in Italy now? There, too, after all, there is army and SS (Camicie nere). What about the people? The royal house? Where are the Duce and his party? Why did he go? Nothing is clear. And so no conclusion can be drawn as to the new German situation. — The night was sultry and exhausting, the day brought only heart complaints and a minimum of sleep. [ . . . ]

### July 29, Thursday afternoon

Absolute ignorance. In the press there is nothing about the Duce anymore—and yet today is his sixtieth birthday; I know that from a recent book review in the *Reich* or the *Frankfurter Zeitung,* which praised a German biography of Mussolini [ . . . ]. Naturally there are hundreds of rumors and secret "facts": A big bookshop here has not only removed pictures of the Duce, but also those of Goering. "Hermann" is in Sweden, in Switzerland, shot, Emmy Goering is in Sweden, in Switzerland, she shot at Hitler, she shot his chauffeur . . .

Yesterday lunchtime, while I was sleeping, there was a daytime air-raid warning here for the first time. Very brief and nothing happened.

[ . . . ]

### July 30, Friday, 8:30 P.M.

Stern turned up just now: Night shifts today and tomorrow are canceled because of lack of supplies. Tomorrow morning "labor deployment" ("sacking herbs") at König Albert harbor: I am excused because I would have to travel more than seven kilometers [4.3 miles] and cannot obtain a travel permit in time.

### August 1, Sunday toward evening

Since Saturday afternoon I'm facing death. Card from the Gestapo: "Requested to appear at 16 Bismarckstrasse, third floor, Room 68, at 7:30 A.M. on Monday, August 2, 1943. Concerning: Questioning. With reference to goods in storage. Transport and Warehousing Ltd." Yesterday I talked to Jacobi and Steinitz: The fact that they give a reason for the "questioning," as well as Room 68, makes it likely that the danger is small. But nothing can be said for certain, and few of those "questioned" have come home again. Perhaps they want only my furniture, perhaps my life. I have so far successfully managed to maintain my composure. I have worked hard and put creature fear aside. [ . . . ] We also had visitors, Glaser in the morning, Lewinsky in the afternoon. I said nothing to either about what was impending.

Perhaps this is my last entry, perhaps everything I have worked at over these years is lost.

I do not intend to take sentimental leave of Eva. We know what we feel for each other. I hope I shall maintain my composure to the end. Before Eva, before the Gestapo, before the gallows. A pity that I lack belief in a life to come; I find it so hard to part from Eva. She herself is stoical again, but I know that her life, too, is at stake.

### August 2, Monday morning, 11 A.M.

It was all quite harmless: "You have furniture at Thamm?" — "What?" — "My Aryan wife's marriage portion, an organ belonging to my wife, specialist scholarly library." — "Can't you put it somewhere else? We are supposed to free as much storage space as possible." — "If you order me, I shall of course try to do so—but where can it go? There would be room at Lothringer Weg, but I don't know how long I shall remain there." — "All right, the matter's closed. Do you know a Frau Huberti in Pirna?" — "No." — "Do you . . ." two further names, one of which I had noticed among the suicide graves. — "No, I never belonged to the Jewish congregation; I don't know anyone." — "The matter's closed." — "May I go?" — "Yes." The interrogation had lasted five minutes, the waiting a good fifteen minutes: at 7:40 I saw the railway station clock again and life again, from which I had felt quite removed since Saturday. (How distant the war news and Eva's appointments for the week had already seemed to me, how greatly I had been annoyed by Glaser, to whom Eva played Beethoven sonatas on the piano, he had been offered them for his record collection!) Now all life was mine again, all interest there again; I was really looking forward to the afternoon at Schlüter with the radio and food.

I really did behave bravely this time, perhaps it was also no more than lack of feeling. This time I did not even have serious palpitations, real feelings of fear. Simultaneously I dreaded the prison cell, weeks of imprisonment, murder. All that was so very close. —

The treatment at Bismarckstrasse was like that two years ago. The caretaker quite impersonal: "Wait there behind the stairs." A Gestapo fellow by the counter: "Get back there, you swine!" Upstairs in the "more lenient" Room 68, a tall junior officer at a desk fairly impersonal, not aggressive, a small fellow at the door sneering and coarse: "You can't have been here before, did they forget about you? You have to say loudly and clearly: 'I am the Jew Victor Israel Klemperer.' Now go outside and say it . . ." I do so. — "What were you before?" — "Professor? Studied for twenty semesters! Don't look at me so stupidly, otherwise I'll hit you so hard, you won't tell Whitsun from Easter." — "Were you in the war?" — "Volunteer? With decorations?" — "Bavarian Service Cross with Swords." — "As a volunteer not even the Iron Cross?" — I am standing close by the door, he wants to leave, he knocks me in the side with his notebook so that I fall a little against a bolt, pushes me with a blow to the back closer to the desk of the questioner. But these buffets are jocular more than anything else, these are the Gestapo's jokes. When I give Jacobi the promised brief report at about nine, he says: "That was First Secretary Müller who had fun with you. A good sign of the innocuousness of your interrogation. If it's important, then these people are deadly serious. — Don't say anything to anyone, in particular don't tell anyone the name of the woman in Pirna. You were presumably summoned because of her. If it emerges that you talked about it, you will be summoned again, and then things will go worse for you." —

[ . . . ]

With respect to Gestapo jokes: At the beginning of the week they were at the Jewish cemetery, sequestered the vegetable plots of the reserve strip, found some cabbage from there in Schein's briefcase. One pulled his revolver: "I could shoot you, then your grave would be handy. — You're all thieves!"

When I was back home again, Eva said: "Back from the trenches, proprio!" I: "From a particularly dirty one!"

[ . . . ]

## August 5, Thursday morning after six o'clock (and later)

[ . . . ] I felt my spirits raised, despite the hardships of recent days, on the
one hand by the constantly renewed comparison with what might have
happened if the Gestapo had not let me go again, and by the constant hope
of an imminent end—it really does look as if it were imminent, because we
are still being kept in the dark about the Italian business (there is not the
least attempt to allay disquiet, and no explanation; all communication between the new Italian government and the German government appears
to have been cut off, there is said to be *no* article by Goebbels in
the latest issue of the *Reich*), and in the East the Russian offensive is advancing ever farther.
    [ . . . ]

## August 12, Thursday late afternoon

The irregular early shift week from 7:00 A.M. until 4:00 P.M. with two half-
hour breaks at nine and half past twelve, once with overtime until five. On
Tuesday, in the packing room on the first floor, filled paper bags with 6½
ounces of natrium each, just as I had previously filled tea, except that this
stuff (ingredient of a medicinal bath) considerably irritates all mucous
membranes. Began just as peaceably on Wednesday. Schlüter appeared in
the first break, talked emotionally; on Monday a committee from Berlin
would decide on the continued existence of his factory; all the smoky and
dilapidated rooms would have to be whitewashed by then; there were no
craftsmen to be had; if we helped him, he would keep faith with us!

## August 14, Saturday afternoon

I was so tired, I fell asleep over the previous entry; all this week I have not
gotten around to any reading or any reading aloud after work, out of exhaustion. Constant heavy physical effort until four o'clock, once until five;
today, Saturday, only until half past twelve. It was all in aid of the
Potemkin village that Schlüter wants to show the Berlin committee on
Monday. The Party here will close his factory from August 31 for sanitary
reasons; he telephoned the economics ministry, which has greater authority, and in the meantime that jack-of-all-trades and Goebbels double,
Neufels, and a couple of others are whitewashing all the rooms—who
cares if the old blotches show through again on Tuesday!—and the rest of
us in the Jewish group are shoving heavy stuff around the crowded cellars, which likewise must be tidied up by Monday and stay that way until
Tuesday. There's an endless shifting about and piling up of sacks, interrupted by the loading and unloading of new merchandise and supplies,
which are constantly moving in and out. Everyone lends a hand, the boss
in shirtsleeves, likewise Schnauder, the head clerk; once Schlüter's son,
who is perhaps eighteen, was part of a chain. The atmosphere was

friendly, almost comradely—no anti-Semitism at all. Once, during the hot days—now, after the thunderstorm, it's cool—Schlüter arrived with bottles of soda water for our group; beer was not to be found. It would almost be pleasant if it didn't strain the heart and do away with my free time because of extreme tiredness. Whether the operation will be successful remains doubtful. The hygiene complaints here were presumably a pretext [ . . . ]. Schlüter is a former Stahlhelm man and not much liked; Hirschel once told me he had already been inside. And now there may be someone in the Party who bears him a grudge. — Today Schlüter went through the half-finished rooms and said to Schnauder in a serious, zealous voice: "Before I forget, we need another half-dozen pictures of Hitler; they must be *everywhere!*" (Hitler and Mussolini were hanging in our tea-filling room; the Duce will presumably disappear now.) [ . . . ] A wild war-profiteering company—primitive, unhygienic, the whole place thick with dirt—but the most humane boss, equally human and bighearted to Aryans and non-Aryans in paying wages, giving days off, etc. "The first ham I can buy goes to Schlüter," says Konrad, who used to trade in meats.

### August 15, Sunday evening

[ . . . ] Today Eva went to see Frau Richter for whom she had made a pair of little blouses for the newborn child. The woman was optimistic. Her husband has been in custody for three months—some political denunciation, followed up by the Gestapo; more cannot be ascertained. She is allowed to talk to him every two weeks in the presence of a police officer. The trial is supposed to take place at the middle or the end of September. By that time, says Frau Richter, who made a very good impression on Eva, the regime would collapse, that was certain. —
    [ . . . ]

### August 17, Tuesday toward evening

Today Eva suffered particularly acute and persistent pains. I mistrusted Annemarie, this time had her go to Fetscher, who was on holiday recently. (My much younger colleague from the TU; later he was considered a friend to the Jews; he once offered, through Kätchen Voss, to hide my manuscripts, then the Gestapo forbade him to treat Jewish patients. I cannot recollect him.) He examined Eva; it seems that her stomach has suffered a prolapse due to loss of weight; an X ray is to be made, she has just left to go to the radiologist. I was really worried, feel more at ease now. Fetscher immediately put his hand on Eva's shoulder and said: "It's coming to an end." [ . . . ] He said of the radiologist, to whom he sent her, that he was "a decent man." He again offered to take my manuscripts for safekeeping.

Yesterday, Monday, was similar to last Monday: Work until eleven, then to Simon, then to eat at the Glasers'. We stood [ . . . ] around in the cellars, there was nothing to do, we feigned work, as in the army. The mood was mixed. Happy, because English broadcasts were reporting a battle for Kharkov [ . . . ]. Unhappy, because despite the Potemkin village, we feared the factory would be closed. I shall find out more this evening. [ . . . ] Glaser would not have any of it and still believes in German invincibility.

On the way home I was wounded by the abuse of a well-dressed, intelligent-looking boy of perhaps eleven or twelve years of age. "Kill him! — Old Jew, old Jew!" The boy must have parents who reinforce what he is taught in school and in the boys' organization. —

[ . . . ]

Here in Dresden there is also fear of English air raids. Hamburg—many of the refugees come here, women in their nightgowns, only a coat on top—disturbs everyone. I can see it in our caretaker. The Jews say: "Now the Aryans know what we feel like when we are driven out in just such a state of nakedness!" [ . . . ]

### August 23, Monday morning

[ . . . ]

On Thursday I found everyone very excited: An official from the labor exchange had signed off eighteen women with immediate effect and transferred them to a sack factory; he said he would come again on Monday (today), to fetch another twenty; this factory was going to be wound up anyway, and "everyone" would be sent elsewhere. At that there was great despondency, especially among the Jews, because for us things can *only be worse*, and the box factory, to which we shall probably be sent, is particularly notorious. On Friday hope rose a little again. Schlüter came and told Konrad, in my presence, that the committee from Berlin, which had not put in an appearance recently, would arrive after all on the twenty-third (that is, today) and make a final decision, perhaps a deferment. He added: "Sometimes, gentlemen, I sleep *even* worse than you." Curious, that he makes *us* his confidants. Curious, how the most humane attitude and fairly unscrupulous war profiteering are reconciled in him. (Admittedly he loses a great deal in tax—but something must be left over.) [ . . . ]

### Afternoon toward six o'clock

Simon and Glaser over and done with, in the rain in my coat—a considerable exertion. As always, Simon chattered as he dealt with me (root treatment), I learned nothing new. At the Glasers' a peaceful lunch and the cigar which, after a little sleep, I am only now smoking, just as on the previous Mondays. [ . . . ]

I said to Konrad, who, as chargeman, has to put up with a lot of unpleasantness: "You are helpless, because your authority lacks any appropriate sanction. If you wanted to reprimand someone for an offense, report an act of insubordination, then the punishment for anything and everything would instantly and only be death, because the merest trifle leads one into the clutches of the Gestapo and so to a certain death." (Into prison and from there to "suicide" or to "shot while attempting to escape" or to Auschwitz with various causes of death.) It is asserted, moreover—I don't believe it, at least I didn't notice anything of it at the Gestapo recently—that the authorities—even the Gestapo!—were lately treating the Jews more gently: The junior ranks were beginning to fear approaching vengeance. A change of mood in this respect can already be noticed in the population. The behavior of a certain Leuschner is characteristic; he is a very anti-Semitic businessman who lives in the Community house, and who until now has displayed the greatest brutality and literally "has several Jews on his conscience"; lately he has presented himself as a friend to the Jews; "he has declared, that for him, the Jews too are human beings," etc. Eisenmann senior, usually very pessimistic, told me about it in the garden yesterday evening, [ . . . ] as well as about a number of corresponding incidents on the tram. (He inadvertently steps on a gentleman's foot and apologizes, whereupon, without saying a word, the gentleman pats him on the shoulder. A conductress says to him: "Why don't you come over to this corner, there's less of a draft." . . . A worker: "Do you still have to wear that rag [i.e., the star]?" Another: "Come on, mate, cheer up! One of the swine [i.e., the Duce!] is gone now!" I: "But the children on the street torment me more than before.")

Also welcomed as a mitigation: The Aryan wives of nonprivileged marriages have recently received a normal household card and with it entitlement to "scarce goods," at least for themselves. The first result was a tin of sardines and was greatly celebrated. Otherwise the food shortage is getting worse. The potato harvest is said to be turning out a poor one, and a stricter rationing of potatoes to be imminent.

[ . . . ]

### August 25, Wednesday afternoon

[ . . . ] Yesterday I heard new, favorable news about Schlüter. The top boss in Berlin has decided that the liquidation of the factory is to be provisionally deferred for two months and the workforce reduced. [ . . . ] and who now can plan more than two months ahead? [ . . . ] The majority of the Jews will remain; at most those who are physically and psychically "undesirable" will go, [ . . . ] that is Levy, Joachimsthal, Witkowsky, perhaps Berghausen. The rest of us will be employed only on mixing and cutting, i.e., for such *heavy* work we shall receive the "*long*-hours ration card." Admittedly most of us will be transferred to Mackensenstrasse, which is less well liked, but it is very possible, that I shall stay at Wormser Strasse, which is more conveniently located for me and less supervised. (At Mackensenstrasse the feared foreman and half boss, Hanschmann, holds sway.) [ . . . ]

### August 26, Thursday afternoon

Yesterday the news that Himmler has been appointed minister of the interior. The most radical, therefore, the Party's most notorious bloodhound, the police chief, the opponent of Goering, the exponent of the truly bloody tendency! How must matters stand in Germany, if the hangman (χατ' εξοχην!) is made minister of the interior! Fetscher's view was, yes, it was certainly an omen, but the end will not come quickly. He told the latest joke: "Anyone who recruits ten new people for the Party is allowed to resign from the Party; anyone who introduces twenty new people receives a certificate that he never belonged to it."

### August 31, Tuesday morning

[ . . . ]

Is the end approaching? Yesterday the certain news—German broadcast—of the fall of Taganrog: Is that a significant withdrawal? Confusing reports, partly from German newspapers, partly from Radebeul about a Scandinavian crisis. I myself was unable to read anything or listen to the radio. It is said supergiù: Uprising in Denmark, King a prisoner; Swedish fishing boats sunk by the Germans. What follows from all of that, how is it to be assessed? In the factory they laugh at my "optimism." D'altra parte: In the next few days Frau Winde is going to send me a bicycle, so that, if there is trouble, I can leave Dresden quickly, and Eva thinks the arrangement with Richter still stands. —

[ . . . ]

### September 2, Thursday midday

Yesterday the dreariest day for a long time at Schlüter. Mercilessly monotonous, uninterrupted filling of bags of tea, ounce by ounce ad infinitum. Feder beside me at the scales. Clock crawling around. The radio: interference, fading, tootling. The same mendacious and reticent military bulletins repeated half-a-dozen times [ . . . ]. The previous night's raid on Berlin minimized, in the East shot up Soviet tanks counted, Italian reports si de rien n'était. One could despair and believe in a whole fifth year of war.

[ . . . ]

### September 4, Saturday

[ . . . ]

Before leaving yesterday I heard the military bulletin on the radio; English troops have landed in southwest Calabria; German *and Italian* troops in action. I found it difficult to be really pleased; it's all going far too slowly. If the war alone is to be decisive, it can go on for years. Especially as the Russian offensive must soon pause for the autumn. Very unpleasant cold, rainy weather reminds us of that.

[ . . . ]

### September 9, Thursday afternoon

In the morning I dropped off to sleep as I was shaving; my knees gave way, I fell against the electric kettle, spilled hot water on the felt cover, it soaked through and ruined the varnish on the piano. During the night, while we were mixing, we had puzzled over Italy, I said it *had* to give up soon. As I was preparing breakfast, Frau Rasch appeared: "Have you heard, Professor, the Italians have capitulated! They are supposed to have signed on the third of September, it's in the *Freiheitskampf*, Herr Milke has taken it upstairs." [ . . . ] I ran up to our rooms, passed on the news to Eva in the bathroom. Then I intercepted Frau Rasch in the garden: "Do you know anything more? It is so tremendously important, the most important news since September 3, 1939 (beginning of war with England and France, *the* beginning of the war for the 3rd Reich because on September 1, 1939, Germany carried out only a 'counteroffensive' against Poland!). Really September 3? Yesterday's military bulletin talks about German *and* Italian troops fighting in *Calabria*." — "I don't know anything more, Professor; Herr Milke took the newspaper upstairs. They are supposed to have signed on September 3." Frau Eisenmann came into the cellar; I told her; with tears in her eyes she patted my shoulders, she said: "If God perhaps after all . . . ?" I lied: "It almost looks like it." While I went to bed, Eva went into town to find out more. Result: So far—Eva saw a number of newspapers at the Deutsche Bank—the news is only "in one section" of the *Freiheitskampf* under the headline: "Cowardly betrayal by Marshal Badoglio and King Emmanuel." The armistice signed on the third had been kept secret provisionally at the request of the Anglo-Americans. For the moment nothing more can be found out. As yet I cannot rejoice; it is also more than uncertain, whether anything further will follow quickly, and whether this further will not first of all be a pogrom. [ . . . ]

### September 13, Monday morning

[ . . . ]

That Thursday evening my optimism was indeed somewhat shaken. I had not thought that Germany would assert itself so powerfully and so far south, at least as far as and including Rome. Did the other side come too late yet again? Then on Friday evening I heard about Hitler's speech (given on Friday, September 10), read it on Saturday; Eva bought the newspaper, which normally we never dare do. [ . . . ] When I thought through the whole situation my hopes rose again: The ally has become the most furious enemy; the *whole* army has undoubtedly not been disarmed. A part will be fighting with the English. The disarmed Italians have to be replaced by German troops. The Pope (Pacelli!) will regard himself as a prisoner. Then there is the effect on the internal situation in Germany. (Himmler!) The German position is undoubtedly desperate. But how long will the regime hold on? Again and again Hitler declares there will be no July 25, no September 3—i.e., fall of the Duce and capitulation—here! But saying "there will not" is hardly enough, and one cannot rule permanently with the hangman and Alba of the movement as minister of the interior. The same newspaper that prints the speech reports the carrying out of two death sentences for defeatism and betrayal of the people. How many have been carried out? How long can they act as a deterrent? [ . . . ]

### September 14, Tuesday morning

[ . . . ]

Our conversations at Schlüter, particularly at night. On the one hand they often go very deep. Recently I had an argument with Feder, which came to a more or less amicable conclusion. I justifiably accused him, as I have done before, of anti-Semitism; I said he generalized from his bad experiences with eastern Jews in Chemnitz. I became extravagant: "What would Germany have become without the Jews?" He called that typical Jewish arrogance. We recognized our overwrought state and our extremism in time. The following night, during the big meal break, matters got to the point where I delivered a lecture. Is there such a thing as *the* German, is there such a thing as *the* Jew. Feder, the student of Lamprecht, was defending my books, my life's work against myself. [ . . . ]

Frau Winde really has brought her son's bicycle here and handed me the key. In the event of an air raid the bicycle is supposed to be safer here than where they live (close to the station); and in the event of terrorism I am supposed to use it to flee. —

[ . . . ]

### September 15, Wednesday morning

*LTI.* Two people, another two!, executed for "undermining the fighting strength of the armed forces."

[ . . . ]

Yesterday the hand on my clock of hope moved from October 1, 1943, to April 1, 1944. The Italian catastrophe has been turned into a German victory by military strength, by superb propaganda. According to it, the English and the Americans have achieved less than nothing, they "have utterly squandered their great effort," for they are making no advances in Italy; they have lost time, which *we* are winning, because now they will need a big breathing space before they are able to attack a "soft spot" elsewhere on the German ring around Europe. That was the sense of reflections by Lieutenant General Somebody yesterday; he summed up what was to be heard on the radio all day long and what the press was dragging out. Besides, in Sicily, where the Italians went over to the enemy, we had committed only *one* division of German troops. And even now we are defeating two Anglo-American armies at Salerno, and the freeing of the Duce is a very great victory, "a lost battle" for the enemy. — In all of that there is a little grain of truth mixed with an infinite amount of lies, but it all helps to consolidate inner resistance; there has been no "landslide" (press catchword). — In the evening Jacobowicz, the tailor, brought news of the continuing Russian advance, but it was small comfort. —

[ . . . ]

### September 16, Thursday morning

In the last two weeks, the labor exchange has on three occasions simply fetched large groups of workers from the Schlüter factory. Women under fifty, men under sixty. They are put in factories essential to the war effort. [ . . . ] For the rest of the Schlüter workforce, in particular also the Jews, a general roll call has been set for 2:00 P.M. today at Mackensenstrasse to "redistribute the work." (There have been rumors about it for a long time. I look forward to it with hope rather than fear.) — Konrad, always well-informed, said: Schlüter pays 85 percent of his profit in taxes but nevertheless retains at least 30,000M as annual net profit.

[ . . . ]

### September 17, Friday morning

Gloomy. My mood both yesterday and today, the autumn weather, the military situation, the reallocation of my factory work—all as depressing and dismal as possible. I was at Wormser Strasse for almost five months to the day (starting April 19), and it had become my familiar pigsty. — At the "roll call" at Mackensenstrasse yesterday it was all torn apart, and one was as quickly alienated from it as under similar circumstances in barracks or at school. Schlüter, the boss, sat behind a little table in the work room at Mackensenstrasse, the workbooks in front of him, the Jews to his left, the Aryans to his right and "divided up." The most crippled among the Jews were assigned to "yard duty" (clearing up, sweeping), the weaker ones to mixing, the strong ones to the dreaded cloud- and dust-wreathed work of cutting. To which I was also assigned. Unfamiliar, in part uncongenial, in part sinister faces. We, the old "we," were back at Wormser Strasse toward four, were supposed to continue filling, indeed herbal *baths* in big 13-ounce bags, managed about two dozen, stood around as if we were in a barracks, clearly and rapidly becoming strangers to one another, felt bored until after nine o'clock, left the radio on one last time. — I don't take such a gloomy view of things—advantages and disadvantages of the new situation balance out, the feeling of being part of the herd will quickly return—if only there were not the renewed destruction of my hopes of an end. It looks as if the English will be thrown into the sea at Salerno—what a triumph for Germany, what a strengthening of the regime, what a lengthening of the war! —

Today at 2:00 A.M. cutting duty for the first time. Now on with my notes on Goebbels.

## September 21, Tuesday afternoon

The alarm clock borrowed from Strelzyn goes off at half past three—it wasn't necessary today, because immediately afterward there was a half-hour air-raid warning; again nothing happened, presumably it was for airplanes returning from Berlin. At quarter past five to Mackensenstrasse in the dark, which was just passing over to first light, a waning moon high in the sky. Today there were black knots of people at the stops: The trams were still held up after the warning. At Schlüter I changed in an inhospitable cellar room, as cramped as a cloakroom and with unappetizing washing facilities, a long gutter with a row of faucets above it and a platform in front. I don't wash there but change my shirt. The work is no harder or dirtier than the mixing at Wormser Strasse. Except that everything is simply more factory-like. The pounding of the cutting machines (reminiscent of an express train), the howling roar of the fan motors, which look like huge lampshades; the clatter of the rocker and of the sieve machine resound together and fill the room; one has to shout to make oneself understood. It is dusty, the dust rises in clouds, my goggles steam up, I see the figures and the lights through a veil: A certain romance, more marked than on the night shift at Wormser Strasse, a certain masquerade of factory work, masquerade as far as I am concerned, has a comforting effect and makes the time pass more quickly; or, rather, had, because the spell is already wearing off, and the dreariness remains. I stand by the rocker. — The cutting machine beside it determines the pace of work. If it is going at full stretch and one of the Aryan chargemen is operating it, then I can keep up only with an effort and begin to sweat—but then existence is also at its most bearable and time flies. The good beans into the tub, the bad ones you may eat: What the cutting machine spits out, Strelzyn shovels into a funnel for me; shaken through three sieves, one on top of the other, three separate streams dance and flow toward me; two containers collect the coarse and the very coarse residue, the third everything that has been finely cut. I stretch a sack inside a wooden frame, fill it, label it, tie it up, drag it away; in between I shovel up the residue onto the wooden table beside the cutting machine, so that it can be cut again. There a man is constantly engaged in depositing the herbs on the table with a shovel or a coal fork; the Russians, familiar to me from the week in the yard in summer, drag the huge bales from the yard or the storehouse opposite. With one hand the cutter forcefully pushes the herbs into the trough as far as the cylinder cutters, with the other hand he pulls the herbs from the table and tugs and loosens them. It demands strength, skill and constant attention, for the hand that is pushing is at risk. As already mentioned, when the machine is running at capacity I

almost lose my breath. But it runs at maximum speed for only a few minutes at a time. There is always something that causes an interruption. As
soon as the newly trained Stern and Aris operate it, there are stoppages,
and when the foreman operates it, there are also frequent stoppages. The
knives are very sensitive, a little dust, a skein of herbs that have not been
sufficiently loosened, then again a skein of herbs that is too soft—they take
everything and anything amiss and have to be readjusted afterward. Or: a
bale is finished, a different sort of herb is announced. As a result there are
only minutes of work at a time that are a strain. In between there are
breaks, in which one can get through the residue; in between there is also
constant sweeping, quite apart from the big cleanup, which regularly starts
one hour before work finishes. In contrast to Wormser Strasse there is only
*one* proper break, which is spent in a decent room next to the kitchen and
lasts exactly thirty minutes [ . . . ]. Most have their food delivered "privately," as they say, from a "Bohemian kitchen"; a female clerk takes the orders in the morning. I myself have settled for the "Russian food," which is
fetched in pails from the "public welfare." It is a "dish of the day," without
any fat, but the amount is large and it costs only 30 pfennigs—"privately"
costs 50 pfennigs or more, and coupons as well—I intend to take it regularly during all three shifts, since we are suffering a shortage of potatoes at
home. The greater coziness, but also the greater boredom of Wormser
Strasse is gone. The noise of machinery makes any conversation impossible, also one or two Aryan chargemen are always in the room, the still
youthful Noack, an even younger man with a somewhat coarse face and
tone, but quite a good fellow, and finally the curiously eccentric Kretzschmar, who is a mixture of willingness to help, martyrdom, and vanity.
Fifty-two years of age, wild, deep-set blue eyes in a gaunt face. Skilled precision engineer, watchmaker, bellfounder. [ . . . ] In the evenings he plays in
the band at Wachendorf's on the Weisser Hirsch. "Which instrument do
you play?" — "Cello, violin, piano . . ." — "Where did you learn?" — "At
the Dresden Conservatory." He has a tattoo on the lower arm, served in the
merchant navy and has been to Brazil. He was married; one son is a professional boxer, "he's already been in the newspaper." Your wife is dead?
"No, she liked variety too much; as long as the children were small, I
thought I had to uphold their mother; but now . . . I would like to help you.
I have already been in prison myself; I know what it is like for all of
you . . ." Etc., etc., right on the first day. What of all of that is true? At any
rate the man is like a stage character and extremely humane as a chargeman. — Stern, who has some familiarity with machines from his father's
factory and from textile school, operates the cutting machine; Strelzyn and
I are at the sieve machine; over at the small cutting machine—it cuts only
soft herbs, which do not need to be sieved first, but can be put into sacks
immediately—are Aris and Bergmann, the pharmacist, and Witkowsky; in
the next room Frank, Feder, Lazarus, Lewin, Jacobowicz operate mixers,
which are bigger than those at Wormser Strasse. Thus I am, or rather was,
surrounded by familiar faces. I *was*, because at midday today a sudden re-

arrangement was undertaken; Aris, Strelzyn and myself were ordered to another shift, a notorious one. "The dregs of Jewry," says Bergmann, who has worked on it; "a malicious foreman who doesn't consider that you are old and unskilled," says Kretzschmar. On verra—my situation is altered again, and that is a change to some extent. And the most unpleasant man on the other shift, whom I have seen only once, but often heard mentioned, is changing to my present one. Everything would have been different for me if he had remained there. For this man, a certain Müller, a blond man with deceitful blue eyes, is a Jew, a star-wearing Jew, but before his Jewishness was ascertained he was an SA member, is still friends with his former comrades, is considered an informer, and dangerous at least, and is said to have Gestapo permission to conceal his star on the street.

[ . . . ]

Neumark as "representative of the National Association of Jews in Germany"—it has risen again, after the property of the first was confiscated—announced this "order of the supervisory authority": Every Jew has to name a representative, who will immediately notify Neumark of his decease. This has been ordered, because "after death the property of Jews falls to the state." (There is no longer any mention of "compensation," which "may" be accorded an Aryan wife.) I gave Eva as the required "reliable person in my immediate surroundings," the other people in my group also gave their wives.

[ . . . ]

### September 24, Friday morning

My new work does after all exhaust me far more than that at Wormser Strasse. Shoveling, shoveling, shoveling with spade and fork onto the cutting table, or shoveling into sacks what has been ground. Knoch, the chargeman, sets not only a murderous pace, he often also drives us, and then my heart cannot keep up. On top of that there is no break from two until six. That is to change now: Instead of taking a break from six almost until seven, there are to be two breaks of half an hour. The supervisor is not malicious, but is like an NCO. On the machine, which is very difficult to clean, he shows me a flap of whose existence I could not possibly have known. As he did so, he said: "I have to expect a little intelligence from everyone." Almost more than the pace of work I am depressed by the lack of communication with the other Jewish people on the shift. During the break they sit silently by themselves or play cards. Yet Garnmann, a little man of sixty-four years of age, formerly a businessman, the third worker on our machine, is uncommonly friendly and helpful to me. And Aris, who is far from mastering the cutting, laments the tempi passati with me. Yesterday evening I also became a little friendly with Steinberg, the whisperer, whose vocal cords were damaged in a concentration camp. We walked home together in profound darkness (by way of Gerokstrasse). Nevertheless: The whole thing, I can think of no other word for it, is dreary. I am often very depressed, as yesterday morning. Later my spirits were roused again by the latest war news. The military bulletin is catastrophic; the little threadbare disguise worse than naked confession. In the face of the never-ending backward movement (now as far as Kiev) the word "disengagement" sounds tragicomic. [ ... ] Also, the constant retreats in Italy, which are conducted victoriously and without loss (from Messina, from Sardinia, from Calabria), appear embarrassing. Likewise the strained descriptions that refer to us as victors and creators of order in Italy. Whereas in fact there's civil war and chaos. — Sure sign of a crisis: yesterday's headline in the *Dresdener Zeitung* is "Japan's fighting strength is further increased." [ ... ] Headline of the military bulletin: "Disengagement proceeds according to plan." "According to plan" has been much in favor recently. —

[ ... ]

### September 27, Monday toward evening

On Friday I was told I would be going back to Wormser Strasse. On Saturday, however, I remained on my cutting shift. The work that day was easy, nor was it too much of an effort today, not at all. I held sacks that were being filled with herbs, in the open air of the courtyard at that. Nevertheless, I remain very exhausted. My heart suffers, my mood suffers. I already know the new sounds: The machine pounds, I have to shovel ever more quickly to keep the table full; I feel my heart straining; I shall have to stop. Now the sound of the machine is lighter, the pounding has stopped: I know that the cutter has thrown the lever on the flywheel, the cogwheel is no longer driving the cylinder; a delay of a few seconds helps me; the man has to put the strip in the trough in place again. The noise fades away entirely—breakdown! The motor is switched off, the cylinder has to be raised by laborious turning, the blade cleaned and adjusted—my break lasts several minutes; I can first of all draw breath and then throw a reserve supply onto the table in peace. But the exhaustion remains. — And the sense of dreariness, of lost time, grows from day to day. I can hardly even think of my own work. [ ... ]

### September 28, Tuesday toward evening

The alarm clock went off by mistake for the first time, at three; to be on the safe side I set it for half past and dozed for another half hour. In the morning Noack, the deputy head foreman told me: "You have to go on night shift today, they're a man short, you can finish work here a little early." I worked until a quarter to twelve, changed, gulped down my Russian food in the kitchen, while the Russians were dining next door, was home at one, set to washing up and preparing our afternoon snack. Eva appeared, very tired and embittered by town and begging errands and loaded with over 16 pounds of potatoes from Frau Winde. In addition, she brought the news that the little stand at Schillerplatz (which is friendly to Jews) had set aside a hundredweight of potatoes for us. Immediately after eating (my shopping hour three till four!) I went out with the Rasches' old high-wheeled pram. The heavy sack was loaded very precariously on the rickety vehicle, and other things I had got, apples and tomatoes, were stuffed underneath. It was difficult to keep the pram balanced. At Prellerstrasse it tipped forward, apples and tomatoes rolled out, and the sack was in the street. I did my best; I was unable to lift it up. A man was nowhere in sight. Then a lady, already turning gray, came running up with a little boy. "I'll help you." She must have seen my star—it was a demonstration. Together we really did get the sack up; I was moved as I thanked her. But then I had severe angina pains, only for a few minutes, but still a depressing memento. At home I was kept busy pouring the potatoes into containers—the hundredweight of potatoes: 4.90M, the sack 5M deposit!—after that with washing up again. I am exhausted and the night shift lies before me. I have the tormenting feeling that I am shortening the remainder of my life.

[ . . . ] In place of the *Frankfurter Zeitung,* which ceased publication, Lewinsky is subscribing to the *Deutsche Allgemeine Zeitung* [*DAZ*] and brought a couple of copies with him. It contains exactly the same commentaries on the situation as the *Dresdener Zeitung,* in a little more detail, accommodating its style to the regular readership [ . . . ] aristocracy, senior civil servants, ecclesiastics—but literally identical in all arguments and catchwords and slogans. Quite obviously, every day a central office issues the official blurb, which *all* newspaper authors have to print or paraphrase. Just as Goebbels once said with delight of marching Hitler Youth: The same face everywhere. That, too, is part of the already frequently emphasized *poverty of the LTI.*

### September 29, Wednesday midday

Just like the army! I arrived at the factory yesterday evening; no one knew I was coming, no one needed me, especially as the motor of the small cutting machine had meanwhile broken down. I aroused sympathy, as I had already done on the early shift—"and at your age!" [ . . . ] Finally I was told: "Go home and get a good sleep. *I'll* sort it out. If anyone asks, you were here, and the rest of you don't say anything; he *was* here!" That was the good Kretzschmar, who will now have to forge 8.80M on the payroll for me for the night I have been spared. — I went home under the now milder starry night and found Eva had not yet gone to bed. We were very cheerful together. Thus I have gained a day and a little sleep.

[ . . . ]

Have I noted that Schlüter will finally shut down on October 31? A great threat for the Jewish workers. They will be put in Schwarze's notorious cardboard-box factory. Endless journey (Leipziger Strasse), bad treatment, no heavy worker's card, *ten*-hour shifts. I know that from Lewinsky, who works there, but it is also the general opinion. [ . . . ]

Now at last I want to tackle Hitler's *Mein Kampf,* which has been lying here for weeks. I read the first few pages a long time ago on Glaser's balcony.

## September 30, Thursday evening toward seven o'clock

After the night shift four hours of daytime sleep, washing up beforehand, washing up afterward, and kohlrabi to clean, two meals—what is left for diary and Hitler? I am presumptuous no doubt; in the factory I see how work and daily life for millions of people consists of shoveling, hauling, sweeping; even the skilled worker is restricted to a few manual movements a hundred times over, and for the Jews, who come from higher professions, this proletarian existence has long ago (for at least three or four years) become taken for granted. If they have been in the factory at night, they calmly sleep through the day; they have given up all, all intellectual interests. [ . . . ] Kretzschmar, the famous bellfounder, is shift leader. The night is cold, the heating boiler is not working. Before beginning we usually sit in the dining room next to the kitchen from ten until quarter past. We (Doctor Lang; Müller, the SA man; Bergmann, the pharmacist; Jacobi, the cemetery custodian; old Witkowsky; and myself) sat chatting until half past eleven. Then, until one o'clock, the big machine cut bean pods—Bulgarian produce, in which quantities of beans are always said to be found; one of us always crouched on the floor and looked, Jacobi already had a whole tea caddy full—after that there was a coffee break until about three (I found my public-welfare food was there and shared it with Bergmann). As a newcomer, it was impressed upon me: We started at a quarter past ten and had a break only from half past twelve until one. Kretzschmar is good; if his behavior is found out, then we're all in the soup. Kretzschmar's behavior: he tells us: "I was six years in Dachau concentration camp (Communist, served in the merchant navy; Noack, likewise a sailor and Communist, was in a concentration camp for four years, but Noack is a more disciplined, normal man, a splendid fellow), here, the scar at the base of my neck, that's a bayonet stab wound; here on my face, that's a blow from a gun butt; here, the puckered skin on my forearm, that's an acid burn. There's no fence around the camp, only a white line, every ten yards inside it there's an SS man with a machine gun; if somebody crosses the line, the machine gun cuts him down. The sentry hits somebody and his cap rolls over the line. 'Fetch that cap!' And the machine gun clatters, and the man has been shot 'attempting to escape.' — The Jews are together with the Aryans. Ban on talking in the dormitories, one's only allowed to whisper while working. It's nice and easy for them to talk about 'mutiny.' A squad has to dig a grave, stand in front of it—then the machine gun cuts them down . . . The work: turning Dachau Moor into farmland: every day using ax, spade, and saw on a plot 33 feet by 3 feet to a depth of 2 feet. Anyone who doesn't achieve the target—no matter how old: punishment drill with a sandbag and wrapped in heavy cloths. And the food! [ . . . ] be glad that you've got your freedom

(Relative: our freedom!), put up with the hardest work, keep your mouth shut, beware of Knoch—if he wants to pin something on somebody—he can make people disappear . . . [ . . . ] I know what things are like for you, I want to help you, but you must keep your mouth shut. Yesterday I credited *him* (he points at me) for the whole night (on the payroll); I think on Saturday, you could clear off at ten, and if there's no check—and there won't be— I'll write twelve. But keep quiet!" — After dealing with a number of breakdowns, he then cut at a good pace after the coffee break. Nevertheless: A quantity corresponding to eight working hours on *two* machines could, of course, not be achieved. Filled sacks produced by earlier shifts were standing around everywhere. Noack had new labels in Jacobi's handwriting attached to a number of them and dragged them over to *his* sacks; thus there was a respectable nighttime result. Then the small machine was opened as well, so that it looked as if it had also been in action. I got the impression that this or something like it was normal on Kretzschmar's shift . . .

Aside from him, I found Stephan SA Müller the most interesting man. I should be very surprised if he were really an informer and spy. He makes no bones of his views. Barely seventeen, he volunteered as an airman in the First World War, later he was in the SA and in the Sudeten German Freikorps, ardently German even today, baptized long ago, vehement opponent of the theory of a Jewish race. No one can take his Germanness away from him, and he wants to remain in Germany. "In a year you'll have your little house again, Professor!" — "That's a forbidden political conversation, Herr Müller!" — "Surely there's no one here who's such a wretch that he would denounce anything!" The others calmly discuss war and politics with him. Every conversation is interlarded with Jewish expressions, jargon, and obscenities. *I* am consistently treated with friendliness and a little respect. — Everyone fears the cardboard-box factory. — The supervisor, Dr. Lang, a medical man, born '94, is very proletarianized.

### October 1, Friday

[ . . . ]
This morning the long-expected and yet surprisingly bad news of our "resettlement." We, together with the Eisenmanns, are to be put in the Hirschels' former apartment, 3 Zeughausstrasse. For seven persons an inadequate fish barrel of three and a half rooms, with other serious disadvantages as well. Tomorrow Eva is going to confer with Neumark, the "representative" of Dresden's Jewish remnant. More about this depressing matter then.

### October 3, Sunday midday

Suffering from the damp autumn cold. That makes it easier to leave. It appears that the resettlement will not turn out quite as badly as seemed likely at first. Eva at any rate is facing it calmly. She saw Neumark and then went to Zeughausstrasse. It appears we shall not be crowded together with the Eisenmanns; tolerable space has been found for us. Everything is still in flux. [ . . . ]

## October 7, Thursday morning

[ . . . ]

It is strange how even the smallest group develops its specific group peculiarities and language and retains them even when new members are added and old ones leave. Stern recently told me that at Zeiss-Ikon he had not much cared for the coarse tone of SA Müller, his frequent shouts of "Jew!" Now in Mackensenstrasse *our* shift has its particular tone, which is quite distinct from that of the other groups. Yet only Dr. Lang, the physician and chargeman, and SA Müller are original members of this group, Jacobi, Bergmann, Witkowsky, and myself are newcomers. Language: As joke and banter they are constantly shouting *Jew* at one another, *even* in the presence of Aryans: "Old Jew!" — "Jew Bergmann!" — "Washing Jew!" (that refers to the use, or not, of the uncomfortable and unappetizing washing facilities in the cellar—I and a couple of others do not use them), etc., etc. The shouting is thanks to the noise of the machinery; but the Berger, Rieger, Steinberg, etc., group does not shout, but remains silent. During the meal break at six, while the Berger group remains silent and plays cards, our shift is debating passionately, and about quite different things than we talked about at Wormser Strasse. Not about food, also very little about the military situation; rather always in principle about Germans and Jews. Müller is vehemently German, without being anti-Semitic, although he has an aversion to eastern Jews; he disputes the existence of a Jewish *race*, he disputes that the German people are universally anti-Semitic, he disputes that Hitler and his regime completely correspond to the character of the German people. Dr. Lang is very bitter; to him anti-Semitism is an ineradicable part of the German character, Hitlerism absolutely in conformity with the German character. Jacobi, who is muddleheaded and hardly altogether normal, and Witkowsky take up positions halfway between the two; I, in large part, agree with Müller. Opposition to the constant shouting of "Jew" is making itself felt. [ . . . ] I suggested avoiding the word, at least in the presence of Aryans.

A peculiar position is adopted by Edelmann, the huge, blond heavyweight from Odessa (tobacco master—or blender—by profession: "at the end I had a monthly income of 1200M"), who joined us a few days ago. He curses all the rabbis, who for millennia have upheld Jewry as something separate. "Without them we would long ago have been absorbed into other nations and would not need to suffer so dreadfully, be so cruelly persecuted again and again throughout the centuries! Yes, if they had been able to found a state of their own! But they've never managed that." — "And they never will manage it," jeered Müller. "I'd like to see the state that they set up . . ." Here I contradict him: Disraeli, Stahl, the coming independent federal state within the British Empire . . .

[ . . . ]

## October 9, Saturday morning

On every birthday since October 9, 1934, I have said: "Next year we shall be free!" I was always wrong. This time it looks as if the end must be near. But they have so often prevailed against every natural likelihood, from the Röhm affair onward; why should they not go on conducting war and murdering for another two years? I am without optimism now. Meanwhile we shall move into the third Jews' House and this time stick our necks in the tightest noose. If it suits the Gestapo, the Jewish remnant bottled up in Zeughausstrasse can be finished off in a couple of minutes. [ . . . ]

Following the last deportation of Jews, the clothes store fell to the state and has been confiscated. Now we are informed by Neumark, the representative: "The Senior Revenue Officer of Dresden, who has taken over the stocks of the clothes store, prior to disposing of them, has declared himself willing to give Jews without a clothing card the once-only opportunity to make urgently needed acquisitions . . ." My application, adapted to the conditions of the circular, states word for word: "In accordance with the circular of 10/6/43 I respectfully request the following items from the clothes store: 1) one pair of work trousers (I own one pair, which is completely worn to shreds and past repair). 2) one pullover (I own one, which is completely worn-out and full of holes). 3) four pairs of light socks (I own three pairs, which have been repeatedly darned and are past repair). 4) one pair of suspenders (I own one pair, which is incomplete and supplemented with string). I declare that my statement is true, and that I do not possess a clothing card."

## October 11, Monday toward evening

[ . . . ]

Today a pale, blond, and likeable-looking young man, Hirsch, reported to our shift; he will now be put with the packers at Wormser Strasse. Six months ago he was arrested with Leipziger and others supposedly for concealing the star. Of the others, some are dead, some are in concentration camps. He is the only one to be released. He is said to owe it to his wife, who managed to see some senior officials in Berlin. He says: After a while he got used to the hunger, but the uncertainty and the mental anguish! He spent the whole six months in a cell in the police prison, Jews are excluded from the daily walk in the prison yard. He was in solitary confinement without any occupation for ten weeks before other people were put in with him. Apart from that he had been treated decently. I thought of my eight days of solitary confinement—how long ago!—and I shivered. —

[ . . . ]

## October 14, Thursday morning and later

Eva has been fighting an illness since Sunday, has been in bed a lot. [ . . . ] I informed the very sensible wife of the caretaker—what a good thing that Hildegard Rasch is Eva's pupil!—she was in the picture immediately. I am not allowed to call a Jewish doctor for Eva, an Aryan one is hardly likely to admit me, a wearer of the star, and may perhaps refuse to treat Eva, all doctors are overburdened; Fetscher lives a long way away; if possible I don't want a Nazi . . . Frau Rasch went to telephone. Result: Dr. Poetzsch would come; he had already treated "Herr Alexander" (Jacoby, a deceased son of the owner of the house). He came at about twelve, an upright, homely old Saxon and a typical uncle-doctor of the old school. [ . . . ]

We shall move to 1 Zeughausstrasse on October 30. Eva saw the rooms and conducted the negotiations. The steam heating is not on here and I am freezing beyond all measure; on my icy way to work early this morning I saw hoarfrost under a bright, silvery, full moon and silvery mist. (On the way back, in Emser Allee, where I always pick up a few chestnuts for the Eisenmann children, I found 26 chestnuts.) Our rooms in Zeughausstrasse are supposed to be south facing and sunny and to be heated by a stove; here we are in north-facing holes with the central heating shut off. But I fear the gossip of the crowded-together Jews; I have had a foretaste of that at Schlüter. Each one mistrusts his neighbor, slanders him behind his back. [ . . . ]

## October 16, Saturday evening toward ten o'clock

I left Eva about five hours ago; the ambulance drove into Fürstenstrasse City Hospital, which I was not allowed to enter. She was relatively fresh and heartily cheerful, but I cannot get rid of the terrible thought that perhaps I have seen her for the last time. It's a pressure inside me; beyond that, hunger, boredom, egoistical imagining of my deportation if my Aryan wife dies, certainty that I am too much a coward to commit suicide, thoughts on what I should do *then*—I asked her where she had hidden my manuscripts [ . . . ]—feeling of absolute emptiness, and underneath it all, while eating, reading, whatever my occupation, there is the pure physical pressure. I am nothing without Eva, and if I lose her I shall go on dragging out a meaningless life out of sheer senseless fear of death. [ . . . ]

Yesterday evening Frau Eisenmann said things could not go on like this; I would have to call Dr. Poetzsch again. This morning Eva had a temperature of 103; I had Frau Rasch call him, immediately afterward her temperature rose to 104. He came at midday. [ . . . ] "I urgently recommend hospital; I shall have an ambulance sent for you." [ . . . ]

Cruelty in the 3rd Reich: Yesterday Eisenmann senior traveled to Berlin to the Jewish Hospital for an intestinal operation. The Nazis would rather hurt themselves than forgo an act of cruelty. Eisenmann could very easily be operated on here, in x hospitals. No—a Jew must go to the Jewish Hospital in Berlin, must encumber the railways. Admittedly he's not allowed a seat. He has to stand or sit on his suitcase. In general he's also allowed to use only slow trains. After a lot of to-ing and fro-ing (Neumark–Gestapo), Eisenmann was given a dispensation in this respect. Compare with the case of Jacobi; the man was operated on here, but sent home immediately afterward in poor condition. [ . . . ]

### October 18, Monday toward evening

I sent Frau Rasch to the hospital with the things Eva requested (soap, tooth powder). She was unable to speak to Eva, but the nurse gave her favorable news. Nevertheless I am uneasy. [ . . . ] In the morning, I first went to Mackensenstrasse to register for the night shift and to make sure of my rations. Two portions of Russian food will be reserved for me every day: I shall eat one meal there and take one home in a pot; thus I am catered for, *the rest is coffee*. Then into town to Richter's office. I already knew from Eva that the secretary is on our side; her husband was taken prisoner at Stalingrad. She was really friendly, was touchingly sympathetic. She is going to send me bread coupons. She spoke despairingly of tyranny and many executions. Richter, released by the court, is still "in the hands of the Gestapo." He is held in the police prison—at least his wife is allowed to visit him and supply him with food—he is supposed to be transferred to a sanatorium. Unfortunately, it looks as if the administration of our house is going to be taken from him. The last 60M was handed over to me. Back very tired at one o'clock; on the way it was almost excessively warm, but in the house, in particular in our north-facing rooms, unbearably cold. [ . . . ] Then the business of moving, which is still up in the air, weighs on my mind. Should I take Eva back to these caves of ice as a convalescent? Should I do the move without Eva and create chaos? [ . . . ] I shall talk to Neumark on Wednesday.
[ . . . ]

### October 20, Wednesday afternoon

I am awaiting news by way of Frau Rasch. Today is visiting day. After that I shall negotiate with Neumark to postpone the move; as "representative" he has a consultation hour at a quarter to six in the Community House. The long distances on foot eat up all my free time, and that's good: "One" remains numb and blunted; "one" could not concentrate anyway on work or devotion to Eva. [ . . . ]

### Evening, 8:45 P.M., kitchen

Air-raid warning just now; I am not allowed to leave the house until it ends. Only an hour ago I saw the play of the searchlights practicing and the silvery airplane caught in their beams. I am convinced that Dresden will once again be spared.

News from Eva very good on the whole, almost comically good. She has written down an extract from her clinical record. No temperature since yesterday. Hungry, nothing to eat yet. [ . . . ] I then went to the Community, first spoke to Neumark alone, then waited for Köhler, the Gestapo representative, to arrive. A fat, stolidly brutal-looking lout of middle age, a pasha, who knows very well that literally the lives of those present are dependent on him. Everyone stands up in deadly silence when he enters the room without greeting. Neumark reports obsequiously in a low voice to the man sitting at the desk. Glance at me: "What does *he* want?" Neumark explains. Gracious decision: It was all the same to him, Köhler; if we did not think it better to have the woman come out of hospital to already "well-ordered circumstances" . . . Neumark pleads. I am asked what I live on. Neumark whispers to me, I can go, the move postponed until well into December . . . I came back very tired, slept on the sofa for half an hour, again with the security of the alarm clock. — Downstairs I found 3 ounces of sausage that "a gentleman" had left for me. Presumably a donation from Stern. —

[ . . . ]

### October 31, Sunday evening

On Sunday, October 24, Eva discharged herself "on making a written declaration that it was on her own responsibility and she was not yet recovered" and was brought back in an ambulance. She arrived here about six; I was at the factory (shift from 6:00 P.M. until midnight), our apartment locked. Eva was put to bed at the Eisenmanns', and Herr Rasch fetched me from Schlüter as we were still sitting in the dining room before starting work. Eva carried up on a chair, was very weak, very limp, very blissful to have escaped the hospital. [ . . . ]

All week long, Schlüter's struggle, bordering on agony; yesterday, Saturday, a tremendous farewell speech to the Aryans—"our Jewish fellow workers—I can say that, after all, we are all human beings!—will remain another one to two months." Joy and reassurance. At midday today Strelzyn turns up here: Order from the labor exchange by way of the Community: Schlüter completely closed down, the Jewish group scattered; I myself to Bauer, Neue Gasse, tomorrow morning. So I was at Schlüter's from April 19 until October 30, 1943. Very depressed.

[ . . . ]

### November 14, Sunday midday and later

Eva's protracted convalescence. She can stand up for half an hour at a time, but not yet go down to the cellar kitchen. I am kept busy all the time; impossible to write a single page. Chaos on my desk, everything just piled up in the drawer. A few notes for the diary on scraps of paper, virtually indecipherable. Apart from that, life very monotonous. Repetition of events, moods, thoughts. Endlessness of the war, Russian victories; but not sweeping; "snail's pace"—the latest catchphrase, I think used by Hitler; snail's pace of the English in Italy; executions and fear inside Germany as hunger begins (shortage of potatoes). General opinion, Aryan and Jewish: It can last another year. I am all the more depressed, as 1) the new work is even more deadly for me than Schlüter's, 2) since November 1 no further pension payment is being made. (I first heard of it on the tenth, as a rumor related by Feder, then as fact at the bank on November 11. I am taking it philosophically: Our reserves as supplement to my factory wage will last about nine months—who will want to make provision for longer than that? But of course it weighs heavily.)

Since Monday, November 1, paid as an "unskilled worker" by the company of Adolf Bauer, Neue Gasse, box factory (pharmacy packets and bags, in particular proofed card containers for creams and ointments), but loaned out (see below) to Thiemig & Möbius, Paper Processing.

My day during the first half of this month:

Alarm rings at half past three. Washing up, breakfast, mine usually gulped down, take Eva's first meal upstairs shortly before six. [ . . . ] At 6:15 A.M., in the dark, I get onto the no. 18 tram. Permission for public transport, a Greek gift. In the morning, it's merely cold on the front platform, but the darkness protects me. But at midday, among the crowds and traffic, I am more helpless than a dog. Once, as I was getting on, an SS officer tugged at my sleeve: "You walk!" I had to stay behind. That was bad. Much worse recently, on the eleventh [ . . . ] at midday on Marschallstrasse, the platform fairly empty. A junior officer gets on, fixes his eyes on me. (I am sure I have seen that blond face before. I remember: the Gestapo officer who shouted at me and poked me in the ribs when I was at Bismarckplatz because of the furniture.) After a short while: "Get off!" — "I've got permission to travel." — "Get off!" I got off and, buying a new ticket, went on with the next tram. The midday journey has been torture for me since then. From one stop to the next I expect a new calamity. — Work at Jagdweg begins at seven. Working day 7 A.M.—4:15 P.M. For the first three weeks, thanks to a doctor's certificate on Eva's condition, I have to work only until 12. At the beginning and in the last few days, drudge jobs (flattening paper, counting envelopes and putting them in boxes); in between, for the longest time, at an envelope machine. Morning break, exactly 15 minutes, 9–9:15 A.M.; midday break, 11:45–12:45.

The morning passes fairly quickly; I still have to face the dreariness of the long afternoon. Constant nightmare: if it should last another year after all! I am already so apathetic, that I doze through the day almost painlessly.

After the food, which is now provided off the ration for us—except on Saturdays—the agonizing journey home. Frau Rasch, who has helped us out most loyally, has meanwhile provided Eva with a cup of coffee at nine and with fried potatoes at twelve. I begin to read aloud a little; out of extreme tiredness it very quickly turns into stammering. Then I have to attend to domestic chores (washing up, cooking, carrying up and down stairs); Frau Rasch takes care of the shopping. Then visitors drop by regularly, many visitors and nourishing ones. Most to be praised is Frau Winde, who does everything she can to help and bring things. A pot with cooked food, a pot with potato salad, tomatoes, vegetables, potatoes, bread, cake . . . [ . . . ] Frau Steinitz brings cakes. Frau Gaehde and Frau Kreisler have each got hold of a bottle of wine. (A tremendous gift. I had commissioned Kretzschmar in vain. It is not to be had for money; only in exchange for a ladies' coat or a pair of shoes.) Frau Ahrens, Stern . . . Not a day without visitors and gifts. Then supper has to be prepared, then I stammer another couple of lines. If possible in bed before half past ten and the alarm clock at a quarter past three. —

[ . . . ]

### November 21, Sunday midday

[ . . . ]

Schlüter's gloomy factory floor at Mackensenstrasse was small, bare, and untidy compared to the machine room of the new company. Crowded together on "my" floor are dozens of machines of differing size and construction, but all related and all operated in a similar way: a tight bundle of paper is placed in the machine, a page at a time is drawn off, gummed, pushed down and folded by a metal plate, folded again by side plates and spat out as a finished envelope or finished bag. The operator, usually a woman, has to feed the machine and remove the finished envelopes, put them in bundles of 50 or 100, and pack them in cartons; the operator has to step in if the machine "jams" (which occurs repeatedly because of the poor quality of the paper), he has to replenish the glue . . . Always the same movements, which the women workers carry out with incredible lightness and speed. I still find the movements difficult, and my bundles and cartons never attain the exactness and evenness of the "trained" workers. —

[ . . . ]

### December 5, Sunday midday

[ . . . ]

What is *intellectual work,* where do its limits lie? I talked to Feder about it, often think about it. The work at the machine is completely mechanical. And yet it demands concentrated attention. A woman worker would justifiably be outraged if we were to doubt the intellectual aspect of her work. — We do not sufficiently value a worker's performance. Inexpressible attentiveness, precision, control, dexterity. Each woman worker who finishes one of these bundles of envelopes—feeding the machine, taking them out, bundling, folding, packing in cartons—is something of a Rastelli. And while she is standing at the packing table, she keeps an eye on the machine. Now it runs out of glue, two different receptacles have to be refilled (yet another deliberation and a feat of skill!)—now more paper has to be put in. In front of the machine *I* am always in a rush—the foreman shouts: "It must not run on empty—damn it"; I cannot keep up, the spat-out items do not dry properly, become warped. [ . . . ] As an experience it's all very well—but for a week, not for an endless time, not as sterilization of the remainder of my life.

First of all, I "drew" paper at the gumming machine for a couple of hours, then changed places with Feder and worked envelope machine 49, small formats. My instructress was the agreeable Frieda, humpbacked, thirty years with the company—a foreman came up: "Private conversations are forbidden!" — She laid a pear and an apple on the machine for me: "For your wife!" (And: "How is the wife?"); after that counted and packed quarto envelopes at Gottfeld's machine. Now, for the last three weeks, I have been operating the simple no. 14 machine by myself. I produce document files for the army, Erfurt Procurement Office. Twenty-five thousand of superior paper are finished, 20,000 out of 45,000 made of thinner material are done. For a while I helped Feder count and pack. Little time for conversation with him. The "work slip," which contains the order, materials received, work in the printing and stamping shop, deliveries . . . , the entry in the machine book, the foreman's morning inspection, consultation with the worker at the box machine, the glue barrel, the two mixtures depending on the thickness of the paper to be stuck, all of it not uninteresting—and yet dreary in its infinite repetition.

How much ingenuity there is in a window envelope, such as banks use! The machine required for that, is literally a machine town. And the long gumming machine with its extended drying channels!

The "Employees' Room," in which we Jews sit. "Jews" on the door, "Jews" in the lavatory. Recently we had to leave a quarter of an hour early; there was an employees' assembly. The platform got a red swastika drape, a swastika banner was hung up in front. No doubt the big Hitler portrait was put back on the long wall again, where it was hanging on our first morning. And presumably a man from the Party preached: "Victory will be ours." And hatred of the "terror bombers." [ . . . ] But the majority of the workers, men and women, is certainly not hostile to Jews. On the contrary!

### December 11, Saturday morning

Leave today, Monday and Tuesday, because of the move. I could have had longer, but the money and the canteen food! I hope there will be a couple of hours left for the diary today. Eva out a lot and working, but still weak. Her cold, which *always* turns into a cough, worries me a great deal. *I can't help;* this absolute powerlessness is my only consolation.

Since the last air-raid warning (December 4), which brought a serious attack on Leipzig—people say: There was a diversion and the night fighters went to Berlin; the city was defenseless, very heavy loss of life, Augustusplatz "a battlefield," the university destroyed. . . . people say it's all rumor, there is no truth anymore—since then the fear here has grown immeasurably, is also beginning to take hold of us. For three days now, the no. 18 morning tram no longer picks up its second car at the Pfotenhauerstrasse depot, but at Fürstenstrasse. The driver tells a soldier: "The depot hall is made of wood; if it were hit by a single bomb, the whole fleet would be lost. We distribute the cars along Fürstenstrasse for the night, we are shunting them around till three, the hospitals there are complaining . . . but what can we do?" — Yesterday I was told by several people, who were all in agreement: The children have been given letters for their parents from school, saying that they should be removed from Dresden as soon as possible. There is supposed to be certain news that a raid is imminent . . . The woman worker at the window-envelope machine: "One feels like putting on one's best clothes and bringing a suitcase with things when one comes to the factory in the morning." — The Steinitzes have sent us a card, inviting us for a Christmas afternoon "(nota bene if we live to see it)." [ . . . ]

I started at Bauer on Monday, November 1. An old, inconspicuous house in Neue Gasse, but with side and rear buildings. An elegant director's office or meeting room. Herr Bauer appeared, a man of about thirty-five years of age, accompanied by our chargeman, the economist Dr. Werner Lang. I heard afterward that the two have been friends for a long time, belonged to the same sports club. Bauer said: "It was a lot of trouble getting you here, because we have enough men, are supposed to hire women. We hit upon the expedient of lending you to the Möbius company. You are on our payroll, you are officially employed by us, no other companies apart from those already authorized to do so are to employ non-Aryans. My friend Möbius also belongs to the SS, but you need have no fears because of that, his thoughts on these matters are even more radical than mine. Only I beg you, you must not say that you are well off with us. On the contrary, you must complain about bad treatment; otherwise we will get into trouble, and it will be to your detriment above all. Schlüter essentially failed because he got a reputation for being favorably disposed to Jews . . ." We went to Jagdweg; after a while Bauer also arrived; we were led to our employees' room; a little later Möbius and Dr. Lang appeared. Möbius also a man in his thirties. When he spoke, he was even friendlier than Bauer; he shook hands with each of us, asked each one as to his profession, when he came to me, he said with a slight bow, that he already knew . . . We are now, in all secrecy, given our food gratis, and in all secrecy, potatoes, which Möbius himself has fetched from the country. We get an hourly rate of 68 pfennigs, although we could and should get the 50 pfennigs of the women's rate. (In this respect I liked Bauer even better than Schlüter. Schlüter said: "I do not want my workers to suffer; I have paid them well." Bauer said more straightforwardly: "We would gladly pay you even more; perhaps a production bonus can be arranged later on. We are prevented from doing so by the price freeze. Otherwise—the high wages don't hurt us! On the contrary, businesses do better out of them, because they can deduct the costs from taxes." [ . . . ]).

*The doctors.* On Sunday, October 24, I called on Katz. He talked a great deal about the unpleasantnesses he has to face. Insulted on the tram, he protested: "Would you offend a former officer?" The matter was reported to the Gestapo. The inspector told him: "You know that you're well in with us, but you must not become defiant." Since then he goes out only during the day in extreme emergency. A second subject of complaint was the Eisenmann case. He had transferred Eisenmann to the Jewish hospital in Berlin as being in a critical condition, had wearisomely prevailed upon the Gestapo to permit it, and now in Berlin they were hesitating to carry out the operation—out of lack of professional solidarity? or because there was no surgeon left there?—and he, Katz, and the sick Jews here would have to take the consequences: because the Gestapo would not allow any further transfers at all. But he did nevertheless take account of my need and promised a "friendly visit." He refused to put me down as a private patient in Eva's place. He then came the same evening with a full bag (a sphygmomanometer, drugs, etc.), carried out long and extremely thorough examination, discovered a heart problem, later protein [deficiency], etc. He was just as careful on repeated visits. Dr. Poetzsch was the complete opposite. Katz advised that we make use of him officially, because an invalid diet could be obtained through him. (Which then consisted of a half-pint of full-cream milk every day for six weeks and three pounds of rolled oats.) Good Dr. Poetzsch remained as quick and superficial in his examinations and diagnosis as at the start. Put his ear to Eva for a few moments and e bene. The heart was sound, the kidneys were sound—"I would now start getting used to standing up and to fresh air." Nevertheless: The man gave me an attestation that my wife could not yet keep house; with that I got some respite at Schlüter and three weeks of part-time work at Möbius, and he really did apply for a convalescent diet for Eva. — Did Katz act out of pure altruism? Once he said: It surprised him that Poetzsch proceeded so hurriedly and superficially. "Simply for the sake of one's prestige, one doesn't behave like that with the wife of a professor!" On another occasion we were talking about our prospects in the 4th Reich. He knows that I was a member of the university senate. He would so much like to be a university physician, a sports physician, he says. — He told me: He delivered a Jewess of a child, the father was Aryan. A week later he was called to the baby. He made inquiries of the Gestapo. Forbidden: The child was mixed race and so he was not allowed to treat it. (In the Curriculum I should perhaps add further types to Katz and Poetzsch: Magnus, completely drained of intellect, and Lang, bitter and mocking, calling himself an "abortionist," quoting *Mein Kampf,* as if the words were his own.)

Throughout Eva's illness and convalescence we had regular visits and gifts every week [ . . . ]. That has essentially ceased now, and we are very short of food, especially on those days on which I do not get a meal at the factory. One of the ladies, I think Frau Winde [ . . . ], related the two following informer stories as vouched for, and the very fact that they are related as vouched for, lends them documentary value: 1) In a railway compartment an officer and a lady, reading. Two ladies get on and begin to complain loudly about the government. As the complaints become increasingly unrestrained, the officer says he's had enough now, can they just shut up. The women show their Gestapo badges: "It's bad enough that you as an officer listened so long without saying anything. And the lady there didn't protest at all. You will both be charged." 2) A star-wearing Jew is abused on the street, a small crowd gathers, some people take the Jew's side. After a while the Jew shows the Gestapo badge on the reverse of his jacket lapel, and the names of his supporters are noted.

Poster: A caricatured Jew's face peering out between Allied flags: "The war is his fault!" — At least two months ago I applied for boots and items of clothing, since a once-only provision from the confiscated Jewish clothes store was promised. Two pairs of socks were deleted from my application; apart from that nothing else has happened yet. The uppers of my boots are worn and perforated. Frau Winde gave me suspenders—my own were held only by string.

[ . . . ]

Frequent subject of conversation and argument during mealtime at the factory: the fact that the privileged Jews fearfully keep their distance from the wearers of the star. *I* cannot blame them for it.

Did I make a note of the Garnmann case? His Aryan wife collapsed in the street and died in the hospital. He had difficulty getting permission to enter the cemetery for the burial. He has now been deported to Theresienstadt. Jacobi related in strictest confidence that a large Jewish transport to Theresienstadt passed through Dresden in the last few days. An eighty-six-year-old woman died on the way. The corpse was turned over to Jacobi. [ . . . ]


## December 12, Sunday afternoon

[ . . . ]

Chaos of moving. Eva is doing far, far too much work. So far *I* have packed my books and scrubbed the kitchen. Very tired and very depressed. We would have had to leave here even without being forced to do so by Köhler, the Jews' pope: There is no more coal for the empty house, and we are freezing terribly. But I am moving to Zeughausstrasse in a mood of despair. The house, in which we once attended a Schlachtfest party at the Fleischmanns, is now part of the Community house (1 and 3 Zeughausstrasse). Now we are completely in the hands of the Gestapo, completely surrounded by Jews. And when the expected air raid comes, we are now also right in the center and in the city. Thus the third stage of our via dolorosa through the 3rd Reich begins tomorrow. No. 1 and no. 3 Zeughausstrasse are Jews' Houses squared, so to speak, quintessence of a Jews' House.

### December 13, Monday morning, eight o'clock

Chaos of moving. Up since four o'clock, Eva, too, on whom ninety-nine-and-a-half percent of the huge amount of work falls. I cleaned the shelves of the filing cabinet I once used for my own printed articles and pieces. How proud I was as it filled up between 1905 and 1912. I believed these essays established my name. Wastepaper! I have forgotten them myself. Is it any different with the books I wrote afterward? The "distinguished" scholar of Romance literatures is now a factory worker; no, my pay slip says "unskilled worker." In my copy of Vossler's *Lafontaine* are the words: "on December 13, 1919, the day of my call to Dresden." On December 13, 1943, I am being "resettled" in the Jewish Community house.

### Third Jews' House: 1 Zeughausstrasse (third floor)

### December 14, Tuesday midday

The worst thing here is the *promiscuity*. The doors of three households open onto a single hallway: the Cohns, the Stühlers, and ourselves. Shared bathroom and lavatory. Kitchen shared with the Stühlers, only partly separated—*one* source of water for all three—a small adjoining kitchen space for the Cohns. Great tension between Cohns and Stühlers; the Cohns warned me against Frau Stühler; I should immediately and sharply assert my rights and then keep my distance. But things do not appear to be so bad, the Stühlers are making an effort to be friendly to us; I had to go to their room for a while. A Bavarian couple, still young, a fourteen-year-old son. The Cohns behave like old friends; *he* is in bed with influenza at the moment, *she* helps with everything, makes tea for us, gave us a fire lighter, loaned us bread, let us use her cooking range, until ours is set up.

Nevertheless: the promiscuity. It is already half like living in barracks; we trip over one another, higgledy-piggledy. And all of Jewry crowded together; and of course nos. 1 and 3 Zeughausstrasse are in constant communication. Sommer, the butcher and strong man, came in while I was at the Stühlers [ . . . ]. When I went down to the cellar to get the key from Waldmann, the caretaker, Frischmann, the cobbler-barber, and his wife, Strelzyn junior, who plays the part of foreman at Bauer, and che so io, also turned up. — What I find very bad is the promiscuity and the public nature of life here. — Our bedroom, as cold as the grave and still uninhabitable, is separated from the front room by hallway, kitchen, and small storeroom. That, too, results in everyone getting on top of one another.

Then the little tragicomic difficulties. I need a gas fitter in order to have a connection to the Cohns' gas meter. For that Neumark's permission is required. I need a coal shovel for the tiled stove. I would have had to apply to the distribution office had not Neumark, who has now moved [ . . . ] to 3 Zeughausstrasse, loaned me an old one of his own—loaned, because he is not allowed to give away any of his property.

Berger, with whom I worked in Schlüter's cutting room, came upstairs and offered his help. He put up a ceiling light for us yesterday, today he is going to put up the second light and help assemble wardrobes, etc.

Nevertheless again and again: the promiscuity! Many of the people, with whom we would gladly live in peace, are at daggers drawn, slander one another. Cohn curses the Stühlers—"they're just Bavarians, that's all!"; Konrad and Berger rave at one another.

[ ... ]

### December 17, Friday toward evening

Eva has bad bronchial catarrh and is coughing a great deal, and her nerves are completely worn out. — Thamm has let us down; the piano has not yet been brought here, no one turned up to assemble the cabinets. Yesterday evening, as mood and desolation had reached their lowest point, Berger and Waldmann (who functions as caretaker) came and set carpet, desk, mirror, wardrobe to rights. Now things can be put away tomorrow. On Lang's advice I was going to feign illness, so as to take time off, but avoid the need for official permission from Köhler, the Jews' pope. Today I really felt so unwell—upset stomach—that I did not even have to lie. I reported sick at two o'clock, especially as my foreman had been grumbling again that I was getting too little done, and went to Simon's. From there to Bauer in Neue Gasse. I would like to be taken on there: The journey to Möbius in the morning causes me serious angina pains. Werner Lang would like me to talk to Katz, and so I shall call on him tomorrow. — In itself the route through the city center [ ... ] in morning darkness and mist is pretty enough. But too far, and throat, chest, and left arm always hurt. "*Pseudo-angina*" says Simon, "otherwise you would have blue lips." But Felix didn't have blue lips either. —

[ ... ]

We hear ghastly details about Leipzig. The greater part of the city was destroyed in twenty-six minutes; university, museum, Neues Theater, ruined; the new hospitals at the Battle of the Nations Monument gone. [ ... ]

A new man has turned up at Möbius: Coën—stage name Klaus. My age, looks much younger. Was operetta singer, buffo, dancer. [ ... ] Viennese, of course. His relatives there are recognized as being of mixed race. Here he is not. Was in prison for months for omitting the name Israel. Among other places he was held at Münchner Platz, was near the guillotine. He heard the blade fall "and each time the ringing of the death knell afterward. About sixteen times a week—then; today there is more work for the chopper." [ ... ]

### December 18, Saturday morning

Back from Katz. A kind of death sentence with a small deferral. "Fullblown angina pectoris." He wants to do an X ray on Monday. Blood pressure below normal (140): Cardiac insufficiency. "Keep warm, don't walk much, don't lift anything heavy." All things I cannot arrange for myself. I am utterly exhausted, constantly fall asleep when I sit down, am constantly freezing. Since Eva is in the same wretched state, frictions are unavoidable. The chaos and the promiscuity make everything worse. — I can also stay away from the factory on Monday, but I do it with a bad conscience—we need every day's wages!

[ . . . ]

### December 20, Monday evening

[ . . . ]

The Stühlers, the Bavarians in the rooms next to ours, have a nice lad of not-yet fourteen years of age. His father had the boy, born in 1930, registered with the Jewish Community; so now, despite his Catholic-Aryan mother, he has to wear the star. He received primary school education in the school of the Jewish Community, but even that was not completed, only the rudiments, because the school was closed down. He then had private tuition: started French, English and Spanish; his teacher was sent to a concentration camp and died there. So as not to be idle, he now works at Bauer from eight until twelve, as a "worker," because he is not *allowed* to be an apprentice. I am going to give the bright and cheerful boy a little tuition in French.

I shall go on making notes, even though it has now become very improbable, that I shall be able to turn them to account one day.

### December 22, Wednesday toward evening

E. is in P. for the first time since July 21—codeine!—it is very likely, however, after a card from Annemarie, which arrived here too late, that they will miss each other.

[ . . . ]

At Möbius again since yesterday; I do not appear to be getting the transfer to Bauer. The most numbing and difficult (most difficult for me) work of drawing paper at the gumming machine. [ . . . ] I am clumsy and not remotely a match for the headlong speed at which the machine spits out paper. The foreman shouting; far more unpleasant situation than once upon a time on the barracks square. — My workmate Coën, the new man, cannot keep up either. This former operetta singer is indignant that some in our group do not call him by his official stage name and even leave out the diaeresis on his Jewish name and call him Cohn. Also, his ribbons have been secretly removed from his buttonhole: It shows the hatred and envy the wearers of the star feel for the "privileged." He himself is Catholic since birth and was awarded seven medals for bravery as an Austrian soldier in the World War . . . Make a list of "Jewish characters in the 3rd Reich" as a separate La Bruyère chapter!

Our piano is still at Lothringer Weg. Thamm says he can promise nothing, it is impossible to enter into any binding commitment.

An appeal from Neumark is circulating, calling on the Jews' Houses in Zeughausstrasse to lay in an emergency stock of provisions, since in the event of air attack, Jews are excluded from emergency rations. But where should we get the reserves he requests?

### December 25, Saturday morning, Christmas

Yesterday, December 24. At half past three in the morning, two minutes before my alarm clock: air-raid warning. Down to the cellar. *Our* air-raid baggage once again consists solely of Eva's music manuscripts. I added this one page of notes, which we had in the house. Apart from that, one probably has to believe in fate. The warning lasted almost two hours, once again without anything happening. But fear is growing all the time. [ . . . ]

In the late afternoon Frau Winde arrived as a kind Father Christmas. Food, two cigarillos, which, with a heavy heart, I gave to Berger as a present—I am afraid of smoking, go without and believe going without to be pointless—a pair of ski boots, belonging to her sons, which fit me wonderfully—the shoes, which I recently received from the Community, are just as thin and worn-through as the ones I have. —

The day before yesterday Stühler said to me almost word for word: "The war will last a long time yet. The Nazis' military reserves may be exhausted, their propaganda reserves are far from exhausted. I heard Hitler speak in 1922 in Munich, he has a tremendous effect. If 90 percent here in Dresden were against him and he came here today and spoke, then tomorrow he would have all 90 percent behind him again!"

[ . . . ]

### December 27, Monday evening

Jewish legend about Leipzig [ . . . ]. Jacobowicz relates *credulously:* "In 1938 the Jews of Leipzig were pulled out of their beds at 4:15 A.M. and taken to concentration camps; the English recently attacked the city at 4:15 A.M., and afterward all the electric clocks were stopped at 4:15." — Leipzig dominated the conversation at the Steinitzes yesterday. A married sister of the wife lives there. When the warning came, the couple ran down to the cellar, the bombs started exploding, and most of their house collapsed. They were rescued, but without clothes, even underwear, quite stripped and naked. They were given 500M for the time being. Frau Steinitz also talked about a huge cold storage plant, which was hit. A river of thousands upon thousands of smashed eggs flowed out, likewise a river of melted butter and margarine. Russian prisoners, deployed to fight the fires, had stuffed the fat into their mouths with their hands until they were sick. Soldiers had fallen upon stores of wine, knocked the necks off bottles against the nearest wall, and gulped down the contents . . . Whole streets are said to have been flattened. The number of dead, once recently given as 28,000, once as 18,000, was now reduced to "only" 1,200. Frau Steinitz talked with unutterable fear of the possibility or even likelihood of an attack on Dresden. —

[ . . . ]

### December 31, Friday 7:00 P.M.

[ . . . ]

On the evening of the day before yesterday, December 29, a short alarm from 8–8:45 P.M. We sat almost cozily in the cellar, on which work has meanwhile been finished. Supporting props have been inserted, as in a mine, it is heated, a first-aid box and a stretcher are hanging on the wall, there is a table. But while we were chatting Frau Eisenmann told me: Her husband is lying in the Berlin hospital next to a Professor Heinemann from Leipzig, who knows me. (My pen keeps slipping, I am almost falling asleep.) He was wounded in Leipzig, his Jewish leg had to be amputated in Berlin. And during our uneventful warning, Berlin was badly hit again. Everyone in Dresden is full of unutterable fear. There is surely not a soul here who does not feel that he has one foot in the grave. At the same time, the fact that Dresden continues to be spared is ever more puzzling. The early warning has just sounded again. There is already supposed to have been an early warning 15 (15 minutes flying time away) before noon. But in *Das Reich* Goebbels declares (December 12), that the English "terror raids" only further consolidate German unity and German hate and will to wage war. — An air-raid-protection circular just now: allocation of cellar occupants to exit windows, mustering of helpers, etc. Everything is being prepared "in case of catastrophe." — Eva has volunteered as a "lay helper," Katz is going to give a course.

[ . . . ]

*Résumé 43:* Factory work since April, own work ever more at a standstill; since November 1—change from Schlüter to Möbius—all study and reading ceases. In October Eva falls ill, on December 13 move to Zeughausstrasse. A few days ago my death sentence: Katz confirms "proper angina."

We are both completely worn-out. The factory shut at three. After that I scrubbed the stairs here. And Eva came back shattered from shopping and begging errands. I am simply cooking a few jacket potatoes for the two of us. We have just drunk coffee and intend to go to bed as soon as possible. New Year's Eve 1943!

# 1944

## January 1, Saturday morning

Gloominess of mood. Future historians will praise two features of the National Socialists: their ability to take punishment and their unscrupulousness in misleading the people. In the evening paper they have the nerve to maintain the opposite of what they maintained in the morning paper, and the people swallow both. They have survived Röhm and Hess and Stalingrad and the breakup of the Axis. On the day of the news of Mussolini's fall, someone at Schlüter said: "We don't really need to turn up in the morning now." [ . . . ] Our usual discussion revolved around whether "he" would last another four or six weeks. The always cautious Feder thought: "till the end of October" . . . Today I am not at all certain that "he" will be finished off this year [ . . . ].

## January 4, early on Tuesday about 6:00 A.M.

[ . . . ]

For Sunday evening there is still a first visit by our fellow lodger Stephan Müller to be noted. Müller now works in a rubber factory. He was again full of foreign news: The Russians have broken through at Zhitomir—our counteroffensive against Kiev has therefore definitively failed—England, USA about to land in France and on the *German* coast, the threat of German "retribution" a bluff, Turkey about to march against Germany, military coup against Hitler on its way . . . I have so often heard him talk like that or something like it. Nevertheless: For a little while my spirits were raised.

At Möbius I have, for a little while at least, a break from counting: Klaus and I (as on one occasion weeks ago) have been sent up to a room on the third floor to cut cardboard. An oversized bread cutter, ou petite guillotine. One person cuts, the other holds the cardboard as it unrolls from a bale, we change places. It is very boring, but not quite as deadly as the never-ending counting. In this room, whose tables would accommodate at least seventy women, *seven* are still sticking paper bags. The others fetched away by labor conscription.

Yesterday evening I taught Bernhard Stühler French for the third time. After a fashion. I get cake—Bernhard celebrated his fourteenth birthday on January 1—bread and bread coupons. Yesterday Bernhard said: "Speak quietly, the Cohns must not hear anything." (A denunciation would mean death in a concentration camp for me, prison at the very least for the Stühlers.) — "The Cohns won't do anything to me." — "But to us." The animosity between the two parties appears to be almost deadly. Cohn is foreman at Enterlein in Niedersedlitz, where Stühler works. There was an argument there in the last few days—Stühler refused to sign some unimportant circular, probably because he did not have time at that moment. Cohn is supposed to have rushed up to the manager: "Have Stühler arrested, he is disrupting labor relations!" The affair has caused a considerable stir among Jewry. Cohn has got a very bad press. Klaus Coën has spoken vehemently against him, says not one of his workers talks to him. D'altra parte: Frau Cohn said to me: They and the Stühlers had known each other for twenty years, had long been enemies and were now forced to live in neighboring rooms. "Perhaps my husband struck the wrong note—he was in the field for four years—but he has suffered such insults, and he has such a bad heart. It's been claimed that he denounced the people who were arrested at Enterlein." (A wave of arrests last year, which cost several their lives.) [ . . . ]

### January 5, early on Wednesday after 6:00 A.M.

I try to set down a few lines in the morning; in the afternoon I am so tired I could fall asleep and am kept busy with domestic chores. The time in the factory does not pass so agonizingly slowly; but I am brought down by the mindlessness, the irretrievably wasted final span of my life, by having become mindless. Whether I cut cardboard or count sheets of notepaper—semper idem. In the Jewish workforce there are two aristocracies: the privileged and the machine operators. *I* am neither one nor the other, the foremen have a particularly low opinion of me, I really am "bottom of the pile."

### Toward evening

Last year there were no block calendars, but at least calendars mounted on a piece of cardboard. This time there does not even appear to be that. In the newspapers, which in peacetime published calendar sheets with nice pictures, the sequence of dates is supposed to have been printed on thin newsprint, to be cut out and perhaps mounted. Such a newspaper was presented to the women on the third floor, presumably by the DAF. I told them about my lack of a calendar, and they cut one out for me and carefully put it on cardboard. I was really touched, also a little cheered: I took it as new proof of the limited diffusion of anti-Semitism among the people. — That was yesterday.

Today at lunchtime I exploded, unfortunately. Unfortunately, because something like that affects my heart, and five minutes later I find it shameful and undignified. I am the most steadfast eater of the group. Most are fussy and spoiled; turnips in particular, but also all kinds of other things are left and are thrown down the lavatory. Today there was a thoroughly good onion soup and with it a handful of jacket potatoes. There had often been talk of the fact that I was a particularly undemanding eater, which in these people's eyes was no praise. (I'm also conspicuous in that I eat my bread dry and my potatoes in their skins, and that in the face of the general complaints I always say that we should consider ourselves lucky and be grateful to the company.) Today as I was eating a second helping of the onion soup, which many turned down, Rieger declared he would not throw such badly cooked potatoes to his pigs and he would throw the pot lid at his wife if she set such swill in front of him. Whereupon I: If anyone said anything like that again about what I was eating, I would hit "his mug so hard that Simon would have work to do . . ." Afterward I deeply regretted it. But I should not take it to heart; there are outbursts and heated exchanges every day, and the most recent one always supersedes the previous one in people's minds. —

[ . . . ]

### January 8, Saturday morning

*LTI.* New Year's messages of the leaders. *Hitler:* "Jewish world dictatorship"—"Extermination of the Jews in Europe"—"With the healthy and fanatical hatred of a race that knows it is fighting for its existence, and which, in this case, at least, stands by the old Bible quotation: 'An eye for an eye, a tooth for a tooth' "—"The openly *effected* betrayal of the Duce"—"With the utmost fanaticism and to the bitter end." — "Unparalleled" several times. New in the content: a) The cunning: Those who have been bombed out must see it through with us because we can compensate them only after victory. b) He gets religion. The conclusion is a long chain of prayers. "Our only prayer to the Lord God should not be that he grants us victory, but that he may weigh us justly . . . His justice will try us until such a time as he can pronounce judgment. It is our duty to ensure that we do not appear too light in his eyes, but suffer a merciful verdict whose name is victory and that thus means life." *(New here is the approximation to a religious style.)* — "It is possible to talk of a Bolshevist economy . . . only in terms of organized slavery for the Jewish board of directors in Moscow." —

*Goebbels:* Almost alone "with few, but courageous allies . . . we must take upon ourselves the defense of a continent, which largely does not deserve it." — "The conditions for victory are more than favorable to us."

[ . . . ]

### Toward evening

[ . . . ]

Jacobowicz recommended an article on the military situation in the *Freiheitskampf.* By chance I got hold of the paper from the Stühlers in the evening. Plain confession of the seriousness of defeat. —

My happiness did not last long. Early this morning, after eight, suspicious-looking men with briefcases came through the machine room. Klaus, by my side, Steinberg and Jacobowicz, near me, were "fetched" almost without a sound. Afterward, Bergmann, the foreman, came up to me: "Do you know what they've been up to? They must have babbled something. They must know that you get put up against the wall for that." A couple of workers also said something similar. Neither spiteful nor shocked. That's the way things are. It then turned out, that there is a definite general action under way against those with privileged status, who are widowed (Jacobowicz, Klaus), or divorced (Steinberg), and whose children live abroad or are of legal age. The business shook me. A moment ago I was in constant contact with these three people, and now they are buried. And tomorrow my fate may be the same.

When I am teaching Bernhard Stühler, I notice again and again that he lacks the most elementary knowledge. (He had never heard the expression "superlative," for example.) That is one of the most wicked deeds of the Nazi Party, that it banned *all* instruction for Jewish children.

I have to squeeze out every line, I am so tired out. Now I have to chop the evening turnip.

### January 10, Monday morning before six o'clock

On Saturday afternoon Witkowsky rang the bell here; he beamed and said: "You needn't be alarmed, there's a general action against those with privileged status, who . . ." etc. On Sunday morning—Frischmann, the stopgap cobbler and barber, originally a businessman, cut Jewish hair, as he does every Sunday, in the first floor hallway (recently he secretly cut Eva's Aryan hair upstairs in our rooms); I also had to submit to his poorly skilled scissors—in the busy barber's hallway, therefore, I was able to observe the mood of those who had been spared: They talked calmly of the victims of the recent action (27, among them the widow of the Leipzig lawyer, Wach), as if of people long dead, and there was general satisfaction that we had not been left to tap anxiously in the dark as to the reasons for their being taken away and that for now we had been spared. I remembered once again Chénier's verses: The prison door shuts behind you, and you are like the animal in the slaughterhouse, separated from the herd. — On Sunday afternoon Lewinsky was here after a long gap, still lost in the world of literature, still convinced that the war would last several years yet, was horrified when he heard of the new action, consoled himself as quickly as the rest of us when he discovered he was out of danger.

[ . . . ]

### January 12, Wednesday morning before six o'clock

Travel permit received without further medical examination. How fatal Katz's certificate might prove! I shall take the tram only if the weather is very bad. [ . . . ]

**January 15, Saturday afternoon**

[ . . . ]

Yesterday evening, quarter past seven, I was just beginning to teach little Stühler, *warning*. And a howling siren at that. But it had been announced that the early warning would be indicated by short notes, a howling siren would sound only if there was immediate danger. For the first time, in addition to the music and diary manuscript pages, we took a knapsack, previously packed with underwear and a blanket, with us. The general fear is gradually infecting us after all. We sat for an hour feeling bored—things remained quiet again. The radio is supposed to have broadcast today that there was an unsuccessful attack on Berlin and Leipzig. — The press is now placing great emphasis on the growing strength of German air defense. The day before yesterday it was said: "139 airplanes, mostly bombers, shot down over central Germany, two of our own fighters lost, seven missing; the attack was unable to develop according to plan." Eva overheard a conversation between two soldiers about it: ". . . then they must have attacked with at least 1500 airplanes!" Always the same question: What is the true communis opinio, what is the true vox populi, the true decisive mood of people and army? No one knows. What is decisive is some trigger, some group, some swiftly spreading mood, what is decisive is something one may call God, chance, fate, x—not the conscious actions of people.

Two and three days ago the newspaper devoted a great deal of space to the Italian treason trial. Ciano, De Bono, and a number of others shot; thirteen, among them Grandi, Federzoni, condemned to death in absentia for betrayal of Fascism, of the Duce, of Italy . . . I consider it certain, that the trial was a farce, that the executions were carried out by the Germans, that Mussolini hardly had a thing to do with any of it—he is quite invisible now, is the shadow of a puppet—above all, that the whole business is meant to deter German internal opponents (Paulus, Seydlitz).

[ . . . ]

**January 17, Monday morning before six o'clock**

The air-raid drill was brief. We clambered out into the open through assigned windows. This "open" is the courtyard of the Russian barracks, which will burn like a torch if anything really happens. There was also one, *one* gas mask there, which no one knew how to put on. Before we climbed out, the younger people had practiced forming a bucket brigade. To me it all seems like the most inadequate fooling around, and I face real danger fatalistically. But the general fear is gradually infecting us; we hear too many awful things from Berlin and Leipzig. Now Eva has made a special knapsack out of curtain material, so that yesterday we went to our places with two knapsacks.

At the Steinitzes' a warm welcome and generous hospitality as always.

Frau Steinitz is extremely afraid of air attack (her sister was bombed out in Leipzig). *I* fear only the Gestapo. The Steinitzes gave me the *Reich* of January 9. Goebbels's leading article "Problems of the Air War" presents variations on, pedantically enlarges on, drums in, what was already contained in Hitler's New Year Message: That those who have been bombed out must fight on and win, if they want to get compensation. — That the destruction sows only hate and *strengthens* war morale, instead of wearing it down. (Is it true? And how far true? Always the same question.) — That this is typical of the English conduct of war and of English cruelty—the good-natured German does not do such things (And the attacks on London? And the murders in Kiev? And, and, and . . . ) [ . . . ]

### January 22, Saturday before six o'clock in the morning

From half past three till ten, half past ten at night completely empty passage of time, factory and domestic chores—no reading, no diary, but constant extreme tiredness. In the factory the most excruciating task of all: counting up; I begin with the same packet a dozen times.

The latest: the little warning. Three short all-clear signals. Meaning: Hold yourself in readiness, *without* going down to the cellar. [ . . . ]

### January 23, Sunday morning toward eleven o'clock

Yesterday's "free" afternoon ruined by coaling. [ . . . ] To buy coal I borrowed a handcart from the "cart hire" and wood seller on Hasenberg beside the Russian barracks. From there to Hesse in Salzgasse, from Hesse back to us is not far, but the cart is heavy; there are a couple of small inclines, and my heart rebels. With my three hundredweight, I could not manage the slope up to our gateway. Then one of the young Russian prisoners of war came running up, laughing and shouting, yanked open the second wing of the gate, effortlessly heaved the cart into the courtyard and disappeared. (Contact forbidden! — General good nature or knowledge of the Jew's star? — The Russians down there are always cheerful.) The dealer had emptied my briquettes and the hundredweight of unrationed low-grade coal out of the sacks into the cart. I now carried the stuff down to the deep cellar in pails. A very full-bosomed and very young girl, with the star, appeared, would not be put off, and helped me carry. I asked her name. Ilse Frischmann. (Mixed race. Originally from the Protectorate. Wearing the star since the murder of Heydrich.) Waldmann also appeared, scolded me for not bringing the coal in sacks. The next time he would carry the sacks down to the cellar for me. So there is no lack of friendly help here—nevertheless I am very exhausted, especially as after carrying so many pails down, two had to be hauled upstairs. —

Last week began with a foolish provocation and argument. Lunchtime conversation: our Aryan wives (and we all have an Aryan wife). One praised their willingness to make sacrifices. Rieger, whose rough manner

I had already disliked at Schlüter, contradicted this in the strongest terms. He knew so many nasty cases; these women were not sound—"they should all be struck down, omein" (omein). I refused such generalizations. He insisted. Suddenly I lost my temper. "I should like to smash your face, it's what you deserve—I don't want to sit down with such a person!" I ran out, went into the machine room. After the break, Lang with whom I was unloading cardboard, said to me: "You shouldn't upset yourself so much, none of us related it to *our* wives; Rieger meant cases that he's familiar with." The next day Rieger and I were ordered to clear out a number of cabinets. Very dirty work. By order of air-raid-protection inspectors, old business papers and account books were being removed. [ . . . ] I said to Rieger: "Why were you so offensive yesterday?" He: "I did not mean you. I was talking only about 'old' cases I know; in particular I was thinking of Steinberg's wife." After that we shook hands. But the man is unpleasant. [ . . . ]

At last a letter from Sussmann. The first since October. One is missing. His daughter Käte has married an American bookkeeper. Georg is still alive. All his sons have children, those in the USA all by American women. Our family's fate and the fate of our blood went through my head. Father was born in the Prague ghetto. His sons were important men in Germany. His grandsons are in England, America, Sweden. His great-grandsons have Swedish and American blood and will know nothing of him.

I shall not be able to continue the correspondence with Sussmann. New postal regulations came out on January 15. A police control card is necessary for foreign correspondence, and it is not issued to Jews. I think it is too dangerous to use Eva as a front. I shall contact Änny Klemperer. But I no longer know her address, we have not been speaking for such a long time. And is she still alive? Is her house, her street—close to the Anhalter station—still standing? Eva is going to track down a Berlin address book.

The tightening up of censorship is evidently related to a nationwide anti-espionage drive. There are said to have been raids and many arrests. (With such an immense number of foreign workers it will be impossible to suppress espionage.) For a good week now on all shop windows, on the windows of the tram cars, in the corners of the newspapers, in black, the figure of a bulky man in a slouch hat, seen from behind. He is leaning to the left, the left arm hangs down, the palm half open, he is on tiptoe or listening for something. A white question mark underneath. There is something sinister, demonic about the figure. [ . . . ] At Thiemig & Möbius the picture has been put up as a poster. It bears the caption: "The enemy is listening too!" (There have been posters with this caption before. E.g., a man in a café eavesdropping on chatting soldiers from behind a newspaper.) [ . . . ]

*Heroic hoax.* Among the many death notices of the fallen (swastika inside the Iron Cross at the side of the notice), *Dresdener Zeitung,* January 19, '44: "Ordained by fate, my only dear son, student of chemistry, Lance Corporal Horst-Siegfried Weigmann, volunteer, holder of the Iron Cross, Second Class, participant in the Polish and French campaigns, was suddenly and unexpectedly taken from this life in the midst of his studies at only twenty-four years of age. In deep sorrow Bruno Weigmann, Master Musician, Munich." — Paul Lang, the physician, and Dr. Katz both knew the dead man personally, his fate, which at first I thought to be a legend, is confirmed from several sources. His mother, divorced from his father, was Jewish and was one of those arrested in the last *action* [ . . . ]. The son (like Erich Meyerhof's sons a soldier at first) went to police headquarters, [said] he was a Gestapo officer, wanted to speak to the prisoner and take her somewhere. He actually reached the entrance of the headquarters with her; once outside he would have got her to safety. (There are said to be many Jews in hiding, particularly in Berlin [ . . . ].) There he ran into a Gestapo man who knew him. The mother is now in Theresienstadt, the son hanged himself in his cell. "Hanged himself"—was it really suicide? — And on top of that the death notice with the military decoration! But he has truly fallen on the field of honor and has shown more courage than any soldier in battle. He will undoubtedly go down in history and literature, will be the hero of plays and novels. Katz said: "I knew him and his circumstances, I could write a script about his case in a fortnight."

Katz visited us twice in succession during recent days. He has a patient here, that poor devil Hirsch, who was in prison for so long and whom I got to know as a walking corpse in my last days at Schlüter. The man is on his back, his heart giving out, dying of influenza. (Which is said to be raging here.) Katz was more depressed than ever; he is expecting the mixed marriages to be separated. [ . . . ]

### January 24, Monday morning before six o'clock

Eva is really not well. Often very weak. Regular heart complaints in the evening. Must go to Fetscher again. Yesterday morning depressed atmosphere because of Eva's condition, filled up by diary. The Steinitzes were here in the afternoon. A couple of real beans in the coffee (out of Eva's Christmas one and three quarter ounces), as well as the people's friendliness, had a stimulating effect on both of us.

[ . . . ]

While we were sitting together, Frischmann appeared with a list of names, to make a collection. Hirsch had died during the night, his wife is said to be destitute. Everyone in the house had put down 5M, I could not except myself. After all, we've got enough to live on for another couple of months.

[ . . . ]

### January 27, Thursday evening

In constant fear of death as a Jew and now, without any chance of taking care of my health, at the mercy of the angina (which has been confirmed),

I had believed myself to be beyond all vanity. And I was really astonished, how badly I was upset by a notice in this morning's *Dresdener Zeitung*. Neubert, this utter mediocrity among the Romance scholars of my generation, a schoolmaster without a single idea of his own, has been called to the Berlin chair of Romance Literatures. How good his Nazi thinking must be, how much better and how much more frequently proven than his achievement in literary history. There is a medieval contrast between his elevation and my degradation. And I felt this degradation particularly keenly today: Foreman Hartwig called me worse names than the NCOs on the barracks square thirty years ago. A schoolgirl would produce more at the machine than I (in which he was not wrong). I could not permit myself a response. Lang, the chargeman, would have had to come to my aid and report the foreman's improper behavior. Instead he told me slyly I should sleep longer in the morning, so that I did not fall asleep in the factory. [ . . . ] When I was called to Dresden, Neubert was falling over himself to acknowledge my genius. When he went to Breslau, his friendship cooled, and finally in 1932 or '33 I read a spitefully hostile review of my literary history by him in a Breslau newspaper. He had grown into his professorship and no doubt also into *the* safe new "worldview" of the future. Poor Berlin University: Baeumler its philosopher, Neubert its teacher of Romance literatures.

I came home physically and mentally washed out, and mopped the hallway. Now totally done in.

[ . . . ]

### January 29, Saturday, 7:00 P.M.

Yesterday afternoon, fed up and exhausted, I reported sick (one is allowed to be "sick" for two days without a doctor's note). Hartwig, the foreman, is tormenting me. He is not ill-humored; he came to me on the afternoon of the day he had abused me; he gave me words of encouragement, more or less apologized, fiddled around with my machine. But the peace cannot last, there will be a final explosion before long. Because the man is demanding from me something I cannot do, I am unable to count and box up while the machine is running, as a practiced woman worker does; I am unable to let the machine run without interruption, I am unable to manage 10,000 files a day without help with the packing. Hartwig repeatedly calculates for me that I am not earning my hourly wage; he simply cannot grasp, that I am not a skilled factory worker. "But it's so simple!" . . . And my fellow workers are likewise getting on my nerves. I no longer take a pot of food home, I no longer want anyone examining and interfering with my private life. Lang provided the not entirely inaccurate response: "Jews don't have a private life any more." — So I excused myself for today and did not set the alarm clock. But precisely at the usual time, at half past four on the dot, the siren went. Early warning. We had to get up. The all clear came at half past four, so we were at least spared the trek down to the cellar. I slept until eight. That has never before been the case here, I have never yet risen here with the blackout removed from the windows—the morning view of the Elbe took me unawares. A long breakfast with Eva, scrubbed the stairs, paid a visit to Stephan Müller, who had influenza— room on the first floor where the "bachelors" live, i.e., those Jews whose Aryan wives claim the family apartment, and where Frischmann cuts hair in the hallway; after that I read a weak, poorly translated French novel that Lewinsky loaned us and that I really want to manage during these two free days. Joseph Kessel: *The Prisoners.* While reading, I repeatedly have to struggle against deadly tiredness and somnolence. Make an end, Lord, make an end!

[ . . . ]

For tomorrow, January 30, the day of the "Seizure of Power," meetings have been announced with the slogan: "Toward German victory!" Now, that really is a bit thick! But who can tell me whether it is not really believed by seventy, eighty, perhaps ninety percent of the population? Who can tell me the true mood of the people? Liebscher, the fitter, a decent, not at all Nazi, not at all idiotic thirty-year-old, excused military service because of a stomach complaint, recently told me in the factory that the war would certainly soon come to an end because the others had had enough of it too, and, after all, they were not so "fantastically organized," not so firmly led as we were. — D'altra parte: Today Frau Stühler for the first time heard someone say out loud in a queue of women that the Jews really had been treated too badly, they were "human beings, too" after all, and the attacks on Berlin and the destruction of Leipzig were retribution . . .

### January 30, Sunday toward evening

In the morning, columns of Hitler Youth marched over the Carola Bridge with drums and music; a parade such as I had previously seen only in films. My thoughts as I watched: If only this were the last time they celebrated January 30! And: How long will it take to remove the National Socialist filth from these children's heads?

[ . . . ]

### February 7, Monday afternoon

I was repeatedly advised (by Stühler, by Cohn, etc.): "Get yourself classified unfit for work for a while, get a good sleep!" Yesterday evening I bumped into Dr. Magnus in the hallway, he had been visiting his friend Cohn. He whispered to me: "It's so easy with your complaint! No one can prove that you do *not* have any attacks!" Foreman Hartwig's persecution had demoralized me, there is no desperate necessity to earn money— so . . . I went to see Katz today. Embarrassing scene. He twisted like an eel. He does not want to lose my friendship . . . [ . . . ] Then after a further examination (blood pressure 200 this time) Katz wrote out a doctor's note and immediately sent me, as he must, to the medical examiner. Rule of conduct: I must not be too modest in describing my complaints. At Stern-platz—imposing building!—at least seventy-five to a hundred people in the waiting room in front of the doctors' rooms on the third floor. I was called after an hour and a quarter. No further examination at all in the con-sulting room. A doctor of middle age, his manner kind. "Sixty-two years of age . . . you were formerly a professor . . . nine hours at the machine . . . it is quite natural for your body not to put up with such a change . . . Rest for a week, then we'll see how we go on; you will receive an appointment in writing." With that I was discharged. — So a little holiday before me. [ . . . ]

Voces populi: On my way to Katz, an elderly man in passing: "Judas!" In the corridor of the health insurance office. The only wearer of the star, I walk back and forth in front of an occupied bench. I hear a worker talking: "They should give them an injection. Then that would be the end of them!" Does he mean me? Wearers of the star? The man is called a few minutes later. I sit down in his place. An elderly woman beside me, whis-pering: "That was nasty! Perhaps one day what he wished upon you will happen to him. One can never know. God judges!"

[ . . . ]

During this holiday week, I shall attempt to get into *Mein Kampf*. But I am doubtful whether I shall succeed. [ . . . ] But first of all, now at seven, instruction for Bernhard Stühler.

## February 10, Thursday evening

I am getting some work done during the holiday week, but with an effort, fighting against extreme tiredness and hopelessness, and without any joy. Dozing away at the envelope machine is actually easier. I really have made headway with *Mein Kampf* (the first 250 of 800 pages); it is as inter-esting as it is vile and depressing—this book was available, and yet this man was made leader and has been allowed to lead for eleven years now! The German upper class can never be forgiven for that. As a kind of anti-dote—decent German at least!—I am making a go of Hauptmann's *Emanuel Quint*, which Eva found at Paulig's. [ . . . ]

## February 12, Saturday toward evening

[ . . . ]

Frau Winde was here yesterday afternoon, optimistic and raising my spirits for a couple of hours with her optimism, but in her bag she had a bottle of sparkling wine, which she had won from her husband; he had made a bet that on February 10, 1944, the "Party" would no longer exist, and it still exists. — But ten German divisions, about two hundred thou-sand men, surrounded at Dnepropetrovsk, are said to be lost, and England has given the Finns and the Hungarians an ultimatum to withdraw from the war, otherwise their capital cities would get the same treatment as Hamburg and Berlin, etc., etc.—English reports. [ . . . ] Steinitz was there, too, and invited us for Sunday coffee; it is indeed very depressing, that we are fed everywhere without being able to reciprocate.

In the evening Katz turned up again, purely out of friendship and to chat; I had to translate the German military bulletin from a French newspaper (a Hitlerite one, of course); he has a yearning interest in French. He talked about his son, now twenty-three and married in England and working at God knows what after he studied at the TU here for a semester; he said that he had had him confirmed at the Reform Synagogue in Berlin, had expressly traveled there with him to keep him Jewish and German. — With Katz, as with Neumark an hour earlier, I futilely discussed how I could change from a nine-hour working day to a half day. The health insurance doctor will certainly be in favor, but the Community, that is, Katz and Neumark, must then forward the request to Gestapo and labor exchange, which have ruled out such requests. I thought I could simply use the health insurance doctor as cover, and he could certainly be won over, not least in the interests of his insurance fund. But then I would have to talk to him about the special difficulties of Jews, and both Neumark and Katz consider that to be dangerous. (Atrocity stories, as it were.)

At lunchtime today I was visited by Konrad, who has been working at Bauer for a long time now and whom I miss very greatly at Möbius, one of the most agreeable figures among the Jews here. (I probably wrote about him frequently during my time at Schlüter.) He brought me a couple of zwieback and a little marmalade; it was very nice of him. He left before Eva came home. "My wife is afraid if I'm too late." One cannot tell by looking at the man that he is one year older than I—no one would say he was more than fifty. — In the afternoon I took the no. 3 over to the Eisenmanns. After almost four months in the Berlin Jewish hospital, the man has been released as improved in health, not as cured; his face and body are of deathly emaciation, he is stooped, his speech is broken and depressed: the bad food (he must keep to a diet)—anything extra is at the expense of his children, but the lack of food in the hospital had no longer been bearable. I asked about the air raids. He did not say much: Berlin was so vast, that in one part of the city one knew nothing of the sufferings of another. [ . . . ]

Despite all these engagements I finished reading the first Hitler volume at lunchtime today. —

[ . . . ]


### February 15, Tuesday morning

I did not manage to do any more of my own work yesterday. First Neumark, the lawyer and "spokesman," appeared in the afternoon. Half a long-planned friendly visit, half the unfortunate business of the reduction of my working hours. Such a request must go to the Gestapo via Neumark and will be rejected. Now I am supposed to enlist the help of the benevolent health insurance doctor, but must under no circumstances mention the Gestapo—for that could be construed as atrocity propaganda or as passing on impermissible stories or making impermissible criticism and—like every trifle—have fatal consequences, first of all for myself, secondly for Neumark, for Katz, for every Jew in the clutches of the Gestapo. I should, therefore, be "diplomatic." Ma come? — Neumark's position is not to be envied either.

[ ... ]

### February 18, Friday toward evening

On Tuesday morning Katz found my condition to be more normal; I should wait for the appointment at the health insurance office, he was thinking of certifying me fit for work for the coming Monday. I received notification on Wednesday of an appointment with the examining doctor at 2:00 P.M. on Thursday; I was to bring a report by the physician in attendance. So back to Katz through ice and snow. I asked Katz, although I found it hard, and I told him so, to wangle another couple of days for me. He must have done it in his report. I handed in the sealed note at Sternplatz at half past one—I was already familiar with the waiting and having one's name called out—I had *Emanuel Quint* with me and struggled through another dozen pages. At about quarter to three it was my turn, this time unfortunately with a different, very brusque (although not malicious) gentleman in a hurry. "Undress in the booth." — Brief examination—"Are you feeling better?" — "Yes, apart from the cold air . . ." — "Take another week to recover." I was discharged; the medical certificate said: "Fit for work from February 24." I must be content with that: holidays from the seventh to the twenty-fourth of February, a little recovered, and by then I shall have completely finished with Hitler and made notes.
[ ... ]
[ ... ]
[In one corner of Katz's waiting room] in the best light the windowless space has to offer, in an oval gold frame hangs the portrait of Captain Katz (medical corps) with Iron Cross, First Class, and the badge for wounded in action; in another corner the picture of a beautiful white horse, which is being stroked by an officer in a steel helmet and wearing leather gloves—I do not know if it is Katz himself. Before I knew him, I had already heard Jews complain about the picture with the Iron Cross, First Class [ . . . ]

Before me, Katz had seen Kornblum, the partly crippled former hussar, whom I worked beside at Schlüter in the spring. See at the time the account of his falling ill and staying away from work. Now he is supposed to be put to work again. Someone had squealed, said he had been carrying coal up from the cellar himself—so he must be able to work! Jews to-gether!

## February 19, Saturday evening

The phases of this period: It occurred to me today, that I have not thought about "encyclopedic style," which was so important at the beginning, for a very long time. It no longer exists, it has been overtaken on two sides—in writing, and probably in most cases, even it no longer dares show itself, it is stifled by fear of the guillotine; and on the other hand it no longer suffices, desperate anger now speaks openly. — [ . . . ]

## February 21, Monday morning

[ . . . ]
    Lewinsky was here in the afternoon, again brought all kinds of reading matter (*DAZ* and a little volume by Tumler, with whom I am quite unfamiliar), complained about Schwarze's tyranny and persecution. This Schwarze, boss of a box factory in Leipziger Strasse, is the most notorious and feared taskmaster of the Jews; Herbert Eisenmann, among others, works there.
    [ . . . ]
    In the *DAZ* an obituary notice for Jean Giraudoux. I have a signed copy of his *Siegfried et le Limousin* but have never read it. [ . . . ] When I talked about Giraudoux yesterday evening, Eva said: "I thought of him only today. *In Siegfried he marvels at the objectivity of the Germans, which a Frenchman cannot understand.*" I: "You have no idea how interesting I find that. Hitler is always raging against the Germans' 'objectivity mania.' " — Eva does not like to hear me talking about Hitler; I myself am as intensively concerned with him as a cancer researcher is with cancer. [ . . . ]

## Evening

In the morning, as several times before, but this time especially clearly, we heard marching Russians singing. The marching song repetitive and melodious, the voices soft, a few notes by the powerful principal singer alone, the rest sung in chorus, reminiscent of church music. These are Ukrainians in German uniforms, Russian Vendéeans. A war of "world-views" and not only, perhaps not even in the first instance, one between states. But to what extent has this aspect been artificially created by National Socialist propaganda, by propaganda and force? To what extent are the "European" legions, the French, Flemish, Spanish, etc., stage armies? And—this is no longer a question, but a matter of conviction—how greatly would these states, which gained their "national" freedom under Germany's leadership, be cheated of that very freedom!
    [ . . . ]

## February 24, Thursday evening

The last time I went to Möbius, two and a half weeks ago, I was still grop-
ing my way in the dark. At 6:20 this morning it was day, with a heavy,
quiet frost (twenty below freezing, but at midday there was an emphatic
thaw), which caused my heart less problems than wind at a higher temperature.

Everything went very peacefully at Möbius; I had been "demoted": The
woman worker who helped me pack and count on the last Saturday was
now at the machine—"the girl does eleven thousand," said Hartwig reproachfully, so she does three times as much as I—and I became her assistant. But I have no ambitions in this field and am glad that the foreman is
no longer driving me. Besides the woman is helping out only temporarily
in this department. Of course, counting envelopes all day was tremendously monotonous and tiring; but curiously the day, in its utter emptiness, passed quickly. So I was at least spared the feeling of time crawling
by; it was murdered under anesthetic, as it were.
[ ... ]

## February 28, Monday morning before six o'clock and after breakfast

I was warned against the initially morose and taciturn woman worker at my
machine [ ... ]. She soon turned out to be courteous, even concerned for me.
She began carefully. What foodstuffs did I have? Really *so* few coupons? No
meat at all? . . . I replied cautiously. What had happened to "the others"
who had been here before? . . . "Gone away." — "What does that mean?" —
"I am really not allowed to tell you. Please don't think that I mistrust you,
but my life is at stake, and I have a wife . . ." Etc. Silence for an hour. Then I:
"Do you have next of kin at the front?" After ten minutes she: "A brother."
Then drawing away: "The chargeman is coming—be careful!" The chargeman is feared. At the very beginning I probably noted the scene with
"Frieda," my first instructress. — Frau Loewe, mid-forties, lives in Nausslitz; she knows our wooden house. — Evidently she is just as fearful and as
anti-Nazi as I am. But I am repeatedly gripped by the suspicion that she
could be acting as an informer. Or repeat something out of foolishness.

Bergmann, the pharmacist, the hunchbacked mixer at Schlüter [ ... ]
Bergmann, privileged and very anti-Jewish, was arrested several days
ago. Reason unknown. Since I heard about it, I am especially anxious with
respect to Loewe. —

In this house there lives a huge, good-humored man by the name of
Heim, with whom I occasionally exchanged a few words in the air-raid
cellar. An innkeeper. I have never seen his wife; she was already ill when
we moved in. The man himself has a serious heart condition. His Aryan
wife died yesterday afternoon (cancer). The man must now "pack his
case" immediately: He will certainly be deported very soon, at the very
least to Theresienstadt [ ... ].

Eisenmann, already much recovered, visited us yesterday at about midday. Previously he was a considerable pessimist. He was now very optimistic, making plans for the future, how he could get his former boss to give him full authority by cable from the USA, and how he would immediately reclaim the expropriated coal company in Aussig and get it going again. It was impossible for me to share his optimism. He also said about Berlin, that there one saw no Jew's stars on the street. It was covered up or not worn at all. He himself had used tram and underground with the star covered—one simply could not get around Berlin in any other way, also in this huge mass of people it was not a risk, it was impossible for the Gestapo to recognize individuals, as they did here in the "village of Dresden." (I am almost inclined to believe that the Berlin Gestapo turns a blind eye, so as to avoid disturbances in the street.)

[ . . . ]

### March 4, Saturday morning toward six o'clock

No possibility of reading, of keeping up the diary, of reflection. Slavery in the factory and domestic chores, lack of sleep, deadly tiredness. Newspapers and books, started or not started, on my desk.

Yesterday my good Frau Loewe returned to the printing shop—her foreman has recovered—and I became an independent machine operator again. With her I "produced" 14,000 folders, alone she produced 11,000, alone I hardly manage 4,000 [ . . . ]. I can already hear today's address by Foreman Hartwig as he inspects the workbook. — [ . . . ]

The war is stagnating bloodily. But the destruction of German cities continues by day and by night, and Dresden is still spared. In the newspaper everything is hushed up or referred to only in brief, sweepingly stereotypical phrases. E.g.: ". . . damage was caused in some towns in central Germany." Privately, however, we hear ghastly things. Frau Stühler's father writes, for example, that Augsburg is eighty percent destroyed. Augsburg, that is, Messerschmitt.

[ . . . ]

### Toward evening

It was peaceful at Möbius. The foreman, seeing my workbook, said mockingly: "Now we're back at 4,000," but did not make a longer speech. Later Frau Loewe appeared for a couple of hours, and I was able to print a small reserve. I allowed myself to be sufficiently carried away to say to her: "If I survive the war and get my house back again, both of which are admittedly quite improbable, then you can come and see us and drink the most beautiful real coffee." If Frau Loewe passes on even an allusion to this sentence, then I am a dead man. For how many mortal sins sub specie tertii imperii it contains! Atrocity propaganda, doubt of victory, enticement to racial crime!

Have I noted the slogan painted in big letters above the Tell chocolate factory in Freiberger Strasse? It must be from the first year of the war, now it appears more than unfortunate: "In this war justice is at last victorious and not happiness!" —

An old fellow, somewhere between gentleman and man, addressed me on Zeughausplatz: "Good day, Herr Professor, how are you?" "Forgive me, if . . ." I am no longer used to being addressed in such a way by anyone. "But I am Dehne (or something like it) from the State Library, we often think of you!" And then a handshake. "We understand one another, don't we?" And as he walked away, he raised his arm a little, as he evidently must at work. I think the man was one of the middle-grade issue clerks, not exactly a librarian by profession but not an attendant either.

On *LTI*. At 3 Zeughausstrasse this doorplate is worth noting. Baruch Strelzyn—Horst Israel Strelzyn. The father, a goldsmith, has a first name which is so Jewish, that he is exempted the addition of Israel; the son, born about 1920, to an Aryan mother, is given that most Germanic name, which was rampant then: Horst. — For the postwar period Horst is what Siegfried was for the previous generation. —

[ . . . ]

## March 10, Friday toward evening

Finland is our new hope. For two days now, the German press has confirmed fairly openly what has been known from English broadcasts for at least a week: that the Finns are negotiating with Russia. But that is very far from being a hope of a quick end. Certainly, it lifted my spirits that Fetscher received Eva (whom he declared pretty much restored to health) with the words: "It's drawing to an end!" But it is only slowly drawing to an end. First Romania must desert and Hungary, first Turkey must enter the war, first the Russians must be in Königsberg and Lemberg, first an Anglo-American invasion army must march on Berlin from their "beachhead" at Hamburg or Wilhelmshaven, before the end comes. —

## March 12, Sunday morning

[ . . . ] There have been hours of drama for me in the factory in recent days. My machine jammed and repeatedly broke down; the foreman repaired, dismantled, had me clean everything (this, too, a strain on the heart, because I have to bring hot water in a pail up two flights of stairs from the engine house). But with all of this there was no repetition of the violent barracks-square scenes. Foreman Hartwig, a man in his late sixties, quite emaciated, ailing, became friendly as I helped him with the labeling. (The same ceremony every morning. The foreman has to deliver the previous day's production, piled up on the tables, to the forwarding department. He identifies the individual commissions according to the order notes, fetches the appropriate labels, brushes paste on them out of a pot, whereupon a girl usually sticks them on the boxes. There is a tremendous shortage of workers; I produce little at the machine, so for the moment I am the paste girl. [ . . . ].) So Hartwig asked about my former profession. Then he said: "The Jews may be to blame for something, but *that* is not right . . . There will be nothing good anymore for us old people . . ." — "Foreman, I'm not allowed to say anything to that, I must not make any complaints, it could cost me my head." — "I know . . . I'm not allowed to talk to you either— but what good can the war bring us now? My youngest is in Italy, he was in Africa first, my older boy is in the far north . . ." — "Were you in the First World War, Foreman?" — After that we told each other about lice, rats, hospital train, etc. Since then he has been paternal, merely sighed, merely grumbled, despaired. Now from Monday, there is to be a woman at the machine again, at least in the mornings. Then I shall be able to count, bundle, and pack more calmly and effectively.

On Friday, as once before, two weeks ago, the company gave each of us a piece of horse's heart or liver, i.e., a share in the regular special deliveries for the Aryan workforce. This allowance is given in complete secrecy, because it is forbidden by the Gestapo. We feel happy, but nevertheless the feeling of happiness is a little like that of Hauptmann's weavers at the dog roast.

Heim, the publican, whose wife died a couple of weeks ago, has already been "fetched" in the last few days. Theresienstadt. The night before last, the ailing Frau Cohn had an attack of asphyxia. The first thought: If she dies—though in the meantime she is on her feet again, a doctor was not to be had, Fetscher advised Cohn by telephone—if *she* dies, he has to go, and as he is not quite sixty, not just to Theresienstadt. I call it National Socialist burning of widowers. [ . . . ]

Frau Winde was here just now: a little bag of potatoes—which are in universally short supply—a little packet of dried vegetables, a tin of tomatoes. She asked anxiously, as often before, if I did not know where I could hide when the time came. Her husband too [ . . . ] wanted to make himself scarce during the critical days. I: I did not know anyone, was also unsuited for flight, would entrust myself to fate. Eva: I should go to Kipsdorf, stay in the woods for one or two nights, use Aryan coupons to eat in restaurants. Frau Winde: "He can't do that. He mustn't mix with people, he would stand out immediately. It always hurts so much. I said to my husband: 'Because of all the years of persecution, the professor looks like a beaten dog.' " She repeated it twice, and I felt awful. I have never had good posture, but now I walk with a stoop, my hands shake, and at the least excitement I have difficulty breathing. I noticed it again only yesterday. —

[ . . . ]

### March 15, Wednesday evening

Empty and overcrowded, trivial and strenuous, the days pass so uniformly between half past three in the morning (at latest) and half past ten in the evening that today I truly did not know whether it was Tuesday or already Wednesday.

In the factory it's now like this: the young woman who instructed me in the machine at the beginning turns out 8,000 folders in the morning, which I count and bundle fifty at a time. Then in the afternoon, if I am alone, I finish off what is still to be counted, pasted, packed, and then let the machine run for a while by myself. The morning at the machine is interrupted by the labeling of the orders, which Foreman Hartwig makes ready for forwarding. Always the same business envelopes and paper bags for drugs [ . . . ] by the hundred thousand, again and again small special runs for a number of pharmacies. Sometimes the foreman is merciful, paternal, almost respectful, sometimes he barks [ . . . ] terribly. Today: "You're getting stupider all the time, the label is so crooked—I would be ashamed to produce such shit for work!" I always remind myself of the comic aspect of the situation, but the humiliation does bother me terribly. And meanwhile Neubert is professor in Berlin. My Frau Rudolph is a harmless creature; her father fell in August 1914 before she was born, her husband is a coppersmith and has been reclaimed in an armaments factory. — How nonsensical it is: We star-wearers work with Aryans everywhere, and personal conversations get under way again and again despite all fears and prohibitions. And now—this became known yesterday—we Jews are to be "deployed" for air-raid protection because there is such a great shortage of people, so the company has to have an extra door and separate washing facilities. But if it comes to it, there will of course be no isolation. There are as yet no details of this latest "deployment"; only that it is to take place on one Sunday afternoon every fortnight and on one night every week. [ . . . ]

### March 19, Sunday morning half past nine

No air-raid warning for a long time, nevertheless air attack remains central. Today at half past ten exercise "with full equipment." Yesterday afternoon, immediately after work on Saturday morning, my first factory watch, from 1:30 P.M. to 7:00 P.M., so that I was in the factory for a full twelve hours. On the one hand this watch duty is child's play, but on the other very strenuous. I had a very bad headache after the usual factory work and a need of fresh air and relaxation, but now had to sit out another six hours. In depressing conditions. On the ground floor of the front house there are large office and shipping rooms. A common room with floor heating and a radio has been fitted out there for the men and women of the Aryan watch. We star-wearers (Witkowsky and I) had to sit next door in an office, which was cooling down; we could hear the people in the other room laughing, chatting, eating, scraps of radio music and conversation—we were the shunned. Individuals, men and women, were, as always, friendly to us. But, as always and everywhere, there are a couple of feared watchdogs and pillars of the Party. A workforce meeting was held a couple of days ago at which the "hundred percenters" are said to have vituperated against the Jews, and in particular to have agitated against those of us on air-raid duty.

I got through the time quite well by [ . . . ] reading, in between exchanging a few words with the rather ailing Witkowsky, catching a couple of radio tunes, among them still the same cabaret schmaltz by the same castrato voice that I heard at Schlüter last summer. Meanwhile, hundreds of thousands have fallen, and that man is still singing "A little girl has stolen my heart . . ." After thirteen hours absence I came home completely shattered. Tomorrow I have a night watch, which means I can be home at five and then have to leave at half past six again, and come back only at five o'clock in the afternoon on Tuesday. Straw beds have been supplied for us in the "employees' room," where we usually eat. I shall keep the night watch with Lang, the doctor. We are allowed to sleep, but not to undress. Lang and I are then marked down again for the night of Saturday to Sunday, the twenty-fifth to the twenty-sixth of March. We have not been told what to do, we have not been given any kind of training. We have only to keep ourselves in readiness to help out in some way in case of an emergency—strictly isolated from the Aryans. Foreman Hartwig now fetches me for an hour every day to label the orders; he pastes the labels, and I stick them on. While he's working, he's like a big child, now roaring, now beaming and friendly. The day before yesterday he got to talking. With Thiemig & Möbius for 44 years, before that on the tramp as machine fitter through Germany and Switzerland as far as Geneva. We talked about Geneva; he went into raptures. "The wonderful Tyrol wine; they mix it with water—I said I can always drink the water afterward . . . And watching the sun rise from the Saleve and the Rousseau Island! . . ." Meanwhile I put the wrong labels on a whole stack and he wailed: "That's what comes of blathering!" Silence for a while. Then: "Do you know Hamburg?" The harbor—and now . . . And now: "Human beings are beasts. Worse than beasts of prey. And what's it all for? Only money . . . What is Europe to the Americans? Does Europe want to attack America? Only because a couple of billionaires want to make money . . ." I let the conversation peter out. Behind the couple of billionaires I heard a "couple of Jews" and felt the belief in Nazi propaganda. This man, who is undoubtedly not a Nazi, most certainly believes that Germany is acting in self-defense, is completely in the right, and that the war was forced upon it; most certainly he believes, at least in large part, in the guilt of "world Jewry," etc., etc. The National Socialists may have miscalculated in their conduct of the war, but certainly not in their propaganda. I always have to remind myself of Hitler's words, that he is not making speeches for professors.

[ . . . ]

## March 21, Tuesday evening

I have come through the first night duty. The worst thing was getting there yesterday. I had come home very tired at five, had to go out again to buy bread, ate a lot and quickly, became nervous, when I didn't get a tram right away, and on the short walk to Grunaer Strasse got worse heart pains than I have ever had before. They passed as soon as I stood still, but it was a very melancholy memento. At Möbius at seven; the head watchman who opened up for me was chargeman Eysold, feared as a staunch National Socialist, but he smiled and behaved quite amiably. Lang and I sat in the same room and in the same isolation as Witkowsky and myself recently. Once one of the women workers came in and asked if we wanted beer. But the barrier was strictly upheld. [ . . . ]

## March 25, Saturday afternoon

Between duty shifts: Factory work ended at a quarter to one, watch duty begins at seven. It will be a bad night, because the weather today is exceptionally raw and wintry. The universal perpetual fear. Lang said to me in all seriousness: "Don't bring any writing work with you. It only attracts attention and harms us all. After all, the Jew only writes things that are corrupting." I got to bed only at midnight after the night air-raid warning and got up at four. I fell asleep just now over my writing. —
    [ . . . ]

## April 2, Sunday afternoon

Friday morning, five past one (the night from Thursday to Friday therefore), pre-alert, immediately followed by full alarm. Once again getting up and being in the cellar did not agree with Eva, and robbed me of one hour of my already scanty sleep. There was another warning on Friday morning—only the pre-alert—Friday midday no sirens, but school children sent home nevertheless (pre-alert). The Americans are said to have caused havoc all day in central Germany. Very little of it gets into the newspapers. Matters appear to be catastrophic on the southern Russian front, now already in Galicia and Romania. — Mutschmann in a speech in which once again the Jews are to blame for everything: "We must win, because otherwise we must die."

Yesterday afternoon, immediately following work, watch duty until seven o'clock. I had left my pot of food at home. Eva brought it to me. In the machine room, I showed her my machine, no. 14. We were alone, only Bergmann, the feared foreman and air-raid-protection chief, was still working at something in the semidarkness. He came up, shook Eva's hand, said a few friendly words—the things one lives to see! But downstairs in the office, when he was looking for something by my isolated table, he said not a word. I made notes on Tumler and Ludwig Finckh. From time to time, one or other of the chatting Aryan watch next door would appear: "Are you very bored?" — "It must be very boring to be alone like this?" . . . and quickly walked on. As he was blacking out, Liebscher, the young fitter, explaining, half apologizing: "We are strictly forbidden to talk to Jews." — Where they are together in a group, they are afraid, and rightly so: There is *one* agent of the Party present everywhere. Alone, they come out of their shell. Recently, while we were labeling, Foreman Hartwig: What had happened to the people fetched by the Gestapo . . . It must be bad to be stared at on the street because of the star. ("Foreman, I go only to the factory, otherwise I don't go out on the street: People don't just stare!")

Last Saturday, a young woman worker, whose machine had broken down, was assigned to me as assistant. She was immediately friendly, tried to begin a conversation. "Things may take a turn yet." Since I did not react, she repeated it several times. Then: Her husband had fallen at Orel; he had been a good man, a bricklayer, later they had wanted to build their own house, in Dölzschen; she herself had already been inside once for a political offense, our fate "was breaking her heart" . . . If she goes to the cinema, she avoids the newsreel—"every dead man is my husband." When she left, she pressed my hand, something very unusual among the workers in the factory, and toward us almost a case of race defilement. Since then I see the woman only occasionally at her distant workplace. Then we nod surreptitiously to one another. It was quite similar with Frau Loewe, who works in the printing shop on the first floor. Taken individually ninety-nine percent of the male and female workers are undoubtedly more or less extremely anti-Nazi, well-disposed to the Jews, opposed to the war, weary of tyranny . . . , but fear of the one percent loyal to the regime, fear of prison, ax, and bullet binds them.

*LTI.* In the summer, some boys once called after me: "We'll string him up." — "Nah, shoot him in the back of the head . . ." I frequently come across this phrase now. For the *LTI* the shot in the back of the head is the emblem of terror, the symbol of the Soviet regime, as the knout was of czarism. [ . . . ]

### April 3, Monday evening

On the *LTI.* During air-raid watch I sit at an office desk some distance from the passageway that leads through the office to the Aryan watch room. I hear the "good afternoon" or "good evening" of those passing, and do not know whether it is intended for me or their workmates, and am or appear to be absorbed in my book, so as not to respond or fail to respond at the wrong moment. But recently I heard a "Heil Hitler!," which is quite exceptional here. I thought: They always put in one who's an informer, a hundred percenter. — Today nice Frieda Dittrich, who trained me at the start and sent Eva apples, comes to my workplace. In an apologetic voice: "I didn't recognize you on Saturday, I thought it was the boss sitting there. I thought, then you'd better say 'Heil Hitler!' " — When I consider how things stand with Möbius's membership in the SS, the story becomes even more characteristic than it already is. Möbius also thinks: You'll have to

say "Heil Hitler!" there—and so steers clear of his Jew-infested factory—
[ . . . ]

### April 4, Tuesday evening

[ . . . ]

Propaganda: English novels are banned of course, but there are books by A. J. Cronin in every shopwindow: He's Scottish and exposes short-comings of social and public services in England. — Most lending libraries (Eva is trying them out) are not taking on any new clients: They can no longer replace well-thumbed books.

### April 7, Good Friday afternoon

At Möbius the women have their separate dormitory for the night watch on the first floor. Previously our stairway passed it, now it is closed to us, and we have been assigned other stairs—ever greater segregation. Recently a bedbug turned up in the women's dormitory, gas was used against it, and for the duration of the operation four beds have been put up for the women in our "employees' room." This is no doubt related to the fact that we Jews have been free of watch duty for all of Easter week. Thus Providence has availed itself of a bedbug to give me four whole days of rest.

[ . . . ]

Frau Rudolph, with whom I have been working in recent weeks, has been given a fortnight's leave by the labor exchange to support her mother: Her brother has fallen. Frau Scholz, with whom I am working now, has lost her son in the East; the recently mentioned woman worker lost her husband. Three women affected in *one* machine room, all against the regime, and all keep their heads down when they are in a group. — Frau Stühler was back from Bavaria this morning; she says people there are complaining openly and angrily.

[ . . . ]

### April 8, Saturday toward evening

[ . . . ]

Stephan Müller was here yesterday evening, Frau Winde and Frau Kreisler this afternoon. They are all fairly optimistic. The Romanians and the Hungarians are going to desert, the Russian advance has been momentarily halted by German troops rushed over from the West [ . . . ] the Anglo-American invasion was imminent at several points. —

[ . . . ] Conversation with Stühler senior: "I shall bear witness." — "The things you write down, everybody knows, and the big things, Kiev, Minsk, etc., you know nothing about." — "It's not the big things that are important to me, but the everyday life of tyranny, which gets forgotten. A thousand mosquito bites are worse than a blow to the head. I observe, note down the mosquito bites . . ." Stühler, a little later: "I once read that fear of something is worse than the event itself. How I dreaded the house search. And when the Gestapo came, I was quite cold and defiant. And how our food tasted afterward! All the good things, which we had hidden and they had not found." — "You see, I'm going to note that down!"

Frau Winde was very depressed: Her son's leave ends tomorrow and he goes back to the front.

[ . . . ]

## April 12, Wednesday morning

[ . . . ]

After work, I was at Hahn, the optician, Wilsdruffer Strasse, where Eva had made an appointment for me, by about five o'clock. An elderly gentleman with the Party badge, a full shop. I was thoroughly, almost tenderly examined in a side room. I am getting *two* pairs of spectacles—"we'll put the more expensive pair on the health insurance!"—they will be ready in *one* week. (Three months is considered normal.) Have you heard anything from Arndt, the jeweler, in Theresienstadt?" We got talking. "The swine! . . . But it can't last much longer!" A Party member! At the end I said: "But don't say anything to anyone; otherwise you don't need to bother making the spectacles for me, because it will cost me my head." For all that, my eyes bother me more than ever before in my life. My vision constantly impaired. The optician said: "Left eye only eighty-percent vision, right eye normal."

[ . . . ]

## April 13, Thursday morning six o'clock

The man who was so friendly to me at the optician's recently was Hahn, the owner, himself. His son has fallen, as Witkowsky told me. Hinc sympathia. There appears to be no better publicity against Hitler than a son dying a hero's death. It was the same with Richter's friend in whose villa in Wehlen I was going to be hidden if things started in August 1943. Nothing started, and Hitler rules, and Richter is inside.

Witkowsky, who is dying of cancer, has refused to be "relieved of duty" and is working six hours a day. Because he is clinging to life, and because he is bored to death at home. He sits and works close by me, and while I pack our largest document envelopes, haul them away on the handcart to the foreman, and wheel up more paper, Witkowsky is continually numbering off, numbering off thousands upon thousands of tiny cellophane bags for a sedative powder. It is deadly for the eyes, it is deadly monotonous—but it occupies his time, he is content: He is working, still earning, people and machines make a din around him, he's alive. — [ . . . ]

## April 14, Friday evening

There was an alert in the morning, from about a quarter to eleven until half past eleven; the all clear was the only thing I heard over the noise of the machinery. [ . . . ] Today good Frau Scholz made me a present of two pounds of bread coupons; she could do without them, over the holiday she had eaten with her daughter-in-law in Pulsnitz. Individually the overwhelming majority of the workers, women and men, are like *that*. But fear everywhere. "Don't show anyone, don't tell anyone!" Likewise on my side. Frau Scholz: "Things were best when we had the Emperor and the King, there was peace and quiet, and enough to eat." I: "Frau Scholz, I am not suspicious of you in the least, but if the devil takes a hand a political conversation with you can cost me my head." [ . . . ]

## April 29, Saturday morning

On Wednesday, in Frauengasse, a man with a white beard shouted loudly at me: "Jewish dog!"

## Evening

Like Lang and Rieger I now avoid the main roads and make my way through Kanalgasse, the little bordello street. Doesn't do any good either. See the "Jewish dog" above. And yesterday a soldier threatened even Lang and Rieger, he was going to shoot them both, he had to shoot them both. The public did not interfere. The fellow's woman companion calmed him down. "But the next time I'll do it!" During the Thursday watch, Rieger read to me from the newspaper, that 300,000 Jews had been dispossessed and interned in Hungary. As usual he was terribly pessimistic: We would certainly be shot or gassed. (There has been a very small improvement in our relationship.) Despite all of that and despite terrible exhaustion and wretched physical condition I am no longer quite as desperate as recently. The Germans had certainly expected, and repeatedly asserted, that for the moment the Russian offensive had exhausted itself, and that engagements in the East would be interrupted for several weeks. And now the interruption has lasted less than three days, and the offensive is already in full swing again. Frau Winde was the first to bring us the news; she also obstinately maintained, that the Anglo-American invasion was imminent. Frau Winde came just as I was about to tutor Bernhard Stühler. Hardly had she left, than Paul Lang appeared with a loaf under his arm: In exchange I was to take over his night watch from Sunday, the seventh to Monday, the eighth of May, his wife's birthday. I agreed, with the result that yesterday Rieger also asked for an exchange: He wants to be free on May 1: his own birthday. For the sake of decency I had to agree to that, too—this time without a loaf. On the factory schedule I was down for

Wednesday and Saturday, so instead I took over the two holidays with their six o'clock start. —

[ . . . ]

Today at half past eleven there was an alert, immediately followed by a full-scale warning accompanied by shooting. A loudspeaker in the cellar announced dully: "The mass of enemy aircraft is over southern Branden-burg, stray aircraft are being fired on here." At quarter past twelve a par-tial all clear, the full all clear at half past. Eva meanwhile was in Frau Winde's cellar. I thought repeatedly of our manuscripts, the music sheets, and the diary. All in the hands of fate.

One day recently we star-wearing Jews were allowed to and had to dis-appear as early as 4:00 P.M.; our coats, etc., all had to be removed from the "employees' room"; in their place appeared a portrait of Hitler, decorated with the swastika banner, and flag cloth was also wound around the little lectern. A propaganda meeting as May 1 approaches, there was a Party speaker.

The newspaper reported, emerging specterlike from Hades, a meeting between the Führer and the Duce, of whom not a sound had been heard for so long. The old catchwords of Axis and Final Victory as in days gone by. The Duce inspected newly mustered Italian "divisions," which will fight for the "Fascist Republic," the Axis, and Germany. The next day, a long-winded explanatory article: The enemy plan had failed, the greater part of Italy was Fascist and Germany's ally. Except they should not have published pictures of the Duce at the same time. The man, once solid, plump, self-confidently Caesar-like, is now hollow-cheeked and broken, a humiliated, poorly fed, ailing servant, and slave of the Germans. The whole thing, as I said, a specterlike advertising farce, and a bit rich, far too rich even for the National Socialists.

[ . . . ]

In the yard, as I was shoveling coal, I once again saw the Italian soldier, who had been working for another company. Frau Belka cried out sponta-neously, so it must be a common expression among the women workers: "There's the *Badoglio* again!"

[ . . . ]

### April 30, Sunday morning

In the morning singing, drumming, marching, shouts: assembly and line-up and roll call of columns of Hitler Youth and League of German Girls on the Carola Bridge. Some ceremony in the Royal Mews. I abhor such dein-dividualization and mass dressage. But evidently it is a *mark of the epoch as a whole*. In Fascist Rome, in Soviet Russia, formerly with the Reichsbanner, also in the democracies, in the USA, partly in Great Britain—the same thing everywhere. There was also collectivization before the First World War: in the primary school, universal military service, the sports clubs, the student fraternities—but there were also private, individual, familial counterweights; and besides, the various and antagonistic forces were held in a Montesquieu-like balance. Now on the other hand . . .

### May 1, Monday, half past one

My holiday is over again at five, because the night watch begins at six. My distressing eye disorder has an adverse effect on everything. As for work, that is, reading, I managed Goebbels, but without notes. If my eyes do not recover, I shall have to give up everything, and in that case I could literally just have myself buried. —

Yesterday afternoon Lewinsky here, an empty, boring afternoon. This morning, while I was tutoring Bernhard Stühler, Steinitz appeared and introduced his (half-Aryan) niece, who had come from Berlin for the weekend. A young, robust, somewhat proletarian, very blond and German-looking, lipstick-wearing girl; her lively character rather likeable. What she reported from Berlin shook me, because it *confirmed* what Goebbels repeatedly emphasizes. The Berliners are quite used to the raids—on Saturday, while we were sitting in the cellar at Möbius, they had another heavy one. Serious destruction on every street, loss of life everywhere, but in general the people's mood is good, humorous, prepared to see it through. Special rations and fear help things along, there's grumbling here and there, but on the whole people carry on with self-confident Berlin wit and cockiness. No one is expecting imminent defeat; some say the war will last another two years, others, that the decisive *German* "retribution" is at hand. (For months there was official talk of "retribution," then the public scoffed at it, then nothing more was heard of it. And now it pops up again in this account.) The girl works in some Berlin factory, so hears this and that. Therefore the regime has no need to fear internal collapse or revolt. And on this point Goebbels is undoubtedly correct: As a means of bringing pressure to bear on morale the air offensive is a failure.

The Stühlers say: It is impossible to judge morale today. All have had enough, and everyone trembles and dissimulates. This time nothing will come from inside Germany.

The Steinitz niece also related something very like what Eisenmann said on his return from the hospital. In Berlin there are no Jewish stars to be seen. The Gestapo acquiesces, or at least closes both eyes. The star is not worn or is covered. (As Eisenmann traveled through Berlin on the tram, his briefcase pressed to his chest.) If the Gestapo is forced to take action because of a denunciation, then the person denounced gets a warning the first time, after that a fine . . . Here, on the other hand, concealing the star inevitably leads to death by way of concentration camp. —

### May 2, Tuesday evening 8:00 P.M.

Yesterday as I left the house at quarter past five, Fräulein Rieger, Rieger's daughter and Katz's receptionist, came toward me downstairs and gave me a packet of sandwiches and cake as comfort and thanks. That was nice—but at Neumarkt I was overcome by angina pains, more severe and persistent than ever before. A nitroglycerin capsule did not help at all—the rest of the contents of the box rolled on the ground, I did not grieve for them—and I had to creep along laboriously, step-by-step, halting frequently. I did not feel better until I was some distance down Freiberger Strasse, and as soon as I arrived, all the trouble ceased. But the memento was left. My clock is running down, ma vue baisse, and the war is stagnating. Nevertheless (this time as sole Jewish watchman left quite undisturbed) I made use of the time from half past six until almost ten, apart from my meal break, for intensive work. I went through the Goebbels, pen in hand [ . . . ] now I need a couple of hours for the actual notes. When shall I find the time? [ . . . ]

## May 3, Wednesday evening

[ . . . ]

*LTI.* I have noticed, as a Nazistic feature, the frequency of the word *total* in article headings. "Total education" — "The enemy totally cut off." — The effect of propaganda: Frau Belka has repeatedly asked me: "Do you have a *German* wife?" — "Does Jacobi have a *German* wife?" Etc. That shakes me more than the foreign word "Aryan." It demonstrates how very successfully the Jews have been "totally cut off" in popular consciousness. —

Frau Rudolph with whom I had previously worked very amicably, whose brother has been killed in action, and who consequently was given time off to be a support to her mother, is back again. I offered her my condolences. She said "Yes" abruptly and curtly, and with noticeable coldness, and walked quickly away from me. Fear? Or does she really believe her brother was a victim of the Jews? The one is as awful as the other.

Eva was at Elsa Kreidl's yesterday for coffee. She said the woman was becoming ever more depressed and tearful and inconsolable. The loss of her husband, the murder of her husband—with time the ghastliness of it is getting through to her. In the beginning she did not appear to be firmly on the side of the oppressed. Kreidl has been dead for almost two years now.

At the factory the Witkowsky-Lang affair is becoming ever more embarrassing. Witkowsky, who is mortally ill and evidently no longer right in the head, takes offense at every harmless word, has fits of rage, swears revenge, and could bring ruin on the whole group, as Leipziger probably brought ruin on a number of Jews besides himself.

[ . . . ]

## May 4, Thursday evening

*LTI.* This morning as I was walking past a shopwindow in Amalienstrasse (fighting with the wind, heart trouble) a board game advertised as "The Total Game" (cf. May 3).

## May 6, early on Saturday

Yesterday a death sentence that is more cruel and brooks less delay than the angina diagnosis. An eye muscle, the obliquus inferior of the left eye, is paralyzed. The eye is neutralized with opaque glass, it cannot be mended. "With your reading glasses you can stick tissue paper over the left lens." How much work will I manage with *one* eye? And how much time is left to me? Diabetes probably the cause—hence my terrible thirst recently. Circumstances: my first stroke, a very minor one, but a stroke nevertheless. I had hoped to die of the angina, decently. What will the second stroke make of me? A heap of imbecility in a shitty bed like Grete, like Father? Shall I disgust Eva and be a burden to her? But I do not have any Veronal, I have no courage, and I must try to survive the Third Reich, so that Eva's widow's pension is assured. —

The work of more than ten years is in vain: the 18ième, the Curriculum, the *LTI*—nothing will be finished, nothing will be published. Vanitatum vanitas, but very bitter nevertheless. Perhaps none of it is any good anyway—what can a senile old man produce, what are his judgments worth?

In order to have something to hold on to, however, I shall go on working just as I have done until now. Perhaps a miracle will happen. And if not—I have to get through the time left to me somehow, after all.

Dr. Waldemar Lothar Meyer, formerly a senior medical officer, a graybearded, friendly man with Swabian diphthongs, Weintraubenstrasse. Walking there yesterday morning caused me serious heart trouble. Many petit bourgeois and Nazistic customers (swastika, Heil Hitler . . .). The doctor himself and his assistant took no notice of my star, but it was very unpleasant. Very lengthy, very thorough examination.

## May 8, Monday toward evening

[ . . . ]

Konrad paid us an inaugural visit around midday. He brought a modern ghetto novel, which I have begun to read aloud. (Reading aloud! Once again after months!) He passed on the two latest jokes of the day. (What is cowardice? When someone in Berlin volunteers for the Eastern front. And: The government has ordered X rays of the whole population. They want to see who has Hitler in his heart and who has him in his stomach.) [ . . . ]

## May 9, Tuesday toward evening

[ . . . ]

Neumark told us: 1) Jon Neumann † in Theresienstadt. Probably not murder—unexpected heart failure after a hernia operation—but very sad nevertheless. I would like to have seen him again. The number of the dead grows ever larger. 2) Neumark did not believe in an invasion. The Germans desired it perhaps as a last chance of victory. But the others could wait and save lives. Germany was finished: The very last food reserves were being drawn on (rice and slaughtering livestock), cripples were being called up (à la lettre, case of a one-armed man). Perhaps until the end of the year, it cannot go on any longer. (Eva added the words of Frau Schibilschak, a trader at the market hall, friendly to Jews: Invasion was unnecessary, it was coming to an end and soon—"if I could say what was on my mind, the things I could tell!") 3) New jokes: The Führer was right when he proclaimed that Berlin would be unrecognizable in ten years time. — Julius Caesar, Frederick the Great, and Napoleon in Olympian conversation; Caesar: If I had had the tanks, I would have conquered all of Germania! Frederick the Great: If I had had the airplanes, I would have conquered all of Europe! Napoleon: If I had had Goebbels, even today no one would know that I lost the Battle of Leipzig! 4) Complaint about Stühler's unruliness. He had a serious argument with Katz and objects to unjust, as he calls it, Sunday duty. Katz at Borsbergstrasse, and the Stühlers here have already spoken in the most indignant terms about the business. Katz and Neumark, responsible to the Gestapo and its slaves, are in the most difficult position, cannot do right by anyone, and the Jews are all incredibly overwrought and embittered. I always try to be conciliatory. In this case I find the dispute especially embarrassing, because both emotionally as well as out of pure egoism I run with the hare and hunt with the hounds. (Stühler says that Katz expressly declared him unfit for work but then, to oblige the Gestapo, allowed him to be put on the heaviest Sunday duty of shoveling coal. Katz denies that he declared Stühler unfit for work, and complains about the most violent abuse on the part of the Stühler ménage. Such cases are common here.

[ . . . ]

## May 12, Friday afternoon

[ . . . ]

Katz tested my reflexes, also carried out a Wassermann test (strange, to see the little tube fill with one's own blood). I am now to work in the factory again from Monday for perhaps a week, with a romantic bandage over my eye, since the spectacles that I have been prescribed cannot be so quickly supplied, and after that report sick again. Then the interest of the health insurance fund will be brought into play, my goodwill, my paralyzed eye emphasized, and my release from labor duty applied for. Meanwhile a humble petition is being sent to Herr Mutschmann to grant me part of my pension, as both I and my *Aryan* wife are unfit for work. "We must have regard for Mutschmann's primitive mentality," said Neumark. "Not demand anything, only humbly ask for *a part*! We shall write only "Prof. at the Technical University." On no account "Cultural Sciences Section." That would provoke him—a Jew and German culture! — These are the things we have to take into consideration. Neumark proposed: ". . . to pay *at least* a part of my pension." — I: "at least" would be provocative. So we deleted "at least." That, too, no doubt belongs to the *LTI*. — [ ... ]

Waldmann came early yesterday: He or someone (I don't know which) had heard on the radio, distinctly heard: Landing by Anglo-American troops. But the where had been drowned out by interference. [ ... ]

The barracks below. Immediately in front, or rather behind our house, there's a harmonious and cheerful atmosphere. A group of Russian cobblers, who do outwork and evidently have a degree of freedom although they are prisoners of war. They wear decent green uniforms, they play ball in the courtyard, they are always cheerful; they squat in groups, one plucks the balalaika, they sing, one cuts a comrade's hair. Cheerfully good-natured among themselves, friendly with the guards. [ ... ] On the other hand the barracks in the yard of 1 Zeughausstrasse: gloomy, closed, screened window slits high up, a sentry with a rifle constantly in the empty courtyard—one sees the people only as a single column coming from work or fetching food or pushing vehicles. These are civilian prisoners, this is a Slav annex of the police presidium prison.

[ ... ]

### May 19, Friday afternoon

"On the sick list" again since yesterday. [ ... ]

It had been agreed with Katz, that I should work for "ten to twelve days," then report sick again, he would then initiate my "release." [ ... ] So I went to see Katz on Thursday morning; he was very sure of the matter and gave me a sealed letter for the medical assessor. "Set your mind at ease, leave it to me, your release is under way." Since the English offensive in Italy was also "under way" and since the German military bulletin was talking of imminent invasion in the West, I believed—as I said—that the factory work chapter was finally behind me. — At Sternplatz—the usual waiting—I found myself in the hands of a doctor new to me, a plump man in his forties, he appeared to be a specialist in spectacle prescriptions; a table of numbers hung on the door. The man read Katz's letter, shook his head, waved his hand dismissively, and said—without pausing, almost word-for-word: "That's out of the question. Release from duty! We are at war, you are only sixty-two, even the blind are working ... Release from duty? Out of the question ... Within the terms of the Reich Insurance, it is not an illness at all—you will get used to it, even the blind are working. Rest for a week, I shall put you down as fit for work again from next Thursday. Heil Hitler!" He really did say "Heil Hitler!" at the end of his speech. There was not the least attempt to examine me, not a trace of it. — This morning I reported the business to Katz. There was nothing to be done, I simply had to go back to work on May 25, report sick again after a while, and then we would try with my heart, instead of my eyes. — So my situation is not a whit changed, my eye not a whit improved. (Eva has procured an eye patch for me, which, however, is very irritating.) My release from work duty is "under way"—it is progressing as quickly as the English offensive. But I intend to make good use of my new holiday. —

## Evening toward eight o'clock

Eva has just returned from Frau Kreisler-Weidlich, with whom she plays music. Herr Weidlich brought the news, that at five o'clock a *German* broadcast had confusedly but clearly announced that "landings" had taken place on the west coast. We, likewise the Stühlers, are extremely tense with anticipation. And skeptical. There have already been far too many disappointments. —

We passed May 16 in very melancholy mood, almost without hope. Eva's present to me was two nightshirts, which she had made out of old curtain material. I had *one* cigarillo for her, which the Glasers had recently intended for me. She had to fetch it from them, however, because Glaser had not dared let me take it away. It could be found in our rooms, its origin be guessed. — The day was doubly gloomy for me: because of my eye and because of the news of Sussman's death, which arrived the day before.

Martin Sussmann † April 8, 1944, of cancer of the stomach and the liver. I had expected the news, and yet it hit me very hard. Quite egoistically: Sussmann was my last contact with the outside world, also I would so much have liked to exchange experiences with him after the war. But I was also truly fond of him. He always demonstrated his friendship and loyalty to me, and in our moment of greatest need he stood up for Eva, when we were still quite illegitimate. — [ . . . ]

## May 20, Saturday morning

[ . . . ]

Eva was at the office of Richter, the trustee of our house. He is no longer in the police prison. But he has not been taken to a sanatorium, rather to Buchenwald concentration camp. The secretary, Frau Streller, is carrying on the business; his wife, with the child born after his arrest, has moved into a little house, the older boy is attending school here in Dresden. —

I recently asked Steinitz, why Jacobi's daughter had to wear the star. The child was born after the Nürnberg Laws, her mother is Protestant, her father has an eye to his own interests. A child "raised as German" would have given him privileged status. Steinitz gave me the definite answer, that at the time Jacobi had hoped to be able to emigrate to the United States; the committees there would have received him more warmly, would presumably *only* have favored him, if he emphasized his Judaism through his child. — The Jews are certainly visited by misfortune and are in the right; but altogether likeable? I think not. [ . . . ]

**May 21, Sunday morning**

The news of the "landings" in the West was again mistaken. Deep disappointment made even deeper by the poor state of health we are both suffering. My eyes let me down more and more.

[ ... ]

**May 23, Tuesday morning**

[ ... ]

I envy Steinitz, who frequently comes to see us now. He is half-blind following a cataract operation, he works all day at the cemetery, he occupies himself intensively but unproductively with English and yet is absolutely content, evidently certain that he has another twenty busy years before him—he is especially proud of his grandmother's grave, which he tends; she lived to be one hundred and four years of age and still went to the opera at a hundred—but evidently also completely calm and composed at the thought of death, although he will be seventy this year.

I also envy Lewinsky, he puts on such a nice act for himself. "In the factory I must have a book with me, in front of me, I do not have the opportunity to read, but I must see it, stroke it ..." — "I said to the medical assessor: 'Doctor, I'm simulating health.' " He also simulates a constant floating in Goethean regions. [ ... ]

**May 24, Wednesday morning**

The eye problem gets ever worse. Working through a pile of issues of the *Reich* even more agonizing than if I stick to a single page of a book or a page of notepaper. Wearing spectacles and eye patch together is torture. On top of that the diffuse, dazzling light of a rainy sky. Goebbels's editorials repeat their few ideas with ever-greater extravagance. "We are after all the elite nation of Earth, whether the others want to admit it or not." And we are protecting Europe. For otherwise Russia alone will be the victor. [ ... ] "The nations of Europe should get down on their knees and thank us ..." ("Our Nation," April 23, '44)—"Our Socialism," April 30, '44: We and we alone have the best social welfare measures, everything is done for the nation. We have clean hands. "Why have millions of foreign workers come into the Reich" and during terror attacks, etc., here, "behave as if they were defending their own property? Because they are convinced that we are right ... Many of them live better in Germany in wartime, than they did at home in peacetime." D'altra parte: "The Jews are the incarnation of capitalism. Dependent on situation and conditions, they cultivate it in plutocratic or Bolshevist form. The effect in both cases is the same ..." We on the other hand: "The leaders of the Party exclusively serve the welfare of the nation ..." What an immense quantity of lies to a tiny, tiny grain of truth. Absurd: The workers who have "come." They have been dragged here and kept here as slaves. [ . . . ] "The Uncertain Factors," May 7, '44: The fortune of war is still in the balance. An unsuccessful invasion would mean final defeat for the enemy. (Why???) And he will not be successful! "The German nation is more worried in case the invasion does not come, than if it does come . . ." Our preparations make us superior. "Should the enemy . . . really intend starting an operation, on which everything depends, with such unbounded frivolity, well, good night!" And then: On our side soldiers are fighting for homeland and a "world-view," on the other side: Mercenaries of "international plutocracy." —

*Reich*, May 7, '44, "A Thousand Words of Soviet": Badoglio has introduced Russian as a school subject: But the Italians are not learning real Russian at all, not the language of Gogol, Dostoyevsky, Turgenev, Tolstoy. "The Bolsheviks have buried the Russian language under a flood of discordant abbreviations and artificial words: The schoolchildren of southern Italy are learning slang." Short article, signed "fr."

France. Article of April 30 in the *Reich:* "Army of Crime. Terrorism in the West" by SS war correspondent Georg Wilhelm Pfeiffer. Here *maquis* is explained as "the thorny-hedged hiding places of southern France." Words new to me: *armée secrète* is what the "callous Gaullist bourgeoisie" calls terrorism as a whole. They also talk about "army of liberation." But the national milice says *armée du crime*. Its starting point is the MOI (Mouvement d'ouvriers immigrés), the Soviets' "Trojan horse." In addition Red Spaniards, Italian Communists, Poles, and, overwhelmingly, Jews, Jews, Jews. [ . . . ] On April 24 an article about Marcel Déat, signed "ar." Normalien, lycée teacher, war veteran, 1926 deputy of the Socialist Party. Wrote against French involvement in the war in the newspaper *Oeuvre*, 1939: "Mourir pour Danzik?" In 1933 he founded the New Socialist Party, was then one of the first *Munichois*. His daily leading articles in the *Oeuvre* warn the Vichyssois. Now Minister of Labor in the Laval cabinet. Broke with Léon Blum as Darnand, originating in the Action Française, broke with Maurras. The third member of the gang is Henriot, previously on the extreme Right. Déat is a "good Frenchman, a good Socialist, a good European," he is also "the first French minister to speak fluent German." (When will I ever hear about the "other France"?) —

[ . . . ]

**Evening**

[ . . . ]

My holiday week is over. Intellectual result: one Johst read, notes made on two Johsts, the Stresemann, and a few notes on *Das Reich*. My poor paper soldiers of the Third Reich! —

The German military bulletin is said to report "major inroads" on the Nettuno front. If we could only understand what is the point of *these* efforts by the English. After all, nothing will be decided *here*.

**May 26, Friday morning, six o'clock**

Machine 49 exactly as I left it a week ago. Except the envelopes have a different company name printed on them. The woman on the next machine helps draw the paper; I managed 23,000 altogether, I got through the day well enough, only the day is an absolute emptiness, hardly distinguishable from death. Jacobi meanwhile has gone to Bauer as a transport worker. We are only four now, and Witkowsky is still grumbling unpleasantly and dangerously about Lang, and nothing, nothing of any importance at all has changed, nothing. A midday meal is no longer delivered, which certainly makes things more difficult, and double vision and the many eye-aches and headaches make things very much more difficult.

On the evening of the day before yesterday, the news of a number of English successes in Italy raised spirits in the Jews' House to some extent (but of course it did not last). Waldmann brought up the food-ration cards for the individual households. He knocked at the Stühlers': "May I come in?" — Since when had he been so polite? asked Stühler. "I am preparing to attend to my customers once again!" He was a well-to-do fur dealer. As caretaker he now hauls coal, he transports furniture for the tax office and gets pocket money for it. [ . . . ]

**Evening**

Today, after a long interval, foreman Hartwig bellowed dreadfully at me again. It very much gets on my nerves. *The Last Laugh*—I remember the Emil Jannings film about the grand-hotel doorman degraded to a lavatory attendant. And at such moments of humiliation I remember that Neubert is professor in Berlin. I already know beforehand that Hartwig will repent and attempt to show me in a paternally affectionate way how simple the required task is. "As simple as that!" Two easy manual movements, and the envelopes are lying flat in the carton. "I don't understand why you can't learn it!" But my fingers won't do it. —

My eyes torment me more and more every day, and I have no hope of an improvement.

**May 29, Whitmonday morning and later**

On Saturday Eva was in Pirna for the first time since Christmas and found everything unchanged. Annemarie remains a puzzle to us. At once loyal and disloyal, affectionate and cold, indifferent to life and the war. Incidentally, even Stephan Müller, who came to see us on Saturday, had nothing to say about the military situation. He merely maintained, that there would very definitely be an invasion in the coming weeks, eight million Americans, English, etc., were in readiness. But where, and whether the war would last months or years yet, he couldn't figure that out either. The more my eyes torment me and the more I loathe the factory, the more gloomily do I go on waiting. Next week stretches out before me at even greater length than usual: two night watches.

On Saturday I had the afternoon watch with Rieger. I read, tant bien que mal, the *Fischmanns*, which I then finished yesterday. — In addition yesterday, that is Whitsunday, at a quarter past two, just as we were beginning afternoon tea, there was a pre-alert, immediately followed by the air-raid warning itself. A privileged Jew with a radio brought the news: "The enemy airplanes have reached the northern edge of Dresden" (so Klotzsche perhaps). For a couple of minutes we heard a loud humming of propellers and intense antiaircraft fire. For a moment I did feel uneasy. But again it all passed us by. — Dresden remained puzzlingly taboo. Really promised to Beneš? The latest joke: Churchill's grandmother is buried here—another version: Churchill's aunt lives here. — At the same time the use of terror is increasing all the time. The public is told only: Low-flying English and American airplanes are firing at people walking, at trains, at workers in the fields. English broadcasts accuse the Germans of having shot captured airmen as hostages for escapees. Now (on Saturday presumably) an official article by Goebbels circulated everywhere, the government will no longer call up military help to protect English pilots who have bailed out from the just anger and retribution of the public, which was much more "radical" than the just and lenient government. Which means therefore: We abandon the captured airmen to the seething populace. [ . . . ] What will be the English reply to Goebbels's notification of murder?

On Sunday afternoon at Steinitz: the longed-for cake and sweet coffee. Our fellow guest was once again the hysterical, very anti-Nazi Frau Dr. Richter, widow of a physician, a Baltic aristocrat, a Baroness Maydel by birth. [ . . . ]

In the evening, in beautiful, almost too-warm weather, an idyllic picture: The Soviet prisoners making music (trumpet, guitar, balalaika, mandolin) down in their barracks yard, singing even more beautifully, Russian songs, leading voice, chorus. In the background the gardens in full leaf, a giant chestnut tree in blossom. Where is the Soviet bestialization, pauperization, etc., in these young, strong, cheerful, good-natured men? Admittedly this group of cobblers appears to be in a particularly fortunate position.

[ . . . ]

### Evening

Today I tutored Bernhard Stühler from eleven until twelve. We had hardly finished when there was the pre-alert and the warning itself. Eva was just eating a meal [in town] and sat in the cellar of Altdresden on Neumarkt. I spent a good hour in [the cellar of] 3 Zeughausstrasse. Everything remained quite calm. The radio, however, reported: "Since seven o'clock this morning large formations over Brunswick, Magdeburg, Brandenburg, northwest Saxony." So presumably to Berlin and Leipzig. —

[ ... ]

### May 31, early on Wednesday after six o'clock

Great heat since yesterday. Up since quarter past three, worn out. Very tired, stomach upset. The usual dreariness at the factory: aggravation. The foreman bawled me out once again, a young girl of sixteen at the next machine gives me orders very disrespectfully (helps me, but does so in an awkward way). Added to that, the worry about my eyes. Eva's state of health also poor. Today I have a night watch before me.

Yesterday at quarter past eleven immediate full air-raid warning, all clear after only twenty minutes. On the radio: "Northwest Saxony," that is, Leipzig. This has been going on now since Whitsunday—over Germany night and day. But in Italy extremely slow advance, and elsewhere not the slightest movement. I am without hope.

### June 3, Saturday afternoon

On Monday morning after completing the night watch—as has already been agreed with Lang—I shall report sick. Renewed attempt to be released from labor duty; if it fails again, as may be assumed, it at least means a couple of days to draw breath. The dreariness weighs on me more and more. I have had very little to do since Wednesday, but am all the more tortured by the slow death of these nine and a quarter hours. [ ... ] I have still not learned how to bundle the paper, to order it in even sheaves, and I shall never learn it. But now I put all the blame on my eyes, and after the foreman's first bout of bellowing, Frau Hippe, the fat master machinist, gave me a hand, and in a few minutes of break she caught up with and finished off what I had not managed at all or only very incompletely. It is very pitiable and very depressing and does not help shorten the hours. [ ... ]

### June 4, Sunday midday

Over Whitsun the Windes visited their navy twins in Swinemünde. Frau Winde said: "It" would start in the navy as in 1918. Unpopular officers had been thrashed, one disposed of during an engagement with airplanes, the crew of a U-boat, which had just returned to port and immediately been ordered to go to sea again, had refused, including the commander, a holder of the Knight's Cross; the officer, reduced to the ranks, was now doing hard labor in a punishment unit in Norway ... The coastal and harbor smoke screens during air raids were causing all the trees affected to perish ... Emergency slaughtering of livestock was now being carried out

on a large scale, food for the winter was no longer assured, the government was staking everything it had.

[ ... ]

Frischmann business. Frischmann is hairdresser, cobbler, ration-
coupons dealer, jack-of-all-trades in the house. His daughter, early twenties, full-bosomed, fresh-faced, mixed race and brought up as Jewish,
therefore wearing the star, once helped me carry coal. Two days ago
mother and daughter were arrested: correspondence between Ilse
Frischmann and one of the cheerful Russian prisoners discovered. The
Russian was immediately taken to the adjacent barracks; the two women,
at least the daughter, irretrievably lost. The barracks yard is silent, no
more tootling and strumming, no playing ball, no gymnastics.

The Jews' mistrust of one another: The pair of us only learned of the
business long after the event, everything was passed on furtively as whispered gossip; not only our house, but also the cemetery already knew it a
day and a half ago.

[ ... ]

In the factory, as in the army, much is pretense. Saturday cleaning. Blind
corners can remain dirty. Even if there is nothing left to be done, you must
remain at your place of work until the bell. You must, even if you have
nothing at all to do, be occupied when the foreman is there. Good Frau
Hippe a hundred times: "Stand here beside me, *over there* the foreman can
see you . . . Pick up a sheaf of paper . . ." Yesterday she hauled over a couple of huge bundles of ungummed paper from the other end of the stock
table and piled them up in front of me: "There, you've got a wall, so that
no one can see you."

### June 5, Monday evening

[ ... ]

This morning [ ... ] after breakfast the now familiar Katz-Sternplatz
round. This time it worked: I was put on the sick list indefinitely. Then, as
arranged with Katz, I went to see Neumark, and now the request to be released from labor duty is taking its course. With what success and
whether to my benefit, God alone knows. —

The evacuation of Rome was announced today, and simultaneously
there appears a proclamation by Hitler, that the invasion will bring about
the final defeat of the enemy. —

### June 6, Tuesday morning

So perhaps Saturday, June 3, 1944, will mark the absolute end of my time
as a factory worker. But I am constantly plagued by doubts as to whether
I have done the right thing with my release application, and today I was
several times on the point of running over to Neumark and stopping my
petition. [ ... ]

**Toward evening**

While I was tutoring Bernhard Stühler, Eva brought the news that the invasion had begun last night (from June 5–6) near Cherbourg. Eva was very excited, her knees were trembling. I myself remained quite cold, I am no longer or not yet able to hope.

**June 8, Thursday toward evening**

Now the English have already held on for three days and are near or in Caen and Bayeux; the landing itself, therefore, has succeeded. But how will it go on and at what speed? I can no longer hope for anything, I can hardly imagine living to see the end of this torture, of these years of slavery. —

The force of facts. Until Tuesday people were saying: They probably won't land, they've got time, they don't need to make this sacrifice. Or if they do come, then probably not at the Atlantic Wall. It's much more likely to be Denmark, Spain, the south of France, the Balkans . . . Since Tuesday people are arguing, that they *had* to come, and indeed that they had to come at the Atlantic Wall. After the event one always finds the most plausible reasons for what has actually come to pass. But had things turned out differently, then equally plausible reasons would have been found.

Yesterday to see Katz. He gave me an official examination for the release application and found, at the most inopportune moment, my heart somewhat better. He now wants to request that either I get a clerical job (which can be managed with *one* eye) or that I be released. General regulation: No one under the age of 65 may be released, regardless of illness. Extra clause: Jews may not be employed in offices or on clerical work. Which exception will the Gestapo find easier, violation of point 1 or 2? I very much fear that this application will end badly for me. —

[ . . . ]

"Legal adviser" Neumark informs me in quotation marks, "that 'the Reich Governor has refused payment of a part of retirement pay to Victor Israel Klemperer.' "

[ . . . ]

**June 10, Saturday morning**

[ . . . ]

I fear that if the release petition is refused I shall be falling out of the frying pan into the fire, and be sent from Möbius to Schwarze, a cardboard box factory, in which one works ten hours for the poorest wage and with the most atrocious treatment. So I went to see Neumark as a precaution. He was somewhat put out when he received me. Why had I talked to other people about my release; everything to do with the authorities was confidential . . . The Jewry, which still exists here, consists of gossip and moire in equal parts. —

The merry camp life of the Russian cobblers below is at an end, the music is silent. Is the Frischmann case to blame or the invasion? At any rate they are kept more strictly; yesterday a shocked Frau Cohn reported, that from a stair window she had seen and heard the brutal beating of a Russian by a sentry.

The invasion appears to be making progress. Yesterday's report: Advances in Normandy. But I still cannot hope. There was repeated talk of "retribution," of new weapons. Goebbels wrote he had greater fear of the invasion not taking place than of its occurrence; Hitler one day before the landing: The most crushing defeat would be inflicted on it at a decisive point. It would be far too rich, even for the LTI, if all of this turned out to be no more than bluff. Is it a cunning ruse, do they want to lure the whole of the enemy force into a trap? Perhaps gas? On the other hand: The English are cautious and well informed and the impregnable Atlantic Wall has evidently been breached. We rack our brains, and I cannot hope. Which means: I am certain of German defeat, have been certain of it since September 1, 1939—but when? Even the annihilation of the invaders would not lead to German victory, only to prolongation of the war. — [ . . . ]

## June 13, Tuesday toward evening

[ . . . ]

Yesterday evening Rieger's daughter, who is the technician for Dr. Katz, brought the latter's medical opinion for the health insurance office. Since my eyes are failing me so badly, I have actually become quite indifferent as to whether I shall now be released or put in a factory again. Besides probably nothing will be decided tomorrow. — Filia Rieger, an intelligent girl (mixed race with star), who wants to study medicine after the war, i.e., in the Fourth Reich, was very optimistic on the strength of English announcements: Rouen in English hands for days; Churchill, who is not at all boastful and always weighs his words carefully, had declared they expected to be finished in three or four months. — Today's military bulletin, which Eva heard on the radio, is vague and has nothing to say. — [ . . . ]

Eva, at present somewhat better supplied with tobacco things, has been given a paper bag of cigar butts (presumably collected to combat aphids) by Frau Winde. Every day I allow myself one in my pipe. No more, because Eva uses them to roll mixed cigarettes (tobacco + blackberry leaves). One of my early memories from Berlin is of poor people on the street spearing thrown-away stubs on the points of their walking sticks. I thought it pitiable and repulsive. A few months ago I was shocked when Eva brought back a couple of cigarette ends from the restaurant. And now I am smoking the stuff myself with pleasure and with a bad conscience in relation to Eva. —

[ . . . ]

## June 16, Friday morning

Scrubbing the stairs, which affects us every three weeks (added to by having to clean the windows of the stairwell). Not only a dirty job, but a double martyrdom, typical of the times. Because 1) I am reluctant to exchange the completely tattered cleaning rag for the better one, because no replacement has been obtainable for months; and 2) there is the torment and fear of being observed, gossiped about, denounced. One is not allowed to work if one is a patient or has been released from labor duty. There are very real grounds for my fear. A few months ago, when I was at Katz's, I by chance overheard him defending the half-crippled Kornblum—cf. the early days at Schlüter—to the Gestapo; the man had fetched coal from the cellar, because he was a bit henpecked. The defense did no good at all; Kornblum, released from labor duty long before, had to go back to work. Reason: "If he can haul coal . . ." He was given "light" work, i.e., *ten* hours slavery at Schwarze. When he could not endure it any longer, his hours were shortened; that meant and still means: eight and a half hours at Schwarze.

[ . . . ]

## June 17, Saturday midday

[ . . . ] Very disquieted by yesterday's military bulletin, which Eva heard on the radio: A wedge has been driven into the English positions; the English coast bombarded with new types of weapons. If the invasion miscarries, the war will continue for years. I shall go to the Jewish cemetery information center; simultaneously my obligatory walk. (There always has to be some pressure to drive me—wearing the star—onto the street. It is a long time since I dared stop in front of a shopwindow, still less a newspaper display.)

## June 18, Sunday morning

My walk yesterday was short; I came upon the Jewish cemetery employees in the neighborhood of Sachsenplatz. Some were more, some less anxious on account of the "new weapon," but knew no further particulars. Meanwhile (radio heard by Eva) it seems to be more a means of reassuring Germany than a truly decisive weapon. Rocket projectiles, with a range as far as London, just as "Long Max" shot at Paris during the First World War. And the battle in Normandy appears to have stalled.

[ . . . ] Big essay in the *Reich* of May 14, '44: "Europe's Prior Question" by Hermann Raschhofer. The "prior question" is the defense of Europe from the fate "of becoming a tourist area for Americans, provided they hold a Soviet entry visa." Only Germany is in a position to do that; the small states must fall into line and subordinate themselves [ . . . ].

**June 19, Monday toward evening**

[ ... ]

The new weapon appears in the military bulletin of June 16 as a "new type of very heavy caliber explosive device." On that day and the following one the newspaper was full of mysterious reports, of publicity for the new weapon. "Shock effect and mass flight from London," "merciless retaliation," etc. But already there are dampeners, too. We cannot expect too much; the English, to adopt their sporting language (as if Goebbels did not do so all the time!), could "take a lot of punishment"; we would make use of further new weapons, this was only the beginning of the surprises and retribution . . . Has not the whole thing largely been put up to distract and mollify the German public, and is it not, at the same time, managed less confidently than was usual before? Or do I see things in too rosy a light? — The battle in Normandy is undecided; in Italy, England is advancing rapidly; in southern Russia, things are still quiet; in Finland, the Russians are gaining ground—how should I sum it all up? I judge things according to my mood of the moment, and it changes every couple of hours. —

[ ... ]

I called on Neumark for a couple of minutes in the afternoon. To my surprise he told me that my release is regarded favorably. Only it is doubtful, whether everything can be settled by Friday. So I shall probably still have to do a few days factory work, but with the hope nevertheless of soon being free. — [ ... ]

**June 21, Wednesday midday**

The first air-raid warning since Whitsun, also probably the longest. Began after half past nine; we soon had to go down to the cellar, were not up here again until half past eleven, and half an hour later there was a pre-alert. They must have mounted a heavy attack nearby—Dresden was spared once more; I am now almost convinced that Beneš has been given a promise. In the cellar only a little band of people, very few men among them. Cohn, Eisenmann senior, and Neumark chatted to one another. Naturally about their own war experiences 1914–18. A grotesque conversation, really, in a Jews' cellar. But it goes without saying that each one of us is attached to the German army of the First World War and to its opponents in this world war with the same degree of passion. We chatted calmly; except from time to time we thought of how things probably looked in neighboring cities.

Factory work begins again tomorrow. Fear of the horrible loss of time. Certainly, the length of the day at home often weighs on me, because I have no distraction at all and shrink back from every errand—yesterday I literally had to force myself to walk to the Jewish cemetery, where in the gardener's shed, with its threesome, the same old things were being talked about—I also fall asleep repeatedly, but despite all that, the day does have an intellectual content; it is lived, there is not the dreadful feeling of killing time, which I can truly no longer afford.

On Saturday Neumark had said: Come and see me on Wednesday, by then I shall have telephoned the employment office about your case. Yesterday he had me called over: He had thought it over, telephoning the employment office might be harmful. "Because if the primitive official over there hears that you have been declared fit for work by the insurance fund . . . It's better if you work for a couple of days; once it has passed the Gestapo, your petition will certainly go through without further investigation. The employment office will then inform your company directly before your release from labor service. . . ." Then after a while: "The employment office sometimes dawdles so much; if nothing has happened by Saturday, I shall call them." And then: "But say nothing about all this to Katz. He wanted *everything* to be kept secret from you. We are not allowed to talk about anything to do with the authorities after all." Katz and Neumark: Each hides behind the other, calls the other prevaricator and jellyfish, lays the responsibility and the decision on the other. Basically one cannot hold it against them, because both are powerless and tremble before the Gestapo, which can destroy them at any moment and under any pretext.

I have now lived more like a human being for seventeen days, I have had the faint hope of at last escaping the factory slavery. All I know is that tomorrow it holds me fast again, and not when it will let me go.

*LTI. Dresdener Zeitung* of Monday, June 19, '44, article "Women at the Searchlight." ". . . Here we have seen the 'antiaircraft-gun women auxiliaries' on duty and in their free time. They are not 'members of the armed forces,' but 'members of the armed forces auxiliaries' . . . It is in accordance with a policy instruction of the Führer that German women are not trained in the use of firearms, as, for example, has long been the case in England and the Soviet Union . . ." What Jesuitry. The women here do not directly serve the "firearms" of the battery, just as the clerical courts of the Inquisition did not carry out death sentences. Also, a woman at a searchlight is directly under fire and in any city under attack is literally at the front—because she is not allowed to go to the air-raid shelter. But if she is killed, then she has not fallen in battle, but has been murdered by "air gangsters."

### June 22, Thursday evening

As if I had not been absent for a single day. World history has moved on during these two and a half weeks, but for Thiemig & Möbius and its Jews absolutely nothing has changed. Paul Lang is still doing his utmost to provoke Witkowsky, and Witkowsky is raging at the "defamation" of Jews by Paul Lang; the nine hours still expand into an eternity and grind me down, I am still tormented by the murder of my time. — I counted and packed 14,800 large folders, that was my day's work. Night watch tomorrow. If and when my release is going to come, God alone knows. — All reading, all study is of course over again.

## June 24, Saturday toward evening

A historic date in my life: Yesterday, on June 23, 1944, I was finally and truly "released from duty." I no longer had to do the night watch. Now the factory work, which I had to perform for fourteen months and which cost me a part of my health and so much wasted time, is truly at an end. I am still too tired to be really glad. — The news reached me in the morning. If Herr Möbius had really been concerned about me, I could have gone home in the morning. But he did not bother himself about anything. Witkowsky came to me: "I just met Möbius on the stairs, and he told me: 'I have good news for you, Professor—you have been released from duty!' I replied, unfortunately I was not the professor." I now waited hour after hour, for Möbius to call me—nada. At midday Herr Hartwig said to me: "You want to leave? I shall find out when." Afterward: He did not know, it was up to the Bauer company to issue the instruction.

Lang, the chargeman, who is of very little use as a chargeman, thought I should continue working until the end of the week. I declared, that I would get in touch with Neumark. I called on him at five; he telephoned Bauer—I was free.

During these last two days Frau Wittich was at the business files machine, and I counted and packed for her; she is a fat, determined, reserved, but good-natured, decent person, has worked in the factory, where her father is also employed, for many years. When she heard that I was leaving, she became a little friendlier. "If only the war were over at last." Her only child, an eighteen-year-old son, a submariner—all the work in the factory, and in the evening her husband comes home from the factory, too, and can't wait to get something to eat . . . "*You* will be able to have a rest now and see something of the summer!" I told her that with the star, walks were best avoided. Whereupon she quite innocently and unwittingly: "*But then I just wouldn't wear it outside!*" She was amazed and disbelieving when I told her that that would literally cost one's life. —

For a while I had very much wanted to move to Bauer. Now I can count myself lucky that this wish was not fulfilled, because in recent weeks things have been more unpleasant at Bauer than at Möbius. Dr. Werner Lang, the chargeman and Bauer's personal friend, appears—nothing is clear—to increasingly have displayed an all-too-overbearing manner toward Aryans as well. At any rate he was dethroned, is no longer chargeman, no longer the boss's deputy floating above the waters, but an ordinary worker. Now, whether this demotion has led to the worsening of measures against the Jewish workforce, or whether it itself occurred in the course of measures initiated elsewhere, remains obscure. At any rate

Bauer has remembered his membership in the SS and the risk of favoring Jews—two arrests in his factory, made by the Gestapo, will have scared him (a woman I do not know, and Neufels, the little Goebbels)—and for some weeks now things have been getting worse and worse for the workers over there. No more food, isolated from the Aryans, all kinds of inspections, prohibitions, threats of punishment—I am glad to have escaped it all, and it will surely affect Thiemig & Möbius. Above all, however, the weight of the dreadful or of the endless eight and half hours has been lifted from my soul. — Does Katz really believe me to be at death's door, or does he really harbor true friendship and especial respect for me? — Admittedly, if I could exchange the health of my eyes for further slave labor, I would do so immediately. —

[ . . . ]

## June 28, Wednesday midday

I repeatedly drop off to sleep, particularly in the morning, sometimes on the sofa, sometimes while sitting reading. The two pairs of spectacles, one over the other, my exhaustion, the ever-worsening diet, senility . . . che so io? Nevertheless, in the course of the day I rouse myself and always accomplish something. What is accomplished? — Paper soldiers, Danes, Russians, Indians, all mixed up together, as chance will have it. And yet something may come of it one day—after all; I am constantly obsessed by the one idea and discover something that bears on it in everything. The Cohns provide us with the newspaper, occasionally with reading matter; in return they cheat us badly on the shared gas bill [ . . . ].

*On the LTI.* The dynamite meteors are now called, since Monday, V-1 explosive devices; it is being explained at great length: Vergeltung—retribution—number 1, means that a V-2, etc., can be expected with certainty. With all of that they are trying to drown out the rapid fall of Cherbourg and the defeats in Russia and Italy. But when will these defeats turn into a real debacle, *the* catastrophe? It can take a long time.

## June 29, Thursday toward evening

Forty years! Unimaginable length of time. And yet I cannot reconcile myself to the thought that my life is drawing to an end. — Nothing but banal thoughts the whole day long, all of them tormenting ones. The only novelty of this wedding anniversary: an air-raid warning from quarter past nine to quarter past ten, no pre-alert, sat it out in the cellar. At one point there came the news—some soldier had it from the radio outside—"Aircraft approaching Dresden, low-level attack can be expected." A few moments of anxious suspense. But everything remained utterly quiet. Dresden appears to be taboo.

Any kind of celebration is made impossible. Day drags on. — [ . . . ]

## July 1, Saturday morning

To go out in the open air a little every day—despite the star—is the hardest thing. Once along the river to Sachsenplatz, once to the cemetery, the news center with its unchanging routine, once to Steinitz with the now-fulfilled, now-unfulfilled hope of a cup of sweetened coffee, a piece of cake . . . At home reading, falling asleep, reading, falling asleep. In the evening, however, the day was never quite as empty as in the times of the factory. [ . . . ]

About a month ago I noted: Ilse Frischmann and mother "fetched," because despite repeated warnings the girl had carried on a love affair with a Russian prisoner. A week ago the mother returned from prison. She had fared not badly, and there was also hope for the daughter: The Russian, an engineer, wanted to marry her, and she herself, being of mixed race and half-Czech, from the Protectorate, would not be regarded as German, but as a foreigner. — The day before yesterday the drastic reversal: The Frischmann couple were now arrested and at the same time Ruth Spanier and Edelmann from our house. Spanier as the girl's friend, Edelmann—I worked with him at Schlüter: tobacco master, giant Russian Jew, I think from Odessa—because he was friends with the Frischmanns, and because he had conversed with the Russians in Russian. At least, that is how it is told and explained at the cemetery, and there they know everything, always know everything, know it first and in a mysterious way. At any rate the business appears to have taken a political turn now, and so there is no limit to its further spread and to its deadliness.

[ . . . ]

## July 2, Sunday midday

While I was tutoring Bernhard Stühler, furious ringing of the bell, animated, not hostile talking outside. A little sergeant, more Russian- than German-looking, in khaki: "Please open the wardrobes, push the clothes apart . . . Thank you." (Eva afterward: "Did he remove the blanket behind the desk? No?!! Three Russians could fit into the recess there—it leads to the Cohns' room.") Two of the cobbler Russians, the prisoners of war, have escaped. Taken together with the Frischmann business, that could turn out to be catastrophic for all the Jewish residents of the house. We *all* have to reckon on interrogation and arrest. [ . . . ]

Frischmann is very much missed, because today is haircutting day. He is also indispensable as a cobbler and for us wearers of the star truly "one of a kind." He was talked about at the Stühlers', at the cemetery, and yesterday at the Steinitzes'.

[ . . . ]

After an interval of very many months, Eva once again ran into the dubious Carpenter Lange, who as a technical worker gets about a great deal. He said it would be over by the end of November; he had a good way of putting things: We did not have three fronts now, but five: Russia, France, Italy, in addition the *home front* of the bombing raids, and the *partisan front*.

## July 5, Wednesday afternoon

*LTI.* Military bulletin of July 2: "In the course of a number of mopping-up operations in the French area 80 terrorists were *liquidated*." Of June 3: In southern France a number of terrorist groups were engaged and *put down*." Note the "terrorists"; the usual word for francs-tireurs is "gangs." Note the way the verbs make contemptible, reduce [people] to objects, place outside military rules. In particular the foreign word *liquidate*. —
[ ... ]

I went through accumulated newspapers of recent weeks, *DAZ* and *Reich*. Reading them bores me, I no longer find anything new, everything is worn-out. Very few ideas, very few stylistic changes. Always the same thing ad nauseam. The Americans and the English are bleeding to death for Moscow on Jewish orders; Germany must make terrific efforts and endure a great deal, but "final victory" is certain—for Europe.
[ ... ]

## July 7, Friday toward evening, in very great heat

Yesterday [ ... ] I tutored Bernhard Stühler at five and then went to see Steinitz for a while. Both the Steinitzes in very high spirits, which infected me—yet I was most anxiously implored not to say anything to anyone else. Mortal fear everywhere! The Steinitzes knew from a "reliable source," from accounts by railway men, who were always well-informed, that the situation in Russia was very bad, catastrophic. The Germans were retreating in haste, abandoning matériel; Wilna and Dünaburg were likely to fall in two or three days, the enemy would be in Germany in two weeks, it would be "over" in September. Since the German military bulletin itself sounds very gloomy, I was—as I said—very credulous and optimistic. That lasted until this afternoon. I read *Das Reich*, I read Franzos's *Der Pojaz*.

In the morning, I was just scrubbing the stairs, there was an air-raid warning; from quarter past nine until a quarter past ten there was the usual meeting in the cellar, sparsely attended because it was morning. We are all quite convinced that Dresden will continue to be spared, and feel the trip to the cellar to be an unpleasant and unnecessary disruption. A time-wasting game. Just as every couple of days they play fire brigade below our windows. A huge basin has been excavated in the gardens on Zeughausplatz and filled with water; every couple of days uniformed men with endless hoses and shiny connecting pipes appear, lay the pipes into various houses to the accompaniment of much shouting of orders, presumably also lay a pipe down to the Elbe and after a short time roll up their hoses again. — [ ... ]

**July 9, Sunday morning**

Circular from Neumark to the factory chargemen: In future haircutting
will be performed by Bär, the cemetery gardener, and shoe repairs by
Saslawski, whom I do not know. With that Frischmann, the imprisoned
barber and cobbler in one, is replaced and can be forgotten. How often do
I think of André Chénier's verse about the animal for the slaughter, which
is no longer counted as part of the herd. How many circulars, prohibitions,
and commandments there used to be! Only very rarely now—everything
has already been prohibited, and there are hardly any Jews left here. It is
also about two years and more since the period of the house searches. (But
the threat is present every day.) Every single thing again and again turns
my mind to the endless length of our slavery, to the very long list of those
who have disappeared, who are dead, who all hoped to survive. And
again and again I tell myself, I, too, shall not survive, deep down I, too, am
apathetic and quite without hope, can no longer imagine myself transformed back into a human being. —


**Afternoon**

Eva is in Pirna. Propter pecuniam nigram. She also has to beg for bread
coupons, we are in very great need. Only yesterday she said we were living on what we could beg, today she lamented: If only the begging errands were at an end! It depresses me greatly. —
    [ . . . ]


**July 10, Monday afternoon**

*LTI.* In the Sunday edition of the *Dresdener Zeitung* a "poet and philosopher" by the name of Werner Deubel, of whom I have never heard, is glorified on his fiftieth birthday in an effusive article by a certain Dr.
Doering-Manteuffel. The epithets German, heroic, and tragic occur in
every sentence (literally). I learn [ . . . ] that he has written plays [ . . . ] and
monographs ("The German Path to Tragedy," etc.). Also novels. That he
uncovered the truly German, anti-Christian, antihumanist, anti-Latin
character of Goethe and Schiller. That we still lack the utterly unique German tragedy. "It demands a new, heroically tragic appreciation of the
world and a tragic culture to emerge from it, opposed to the Europewide
Latin culture shaped by Humanism, Christianity, and Philosophical Ideal-
ism, which still sets its stamp on our lives today. [Such a] culture is the
condition for a German Empire freed from all alien bonds." [ . . . ]


**July 11, Tuesday toward evening**

During the night, more precisely at half past one in the morning, there was
an alert, soon followed by the warning itself. It was the first nocturnal trip

to the cellar for months. We sat there for only a little while, before the all clear sounded. Presumably the main force had been in Berlin again with only a stray particle floating around here.

Goebbels's leading article in the *Reich* of July 2: "Are we conducting a total war?" Sounds desperate. Each one of us must feel himself to be in mortal danger, since the enemy wants literally to exterminate the Germans. Hence each one of us must give everything of himself, must forgo everything, live as "primitively" as those who had been bombed out. We can in no respect "be falsely indulgent to ourselves" . . . "That is Bolshevist?" Why? . . . "One must adapt to the methods of a tough opponent . . . Even the most refined gentleman will finally have to take off his jacket and roll up his sleeves if he is assaulted in the street by three vulgar louts who are boxing not according to the rules, but to win." (So gas? V-2 and 3, etc.?) . . . "We have a great advantage over our enemies because of our better *national race.*" But they are stronger in numbers and resources. "We cannot allow matters to reach the point where our racial superiority can no longer tip the scales against our enemies' numerical superiority." Ergo: "We must exploit our human and material resources even more rationally . . . than before." [ . . . ]

In the afternoon I fetched a new iodine prescription from Katz. He also appears to be expecting the end to come more quickly now. Caen and Wilna . . . From Wilna to the German border is only another 110 miles. Katz measured the distance with compasses. He does not really believe in the "accidents" that have killed Dietl and two other generals so soon after one another, he also considers the resignation of Field Marshal Rundstedt to be significant. — But he has as little real optimism as I do.

## July 12, Wednesday evening

Eva's birthday. My hands quite empty again, not even a flower. [ . . . ] In the afternoon guests (which means ¾ lb. of white-bread coupons): Glaser, Frau Winde, Frau Kreisler. Frau Winde came after all: "but for only a short while, and not often anymore. My husband is anxious, he is drawing a pension after all and hopes for a new appointment . . . and then my sons!" [ . . . ]

Frau Winde told us: 1) *Das Reich* appears regularly on Saturday with Sunday's date; Fritzsche reads Goebbels's leading article on the radio on Friday evening (I often heard it at Schlüter's). Twice now the English have already broadcast this leading article on Thursday. So there must be a spy or traitor in National Socialism's innermost circles. 2) Polish women workers (forced labor) were repeatedly sent home if they were expecting. Many wanted to go home, so many became pregnant. Now abortions have been carried out on five hundred women: because they are needed as labor and because an increase in the Polish population is not wanted. I assume it will be a matter of no more than fifty cases. But even if it were only five—what unheard-of tyranny!

[ . . . ]

**July 17, Monday toward evening**

Monotony of the day; toward evening—as almost customary—a half-hour dutiful boring walk up the Elbe, a few yards past Sachsenplatz.

Reading Rosenzweig with a feeling of despair.

If one reads the military bulletin, then matters look almost lethally bad for Germany, falling ever farther back in the East (Grodno evacuated today, less than 40 miles from the German frontier), heavy fighting in the West, Anglo-American "suction pump" [ . . . ], falling ever farther back in Italy (Arezzo), "gangs" and "terrorists" everywhere . . . If one reads the newspaper articles—I am just leafing through a whole pile of the *DAZ*, which Lewinsky brought yesterday; he was here in the morning, Steinitz in the afternoon—then things are going very well for us: Our enemies are bleeding to death in Normandy, suffering terribly because of the V-1 (which I consider to be nine-tenths B-1 = Bluff 1), are not achieving anything decisive either in Italy or in the East. Eva's spirits are very much raised every time she hears the military bulletin, which she catches at five o'clock at Pirnaer Platz; I can no longer really hope, can no longer be satisfied by small successes, wait for the catastrophe. It is inevitable, but whether it will come tomorrow or in a year's time, God alone knows. And in the background always the fear: What will become of me *afterward*? Can I still produce? Etc.

**July 19, Wednesday morning**

I repeatedly fish something important out of the Rosenzweig ocean of incomprehensibility, and so I cannot get away from it. Yesterday I had hardly any time to go angling: In the morning Katz arrived for a long, chatty visit; in the afternoon severe pain drove me to Simon: an inflamed, festering root inflammation, lengthy treatment.

This affects me financially: After both Neumark and myself had been told that insurance continued to exist *also for Jews*, and I had been handed an application form, today I received a rejection of the application on a postcard, "since you are non-Aryan."

Yesterday Katz was at once optimistic and scared. He *knew* that the Russians had taken Kowno—an hour later Eva came from "Gertrud Schmidt" with the definite information that Kowno had been in Russian hands since Sunday, and Russian troops had already reached the border of eastern Europe—he thought the débâcle was imminent, but there was the simultaneous possibility, if not probability, that we would be butchered in the course of evacuations. [ . . . ]

The more disastrous the situation is, the more shameless are the superlatives of National Socialist language. In the *Dresdener Zeitung* of July 17, the commentary on the "NSDAP word of the week" concludes thus: Today "our faith in victory has hardened into unshakable certainty. No power in the world and no devil from deepest hell can snatch it from us now, because we have become a race of iron." The quotation itself, by Goebbels, reads: "Only a race of iron will be able to hold its own in the storms of our time. It must possess innards of iron and a heart of steel." (Chapter: The superlative and the curse of the superlative.) Still no word about Kowno in the military bulletin.

### Evening

Still no word from the Germans about Kowno. False English report? But for all its concealment the German military bulletin is catastrophic enough. "Large-scale attacks" on all three fronts and loss of terrain somewhere on all three fronts.

[ . . . ]

### July 20, Thursday morning

*LTI.* Editorial in the *Dresdener Zeitung* of July 18. "Jews in Normandy." The battle was still going on, when there appeared the "ever-grasping," the "hook-nosed," to take possession. After all, it's "their" war, "All of Judah's war." The reader awaits some fact to substantiate the article. It consists solely in de Gaulle's decree abolishing the Jewish laws. In addition, one is told, that a chief rabbi is once again officiating in Rome . . . Important to *me* is this: 1) The Allies' first decree everywhere is abolition of the Jewish laws. 2) The campaign against the Jews, the reduction of all enemies to *one* enemy called Jew becomes ever more grotesque on the German side. 3) My conclusion from 1) and 2) and the rest: However much I resisted it, *the Jew* is in every respect the center of the LTI, of its whole view of the epoch. — Note in this article also: "Eisenhower's hordes."

*Jewish psychosis.* Conversation between Cohn and myself. "I have good news." — "I don't want to know it!" Looks around anxiously. "Someone could be outside, listening by the mailbox . . . The window's open, it could be heard downstairs . . ." His wife complains he is always like that now, the fear of being watched does not let go of him for a single moment.

### Evening

There was a pre-alert at 11:00 A.M. Eva was about to go to the Windes'. I advised her to go nevertheless; she can go into any cellar, and her chances are the same everywhere. The air-raid warning itself came before she could catch a tram, and so we after all spent an hour sitting together in the sparsely attended Jews' cellar. Two, three times we heard the loud hum of the enemy aircraft, once also antiaircraft fire. And I did get palpitations, despite philosophy and despite faith in Dresden's Beneš protection, because we had just heard ghastly things about the last heavy attacks on Leipzig and Munich. But again everything peacefully passed us by. —

[ . . . ]

## July 21, Friday toward evening

I was sitting and ordering my Rosenzweig notes—wearying work, still not finished and will not be so for a long time—when, as the day before, there was an air-raid warning at half past eleven, first pre-alert, then the proper thing. This time our stay in the cellar was a little shorter and quite unsensational, i.e., it was completely taken up by another sensation, by the attempt on Hitler's life. Perhaps in a few years it will appear as remote to me, be as shadowy a business, as the Bürgerbräu affair of '39 is remote to me now. What was it about, who was the perpetrator, what was the intention, etc., etc.?? Neither Eva nor I can remember, because it simply was without effect and so was painted out, displaced by what came after. Perhaps it will be just the same with this plot, but perhaps it is the turning point. The person who lives through things knows nothing. I put on record: On the stairs Frau Witkowsky told us: It had just been announced that an attempt had been made on the Führer's life, at General Headquarters, by *named German officers, who had already been shot*. In the cellar, I turned to Neumark with this piece of news, believing it to be something absolutely new. Whereupon he: It was already in the *Freiheitskampf*, had happened yesterday, the Führer had spoken on the radio in the evening. He gave us the newspaper. There was the assassination attempt, the names of those officers present and of those wounded—but nothing about the perpetrators, only the conjecture that the [British] Secret Service was the culprit. Neumark added, there were rumors of German officers (but the Jews had to be especially cautious, because they were certainly being watched); Frau Witkowsky said: But special editions with the names of those shot had just come out. Until now, seven o'clock in the evening, I have been unable to find out anything more and anything more reliable here in the the Jews' House. The Stühlers, too, are puzzling over things. He said: Perhaps it was all lies, because HE wanted to give himself the aura of holy invulnerability. I: It would be suicide to say that the army had turned against the Führer, that had not even happened on November 18. Stühler: Perhaps the information that German officers were the perpetrators is false. How would they have been able to, in the middle of General Headquarters? And why would German broadcasting have admitted it? — That is how little we in the Jews' House know what is happening. — Eva is at Frau Kreisler's, perhaps she will come back with fresh news. And I hope of a kind that will console us and tide us over the awful hunger of recent days. — Just now music and soldiers marching by; the Stühlers report, that a mass rally for Hitler has been announced on posters. —

## After eight o'clock

Then [ . . . ] first of all Katz, who has a patient in the house and often uses this as an opportunity to visit us, came, and after that, Eva. Thus far we know: This evening Hitler said (it is in the newspaper), a "small clique of stupid officers" had wanted to get rid of him, but had already been eliminated, he himself had been saved by "Providence." And then despite the word "eliminated": He ordered the army to accept no instruction whatsoever from the *usurpers*. The expression "usurpers" repeated. [ . . . ] Further, he transferred supreme command of the Home Army to Himmler. That much is fact. In addition rumor: There were disturbances somewhere—location unknown, aircraft used against rebels. English broadcast: There was "civil war" in Germany. Joke from Professor Winde (his own?): All Germany was standing in mourning at Hitler's empty coffin. — Katz told us: Neumark, who is very nervous, and several other Jews had already packed their suitcases last night. To that I said, and Katz agreed: Why pack suitcases? If they come for us now, we won't go to Theresienstadt, but against the wall or to the gallows. Katz also said: Kowno was really supposed to be in Russian hands and German border areas to be under Russian artillery fire. —

I want to go on observing, taking notes, studying until the last moment. Fear is no use at all, and everything is fate. (But, of course, despite all philosophy I am seized by fear from time to time. As yesterday in the cellar, when the Americans were droning up above.)

[ . . . ]

### July 22, Saturday afternoon

Yesterday evening, at about ten—Eva was already asleep—Cohn brought me the newspaper with Hitler's speech, the proclamations of Goering and of the commander of the fleet, etc. Even now it is still not possible to say whether this is really the beginning of the end—how many such beginnings have there been, which then got no further than the beginning! — Linguistically all the characteristics of the LTI are present again: the portentous foreign word "usurpers," the undignified abuse, the courting of Providence, the closeness with which everything sticks to the vocabulary, style, imagery of its models. The predictable, impoverished LTI! Only as a result of the stupefaction of the first moments can the following contradiction be explained: A small *clique* of officers has been hunted down and has already been *liquidated* or *put down* (note these two verbs of the trashy press, which are now turning up in descriptions of the Maquis and have spread from there to the latest press material), and on the other hand there's the order not to take commands from any headquarters—ergo the liquidated and the hunted down must still hold something they usurped. — All in all a worse defeat than the loss of a battle or even of a province. —

The *Jews' boundless fear.* I was at Simon's (protracted treatment) and afterward called on Glaser. Glaser was so distracted with fear, so pitifully spineless—begged me never to tell him anything about foreign reports—torture could force one to make statements [ . . . ], he did not want to know anything he was not allowed to know . . . I told him, we all had one and a half feet in the grave anyway, as old people we had to resign ourselves to fate . . . All in vain, he remains an unlovely trembling aspen leaf. [ . . . ]

The *Dresdener Zeitung* of July 20 printed an appeal by the Frankfurt Hochstift [Foundation]: Contributions to the rebuilding of the Goethe House; the foundation stone, which has survived and which, as a boy, Goethe himself laid, will be incorporated . . . etc. The most repulsive fetishism, a vulgarity without parallel in this time of blood, much worse even than the [Catholic] Church's cult of relics. —

In the *Reich* of July 9 an already routine but especially pathos-laden article by Goebbels addressed to the English: Ally yourselves with us, because Russia will also overwhelm *you!* Linguistically interesting to me is the following: a) The occasional reemergence of obsolete LTI words, which had gone out of fashion, were no longer heard: When the defeats began, we were in possession of a most extensive area, completely invincible, "vulnerable" only on the periphery: Then there was no more mention of that. Now the word is: "After so many retreats and reverses" we are militarily more effective than at the time of our great victories; "then we were sensitive and *vulnerable* to even minor misfortunes." There is again talk of the future of "Western man" and of the threat of the "loss of individuality." [ . . . ] b) even in the pathos of despair he cannot desist from the language of sport. Concluding sentence, exhortation to hold out: "The competitor who breaks the finishing tape before the others, even if only by a head, wins the race." [ . . . ] For how much longer will the *Reich* appear?

### Evening

Without the least bit of news (while world history is rushing by) all day. Did not pick up the military bulletin, nothing about the internal situation, did not see the evening newspaper—absolutely nothing. And I do not believe that anything decisive has happened anyway. They can take punishment, even July 20 will remain an incidental date, far removed from the actual beginning of the catastrophe. I find my way back to Rosenzweig by arranging my notes. He is not worth the misery and the time expended.

### July 23, Sunday morning

No news. But since everything in Dresden is calm, it can be assumed that the NSDAP has remained victorious this time also. We must be another little bit closer to the end, but only a little bit closer to the distant end.

How greatly everyone, but absolutely everyone, is imbued with Germany's military superiority: yesterday in conversation with Waldmann, I: The Russians are evidently better led than before; he: Yes, no doubt it is *German* leadership, after all German generals had deserted to the enemy. —

Simon told me his wife says Hitler must not be allowed to die, he can be used to earn money by taking him around the world in a cage—one dollar to look at him, two dollars to spit at him, three dollars to smack him in the mug. —

Now I have been infected by Glaser's fear after all. It occurred to me: The Windes are not cautious with the radio. — Annemarie's brother is close to the conspirators in his views at least. Annemarie herself is politically unpopular. Eva is a frequent visitor at the Windes', my manuscripts are with Annemarie. Be a fatalist!

[ ... ]

**Toward evening**

[ ... ] Steinitz was here for a long time in the morning. He, too, knew nothing. Only rumors. According to them five thousand officers, etc., are supposed to have been arrested and shot, numerous Berlin *workers*—and that would be tremendously important—are also said to have been arrested. — Cohn has just brought the Sunday newspaper: According to it the last conspirator was eliminated within "six hours," and now the jubilant nation felt doubly strong and optimistic—and so we shall not find out more until the "final victory" or until the next time. (When, therefore?) Eva heard the military bulletin on Pirnaischer Platz: small advances by the Anglo-Americans in Normandy, large ones by the Russians in the East, Italy quiet; unchanged tone of the German bulletin: "warded off" . . . "blocked," etc.; I am sick and tired of it. — I am in fact very depressed. For sure, it may not be entirely true that the threat has been completely eliminated, and even if it is then there are certainly metastases remaining in the body of the army; but nevertheless: They still have the press and the power and all that goes with it; contrary to every natural law they have once again maintained their invulnerability—"Providence!" "within six hours," *spontaneously* (also resurrected!) jubilant nation—in terms of propaganda they have drawn something rousing, a mood of victory out of a most serious defeat, millions will once more believe in final victory. And meanwhile some gauleiter or some other Party boss has given a speech, the army was about to be completely reequipped with new weapons and would be victorious in "the last round" with these new weapons; and in the latest issue of the *Reich* Goebbels is supposed to have written he shuddered at the thought of the fate to which London was sentenced; and so millions of "national comrades" have been given new hope, and so there is little point in the Americans scattering leaflets over six-times-bombed Munich: "For the V-1!" and over devastated Budapest: Reply to the persecution of the Jews! — the German side will endure it (partly whipped up, partly intimidated), and the swastika still rules. — [ ... ]

**July 26, Wednesday toward evening**

Yesterday Katz was here for a while [ ... ]. He told us: Many shootings had occurred, including in Dresden; the whole army was now allowed to use only the Party greeting (he had seen an officer begin to salute and then correct himself by raising his hand into the air from his cap), the whole army had renewed its oath of loyalty (had sworn for the second time, therefore!) to Hitler. All three of us considered this second oath to be utter madness. (An oath of loyalty is completely pointless! Outwardly it is unnecessary; the law, compulsion is binding. It is only of special significance with regard to one's conscience, and that cannot be affected by an imposed oath.) Katz concluded, therefore, that this business was not over, rather it was only just beginning. — [ . . . ]

## July 28, Friday toward evening

[ . . . ]

*LTI:* In the military bulletin of July 26 on the fighting in Normandy: "Our troops fighting fanatically . . ." For the first time the word "fanatically" is in a military bulletin! After the introduction of the German greeting, this word has now been taken into the official language of the army! Until now only at Party meetings or in individual proclamations of National Socialist generals, but never in the army bulletin. As already mentioned, I set it beside the greeting and the second oath of loyalty.

[ . . . ]

## August 2, Wednesday morning

Since yesterday dominated by the feeling: thirty years ago! Linked to that is always the contemplation of being old, of standing at the end of something, of having no entitlement to anything. But I am so utterly lacking in what I always imagined to be the maturity of age, I am neither satisfied, nor tired, nor in any way calm in the face of death. Only absolutely skeptical. — As far as the war is concerned, it appears to me a cruel irony of fate that the Russians occupy exactly the same positions with respect to East Prussia as they did on August 1, 1914. Who is there, who could inflict a Tannenberg on them today? If one looks only at the military bulletins of the last few days: Normandy, Augustow, Warsaw, in addition since yesterday the Beskidy Pass and Turkey's irresolution—then one has no choice but to say, that the war can last only a few more weeks. If one reads the newspaper articles, speeches, decrees, then provision has been made for years to come, the tyranny unshaken and unshakable, "final victory," despite all momentary "crises"—crisis is the current euphemism for "defeat"—absolutely certain. And since even I am influenced by this iron impudence and this relentless repetition, how can it not have an effect on the mass of the population? I tell myself again and again: They have maintained themselves for so long in the face of all nature and every calculation, why not yet another year? —

[ . . . ]

## Evening

Today stagnation on all fronts; nothing remarkable, but it shows never-theless, that the German army is offering resistance, that it is by no means demoralized and disintegrating. And at some time or other the Russians will have to pause. I already see the sixth winter of the war before me. And since war and armaments and labor deployment have been even further "totalized," and since a new questionnaire on labor duty arrived today, I am expecting a reexamination and see myself in the factory again. And since I have for days been plagued by a stomach and intestinal disorder, which appears to be very widespread at the moment, and since Eva also has a lot of heart trouble again, everything looks very gloomy.

## August 4, Friday toward evening

I am bored by exhaustion and despondency. No end in sight. The stagnation in the East is more marked; troops are said to be constantly moving through Dresden, being rushed from Italy to Russia. And in Italy, too, the English are advancing only very piano, piano—they have been just outside Florence for at least two weeks and have not taken it. On the other hand: The famous "bridgehead"—does it, too, not belong in the superlatives chapter of the *LTI*? —is now expanding from Normandy to Brittany and extending in depth toward Rennes. And likewise on the other hand: Turkey has broken off relations with Germany. Does it signify nothing, or does it signify only a symptom (the rats leave . . . ), or does it perhaps, as a fourth front, as a rolling up of the Balkans, signify the decisive blow? At the moment one can say just as little about the significance of the Turkish factor as about the sig-nificance of the officers' putsch. Yesterday and it certainly belongs to the *LTI*—brief newspaper item. Lord Mayor Goerdeler (Lord Mayor of Leipzig, Commissioner for Prices, retired from both, but not so very long ago), a fugitive since July 20, a participant in the plot. *One million marks reward.* What belongs to the *LTI* here is the amount. Curse of the superlative, in this case the form determines the content: If everything is expressed in huge numbers, then the price on someone's head has to have the requisite zeros as well. But they harm only themselves as a result, because people will say to themselves: How dangerous must a wanted man be if they are willing to part with a million. Quite absurd also is again the cool brazenness of the thing: Yesterday only a few officers, *only* officers, were involved, and they had all been "liquidated," and today they are hunting a lord mayor. —
[ . . . ]

## August 7, Monday morning

On Saturday afternoon Lewinsky, who was expected the next day, turned up unannounced. Full of indignation: He has to do Sunday work duty

("Sunday deployment") and help unload goods at the station. It's one consequence of the new supertotalization: Sunday deployment with the age
limit raised from sixty to sixty-five, ten-hour working day in all factories, including Bauer, of course, and Thiemig & Möbius. In the event of a reexamination, therefore, I must expect the worst. — Steinitz was here on Sunday
morning; later, at a quarter to twelve, the usual Sunday alert sounded, but
no more than a pre-alert, and it lasted only thirty minutes. In the afternoon
I visited Eisenmann senior, and when I came back I found Berger here. Naturally "the situation was discussed" again and again with Steinitz, with
Eisenmann, with Berger. With Steinitz I was the active party, encouraged
both him and myself, by listing everything that indicates collapse. In particular the new threat of a Turkish front and the ever-wider circles made by the
plot business. This new bulletin; the list of "cashiered officers" ("The army
purges itself!" At its own request, which Hitler complies with, the following
are handed over to the "People's Court" . . . then the list. The bloody court,
therefore, which was recently defended in the *Reich* as not passing *only*
death sentences, one case had even ended in acquittal, although since it
dealt solely with high treason . . .) — With Eisenmann and Berger, however,
it was they who set me to rights. Eisenmann said thus far he had believed
the outcome would be decided in the East, he was now of a different opinion and justified it like this: The army knew that the war was lost, that Germany was defeated. In that case the soldiers preferred the Anglo-Americans
rather than the Russians to enter the country, and consequently—proof was
the rapid success of the enemy in Brittany!—they would run away as fast as
possible, so that the Anglo-Americans would reach Germany before the
Russians! He held forth about this in all seriousness and with great certainty. He was convinced that a complete and final German collapse would
take place within a few weeks. [ . . . ]

*Voces populi.* In a restaurant, Eva overheard a gentleman reading the list
of those "cashiered" to two women. The first woman: "And they are supposed to be German officers?!" The other, a postal worker: "Well, they
must just have had enough!"

*LTI.* 1) Eva drew my attention to "action." I don't believe I have ever
made a note of it, and yet it is one of the very oldest catchwords. From the
very beginning, every form of activity, against the Red Front, against Jews,
against other parties, etc., is an action. Cf. Goebbels' HIB action. [HIB—
"Hinein in die Betriebe!"—Into the factories.]

2) Large amount of space in the press devoted to Knut Hamsun's 85th
birthday. He visited a German submarine and expressed the hope that
Germany would be victorious over Bolshevism and Jewry for Europe. I
have never read anything by Hamsun, but after reading the few remarks
in R. M. Meyer and Stammler, and after what Eva tells me, I can find absolutely no clue as to how this psychologist and follower of Naturalism
finds his way to National Socialism, finds his way to it *now,* or stands by it,
when his country is subjugated, when all the criminality of the National
Socialists is plain to see. [ . . . ]

**August 8, Tuesday toward evening**

Yesterday evening, Eva was already in bed, Stephan Müller was here. He confirmed from Swiss broadcasts what Berger had reported the day before, added that the Americans had turned east and were advancing on Paris from Laval. He said, among those shot for participating in the plot were Schacht and Neurath; there's a certain "Commissioner Nebe," who, according to a newspaper item, is roaming around in a state of mental derangement, and whose finder receives a fifty-thousand-mark reward. Nebe was the fugitive head of the Berlin detective force. [ . . . ]

**August 9, Wednesday morning**

The military bulletin continues to obscure, to conceal, to pass over in silence. But the newspaper reports and articles, etc., are now becoming more plainspoken. (I get to see newspapers only late and irregularly—now from the Cohns, now from the Stühlers, although each is afraid of the other; and the radio broadcast on Pirnaischer Platz, which Eva listens to at five o'clock, is often unclear and affected by interference; if she tries to buy a newspaper, it is mostly sold out; occasionally Frau Winde gives her a copy . . .) In the *Dresdener Zeitung* of Monday, August 7, there is: 1) Reception for SS and Party leaders, Reichleiters, and gauleiters, at the Führer's headquarters. Himmler talks of a "holy people's war." Hitler says he is protected by fate, because "the nation . . . needs a man who does not capitulate under any circumstances but unflinchingly holds high the flag of trust and of faith, and because I believe that no one else would do it better than I do it. Whatever blows of fate may fall, I shall always stand straight as bearer of the flag!" (Style! Worn-out petit bourgeois phrases. — [ . . . ]) 2) Article: "East Prussia sets an example of supreme preparedness for battle. (Unique effort by the whole community to protect the frontier—beacon of German readiness.)" [ . . . ] "With an ardent will to prevent the deadly Bolshevik enemy from violating German soil . . . hundreds of thousands of East Prussians" are working to throw up ramparts. (We hear that large numbers of Hitler Youth have been sent to do digging in East Prussia.) Thus is propaganda capital made out of the report of the Russian advance [onto German territory]. The article is taken from the "National Socialist Party Correspondence"; it is therefore undoubtedly in all the newspapers.
     [ . . . ]

**August 10, Thursday toward evening**

[ . . . ]
     Yesterday Eva ran into Natscheff in town, they greeted each other spontaneously. He was in prison for a whole year. He had been denounced by

a middle-class person, said it was an exception, most denunciations were made by the lower class of people. He was unchanged in appearance, but said his nerves had suffered badly. He was not allowed to open a shop for five years after the sentence—but thought he would be able to, "in two to three months time." Bulgaria is negotiating. —

[ . . . ]

### August 13, Sunday midday

Four Jews have been arrested at the Schwarze factory, one woman is supposed to have been "gabbing," three people are supposed to have been "listening." That is sufficient. I know only one of the four, and him only slightly: the singer and chargeman Kosciollek, I talked to him once at the hairdresser's. Stühler, dismayed and shaken, told me about the business yesterday. "Let's just keep very quiet—we don't want to lose our heads now, at five minutes to twelve." — At that I remembered: A good ten years ago Grete Blumenfeld said to me: "Walter has been dismissed, it is so sad—now, at just five minutes to twelve!" There are hours in which I assume the "last five minutes" could stretch out terribly once more. At any rate things are at a standstill in the East.

### Evening

Stagnation in Russia and Italy; there will be no conclusion this year either. Tremendous internal measures in Germany, new troops mustered, new enlistments for labor service, closure of theaters, postal deliveries only six days a week and only once a day, etc.

[ . . . ]

### August 14, Monday evening

*LTI.* The new regulations for the mail are notified under the heading "Urgent measures." Among them is also the abolition of the "packet." Packet has been the word used for years now for "sample of no commercial value." Packets play an important part in communication with Theresienstadt. The Jews there are said to suffer much more from hunger than we do here, and whoever can do so sends them packets, mostly bread, zwieback. Now that is no longer possible. It has never been quite clear *who* among the people in Theresienstadt is allowed to correspond with whom. In all these years we have not heard a word from Trude Scherk. News of the Hirschels has often reached one or other person, and we heard of the death of Jon Neumann, and that Frau Ida Kreidl was well. Now it is said that a great number of the Theresienstadt people have been transported, perhaps to Auschwitz, perhaps to their death.

[ . . . ]

## August 16, Wednesday morning

Two humiliations yesterday, which brought home to me once again the ghastliness of my situation. — One of the salesclerks in the always-crowded Amalien pharmacy is a pop-eyed creature with thick glasses, whom I have long suspected of hostility to Jews. She has often made me wait, served people first who came in after me, or chattered endlessly to a customer in front of me. I refused to believe it, thought I was oversensitive. Yesterday an elderly gentleman indicates me in a friendly fashion: "Was here before me." — "Yes, and can I help you?" serves him first. It is ridiculous how bitter such a trifling matter makes me. And instead of becoming more indifferent, I become ever more raw. Then in the evening, around ten, the Cohns and the Stühlers, Eva as well, were already in bed, the usual police check and, as also fairly usual, on the first floor. Unusual was simply that Waldmann, instead of ringing once as normal, rang repeatedly and furiously. I thought: Gestapo! and had a brief bout of palpitations. — But a new hope squeezed between these two humiliations: the Anglo-American landing in southern France. There is a psychological reversal inside me: My mind hopes, but my heart is no longer capable of believing.

The frequent LTI observations about "sunny," etc., death notices will now probably cease. Since Monday the *Dresdener Zeitung* is printing only mass graves, so to speak, or memorial tablets. I.e., the individual notices are contained within a large black-framed panel and are as compressed as classified advertisements; only the scantiest particulars and even these with abbreviations, so that all decorative adjuncts are dropped and not much more remains than the earlier lists of the fallen.

## August 17, Thursday toward evening

During the afternoon I was unsettled, half concerned—arrested? taken ill?—half irritated, that Eva stayed out for so long, and appeared only toward half past three instead of toward two, as expected. Reason: Frau Winde's cat was just giving birth to the kittens, about which we have been talking for weeks: Two of them, once they have spent three months with their mother, are to come to us—*if* we can take them by then. *If*, therefore, by November 17, 1944 . . . Will that be the case? From the Winde source, from Simon, but also from the German military bulletin, and not *only* between the lines of the latter, we deduce, that things are going extremely badly in France. But is it a real débâcle, is it *the* débâcle, is it *the* moment of decision? Katz, who has patients in the house and frequently drops by— as yesterday evening, as at lunchtime today—is halfway certain that point has been reached; Paris will have to be evacuated in the course of the next few days, the "small pincers" at Falaise were cutting off the southern wing of the German Atlantic army, the Americans, who had landed on a front of 100 miles from Nice to Marseilles, were meeting little resistance and would dash up the Rhône toward Germany—a snap change in the weather: My mind believes it, and my heart does not believe it. —

Yesterday morning there was a full air-raid warning for nearly all the one and a half hours between half past ten until almost twelve; the Americans were in x places again and left Dresden alone once again.

[ . . . ]

### August 18, Friday morning

[ . . . ] We had imagined, as a kind of caricature, what the newspaper would write about the new French situation, and now there it is, word for word and in all seriousness in the situation report: Eisenhower had undertaken his large-scale offensives in Normandy and Brittany, hounded by the V-1 and out of fear of the V-2 and V-3, and the landing in the south of France, in despair at the lack of success in Normandy and the deadlock in Italy; despite tremendous losses of men and matériel and small gains of territory, all the French enterprises have thus far entirely failed to achieve the real success that was anticipated . . . Do the mass of readers really believe it, and for how long will they go on believing it? But do I myself not believe a little bit of all of that, when it is repeated so brazenly and impudently? — Nevertheless: Suddenly the enemy is in the Chartres-Dreux area, when only recently (according to *German* reports and in contradiction to other reports) he was so hopelessly far away from there. — [ . . . ]

### August 19, Saturday afternoon

[ . . . ]

A pompous article on guerre totalissime: "Renunciation of peacetime habits; mustering of the nation's reserves of strength." In it a) The cities badly affected by the *air terror* were "very rightly described as *frontline cities.*" b) It was now the "unyielding demand of the hour" "to change from the more bourgeois way of life of yesterday to the revolutionary and soldierly lifestyle of today." ("Revolutionary" is the stamp of holiness here.) —

In the same paper a ban on adhering to old house regulations made obsolete by the war: Domestic stairs, like those in shops and factories, were to be scrubbed only once a week—cleaning rags had to be saved.

Two Jewish rumors: There had been mass murders in Poland in the course of withdrawals. On the other hand Jews had been allowed out of Hungary after a Hungarian agreement with the USA. We consider point 1 very likely; point 2 can be correct only if Hungary has broken away from Germany. *Did it?* We are tapping in the dark. —

### August 20, Sunday afternoon

[ . . . ] After hours of work making notes on Stresemann, I had forced myself to take a long walk for health reasons. On Saturday afternoon one encounters only the Jacobi family at the cemetery, it's *weekend* for the trio of workers. I was sitting with the Jacobis on the bench in front of their house, when Werner Lang turned up, and I walked home with him afterward. Naturally we talked about the situation: Matters appear to be catastrophic in France. But four weeks ago they appeared to be similarly catastrophic in Russia, and suddenly the Russians were checked. I learned: A little while ago many elderly Jews (Three hundred? Three thousand?) had been transported from Theresienstadt, and afterward an English broadcast had announced that this transport had been gassed. Truth? Forsechè sì, forsechè no. — On the way home Werner Lang also told me: A soldier had addressed him on the platform of the tram: "You're still here, why is that?" (Without any aggression in his voice) — "Because I am in a mixed marriage." — "Well, that's decent; but I've seen such awful things in Poland, such awful things! It will have to be paid for!" This very loudly, while other people were listening. The man was risking his head. — And this morning Steinitz was here and told us his wife had come from the bank in a cheerful mood. She had asked for application forms for the currency office. "Take as many as you like (the woman clerk pushed a whole pile toward her), soon no one is going to need them anymore. You'll see, in two weeks!" Our hopes are raised for an hour at a time by such talk, a little longer by the situation at the front—but even then not for very long and not always consistently. Only one thing is surprising about the talk: People's courage and lack of caution, because the newspapers are full of prison and death sentences for every kind of "defeatism." — [ ... ]

### August 21, Monday midday

Exhaustingly hot and humid days, for the first time this summer really. Yesterday evening instead of taking my obligatory walk I lingered in the Waldmanns' cellar apartment. Berger was there. Of course: the situation. In addition the gossip about individual Jews and the deep mistrust of one for the other and the tremendous fear of being betrayed even at the last moment. All of them are demoralized and frightened, each warns against the other, counsels silence and caution and is himself incautious. I myself always argue for an attitude of fatalism absolutely without dread (*not* fear). Berger quoted something, which is supposed to be old, but was new to me: "We passed through the Red Sea, and we shall pass through the brown shit!" [ ... ] Aside from that, the newspaper articles about the war again and again attempt to deflate the Allied victories by emphasizing the V-1.

[ ... ]

Among Jews the idea of owning books has disappeared. Too much is floating around masterless, too much has been stolen, been left behind, has passed from hand to hand; no Jewish property is safe. Months ago I lent Berger two books, which I myself had found somewhere or inherited. The collection of criminal reports I had found left behind in the uncleared rooms at Lothringer Weg; where the "Singermanns" came from, I no longer know. When I asked Berger to give the things back to me, he was embarrassed; evidently he had long ago loaned them to someone else. Books are masterless, Jews' books. He came a week later; he wanted to put back what he had borrowed [ . . . ]. I immediately saw that there was a mistake but pretended not to notice.

I am now worried about my reference books. An appeal in the newspaper: Books, especially dictionaries in private hands, to be given up, since many public libraries have been destroyed by air terror. What is *requested* from Aryans, is usually taken from Jews. On the other hand Steinitz thinks: After all the robberies that have already taken place, they imagine we don't have anything anymore; after all, we've also been spared the latest fabric collection. I am undecided, whether we should get the reference books to Gertrud Schmidt or leave them here. They would be a heavy load for Eva to carry, and I should miss them greatly. —

[ . . . ]

### August 24, Thursday morning

[ . . . ]

Yesterday afternoon, on the tram line grade crossing in front of our house, a wild-looking worker passed close by me and said loudly: "Chin up! The scoundrels will soon be finished!" — Stühler had a similar experience. But for years now we have had such experiences every couple of days, and for years now we have had quite opposite experiences every couple of days. No conclusions can be drawn from them, nor from the military situation, desperate as it is for Germany, both in the West and the East.

### August 25, Friday morning

Yesterday afternoon Frau Stühler: Customers said German broadcasts had reported the defection of Romania. In the evening (during the air-raid drill), Stephan Müller told me it was already in the newspaper. Today Cohn saw a copy of the *Freiheitskampf*, which was displayed; according to that, the position was analogous to the Badoglio business. Naturally a National Party had already emerged with a proclamation and a civil war was in progress. — For a moment my spirits were greatly raised—but from the first moment also muted and skeptical. Really Germany should collapse now; but "really" it should already have done so in July '43, when Italy defected. — The Jews are afraid and skeptical. Stühler rebuked his wife for having talked about it [the defection of Romania]. "I am afraid, at five to twelve I don't want to . . . if you had seen the people who recently returned from Gestapo interrogation, then you would be afraid, too." Fear is the dominant feeling, apart from that apathy. People can no longer imagine an end. And yet the whole Balkan front seems to be collapsing: Bulgaria, Turkey, Romania, and fifty to sixty percent of our oil comes from Romania. But in Berlin "they" will still offer resistance. Yesterday during the air-raid warning some bombs fell on Freital; Eva, who was in the cellar of the Albert Theater, went to see Glaser afterward, saw the columns of smoke of the fires. On the tram people drew each other's attention to them, but *only* by glances, *no one dared speak.* — [ . . . ]

Yesterday evening from half past seven until half past nine, i.e., until well after dark: air-raid drill. An imaginary phosphorus bomb (a tin can) and splashes of phosphorus marked in chalk were disposed of with fictitious sand and fictitious water. Before and after, endlessly, the by-now-familiar instructions, admonitions, threats. On this occasion something became very evident, which was already evident long ago: The Jews are not very attentive, even a little refractory in a passive way, because they know they are not well trained and well protected. There is a lack of gas masks; there is a lack of first-aid attendants, because Katz is not allowed to train any Aryan women and because Aryan wives of Jews are not allowed to attend any general training course. One of us, Waldmann indeed, who plays an important role in the house, after all, posed the question: "If our Jewish cellar collapses—will anyone pull us out?" Kautzsch, a decent man, replied, half indignant, half uncertain: "As long as *I* am Group Leader here, certainly!" Yet earlier, when there was talk of the missing "lay nursing attendants," he had said very dolefully: "I should very much like to help you, but as you know, my hands are tied." It is tragicomic and turns into pure LTI when the man attempts to make us fit into the general "effort," when he inevitably slips into the stock of phrases he has learned by heart, which are like an insult to us: Three times yesterday we were told that we had to play our part, for both our own and the general good, ready for action as a "community bound by oath." Pretty to hear, when one wears the star and is an "enemy of the state." [ . . . ]

### August 26, Saturday afternoon

The very exhausting heat has now lasted for something like a week. The sun shines on our living room for the greater part of the day. —

I had to have my wretched shoes sewed up again. I went to the third Jewish cobbler. The first, a giant Russian Jew, who had his workshop in Sporergasse, hanged himself in prison. The second, Frischmann, has been inside for weeks—I made a note of the affair in which he was involved. The third, Saslawski, has set up his workshop next door to Waldmann; I made his acquaintance yesterday, saw and listened to him while he was working. A lean, dark man, fifty-one years of age, eastern Jew, an eastern accent to his speech—that is what a Galician craftsman must look like and talk like. Previously he did locksmithing; in peacetime he had done "everything," as he says, film and traveling salesman. His mother is in Theresienstadt, one son (cobbler) is interned in Australia, one daughter, a trained nurse, is in England. He was sensitive and respectful toward me, the professor whom "they hounded from his chair" (*sic*); he could not be persuaded to accept money for his stitching. What did I know of "Judaism"? I said, unfortunately I had no knowledge of Hebrew. — "But you must know words like *broche* and *mitzvah*." I showed sufficient knowledge. Incidentally this man, too, is of course in a mixed marriage. And then: As a consequence of being buried alive during the First World War his whole head and half the upper part of his body twitches terribly while he is speaking and working. [ . . . ]

### August 27, Sunday midday

Steinitz was here yesterday afternoon. He said the cobbler Saslawski had not been a German front-line soldier and had not been buried; his trembling originated in a concentration camp of the Third Reich. —

The bombs dropped on Freital-Dölzschen-Birkigt are supposed to have caused greater damage than was at first assumed; according to an optimistic rumor sixty-four corpses are buried in a bunker; according to a gloomier one, it's two to four hundred. Since no details are ever published, the most disquieting rumors are naturally going around. I have been scared out of my complacency about Dresden a little. Now I also fear for our little house. One of the targets of the attack, if not *the* target, was the railway line in the Plauenschen Grund [below Dölzschen].

[ . . . ]

### August 28, Monday evening

This morning [ . . . ] Waldmann was supposed to repair one of our roller blinds. (Troublesome business, procuring the necessary cord: written confirmation from the landlord is required.) At the last moment: impossible, he [Waldmann] has to fetch a corpse. (That is his office, together with Jacobi.) At once there was the fearful rumor, someone will have met his death in the police prison. It then, however, turned out to be the Jewish wife of an Aryan in Niedersedlitz. The corpse was brought back in a handcart—for Jews there is no proper vehicle for conveying corpses.

In Saturday's newspaper there was an announcement—"the burial" (no more than that!) will take place in Freital at 5:00 P.M., delegations with flags should, etc. . . . A great mass of people is said to have gone out there, but no one is allowed to talk about it. There are said to be many dead still in a destroyed bunker. All of it is hushed up, the military bulletin long ago ceased to concern itself with such trivia. For weeks now it has stated: large formations over central Germany (e.g.), in particular over . . . there follow the names of two cities, where the losses were evidently far too great to pass over in complete silence. How many Freitals with dozens, perhaps with two hundred, dead may there be in Germany every day?

The newspaper lavishly celebrates the organizational achievement of the gauleiter of East Prussia, who in twenty-four hours mobilized hundreds of thousands to dig trenches. The whole thing is once again a National Socialist triumph, a defeat for the Russians, who cannot and will not be able to invade East Prussia. Thus everything is turned into a German victory. For how much longer will it work? All measures are taken with such effrontery and emphasis, as if the war were going to last years yet. It is repeatedly emphasized that a new field army would be made available by the new measures [ . . . ]. (Have I noted that from the first of September, no more "belletristic" and "related" books may be printed anymore? Only natural science and technology! That commercial schools, etc., are being shut?) — [ . . . ]

### August 30, Wednesday morning

[ . . . ]

From individual editions of the *Deutsche Allgemeine Zeitung*, mid-July until mid-August. [ . . . ] On July 15: "The Self-Assertion of the Theater During the Air Terror." Report by the "Reich Dramaturg," Ministerial Councillor Dr. Schlösser, on how, despite all the destruction, "the uplifting and relaxing art of drama" was being sustained for the population through amalgamation and mutual assistance. Four weeks after this speech, Goebbels extinguishes *all* theaters from September 1. — An item about forthcoming symphony concerts in Bucharest, a German will make a guest appearance. Two weeks later Romania declares war on us. — [ . . . ] On August 16 a leading article, "Our Nation in the East," a hymn to the Upper Silesians' love of Fatherland, from which it emerges that there they are just as anxious and are digging trenches just as in East Prussia. [ . . . ]

### September 1, Friday morning and later, five whole years of war!

[ . . . ]

I do not believe I have ever noted this: At every door of the apartment, fixed at an angle and at eye level, there is a mezuzah. Lewinsky says the rabbi lived here. Recently he opened one of the little rolls and showed us the splendid, regular, but minute handwritten verses from the Bible.

[ . . . ]

Since the destruction in Freital I cannot get rid of the thought that a bomb could fall on Annemarie's clinic. Industrial Pirna, Küttner's nearby, which makes parachutes! Then every one of my manuscripts, which are all in the same suitcase there, would be destroyed at one fell swoop. Yet I fear the Gestapo more than the Americans. But everything is fate, and there is no safety anywhere.

On August 28, together with detailed news of the complete abandonment of Paris—one now saw that apart from "strong points" it had really been in the hands of the others for days—the *Dresdener Zeitung* (and certainly not it alone) printed an article: "Secret of the Final Phase of the War" by SS war correspondent Achim Fernau. It is the most absurd thing they have come up with so far. Popular and mysterious. Yes, for months we have been losing area after area, army corps after army corps in every theater. The spectator is like someone watching a game of skat through a glass door. Two players have all the trumps in their hands, the game appears to be up for the third. And suddenly—the third player is being congratulated. Because the spectator did not see the grand coming at all. — Or: Two cars are racing each other. What counts is which one was last to tank up, which one is able to tank up last. The Allies want to reach their goal now, must reach it now—because afterward! The English Minister of the Interior has said: "I know of terrible things!" The V-1 is only the beginning of these terrible things. Churchill knows that, hence the tremendous exertion now, the desperate push forward! Churchill has said in an interview: "We must end the war by the autumn, otherwise . . ." Ominous dots in the text. [ . . . ] In short: At the moment our enemies are winning out of fear and desperation. *We*, we have to hold out only until autumn. And we shall do it too. "With all our means and all our strength. Victory is truly very close." (Conclusion of the article!) — This has been going on for weeks now on an ever-increasing scale. Germany is *keeping its cards close to its chest*. Is it bluffing, or does it really still hold trumps? [ . . . ] Anyhow: With the slogan "time in exchange for territory" and with the mysterious weapons the nation is kept in line.

[ . . . ]

### September 3, Sunday midday and later

[ . . . ]

All morning beating drums, fanfares (wrongly played, just as all the notes of the 3rd Reich are wrong), Hitler Youth marching, singing, in position on the Elbe bridge, waving their flags at the sound of the fanfares, in a word: the same old carry on. Reason: According to the National Socialists the war began today, on September 3, 1939, as a result of the groundless declaration of war by the English and French. On September 1, 1939, we merely "returned Polish fire."

[ . . . ]

### September 4, Monday morning

Lewinsky stayed away yesterday. But Eva played very nicely on the piano; now I often do not listen to her for weeks; but away from home she plays a little with Glaser and with Frau Kreisler—at the same time there are all kinds of things to eat, to smoke and also food and things to smoke to bring home.

*LTI.* On every house, beside a chalk circle and arrow, the letters LSR [Luftschutzraum—air-raid shelter]. As a new explanation we heard: "Lernt schnell Russisch" [Learn Russian quickly].

On Saturday evening Katz was here for a while. He maintained, that the Gestapo were becoming a little more courteous and reasonable; at any rate they did not want to make themselves *even* more hated. (I don't believe it, it's not in their character, does them no good now anyway.) [ . . . ]

## September 5, Tuesday morning

Yesterday Eva brought home from the *Freiheitskampf* that Finland has capitulated and Bulgaria has got a "suicide government" (i.e., one turning toward Russia). Frau Cohn brought the news, Waldmann whispered it to her on the stairs, Brussels had fallen. Toward evening, during my health walk by the Elbe, a fat gentleman, coming up from the river, crossed my path and said: "Now it will soon be over!" And when I walked on without reacting, said behind me: "Thank God! . . . You must not misunderstand me!" — For all of that it goes on and on. The last newspapers I saw declared: In the West we are establishing the same *elastic* (*LTI:* Since Stalingrad the line in the East has been *elastic,* and the enemy never achieves a *breakthrough*)—so the same elastic front line as in the East; we are avoiding the decisive battle and will fight it only when the prospects are favorable to us again. Do people believe that? Goebbels has dampened hopes in the *new weapons,* one must not expect any sudden miracle from them, and in the last military bulletin, says Eva, the V-1 was *absent,* absent for the first time in weeks! Thus I vacillate between hope and an inability to believe, but am, for all that, diligent in storing things away. I now make a virtue out of the misfortune of no longer being able to stick to *one* theme: I tell myself, I *still* have time to catch up a little on the general education, which I neglected in recent decades.

[ . . . ]

On *LTI.* National Socialism is a most poisonous consequence, more properly overconsequence, of German Romanticism; it is just as guilty or innocent of National Socialism as Christianity is of the Inquisition; Romanticism makes of it a specifically German matter and distinguishes it from Fascism and Bolshevism. It finds its strongest expression in the racial problem, and this in turn emerges most strongly in the Jewish question. Thus the Jewish question represents the "essential core" and the quintessence of National Socialism. And it is precisely this kernel that demonstrates the mendacity and absolute loss of intellect, the absolute descent into the Hell of Romanticism in the Third Reich. The Jewish problem is the poison gland of the swastika viper.

## September 6, Wednesday midday

[ . . . ]

In the evening I succumbed to temptation, as I have done occasionally, and did not go for a health walk, but to Waldmann, caretaker, undertaker, and removal man—for the revenue office, public sale of confiscated Jewish property; he said: "They're in a hurry now, they're probably afraid"—formerly a fur dealer, vigorous man in his early fifties, much younger, very blond wife, likes to talk politics, very well disposed to me—went to see him therefore under the pretext of reminding him that a torn rollerblind cord has long been in need of repair. Down in the cellar he has a pleasant sitting room with four club chairs around an elegant oval table; apart from the couple I have sometimes found Berger there, with whom he is on very friendly terms. First the men are quiet, then they warn me to be cautious, then they reveal the Allied reports and give their own views. Berger says the most, but Waldmann is not sparing with interpretations and suppositions.

[ . . . ]

The *Reich* of August 20; Goebbels's leading article: "In the Storms of Our Time." Naturally we have become stronger in every respect because of July 20 (the assassination attempt). The culprits—incomprehensible, "that there are men with German names and born of a German mother, who raise their hand to extinguish the life of the Führer"—are ultrareactionaries, and in their character "the powers of a diabolical intellect have overwhelmed the powers of instinct." [ . . . ] An article by Hans Schwarz van Berk: "The impatience of the enemy. The morass of his policies." The same old tune: Our opponents do not have any positive cultural war aims—their soldiers are war-weary and want to go home, so matters must be brought to a conclusion. We on the other hand, we are defending our culture, culture as such, that is our mission, otherwise we shall go under. That is why we shall "fight for every inch." Among the familiar awful visions of defeat there is also the following: "Instead of the German school for our children there will be foreign institutes, in which they would be 'reeducated' and have to deny what their parents thought and did, where in the history class men like Prien, Mölders, Dietl would be condemned as criminals, while Dürer, Leibniz, Beethoven, and Goethe would be declared citizens of the world . . ."

("Citizens of the world" as a derogatory term! Equivalence of Prien and Leibniz!)

[ . . . ]


### September 7, Thursday midday

Undoubtedly in *all* newspapers of Tuesday, September 5—I got hold of the *Dresdener Zeitung* from Cohn only yesterday evening, but everyone had already been talking about it before that—Article: "Readiness is everything! Within Germany's borders: People's War. By Helmut Sündermann, Deputy Reich Press Spokesman." (An official statement therefore.) Tone of the proclamation. The word "Heckenschütze" [lit., hedge shooter, i.e., guerrilla]—which is the LTI's word for franc-tireur—is avoided, but the thing itself is promoted in the most bloodthirsty manner and with a fanaticism extreme even by National Socialist standards. The enemy is approaching Germany's borders; his plan: "The German state is to be wiped from the map, the Germans are to be dispersed over the whole globe as labor slaves." "Driven on by insane Jewish fantasies of hate" the enemy wants to exterminate us entirely. [ . . . ] We, for our part, "we do not want to win, in order to extirpate the British nation or to conquer America; we have to win, in order—whether as nation or individuals—to continue living in freedom. We shall achieve this victory, even if by the mobilization of every German, for whom the heroic state of freedom has become the highest law of life . . ." "A nation that has absorbed the slogan 'better dead than a slave' and has fanatically made it the guiding principle of its whole heroic mission, such a nation will never be servile, and it will live forever!" Concluding sentences: As yet our soil is "not directly threatened"—but "readiness is everything!"

Further to this: The content is less criminal than stupid, because for the first time this is naked desperation speaking. And who will be inclined to a "people's war," when every town is exposed to enemy airplanes? And must not everyone say to himself: Why should the others not be "invaders," why is their invasion a crime, when we had occupied so many countries? Stylistically: Once again there are the few, ancient LTI raisins baked in with the mix. But the tenor of the whole thing seems to me more extravagant than all the earlier scribblings. (Admittedly, they used all kinds of superlatives for the cruelties of the Poles, Czechs, Soviets, Jews.) I do not believe that it still goes down well.

### September 10, Sunday morning

[ . . . ]

What is happening in the war? This morning Frau Cohn relates: "They fetched five women (Aryans, that is) from the Sachsenwerk plant, because, they said, [the Allies] had already reached Metz; a soldier's wife denounced them." In the afternoon Eva reported from the military bulletin: "Engagements at Metz." And Eva reports via Winde and Simon: The English have declared the larger part of the island is no longer being blacked out, it is no longer necessary. They have also declared, however, that there is a pause in the advance, troops have to be brought up.

And Lewinsky, who is always absolutely pessimistic, has heard from a "most reliable source," that Aachen is already in enemy hands, about which, however, England is keeping silent. And not a soul knows what is happening in the East, and what in the Balkans [ . . . ] and what in Italy, and what in Finland, and what in Germany itself; no one knows, and everything is obscure.

New "totalization" decrees have come out: University departments have largely been closed down (theology and philosophy completely), the senior classes of secondary schools have been dispatched to factory work, all periodicals apart from those "important to the war effort" [ . . . ] have been suppressed [ . . . ]. The weekly article on the military situation paints a very dark picture. Naturally: We shall manage *nevertheless,* and "time is on our side," but that is the most transparent of veils, contradicted by everything else in the article.

A particular characteristic of the *LTI* is the shameless short-windedness of its lies. There is a never-ending impudent abandonment of assertions that have been made the day before. "They cannot land. — They will not scale the Atlantic Wall. — They will not break through . . ." And now: "It could all be foreseen and given their superior strength occurred astonishingly late. But they cannot impose a decisive battle on us, because our lines are on the terrain we have chosen; we are disengaging with great skill . . ." Nothing more about the V-1. Once in recent days we were told: [firing] has become "irregular because of events in northern France," but resumed. Now silence.

### September 11, Monday morning

Shortly after nine yesterday, as Eva was getting ready for bed (I tend to follow her an hour later, but to begin the day at half past four), Stephan Müller turned up and stayed until around eleven. He said it can last no longer than mid-October at the outside. He talked about the English and the Russian "Freedom Broadcasting Stations." Everyone was listening to these broadcasts, the government was powerless to stop it. Officers and men of the Paulus-Seydlitz army speak on the Freedom Station: Three-hundred-thousand strong they stood ready to serve Germany, they wanted to establish a "democratic" order. The English also allow German prisoners to speak and solicit support. Germany's army in the West was very demoralized and tremendously weakened. Kluge, the commander in chief, had shot himself in the express train on the way to Hitler. [ . . . ] The collapse in the Balkans was absolute and entirely analogous to the débâcle of 1918. The V-1 was finished, likewise V-2 and V-3, the latter were "one-man" torpedoes and some kind of electrically remote-controlled boats with a huge explosive charge . . . (A card dated August 28 has just arrived from Hilde Jonson-Sussmann in Stockholm; she, too, twice hints very clearly that in Stockholm they believe the end is near.) — So we did not get to bed until around eleven; half an hour later—the first nighttime alert for many months—the sirens wailed. Müller had said the Allies had announced increased air bombardment; all the air force units, which so far had been deployed against the V-1, were now also available; in addition we remembered the four hundred dead in Freital: It made me feel rather uneasy. The air-raid warning itself came after about twenty minutes. But as I was shouldering the knapsack the all clear sounded—evidently the air-raid warning had been given by mistake. [ . . . ]

## September 14, Thursday afternoon

[ . . . ]

In the evening, without having heard or read the reports herself, Eva came home with the [contents of] the latest bulletins: In the *German* military bulletin: English attack on Aachen; in the English one: in the course of the attack on Trier, the German frontier crossed on a 22-mile front. A new offensive is also said to be under way in the East. — The fact that the enemy is on German soil will make a tremendous impression. How will the LTI respond? — In the cellar, Neumark had an old copy of the *DAZ*, which he had found by chance and which included a page summarizing the events of 1943. In February 1943 the fall of Stalingrad, in the spring the Führer holds discussions with the King of Bulgaria, with Antonescu—Count Ciano is appointed Italian ambassador to the Vatican . . . What an impression it all made on us! Ciano shot, Bulgaria and Romania changing sides, Stalingrad as remote as a fairy tale . . . But something else made a greater impression on us—it was the same for both Neumark and myself: the impotence of memory to fix all that we had so painfully experienced in time. When—insofar as we remembered it at all—had this or that happened, when had it been? Only a few facts stick in the mind, dates not at all. One is overwhelmed by the present, time is not divided up, everything is infinitely long ago, everything is infinitely long in coming; there is no yesterday, no tomorrow, only an eternity. And that is yet another reason one knows nothing of the history one has experienced: The sense of time has been abolished; one is at once too blunted and too overexcited, one is crammed full of the present. The chain of disappointments also unfolded in front of me again. [ . . . ] Ever since Stalingrad, since the beginning of '43 therefore, I have been waiting for the end. I remember asking Eva at the time: Do you think it is *a* defeat, or do you consider it to be *the* defeat, the catastrophe? That was in February '43. Then I had not yet done any factory duty. After that I was a factory slave for fourteen months. And now it is almost three months since I was released, three months in which I find it ever more difficult to wrest useful work from my so-called free days. —

Eva draws my attention to a characteristic feature of the times, the way that individual serviceable maps of the theaters of war become family relics. Eisenmann is proud of a large map of Europe, in which a parcel was once wrapped; the Windes have a "good" map of France, which was sent to them a long time ago; Gertrud Schmidt also possesses something similar. Naturally it has long been impossible to buy such a thing.

[ . . . ]

Cohn, usually so fearful, pessimistic, was quite elated yesterday: In the factory an Italian worker had spontaneously said to him in broken German: "In a few weeks finish . . . Like so," and had pointed upward and silently indicated, that the end would come through air attack. And that same day, on the tram, a young, well-dressed gentleman with several military decorations had wanted to press two meat coupons on him, assured him of his philo-Semitism, and that now it would soon be over. —

[ . . . ]

### September 15, Friday morning

The lethargy or bluntedness of the imagination! I am so accustomed to news of cities destroyed by bombing, that it makes no impression at all on me. Yesterday at the Steinitzes—I had to call on the watchmaker, who lent me a bulky alarm clock until the repair is completed—I was moved by a letter that a friend had written to him from Königsberg: Eva's hometown is 75 percent destroyed, according to official reports 5,000 people are dead and 20,000 injured; the writer and his wife had saved nothing except the clothes they were wearing; three relatives of the man, an old district judge, are dead. That shook me, and in the morning—dark, glowing, deep-purple dawn—as I washed myself and looked out at the Carola Bridge and the row of houses on the other side, I could not stop imagining that this row of houses was suddenly collapsing before my eyes—as indeed could happen at any time, as something like it really does happen every day somewhere in Germany. But unless there happens to be an air-raid warning in the next few hours, this image naturally fades, and I go on placing my hopes in "Churchill's aunt." Until now Dresden itself really has been spared; the threateningly clear bangs recently were not produced by bombs, but by our antiaircraft guns. —

Waldmann reported yesterday, a foreign station had broadcast this: When the Russians entered Larusha (Warsaw front), they found the SS engaged in shooting 1,000 Jews (men, women and children). They liberated the Jews and put the SS people up against the wall. I believe this report without hesitation, none of us doubts it. And each one asks himself, how many Jews are still alive in Poland? In the evening, when I passed on the news to Cohn, he relapsed into his literally quaking fear—he did not want to know anything about foreign broadcasts, the Gestapo, etc., etc. The same fright as with Glaser, as with Stühler. There is nothing more ghastly than the Jewish fear of the Gestapo. —

Leading article in the *Reich* of September 3: Goebbels: "The strength of our confidence." It is shameless and criminal and amazing in equal measure, how again and again, in defiance of all contrary events, the same phrases about certain final victory, of "time working for us," of the new weapons still to come, are hammered into people. How the same words are used again and again: The "reversals" are conceded, but our "morale" is higher, we constitute a "community bound by oath," "we shall not weary of again and again making clear to our nation that all the chances of final victory lie in our own hands. What counts today is not where we are fighting, but that we are fighting and how we are fighting . . . We shall not get out of breath, when it comes to the *final spurt*." The most absurd of these phrases is probably this one: it's all the same *where* we're fighting!

They know that the war is lost, and allow city after city to be destroyed, so as to gain another few weeks or months for themselves. To be noted in terms of language is the cramped uniformity and monotony of the LTI to the very last.

## September 16, Saturday morning

[ ... ]

## Evening

[ ... ] Glaser wrote to Eva today—no longer to me!—that he had been ordered to do labor duty, despite his 68 years. I repeatedly ask myself, why I am released from duty. Katz is exceedingly fearful and scrupulous; Aryans and Jews with serious heart problems are doing labor duty (e.g., Cohn, who has bad attacks every couple of weeks)—why was I let go? Does he consider me at death's door, am I at death's door? Sometimes I believe I am, sometimes I think he was impressed by my former professorship and the books I produced and that he wanted to conserve me and allow me to go back to my work. The question frequently preoccupies me, although it is really of no importance. During the day I push it all into the background and read, study, collect whatever I can, and occasionally fall asleep and then go on reading again. If one day I can turn it into a good book, then it was heroism—if not, then a senile pastime. I force myself to repress the absolutely fruitless thought of death, the absolutely sterile What for?—and even succeed in doing so again and again.
[ ... ]

## September 18, Monday afternoon

Frau Cohn (the Aryan half) told me at a quarter to five in the morning—I was washing up, she was making breakfast for her husband as every morning: "Today is your high holy day, today is New Year. My husband has worked it out." There was sometimes talk at Thiemig & Möbius that no one here knew the dates of the Jewish holy days—a calendar has not appeared, there is no longer any religious practice; the Jews left here are only those in mixed marriages, those who have more or less broken away therefore. Even Lewinsky, who has various memories of orthodoxy, did not know the date—otherwise he would certainly have mentioned it yesterday afternoon. I pictured to myself with what rejoicing this Jewish New Year will be celebrated in Italy, in France, in all the countries from which the Germans have had to retreat. It has truly become "the Jewish War"; abolition of the Jewish laws is everywhere one of the Allies' first acts. —
[ ... ]

### September 19, Tuesday morning

Yesterday evening, shortly after falling asleep, 11:00 P.M., alert, immediately followed by air-raid warning. Down to the cellar; Eva's heart in a really bad state; hardly there for a quarter of an hour: the all clear. Everything had remained quiet. But lately the strain has become very great. The English have issued a warning: Go into the open, our new bombs go right down to the cellar! And in Königsberg they appear to have substantiated the warning. —

Printed close together in the newspaper: Air raid on Auschwitz (concentration camp); "air raid on Buchenwald Concentration Camp near Weimar: the prisoners Thälmann and Breitscheid are among the dead." How much of that is true and how much the covering-up of murder? An attack on Buchenwald is in fact said to have taken place. (Letter from there from Pauly to his wife.) But were Thälmann and Breitscheid still alive then? And *who* dropped bombs on Buchenwald? And . . . there are so many possible ways of mixing an atom of truth with lies, of hushing up murders . . .

### September 20, Wednesday evening

The "NSDAP's Word of the Week" (*Dresdener Zeitung,* September 18) goes: "The coming victory will be a victory for us all. Today we must assume responsibility for it, fanatically and unconditionally. Dr. Goebbels." (Always: "Dr.," their famous university man, always the worn-out "fanatical.") The headline above this text, which also sets the tone for the subsequent commentary: THE CREED OF THE NATIONAL COMMUNITY. Final words of the commentary: "Now more than ever!" — This, while there are battles on German soil, the English are 20 miles from Cologne, and in Holland their airborne troops are on the right side of the Rhine delta! I ask myself again and again what kind of effect it has, whether it rouses people against the Allies or against the Nazis, whether it is the height of stupidity or the height of cleverness. Only success can answer that question. [ . . . ] I believe by turns (changing my mind six times a day), that Germany must collapse in the next few weeks, and that Germany will stand its ground. And again and again: My reason hopes and believes, but my heart doubts. — [ . . . ]

### September 21, Thursday late afternoon

[ . . . ]

On the *LTI.* [ . . . ] In Rampische Strasse I saw new banners (big, printed strips of paper) on shopwindows and doors: "Our will to live is stronger than our enemies' will to destroy." And (roughly): "Only a strong heart withstands the harshest test." Posted in a watchmaker's: "When there's an alarm/Put a watch on your arm!" It must be very old, because it is a long time since there were any watches to be bought, and even repairs are no longer carried out. —

In the *Dresdener Zeitung* (and no doubt also in all the other German newspapers) of September 19, three articles at once, of which I ask myself, whether they are the height of stupidity or cleverness. 1) A moral reflection by a certain Lieutenant Colonel Ellenbeck: "Daily reflection. What can I do to help my nation?" Content: One minute of reflection every morning. Then weigh every word, show no weakness, be convinced of victory. Encourage those who show weakness, denounce defeatists. The really interesting thing about this sermon is its style. For the LTI there is only the Goebbels-Hitler pattern—all the run-of-the-mill is imitation of that. [ . . . ] As consolation we are told that after all the [Russian] offensive in the East was stopped six weeks ago. — 2) Article ("Berlin. The High Command of German forces in Northern Finland announces"): "Germans are still shielding Finnish soil. "(Below in smaller print:) "Only where the Soviets attack is firmness unavoidable." Everything Germany has done to protect Finland is noted. Accordingly it is "completely absurd" now to accuse German troops of arbitrary devastation of Finnish towns. Only: Whatever is of use to the enemy in his fight against the withdrawing German army, must be destroyed. "Where destruction is undertaken, it is not directed against the Finnish people, but against the mortal enemy of the Finnish people, Bolshevism." (With which Finland is just concluding peace!) 3) "Transparent enemy lies about the Waffen SS. The steel spearhead of liberation in the battle for freedom." Here, everything that for years has been said about the SS and has been substantiated by examples is collected together as "enemy lies." (No, not *everything*: the atrocities, the firing on their own troops, the murders of the Jews are missing.) They were not against the family, on the contrary, "care of the kinship ideal" [was in their hands]. They provided for the women in exemplary fashion, as well as for their illegitimate children. "The enemy's imagination has expressed itself with typical Jewish cynicism on the subject of the 'Lebensborn' homes. The nasty rumors about fathering occurring by choice, by force, or serially, characterizes their author only too clearly." They did not have a superior attitude to other elements of the army. They were not opposed to religion, they did not have to leave the Church, they believed in Divine providence. Nor did they have higher losses than other branches of the army. (This presumably refers to the well-known fact that in the East, at least, the SS is given no quarter.) In conclusion the article emphasizes that "today the best of every European country voluntarily serve at the front under the sig runes for the reordering of their continent." — I find the article especially stupid. It is virtually a compendium and repetition of all the accusations that have been made for years. And the final sentence is especially awkward, since one repeatedly hears that people are *pressed* into the SS. This whitewash article is no doubt related to the recruitment march we saw and heard last Sunday morning, without knowing what it was about: Long columns of troops in field-gray and SS-black uniforms, with two noisily blowing military bands, marched across the Carola Bridge, onto which our kitchen windows look out. Then the next day we read that there had been a propaganda march through town.

### September 23, Saturday morning (and later).

[ . . . ]

Internally they act in every way as if their rule were still assured for a "thousand years." But militarily, too, the fact that they are holding out is completely incomprehensible. Where do they get the gasoline, the people, where the morale, the ability to resist? Perhaps the annihilation of the English "airborne landing division" at Arnhem is an unimportant, soon-to-be-forgotten episode; but it is extremely important to me today and pushes back my hopes of an end from September '44 to Easter '45, precisely because it is proof to me of unbroken powers of resistance. [ . . . ]

### Evening, 9:30 P.M.

[ . . . ] Eva came back late from the Windes'. One of their twins appears to be lost. Yesterday evening the English announced the sinking of his torpedo boat; nine men were named as saved—the crew numbers about twenty—young Winde was not among them. A supplement is supposed to be broadcast today; there is a very small hope (very small) that the boy has been picked up after all. It was his first engagement. The other twin has already seen action often and can at any moment be overtaken by the same fate. Their parents sent both seventeen-year-olds to the navy, because the training period lasts longer. It did not last "longer" or at any rate not long enough. As soon as the great dying comes close, it becomes impossible for me to say, "I can show no pity." The Windes, who have now lost the second of four sons (and the other two are still in danger), are absolute enemies of Hitler. —

[ . . . ]

### September 25, toward evening

*LTI.* On the subject of the unfathomable hatred of Jewry: I have had lying on my desk for a long while now an article by the vile and without doubt knowingly mendacious anti-Semite Prof. Dr. Johann von Leers of Jena (whom I repeatedly encounter in newspapers), "Hero Worship and the Jews." I came across the page as wrapping paper, and it was impossible to ascertain which publication it came from; it must have been printed in a specialist or members' periodical, perhaps of the veterans' association, and probably dates from 1942. Leers assembles a number of Jewish quotations, all of which disparage German heroism, German love of Fatherland, German ideals. He asks himself how one could even have thought of giving such people German citizenship. He asserts that *the* Jew deliberately disparages German heroism, "deliberately . . . to uproot us, to rob us of the blessing of the dead and their deeds," while they on the other hand demand that all the nations worship *their* dead heroes. — In fact the quotations are in every case heartfelt expressions of pacifism and humane internationalism made shortly after the First World War. In the light of the war, they were prevalent in every country and by no means uniquely Jewish in character. Naturally there is not a word about Jewish volunteers and Jewish dead.

[ . . . ]

## September 27, Wednesday morning

Yesterday evening at a quarter to seven an air-raid drill in the cellar and the courtyard of no. 3 Zeughausstrasse. Chalk circles on ground and wall represent burning phosphorus—"anyone who puts his foot inside, falls out!"—a stone, the phosphorus incendiary bomb. The fire-fighting group scratches away at the walls, throws sand on stone and circles, plays water—"when spray jet, when full jet?" Second assumption: There are two stick incendiary bombs in a room; as yet only a little flame is burning on the first, the other has already burned a circle around itself. The fire-fighting group shovels up no. 1 and throws it out onto the yard and now fights the supposed fire in the room. "What do you do with the curtains? . . . Do you tackle tables and chairs first or wardrobes?" The group mimes its work, the rest of us are called on to make criticisms: "He scratched the phosphorus toward himself, instead of away from himself." — "He stepped inside the burning circle" — "The curtains should be torn down first." Kautzsch, the upright air-raid warden, definitely an old SPD man, definitely no Jew-hater, former sergeant major (silver wounded-in-action medal, long decorations bar), Saxon, doing his best to speak proper German, not quite steady grammatically, good at explaining, usually good-naturedly pleasant, sometimes threateningly disciplinarian, repeatedly entreats: "It's *your* life, *your* blessed limbs, that are at stake!" — Above all Kautzsch shouts: "None of the firefighters was wearing eye and mouth protection! Either a mask or goggles and a cloth tied over your mouth!" There are a couple of gas masks, very few have such things. [ . . . ] The practice is comical, not quite without value as instruction—I now know a great deal about fighting fires and about bombs, about the organization of air-raid protection—only it's much too long-drawn-out, which is even more the fault of the Jews than of the Aryans, because whenever Kautzsch wants to wind up: "Does anyone still have a question?" a Jew looks self-important and really does have another question, whereupon everything starts again from the beginning. — Repeatedly the question goes through my head: It's all a comical game, but matters have already turned horribly serious very close by; will it remain a game for us?

[ . . . ]

Eva intends to go to Pirna this afternoon. The last time she was out there was on July 8. In these barely three months there has been the whole collapse in the West, the Hitler assassination attempt, and the hanging party, and the Balkans and Finland have been lost. In retrospect a tremendous amount in a very short time. And yet for us right in the middle of things the hallmark of each day is: too slow, stagnating too much! — Actually there is something a little ridiculous about removing the manuscript pages: In industrial Pirna the things are *at least* as unprotected against incendiary bombs as here. And are they so *very* much safer from the Gestapo? Annemarie is not in their good books, has often incurred displeasure. To be sure, she has gradually become cautious: I have been wearing the star since September '41, she visited us for the last time on October 9, '41. Nevertheless! And I do not wish to deny how far she is sticking her neck out for us. She not only knows that she is looking after my manuscripts, she also knows that these are diaries. She has known for months that for such behavior it is no longer a question of prison, but quite plainly of one's head.

My diaries and notes! I tell myself again and again: They will not only cost me my life, if they are discovered, but also Eva's and that of several others, whom I have mentioned by name, had to mention if I wanted them to have documentary worth. Am I entitled, perhaps even obliged, to do so, or is it criminal vanity? And again and again: I have published nothing for twelve years, been unable to complete anything, have done nothing but record and record. Is there any point to it, will any of it be completed? The English, the Gestapo, the angina, my sixty-three years. And if it is completed, and if it is successful, and if I "survive through my work"—what is the point of it all for me? I have so little talent for faith, in fact none at all; of all possibilities nothingness appears to me, as far as the individual personality is concerned, and that is all that counts, because what do I care about the "universe" or the "nation" or anything else that is not I myself?—nothingness appears to me the most likely. And I recoil from that alone, not from the "eternal judge," in whatever shape. But I am writing all this down (which goes through my head every day, *several times* a day) only because I do not want to send away an empty page. And immediately afterward I shall go on working, i.e., reading and taking notes. Not because I am so full of energy, but because I am unable to do anything better with my time. —

[ . . . ]

## Afternoon

The familiar feeling of anxiety until Eva's return. Later I shall visit Steinitz; that helps pass the time. Eva used to wait for the bus at Caspar David Friedrich Strasse; that was far away from the hurly-burly at the station and from the Gestapo building. I wish she were back already. —

A few months ago Frau Cohn related that she had told a woman friend about us as sharing the same apartment. "At the university I once attended a lecture on Dante given by a Professor Klemperer; is it the same person?" I told Frau Cohn, yes, I was the same person, only twenty-three years older. Now today Frau Cohn brought a bag of apples. The woman friend had asked her, whether things were as short at the Professor's as at the Cohns'. Yes? Then she should present him with these apples "from an unknown well-wisher"! Dante apples, as it were, late fruits. I thereupon read a couple of pages of my "Dante the stranger." Like the book of an author I did not know.

[ ... ]

**7:30 P.M.**

Eva not yet back, and the feeling of anxiety is beginning to rise. I tell myself: "It always, always turned out well before," but I also tell myself, it need not always turn out well. — The feeling of anxiety exacerbated by bad, hampering pain in my eyes; for days I have been struggling against inflammations and against the horribly diffused and glaring light. As there was no one at home at the Steinitzes, I have tried to read too much and have overstrained myself. —

Eva has meanwhile just returned safe and sound. Annemarie sends me four pounds of bread coupons as a birthday present—a blessing and a necessity given the terrible food shortage. (Frau Stühler sometimes puts a little bowl of potatoes or some other leftover on the kitchen table for us; she gives me a single slice of bread, which Bernhard has brought back from the factory—I take everything without shame. My fee for French lessons! This misery is degrading: The Stühlers live very well, thanks to their Bavarian parents; the Cohns have their connections—and *we* are stripped and naked. Today I have not yet had much more than black ersatz coffee and dry bread.) — Apart from that—Cohn said so— today was Yom Kippur. In many countries the Jews will be in seventh heaven. Here, on the other hand . . . Who is still alive? And who will survive? — [ ... ]

**September 29, Friday morning**

[ ... ]

In the late afternoon visited Steinitz for a couple of minutes. There I was told that the 1897 class, that is men of forty-six—Frau Steinitz's brother-in-law is among them—is already being deployed at the front itself. That did not happen in the First World War. By contrast the English broadcasts declare that the balance of forces between the Allies and Germany is now 10:1 in terms of men, 40:1 in terms of airplanes. But in the *Reich* of September 17 (so it can still be obtained after all!) Goebbels writes: "Resolute and prepared for everything" and is still proclaiming confidence in victory; and two or three days ago there were three death sentences in the newspaper (which had already been carried out): for the treasonable offense of having listened to foreign broadcasts and discussed them in a manner hostile to the state—"I'd rather believe in victory than let myself be hanged!"

[ . . . ]

### October 5, Thursday evening

[ . . . ]

This morning I accompanied Eva and waited for her at Steglich, the butcher's in Marschallstrasse, to carry three cans of broth for her; two for us, one for Frau Stühler, eleven and a half pints altogether. Women and men were coming with cans and other containers all the time. But, and this is progress under the 3rd Reich, one no longer sees a queue on the street. People line up in the courtyard. Hic et ubique.

[ . . . ]

### October 8, Sunday morning

[ . . . ]

I now take note of everything with a very different underlying feeling. Yesterday for the first time "it was very close to us." Freital recently was not yet Dresden. This time we were really hit. The alert sounded at 11:45 A.M. I was working on my Göring notes and went on writing, Eva was at Frau Winde's (corner of Bamberger and Chemnitzer Strasse). At 12 the air-raid warning. I took *Tonio Kröger*, a tiny volume (from Steinitz), down to the almost-empty cellar and read for a while. Then there was antiaircraft fire, then we heard clear, loud explosions, evidently bombs, then the light went out, then there was a swelling rumbling and rushing in the air (bombs falling a short distance away). I could not suppress violent palpitations, but retained my composure. It became quieter, from the entrance to the cellar we could see white streaks ("vapor trails") snaking and curling in the sky, there were said to be columns of smoke rising near the Wettin Station ("presumably the Shell tanks"), we heard the sound of the fire brigade. Then the noise of a squadron again and more explosions. An old woman had a heart attack and was taken to her apartment. The electric light flickered, came on again. More antiaircraft fire . . . The all clear not until half past one. No one knew what had happened. All anyone said was: Around Wettiner Strasse, Postplatz. Now I began to worry about Eva. She could very easily have been at Postplatz. (Later it turned out that she was within a hairbreadth of having to go down to a cellar there; she was still on the no. 6 tram when the pre-alert sounded.) People from the factories brought news. The tram service was not running, rails had been destroyed close to the Annenkirche, a big crater . . . I had to wait for Eva until five o'clock. She had carried two heavy bags from the Windes' to "Gertrud

Schmidt," Winckelmannstrasse, deposited them there, and returned on foot. She had eaten lunch with Frau Winde on the cellar steps, she had seen the columns of smoke from the Windes' roof. A dud bomb had fallen [ . . . ] nearby. Eva had heard the rumors on her way back. A worker said loudly that the Playhouse was "gone" and the Zwinger gallery damaged. Frau Ahrens received her with the question, whether all of Chemnitzer Strasse had really been destroyed. Not even the smallest bomb fell on Chemnitzer Strasse, and Frau Ahrens is an air-raid warden. — What was actually hit and whether there were dead, we do not yet know. Nevertheless: Dresden has been bombed for the first time. And it can be repeated at any moment. The newspaper says the real attack on the West Wall is imminent, so in preparation the whole of Germany was being bombed to stop reinforcements—yesterday and the day before yesterday "they" were everywhere again, at the coast, in Munich, in Berlin. There appears to be nothing after all to Churchill's aunt and the promise to Beneš. Today Eva had to fetch her bags with sauerkraut and a present of fruit from Winckelmannstrasse; she left at ten, since the air-raid warning usually comes around midday and by then she should no longer be in the vicinity of the railway station. It is now almost a quarter to one, she is not yet back—she will have heard the radio "air situation," and there was no alarm. Nevertheless: Our relative calm (and presumably that of all Dresden) in the face of the air war is gone. Thus Bernhard Stühler came into our room at three o'clock yesterday to ask whether he had missed the warning. No, why? — "People are running into the air-raid shelter down in the park." Later we heard: The pre-alert (announced on the radio and not by sirens), which normally no one bothers about—people take notice only at the first siren warning—had been spread by word of mouth, and people in the streets had started running.

Katz visited us yesterday evening; a different worry was weighing on him: If it came to an evacuation of Dresden, then Buchenwald concentration camp would be in store for those of mixed race and the men in mixed marriages; that is how the Jews in other evacuated cities had been dealt with. Katz called it the "narrow pass." If the German front collapses, we Jews would have to go through the "narrow pass." — [ . . . ]

### October 9, Monday morning after nine o'clock

Very curious: My first frontline birthday (because during the First World War I was safely at home on every October 9). All kinds of news and rumors mounted up about the attack the day before yesterday. From the Stühlers, the Cohns, from Eva, who had been to visit Frau Winde and gone home via Postplatz; she had seen a crater in Annenstrasse and damaged houses. There are said to be quite a large number of dead, who were laid out in Freiberger Platz (cordoned off). [ . . . ]

Congratulations from Annemarie. The modest hope that a bread coupon might also be enclosed was disappointed.

## October 10, Tuesday morning (fog and rain)

Yesterday was quiet—but will today be quiet? One's entire awareness of life is altered. Uneasy waiting until almost one o'clock; the Americans do not usually appear here later than that. Then in the evening: Will the English let us sleep? Somewhat calmer—unjustifiably in fact—in the afternoon. I think: we shall get used to it, I got used to the angina, too. Seidel and Naumann is said to be almost completely destroyed, Wettiner Strasse more badly hit than at first assumed; the number of dead—a Russian barracks!—seems to run into the hundreds. But it's all "is said to" and "seems": The most definite accounts contradict one another, each one is exact and incontestable, one man adds zeroes, the other crosses them off. The only certain thing is that there have been great destruction and slaughter in our immediate vicinity. Anger at the newspaper. The military bulletin mentions various towns that have been attacked, but not Dresden. What happened to us is evidently a trifle, occurs every day in x places, which also go unmentioned. Unless whole streets have gone, unless there are over a thousand dead, they no longer devote any space to it. (England announces that there were 5,000 aircraft over Germany on Saturday.) The raid even goes unmentioned in the local press—we saw the *Freiheitskampf,* the Stühlers say the same about the *Dresdener.* [ . . . ]

Waldmann, to whom I talked yesterday evening, knew "for certain," that in the event of evacuation we mixed-marriage people would be put in an Organization Todt labor camp.

## October 11, Wednesday morning

The Stühlers said: "Every day we wait for the airplanes as we used to wait for Clemens and Weser" (the Gestapo bloodhounds). I: Then I prefer the bombers. — Which is also true. But the present state of affairs also gets terribly on one's nerves. One hears awful details about the mutilations and deaths on Saturday, but the most divergent figures as to the number of dead. — [ . . . ]

## October 12, Thursday morning after seven o'clock

At about four o'clock in the morning the alert sounded; hardly five minutes later the air-raid warning itself, but by half past four we were up here again, without anything having happened. I simply didn't go back to bed. Eva is still asleep, and we don't anticipate anything unpleasant before midday. Physis and Psyche! It was the first air-raid warning after the deflowering of Dresden. [ . . . ]

*LTI.* In the *Dresdener Zeitung* of October 10 and 11, along with the other dead heroes of Greater Germany, there are twenty-six names together, about twenty of them women's names; accompanied by the stock phrase: "were taken from us by a tragic fate," followed by the date of the burial. These are of course some of the victims of the air raid. In previous notices in the *Dresdener Zeitung* as in the *Deutsche Allgemeine Zeitung*, I repeatedly saw the words: "during the terror raid on Munich" or something similar. Here and now they have to keep quiet about trifles. If it does not make it to the military bulletin, then a town simply has not been hit. — Hitherto only Dresden and Breslau of all the big German cities were supposed to have escaped unharmed. — A few days ago Breslau was mentioned in the bulletin and is said to have been terribly devastated. —

### Quarter past eleven

When I fetched broth with Eva, she was told in the shop, that the air situation was "rotten," "they" were close [ . . . ]. Eva took the tram to the hairdresser's, I hauled home the cans for ourselves and for the Stühlers, boiled some milk—then Waldmann came up, he had got four hundredweight of coal for me. We went down to the cellar. "Air situation?" — "You must have heard them droning (we had)—a reconnaissance plane has again marked out the white square [target area], which was above us on Saturday . . ." When I came upstairs, Eva was already back from Racknitzstrasse; the hairdresser wanted to close right away, "they'll be here any moment." — One becomes deadened: Once I have finished my entry, I shall go on with the Wilhelm II book.

### Evening, seven o'clock

They did not come, despite the square, which other people also saw; they were in Brunswick and Hanover. I believe the psyche of the city has changed since Saturday. Frau Waldmann, a robust, blond, younger woman, says: "We are sitting here and waiting for death." Frau Cohn had the same experience at her hairdresser's as Eva. — Shall we really become accustomed to it? At this moment, of course, fear of the night is beginning again. One really feels calmer only between 3:00 P.M. and 8:00 P.M. —

Witkowsky moriturus is traveling to Berlin tomorrow for an operation (intestinal cancer). I brazenly told him that it was a light operation, and that afterward he would be full of life again. He really seemed to believe it.

[ . . . ]

### October 16, Monday afternoon

[ . . . ]

At about eight in the evening a Hitler Youth appeared, and in a fairly peremptory tone passed on an order to Cohn and Stühler to carry out clearance work in the destroyed houses on Sunday. The instruction, from the police, also went to a whole number of long-deported and murdered

Jews. There was something wrong about the list. A little later Lang and Neumark, who are responsible for the Sunday deployment, turned up on the same business. People over sixty (including Konrad) were not required ... Toward eleven, we were already asleep, I was roused by thunderous knocking: Neumark and Werner Lang once again, new instruction: *everyone*, every Jew without exception, had to report at 7:00 A.M. at 33 Wettiner Strasse. I was given a travel permit (which I then did not even use), and I went back to bed. Stühler senior, as I learned later, had a serious argument with Neumark and Lang because he did not want to send his fourteen-year-old boy, Bernhard. — On Sunday morning, I got up at four; half the house set out together. Wettiner Strasse was closed to passersby. A number of houses on the street terribly devastated. [ ... ] We stood in two rows at the edge of the road for a roll call; besides the large Jewish group there were also many Aryans; also a little group of women. A squad of Italian prisoners with spades marched past. SA officers, among them Köhler, the plump and brutal overseer of the Jews—abuse and Gestapo tone—made lists and divided people up; the groups that had been formed moved off. About a dozen people were left behind, myself among them. "Can go home!" Today I heard from Neumark, Köhler had decreed he had no use for the "band of cripples." [ ... ] I was back again at eight o'clock, had seen the otherwise inaccessible destruction, and saved the day for myself ... The men who were deployed did not come back until six in the evening after exhausting shoveling of rubble. They had received a large meal from National Socialist Welfare, millet gruel in milk. And Konrad had brought a potful for us. I have just been downstairs to thank him. [ ... ]

Envy, ill will everywhere, not only among Jews. Frau Witkowsky, just back from Berlin, tells us: People, both Aryans and Jews, had again and again said to her, almost malevolently: "You should get a proper raid for once, you should find out what it's like!"

Eva has just come from listening to the radio at Pirnaer Platz: The military bulletin is colorless, says nothing about Hungary. Eva said: Evidently everyone had listened to the English broadcasts, a much larger crowd than usual waited much more patiently than usual through all the miscellaneous news, "even from Tokyo." In vain.

### October 17, Tuesday morning

It worries me greatly that our personal situation has been so very much altered by Hungary's elimination. Now Dresden may become a transport junction behind the front, which is most threatened, and that in a very short time. Then we shall get heavy air attacks. [ ... ] Then there will be an evacuation, and at the same time the mixed marriages will be separated, and the Jewish parties gassed—who knows where?—then my manuscripts, the yield of so many years, will burn in Pirna ... These are the "horrors" my imagination has been painting since yesterday, without even piling up any improbabilities. — [ ... ]

**October 21, Saturday morning**

Yesterday at 1:15 P.M. immediate warning of an air raid, but nothing followed, except that we spent a good fifteen minutes in the cellar. The feeling of dread has already (after a few harmless alerts) abated again, but the sirens are always a shock now. [ . . . ]

**October 24, Tuesday morning**

[ . . . ]

On Sunday evening Konrad was here for a couple of minutes. He spoke very pessimistically—and there is a great deal of probability behind his assumption and evaluation—about the fate of the Jews fallen into Hitler's hands, those from Poland, Hungary, the Balkans, and those deported to the East from Germany and Western Europe. He believes (to judge by soldiers' reports) that before the retreats everyone was murdered, that we shall see no one again, that six to seven million Jews (of the fifteen million that had existed) have been slaughtered (more exactly: shot and gassed). He also considered that the prospects of us, the small Jewish remnant left here in the clutches of the desperate beasts, remaining alive were also very slight—and his judgment is largely shared by Dresden Jewry as a whole. —

We now also hear complaints from Aryans about the worsening hunger and the increasing danger. I always tell myself: We, the Jews, get a generous double measure of both: We get shockingly smaller amounts of food, and our lives are threatened not only by bombs, but even more by the Gestapo. The rumor of the separation of the mixed marriages continues to circulate and grows stronger. —

Yesterday from around 12:30 to 1:30 P.M. there was a pre-alert immediately followed by a warning. There was heavy firing for a couple of minutes, two or three times we heard the ringing sound of shell splinters falling to the ground, but otherwise nothing happened. [ . . . ] The Japan news of recent days belongs directly to the *LTI*. Japanese victories always appear when things look bad for us, and the Japanese victory statistics are always pitched almost as high as those of Goebbels. In the last few days therefore the Japanese won the very greatest air and sea victory, in the course of an unsuccessful American attempt to land on Formosa, and annihilated almost the whole of the American fleet; the fleeing remnant was pursued and also appeared to be sunk. Meanwhile it has become clear—German report; so how clear must it have become!—that the Formosa operation was a diversion by the Americans and that they have now landed in the Philippines with a huge fleet and a huge army. And "a German naval reporter" writes of the sinking of the American fleet (the *Dresdener Zeitung* of October 22 quotes him), it is possible that "the high figure for American ships sunk will subsequently be somewhat reduced—since given the great speed and intensity with which sea-air battles are con-

ducted, reports [of sinkings] can, in certain cases, very easily be dupli-
cated."

[ ... ]

The Sunday newspaper also reported the disbanding of "the music corps
of the army in the field"; the musicians will be sent to the front line. In addition numerous reflections on the Volkssturm, in which parallels are repeatedly drawn with the Landsturm of 1813. The leading article—evidently
an all-German one—states, the German leadership firmly rejects "the underground and underhanded fighting methods that our enemies have
adopted in many theaters of war. The German Volkssturm has nothing in
the least in common with partisan fighters." [ ... ] (What folly and what un-
masking through language itself is contained in this "nothing in the least"!)

I have never before encountered such a wholesale use, such a
squadron-scale "concentration" of "fanatical" and "fanaticism" as in this
Sunday's edition. The word is repeated in every article, used at least a
dozen times altogether. [ ... ]

### October 27, Friday morning

Clinging to any hope. It occurred to me, Frau Kreisler told me recently,
that her husband, [ ... ] her Herr Weidlich, head clerk or junior director at
Wachs & Flössner, a foodstuffs factory (jams, etc.), himself quite unpolitical, reports what his bosses, who from time to time have dealings with
government offices in Berlin, say: There they are expecting the end to
come soon, not because of the military situation, but because of the extreme shortage of food and of gasoline. — In any case, between the lines of
the military reports and the commentaries, matters sound desperate
enough, for all the covering up and straightening out and "fanatical" belief in victory. But the waiting grows ever more agonizing; one's strength
is weakening too greatly.

Yesterday morning to the labor exchange in Maternistrasse. They wanted
my employment book to make a correction. It was a good thing I went myself instead of sending it in, because there—by the way: courteous treatment—they were not aware that I am permanently released from labor
duty. My route (with a few diversions) took me by way of the bombed district (Queckbrunnen, Freiberger Platz). The picture was the same as recently
in Wettiner Strasse. Everywhere the destruction was just as it had been on
the first day. How must things look in towns that have been seriously hit?

[ ... ]

### October 29, Sunday after 1:00 P.M.

Now they probably won't come today. The Americans are in the habit
of appearing here on Saturday, Sunday, or Monday, truly: in the habit, as
if, like traveling salesmen, they were doing certain areas on certain days. I
can no longer stop thinking about them. Not until about 2:00 P.M. do I tell

myself: probably not today. Then in the evening I look out of the window before going to bed: If the sky around the Neustadt station is bright, if it is lit up, then in all likelihood, a quiet night can be expected. —

Yesterday afternoon, as is usual by now, Steinitz was here; he brings Eva unfermented tobacco leaves taken from plants that he has grown on the grave of a Jewish tobacco dealer. [ . . . ]

### October 30, Monday afternoon

[ . . . ]

At midday Katz was here for a while. Very depressed. Yes, if only the English had not been beaten at Arnhem! Then they would have the Ruhr by now, and the war would be over. But now . . . The mixed marriages will be torn apart. Mutschmann has been stirring up dreadful hatred against the Jews again, and the Bolshevist atrocities in East Prussia, in which people presumably believed, may be taken out on us.

[ . . . ]

### November 2, Thursday afternoon

The stagnation of the war weighs heavily. Another winter, that is a dreadful thought.

There was an alert at quarter past twelve today, soon after that the air-raid warning itself; we were in the cellar until one o'clock, heard firing very far away, otherwise nothing happened. I, all of us are already forgetting the recent attack, and we are beginning to hope again, that Dresden is essentially taboo. But a little bit of dread has remained nevertheless.

[ . . . ]

### November 6, Monday toward evening

Yesterday morning I was considerably annoyed by Steinitz. He frequently comes to see us on Sunday after his haircut. (Since Frischmann was sent to labor camp, this is now performed by Bär, the cemetery gardener, who lives on the first floor.) Steinitz said: "You are a hysterical optimist. In fact, at least 80 percent of the Germans still believe in Hitler, and it is National Socialist ideology that makes them offer such tremendous resistance," that no end at all is in sight. — I am an optimist only when I talk to others, inside not at all. I responded fiercely: "That is Jewish fear speaking—where do you get the figure of 80 percent from?"

[ . . . ]

### November 12, Sunday evening

This morning the two former coal merchants from Aussig—Steinitz and Eisenmann—met here. Both saw the situation, with respect to the length of the war, the shortages of the winter, and the danger to the Jews, as very gloomy. Eisenmann has been working at Thiemig & Möbius since yesterday and for the time being is helping out at the machine for big document files, just as I did. [ . . . ]

Yesterday Eva reported something else from Frau Kreisler: There is a female interpreter from the Crimea living with her now; she did or still does duty with the mysterious Moslem labor detachment now quartered at 2 Lothringer Weg. The girl related from her own experience that when the Germans invaded the Crimea, the younger villagers fled. The older ones said: "We know the Germans from the First World War; they're decent people, we're staying." The younger ones warned, these were no longer the same people. The Germans came and looted ruthlessly. She, the interpreter herself, had all her things on her bed and sat on top of them. That was a help. But the old woman she was staying with had to open her cupboard and, weeping, hand over what the soldiers wanted. That tallies with the recent accounts of the withdrawal from Riga. — [ . . . ]

### November 14, Tuesday morning

[ . . . ]

Many things got in my way yesterday. In the morning I again underwent martyrdom three times over fetching a hundredweight of briquettes from Hesse in Salzgasse. Every day the coal supply is more endangered, and we have only a third of our ration in. However, I can hardly enlist Waldmann's help yet again, as he is suffering from an eye injury. I can feel this work breaking my heart, but I have to do it. Finished with the hundredweight of coal, I went to fetch potatoes with Eva. When I wanted to make use of the remainder of the morning to write, my tired hand failed me. — In the afternoon I had to go to Simon's (who this time wants to complete the treatment on Saturday), and after my return my hand was still on strike. I began Lamprecht's *1809, 1813, 1815*, but did not get far, because Katz was here three times, at midday, in the afternoon, and in the evening, and he made us party in detail to the closing act of the Cohn affair. The poor, tall devil, who has had serious heart disease ever since we've known him, has been suffering from an abscess in the tonsils for a couple of days.

Katz lanced it at midday yesterday and told me in the evening, when I opened the door to the house to him, that it looked almost hopeless. Then today Frau Cohn, weeping copiously, told us that her husband had died at a quarter to twelve, in his sixtieth year. Once again I was struck by my own shockingly unfeeling coldness. I thought only of myself—"Hurrah, I'm alive!" and "When will it be my turn?"—and of collecting material for my book. Several features can be added to this collection: When Frau Cohn brought us news of the death at eight o'clock in the morning, Frau Jährig, who had been sent by Neumark, was here [ . . . ]. Frau Jährig (Neumark's secretary) began to weep and asked Eva for a handkerchief. Afterward Eva said to me: "What wretched times. I am not going to iron my handkerchiefs anymore. I still had a good ironed one; it's one of the couple of things that Kätchen Voss gave me for safekeeping when she was put in the barracks camp. She has almost certainly been murdered in Poland long ago." — Frau Stühler—the Stühlers set the mortal feud aside and behaved in a friendly manner; yesterday they lent a heating pad, gave a few leaves of real tea—Frau Stühler said: "Who knows what *he* has been spared and what is in store for *us*? At least he wasn't separated from her." That had also been emphasized by Frau Cohn: "At least he died here and with me." Later I encountered a terrible companion piece. I was fetching coal from the cellar. Working close by was a woman from the house, with whom I have exchanged a few words without knowing her name. I told her Cohn was dead. Whereupon she, upset: "But at least his wife knows how he died, she was there! But I! But I don't know how my husband and my child died!" So that is Frau Bein, whose husband and son were shot "attempting to escape," i.e., were murdered in a concentration camp and who goes to the urn graves at the cemetery every day. — Then on the stairs I also met little Frau Spanier, who looks like Eva's mother; her husband has been in a concentration camp for years, her daughter was recently "fetched" in the Frischmann business. She responded abruptly: "He hasn't missed anything; we won't live to see it anymore." —

In the kitchen Frau Cohn to Frau Stühler: "I would so much have liked to pray with him. But I can't say the Lord's Prayer—they've got different prayers, after all. I folded his hands." To that Frau Stühler said with conviction: "There was no reason not to pray with him. We are all God's children." I, out of respect, but without conviction: "There's no reason not to say the Lord's Prayer for him. Every line is taken from the Old Testament." Again I was struck by the widespread belief, despite everything, in the Lord above and by how impossible this belief is for me. Likewise for Eva, but she is much more stoical in this respect, much more indifferent. — [ . . . ]

### November 15, Wednesday evening

[ . . . ]

There was a depressed mood at home, because now Frau Cohn has fallen ill with a high temperature and appears to have been infected by her husband. A threat to us all here in this apartment shared by three parties. An Aryan doctor is much harder to get hold of than Katz, who is not allowed to treat Frau Cohn. Meanwhile, however, after a great deal of to-ing and fro-ing, Fetscher was here; reassuringly (but was he being honest?) he concluded that it is not an infection, but rather a simple inflammation of the throat.

### November 16, Thursday toward evening

Content of a day: Washing up, fetching broth. In six difficult trips hauled two hundredweight of low-grade coal, the unrationed fuel, from Salz-

gasse to the cellar. Washed up and made coffee. Fell asleep out of tiredness. Tutored Bernhard Stühler in rough-and-ready fashion. In between
not even five pages of Lamprecht. During all this time Eva was here, there,
and everywhere, begging more than shopping. — Rumors about Hitler
and Himmler on all sides, safety nowhere. But together with the big offensive they give grounds for hope nevertheless. —

Stephan Müller was arrested yesterday. He may have felt himself too
secure because of his understanding with the Gestapo, because he was
recognized as a former Freikorps lieutenant, may have concealed his star
too often. Perhaps also he was incautious with respect to the radio. If it's
the first, then concentration camp, if the second, death.

[ . . . ]

## November 21, Tuesday morning

Warm *Föhn* weather again; I look at it solely from the point of view of
whether it hampers operations. The Anglo-American offensive appears to
be making a little headway in the West, but all too little. —

[ . . . ]

I inherited from Cohn: Three pairs of socks, one pair of gloves, suspenders, and garters. I accepted these precious things gladly and without
qualms, because all personal effects of a Jewish spouse must be surrendered. Strangely Frau Cohn had no idea, that her husband's will is invalid—the state takes *everything*. She has no other choice, except to claim
compensation afterward. Afterward—that may be tomorrow or in a year's
time.

[ . . . ]

## November 23, Thursday morning

From ten until after one o'clock yesterday morning I hauled a hundredweight of briquettes and two hundredweight of coal from the shop in
Salzgasse across Zeughausplatz and down to our cellar in nine two-pail
trips and afterward was angry and *down*. Thus I shorten what is left of my
life, and nothing will ever be finished. [ . . . ] At the coal merchant I was
busy for a longer time filling my pails. At the same time I listened to the
conversations of the women customers—the men are all in the army or in
the factories; the women fetch what they need in handcarts or also in
pails—with the friendly, not-at-all-Nazi Frau Hesse. (Her husband in turn
had business at the railway station; his most characteristic entrance is as
cyclops, when he rolls up, standing at the front of his little electric trolley.)
"Now I've got a ration ticket for overalls for my man, but I can't get a pair
anywhere." [ . . . ] "My man is in Italy, near Verona. I'm allowed to send
him 75M a month. He still manages to pick up all kinds of things. Two and
a quarter pounds of chocolate 27M." — "I'm being sent a rabbit for Christ-

mas." — "Won't it smell?" — "I'll wash it down with vinegar." — "It varies with the men abroad. Some can send food. Others have to be sent something extra to eat." None of them thought of peace. The war just goes on. "Mine is getting Christmas leave." — "He's doing a course now, which last eight weeks, then he goes to the front again." [ . . . ]

Horribly grotesque death. In our house there lives an ancient white-haired, white-bearded Jew, capable only of creeping shakily along, Grünbaum, eighty-eight years of age. I saw him downstairs once, when Frischmann was still hairdresser; another time being led along the street by his twelve-years-younger wife. A couple of weeks ago he seemed to be dying. Katz came frequently and described to me most graphically how swollen by edema he was. ("One can no longer see his penis.") The man recovered, and during the night of November 21–22 his wife died of a stroke. Now the helpless old man is quite alone and will presumably be sent to Theresienstadt, that is, if they don't save themselves the detour and do away with him at police headquarters. [ . . . ]

### November 26, Sunday late afternoon

Yesterday at midday, a warning from quarter to twelve until half past twelve, in the cellar after a few minutes. At a great distance, but it was very clear and thus not so far away, there was uninterrupted heavy firing for a good half hour. So there must have been a very big raid and once again destruction and death in our neighborhood—but no one can find out where, everything is kept secret. [ . . . ] We are in the dark in other respects also. English broadcasts claim the Americans have crossed the Rhine near Mulhouse; German broadcast: They have been cut off near Basel and encircled.

Cohn died of a tonsil abscess and sepsis, and now Stühler is on his back with a tonsil abscess and influenza. Katz, who lanced it today, is here twice daily and then almost always sits with us for a long time. He says influenza and tonsil abscess appear to be widespread; he is very pessimistic about the future: epidemics, malnutrition, shortage of doctors and medicines, and no end to the war—Hitler appears to have been pushed aside, Himmler is even worse. "He is capable of setting Dresden alight himself, if it is the only city the Allies spare!" He also foresees death for us, the wearers of the star, and bloody civil war for everyone. — At the Windes' parts of an account by a man on leave were once again related: horrible murders of Jews in the East. The troops had to be given schnapps. "When we got schnapps, we always knew what was coming." Some men had committed suicide, "so as not to see it a second time and have to have it on their conscience." That has now been reported too frequently and by too many consistent Aryan sources for it to be a legend. And of course it also tallies with what we have experienced here. I heard about the fate of the Frischmann family: The girl together with her friend Ruth Spanier presumably in Auschwitz, sent to certain death therefore; her father in Radeberg labor camp; her mother, an Aryan, sentenced to two and a half years in prison.

In the newspapers a propaganda picture of awful stupidity: Four children, boys of eight to fourteen (their ages are given!) defended a position in Aachen with a German rifle and a captured American one and are now prisoners of the Americans. Picture and caption and accompanying article are of course intended to demonstrate and publicize and inspire fear of German heroism. What effect do they really have? 1) the Allies have a document that provides proof that the Germans are fighting with irregulars, gangs, francs-tireurs; 2) they have a document of German weakness—the *DAZ* says Eisenhower is attacking with seven armies, with two million men (men not children!); 3) it must turn the heart and stomach of all parents, all German parents; 4) the Allies must feel confirmed, and rightly so, in their plan of taking the education of German youth into their own hands. Thus the heroism propaganda trips over itself, that, too, is like the *curse of the superlative*.

[ . . . ]

### November 30, Thursday late afternoon

Only now, after six o'clock in the evening, have I managed to complete the questionable notes on Paul Ernst—leaving Dostoyevsky aside. Yesterday morning I again hauled up another two hundredweight of coal; that not only tires me out very greatly, but also has the effect of crippling my writing hand afterward. So then I was essentially restricted to reading (Dostoyevsky monograph, from Lewinsky; and Stefan Zweig, from Steinitz), also called on Steinitz, as I usually do once a week.

But the case of Stühler, above all, has been and continues to be ever more distracting and depressing. While his wife's and the doctor's hopes go up and down, the man is hopelessly ill and quite mysteriously so. Overcoming the Gestapo's resistance, Katz consulted a throat specialist yesterday: The angina is subsiding, the puzzling sepsis remains: The second case in the house. The third, if one includes the sickness of Frau Cohn's sister-in-law; a fourth is in Katz's care elsewhere. Hence suspicion of an epidemic. But the public health department has made no announcement. Anyone who made the suspicion public would be a defeatist. Also, now that death is raging at the front and over the cities, it makes no difference if one more rider of the apocalypse joins the others. Also there is a shortage of doctors, hospital beds, and medicines. [ . . . ] We found Frau Stühler, normally so active, in tears, especially worried about Bernhard. We promised to put the boy up in our bedroom and to sleep here in the front ourselves. This was to be organized today. [ . . . ]

Then, hardly was Katz out of the house than the alert sounded, followed very quickly, from half past twelve until half past one, by a full air-raid warning, threatening news, bomber formations approaching, attack on Dresden possible. We heard humming, heard a great deal of very distant firing, but otherwise nothing happened. Meanwhile I discussed the unpleasant Stühler business with Neumark. He wanted to think over with Katz, whether perhaps Frau Cohn and ourselves should be got away from here and put in temporary quarters for the critical period. We are now awaiting the doctor's evening visit. Thus at the moment the usual two sources of danger—Gestapo and bombers—have been augmented by a third and, perhaps, probably even more dreadful one. [ ... ]

## December 1, Friday morning

Stühler died last night—it could make one's flesh creep. Whatever happens, however, I intend once again to report quite coolly and until the very last. — Katz came yesterday evening; I was expecting him to talk to us in detail about the question of sterilization. But when he had finished his call, at about quarter to eight, there was an alert, the second yesterday. (The all clear was sounded at half past eight, without our having to go down to the cellar.) Katz hurried off—absolute reversal of mood!—we should not be too anxious for ourselves. Stühler himself, to be sure, whom he had injected with camphor, was "far from turning the corner." At about ten in the evening, Frau Stühler had to go to the pharmacy, meanwhile I had to keep watch. I heard the light switch and steps in the sickroom; when I opened the door, Stühler was already in bed again, but very restless and breathing heavily. I asked him, if he wanted a drink. — Yes. — He sat up, I first supported his pillow, then his head, which was soaked in sweat, gave him a little mineral water. He was terribly thin, his eyes were glassy, his voice rough; it was an effort for him to speak, but he was completely lucid. Where was his wife, when was she coming back, thanked me repeatedly. I washed hand and sleeve in the ersatz Lysol, which Eva had finally managed to get hold of, lay down to sleep at half past ten. Frau Stühler woke us at half past one: She could not hear any breathing, feel any pulse. Stühler lay on his back, his eyes open but not glazed, his face pinched and stiff—not really peaceful, but not suffering either, merely cold and distant. Obviously dead, but I could not say so with certainty. We knocked at Frau Cohn's door [ ... ]. I felt afraid as I went to sleep, came into the front room at six, found Frau Stühler on our settee, and continued to feel afraid, realized the complete pointlessness of the attempts at disinfection, and let fate take its course. [ ... ] I went to see Neumark before breakfast and telephoned Katz. [ ... ] Overnight Katz's mood had changed entirely. I should not be excessively anxious, today, in wartime, there was no question of disinfection by the authorities; the "house community" should protect itself by mopping the floors with Lysol. He, Katz, had no "official" reason, indeed, no right to make a report—if he did so nevertheless, then the consequences for all of us were incalculable—officially Cohn and Stühler had died as a result of septic angina; he, Katz, had expressed the suspicion of contagious disease (with bread perhaps the

source) to me and to me alone, privately, in "friendly conversation," and
he was binding me to silence. [ . . . ]

### December 2, Saturday morning

Central from morning till evening is the frightful threat of infection. A
bowl with stinking ersatz Lysol on the kitchen table—but what good is the
holy water, with all this promiscuity? [ . . . ] Perhaps the pestilence is already inside us, perhaps a bomb will hit us before it breaks out.

### December 3, Sunday evening

Our mood is no better, even though a degree of apathy in the face of the
naked fear of death has set in. Yesterday we still got rid of bread and cake
from the Stühlers—today I ate a piece of bread that Frau Stühler had given
us. In between admittedly every kind of thing has been disinfected, including the crockery. [ . . . ]

### December 5, Tuesday toward evening

[ . . . ] Eva has just come from Gertrud Schmidt with the news, halfway
confirmed by the German military bulletin, that the Russians have broken
through at Lake Balaton. If that is true, Vienna is threatened, and then
there will be air raids on Dresden. In the West everything is being slowed
down by flooding in Holland.

Yesterday the Gestapo fetched the eighty-eight-year-old Grünbaum,
whose wife died recently. Will they still take him to Theresienstadt, or will
they just do away with him here?

It touched me very much, when Frau Cohn told me today, that on his
last healthy Sunday her husband had so much wanted to take a walk with
her, it was such fine weather. She had refused: "On Sunday people stare
even more than on a weekday. — You'll just be annoyed. Wait!" He had
complained bitterly, "I'm a prisoner" and now she was reproaching herself. How often have I, too, had this feeling of "Imprisoned!" and no doubt
also made a note of it.

### December 7, Thursday morning

Yesterday was a day that shattered both of us physically; it was marked by
two alerts. In the morning another two trips to Hesse to fetch two hundredweight of coal, and from the start it strained my heart very badly.
Toward the end of the procession back and forth, distant firing was audi-
ble. [ . . . ] "They're already banging away, we'll get an air-raid warning in
a minute," said Frau Hesse. So I completed my coal business in a great
rush, especially as afterward I still had to wash and change some of my

clothes, also pack the manuscript in the air-raid bags. While I was doing that, shortly after twelve, the siren went. Heavy firing continued in the distance, but there was no more than an alert, which was called off soon after half past twelve. My heart is no longer up to this tension, although mentally I remain quite calm. The second alert was worse. [ ... ]

From the *Dresdener Zeitung* of recent days: 1) Official: The little piece of soap, which in the past five years and four months of war had to last four weeks—but it always lasted only for a few days—has now to last eight weeks. Corresponding extension for detergents. 2) Call by the Reich head of the BDM [League of German Girls—equivalent of the Hitler Youth for girls] and by the "Reich Women's Leader" to "German women and girls" to volunteer for the "Wehrmacht Women's Auxiliary Corps," which is to be the expanded form of "the already existing *deployments of women*" (in particular the "women's antiaircraft gun auxiliaries"). The "German woman *who is ready to do her duty*" joins the "*Wehrmacht personnel*" and wears a uniform. Each auxiliary "*releases* a soldier." Certainly, the auxiliaries do not carry arms, but do serve under fire, like doctors. Is there such a great difference between that and the "gun woman"? The difference is made up by the Volkssturm proclamations and the glorification of the children who joined in the fighting at Aachen. 3) *German memorandum against De Gaulle's terror.* The De Gaulle government is behaving "brutally" toward German nationals and French citizens "*who did their duty in accordance with the instructions of the legal French government of Marshal Pétain.*" Threat (officially via the Geneva Red Cross) of countermeasures. 4) From time to time a Lieutenant Colonel Ellenbeck writes moralizing articles in a *most popular* style in order to strengthen resistance. Three or four days ago he was inciting people to reduce to silence anyone (in fact, of course, it is an encouragement of denunciation), who says, for example, perhaps the Russians are not so murderously bad after all, perhaps one could think of giving in. That was "damned stupid," that was a crime committed out of stupidity.

[ ... ]

### December 8, Friday toward evening

After wearisome reading—admittedly almost the whole morning was taken up with scouring and other housework—sparse yield from the *Reich*.

[ ... ] Article "The Foreigners Among Us" by Hans Schwarz van Berk. Their huge number, in some factories only a tenth of the workforce German; in some villages "only prisoners of war behind the teams." Why does the uprising, the sabotage, on which Eisenhower counted, not take place? Some may think of it—but they also think of the annihilation of insurgent Warsaw! (Yesterday, in Hüttig's, Eva had a conversation with a watchman from a private company. He told her, twelve-hour turns of duty in a nearby Polish camp, in which ten thousand prisoners are guarded by a very few hundred police officers. Recently they had "mutinied" — they had used every stick, every piece of iron as a weapon—and "we nearly got *our heads done in.*" [ . . . ] So how far is the *Reich* article right? At any rate as regards the main point, that thus far there have been no major acts of sabotage or anything similar. And it is certainly also right that only a small proportion of these foreigners of very mixed origin are really hostile to Germany and have a real will to fight it.)

[ . . . ]

### December 10, Sunday toward evening

Steinitz visited us in the afternoon. Gloomy mood as with all the Jews, as also in the Winde-Kreisler circle, because of the stagnation of the war; rumors of new German weapons are also turning up again: They are supposed to be building turbines, which can suck airplanes out of the sky! I myself am gradually being influenced by the sentence, which one hears everywhere: "the war is not yet decided." [ . . . ]

Yesterday in the late afternoon I also tutored Bernhard Stühler. He asked me to teach him history, because it is his favorite subject. I have repeatedly observed that the most common foreign words are unfamiliar to him or at least unclear; so, in a lesson somewhere between French and history, I explained the concepts dictator, republic, monarchy, oligarchy, constitution to him. This lesson and the Bernhard Stühler case in general—fifteen years old on January 1, 1945, almost no schooling, but fed with a few scraps of English and Spanish (a couple of private lessons, his teacher ended up in a concentration camp; before that some makeshift primary school organized for Jews, factory worker for some time now)—this case is, therefore, extremely important to my account, whether the *LTI* or whether the Curriculum.

[ . . . ]

### December 11, Monday morning

Berthold's birthday. He would be seventy-three now, he has been dead for fourteen years, died at fifty-nine. The affection and the conflict between us filled so many years—what did it leave behind, do his sons have the faintest notion of it and of the life and thoughts of their father—how far did even his wife penetrate his real essence at all? His whole life he desperately wanted to be someone else to her, to himself, and not who he really was. Perhaps we Jews always want to be something else—some Zionists, the others Germans. But what are we really? I do not know. And that, too, is a question to which I shall never get an answer. And as a scholar that is my greatest fear of death: that in all probability it will give me no answer to all my questions.

[ . . . ]

### December 14, Thursday toward evening

Yesterday at midday two alerts with only a short interval between them, from half past one until two, and from 2:25 until 2:40, both without cellar, both very nerve-racking and also disquieting.
[ . . . ]

### December 18, Monday morning (and later—during the day I shall probably be busy with notes)

On Saturday morning I got only a hundredweight of briquettes from Hesse. He said, there was now nothing more to be had before January; he said, there will be a coal catastrophe. Meanwhile serious frost has set in. It almost, no truly makes me glad: Because that will get the Russians moving.
[ . . . ]
Early this morning, as I was washing up, Frau Stühler related: She had had a letter from Heidelberg; there, although not yet declared a war zone, people were living as if in hell. Several days a week completely without gas, constantly in the cellar—here we didn't have a clue about the war. Then: Yesterday during her air-raid duty (in the Böhme Fashion House in Waisenhausstrasse) she was again struck by people's obtuseness (the people—that is the insoluble puzzle): A couple of the staff, not entirely uneducated, were still firmly convinced of Germany's victory; after it had survived the difficult summer months, it was now making headway again. — So is the propaganda of the press, etc., having an effect after all? But on what percentage of the population? And how far is Saxony, how far is unbombed Dresden, how far is this little group of three or four people characteristic of the whole? Again and again the same impossibility of knowing.

### Midday, 12:30

Wild wartime day. We had to fetch broth before midday, because the Monday supplier in Pillnitzer Strasse opens at nine o'clock, and by ten there is nothing more to be had. I was up from half past five and had three cold potatoes in my stomach. At nine on the dot Eva was standing in the queue that had already formed; I waited a house away and then carried the liter she had secured. [ . . . ] When Neumark left, it was about 9:45, and Eva went into the kitchen to heat up the soup. Two minutes later the alarm sounded. We nevertheless stubbornly sat down to eat, except I first of all made the air-raid bags ready. After the first plate Eva said: "So—we've had one plate of soup." The second plate and half a cup of tea followed after, then, at 10:15, came the air-raid warning: A quarter of an hour in the cellar without firing. [ . . . ]
At half past ten we were upstairs again, drank another cup of tea, then I

took my diary out of the air-raid baggage. Then came the second alert, and I had to pack again. This time there was no warning, but the alert lasted a good half hour. — Now I shall see whether during the afternoon I shall manage to make a few notes on my copious, but for me not very profitable, for the *LTI* almost completely unprofitable, reading of recent days.

[ . . . ]

### December 19, Tuesday morning

[ . . . ]

Yesterday evening Frau Stühler brought the military bulletin in the newspaper—it had already appeared as a special announcement—the first time in years!—at midday: A major offensive started unexpectedly from the West Wall on the morning of December 16, American forward position overrun "after brief but tremendous preparatory fire," the attack continues . . . For me it was truly, and this is no mere phrase, a bolt from the blue—or at least it now appears to me that *before* this announcement the sky had been almost blue. Because it did hold out hope of an end. But now . . . a German victory delays it for many months. During the night it occurred to me: The surprise might consist of gas. Eva has now gone to the Windes'. Perhaps they know something.

### Toward evening

From 12:45 until 1:40 there was another alarm, but this time without the cellar. [ . . . ]

Today I again went through umpteen issues of *Reich* and *DAZ*; it now always really wearies and bores me to do so. The yield was, almost gratifyingly, very slight—it is all so familiar to me.

[ . . . ]

### December 21, Thursday morning

[ . . . ]

A new Talmud question, but a perilous one. The Jews are ordered to use *only* the front platform of the tram, and not to enter the carriage. Since the day before yesterday a new regulation has been displayed on the trams in large letters: Entry at front only. Exit at rear only. Now, which command should a Jew obey when he alights? Any transgression of a command costs him, by way of prison and camp, his life. There is impassioned discussion of this question; I shall note the outcome.

[ . . . ] I was supposed to get a pair of Stühler's shoes; they fit me, I had them in our room for a day, then I gave them back—I found it all too repulsive to be running around in front of the widow wearing her husband's shoes. Shoes are more visible, more evident than gloves and socks.

[ . . . ]

## December 22, Friday afternoon

[ ... ]

Today, on behalf of the tax office, Waldmann removed—that is his office—two dress baskets containing the personal clothing of Cohn and Stühler, including hat and walking stick. Naked robbery, and loathsome in its contemptible shabbiness, as well as its brutality to the widows. — How little thoughtfulness there is: Frau Cohn lost her husband to a throat disease. She said of the tax official: "He told me his child died of diphtheria a few months ago; I regard that as God's punishment!"

## December 23, Saturday evening

The German offensive in the West is making progress and depresses me greatly; nevertheless I hear on all sides (the Windes, Stern, Katz), it should not be viewed too gloomily, it is an act of desperation, perhaps it does not mean a postponement, but perhaps even an acceleration of the inevitable end. Anyhow I am heavy at heart. Especially as it has turned very cold, and our diet gets worse every day, and Eva's strength is failing.

Stern was here and invited us for tomorrow afternoon, Steinitz came and brought an invitation for Tuesday. That will be our Christmas celebration: a little bit of home-baked cake twice over. *We* can give no presents, neither to ourselves nor to others. This year the only Christmas trees are given by the Party to large families. The special rations—the first for several months and naturally only for Aryans—consist of half a pound of meat and two eggs. This sorry situation is now supposed to be improved by the victory in the West. Goebbels writes we will fight to the last regiment and not give up "because of some butter ration."

[ ... ]

## December 31, Sunday evening, half past seven

Just now, I was reading aloud, there was an air-raid warning. A very brief one, 6:50 until 7:10, but we immediately had to go down to the cellar across frozen snow and in the darkness. Each of these warnings does shake my nerves a little: Dresden has been spared, yet on two occasions this year has had a couple of hundred dead nevertheless. Today—I already noticed it in the morning, when fetching coal—the march up and down stairs with baggage was particularly hard for me; my heart has its say in my New Year's Eve résumé. The only really important date of the year for me was June 24. The day of my release from labor duty. Since then I have been rid of the factory slavery, since then I have—at first I found it hard, now I am used to it again—been able to work more extensively for myself, i.e., to carry on reading indiscriminately with respect to *LTI*. But since June 24 I am also very conscious of being under a double death sentence: If I were not suffering from very serious heart disease, Katz would have been unable to apply for and unable to get his way with this release from duty. (Admittedly the eye paralysis, which has meanwhile unquestionably improved a little, probably also helped a bit.) After that: If Dresden is evacuated, and I were classified fit for work, I would have to dig trenches somewhere, while as a useless old Jew I will undoubtedly be disposed of.

I face the future apathetically and with little hope. It is very uncertain when the war will come to an end (although at the moment, with the offensive in the West at a standstill and Budapest lost, German prospects have sunk again). And to me it is even more uncertain whether I shall be able to benefit from the peace, since I have evidently come to the end of my life. —

I am incapable of somehow becoming reconciled to the thought of death; religious and philosophical consolations are completely denied me. It is solely a matter of maintaining one's dignity until the very end.

The best means for that is immersion in study, to behave as if the accumulation of material had a real purpose.

My financial position is also gloomily depressing: My bank balance will last until April, certainly no longer. But this worry about money does not depress me too much. It seems of minor importance, since I always see myself, and twice and three times over, in the direct proximity of death.

The year draws to an end very disappointingly. Until well into autumn I, and probably the whole world, thought it certain, that the war would be over before the end of the year. Now the general feeling and mine also: perhaps in a couple of months, perhaps in a couple of years.

Second New Year's Eve alert, without cellar, 10:15 until 10:30. We were about to go to sleep.

# 1945

## January 1, Monday, 7:00 P.M.

In the *Reich* of December 31, an article by Goebbels, "The Führer," which contains such extravagant glorification that the title could just as well have been "The Savior." "If the world really knew what he has to tell and to give, and how profoundly his love goes out to the whole of mankind beyond his own nation, then at this hour it would bid farewell to its false gods and render him homage." But something else is more important than this deification: Twice it says he walks with a slight stoop, which is due to his study of maps; once, his hair has turned gray; once, at the same age Frederick the Great was already known as "Old Fritz." But nevertheless, and that must be emphasized most strongly, it was a lie if enemies spread rumors that he was ill: He was healthy, his eyes still gleamed youthfully, and he would break his silence, when it suited him, and not when it suited his enemies. — After this article I thought it certain that Hitler was ill. But just now at the Witkowskys', I heard that yesterday evening he really had spoken on the radio. —

## January 4, Thursday 7:00 P.M.

Today Eva was at the Windes', who visited their son in Flensburg over the New Year; he is at the Naval College there and has just been made a midshipman. They told of the extreme difficulties of the journey—reason: the lack of locomotives, the constant air attacks on the latter—but they also related that now "midget U-boats" were being mass-produced, which a few days ago were praised as the newest of the new weapons. One thing is unquestionable: the tremendous tenacity and repeated ingenuity with which the government carries on the war. They do indeed have a right to talk about a "German miracle," and I am truly no longer so certain of their defeat; at the very least they will continue resisting for all too long. They do not keep the mass of people in line by tyranny alone. But above all by the ever repeated (and believed even by people like Frau Stühler!): Our enemies, and in particular the Bolshevists, want to annihilate you, literally kill you. They owe everything to the bogeyman of Bolshevism, even though they themselves are the most Bolshevik of all. —

[ . . . ]

## January 5, Friday afternoon

Steinitz and Lewinsky, my fellow tenants, supply me with newspapers (*Dresdener, Reich, DAZ*), but I find it ever more distasteful to plow through them. They are utterly sterile; the style and content are endlessly repetitive. With respect to the *LTI*, I can learn nothing more from them.

The sole new feature of Hitler's speech broadcast at midnight on New Year's Eve was the invocation of the Almighty, who will lead the just cause to victory. "He's got religion." Stylistically there are two stages to this getting of religion. First "Providence" appeared, now the good Lord in person has followed. [ . . . ] Despite its jaded tone, the text of the speech gave me something of a jolt. I said to myself that perhaps (probably, even) its obstinacy will, despite everything, be believed by millions and be experienced as invigorating. Especially as Hitler can say with justice that all the Allies' deadlines were false prophecies and that after the catastrophes of the summer Germany has after all pulled itself together. (Here the National Socialist superlative triumphs once again: "Thousands of *Volkssturm* battalions have been raised and are in the process of being raised. Division after division has been re-formed, People's Artillery Corps, rocket launcher and assault-gun brigades have been created overnight . . .")

My spirits were raised a little by Katz. He said: If the recent offensive in the West had had the least real success, just think what a part it would then have played in Hitler's speech! Because it was undertaken solely for this speech, solely to rouse the people. And Hitler did *not mention it once.* —

[ . . . ]


## January 6, Saturday morning

[ . . . ]

Eva, who had spoken to Frau Richter, when she visited the Kreisler woman, brought good news home from "Kötzschenbroda": Hungary has declared war on Germany—in the Hitler speech Hungary was placed among the "apostate nations"—in Budapest 50,000 men are besieged in the citadel, the city was shot to pieces, after the garrison had shot Russian truce envoys. In the West the German offensive has been completely stopped. — For all that: how much longer?

[ . . . ]


## January 10, Wednesday morning

For days, after a very short period of thaw, frost again. But no Russian offensive. On the contrary. The Germans have attacked in Hungary as well as in Alsace. Yesterday morning wretched coal business with the usual memento mori. First a load up from the cellar. Later Frau Cohn, for whom the lugging is just as much a strain as for myself, and for the same reason, announced that Hesse had briquettes. There, I found a whole heap piled up on the street, the scales set up in front of it; Frau Hesse did the weighing, Herr Hesse dealt with the queue of women (ration-card entry and payment). Half a hundredweight for each customer. [ . . . ] A woman in front of me got a whole hundredweight. A woman behind me, more wistful than irritated: "*She* gets a whole hundredweight." Immediately the one with the whole hundredweight, very agitated and half weeping: "I would happily change places with you, I have been bomb damaged—for five weeks now—I've no strength left—but if I say that, then I'm told I'm complaining!" The other: "But I didn't know that, I didn't mean it *like that . . .*" Frau Hesse: "You see, if only you'd kept quiet!" Herr Hesse, in front of his desk, at once warning and telling off: "Quiet! Quiet out there!" That is the most characteristic thing about the scene: Everyone is afraid. Someone could denounce something, the complaint of the bomb-damaged woman, the complaint of the envious woman, the trouble in the queue outside the Hesses' shop; each one of these denunciations would lead to punishment. The war will go on as long as this fear is the strongest emotion among the populace. — [ . . . ]

## January 14, Sunday morning

Each day teaches one anew that for the 3rd Reich this war really is the *Jewish War,* that no one can experience it as acutely and tragically as the star-wearing Jew, who is held prisoner in Germany and who in his upbringing, education, and sentiments is truly German; each day therefore validates my work. Lately I have been thinking of it as a double volume under the title *LTI.* Volume or Book I—the diary 1933– ?, volume II—the philological studies, sketches, problems. In that way the opus could become the pacemaker for the whole Curriculum. "We lack only time," the poet Dehmel, I think, says somewhere.

On the Jewish War. The *Dresdener Zeitung* of January 12 has a little article from Stockholm about the planned "Reeducation" of German youth (which, of course, will never happen, since Germany will be the victor). A five-volume history of the world is due to appear in April, a series of six German readers is under way and will be published in large editions; the authors are "without exception Jews," almost all émigrés from Germany. Headline of the article: HISTORY, FALSIFIED BY JEWS [ . . . ]. *Dresdener Zeitung* of January 11, article: "The Right Language. Churchill in Hebrew." For some years without a ministerial post, Churchill "had lived by the pen" and now the "works" (mocking quotation marks) are being translated into Hebrew. "Now at least they will be in the place, where they are best understood. They will be put on the shelf beside Talmud and Shulhan Arukh." — *Dresdener Zeitung* of January 13–14. (Sunday edition) big headline: JEW LORD PAYS HUGE BRIBES. HENRY MELCHETT-MOND IN HUGE CORRUPTION SCANDAL. Boss of the biggest English chemicals company, lord, member of the upper house of Parliament. The man was predestined for it: "Because his title is nothing more than the mask concealing the ugly Jew's face of the son of Alfred Mond, who became a Sir and a Lord because of his money and was the model of a Jewish upstart." To that is added the usual stuff about the "international goal of the Jews," "profits through corruption and prolongation of the war." [ ... ]

### January 15, Monday morning

At night in the cellar, Schwarz, a star-wearer, who has a bad heart and is released from labor duty, with whom I sometimes exchange a few words without knowing very much about him, told me that yesterday's military bulletin had reported the beginning of an East Prussia offensive and also "heavy fighting" in the Vistula offensive. The English reports, however, give the most detailed information about the Vistula offensive: The Russians had advanced from Baranow and Sandomir; on a front 40 miles wide and 25 miles deep they had broken through three German positions, had passed Kielce, and were now 40 miles from Krakow and advancing toward Upper Silesia. Also, after a considerable interval, Thomas Mann had spoken on the radio from the USA—"splendid—it gave my spirits such a lift!" He [Mann] had wanted to wait until he was sure of his ground, but now that the German offensive in the West had failed utterly, that National Socialism had undoubtedly been granted only a brief reprieve, he wanted once more ... well what? That I didn't elicit from Schwarz, he repeated in fervent voice only that it had been so "uplifting." He didn't want to believe me when I told him that Mann was Aryan through and through and from an old patrician family; he had always thought him to be a Jew. I enlightened him—only his wife was Jewish. This morning, when I passed on my news to Frau Stühler as morning consolation, it turned out that she already knew it all. She also knew that Mann talks frequently and is considered an outstanding speaker—(quite new to me!). She is much more discreet than I am, when it comes to these matters. It also turned out, however, that the news did not give her any pleasure. Again and again this: We have been disappointed too often, *they* just will not stop! The mood down in the cellar was similar. —

Lewinsky here yesterday afternoon; Witkowsky, the indestructible moriturus, also stayed for a long time. Lewinsky had heard again from an Aryan source what we have now heard in the same words from so many different people, and which can therefore not be an invention: that in Poland the Germans have carried out the most dreadful murders of Jews. A soldier had told how small children had been taken by the legs and their heads smashed against the wall of a house. Immediately after that Lewinsky read out from the *DAZ*, with considerable indignation and in a voice full of histrionic pathos, what infamous destruction of culture had been caused by the last English terror raid on Nürnberg, how many patrician houses, churches, etc., had been destroyed. I asked him whether he knew who had destroyed the synagogue in Nürnberg and the Tower of London, whether he knew how many factories in Nürnberg were working to keep the war going. I told him I began to see red if I just heard the words "German culture." — [ ... ]

## January 16, Tuesday

[ ... ]

Four pounds of bread coupons arrived, addressed to Eva "with kindest regards and in haste your Käthe." I said to Frau Cohn: "We cannot figure out who sent them; our friends sign only with their first names, and even then they don't use the right one." To which Frau Cohn (who, by the way, is curiously full of life as a widow and is becoming ever more youthful and cheerful): "It was exactly the same with us."

[ ... ]

## After eight in the evening

Hurrah, we're still alive! Dresden had a heavy raid for the third time. The alert sounded at 11:30 A.M. I calmly went on reading [ ... ]. At twelve the siren sounded again, I thought for the all clear, but it howled a full-scale warning. Slowly down to the almost-empty cellar. Then others came: The radio reported formations approaching, 30 miles, 20 miles away. I stood at the cellar entrance with Werner Lang and Neumark. I guessed Eva to be at Maxe, the Berlin cafeteria in Walpurgisstrasse, or at Gertrud Schmidt's in Winckelmannstrasse. We heard approaching aircraft, a series of detonations, single explosions, not the double bang of the guns. We went into the cellar. Very loud humming of the aircraft directly above us, the blast shook the cellar door, a couple of times it went dark for seconds, we waited in unpleasant suspense. Then we went up to the cellar door again. Smoke in the sky. Werner Lang went through the house onto the square and reported: big clouds of smoke over Friedrichstadt. We heard humming again, more explosions. It went on like that for a good hour before the first all clear sounded. I was upstairs again at a quarter past one, the final all clear did not come until half past. I had not been very agitated, at any rate much more impassive than the previous time. I had no worries about Eva. For a long time there were no trams running, and she did not return until about half past four. Again she had been closer to the mischief than I thought. Because the Americans bombed not only the Friedrichstadt station, but also the railway tracks at the main railway station, at the Hohe Bridge, and at the Nossen Bridge, and during the actual attack Eva was at Frau Winde's, at the corner of Würzburger and Chemnitzer, and heard the bombs whistling down and exploding very close by. — [ ... ]

Second alert from 9:45 until almost 11, one whole hour of that time in the cellar. After a late meal, we were fortunately not yet in bed. Sparkling starry sky, but very dark. Very bad heart trouble. Distant, but prolonged and heavy firing, probably in Riesa and Grossenhain again, as on Sunday. In the cellar many very downhearted, indifferent to the Russian successes, pessimistic, fearful. Eisenmann senior was dismayed and warned me to be cautious when I talked about the English report. Incidentally, the English are said to have declared, if Germany still would not yield, that the air raids would "become serious." [ . . . ]

### January 18, Thursday morning

Everything is kept secret, for everything one is dependent on rumors, on what is passed on by word of mouth, on what cannot be controlled. What is certain today is that this time Dresden was hit much more badly, in many more places than in the earlier raids. Thiemig & Möbius in Jagdweg, close by the railway line, got shrapnel on the third floor (where I cut cardboard); the house opposite was destroyed—28 dead [ . . . ]. Eisenmann père talks of around 1,000 victims; how he arrives at this figure, I do not know. —

Yesterday Eva went to customs to fetch a package from Stockholm, of which we had been notified. Fabulous things: four tins of sardines, more than two pounds of plain cake, pralines, a pound of yellow peas, soup cubes, dried fruit. The Eisenmanns were invited for the cake—a necessary return match!—they also got the dried fruit; with that we're fishing for cigarettes. The candies go to Frau Winde as a small expression of thanks and to cheer her up, the pralines went into our air-raid bags, the sardines were attacked immediately. For who knows what is going to happen tomorrow, what will happen this evening . . . Our guiding principle in everything is now: At least I've had a piece of cake. —

At Steinitz's yesterday afternoon feelings were mixed: Close to death and close to deliverance: the Russians outside Krakow, the Anglo-American bombers above us, the Gestapo behind us.

[ . . . ]

### January 20, Saturday morning

Yesterday a thaw with a mild wind and almost 44 degrees, today frost and snow again, which doesn't bother me, because it helps the Russian offensive. It has broken terribly upon Germany: Warsaw, Krakow, Lodz, Czenstochau have been taken, the border of Upper Silesia has been reached. "Over 150 divisions" have been committed against us, says the bulletin; perhaps it exaggerates the number, in order to diminish the defeat. Made wise by events in August, I am still reining back all hopes. First it remains to be seen, whether the extraordinarily rapid German retreat means a real collapse. I still believe it to be strategic calculation: They will bring the Russians to a halt at prepared positions on the frontier, as they did in East Prussia in August and as they did with the Anglo-Americans in the West. And the when and how of the end of the war is still unpredictable.

Admittedly Steinitz relates: Recently Jacobi had to go into a public air-raid shelter and hesitated on the threshhold. But people had been friendly, and a worker had called out: "Come on in, mate!" Jacobi: "But you mustn't say that." The worker (loudly): "We're all mates—and soon we'll be able to say it out loud again." But I, too, have heard of and myself experienced similar scenes for ten years—and the word was always "soon," and we were always disappointed. —

Frau Cohn has just come: There's coal at Hesse's, probably half a hundredweight.

## Afternoon

Just now there was the most unpleasant counterpart to Jacobi's experience; now which is the vox populi? There was a whole hundredweight of briquettes to be had at Hesse's; that meant three two-pail trips, aggravated by terribly slippery ice. I carried the first two pails, piled high with coal, down to the cellar, the second load up to us. Then, at about 11:50, there was an alert. Since things remained quiet, I ventured to go to Salzgasse once more, without waiting for the all clear. I reached our house with the last two pails just when the warning itself sounded. As I made my way to our cellar, the Russian prisoners were standing in the courtyard; they stared up at the sky and then crowded into the passageway in front of our coal cellar. "Many, many" one called out to me. (There were 46 airplanes; Eva, at the Windes', counted their vapor trails. They merely flew over Dresden; again there was no antiaircraft fire to be heard.) I was agitated and very tired, so I went past the landing with the empty pails and down to the Waldmanns' apartment. I did not know that their large hall represented the building's "Aryan" air-raid shelter. All kinds of people were standing around; I squeezed into a corner without saying anything. A small black-haired woman immediately came up to me: "You're not allowed to stay here!" [ . . . ] Immediately after that, old Leuschner also turned to me: "What are you doing here?" I pointed at my two empty pails, said I had fetched coal and just had to catch my breath for a moment, then dragged myself up here despite the most severe angina pains. Then I remained here, very much the worse for wear, physically and spiritually. Nothing more happened, and the all clear came exactly one hour after the first siren. I am very depressed: The bout of pain was the price of exertion and agitation—the slightest upset clutches at my heart, even before it touches my thoughts, and before I can at all consciously ward it off—and its severity was once again a very bitter memento. —

Eva was in a hurry when she returned from the Windes'; she had to catch the half-past-three train to Pirna, the first visit there for three months. As I was making up the manuscript package, I was again tormented by the question, whether I shall ever be able to turn to account everything I have collected. But of course I must not think about that, unless I want to sink down into utter nonexistence.

[ . . . ]

**January 21, Sunday evening**

Eva returned from Annemarie in a rather depressed state: "a dead person." That was already my impression when I could still get out to Pirna in the early days of the war. She is apathetic about everything. Apart from that, very friendly to us, helps out with money and by looking after manuscripts. I continue to be of the opinion that she was broken by the Dressel affair.

[ . . . ]

**January 25, Thursday evening, 7:30 P.M.**

Frau Stühler often complains about the rampant National Socialism and credulous certainty of victory of her female colleagues in Böhme's clothes store on Georgsplatz. Today she told us the women were scared, expecting the Russians to march in, arguing whether it was better to stay or to flee—flight is preferred by the majority, the Russians are represented as particularly cruel and murderous. — I went downstairs just now, to see Waldmann to ask about the military bulletin and to probe the Jewish mood. Berger was there and Werner Lang—the elegance of the lounge chairs in this cellar room beyond the inhospitable hallway is very curious. The Russians have crossed the Oder at Brieg, they are (German report!) close to Breslau, there's street fighting in Bromberg, they appear to have reached Elbing, Oppeln has been taken. Our people also expect a Russian advance on Dresden. There are already said to be crowds of refugees from Silesia here. It really does appear, that the end is rapidly approaching and can no longer be halted. —

[ . . . ]

Astonishing and almost disquieting that there has been no air-raid warning for many days now. Now, when the Russians have reached Breslau! What is in the offing?

**January 27, Saturday morning**

The mood of catastrophe, for us as wearers of the star, nine-tenths joyful, one-tenth fearful—but even when it comes to fear people say: "Better a terrible end!" — is growing stronger. I note some of the signs of the mood. Sources: Yesterday I got a hundredweight of inferior-grade coal from Hesse (am supposed to get a half-hundredweight of briquettes today), in the afternoon I tutored Bernhard Stühler, toward evening went to see Witkowsky, who is now in bed and has been given up—weeping Frau Witkowsky had asked me to visit him, Katz had informed her of the hopelessness of the case and of the probable imminence of death—but whom I found remarkably fresh, buoyant, and certainly unsuspecting; Eva visited the Kreisler woman, met Frau Winde and Frau Richter there; Frau Stühler reports from Böhme's; and "Leni," Frau Cohn's gray-haired, thin and tiny sister, whose hip is badly dislocated and who works in a big linen factory in the Neustadt, also reports this and that. —

The actual situation: Battles in Breslau, the Oder crossed, English offensive imminent in Holland. (English source, I am still ignorant of yesterday's German bulletin.)

Leni: In the room with her seamstresses, a group of twelve women, they say that Dresden will remain spared, because the Russians would be in Berlin very soon, "in eleven days." Where they get the eleven days from and from what point they were counting, could not be ascertained. Frau Richter had more details. On January 19, the Russians had broadcast a declaration that they would be in Berlin on the anniversary of the "seizure of power" on January 30. There was no need to wait for supplies, as huge German stores had been captured when western Poland was overrun, and the troops could be supplied from there. — At Hesse's I heard a woman grumbling more loudly and openly than anyone usually dares to: She could knock "their" heads against the wall, it could make her "really sick," was one supposed—the coal shortage, the gas cut off!—"to cook on snow" [ . . . ]

Curious sign of the wind turning, reported in the same way by Bernhard Stühler and at the Witkowskys': Jacobi and another couple of Jews were to prepare a mass grave at the [Aryan] cemetery. (Every day long columns of the air-raid dead in the newspaper.) An Aryan worker was supposed to dig with them. He refused, he was a "skilled worker." The cemetery inspector ordered him to do it. "No, not with Jews." At which the inspector: "Then do it yourself!" and sent the Jews home. [ . . . ]

In the *Dresdener Zeitung* of January 25, Walter Lippmann is once again quoted and reviled as "one of the inspirations of Roosevelt's foreign policy ("Yid Lippmann's cynical confession," that is, on the "surrender of Europe to the Bolshevists"). He is presumably the editorial writer of the *New York Herald Tribune*. [ . . . ]

### January 29, Monday morning

Yesterday tension and hope rose all day. Waldmann was here in the morning; English bulletin: Russians in Liegnitz, in the whole of Upper Silesia, in Danzig [ . . . ]. Waldmann was convinced of complete collapse in a few days, of the occupation of Berlin and Dresden within a very few days. He told us—incidentally not always on a friendly footing with foreign words—about a speech by Thomas Mann; according to it the Germans murdered one and a half million (the figure was given down to the last hundred) Jews in Auschwitz and ground down their bones to use as fertilizer. The exact figure was owed to German thoroughness, a record had been kept of every single dead Jew, and thanks to their surprise advance the Russians had found the books. Waldmann related further that havoc was also being wreaked among non-Jews. He is employed as a furniture remover by the tax office. In the last few days he had to clear the contents of an Aryan apartment. At the tax office he was told that the tenants of the apartment, a lawyer and his wife, had been executed. — In the evening during the alert Schwarz (or Schwarze), who exactly two weeks before had informed me of the victorious beginning of the Russian offensive and told me of Mann's speech, paid a friendly visit. He had never called on us before, he felt a need to talk about the situation. [ . . . ]

Immediately before Schwarze's visit, and after the alert had already started, we had the most astounding Jewish inspection. While we were eating, a middle-aged police officer (two stars, probably the most elevated lower rank) appeared in our room accompanied by Waldmann. Very friendly "Good evening—well we've got our little inspection to do—don't interrupt your meal, dear!" Waldmann, evidently already well-acquainted with the policeman, whom he was taking around—usually those carrying out the inspection set up their tribunal in the hallway on the first floor, and I had to go down to them. Waldmann said: "The professor here is an eminent man, his name is in every reference book!" The policeman asked me sympathetically, whether I got a pension. "Not a penny since November '43." Embarrassed silence. He then shook my hand. "So good night, professor. Things are going to change, you will get your post back!" That in uniform, on duty, in front of witnesses! One is executed for less. —

On the subject of "refugees." [ . . . ] Frau Cohn told me, that the railway station here, overflowing with refugees, looks terrible. I asked, what was it, that looked so bad. She: A public passage leads from the inquiry desk to Bismarckplatz. There, in broad daylight a man was squatting by the wall and "doing his business." The whole stretch along the wall looked like a pigsty. They all squat down there, men and women together. Where can they go—all the toilets are occupied, and who knows how long they've been traveling. [ . . . ] In yesterday's Sunday newspaper: A poorly covered mass grave with 274 bodies was found in a recaptured Hungarian village. A slightly wounded worker said: The Jewish village shopkeeper, Isidor Kober, had denounced the inhabitants as anti-Bolshevistic to the commander of the Soviet regiment passing through, whereupon they had had to dig their own grave and all, apart from the lightly wounded witness, who had escaped, were shot. — The Jewish denouncer naturally interests me most in this story. He need not even be invented. Because if we were asked whom we could name here as particularly unpleasant Nazis, we wouldn't exactly hold back either. Ergo: What will become of us?

Chaotic issuing of orders: A few days ago the hours of the blackout were extended; today they have been reduced again. — A few days ago letters were prohibited altogether. Today they have been permitted again. — New orders: The newspapers, which recently were limited to four pages in a smaller format, are now to be restricted to a mere two pages four times a week. —

Eva said I must not mention *any name*, must not put anyone at risk. Right—but how could I keep a precise record without names? I think there will be no house searching of the air-raid bags; I hope that now there will not be enough time and people for house searches at all anymore.

[ . . . ]

### February 2, Friday afternoon

[ . . . ]

From yesterday to today, two alerts, no cellar, the first as we were at supper, 8:10 to 8:35, the second toward morning today, 3:40 to 4:05.

Elated and extremely tense mood: According to yesterday's German military bulletin the Russians are northwest of Küstrin, according to the English one: in Landsberg and in Küstrin. But serious food problems tug at one's nerves. For one thing all our reserves are exhausted, and there's a shortage of potatoes, also Eva does not get anything to eat in crowded restaurants and still less anything to take away; and for another the gas now almost completely fails even at times when it is available. We can hardly boil water, potatoes cannot be cooked at all. Since yesterday we have been experiencing the nadir of our diet. With a bad conscience and plagued by pains in my belly, I stuff dry bread into myself, and Eva practices going without. I hallucinate having enough to eat.

[ . . . ] At the sight of the refugees Frau Stühler said with complete conviction: It was heaven's just punishment for the deportation of the Jews, she felt no pity at all. — I do not feel pity either, on the contrary—but God's punishment so readily strikes the wrong person, it is at any rate not much bothered about the individual.

### February 3, Saturday morning

We do not know yesterday's military bulletin. Frau Stühler brought home from her shop: Russian tank spearheads had entered Berlin; Eva from Kreisler (+ Winde and Richter): in Berlin everything was chaotically congested, masses of refugees colliding with troop convoys, and two air raids (the cause of our two last alerts) had come down on this chaos. Both the Stühlers and the Kreislers had known of people who were expecting the final collapse in the next few days.

Meanwhile the shortage of food and gas is driving us to absolute despair; this morning was a nerve-racking tragedy. At times only one little flame was burning on the Cohns' and the Klemperers' two stoves, even that only with popping interruptions.

### Evening seven o'clock

Mood has sunk greatly again. News came, that the Russians are *not* in Berlin, and that their advance has been halted. News came, that the four-week ration card has to last for four and a half weeks—when as it is we cannot make the bread last anything like four weeks, and when during the last few days, almost completely dependent on dry bread and jacket potatoes without any accompaniment whatsoever, we have already become familiar with hunger.

[ . . . ]

### February 5, Monday morning

[ . . . ]

I wrote about Kornblum during my time at Schlüter. He is on his back, fairly given up for lost, paralyzed and with a serious heart problem. On the stairs, his wife, a feared Xanthippe, not unfriendly to me, asked me to visit him. When I went down, the daughter, without makeup and more presentable than usual, opened the door. The mother was in the kitchen; she was praying for her husband. So Kornblum seriously and piously told me. Otherwise there was innocuous talk of his good times as a shop owner in Dresden. Eva came to fetch me upstairs again. She was admired for her courage. — Why courage? — It was said that Aryan wives were forbidden to visit Jews, even those in mixed marriages. We had not heard anything about it. On the other hand we had already been warned—secret order, issued by Neumark—Jews not to talk in groups, not even in twos, on the street, above all to display a cheerful and even "triumphant expression." —

[ . . . ]

In the afternoon Eva went to listen to the broadcast on Pirnaer Platz: The Russians at Arnswalde, i.e., less than 40 miles from Stettin, the English offensive against Cologne is imminent (artillery exchanges). More threatening—other people had noticed it, too—military patrols on the streets. Then in the evening Schwarz said: Another two weeks at the most. Chaos in Berlin, in which refugees and troops jam the streets and which had the most atrocious air raid during our last alert (center and Wilhelmsstrasse destroyed, many dead); the Russians in position on the Oder for a frontal attack on Berlin, the infantry already brought up behind the tank army in thousands of American trucks. In two weeks there would at most be guerrilla fights with Nazi remnants in Upper Bavaria. Eisenmann, Schwarz, Frau Stühler also knew what the patrols were for. The army has been confined to barracks, from today the police also, no policeman is allowed to sleep outside barracks anymore. There was so much desertion from the Volkssturm here and from the Eastern front. They were looking for fugitives, making checks. [ . . . ]

### February 6, Tuesday afternoon

[ . . . ]

Since yesterday all cinemas have been shut. Officially, and it's very likely, because of lack of coal. Frau Stühler thinks, to avoid people gathering. But I don't know: Cinema is a distraction; reflection and anger grow where distraction and gathering together are absent.

[ ... ]

### February 8, Thursday evening seven o'clock

At lunchtime today—queuing for broth, queuing again at Maxe (Berlin canteen)—Eva had a fainting fit and came home feeling very unwell. She is too worn out, too poorly fed, unlike myself she cannot substitute quantity for the missing quality. I cannot help her, I am very depressed and have a bad conscience as I still my own hunger.

No news about the war for 48 hours. It is going too slowly for us. — Everyone is afraid. The Jews of the Gestapo, who could murder them before the Russians arrive; the Aryans of the Russians, Jews and Aryans of evacuation, of hunger. No one believes in a quick end, and Jew and Christian alike fear the air raids. This morning Eva had something more up her sleeve. When the Russians come, she said, the bridges will be blown up; then we shall certainly have to leave our house; either because of the explosion itself, or because it will be made ready for the defense. — We both had to laugh, because we were discussing, as such a matter of course, what would once have appeared to us like something from a novel. At bottom we are afraid of nothing anymore, because we constantly, at every moment, have everything to fear. One becomes blunted. [ ... ]

Today as I was waiting for Eva by the broth queue, an ordinary woman wanted to give me a bread coupon. "I would really like to give you something." I declined with heartfelt thanks. Eva also experienced an expression of sympathy. At Butcher Nacke in Pillnitzer Strasse, where we fetch broth on Thursday and where Eva usually buys sausage, the shop was empty, and the butcher's wife asked to whom the Jew's ration card belonged, emphasized her long-standing friendship with Jews, in particular with Konrad, and wanted to hand Eva the latest *Dresdener Zeitung.* "There's someone looking through the shopwindow—I'll wrap the bacon in the newspaper." The bacon was very generously weighed.

### February 9, Friday morning

Yesterday's "conversation from a novel" about the possible blowing up of the bridges! In the evening Schwarz came upstairs: the English and the Americans both announced the Russian intention of taking Dresden; Waldmann had seen civilians marching to Ullersdorf to dig trenches; he himself, Schwarz, was on good terms with a friend of the chauffeur of the local head of the SS, von Alvensleben; his acquaintance reported that Mutschmann was preparing to flee; he himself, Schwarz, had, by chance, heard the order being taken around an Aryan tenement block to hand over spade and pickax from the air-raid-protection equipment ... [ ... ]

Keep on making notes to the last: Frau Cohn's curious psychology. Her eyes full of tears, she had stood loyally by her husband, she remained a friend of the Jews, she was not clinging to life—but she did not want to die in *this* community, she wanted out of *here*. (Particular cause of bitterness: that the Aryan air-raid shelter was refused her, that she had to fetch her ration coupons at an office for those of mixed race!) Curious psychology of Frau Cohn and Frau Stühler: They always already know everything that we tell them from forbidden sources; but they always mistrustfully keep *their* knowledge to themselves. Everyone is afraid of everyone else.

Yesterday, however, Frau Stühler divulged a curious fact: Order relayed to Aryan houses not to give bread to begging soldiers, still less a bed, and to chase away any who were persistent. (Schwarz said that in Dresden alone, patrols were said to have arrested about 700 deserters.)

[ . . . ]

### February 10, Saturday midday

[ . . . ] Today Jacobi came to visit me for a while; Katz has got him declared unfit for work because of a weak heart. He said that the Volkssturm was being put in secondhand SA uniforms, which made the men afraid and angry. Further, that many *treks*—the latest *LTI* word—had been overtaken by the Russians and well treated; just to keep up the anti-Russian atrocity propaganda, it was now being spread about (we have already heard it, too), that the Russians say: "*We* won't do anything to you, but keep running, because after us comes the commissar!" The commissar, that is, the "Jewish-Bolshevist Commissar," that is, the bloodhound. χατ'εξοχήν [in person]. [ . . . ]

### February 11, Sunday morning

[ . . . ]

Latest rumor, based on the fact that everywhere on the streets stringent checks are being carried out by soldiers and by SA: Russian parachutists in German uniforms have landed and are in hiding. I believe it *almost* as little as in 1914 I believed in the poisoned wells, but given the mass of Russian people here who are on the German side, serving in German uniforms, it is, of course, not completely impossible for someone to find shelter. On the other hand: What could single parachutists accomplish here? And, says Eva, what good are the checks? These parachutists would surely have convincing documents. Admittedly Eva also says: What good is digging trenches? It won't stop anyone anyway.

### Evening after seven o'clock

Eisenmann senior and Steinitz were here this morning. Steinitz: At the mailbox an individual, something "between man and gentleman," had stared at his star and told him in broken Slav German he had "better stay at home in the next few days." Weighing the matter, the four of us came to the conclusion that it was more likely to be a reference to an uprising by the many Eastern workers than to a pogrom, and that perhaps there was some truth after all to the parachute Russians. But everything is mysterious and in the hands of fate. — Have just spent a little time with Witkowsky, the vigorous moriturus. There Frau Spanier arrived with this news, she had spoken to refugees at the railway station, who said the Russian tank spearheads (*LTI.* New!) were at Görlitz. And Frau Stühler brings from town: Liegnitz in the east and Cleve in the West have been taken. — Eisenmann senior taught me: *Ja Gewrej*—I am a Jew. He talked of three sources of danger: the first: looting Eastern workers, the second: retreating German troops, the third: invading Russians. He forgot to mention, what I fear the most: the Gestapo.

### February 12, Monday morning

Rumors, which at least are characteristic as such, and which are more in the realm of the probable than of the possible. In the afternoon Frau Stühler was at Aryan friends with important connections, among them "a big Nazi swine in the SS." His wife had been wailing: "My husband says, we have to shoot ourselves, but we can't shoot the children!" — Everything has been prepared for the evacuation of Dresden. — The Aryans have been evacuated from Breslau, but the Jews have been left in the city. — Foreign broadcasts have announced that we should provide ourselves with provisions for three weeks (tu parles!) and if possible bury them, at any rate not keep them at home. — The number of deserters detained in Dresden already stood at seventeen thousand (*sic,* it was seven hundred two days ago!), they are put in assault battalions(!), behind them guard units ready to open fire. — Freisler, the chief judge of the People's Court, the man who treated the assassins of July 20th in such scoundrelly fashion, and who in the newspaper was announced as one of the victims of the most recent "terror raids" on Berlin, was in truth hanged by officers, and in exactly the same way as he had ordered the execution of the condemned: slowly, and with the rope loosened a couple of times. — There had been disturbances in Berlin, but the rebels had been shot to pieces. — In the coal cellar just now Waldmann added an indisputable report to all of this: He had seen soldiers working at the pillars of the Carola Bridge, had inferred they were mining it. He believes that the next few days will decide our personal fate. He also thinks any attempt at avoidance is impossible. In the hands of fate. [ . . . ]

An old lady came to visit Frau Cohn yesterday. She said, she had been advised to remove the picture of Hitler from her apartment, best of all, to take it out of the frame and put something else in it. "I cremated him." [ . . . ]

**February 13, Tuesday afternoon, perfect spring weather**

Odysseus in Polyphemus's cave. — Yesterday afternoon Neumark had me called over; I had to help him deliver letters this morning. I was quite unsuspecting. In the evening Berger was up here with me for a while, I told him, and he was annoyed and said, it'll be for digging trenches. I still did not grasp the seriousness of the threat. So today at eight o'clock I was at Neumark's. Frau Jährig came out of his room weeping. Then he told me: Evacuation of all those capable of work, it's called outside work duty; as I myself [i.e., Klemperer] am released from duty, I remain here. I: So the end is more likely for me than for those who are leaving. He: That is not the case; on the contrary, remaining here is a privilege; there will also remain a man who lost two sons in the First World War, further, he himself, Neumark, then Katz (presumably as holder of the Iron Cross, First Class, not as physician, because Simon is going), Waldmann and a couple of those who are seriously ill and released from duty. For the first quarter of an hour my heart almost let me down completely, then later I was completely blunted, i.e., I made observations for my diary. The circular to be delivered stated that one had to present oneself at 3 Zeughausstrasse early on Friday morning, wearing working clothes and with hand luggage, which would have to be carried for a considerable distance, and with provisions for two to three days travel. On this occasion there is to be no confiscation of property, furniture, etc.; the whole thing is explicitly no more than outside work duty—but is without exception regarded as a death march. The most cruel separations are taking place: Frau Eisenmann and Schorschi stay here, Lisel, the eleven-year-old, who wears the star, has to leave with father and Herbert. No allowance is made for old age or youth, not for seventy nor for seven—what they mean by "capable of work" is quite incomprehensible. — I had to inform Frau Stühler first, she was far more shocked than on the death of her husband and rushed out to alert friends on behalf of her Bernhard. [I.e., in the hope, that they could intervene.] Then I went by tram, I was permitted to do so, to the Station and Strehlen quarter with a list of nine names. Simon, not yet fully dressed, maintained his composure, whereas his normally sturdy wife almost collapsed. Frau Gaehde in Sedanstrasse, very much aged, eyes staring, again and again opened her mouth so wide, that the handkerchief she was holding in front of it almost disappeared inside; a desperate look on her face she protested wildly and vehemently: She would fight to the last against this order, she could not leave her ten-year-old grandson, her seventy-year-old husband; her son-in-law was a prisoner of war "for the sake of the German, of the *German* cause"; she would fight and so on. Frau Kreisler-Weidlich, of whose hysteria I had been afraid, was not at home; relieved, I dropped the sheet in the mailbox. Also in Franklinstrasse I had to call on a Frau Pürckhauer. I met her with her Aryan and deaf husband. Ordinary people. They were the calmest of those on my list. A Frau Grosse in Renkstrasse—a handsome villa by the Lukaskirche—was bad despite her self-composure.

A woman of middle age, rather ladylike; she wanted to call her husband, stood helplessly by the telephone: "I have forgotten everything, he works in a confectionery factory . . . my poor husband, he is ill, my poor husband . . . I myself have such bad heart trouble . . ." I comforted her, perhaps things would not be so bad, it could not last long, the Russians had reached Görlitz, the bridges here had been mined, she should not think of death, not talk about suicide . . . I finally got the necessary signature acknowledging receipt and left. Hardly had I shut the corridor door than I heard her weeping loudly. Even more pitiful was Frau Bitterwolf in Struvestrasse. Again a shabby house; I was vainly studying the list of names in the entrance hall when a blond, snub-nosed young woman with a pretty, well-looked-after little girl, perhaps four years old, appeared. Did a Frau Bitterwolf live here? She was Frau Bitterwolf. I had to give her an unpleasant message. She read the letter, several times said quite helplessly: "What is to become of the child?" then signed silently with a pencil. Meanwhile the child pressed up against me, held out her teddy bear, and, radiantly cheerful, declared: "My teddy, my teddy, look!" The woman then went silently up the stairs with the child. Immediately afterward I heard her weeping loudly. The weeping did not stop. — 29 Werderstrasse was also a very shabby house. Women on the stairs told me that Frau Tenor was not at home, but I should call on her friend right at the top. A sickly, almost delicate-looking young woman in a very wretched attic room. She spoke very anxiously, her friend had always feared this, would commit suicide. I urgently preached courage, she should keep her friend's spirits up. — At 52 Strehlener Strasse, where we had frequently visited the Reichenbachs and the Seliksohns, I had to deliver the letter to a Frau Dr. Wiese. Instead of her the door was opened by an imposing matron in trousers, a Frau Schwarzbaum. She told me, and I remembered the case, that the previous year, her own husband, together with Imbach, had committed suicide (cf. the diary of Lothringer Weg), in order to escape arrest by the Gestapo. — Finally at 7 Bürgerwiese, a tiny, white, shabby old house, with stately buildings on either side, I searched in vain for a Frau Weiss. Star-wearing Jews are permitted to cross Bürgerwiese only by way of Lüttichstrasse, and must not walk along it otherwise; consequently it is years since I have been there. — Frau Jährig was here just now with her young daughter, from whom she must part. Instruction from Neumark: Frau Weiss lives with her mother, Frau Kästner; I must immediately go there once again.

**Toward 7:00 P.M.**

Frau Kästner lived in the cellar of the side wing in the back court; behind the courtyard one can see a curious little old church. A dark young girl opened the door, she read the letter with complete resignation. Yes, it was all the same to her now, only she didn't want to sign before her mummy had read it. Could I not come again. I said that was impossible for me. I then had to urge her for quite a while before I got a signature acknowleging receipt. —

At Neumark's the whole office was crowded with those to be deported, I shook hands with Paul Lang, Rieger, Lewinsky—"You're coming, too? No?" with that there was already a gulf between us. I went upstairs to the Eisenmanns for a moment, the whole family had assembled—extremely upset. I went to Waldmann, who remains here. He set forth the gloomiest hypothesis with very great certainty. Why are the Jewish children being taken as well? Lisel Eisenmann can't do work duty. Why does Ulla Jacobi have to go *alone*—as cemetery superintendent her father is still classified indispensable. There are murderous intentions behind it. And we who remain behind, "we have nothing more than a reprieve of perhaps a week. Then we'll be fetched out of our beds at six o'clock in the morning. And we'll end up just like the others." I threw in: Why are they leaving such a small remnant here? And now, when they've got so little time? He: "You'll see, I'll turn out to be right."

### The Destruction of Dresden on February 13 and 14 (Tuesday, Wednesday), 1945

### Piskowitz, February 22–24

We sat down for coffee at about half past nine on Tuesday evening, very weary and depressed, because during the day, after all, I had been running around as the bearer of bad tidings, and in the evening Waldmann had assured me with very great certainty (from experience and remarks he had recently picked up) that those to be deported on Thursday were being sent to their deaths ("pushed onto a siding"), and that we who were left behind would be done away with in just the same way in a week's time—then a full-scale warning sounded. "If only they would smash everything up!" bitterly said Frau Stühler, who had chased around all day, and evidently in vain, to get her boy freed from the work duty. — Had there been only this first attack, it would have impressed me as the most terrible one so far, whereas now, superseded by the later catastrophe, it is already blurring into a vague outline. We very soon heard the ever-deeper and louder humming of approaching squadrons, the light went out, an explosion nearby . . . Pause in which we caught our breath, we kneeled head down between the chairs, in some groups there was whimpering and weeping—approaching airplanes once again, deadly danger once again, explosion once again. I do not know how often it was repeated. Suddenly the cellar window on the back wall opposite the entrance burst open, and outside it was bright as day. Someone shouted: "Incendiary bomb, we have to put it out!" Two people even hauled over the stirrup pump and audibly operated it. There were further explosions, but nothing in the courtyard. And then it grew quieter, and then came the all clear. I had lost all sense of time. Outside it was bright as day. Fires were blazing at Pirnaischer Platz, on

Marschallstrasse, and somewhere on or over the Elbe. The ground was covered with broken glass. A terrible strong wind was blowing. Natural or a firestorm? Probably both. In the stairwell of 1 Zeughausstrasse the window frames had been blown in and lay on the steps, partly obstructing them. Broken glass in our rooms upstairs. In the hallway and on the side facing the Elbe, windows blown in, in the bedroom only one; windows also broken in the kitchen, blackout torn in half. Light did not work, no water. We could see big fires on the other side of the Elbe and on Marschallstrasse. Frau Cohn said in her room furniture had been shifted by the blast. We placed a candle on the table, drank a little cold coffee, ate a little, groped our way over the broken glass, lay down in bed. It was after midnight—we had come upstairs at eleven. I thought: Just sleep, we're alive, tonight we'll have peace and quiet, now just put your mind at rest! As she lay down, Eva said: "But there's glass in my bed!" — I heard her stand up, clear away the glass, then I was already asleep. After a while, it must have been after one o'clock, Eva said: "Air-raid warning." — "I didn't hear anything." — "Definitely. It wasn't loud, they're going around with hand sirens, there's no electricity." — We stood up, Frau Stühler called at our door "Air-raid warning"; Eva knocked at Frau Cohn's door— we have heard nothing more of either—and we hurried downstairs. The street was as bright as day and almost empty, fires were burning, the storm was blowing as before. As usual there was a steel-helmeted sentry in front of the wall between the two Zeughausstrasse houses (the wall of the former synagogue with the barracks behind it). In passing I asked him whether there was a warning. — "Yes." — Eva was two steps ahead of me. We came to the entrance hall of no. 3. At that moment a big explosion nearby. I kneeled, pressing myself up against the wall, close to the courtyard door. When I looked up, Eva had disappeared, I thought she was in our cellar. It was quiet, I ran across the yard to our Jews' cellar. The door was wide open. A group of people cowered whimpering to the right of the door, I kneeled on the left, close to the window. I called out several times to Eva. No reply. Big explosions. Again the window in the wall opposite burst open, again it was bright as day, again water was pumped. Then an explosion at the window close to me. Something hard and glowing hot struck the right side of my face. I put my hand up, it was covered in blood, I felt for my eye, it was still there. A group of Russians—where had they come from?—pushed out of the door. I jumped over to them. I had the knapsack on my back, the gray bag with our manuscripts, and Eva's jewelery in my hand, my old hat had fallen off. I stumbled and fell. A Russian lifted me up. To the side there was a vaulting, God knows of what already-half-destroyed cellar. We crowded in. It was hot. The Russians ran on in some other direction, I with them. Now we stood in an open passageway, heads down, crowded together. In front of me lay a large unrecognizable open space, in the middle of it an enormous crater. Bangs, as light as day, explosions. I had no thoughts, I was not even afraid, I was simply tremendously exhausted, I think I was expecting the end. After a moment I scrambled over some vaulting or a step or a parapet into the open air, threw my-self into the crater, lay flat on the ground for a while, then clambered up one side of the crater, over the edge into a telephone kiosk. Someone called out: "This way, Herr Klemperer!" In the demolished little lavatory build-ing close by stood Eisenmann senior, little Schorschi in his arms. "I don't know where my wife is." — "I don't know where my wife and the other children are." — "It's getting too hot, the wooden paneling is burn-ing . . . over there, the hall of the Reich Bank building!" We ran into a hall, it was surrounded by flames, but looked solid. There seemed to be no more bombs exploding here, but all around everything was ablaze. I could not make out any details, I saw only flames everywhere, heard the noise of the fire and the storm, felt terribly exhausted inside. After a while Eisen-mann said: "We must get down to the Elbe, we'll get through." He ran down the slope with the child on his shoulders; after five steps I was out of breath, I was unable to follow. A group of people were clambering up through the public gardens to the Brühl Terrace; the route went close to fires, but it had to be cooler at the top and easier to breathe. Then I was standing at the top in the storm wind and the showers of sparks. To right and left buildings were ablaze, the Belvedere and—probably—the Art Academy. Whenever the showers of sparks became too much for me on one side, I dodged to the other. Within a wider radius nothing but fires. Standing out like a torch on this side of the Elbe, the tall building at Pir-naischer Platz, glowing white; as bright as day on the other side, the roof of the Finance Ministry. Slowly thoughts came to me. Was Eva lost, had she been able to save herself, had I thought too little about her? I had wrapped the woolen blanket—*one*, I had probably lost the other with my hat—around head and shoulders, it also covered the star. In my hands I held the precious bag and—yes—also the small leather case with Eva's woolen things, how I managed to hold on to it during all the clambering about is a mystery to me. The storm again and again tore at my blanket, hurt my head. It had begun to rain, the ground was soft and wet, I did not want to put anything down, so there was serious physical strain, and that probably stupefied and distracted me. But in between there was constantly present, as dull pressure and pang of conscience, what had happened to Eva, why had I not thought enough about her. Sometimes I thought: She is more ca-pable and courageous than I am, she will have got to safety; sometimes: If at least she didn't suffer! Then again simply: If only the night were over! Once I asked people if I could put my things on their box for a moment, so as to be able to adjust my blanket. Once a man addressed me: "You're also a Jew, aren't you? I've been living in your house since yesterday"—Löwen-stamm. His wife handed me a napkin with which I was supposed to ban-dage my face. The bandage didn't hold, I then used the napkin as a handkerchief. Another time a young man, who was holding up his trousers with his hand, came up to me. In broken German: Dutch, impris-oned (hence without suspenders) at police headquarters. "Ran for it—the others are burning in the prison." It rained, the storm blew. I climbed up a little farther to the partly broken down parapet of the Terrace, I climbed down again out of the wind, it kept on raining, the ground was slippery. Groups of people stood or sat, the Belvedere was burning, the Art Academy was burning, in the distance there was fire everywhere—I was quite dulled. I had no thoughts at all, no more than occasional scraps rose up in my mind. Eva—why am I not worried about her all the time—why can I not observe any details, but see only the theatrical fire to my right and to my left, the burning beams and scraps and rafters in and above the stone walls? Then the calm figure of the statue on the terrace made a strange impression on me again—who was he? But most of the time I stood as if half asleep and waited for dawn. Very late it occurred to me to jam my bags between the branches of a bush: Then I could stand somewhat more freely and it was easier for me to hold my protective blanket around me. (Incidentally Eva had had the leather case after all; anyhow the bag and the knapsack were burdensome enough.) The feeling of the encrusted wound around my eye, the rubbing of the blanket, the wetness also had a numbing effect. I had no sense of time, it took forever and didn't take so long at all, then dawn began to break. The burning went on and on. To the right and left of me the way was still blocked—all the time I thought: To have an accident now would be wretched. Some tower glowed dark red, the tall building with the turret on Pirnaischer Platz seemed about to fall—but I did not see it collapse—the ministry on the other side burned silvery bright. It grew lighter, and I saw a stream of people on the road by the Elbe. But I did not yet have the courage to go down. Finally, probably at about seven, the terrace—the terrace forbidden to Jews—was by now somewhat empty, I walked past the shell of the still-burning Belvedere and came to the terrace wall. A number of people were sitting there. After a minute someone called out to me: Eva was sitting unharmed on the suitcase wearing her fur coat. We greeted each other very warmly, and we were completely indifferent to the loss of our belongings, and remain so even now. At the critical moment, someone had literally pulled Eva out of the entry hall of no. 3 Zeughausstrasse and into the Aryan cellar, she had got out to the street through the cellar window, had seen both numbers 1 and 3 completely alight, had been in the cellar of the Albertinum for a while, then reached the Elbe through the smoke, had spent the rest of the night partly looking for me [ . . . ], had in addition observed the destruction of the Thamm building (thus of all our furniture), and partly sitting in a cellar under the Belvedere. Once, as she was searching, she had wanted to light a cigarette and had had no matches; something was glowing on the ground, she wanted to use it—it was a burning corpse. On the whole, Eva had kept her head much better than I, observed much more calmly and gone her own way, even though pieces of wood from a window had struck her head as she was climbing out. (Fortunately her skull was thick and she was unharmed.) The difference: She acted and observed, I followed my instincts, other people and saw nothing at all. So now it was Wednesday morning, February 14, and our lives were saved and we were together.

We were still standing together after our first greeting when Eisenmann appeared with Schorschi. He had not found the other members of his family. He was so low that he began to cry: "In a moment the child is going to ask for breakfast—what can I give him?" Then he pulled himself together. We would have to try to find our people, I would have to remove my star, just as he had already taken off his. Eva thereupon ripped the star from my coat with a pocketknife. Then Eisenmann suggested going to the Jewish cemetery. It would be undamaged and be a meeting point. He strode ahead, we soon lost sight of him, and we have not seen him since. We walked slowly, for I was now carrying both bags and my limbs hurt, along the riverbank [ . . . ]. Above us, building after building was a burned-out ruin. Down here by the river, where many people were moving along or resting on the ground, masses of the empty, rectangular cases of the stick incendiary bombs protruded from the churned-up earth. Fires were still burning in many of the buildings on the road above. At times, small, and no more than a bundle of clothes, the dead were scattered across our path. The skull of one had been torn away, the top of the head was a dark red bowl. Once an arm lay there with a pale, quite fine hand, like a model made of wax such as one sees in barbershop windows. Metal frames of destroyed vehicles, burned-out sheds. Farther from the center some people had been able to save a few things, they pushed handcarts with bedding and the like or sat on boxes and bundles. Crowds streamed unceasingly between these islands, past the corpses and smashed vehicles, up and down the Elbe, a silent, agitated procession. Then we turned right toward the town again— I let Eva lead the way and do not know where. Every house a burned-out ruin, but often people outside on the street with household goods they had saved. Again and again fires still burning. Nowhere a sign of attempts to extinguish them. [ . . . ] Not until we came to the hospitals was I able to orient myself. The Bürgerspital seemed no more than a façade, the hospital only partly hit. We entered the Jewish cemetery. Only the outer walls of the little building that had contained the dead house and the Jacobis' small apartment were still standing. Inside there was a deep hole in the naked earth, nothing else, everything was gone. This space appeared remarkably small; puzzling, how it had managed to contain the hall, the apartment and several side rooms besides. I walked down the avenue to the gardeners' shed, in which I had often come across Steinitz, Schein, and Magnus at their game of cards. Many gravestones and slabs had been thrown over or pushed aside, many trees snapped, some graves as if dug up. (Later, in a street quite some distance away, we found a piece of gravestone, Sara . . . could be deciphered on it.) The gardeners' shed was hardly damaged—but no one to be seen anywhere. There was no cellar at the cemetery—what can have happened to Jacobi and his family?

Now we wanted to go to Borsbergstrasse, to Katz, partly to make contact, partly because of my eye, but there was rubble and smoky dust everywhere on the streets, everywhere individual houses were still burning. When one building collapsed only a few steps in front of us, naturally raising an incredible amount of dust, we gave up the attempt. Slowly, halting frequently, very exhausted, we went back the way we had come. There the same procession flowed as before. Then we went to the square in front of Zeughausstrasse to see whether any of our people were there. No. 3 Zeughausstrasse was nothing but a heap of rubble, a single pillar of no. 1 Zeughausstrasse stood facing the town, with a little piece of wall hanging from it, as if from a gallows. It stuck up eerily and dangerously and only emphasized the picture of absolute destruction. Again not a soul. We now settled down against the outer wall of the Brühl Terrace, the narrow side. There we found the Waldmanns and Witkowskys, as well as the Fleischners, an elderly couple. Waldmann boasted of having saved some forty people, Jews and Aryans, from 1 Zeughausstrasse, no one had died there. He also knew from somewhere, that both the Steinitz and Magnus ménages were safe—he knew nothing of all the others. I was curiously moved by the fact that Witkowsky, who had been quite given up, was tenaciously and nimbly among the living.

An ambulance stopped on the open space in front of us; people surrounded it, stretchers with wounded lay on the ground nearby. On a little bench by the door of the vehicle an ambulance man was dispensing eye-drops; there were a great many people whose eyes were more or less badly affected. It was very soon my turn. "Now, dad, I'm not going to hurt you!" He removed some dirt from the injured eye with the edge of a small piece of paper, then put stinging drops in both eyes. Feeling a little relieved, I walked slowly back; after a few steps I heard the ugly hum of an aircraft above me coming rapidly closer and diving. I ran toward the wall, where there were already some other people lying, threw myself to the ground, my head against the wall, my arm over my face. There was an explosion, and little bits of rubble trickled down onto me. I lay there for a little while longer, I thought: "Just don't get killed now!" There were a few more distant explosions, then there was silence. —

I stood up, Eva had meanwhile disappeared. The Fleischners had only just seen her, there had been no calamity here. So I was not especially concerned. Nevertheless it was probably two hours before we found each other again. When the first bomb was dropped, Eva had, like myself, taken cover against the wall, afterward sought out a cellar by the river. I looked for her along the wall, then, together with Waldmann, in the Albertinum. At the wall I left my address, so to speak, with an elderly man, who had turned up and with whom I found Waldmann in relaxed conversation. "Leuschner's brother-in-law." — "But he must know, that you and I were wearing the star." — "That doesn't matter at all now. All lists have been destroyed, the Gestapo have got other things to do, and in two weeks everything will be over anyway!" During the next few days that was Waldmann's frequently repeated conviction. Löwenstamm and Witkowsky judged likewise. Leuschner's brother-in-law at any rate remained harmless, I chatted with him often during the night, and the next morning we shook hands on parting.

After some time, therefore, Eva had got to the cellar of the Albertinum, familiar to her from earlier days and from the beginning of the night of terror. The upper stories of the big building had burned, but I know that only from Eva's report. For the cast-iron queen reigned unharmed up above, and there was no damage to the solid range of cellars, real catacombs, to which a broad flight of stairs led from the gateway. The numerous high rooms, lit by electric light, were very full. It was difficult to find a seat on the benches. The seriously wounded lay on the ground on stretchers, blankets, or mattresses, some rooms were organized as a hospital, filled only by people lying there. Soldiers and ambulance men came and went, more stretchers were brought in. Where I found a place, it was perhaps in the middle room, there was a soldier on the ground groaning terribly, a strapping fellow with big legs and feet. Everyone who passed stumbled over his boots; the man, completely unconscious, was no longer aware of anything. Close by him, two women were lying under bedding, and for a long time I thought they were dead. Later one of them began to groan and asked me to stuff the blanket more firmly against her back. A generator stood on a low platform in a corner of the room, a big flywheel with a handle. When Eva came, she stretched out on this platform and slept. I myself wandered around a lot, chatted, in between I huddled on a little bench and slept. After the night of catastrophe and after the morning's lengthy march with baggage, I was so exhausted that I no longer had any sense of time. It was no later than four o'clock, yet it seemed to me as if it were already late on the second night. My exhaustion was made worse by hunger. We had not had a bite to eat since the small amount of food with our coffee on Tuesday evening. We were constantly being told the National Socialist Welfare was going to bring food. But nothing came. The army medical orderlies had their own rations of bread and sausage. They gave some of it away. I went up to one to beg something and brought Eva a slice of bread. Later a woman came by, broke off a piece of her sandwich with her no doubt dirty hand and gave it to me. I ate the piece. Much later, it was already late in the evening, a senior medical orderly announced that everyone would now get something to eat. Then a basin appeared with white packets of bread, two double sandwiches in each packet. But after a few minutes we were told: Each packet must be shared between two people. I shared with Eva. But what most people—though not, curiously enough, ourselves—missed more than food was something to drink. At the beginning people had got hold of a little tea somewhere and distributed it by the mouthful. Soon there was nothing at all, not a drop of water, not even for the wounded and dying. The medical orderlies complained that they could not help anyone. The vigorous Waldmann felt tormented by thirst to such a degree that he literally began to fade away. He fell asleep, started up in a wretched state, he had been dreaming of drinking. New medical orderlies came. One put a bottle to Waldmann's mouth. Another, evidently a doctor, stood in front of the man groaning on the floor. "The lungs?" I asked. — Edema, came the indifferent reply. After a while the groaning stopped, a little foam came from his mouth. But the man's face went on moving for a long time, before he lay still. Later the corpse was taken out. There were said to be many dead lying in the courtyard. I did not see them, I only (like x others) relieved myself up there. At some point the lights went out, we were sitting in the dark, immediately a wail went up: They're here again. And indeed we could hear the humming in the air, and indeed the airplanes were back again. Candles were lit, and someone called out there were no airplanes after all, we simply had to generate new current for the lighting and the ventilator with the hand machine. The big wheel was turned, and the huge shadows of the men working it, rising and falling on the wall, looked fantastic. After a couple of minutes the lights gradually came on again, and the ventilation machine began to sing again. The whole scene was repeated a few hours later . . . Eva slept soundly, I walked around, slept again, walked around again, was without thoughts or sense of time, but nevertheless somewhat less strained than the night before. The wounded were constantly being carried in or transferred from one room to another, new medical orderlies, also more civilians were constantly coming in. A girl told me she had been waiting tables in the Trompeterschlösschen, which had a particularly good cellar. During the first attack the Zentraltheater and a nearby hotel had been hit, and the people from there had come down to the cellar of the Trompeter, they had also been given wine down there. Then the Trompeter, too, had caught fire, it had become terribly hot in the cellar. She herself, a cook and another two employees had kept the ventilator going by hand, and holding damp cloths over their mouths, had managed to get outside; but all the rest had collapsed, those who escaped had climbed over whole piles of corpses. Very late at night or early in the morning, Witkowsky came excitedly up to me: "We are all being taken out of here to Meissen, to Klotzsche." I woke Eva, she agreed, but it was a while before she was ready. Then we were told the truck was full, but others would follow at short intervals. We remained outside on the bench in front of the cellar—it was very hot and stuffy inside. [ . . . ] We sat for a long time, dawn broke. Then another truck was ready, several wounded on stretchers were put on, then we, the healthy ones, were pushed between them and to the back. A bumpy drive past ruins and fires. I could not see much from my seat, but the complete destruction ceased on the other side of Albertplatz. We were at the air base fairly early on Thursday morning.

### Klotzsche

#### February 15, Thursday morning–February 17, Saturday evening

The first delight was the huge pot of noodle soup in the dormitory. I calmly took the spoon of an old man, who had eaten before me. I ate three big bowls. Then we went to look for our people and soon found them in an identical room in an identical building. I always lost my way in these uniform labyrinths. We found the Waldmann couple and Witkowsky and Frau Bein, whose husband and son had been shot in the concentration camp. Good people, but in the long run—by Saturday I had had enough—a little too populusque. Likewise the Aryans quartered there. What had happened to the educated people? We both asked ourselves the same question. Presumably there are so few of them that in such a catastrophe they disappear from sight altogether. One gray-haired man looked like a vagabond from a Hauptmann play. During the night Eva's woolen jacket and skirt disappeared under his pillow. When Eva energetically searched for and found them, he declared that he had made a mistake in the dark. The inconstancy of the popular mood was demonstrated on this occasion. First people were scandalized by the attempted theft. But then a female piped up: "Why's she sleepin' naked? Why don't she look after her things?" And the mood veered around. The populusque—the Jewish included—was more demanding than we were: Now the soup was too monotonous, and it was impossible to eat one's fill!, now there was too little "welfare," now people were longing for a room of their own and "being able to cook for themselves." Frau Bein was the most plebeian soul in our group; in the morning she woke up weeping: "All the furniture, all gone," immediately afterward she was cheerful. People probably took it a little amiss that we went our own way during the day. Also that we didn't find fault with the food. Of course we found it really monotonous, always the same soup (no longer the nice noodle mixture of the first morning) and bowls of crumbled bread with it—crumbled by whose dirty fingers!—but we were simply grateful to have enough to eat.

There was an alert even before lunch on Thursday, and the air-raid shelter was a very flimsy affair, which would certainly not have withstood a direct hit. But strangely enough Klotzsche had thus far always been spared and remained so this time also—the airplanes were over Dresden again.

In the afternoon I went to the military hospital. I had already noticed the great number of eye injuries in Dresden. Here a special eye ward had been set up. It was soon my turn, the young doctor was very kind, asked my profession and became even more kind and attentive. Findings: A cursory examination (and there was not the equipment here for anything else) showed that the hemorrhage was under the conjunctiva and harmless; but a tear in the retina could not be ruled out, I would have to see a specialist. How speedily I would have done that in normal times. Now I had no choice but to add this danger to the rest. The eye has meanwhile almost recovered, and now there will probably be no further problem. — [ . . . ]

During Friday night, the sound of aircraft was uninterrupted. During that same night the thought occurred to me: Piskowitz. [ . . . ] In the morning we went our own way again. At lunch (Saturday midday therefore) we learned that all civilians would be evacuated from the air base on Sunday, the bombed out would be taken to places in the neighborhood like

Coswig and Meissen. But we thought that Piskowitz might be a place where we could disappear more completely and so made ready to leave.

[ ... ]

It was in Klotzsche that I first began to think of what we had lost. All my books, the reference works, my own works, *one* typescript of the 18ième and of the Curriculum. If there is an accident in Pirna, then the whole of my work since 1933 will be destroyed. — In my desk were all the pieces for the third volume of collected essays. How can I put that together again? All my reprints were destroyed at Thamm's ...

None of that bothered me very greatly. I would reconstruct the Curriculum in a more condensed and perhaps better version. [ ... ] It would be forever a shame only because of the collections of material on the LTI. — Every time I thought and think of the pile of rubble of nos. 1 and 3 Zeughausstrasse, I nevertheless also had and have the atavistic feeling: Yahweh! That was where the Dresden synagogue was burned to the ground.


### Piskowitz, February 19, Monday afternoon

I have a catchword outline, which I am continuing with; here I shall enlarge upon certain details depending on time and mood.

I am again and again concerned about the double danger. The danger of the bombs and the Russians I share with everyone else; that of the star is my own and the much greater one. It began during the terror night; at first I covered the star with the blanket. In the morning Eisenmann said to me: "You must remove it, *I* have already done so." I took it from my coat. Waldmann reassured me: In this chaos and with the destruction of all offices and lists ... Besides I did not have any choice; with the star I would immediately be picked out and killed. The first step was of necessity followed by the others. In Klotzsche I registered as Victor Klemperer and nothing else. At first I carefully dictated it. Later, when food coupons were distributed, that is what I signed. After that I needed an entitlement permit. Now detailed statements and signatures at two offices in the town of Klotzsche. Eva also took a smoker's card for me. I signed twice. I sat in restaurants, I traveled by train and tram—as a Jew in the 3rd Reich all of it punishable by death. I constantly told myself, who could recognize me, especially as we were going farther and farther away from Dresden. Kamenz is a separate district. Here [in Piskowitz] we first of all asked Agnes whether she had ever told anyone in the town that ... Reply: no one. Now the young mayor wanted to know why we had thought of Piskowitz. I: Agnes had been in service with us for many years. "Oh, then you are Herr ..." — "Klemperer." — "Did you not live somewhere else before?" — "Yes, in Hohe Strasse." — "Anna Dürrlich was with you there, wasn't she." We talked freely about everything, asked after Anna—she was married in Vienna. Then when our details were taken down, the question that had not been put in Klotzsche: "You are not of Jewish descent or of mixed race?" — "No." A friendly shake of the hand on leaving; we shall have to go there again because of the food-ration cards and the entitlement permit [ . . . ] with the entry that we have been bombed out. I am just as close to death as on the night of the bombs. —

*Voces populi.* In Klotzsche. A young woman from Lübeck: "They are trying to use terror to force us to capitulate. (With genuine indignation:) They have made a mistake!" A pair of blathering females, very plebeian, who were in Dresden and have rescued something from the cellar. "Mutschmann was there." — "You should have smashed a stone in his mug!" At table, an elderly woman: She could not understand the military bulletin, because the young woman opposite was talking so loudly. The young woman: "No one is going to tell me to shut up. I've heard enough Führer speeches!" On another occasion a matron: "Our good Führer, who sooo much wanted peace—but our enemies, and now the traitors among us, who are to blame for everything, only the traitors are to blame!" —

The situation is just as unclear and contradictory as the vox populi. The impression made on me by Klotzsche air base was one of great solidity in every respect. I repeatedly thought, they are invincible. For one thing, the military aspect. The solid, unpretentiously elegant and formal layout of a whole military town. [ . . . ] Where here is there a lack of men or resources or morale or is there sluggishness or lack of zeal? What evidence is there of five and a half years of war and imminent collapse? But much more impressive even than the military element was the other side of it. The homeless of Dresden flocked here, a thousand are said to have been brought here, and the sudden strain was borne without difficulty. [ . . . ] "Things ran smoothly," only a few miles from the chaos, the spirit of organization, which seemed to be collapsing, recovered itself. Going by that, Germany really will have to be destroyed yard by yard, before it is completely defeated. Going by that, it can go on offering resistance for a long time yet. — But then we went into the town of Klotzsche. Three forms of life pouring uninterruptedly along the highway. First of all military vehicles, all kinds of supply columns. Little Russian nags and Russian soldiers, often with Asiatic faces—that is the German army saving Europe. Then people coming from Dresden with loaded handcarts, with bits and pieces found under ruins in cellars. Moving in the opposite direction refugee treks from the East. Trucks, some transformed into homes with ingenious straw roofs, occasionally a small vehicle or a buggy being towed by the first. Here again I thought, it cannot last much longer.

### February 20, Tuesday morning

All the reflection in our group on the mood of the people and on the situation naturally led again and again to the question of personal safety. I was the only one who was anxious. Then on Saturday we learned: 1) a new surrender ultimatum would expire on Sunday, 2) all civilians would be evacuated from the air base on Sunday. At that Eva, considerably perturbed, took the Piskowitz plan in hand with wild energy. We were back at the air base with all the papers we needed at a quarter to seven, our train was supposed to leave Klotzsche station at 7:10, and we got there with our luggage and plain slices of bread at 7:20. "Train will be announced—uncertain when." Crush of soldiers and civilians. We ate our bread. The train came at about 8:30. Set off into the dark with endless stops and an unbelievable trail of sparks from the engine. In Kamenz at midnight precisely. The railway station overcrowded. Troops and refugees. The welfare organization's room. Two tiers of bunk beds, one above the other, as in a dugout, six to eight small children on each, some sleeping, some crying. Diapers drying on the tiled stove. In the middle, long tables and benches. Helpers handed out a ghastly herbal tea and bread and jam. Baby carriages. A child's diaper was taken off, the inflamed little backside given an airing. Coming and going, hot stuffy air, overcrowding. Eva drank a mouthful, I ate a slice of bread, then we went into the booking hall, where one could breathe. German-Russian soldiers—one of them just as pure Mongolian as his comrade from the supply train on the main road in Klotzsche—lay stretched out on the ground on their coats and kit bags, two nuns with big white cowls sat on a bench. Eva slept for hours on the long, metal-covered surface of the baggage counter, I walked up and down a lot and studied the advertisement of a department store, Lahmann am Markt, which promised to supply crockery of the previous quality "after victory." Toward morning we went into the somewhat thinned out and ventilated rooms inside. A young, short, thickset man with a good-natured negroid face, a touch of Dumas père, asked for a light, sat down beside us, talked. His father, partner in a large circus, he himself an animal tamer, had served as a parachutist, discharged from the army because of his health, now called up for the Volkssturm. He spoke very critically about the situation, it *could* all be over in a few days, *had to* be over by the spring. The soldiers had had enough. [ . . . ] Everything in Cologne dialect, not all of it comprehensible. Sometimes I had the impression that he was an informer, but probably did him an injustice. He talked about the corruption in the country, all the good things were still to be had, one simply had to know where and have the money to spend. He offered Eva a cigarette from a full pack and slipped me a cigar. Afterward we lost sight of him.

I inquired in the welfare room whether there was any public transport to Piskowitz. Unlikely on a Sunday, I was told; but I should inquire at the barracks of the armored infantry, also I could flag any military vehicle on the main road.

We began the march with baggage after seven o'clock. Much on the way was familiar to me from our drives. They were extremely courteous to us at the barracks, but there was nothing going to Piskowitz, nor did we have any luck flagging down vehicles. (Every time I had anything to do with the National Socialist Welfare or the army or any government or Party official, it gave me a small jolt to the heart as a memento. Ever since the mayor here

asked his question, the jolt is no longer small, and in fact I have death constantly before me, although Eva's soundings this morning suggest the man
is harmless.) We had to walk the whole 5 miles slowly, slowly. Flat fields alternate with perfectly rectangular pieces of woodland, which consist of
closely planted, uniform, and unromantically scraggy pine trees. In Grossbaselitz the inn was open, but occupied by a troop of laborers. We went to
the kitchen, related our misfortune, were immediately made welcome, got
coffee and rolls and butter at the kitchen table, for which coupons and
money were refused, and had to report. An old man, very vigorous, with a
finely chiseled and freshly shaven face, the landlord or the father of the
landlord, sat down at the table for his own breakfast and spoke loudly and
plainly of the untold misery, for which *he* was to blame, *he* alone, and that
he, the landlord, had seen it coming a long time ago. Now the end had
come. We took this hospitality as a good omen. —

Thus far we had had pleasant lines of hills to our right; at the beginning, on and between the hills there had been Kamenz, drawn-out, but
clearly defined. Now there was only flatland, after a while a wood and
then, with a few houses emerging behind the wood, Piskowitz. A large village, a scattered cluster of half-timbered houses, a large farm building of
yellow-brown stone, *buildings* really, which are set at odd angles to one another, in front of it a large manor house, with an imposingly solid, yellow
wall. One wing of the building is now used by the Wehrmacht as a military hospital. Close by the farm a long row of bright green barracks, a
camp for girls on land-labor service, which will be evacuated tomorrow
and occupied by troops. Principal characteristic of the place: the large
number of images of the Virgin Mary and of Christ on houses, on rocks
everywhere. A Christ with a stone pillar on the little bridge. We easily
found "our house" on the other side of the stream.

### Afternoon

Knocked out, but in fact more by a cold suddenly coming on and by tiredness than by the fear of death, which now weighs on me only as a general
dull pressure now heavier, now weaker. I am probably sustained a little by
the romantic strangeness of the situation. Eva went to see Krahl, the mayor,
early this morning, showed him her passport, which she had found, and
her clothing card, asked if anything could be obtained with it, chatted with
him, found him harmless, does not believe that he suspects us.

We arrived early on Sunday afternoon. A little girl, the eight-year-old
Marka (Maria) by the door: Her mother was ill. Agnes sat in a bed made
up on the sofa in the familiar room; she was very little changed, her face
ruddy as ever. Shock and joy and shock again—she had thought us lost
years ago [ . . . ]. Then in the plaintive voice that she always had: Now she
was on her back—but it was only influenza, which was passing, and the
next day she pulled herself together—after all too much misfortune: Her
youngest child, a three-year-old, had died in December '43, her husband,

Michel, only forty-six years old, had died in September '44 of influenza and inflammation of the lungs—no doctors, no medicines, not enough time in the hospital!—at eighteen her hardworking foster son (her husband's illegitimate son) was an American prisoner of war; Jurij, the thirteen-year-old, was harum-scarum and unwilling to work; Marka, who was good, was still too small. Only her sister-in-law helped her. And then the refugees, and then the soldiers, and then the threat of starvation, and the threat of evacuation. But it was a matter of course for her to take us in; she said, much sorrow and *one* joy had been foretold her, and the sorrow had come true, and now we were the joy. She immediately understood our situation or constellation. The members of her family also greeted us as a matter of course and with warmth, and they were immediately in the picture about us (whether about the star also, I do not know; they speak Wendish to one another). Agnes's father, old Zschornak, who brought her to us in Dresden a good twenty years ago, occasionally came from the next village to help and greeted us as old acquaintances, a giant, hardly bent seventy-six-year-old, who earns plenty of money and food with casual work. Frau Rothe, her sister-in-law, is busy for hours with the farm work; her husband, worker in a sawmill somewhere, sits here in the evening and talks politics. Vehemently anti-Nazi, Catholic, Slavophile, and pro-Czech. He of course listens to Radio Beromünster—he was allowed to do that, it was neutral—"it can cost you your head, Herr Rothe!"—the country from here to the island of Rügen belonged to the Sorbs, he would not flee from the Russians, he and Agnes did not believe the propaganda and atrocity stories, the war must be over in a very short time, Herr Hitler had forgotten about "General Hunger" . . . On Sunday evening two tall soldiers, stooping, entered in the middle of his talking politics and in Bavarian dialect demanded quarters for themselves and four horses. They are still billeted here, but are extremely pleasant and obliging; they gave the two of us cigars and cigarette papers. Whether they belong to the service corps, to the infantry, or the artillery is not quite clear—there appear to be all three in the village. — Refugees, soldiers, the building of antitank obstacles, trenches, horse-drawn supply wagons with sacks of cement and other equipment mark the whole district.

[ . . . ]

### February 21, Wednesday morning

The Scholze property [ . . . ] is perhaps the tiniest in the village. There are two rooms in the little half-timbered house. Downstairs the familiar low living room with all the Catholic ornaments, upstairs a bedroom with two beds for the married couple and a child's bed. Both upstairs and downstairs a very tiny kitchen recess with stove, cauldron, a faucet (but no sink). Behind the house, the stall and the impossible toilet, behind the stall, the barn. In the kitchen everyone—ourselves included—washes from a *single* washbasin (but there is always hot water on the stove); using the toilet is an excruciating feat because it is so cramped, there is a lack of paper, since no newspaper comes from Dresden. Agnes sleeps on the sofa in the living room, the boy on the floor. On the first night Eva and I slept in one bed upstairs, Marka in the other. After that we were supposed to get the closet next door, in which corn is stored at the moment. But since people are constantly expecting evacuation, Agnes is not shifting things around: Now Marka sleeps in the child's bed upstairs, and we sleep in the marriage beds. Since the room cannot be blacked out or illuminated, and dressing in the pitch darkness is difficult, I sleep in my trousers. The closet downstairs is occupied by the billeted soldiers [ . . . ]. I spend hours writing my notes—the ink, the paper, the pen from the grocer's shop are torture to use—in the living room, where everything happens: Jurij winds on his footcloths, Marka is dressed, Agnes combs her hair, I myself shaved here yesterday, freed myself of the thick one-week beard with the shaving things that have come down to me from the late Michel (I have also inherited a fine hat from him). At the wooden table, which is never covered, but is frequently wiped with a damp cloth, *every* kind of work is carried on: Playing and school exercises, sewing, eating. People wash themselves little and bathe not at all. Everything civilized and urban, everything that is taken for granted in the city, is absent here, probably even in normal times and certainly now. (But there is a water supply and electric light.)

But against all that the food is heavenly. It is not as if Agnes treated us as guests and prepared treats, rather we get exactly what she and her children eat. Except the two of us probably ate especially badly in Dresden; we already appreciated the board in Klotzsche as a feast. But here one is truly living on butter and cream and gets more calories in a day than one got in Dresden in a week. Morning and afternoon we get any amount of the lovely rye bread with butter and curd cheese or honey. At midday we get a rich soup and almost always meat in the evening, too. They have rabbits and butcher them, they have milk in abundance (from two cows), do not deliver everything they are supposed to deliver, and make a little butter on the side. Yesterday afternoon we got pancakes with our coffee. Eva ate two and a half and followed them with a slice of bread with meat. I ate three and a half. [ . . . ]

Yesterday the neighbor slaughtered a pig, from that we got fatty boiled pork at midday and a fatty sausage broth in the evening. For many years midday meals had no longer agreed with me; now I am so starved, that at every mealtime I can devour large amounts with a good appetite, at breakfast at eight, at lunch at twelve, at coffee at five, and at supper at eight. In this tremendous emergency the peasant is indeed—a thought I used to resist—the most important and the happiest man. Getting enought to eat is the most important thing of all, even somewhere to live comes second.

Apart from a little arable land and woodland, Agnes owns two cows, a goat, a pig, rabbits, pigeons, some geese and hens, about 30 swarms of bees. The supervision of the deliveries is supposed to be exceedingly strict, nevertheless some things are put aside. The milk pail in the morning would be what one of our ordinary town shops has to make do with. And here there is no such thing as skimmed milk. This morning we came upon Agnes with a large brown stoneware jug; she was secretly making butter in it with silent rocking movements.

Yesterday the stove fitter greased the cauldron in the little kitchen, because "our" pig (between two and three hundredweight) is also to be slaughtered.

*Children's schooling.* Yesterday Marka went to Grossbaselitz for her lesson (every second day in the inn). Today Jurij likewise to Kleinbaselitz; but he rejected the name; it was Deutsch-Baselitz and Wendisch-Baselitz. They don't allow the Wendisch words to be taken away from them. Jurij came back without having been taught anything. Refugees from a trek were encamped in the inn; the teacher had said the smell was too bad. Yesterday evening Eva helped Marka do counting on the slate. 5+2, 3+4 . . . Incomprehensible how hard it was for the little one to count off the numbers on her fingers. The *German School Atlas* by Philip Bouhler (facsimile signature) with the date September 1, 1942, has been republished. The most terrible hubris. From the contents: Greater Germany within Central Europe; Greater Germany as living space [Lebensraum]; the regional divisions of the National Socialist Party; German colonies; Nürnberg, City of the National Party Rallies; Munich, Capital of the Movement . . . A "German Counting and Arithmetic Book" takes its exercises from Winter Aid 1938–39, the Versailles Diktat, the abolition of unemployment by Adolf Hitler, etc.

Now and then a soldier comes into the room: "Mrs., can I have a little flour?" Then there's a little chat. The men are resigned—it's not war anymore, only slaughter, the Russians' overwhelming numbers could no longer be stopped, etc., etc.—but that's just it, they are *only* resigned and weary—one of them has been a soldier for seven and a half years—and by no means defeatist or even rebellious. They will undoubtedly go on letting themselves be slaughtered, they will undoubtedly go on offering resistance. —

From his vain walk to school Jurij brought back some bullets he had found, including a whole clip. We said the Russians would shoot everyone in the house, if they found the bullets here. At that, his mother took them away from him, which put him in a terrible huff.

**Toward evening**

It rained for the best part of the day. As a result the continually passing refugee treks made an especially sorry impression. Horse and oxen teams drawing open wagons, also horse and ox together, horses and ponies tied on behind. Like something from earlier centuries. And that in conjunction with the horrors of air attack. In the afternoon we went for a short walk. The highway and the edge of the woods churned up. Treks again. They are building a second antitank barrier in the village: narrowing (not closing!)

the road with stone ramparts and tree trunks in front of them. In the farm-yards soldiers with well-looked-after horses—a curious infantry! At the edge of the wood, as elsewhere on the roads, strips of tinfoil, dropped by aircraft to distract the locating devices. (N.B. Jurij showed me leaflets that had been dropped.)

At home we met a shopkeeper from Dresden who had lived through the night of terror on the Wilder Mann without being bombed out and who had left Dresden on Monday. Her relations, the Kuskes (our suppli-ers, when we lived in Holbeinstrasse), mother and daughter, were dead. There was a dreadful smell of corpses, the authorities estimated 200,000 dead, there was a thin supply of water, no gas, there were no newspapers, instead a leaflet from the *Freiheitskampf,* which threatens shooting for "everything"; narrow alleyways had been cleared through the rubble, one sees slips of paper put up: I am safe . . . I am looking for . . . —"Have you perhaps heard anything of a Dr. Lang, a Jewish doctor—he had a practice until just before the war, later I sometimes saw him at the Goehle plant . . . ?" — "I don't know him, but if he was a Jew, then he was cer-tainly taken to Poland long ago, they were all deported . . ." The woman was incensed, there were no bounds to her reviling of the murderous gov-ernment, repeatedly interrupted, however, by outbreaks of fear and en-treaties not to betray her. She gave me a razor blade—from a safety razor left behind by a soldier—and a little comb. In Dresden, and this made us take a particular liking to her, she had picked up a cat and brought it to Piskowitz. The soldiers are calling the children to eat with them, there's meat. You find them in every army: decent people and murderers. — [ . . . ]

### February 22, Thursday morning

Yesterday evening, young Rothe, a bright boy of about seventeen years of age, brought a few editions of the *Kamenzer Tageblatt* [Kamenz Daily Paper]. The military bulletins gave us no encouragement whatsoever: The enemy is making no progress either in the West or the East, there is no question at any rate of panic on the German side. *Like this* it can go on for months. On the other hand: Under the date of February 16, summary courts-martial have been set up. Every weakening of resistance is punish-able by death. I link that with the desertions during our last days in Dres-den. But for how long can a despairing nation be forced to resist? —

The brief items on Dresden are shameless. Nothing but the irreplace-able works of art, not a word about the 200,000 dead. [ . . . ]

### February 26, Monday after supper

All night long and all day a most violent storm, usually with rain. Toward morning I lay awake with gloomy thoughts. I am in greater danger with every day that passes; tomorrow, two weeks will have elapsed since the catastrophe, everything is still functioning, an end to the war is not in sight neither in the East nor in the West nor internally. Hitler is supposed to have spoken again and to have predicted a turnabout in the fortunes of war for this year. How long can I remain here unmolested? — The house was astir very early, because the soldiers moved out. Remnants of a destroyed division, which is to be re-formed somewhere. I asked our man whether he knew the latest military bulletin. Reply: Yes, Breslau was holding out for the tenth day since complete encirclement, there was no mention of our section (Görlitz). — [ . . . ]

### February 27, Tuesday morning

Still the noise of rain and wind, although not quite as bad—but with the roads muddy, no weather for an offensive. — Eva is making all kinds of contingency plans for flight, we have also written a line to Annemarie. Agnes drops the letter in the mailbox in Grossbaselitz: But at every moment there is nevertheless the awful threat, that someone comes in here: "You are . . . Come with me." How do I know whom they are searching for from Dresden? Perhaps not a soul is bothered about me, perhaps I can live here quietly for many weeks [ . . . ]. It torments me literally day and night. [ . . . ]

### Afternoon

Tomorrow the pig will or was to be slaughtered; a big event, Agnes went as far as Kamenz for condiments, the children are reveling in it, Jurij would like to do the slaughtering himself, Marka: "I told the pig, tomorrow you're going to be slaughtered!" Then Agnes came home in despair, the butcher, whom it had been such an effort to obtain for tomorrow, has suddenly been called up! Now she is running from pillar to post, to find a substitute. —

I feel I am like the pig. A brief stay of execution, no more, and the deliverance on February 13 will have been for nothing. The Russians appear to have been pushed back everywhere, it's supposed to say in the newspaper, that eastern Saxony is no longer in danger. Also the newspapers are calling on all inhabitants of Dresden whose homes were not destroyed to return to the city, so order is being reestablished there. I feel I am lost. Thus far we have not thought of a way out. —

Short walk along the country road. At the milestone we came upon a large family, decent petit bourgeois people with small overloaded handcart. They asked us if there were accommodation in Piskowitz. They had been walking for a week. Bombed out in Cologne, they had gone to Muskau, which they had now left as refugees. The Russians had been thrown back 40 miles at Guben(?!), but how long would that last? "It could drive one to despair," said the oldest of them, probably the granddad, sixty-six years of age. I consoled him and thought *he* need not despair. But

*I* could. I saw the Gestapo swine, the vicious Müller, the brutal Petri, the arrogant mountain of flesh Köhler literally before my eyes and wished I had Veronal. Anything but fall into their hands!

During lunch the sound of an alert in Kamenz.

## February 28, Wednesday morning

[ . . . ]

Eva went to see the mayor early today. Harmless and overwhelmed as before, and in Dresden things still appear to be fairly chaotic. But he read Eva new orders from the Kamenz newspaper, and Agnes has just now brought the newspaper with decrees issued by Mutschmann: The rope is drawing ever tighter around my neck, there is no way out to be found. And the war is continuing downright successfully for Germany: It is standing firm everywhere, even recovering ground. After breakfast I was in the grocer's shop, got some ink—but it is hardly any better than what I have been using so far—and some toilet paper. A woman, speaking in a strong East Prussian accent, was lamenting: She was from Tilsit, she had been able to rest here for a little while, now at midday today the refugees were being moved out, all the evacuees *had* to leave, presumably for Bavaria. A young woman said: She was from Görlitz, was living with her aunt here and hoped to be able to return to Görlitz, because no doubt the Russians would be pushed back. — All of that worsens *our* position here, because in our isolation we shall inevitably be ever more conspicuous, in next to no time we shall inevitably be sent back to Dresden. [ . . . ]

## After lunch, two o'clock

Eva's steadfastness always raises my spirits. Her plan of appealing to Scherner appears to me quite fantastic, not to say impossible; but we would go there by way of Pirna in any case, and I pin something like my very last hope on Pirna. —

[ . . . ]

## March 1, Thursday morning

Extremely mild early spring weather. Lay awake for a long time this morning with a little spark of hope from yesterday. Benko Rothe, the seventeen-year-old, had been here to ask if we wanted to come over and listen to the radio at seven o'clock in the evening. A speech by Goebbels had been announced, and we said, that didn't tempt us. Whereupon he: "No, *it's the other one.*" So we went over there at seven o'clock, i.e., Eva literally led me by the hand through deep darkness. I had bad heart trouble—my cold, the dull agitation?—as I have had for much of the last few days. This time we found the Rothes, including Maria Scholze, alone; later another girl came by herself. Over and above the roaring rise and fall of interference, interrupted by individual scraps of words and melody from various countries, we could clearly hear the speech of a network addressed to the German forces, which compared the Party program with the actual conditions and achievements, then again the accusatory speech of a prisoner of war in England, calling for the pointless war to be brought to an end and the criminal regime, which had murdered "millions of Jews, Poles, etc.," to be brought down . . . Listening to these speeches I had, as before (and as with all the reports, of which I have heard so many via Winde), a sense of their utter futility. Millions have been listening to them for many months and don't lift a finger. "You are too cowardly to stop!" said one of the speakers. Then we heard, sometimes drowned out by the noise of interference: News from the front. "Marshal Stalin" announced the capture of Neustettin and Prenzlau in Pomerania; the English say that in the last 24 hours they have advanced 10 miles near Cologne, there had been heavy air raids on Berlin again. And then suddenly Goebbels's speech was there after all, the crudest antithesis to the earlier accusations, and I drew hope precisely from that. Goebbels spoke differently than usual. He largely dispensed with rhetorical tone and structure and instead let the individual words fall very slowly with a strong, even emphasis, like hammer blows, with a pause between every blow. And the content was utter despair. The language of sport even now: We are like the marathon runner. He has put more than 20 miles behind him, he has another six miles to go. He is covered in sweat, he has severe stitches, the sun is blazing, his strength is giving out, again and again he is tempted to give up. Only the greatest willpower keeps him going, drives him on, perhaps he will collapse unconscious at the winning post, but he must reach it! . . . How often has a dying man overcome death through his sheer will to live! . . . We are strained to the utmost, the terror attacks have become almost unbearable—but we must stay the course. Only a very few inferior characters think differently. We shall "coldly and calmly put a rope around the neck" of anyone who tries to sabotage us. And now the old tune, history would lose its meaning, if we were not victorious over the hordes "from central Asia." Then as practical consolation: Our enemies were "just as tired as we were." And as future prospect: We had to "economize and improvise" and "reconquer" German territories as soon as possible." — All in all: This marathon runner speech was totally despairing, and in conjunction with the English report, that the pace of the advance on Cologne had quickened, it gave me at least a little spark of hope, that the next few days could perhaps after all see a change.

Apart from that the speech was also in marked contrast to a proclamation that Hitler had read for him a few days ago—I saw it in the Kamenz newspaper yesterday—and in which he intends to achieve a reversal in the fortunes of war "this year" and rout the "Jewish-Bolshevist plague" and its Anglo-American "pimps." There is no lack of "fanatic" and "fanaticism" in either Hitler or Goebbels, and Goebbels, in the manner of the old myth of the battle against the Huns, has the dead go on fighting in the

skies and will himself rather die than see defeat. — "Let him!" cried Maria
Scholze, who repeatedly interrupted the speech loudly and vehemently.
[ . . . ]

### Falkenstein im Vogtland
### In Scherner's pharmacy
### March 7, Wednesday morning

Since we arrived here, my chances of survival have probably risen something like 50 percent. My manuscripts in Pirna, however, of which there
are no copies anymore and which include all my work and all my diaries,
I give at most a 10 percent chance.

### Now in order:

On Sunday in Piskowitz I had just finished my notes, when the mayor
came into the room and told us without much ado, well we had to leave at
two o'clock; when we objected and pleaded that we were accommodated
"privately," he replied that it was a strict order, he was sorry, but . . . If we
had friends somewhere, we did not need to join the mass transport going
to the Bayreuth area. Eva said these transports meant certain murder, the
bombers destroyed them at the railway stations and in communal quarters (as in Berlin, as in Dresden at the Technical University and at the main
railway station). Krahl, the mayor, agreed. Eva then got some food-ration
cards from him, he was friendly, he was willing to send on an entitlement
to purchase a pair of trousers, as soon as we informed him of a new address. Agnes was shattered, principally out of true affection and concern
for us, but also out of fear that now soldiers would be billeted on her.
[ . . . ] At two o'clock, during an unpleasant snowfall, Agnes and Marka—
Jurij was somehow absent—took us to a neighbor's house. A refugee
woman was already waiting there. Then a small, half-full open wagon,
preceded by an already completely full one, rolled up. On our wagon we
pushed our way between suitcases, bundles and, above all, making up an
all-too-wide middle axis, three baby carriages. Eight adults (including the
wagon man) and four children; there were also three well-wrapped infants in the baby carriages. The women—there were no men with us—
were agitated, slovenly, and coarse; it would not have been pleasant to
remain in their company. Together with the first wagon we formed just
such a trek as we had often seen. So now we ourselves were also bombed-
out and evacuated refugees. We crawled along, the journey lasted longer
than we had taken on foot from Kamenz to Piskowitz. [ . . . ] At the railway station the crush we were already familiar with. It was 4:00 P.M. Eva
bought tickets for Pirna, and soon afterward the train set off at a snail's
pace and with repeated stops. [ . . . ] Finally toward eleven in the evening
we reached Pirna. We trotted along the dark, wet street. Eva knew the way.

We had to knock for a long time at the locked door of the house and look for the bell. Then Dr. Dressel and Annemarie came downstairs at the same time, both hardly changed, both not overly surprised—I had after all recently sent Annemarie a penciled note from Piskowitz. [ . . . ] I told my story and what danger I was in (for the sake of simplicity, that I myself had already been part of the transport intended for gassing, set to leave on Friday, February 16), that I was an outlaw and had to have shelter. [ . . . ] Dressel gave us the marriage bed in his apartment for the night and slept next door on the sofa, he gave me a pair of shoes (which fit) and trousers [ . . . ], he gave Eva smoking things. Next morning Annemarie made breakfast for us—after that we starved—she took charge of my documents ("without any guarantee, of course!"), she gave me 250M. Later she came rushing after us at the railway station, because she thought we had forgotten a couple of keys, but we had deliberately left them behind, because the house to go with them is no longer standing! [ . . . ] While I was shaving Eva went to the station. One was allowed to travel 50 miles without confirmation in writing from the Party district office. For the time being we did *not* want to call on the Party, but see how far we could get toward the Scherners without its help. Eva returned: Everything seemed to be simplified; on showing the document issued in Klotzsche she had got tickets to Falkenstein im Vogtland without any problem. [ . . . ] The success with buying tickets heartened me a little; should things not come off with the Scherners—perhaps he was long dead, he had already been apoplectic enough in the thirties, and Annemarie had not heard anything from him throughout the war years either—then we would go on to Bavaria. Our goal Schweitenkirchen near Munich, where the Burkhardts, Frau Stühler's parents, live. They do not know us, we know nothing of them, it is less than a straw to a drowning man, but yet it is an extension of our vanishing line . . . [ . . . ] The train departed at 1:45 P.M. almost without any delay. [ . . . ] We set off without feeling particularly afraid of aircraft; the Americans had already completed their daily quota, the English came only at night, and we should have passed Dux and Brüx, their usual target, a long time before. But the train went ever more slowly, with ever-longer stops, and when we reached Dux, it was already completely dark. The synthetic petroleum plants were supposed to be between Dux and Brüx, the whole area as far as Komotau was a coalfield and the target of raids. Hardly had we left Brüx than there was an alert. The train stopped, went backward for a bit—into a strip of woodland, said Eva afterward—stopped again. We heard the sound of aircraft, we heard relatively close explosions, perhaps antiaircraft guns, perhaps bombs. Suddenly everything around was very bright—the brightness of flares, as I remember it from Flanders. "Damn," said Eva, "flares above us!" and crouched down between the benches, I crouched down, too, and opened my mouth. My heart beat fast, I felt death above us. Two, three explosions nearby. Someone said: That looked like three strips of burning oil, and now something is burning on the ground, about thirty yards away from us. The great brightness was still all around us. But the humming was gone, neither did we hear any more explosions. Then darkness fell again, and a little while later the train crept farther on. [ . . . ] Then at eight o'clock in the morning we were in Zwotental, a little dump among wooded hills covered in deep snow. We had thin shoes and shivered and starved. (We have done so continuously since then.) An ill-humored station official said: A train went to Falkenstein at seven in the evening. [ . . . ] As soon as we alighted we heard that a freight train [for Falkenstein] was passing through at half past ten; but the official we asked had also immediately and categorically told us that on no account would he allow us to travel on this train. [ . . . ] When the train pulled in, we ran after it through the deep snow to the baggage car. The official kept on shouting, he would not let us travel on it, we were old people, alighting without a platform was dangerous . . . I was about to give up, but Eva didn't stop. At the train itself, the engineer told the same story. [ . . . ] I was already convinced it was quite pointless—we had all the time protested, we were agile, were not stiff, had also had to clamber around on the night of terror . . . —the guard suddenly said (and the official didn't contradict him), well, now that we were here and weren't giving him any peace, we should get on. [ . . . ] We went very slowly, but nevertheless faster than on the passenger train, through the snow-covered timber and over bare hilltops [ . . . ]. There was loading and shunting at several stations. Once a quantity of cartons, Knorr soup noodles, were passed from a freight shed to the wagon by a line of men, as we had done at the factory. I wanted to join in like the soldiers, but: "The army is allowed to, but not civilians—if you ruptured yourself" . . . Twice we had to get down during the shunting, into deep snow (in our low shoes!). Once we heard an alert far away. But at one o'clock without any trouble we reached Falkenstein behind the pounding locomotive, halted pretty much out in the open, were brought to the station by the guard, and ended up in the waiting room with rice soup. An ordinary woman at our table immediately told us where the Scherners' home was. He was such a good man, unfortunately he had had a bad stroke a couple of years ago and had to go to a sanatorium, but now he was all right again. Then as we slunk toward the town with our bags—wintry scene, snow and ice—a woman called out to us, her sledge was empty, I could load our things on it. I did so and helped pull. She also immediately sang Scherner's praises: "You will be in good hands there!"

## March 8, Thursday morning

I spent all day yesterday and early this morning noting down the last entry. With some effort and a degree of pedantry, because there is so little hope that I shall survive, and even less hope that my manuscripts will survive in Pirna. The destruction continues unceasingly, day and night.

At Scherner's apartment an elderly lady, who was very kind and immediately grasped the situation, a sister of Trude Scherner, opened the door for us. We left our luggage in the corridor and went to the pharmacy. Friendly, circumspect welcome by female assistant, the boss has to sleep until three o'clock—it was half past two. We sat in the room joining private office and shop. After a while Mommy stuck her head out, recognized me—astonished greeting. Hans Scherner got up from the sofa with considerable difficulty. An excessively fat wreck, every movement ponderous, a thick cane always in his hand, usually—on the street always—guided. Yet in many respects unchanged. Extremely warm, obliging, lively, at heart evidently quite content. Yet then again not only even-tempered, but indifferent, apathetic, not granting events any very great importance. About himself: Yes, he had had a stroke in 1940, but then a cure at Bad Tölz and some other cure, and now he could manage again, even with the arm, and gout and rheumatism were evidently to blame for a great deal . . . Bubby? — But he's dead, five years ago by now, pernicious anemia, he got to forty-five. Harms? Still, in his eighties, an editorial writer, very, very Nazi—God knows, he has to earn a living—and perhaps he even believes it. Scherner himself wears the Party badge and the picture of Hitler hangs in the private office, "and you must be careful, my little assistant, a good, charming girl, but after all she has been brought up . . ." etc., etc. Our own story is heard with sympathy and revulsion, but then again also with a degree of insensibility. But perhaps the apathy is only not knowing, an inability to imagine. Because the same indifference is displayed in the face of the danger from bombs. "Down to the cellar? Never. There are barrels of gasoline down there, also the way out isn't very easy. We always sleep through it." But the apathy was again and again followed by warmth, pleasure. At the same time the business of the shop was being conducted at a furious rate. "I have been completely free of debt for five years now, I have an annual turnover of 250,000M, I have nine employees, including two certificated pharmacists, I pay 50,000M in tax and 2,000M a month in salaries." — "Of course we'll put you up, we just have to think how. At home we had to rent one room to a Berlin engineer, then Mommy's sister is there, then we're expecting Norma Schingnitz with three children. (Schingnitz? — Oh, she got a divorce from the Nazi, she is the wife of a Leipzig doctor, completely anti-Nazi) . . ." After a while—Mommy had made some tea for us—he stuck his head in again: "You will sleep here in the private office on the two settees. You have to leave it at eight o'clock in the morning; during the day you'll have the night-duty room upstairs." And so it was done, and so this is where we live and we have almost got used to it. [ . . . ] The food is the gloomiest point and the greatest disappointment here. Less than nothing remains of Scherner's former pleasure in eating and hospitality with respect to food. [ . . . ]

Again and again I go over my chances: My trail as a refugee has been covered, the constantly growing chaos is too great for any inquiries to be made about me. On the other hand: Every movement can cost me my life at any moment. And for how much longer? We do not find out very much, the Scherners are absolutely uninterested, the newspaper from Leipzig is

said to arrive irregularly, we have had no luck with the broadcasts on the
town hall square. Still: The allies are certainly in the suburbs of Cologne.
Forsechè sì, forsechè no . . .

## March 9, Friday morning after seven o'clock

Shaved and made myself ready in the laboratory-kitchen. Eva splashes on
some water in the room between shop and private office. She then packs
things up down here, we breakfast, and at eight, when Scherner appears,
we move upstairs. Already familiar.

But a new oppressive anxiety. When we come downstairs toward
evening, there is a crowd of people here. Scherner is friends with all of
them, immediately introduces us to all of them. "Herr and Frau Professor
Klemperer" here and there, on everyone's lips. For sure, friends, harmless
people. Yesterday a fat woman offered me a pair of woolen socks; I declined, but as she left she dropped two "fingers" of cheese on Eva's handbag, "so that you don't starve completely!" But all these harmless people
have relatives, friends, all of them have connections with Dresden. After
that and a thousand times worse: Yesterday we handed in our police residence registration form, signed by Scherner and the landlord's representative. Victor Klemperer, former professor from Dresden. Naturally there is
Gestapo here, too. And naturally they will keep a check on arrivals. What
do they know, for whom are they looking? Klemperer is an unusual and
well-known Jewish name. (The Bank Klemperers.) It is a horrible feeling.

## Morning nine o'clock

The registration form has not been handed in yet, has not yet been signed
by the landlord. Eva thinks the landlord (the branch manager of the Allgemeine Deutsche Credit-Anstalt Bank) is strange, she also considers him
superfluous, as we are only *visitors*, not *tenants*. She will try to prevent [his
involvement]. But after that? Not hand it in at all? Alter it to cover things
up? Everything is made infinitely more difficult by Scherner's double lack
of understanding. For one thing, he is unaware of and fails to understand
the difficulty of our position (and we dare not make him fearful and nervous); for another he is extremely hard of hearing, one has to shout at him.
We are thinking of further flight—but where to? The Burkhardts in
Schweitenkirchen do not know us, the journey there, even if we were permitted to undertake it, would mean night after night of deadly hardship—
and then we shall find everything overcrowded with the bombed out of
Munich and Nürnberg. — Remain here and lie low without registering?
For that we would have to know, how much longer? In the *Leipziger
Neueste Nachrichten* of March 7 a situation report was sufficiently somber
to give cause for hope. [ . . . ]

Scherner repeatedly comes creeping unsteadily upstairs during the
course of the day; with fur hat and cane and wearing his white coat he's

worthy of the stage. I chatted with him as best I could, but he understands Eva better than me; my still-raging cold makes me almost incomprehensible even to people with normal hearing. He has, as I assumed, reconciled himself with the Catholic Church. The Protestants: dull fellows, nothing but Kantian philosophy and the Enlightenment—"In the past I wanted to understand, explain everything with the intellect. Now I tell myself: Whatever I can understand, whatever I can explain, I don't need to know!" Thus one becomes a Catholic or a National Socialist, thus one becomes enviably happy. And thus one makes light of every calamity, of one's own crippled condition, and of the surrounding hell of murder and crime. — [ . . . ]

**Evening 7:30 P.M.**

The situation continues to be completely uncertain. Signed registration forms were returned to us by the landlord. But after consulting with Scherner we did not hand them in. Eva obtained new copies, on which we shall give Landsberg as place of residence before Piskowitz instead of Dresden—a small deception. But it remains doubtful, whether this registration will be accepted without the landlord's signature. Further: A special permit of residence has to be issued, even for visitors. I said we would get that, because he, Scherner, was letting us share his own living space. On the other hand, it is doubtful whether the employment office will not lay claim to me. We do not know whether the age limit is sixty or sixty-five. And every encounter with officialdom is simply deadly dangerous for me. — [ . . . ]

**March 10, Saturday morning nine o'clock**

I still see us outside Brüx, crouching on the train in the light of the flares, waiting for the bomb to drop. Since yesterday I feel exactly like that all the time. The registration business is still unsettled. I wrote Landsberg instead of Dresden with a very heavy heart. (It's done, anyway; everything else, even the haircut at the barber's, could also be the death of me.) The question is, whether we shall be able to hand in the form without getting the landlord's signature again; further, whether the employment office claims me. Eva will shortly go to the town hall. —
   [ . . . ]
Scherner reported yesterday: The district headquarters of the Gestapo is actually in Plauen; in Falkenstein, transferred from Silesia, there were sixty "controllers of harmful elements," presumably a group of observers, spies, informers, police hounds poking around for rebellious refugees and deserters. In Falkenstein, said Scherner, the antagonisms were very sharp, strong Nazism and strong anti-Nazism; the contest will be a bloody one. — [ . . . ]

**Afternoon about four o'clock, private office**

The registration forms were accepted; we keep one, one is kept in the town hall, one goes to the county office in Auerbach. There was no more talk of any special permit, nor of the employment office. It is possible, therefore, that the bits of paper will disappear among a thousand others, that I shall have peace for a while. [ . . . ]

**March 14, Wednesday afternoon, three o'clock**

[ . . . ]

Today, March 14, I am very depressed. I can see no end to it—Scherner's stock phrase is "in three months"; I do not see how I can remain hidden for three months. Why the torture of constant fear and constant hunger, if in the end I am going to be beaten to death anyway? —

The ADCA, the Allgemeine Deutsche Credit-Anstalt Bank, occupies the ground floor below the Scherners' private apartment and is his landlord. Thus far the local branch has been shut; the manager, also the landlord, worked in the Auerbach branch. Today Scherner told me that the Dresden ADCA is being transferred here, to Falkenstein, and will begin conducting business here as early as tomorrow or the day after. I paid the Zeughausstrasse rent to the Dresden ADCA. The people will not neccessarily know me because of that, they will know nothing of my presence here—but some other Dresden establishment can just as easily come here, and I can at any moment encounter someone from Dresden who knows me. I told Scherner about the danger I am in; at first he was skeptical, he asked quite surprised, whether the Nazis were really "such beasts." He will now be cautious no doubt, but also a little frightened. —

[ . . . ]

**March 16, Friday, 7:00 P.M., upstairs**

We return dead tired and very hungry from our walk and find Scherner up here: "I have to tell you something, you must find lodgings somewhere in a nearby village, from Monday I have to accommodate a female apprentice up here, I've been ordered to." — I cannot see things clearly yet, it is like a blow to the head, it is probably a death sentence, certainly a dreadful further worsening of our situation—even less room, even less food, although that is unimaginable, new acute danger—it is probably impossible for us, because the villages all around are completely overcrowded. I have to wait and see what else Scherner has to tell us; he said only a few words in the presence of Uhlmann, who was fetching some article from the cupboard here. Meanwhile I have been reading aloud, I shall at some point set down my notes about this afternoon, the time before the new blow.

**9:00 P.M.**

We had a first alert from 11:30 to 12:30, then, as we were walking after lunch, a second from 1:30 until almost 3, and the third sounded just now at 9 o'clock, but so far no air-raid warning.

As he left, Scherner said that the apprentice he was getting on Monday was from a strongly Nazi Dresden family, her parents, likewise bombed out, are in Rodewisch, she will perform her duties here during the day and sleep with her parents at night—the bus to Auerbach goes on to Rodewisch. Hence it was far too dangerous for us to stay here in the house, and the rest is to be discussed tomorrow morning. I see the danger multiplied a hundred times over—but we are too exhausted to think through the new state of affairs now. We want to go to bed as soon as the alert is over. (Last night was short, today's walk long, and hunger once again our constant companion.)

[ . . . ]

**March 17, Saturday, 4:00 P.M.**

[ . . . ]

When we went up to the night-duty room this morning, Scherner was just receiving his new apprentice. A very young thing, she must have been a child when war broke out. What can the name Klemperer mean to her? The bank people were already out of the country, I myself was knocked out in 1935. A Fräulein Otto; her father, said Scherner, managed nursery gardens; there is no reason either for him to be familiar with the name of Klemperer. Nevertheless we must wait and see what Scherner thinks and decides—he, after all, is hardly any less at risk than I—it was tremendously busy downstairs (the pharmacy is open today and Sunday) and we hardly set eyes on him. —

[ . . . ]

**March 18, Sunday, toward seven o'clock, downstairs**

Brief morning reflection arisen from great love. In fact, the main point after all is that for forty years we have so much loved one another and do love one another; in fact, I am not at all sure at all that all this is going to come to an end. For certain, nothingness—en tant que individual consciousness, and that is the true nothingness—is altogether probable, and anything else highly improbable. But have we not continually experienced, since 1914 and even more since 1933 and with ever greater frequency in recent weeks, the most utterly improbable, the most monstrously fantastic things? Has not what was formerly completely unimaginable to us become commonplace and a matter of course? If I have lived through the persecutions in Dresden, if I have lived through February 13 and these weeks as a refugee—why should I not just as well live (or rather: die) to find the two of us somewhere, Eva and I, with angel wings or in some other droll form? It's not only the word "impossible" that has gone out of circulation, "unimaginable" also has no validity anymore. —

[ . . . ]

### March 19, Monday, 9:30 a.m., upstairs

[ . . . ] meanwhile Eva, in whose hands I now place myself, has already approached Scherner with a finished tightrope plan—I cannot even say that the rope is stretched across the abyss, because Münchhausen-like, it is being thrown up into the air, cut behind us, thrown up again. The goal Schweitenkirchen in Bavaria, changed name, lost documents—a mixture of Karl May and Sherlock Holmes. Our proper documents, our manuscripts (Eva's compositions, my bit of diary) are to be deposited with Scherner, the Jew's star also. I shall be five years older and a secondary schoolteacher from Landsberg an der Warthe. Scherner is to give us money. — It is all absurd and terribly risky. But Eva thinks the apprentice pharmacist from Dresden, working here since this morning, seems *even more* dangerous. She is planning the departure for tomorrow morning. Officially to Aussig. [ . . . ]

### 11:30 a.m.

The secondary schoolteacher Wilhelm Klare and his wife, Ellen Veronika, both resident in Landsberg an der Warthe, from there to Strausberg, from there to Dresden, overtaken by the catastrophe, finally seeking shelter with Scherner, but his house is overcrowded, and now en route to the Burkhardt-Stühlers in Schweitenkirchen, lost their documents, when their briefcase was taken by mistake while changing trains at night — "but we still have our food-ration cards, here they are as proof of identity ([ . . . ] and so far the cards have not even been signed, fortuitously not)—moreover Herr Dr. Scherner in Falkenstein will confirm our statement, you can describe us, a sixty-nine-year-old gentleman, a lady of the same age with short hair and thick spectacles . . . ," this ménage, in every detail Eva's invention, will not go on its travels for the time being. Scherner was up here and said that the dreaded Fräulein Otto was not starting to work for him until April 1—the girl only introduced herself on the Saturday. For that length of time at least we should not tempt fate — "and by then perhaps the war will be over." Accordingly Eva is now also in favor of staying. I feel I am without a will of my own.

[ . . . ]

### March 21, Wednesday morning

During the night, from three until five, so truly for the beginning of spring, there was an air-raid warning. Out of bed for two hours; repeatedly during this time, not deep and close, but nevertheless threatening, there was the humming above us. "Formations over Thuringia approaching Saxony," the young daughter of residents of the house reported as a radio announcement. There must have been big raids again. We spent the longest time sitting in the corridor close to the door to the laboratory-kitchen with Fräulein Dumpier, who was on night duty. She cautiously began to come out of her shell. The never-ending misery—whether there was any point to continuing the war—if not, then why were people being deceived? I said, defeatists would be shot, and this was martial law after all. She gradually came out with strong doubts of National Socialist teaching. She said her grandparents could not speak German, only Lithuanian, she talked of the oppression of the Lithuanians by the Germans. It was then very easy to talk to her about the arrogance of the Germans. About the nature of propaganda, of "bringing everything down to one denominator." She turned the conversation toward the Jewish question. I sidestepped carefully. Anyone who says: *the* German, *the* Pole, *the* Jew, is always wrong. [ . . . ] But I always fell back on saying, that a regime fighting a war *could not be objective, must* suppress criticism of itself. I went through quite a few contortions. The girl's last words were amusing. She understood all of that, she believed in the rights of nations, she found the arrogance and brutalization in Germany repugnant—"it's only the Jews I hate. I think I've been influenced a bit in that." I would have liked to ask her, how many Jews she knew, but swallowed it down and merely smiled. And noted for myself, how demagogically justified National Socialism was in putting anti-Semitism at the center.

In the *Leipziger NN* of Sunday, March 18—four pages in honor of Sunday—there is a lead article signed Hs., therefore written by Harms in Berlin-Dahlem: "The Slave Traders of Yalta." Under Lincoln the North Americans freed the Negro slaves and now they want to sell the Germans into Bolshevist slavery (for rebuilding work). They want to enslave Germany and Japan, but Germany must and will defend Europe . . . Thus far it is the usual stuff here and now, and could possibly be excused an old journalist as a necessity of war, although of course Harms must know that in the National Socialist perspective "the freedom of European living space" is no more than German elbowroom, that France, England, etc., etc., etc., resist. But now: "Moscow is to be the seat of the 'Tribute Commission,' a Jew has been put in charge of it. The powers that had the last word at Yalta are thereby given due prominence: The Kremlin and World Jewry." And again later, the USA has been led astray "by its President and by the Jews, his associates, and his partners by marriage." Harms must know, he really must know, how much he is "wriggling," "reducing things to the lowest denominator," *lying*. There is no excuse for it. When I think how he supported me in 1918–1920, loved and championed me as his colleague, his political friend . . . He is a perfect representative of the decline and of the treachery of the German intelligentsia, of German morals. —

[ . . . ]

## March 22, Thursday, 7:00 P.M., private office

Quiet night without alerts, oppressive sense of hopelessness on waking. It is taking too long.

[ . . . ]

Yesterday in the late afternoon we took a walk over to the station and in the crowded waiting room drank a coffee to go with bread we had brought. [ . . . ] At the station an elderly woman from Tilsit chatted with us, confiding, embittered, and absolutely defeatist. She owned a small farm in the suburbs of the town, and she described all the animals and the produce, is worried about scattered relations in Königsberg, in Stettin, at the front. "If you've got just a little bit of intelligence, then you must know how it's going to end. But before that happens, they'll let us all get killed." — One hears very many East Prussian accents. East Prussians and Silesians form the majority of those accommodated here. Treks from Silesia— the covered wagons often camouflaged with fir twigs—are still passing through.

In the evening we went out again, for soup and potato salad at Mayer's. We heard the military bulletin, the Anglo-Americans are pushing up the Rhine step-by-step—Koblenz, Bingen taken—the Russians are also advancing step-by-step, but it is happening with nerve-racking slowness, and the final offensive itself, against the Ruhr, against Berlin is still to come. [ . . . ]

## March 23, Friday about 9:00 P.M., upstairs

[ . . . ] I have made considerable progress with Wassermann's *Maurizius* and am reading aloud a great deal. I already want to make notes on a couple of points today. "If I live and I'm healthy," Father used to say. If the bombers and the Gestapo permit, I said today. Hunger, the bombs—I would take them upon me in double measure, if only the ever-more strongly tormenting feeling of being hunted would disappear. I *have to* sit in a restaurant several times a day, and every minute is torture. (On the street, while walking and here I feel—in general, not always—a little safer.) I look at every person, trying to judge whether he is a Party official or something similar.

## Evening about ten o'clock, downstairs

Out for much of the day, although in the morning and in the late evening I read from *Maurizius* a lot. At half past eleven we went to the Lochstein. [ . . . ] Hardly had we got to the top than there was a full air-raid warning, which lasted a whole two hours, from a quarter to twelve until a quarter to two. We walked in a westerly direction for a while between wood and meadow and sat down on a bench right beside the entrance to the wood. It was the first warm spring day—still cold in our room naturally—the sun shone very pleasantly on us. After a while an elderly couple joined us and began to chat confidingly and with astonishing trustfulness.

## March 24, Saturday morning, after half past six, downstairs

Extremely tired yesterday evening. The night calm and free of bombers. — The couple [see above]—he talked, she reinforced the important points—were fleeing to the country from the terribly damaged Plauen for a couple of weeks respite, were only waiting in Falkenstein for the next train. It could not last much longer, everything would certainly be over in a few weeks, in the West and the East. They should have foreseen it. The many dead in Plauen. Of course there are bunkers only for the bigwigs. And the way the dead are treated! They are put in paper bags, which tear, head and feet stick out. But recently, when the Gestapo building was hit and there were seven Gestapo dead [ . . . ], then of course seven coffins were immediately requisitioned; yes *they* get taken care of, *they* have everything . . . Poor Plauen, 120,000 inhabitants, there used to be 130,000. We had so many foreigners, such big companies . . . The persecution of the Jews ruined it all, there were such big Jewish companies, the murder of the Jews . . . [ . . . ] But it can't last much longer now, a couple of weeks at the most . . . But how we shall suffer in the meantime! . . . What decent people Hindenburg and Ludendorff were by comparison! When they saw that the game was up, they brought it to an end and didn't let us go on being murdered. But *these people*! Just so they can rule for another couple of weeks . . . [ . . . ] and the National Socialists made so many promises, to small businessmen, to workers, everybody! [ . . . ] Well, in a couple of weeks it'll all be over. If we just manage to stay alive . . .

The man had no doubt been an inspector or some other kind of middle-ranking employee in a big Jewish textile company, a Social Democrat as well and probably an official of his party, because he knew the party's history (talked about Bebel, about the shooting of Karl Liebknecht) and used political clichés like "stronghold" (Plauen became a "stronghold" of the National Socialists). His optimism did me no end of good.

[ . . . ]

## March 27, Tuesday morning

[ . . . ]

During a late and meager supper—we can always go out only when Scherner leaves and hands us the key—we listened to the military bulletin: American tank spearheads at Hanau, that is, close to Frankfurt am Main. That is a prodigious step toward the destruction of Germany; but it does not take the weight from our soul: With this people, this desperado regime really will resist down to the last village. And where shall we go next Tuesday? Into the void, and this void is small and bombs rain down on it. With every hour that passes, I have to pull myself together again, in order to push the thought into the background and make good use of the moment. —

[ . . . ]

Last year I got a bottle of iodine preparation from the Amalien pharmacy in Dresden on Katz's prescription. On it my name was *Kleinpeter*. By altering two letters, one can very easily read *m* as *in* and *r* as *t* [ . . . ] We remembered that now.

**8:00 P.M.**

Walked all afternoon; I have enough strength left to read aloud a little, but not to write.

### March 28, Wednesday, 11:00 A.M.

At eight o'clock Scherner brought news, which he had from an English broadcast; according to it, the Anglo-Americans had already reached Würzburg and Fulda. But he didn't know exactly; when it comes to these things he's like a six-year-old child. He was up here a while ago, a visitor had written down the important points from yesterday's German military bulletin on a scrap of paper for him: Aschaffenburg and Limburg occupied by the enemy. — What affected me most were two quotes Scherner had from the English broadcast: They were in the process of cutting Bavaria off, and, above all, "This is your Easter Week, Mr. Hitler!" [ . . . ]

### March 30, Good Friday, half past twelve at night

At 23:40 we were wakened by an alert; the all clear has just sounded, after fifty minutes; the target will have been Berlin.

Today we heard the military bulletin at five, as we were drinking coffee at Pohlandt. Despite all the window dressing, it is so catastrophic that we tell ourselves again and again, it cannot go on much longer. Then again, the will to resist is whipped up by the most contemptible means, they work on people's fears far more than they appeal to fanaticism. It goes on like that from broadcast to broadcast. During lunch at Mayer's a situation report came on. The speaker formulated thus: "If we resist, we have the possibility of continuing to live; if we capitulate, we shall certainly die. Because not only the Bolshevists want to exterminate us, but the Anglo-Americans want to do so, too, behind both is the Jewish will to destroy." [ . . . ]

### March 31, Saturday evening after nine o'clock

[ . . . ]

So Eva has given notice of our departure from here on April 3. Today also the military bulletin points to the great progress of the Allies in East and West, but even today it does not hold out any prospect of an end, and the whipping up of resistance together with the wildest abuse of the enemy continues. Thus we are setting off into the void with all its dangers for weeks, perhaps months. [ . . . ]

### April 1, Easter Sunday morning, after six o'clock

[ . . . ]

Yesterday I went through a number of Velhagen & Klasing magazines from 1944. (Publisher and editor Dr. Paul Weiglin. Take note!!) In between neutral things and art there are special articles with the most vile, the most loathsome, the lowest, the most idiotic anti-Semitism. Prof. Dr. Johann Leers, who published the most poisonous articles in the Dresden newspapers, has an essay here entitled: "The Moses of the twentieth century." Id est Roosevelt. He is of Jewish descent, his wife also and with a vengeance. He was in partnership with Jewish robbers from the start, was involved in corrupt deals from the start, has no natural gifts, etc., etc. He is to blame for the war. [ . . . ]

### 6:00 P.M.

Scherner consoled me today: "You'll take part in the reconstruction, you'll be rector of the Technical University yet." I said, I believed I would play an active part, if I survived the next few weeks. *If,* that is the big question.

### 11:00 P.M.

While we were eating potato salad at Mayer's, there was a pompous report on the "Werwolves," men and girls taking up the fight against the enemy in the territory occupied in the West. They have a transmitter, Greater German broadcasting will pass on their news. With that, this franc-tireur, partisan group [ . . . ] is not only glorified, but also officially recognized. It was immediately followed by a corresponding appeal by the Party to all men and women. "The supreme test," fight to the bitter end. What will the Anglo-American answer be? Destruction of every house from which a shot has been fired, even more intense air attacks. And no one in Germany puts an end to this murderous government.

### April 2, Easter Monday morning

Storm blowing, today as yesterday. Yesterday evening, when we stepped out of Mayer's into utter darkness, the wind tore the hat Agnes had given me from my head and blew it away. No chance of finding it again, we began to grope our way back, Eva more desperate than I. Suddenly in the darkness I saw something even darker, nudged it with my foot—it really was my hat. I should very much like to take the utterly unexpectedly

rescue of the hat as an omen for the head, which goes with it. But I am
skeptical. Yesterday's Werwolves and Party pronouncements are unquestionably an expression of desperation, but equally undoubtedly they
demonstrate what *we* two can expect, if we don't make it . . . But since, if
discovered, we are lost anyway, then a little bit more or less forging of documents (thinks Eva, and I agree with her [ . . . ]) is neither here nor there.
Our plan, therefore, is this: The Kleinpeters, a married couple from Landsberg, afterward in Dresden (bombed out here), Piskowitz, Falkenstein,
have given notice of departure for Aussig, because they have acquaintances there and also because the Scherners are expecting new arrivals
(two apprentices for the pharmacy and a brother, who is a refugee). But
we shall travel southeast only as far as Falkenau and then turn toward
Schweitenkirchen by way of Regensburg. For Regensburg we give Professor Ritter's name, but do not find him there, have to go on, and for
Schweitenkirchen give the names of Frau Stühler's parents, whom we
shall probably really find there and who would certainly help us with accommodation. On the way we shall turn to the National Socialist Welfare
or the local official of the Party farming organization. Proofs of identity:
The Falkenstein registration of departure and the food-ration cards, which
are in order [ . . . ]. This afternoon I am depositing this compromising
diary, the pages covering exactly four weeks in Falkenstein, with Scherner
in a sealed envelope as a scholarly manuscript, to be retrieved, eventually
retrieved. I am aware that carrying out the plan Eva has devised depends
on Eva; she must everywhere be the one who acts and speaks, my own
presence of mind or calm or courage is not sufficient, alone I would surely
be lost. I am completely aware to what extent she is putting her own life at
risk in order to save mine. While we are depositing the diary, we are keeping—against Eva's judgment—despite the risk of our luggage being
searched, we are keeping our passports and one J star, because we shall
need this evidence to save ourselves, just as much as we need the Aryan
identity. — I now want to go on noting details, comme si de rien n'était.
[ . . . ]


**3:00 P.M.**

We bought tickets to Falkenau before lunch. The only train leaves at 4:52
in the morning and is supposed (supposed!) to be in Falkenau three hours
later. There it will be apparent, whether traveling on to Regensburg is possible without any difficulty.
    [ . . . ]
    Now Eva is going to forge the documents, with this ink and this pen.
And I am closing the Falkenstein diary, in order to take these pages to
Scherner. Coffee somewhere beforehand, to be on the safe side. —
    The dominant memory of Falkenstein will surely be the constant tor-
ment of hunger.

**April 2, evening**

Heartfelt, indeed very heartfelt leave-taking, a little in extremis, of both the Scherners. Nothing new to report. Tea (real sugar and *cakes*!). [ . . . ] Listened to the military bulletin. Three pounds of bread coupons as parting gift.

Now, after eight o'clock, we want to eat at home; I shall then read from Bergengruen, but only until the time when, from previous experience, the hour of the English is over. So until about half past nine. I hope they will not come during the night, and I hope we shall wake up in time, i.e., at three o'clock, of our own accord. We are both very, very exhausted and tired (in every respect). [ . . . ]

**Unterbernbach near Aichach**

**April 13, Friday morning, house of the Ortsbauernführer**

It looks as if, after ten very difficult days of flight, we shall come to provisional rest here. It also looks as if the war were now really and finally coming to an end. [ . . . ]

**April 15, Sunday, 1:00 P.M., at Grubers'**

**Supplementary entries**

During the night from April 2 to 3 we were without an alarm clock. We woke up at one o'clock, at two, at three. Then we got up, drank a coffee, trotted off to the railway station. The dead of night, still dark when the train left. Muldenberg, Zwotental, Falkenau—the same stretch that we had come. In *Falkenau* at half past eight. [ . . . ] Then Eva proved her worth as "tour manager": Without any difficulty and without any phone call to the authorities, she got tickets to Munich; in the town she found a handsome large hotel in which we could breakfast. [ . . . ]

In the early afternoon, now already tired, on to nearby *Eger*. There at four o'clock; for the first time I saw a partly destroyed railway station: part of the building, part of the train shed in ruins. In the course of the next few days I came to take this sight for granted; here, for the first time, it shocked me. A train to Wiesau was due to leave almost immediately, I really wanted to catch it. We reached it just as it was pulling out. It would still have been possible to get on; Eva hung back, I despaired for a moment. Eva pointed to the antiaircraft guns on the last car: "We would have been even more at risk than here." (There was an alert as we left Falkenau, there are low-flying airplanes active everywhere.) So we sat in the waiting room for a while and then from about six to seven o'clock, traveled on to *Markt-redwitz*. Terrible squeeze. A fat woman with a well-informed little boy was thrilled by the deeds of the Werwolves. They had shot thirty horses some-

where, "and killed three officers," added the boy. The woman sitting beside them asked doubtfully whether this would not bring harm to other
civilians. The Nazi cow said nothing.

We went the whole length of the place—a massive town hall building—
looking in vain for accommodation; every hotel refused. Back to the station as darkness fell. Opposite, in the gatehouse of a public building, the
National Socialist Welfare [NSV]. Lots of people there, begging for lodgings like us. Very nice girls helping out, trying to do their best. (As the
NSV everywhere tried to do what it could, but was also everywhere
largely helpless.) We got soup. Then in utter darkness we were led down
the street and through a park to the Josefa convent. An infernal hall. Many
beds, one above the other. Crying children, drying diapers, the air blazing
hot and quite suffocating, dirty, cursing women. One complained her infant was starving, there was milk up to only six months! Another: It
wasn't true that she had scabies, it was only a rash. At that, we said we
preferred a night in the station waiting room. So back there. With many
people in the ticket and luggage hall. At the Josefa convent we had heard
that the previous day's refugee train had been attacked: five dead, a number of wounded. Now the light suddenly went out, no warning. Meanwhile the humming could already be heard in the air. "Where is there a
bunker?" No one replied, no one knew. We crouched down close to pillars
and waited—helpless. A large formation appeared to be flying over the
town. After a while it became quiet. That was at about midnight. [ . . . ]

On the morning of the fourth we were "refreshed" with coffee at the
NSV, and at half past seven there was a train for Regensburg, which left
late and was held up frequently on the way. I was very preoccupied; every
time we stopped, I thought, now there's going to be a raid. I spent the
whole time standing in the corridor. [ . . . ] Two people were interesting: A
very young, boyish waiter, who had to report for call-up and displayed
not the least enthusiasm; and a German from Slovakia conscripted into the
German army, who spoke obliquely but very bitterly about the propaganda of the Nazi Party, which had first created the divisions and tensions
within Czechoslovakia and between Germans and Czechs. Now the Slo-
vaks were completely anti-German and the Germans in Slovakia—he
himself had sworn three military oaths in succession, had had to serve in
three different armies in succession, as a Czech, as a Slovak, as a German—the Germans in Slovakia had been utterly led astray and had no future.

We pulled into Regensburg at half past one. The constant increase in the
degree of misery means that I can no longer quite do justice to the early
stages of the journey. The first waiting-room night in Marktredwitz had
made a great impression on me because of the crowding together and the
different groups mixed up on the floor. Soldiers, civilians, men, women,
children, blankets, suitcases, kit bags, knapsacks, legs, heads jumbled up,
the picturesque centerpiece a girl and a young soldier sleeping gently
shoulder to shoulder. Such sights have now become so commonplace for

me that I forgot this picture of the first night. It occurs to me only now because Eger railway station was nothing compared to Regensburg railway station (and this in turn was a harmless sight compared to Munich). Craters, ruined buildings, destroyed railway trucks and carriages, destroyed ships, which had been run aground, a ship's bow just like that, the railway station itself largely a ruin. Here an alert during the third plate of NSV soup. Possible to continue our journey at 5:45 P.M. To a nearby hotel. An air-raid warning while drinking the first cup of coffee. Spacious, well-equipped cellar. A dozen people. The landlord reports the situation minute by minute. After a while the preliminary all clear. We drink our second coffee upstairs. Radio (without another siren) repeats three times: extreme danger from low-level attack. No one in the street pays any attention. Finally we don't either. Walk through the city. [ . . . ]

Back to the railway station—wretched food during these last days, rarely anything but dry bread or an NSV soup—and a much-delayed start to the journey, as we hoped, to Munich. Instead, at Landshut, at about nine o'clock in the evening, at any rate in complete darkness, we were told: alight, line destroyed, two and a half miles on foot to Altdorf, the next station. That was probably the greatest hardship of these days (although later we had to cover longer distances on a march with baggage). Knapsack and a heavy holdall in each hand. On no account could we lose contact with the hurrying group of passengers. The way was extremely bad, more a raised rough path over wet terrain, in which, one after another, huge water-filled craters shone on either side. Stumbling, going over on one's ankle, slipping, constantly in danger of falling into a crater. Sweating, pains in shoulders and arms, panting forward. From time to time destroyed buildings, mostly only the craters in the ground. What can have occasioned such bombardment here? After a while the group had evidently lost its way, we went through ever more waterlogged fields, and then there was a stream, fairly wide, and only a few beams sunk in the water remaining of a bridge. We had to get across; the water went over our ankles, filled our shoes. After that the ground was drier, and now in the darkness we saw a train in front of us. We clambered on. Somewhere a flashlight, a match, a cigarette lit up always only for seconds. We were in a very large second-class compartment with a lot of space between the benches. All only indistinctly recognizable. We found places on the upholstered seats, could put down our baggage in front of us. Conversations went back and forth in the darkness. A young man beside me: My father still believed in victory, never listened to me. But now even he doesn't believe anymore . . . Bolshevism and international Jewry are the victors . . . A young woman sitting same distance away: She still believed in victory, she trusted in the Führer, her husband was fighting in Breslau, and she believed . . . the train got going at about eleven o'clock; I dozed a little, the wet shoes remained on my feet, a heavy cold, from which I am still suffering, was the result. Eva bore the wet feet, but then caught my cold and turned it into a cough . . . At about four o'clock we were again told to change, in the dark, over tracks, no platform, an electric station light dazzled us, more confusing than illuminating. That was *Moosach*. Standing on the crowded platform of a carriage, we finally pulled into Munich at 4:45 A.M.

So on Thursday, April 5, we were in *Munich* for the first time. The station building, the huge roofs of the station hall fantastically weirdly ruined. At a great depth beneath it, giving a feeling of safety, an immense bunker, whole catacombs divided into a wide lengthwise corridor with big side rooms, subterranean waiting rooms, NSV post, first-aid post, toilets, washrooms. All of it overcrowded with people lying, sitting; staff, railway police often very rough: "Wake up! Legs down! Other people want to sit, too . . . [ . . . ] You're here for the fourth day; if I catch you again, you're coming with me! . . ." The Marktredwitz scene magnified and varied fifty times over. We were there three times. Eva lay on her scabby fur coat spread out on the bare floor of the cooler outside passageway, surrounded by Italians and Slavs (who were restricted to the outer rooms), I sat in the rooms, where it was crowded, stuffy, smelly, but warm. Naturally, for me, sleep was limited to a very few hours. In a room at the very back, one got coffee and bread from the NSV in the morning, soup, very thin soup, and bread at midday and evening. Everything was given out in a very friendly manner, but a record was kept of every ration, and there was unpleasant embarrassment the third time we appeared: "Oh, you're still here?!" A fairly depressing business and yet also no more than a prelude to our experiences in Aichach and Inchenhofen. But now I have run ahead and summarized.

On Thursday, April 5, then, we waited in the bunker until morning. We learned that in the afternoon (4:00 P.M.) we could go on to Pfaffenhofen by way of Dachau. From there—the bus service had been suspended—the milk truck would take us to Schweitenkirchen. The square at the railway station was terribly destroyed. Messina. The more we got to see of *Munich*, the more evident was the dreadful destruction. Whole fields of rubble and great buildings and palazzi in ruins, tumbledown, partly collapsed, badly damaged, boarded-up rows of houses; houses that one can enter, but inside floor after floor is shattered and uninhabitable. The landmark church of the city is still standing, but one tower is without a roof and the cathedral itself smashed, the university is partly ruined, the city gates damaged. Yet it was precisely because of the damage and destruction that I realized (especially on the street leading to the Maximilianeum) what a wealth of massive Italianate and neoclassical buildings there are in Munich. [ . . . ] The whole city is interspersed with classical and Renaissance styles, the whole city has something grandiose and powerfully Roman about it—Dresden by comparison is no more than a little rococo jewel box, a most precious one indeed, but nevertheless a toy box, or rather: it was, because while Munich can perhaps be restored, Dresden is probably totally destroyed.

Extraordinary how in Munich, this city of ruins, life is already "getting going" again. There is no sign of the small-town sleepiness of the place *be-*

*fore* 1914. Shops in half-destroyed buildings, in—Messina!—new wooden huts. Tracks laid *on* the streets, little locomotives, giving off black clouds, pull trains of wagons, each truck converted into a primitive carriage by means of box boards, all the seats packed, also clusters of people hanging between and on the wagons. (Marseilles to the nth degree!) In the city center there are even one or two proper tram lines. Noticeable is the almost complete absence of craters in the streets, noticeable how few traces of fire there are; they must have aimed very well and used only high-explosive bombs, no phosphorus. We said to each other: a dreadfully damaged city, but, unlike Dresden, one that was still alive; but we also said to each other: here there is still much damage to be done; and since then Munich has been repeatedly bombed.

I have summarized the impression made by both stays. On the Thursday we did not see very much of the center, we first of all breakfasted in a hotel close to the station, were then caught by an air-raid warning and directed to the "Party bunker." These are deep catacombs, similar to those of the station bunker, below the open ground somewhere by, between, or behind the museums (I mean the Pinakotheks and the Glyptothek); I was unable to get an idea of which of the museum buildings was still standing, to what extent the open ground was originally lawn, to what extent cleared ruins; and whether they are enlarging the big bunker here, or at what else they are working. Hundreds of people poured in, we were crowded together. News from the radio was relayed every couple of minutes. After less than half an hour the preliminary all clear was announced. Hardly outside, we heard the humming of low-flying airplanes, also the rattle of a machine-gun salvo and with very many other people hurried back into the bunker. A little later the all clear proper was announced—although that is not to be relied on either. When the air-raid warning began, we had just been promised soup in a small public house; now we had strayed far from there, but instead found a proper big restaurant. Only a few were still in business, and mealtimes are extremely restricted everywhere. But compared to Falkenstein there was nevertheless a certain abundance. Above all one gets—everywhere in blessed Bavaria—potatoes *without* coupons. One also has to hand over fewer fat coupons and receives more generous portions. That is, of course, true of Pfaffenhofen and of Aichach to an even greater degree than of Munich; also, prices are rather high in Munich, very low in the small towns. Then in the villages the extremes meet. I.e., everything is evidently there in plenty, but while some good-naturedly share a part of their astonishing riches, milk, bread, spaghetti, sausage, macaroni, semolina (without ration cards and prepared with egg), others hard-heartedly keep everything back, reckon that a famine is coming, and regard the countless refugees flooding across the country [ . . . ] as a swarm of locusts without rights.

During lunch we shared our table with a married couple from Berlin. He said: People were saying Hitler had shot himself, she: They were saying, the "turning point," the new weapon, the new offensive, was coming

in four days. Taken to an extreme, those were the two sides of the vox populi, which one encounters everywhere. Or more exactly: encountered. Because in the last few days the final victory optimism has almost died away
(at least among the people around us), and the defeatist remarks are as difficult to count and tell apart as the air-raid warnings: Everywhere one
hears sirens, low-flying aircraft, everywhere the distant and no longer so
distant rumble of the front, everywhere the sigh: "If only the Americans
come quickly!" — So in the late afternoon of April 5 we traveled to Dachau
and from there to Pfaffenhofen on another train. [ . . . ]

Very early on Friday, April 6, we walked down and into Pfaffenhofen
from the railway station, breakfasted at Bräuhaus Müller, also ate there at
midday, strolled around the place a little. The milk truck was due to leave
at one. We have meanwhile discovered this institution to be a general one
in Upper Bavaria. Somewhere in each district there is a central dairy, every
day the peasants have to supply the bulk of their milk to it (but naturally
keep back enough for themselves—and from the perspective of the towns-
man, not to say Saxon, it's half Canaan—in part openly because they are
"self-sufficient," in part illegally), and get back butter, "skimmed" milk,
etc. The dairy vehicles convey passengers from village to village free of
charge, one clambers up with difficulty, one crouches on the massive milk
cans, one gets down when the cans are loaded and unloaded at the milk
platforms of the various places; these stages or platforms in front of large
farms now constitute a kind of station; the timetable is only very approxi-
mate—but one also has to wait hours for the train. I have got to know these
particulars only here in Unterbernbach. In Pfaffenhofen we waited in front
of the post office for a long time. The van arrived toward two o'clock; it did
not go directly to Schweitenkirchen, which is five and a half miles east of
Pfaffenhofen, but made a long detour to the north by way of the village of
Geisenhaus, a distance of about twelve and a half miles. [ . . . ]

In Schweitenkirchen we quickly found the Burkhardts by asking the
way. A small house, rented for six years (and probably rented only in
part). Modest petit bourgeois people; the husband was a typesetter and
proofreader with Bruckmann in Munich for forty years, then he retired at
sixty-five and yearned for rural peace. The wife not much younger and
with very bad heart trouble. Staying with them a married daughter,
bombed out in Munich, younger than her sister Lisl Stühler, a little disfig-
ured by missing front teeth, which are irreplaceable at present, but pleasant looking. All three people displayed an unsurpassable, charming, most
agreeable warmth when we introduced ourselves as Lisl Stühler's neighbors—they had heard of us.

We learned immediately: Lisl Stühler had been there for several weeks
with Bernhard, but then left again, because she was unable to continue
there without food coupons. Her plans were unclear, her parents did not
know and were very worried. She had wanted to go back to Dresden or
perhaps go to Württemberg, she had somewhere obtained coupons for
herself and the boy, she had wanted to return to her parents, who were

keeping an otherwise requisitioned room free for her. We also learned immediately that the Burkhardts could *not* take us in; they were afraid of a Nazi in the same house, they were afraid that someone knew about Bernhard Stühler's mixed blood, they were afraid of us as Lisl Stühler's neighbors, they had promised to keep the spare room for Lisl Stühler herself.

But we got such a good rest, we could catch our breath and pluck up courage. I was able to dry shoes and socks and sit back in warm socks and slippers, we got coffee, we got a very plentiful warm supper, we were put up for the night, and slept together on a very wide settee; the next morning I was able to shave, there was breakfast as well—and with all of that they were friendly to us, and in the evening we listened together to the English broadcast and drew hope from the advance of the Anglo-Americans.

We decided to return to Munich and to call on Vossler; we had already found out at the university that he was still living in the Maximilianeum. The attendant said he had seen the Councillor and his wife on the street only recently. If Vossler did not know what to do, then we would turn to a [welfare] organization, after all there was nothing wrong with our documents. (Only we would have to use our proper names, since we would of course have to present the certificate attesting we had been bombed out. Little risk at such a distance and in this chaos. — We had registered in Falkenstein under our own names. Then because it was Easter and because of an air-raid warning we had been unable to obtain the notice of departure.)

We had slept well, eaten well, had washed—we had got our courage up. On Saturday, April 7, after breakfast and after lengthy conversation, Herr Burkhardt led us through the village to the entry and exit point of the Munich (25 miles)–Nürnberg (69 miles) autobahn a mile away. Military vehicles and trucks were always passing, they would certainly give us a lift. [ . . . ] There was a strong, bitingly cold wind blowing, Father Burkhardt complained about his coat being too light and about "stomach" trouble, so we took our leave of him and waited alone. And cars did come, three or four, but they paid no attention to our signals. Chilled to the bone ourselves, we gave up and began our march with baggage to Pfaffenhofen, which was another 4½ miles from there. For a while we had to fight our way along the open road, then we entered tall woods. Right at the edge there was a military vehicle, the driver was repairing it, a soldier was watching. Could they give us a lift? — The repair would take hours, we'd be in Pfaffenhofen more quickly on foot. Hardly had we gone any farther, than the soldier caught up with us, as a matter of course took one of my bags and chatted artlessly the whole way. He had only one hand. Lost the other in Normandy: Taken prisoner there, shipped to the USA, and then exchanged. He was eighteen, big and strong, from the Waterkant, the North Sea coast, but he liked it here, he had found a girl here. Only—did he have any future at all? He was in the SS and what would happen to the SS, if . . . But the Führer didn't deserve to be defeated, he had had such good intentions and organized everything so well. And he would not be defeated either. The defeats so far had been the result of treachery, there had been treachery long before July 20, and now, on the Führer's birthday, on April 20, our new offensive would begin and liberate the East. He did not seem quite certain of that, however, and was glad to be consoled by me: As a bricklayer he would always earn a living, and he would surely be able to work with one hand and a prosthesis. I asked him what it had been like in America. "Good," he could not deny it, good rations, decent treatment under German officers . . . But of course the Americans had done that only for propaganda reasons, so that those exchanged would afterward say good things about the USA when they got home. So the lad got natural and reasonable things and what had been drummed into him all jumbled up.

[ . . . ]

We soon reached Pfaffenhofen; at the edge of the town he turned away toward his billet. His last word: If things went really badly, then he would volunteer for the front again. I think, that is the very last pro-Nazi and bellicose voice that I have heard. From that point on, there are only ever more frequent defeatist remarks, sometimes disguised, sometimes openly expressed, until finally, they can no more be kept count of than the air-raid warnings. With very rare, purely official exceptions, one also no longer hears "Heil Hitler." Everyone says, already said in Munich, "Grüss Gott" [Good day] and "Auf Wiedersehen" [Good-bye].

Hardly had we entered Pfaffenhofen, at about 12:30, than there was an alert; hardly had we sat down to eat in Bräuhaus Müller on the big square, than there was a warning, and we had to go down to the spacious cellar. Conversation with one of those present: "How on earth will the war end?" Smirking reply: "I can't tell you that—silence is golden—one never knows whom one is talking to." As I said: There are too many such remarks to note down any more. Refugees, with whom one is together for a few minutes, on the milk truck to Schweitenkirchen, on a railway platform . . . talk bitterly, accusingly, are waiting for the end—and the peasants most of all! When can the Americans get here . . . if only they were here . . . Dig a hole for a bazooka? We'll take a towel with us, so we can surrender right away . . . It's madness, that *we* are supposed to fight! But *he* has every general and every mayor who doesn't go on fighting shot . . . Another one to two weeks, no more, then they'll be here . . . My lieutenant says, the new offensive is coming on the twentieth and then the East will be free in four weeks, but I don't believe it . . . The new weapon? We've heard that for two years now . . . If only they were already here, the Americans . . . Etc., etc., as unceasing as the warnings and the airplanes.

We ate at Müller's, got a cup of coffee (only *one*) at the café next door, then got the train to Dachau. We were supposed to go on from there at 6:00 P.M., but the train was stormed by the crowd and so packed, that we had to wait for the next one an hour later. It was dark by the time we arrived in *Munich* and sought out the already familiar bunker. I have already described the overcrowding, the thin NSV soup, the rough tone of the railway police. I appealed to a first-aid man and was rewarded with a stretcher on which Eva could lie on this second night in Munich.

[ ... ]

On Sunday, April 8, in Munich the cleaners and guards woke us after five o'clock, we again went to the NSV room for coffee, then sought out an early opening hotel (Excelsior) in a heavily damaged building close to the station, sat there quietly for a while over breakfast. Then the trip out to Vossler. [ ... ] Apart from a tiny stretch by tram, we wandered through the city on foot, there was an alert almost the whole way. We arrived at the rear of the Maximilianeum, where it is surrounded by gardens. Painted on the wall in large letters: To the Academy. To Vossler. To the library. A public air-raid shelter. We agreed: Eva would wait for me in the gardens; if there was an air-raid warning, she would go down to the shelter. At that very moment, theatrically, the air-raid warning sounded. Very many people suddenly appeared and flooded into the shelter, the two of us along with them. Several rooms; I looked around for Vossler, in vain. Radio announcements of the position of the aircraft formations were constantly relayed. From time to time a man with an armband emerged from the crowd. After a while I approached him to ask whether there was a separate cellar for people living in the house, I had been about to call on Vossler. — "There's the Councillor's wife now." An imposing blonde woman, in her early fifties, at once dignified and pleasant in appearance. I introduced myself to her as Vossler's oldest student; it afterward turned out, that she had not understood my name, nevertheless she took me upstairs immediately. A vast, elegant room, but evidently everything in one: study, dining room, drawing room. Not an official apartment, despite Academy and library, but given to Vossler privately. He stood in the middle of the room, at first sight little changed—later, however, I noticed the signs of age. The face with the very small, gray mustache was fairly gaunt, often the posture of someone hard of hearing who would like to disguise his ailment, for all his liveliness distinctly fatigued after a while. He received me very warmly: "We have often talked about you, we thought you were in America long ago!" The moment Frau Vossler understood my name, there was no holding her, Eva must come up, she would simply call out her name downstairs. I described Eva: Fur with burn marks, thick spectacles, and after a few minutes both ladies were upstairs. We were kept there for a princely peacetime lunch. The Vosslers still have a maid, still have "sources": we got soup, a peacetime-sized schnitzel with young spinach and fried potatoes, a dessert, Eva got two cigarettes, I got a cigar, which I put away "for the evening" and so saved for Eva. As we ate there was no end to questions and talking. Shoptalk is nice, shop gossip even nicer. Pfandl has died, Hämel bombed out, Gelzer killed in a terror attack on Jena, Curtius has devoted himself entirely to Low Latin, Lerch, whose eldest son has fallen, is staying "somewhere in the Riesengebirge hills." She had never forgiven him his behavior to Sonja, said Frau Vossler, and Vossler and I also pronounced negatively on Lerch's character. Rohlfs, who attacked Vossler and Lerch and myself so fiercely and unfairly, succeeded Vossler in Munich in 1938 and is still his enemy, at the same time an enthusiastic Nazi and race man. "In the department he displays his attacks on me and not my replies," said Vossler. And she: "My husband is completely isolated." I observed in him a degree of vain pride in his (former) successes. "That is the man who made me an honorary doctor," he said of me to his wife. I: "It will not have been the only Dr. h.c."—"Coimbra and Madrid have been added."

[ . . . ]

I told him and his wife of my fate as a Jew and of the risks of my flight. "For me you are Aryan, I know nothing else." Both talked about Cossmann, the editor of the *Süddeutsche Monatshefte*, the nationalist of the First World War. Frau Vossler [ . . . ] was his secretary, had got to know Vossler, the widower, then. Cossmann, a very devout Catholic—he prayed for Hitler, because even Hitler had an immortal soul—was a full Jew and wore the star, was in prison for a year, died in Theresienstadt in his seventies. [ . . . ]

A couple of times the conversation went beyond talk about people. [ . . . ] For all that, however, the Vosslers could give us no advice as far as accommodation was concerned. Frau Vossler offered only to put us up for the night, if we did not find quarters anywhere else, we had to promise her to come back, if no hotel or room could be found. But Vossler himself was very exhausted, even a little indifferent, and immediately took leave of us with a degree of finality. Frau Vossler accompanied us, first of all showing us the view of the city (I think the Maximilianstrasse) from one of the big balconies. The passageway leading to it was damaged, the top floor of the Maximilianeum had been hit and had burned out. Then Frau Vossler guided us to nearby Thierschstrasse, where the Resettlement Office is situated, but which was closed on a Sunday.

[ . . . ]

We walked back into town. [ . . . ] We looked for accommodation, first in hotels—in vain—then in pensions that had been mentioned to us or which we found ourselves. They were all in such dreadfully shattered, partly collapsed, fire-damaged buildings that we became quite alarmed. Frequently no one opened up when we rang. Or we were told the rooms were uninhabitable. [ . . . ] After a while the ruined buildings made us feel quite fearful, and after supper in the Roter Hahn [ . . . ] we went back, for the third time, to the station bunker. At the NSV they said: "Are you still here, people?" and there was only the bare floor for Eva to sleep on. Nevertheless we were glad to be there, because at one o'clock at night there was an air-raid warning, many people poured in, and bombs fell somewhere outside. It would have been no pleasure in one of the pensions.

On Monday, April 9, we already felt so much at home in this situation that I hardly registered life in the bunker and among the ruins as anything out of the ordinary anymore. We again breakfasted in the Excelsior, and as people with a knowledge of the place, old-established habitués, as it were, we were joined by an interesting young couple. They were from Graz, the man, a minor civil servant, was on his way to Berlin to claim his overdue salary; where they were going to come to (momentary) rest or be "redeployed," they did not know. It was amusing to observe how isolated and crumbling scraps of the LTI, which had been dutifully learned by heart, still floated around like islands in the man's disillusioned and embittered head. The bigwigs had fled Graz by car, and the ordinary people had to get out as best they could. And it was ordinary people once again who were left to face the music: the distress, the war . . . But, of course, it would still turn out well. The Führer had said nothing was impossible, and then: We were "Europe's rampart against Bolshevism." We let the couple go on talking and took a friendly leave of them; they will certainly very quickly and very willingly find their way into the Fourth Reich. Now (to the accompaniment of repeated alerts) there were wearying errands, which took us through Munich. First to the Resettlement Office. While Eva was upstairs, I took a look at the River Isar. Eva very soon returned with an allocation to Aichach. Neither of us had ever heard the name before and did not know where the place was. Then back to the railway station; there was annoyance and loss of time because of queuing at various counters. [ . . . ] After dealing with preparations for the journey we had to fetch ration cards at the Food Office, which was in Sparkassenstrasse right in the center of the city. We wearisomely found our way by asking, and we spent an excessively long time at the ration-card section.

[ . . . ]

At 3:00 P.M. out of breath to Dachau. Arriving there at four, we were told that we could probably reach Ingolstadt by late evening, but the waiting room there had been destroyed in the last air raid; it was better if we stayed in Dachau, perhaps there was even accommodation in the town. The town was some distance from the railway station, haphazardly scattered around the not very high, but steep, blocklike and flat-topped hill, which is crowned by the castle. [ . . . ] A few yards below the castle, but still high up on the hill, on the market place of Upper Dachau, so to speak, there is situated, like a massive box, the inn, presumably also an independent brewery, of Aloys Zwicknagel. There, during yet another alert, we ate a good evening meal—naturally there was no accommodation—and after the all clear we resignedly undertook our march with baggage back to the station and once more spent the night in a waiting room, without a bed and without protection against each and every air raid. Naturally also always unwashed.

On Tuesday, April 10, we were supposed to travel on to Ingolstadt at five o'clock in the morning, there we would get a connection to Aichach, by the afternoon we would have reached our goal. We did indeed get on the waiting train at about five and found good seats, but we sat there for almost four hours before the train set off. While we were waiting and during the journey there was a constant alternation of alert and all clear. [ . . . ]

We arrived in *Ingolstadt* at half past eleven, we were supposed to go on to Aichach. Contrary to the information at Dachau, the station was quite undamaged, we even got a good lunch in the restaurant. And another good thing: A painful abscess had formed close to the thumbnail of my right hand; in a little Red Cross room a friendly nurse provided relief with some antiseptic cream and a protective bandage. I was walking content-edly down the platform back to the restaurant when I heard a loud whistling sound above me; I leaped into the dining room and knelt beside a pillar just as there was a bang and panes of glass rattled; half underneath me crouched a very young girl, whimpering, "Oh God! Oh God!"; all around people were kneeling on the floor, chairs had been knocked over; many people ran to the door, others shouted: "Stay inside! Stay inside!" All that in a matter of seconds. I immediately said to myself: a single low-flying airplane. In fact the bomb it dropped had hit a lavatory close to the dining room. Things became a little more calm, I hurried over to our table in the middle of the room; Eva sat there unhurt (like everyone else); she had taken cover under the table, "there was a captain under the next table, we crawled out again at the same time." To get over the shock we ordered another coffee, I made a note on a scrap of paper; then we were told a for-mation was now approaching, we should go down to the cellar. Beneath the station hill, it was fairly deep and inspired confidence, except too small and packed full. I had to leave our bags by the steps in the outer room and I positioned myself close to it, while Eva stood somewhat far-ther inside. People stood squeezed up against one another. A loud bang, chalk dust trickled into one's eyes, the light went out, my hat had disap-peared. Shouting, calls to "Stay calm!," many voices: "My hat!" — "My cap!" — "Has no one got a flashlight?" — "There's someone injured in the outer room!" . . . Meanwhile there was the beam of a flashlight here and there, hats were found, Eva called from faraway: "Victor, I've got your hat!" All of that is a distraction, there must meanwhile have been repeated explosions, even if not quite so close—I don't know. People poured up the stairs, it was over; they quickly ran down again: It was continuing. A while later Eva and I found each other, and we risked going upstairs. [ . . . ] Things did not look too bad—and we heard later, as we took shelter from low-flying airplanes in a house by the road, that there had been only a few injured, and no dead—but now the railway line was destroyed, and we had to undertake a 5½-mile march with baggage to the next station at Zuchering. En route, as already noted, we took shelter from low-flying air-craft for the first time, something that since then has become a daily habit for us. For a while we walked along with a soldier; the man, a complete exception here, still had hopes of April 20. (Today is the nineteenth, Rus-sians and Anglo-Americans are simultaneously closing in on Berlin; I, too, am now almost superstitiously on edge, awaiting what this April 20 will bring, on the German and on the enemy side.)

The hike was arduous and dreary. It was not the typical plain of Upper Bavaria, which we have now been daily and thoroughly getting to know and like for the past week, apart from its dusty, treeless and shadowless grand'routes. Typical of this high plain is its green, rolling terrain, in which again and again there are strips of woodland, often like backdrops, so that one gets a glimpse of more broad meadows and more woodland backdrops or islands beyond. And then far away in the distance, forest-dark or distant-blue, there are real mountain ranges on the horizon. And everywhere, often quite close together, there are villages, each with its own church [ . . . ] and each church has its tower, the simple onion dome, or the one with a radish stuck on, or the pointed tower, or the stepped-gable tower, and sometimes there is a stork's nest loosely attached to the far end of the church roof, and once I even saw a stork standing on it; and fairly often the more imposing tower of a large, yellow, baroque monastery church also appears, usually made of stacked up filing boxes and with a helmet on top. But on the stretch between Ingolstadt and Zuchering all that is missing. Nothing but meadow and arable land, as flat as a pancake, not rolling at all, no woodland at all; it might just as well be a stretch of country somewhere in the province of Posen. "It's there, that's all."

We arrived in the village of *Zuchering* very late in the afternoon, very hungry, very tired. A little outside it there had been a stream with willows along the bank, we had briefly rested there, ducked into the bushes because of a low-flying airplane. Close to us a soldier in a brown uniform had been standing guard at a little bridge. When we asked a question he shook his head with a friendly smile. Afterward we saw several more of these foreigners, and learned that they were part of a Hungarian company. But there were also German soldiers in the village. I was standing in front of a little shop, in which Eva had got nothing to buy, and telling one of them about our fate, and that we were starving, and that Eva was just now in the butcher's shop opposite, making a final attempt to obtain something for us. At that moment the shopkeeper leaned out of her parlor window and said: "If you don't get anything, I'll make you a soup. You can rest in the 'summerhouse,' your train doesn't leave until ten in the evening anyway." Eva came back, having met with no success, and we were led to the summerhouse at the back and a good soup was put in front of us. (Afterward the woman refused any payment.) The soldier mentioned above, billeted here, a Württemberger by his accent, no longer young and of good family, spoke very openly about the war, which was unquestionably lost, about the senseless murder of the continuing fighting, about Hitler's "megalomania." Then he disappeared and brought us a large piece of army bread and a quarter pound of butter as a present. We should just take it, when more than a hundred men were being supplied with rations—he was evidently mess sergeant—there was always something left over. We then slowly walked the last part of the way up to the station. Scattered groups, soldiers and civilians were lying in the meadow around the little station. We did likewise until it became too cool and damp. It was completely dark when the train arrived, and it was overcrowded. There was a crush, anger, literally a night battle. We forced our way into a compartment, were at first made to feel very unwelcome by the military occupants, angrily rebutted a remark that civilians were still traveling for pleasure, stood and crouched very unhappily. But gradually the situation calmed down. We arrived in *Aichach* at half past one in the morning. This now became the seventh and final waiting room or train night of our days of flight, but our odyssey was not yet over.

The next morning, Wednesday, April 11, Aichach greeted us with three cups of coffee each in the station restaurant. That was a beneficent surprise. We then walked into the town itself, and Eva negotiated in the county office. We have since been in Aichach another three times and my impression is always the same. I can distinguish it from Falkenau and Pfaffenhofen almost solely in terms of size—the large small town, the smaller small town, the very small small town. There is always a ring of almost villagelike houses and streets around an elongated patrician and historic main square. Yesterday (April 18) I made a particular effort to grasp the specific character of Aichach. Its long main square is divided in the middle into two squares at an obtuse angle to one another by a big baroque assembly house that leaves a road free to right and left. The dominating church is missing here, there is only a modest ecclesiastical building on one long side; a massive gate with a massive pyramid tower bears a large colorful inscription that tells of battles in the Thirty Years' War. Close to the main square there is a smaller three-cornered square, adjoined on one side by the rear of the main church and its big yellow tower. (It has a stork's nest.) Beside the church is the county office, with which, much more than we would like, much much more! we are very familiar. On the main square there are three big restaurants, of which two are also breweries, and a Café Mayr [ . . . ]. We have already eaten well a couple of times in the Ziegler Inn—but sometimes school classes are conducted in its dining room, then we have to go to the Stieglerbräu. Beer is served only on certain days, coffee almost always, often also lemonade—but only here in town; the village inns decline to serve.

Eva returned with this information: Munich had referred us to Aichach by mistake, the district was already closed to refugees; but since we were here, they would look after us, only we must immediately continue, on foot, to Inchenhofen with a special letter of recommendation. Inchenhofen is a small market town 4½ miles northwest of Aichach. Here the district is not as dreary as near Zuchering, but simply the typical Upper Bavarian landscape. The same is true of Unterbernbach, in which we have now come to rest—rest for those who have become modest.

We reached Inchenhofen toward seven o'clock in the evening very tired and flushed. As a place with a market it occupies a curious position between village and town. Nothing but village houses [ . . . ], nothing but village dirt roads, but several proper streets, long and with houses built close together, the narrow gable ends of the houses facing the street. The whole place high up, on the ridge itself the main square with the yellow church, whose narrow, helmeted tower (the ugly "gooseneck," says Eva) dominates the whole district and thus is also visible from Unterbernbach. Reading my scraps of notes I find that there was a constant alert during the walk to Inchenhofen, that we heard bombs falling, that someone expressed the wish "If only they would come, the Americans!" During the last week (today is April 19) all of it, the constant alert, the formations and individual fighters flying over us, the openly expressed longing for the Americans, all of it has become so commonplace and taken for granted, it dominates completely the atmosphere here—and "here" for us is now Aichach and a good half-dozen surrounding villages we have walked and driven through, so that these things no longer stick in my mind from the hike of April 11. I know only that we ended up at the inn in a quite desperate state and that the young landlady there wordlessly and with an almost mocking shake of the head refused us the least bite to eat and the least drop to drink, although a party of billeted soldiers were getting an ample meal. While I waited resentfully, Eva went to see the mayor and returned with a billeting slip for the peasant Joseph Pulver. Now, this man Pulver is the nastiest fellow we have so far met on our flight. [ . . . ] Pulver, a shriveled up, little old man, hard of hearing or making a pretense of being hard of hearing, accompanied by his wife and a young person, who afterward sneaked away. Pulver sullenly read the slip, then said we could have the closet with one bed, anything more was nothing to do with him, he would not lift a finger. I asked for water. — "Water?" — Yes, for washing, for drinking. No, he didn't have any water, the pump wasn't working. And the young person confirmed that the pump was broken, they didn't have any water. Now I was driven by anger and desperation. Eva gave me the address of the mayor on the main square. A heavy, black-haired man, limping and with a cane. I told him that we had been received with "plain hostility," the man refused to give us water. No doubt my voice was hoarse, tired, desperate, it made an impression. The mayor—at first he had said, it was just for this one night, he would provide something better tomorrow—nodded mournfully and repeated "with hostility, yes: with hostility." Then: "Go to the gendarmerie, the house on the other side of the square, tell the police sergeant on my behalf what has happened." I found the house, knocked, a friendly man, probably in his fifties, in a woolen undershirt, opened the door, listened to what I had to say. "I'll come and help you, wait downstairs for me." After a while he appeared in full green uniform, his revolver buckled onto his brown belt. Joseph Pulver seemed to be well known for his unpleasantness. "I will have to take vigorous action for once, put things straight; these people don't know what others are suffering, they've not had to go through anything themselves, but now things have got to be put straight." By the time we arrived, Pulver had evidently become a little fearful and taken up a pail of water, to which afterward an empty beer mug and a chamber pot were added. The police sergeant argued with the old people. Meanwhile a younger man turned up, an enormous fellow, not in uniform, he must have had some position in the Party, possessed of some more absolute authority than the gentler police sergeant with his "they call themselves Christians." He waved his fists, roared terribly at the old man. Out of the flood of dialect I understood only the repeated, we're not taking any more and: "I'll have you taken into custody, into custody!" Then the two of them departed with us, the bellower disappeared, the fatherly police sergeant led us to the Klosterwirtin, a more modest inn, already closed, opposite the mayor's house. There he negotiated in the kitchen, while we sat in the empty taproom, came back, asked whether we would like the sausage warm or cold—"Whatever is less bother"—made promises for the morrow and left after many words of comfort. A pig had evidently just been slaughtered in the house; we were reminded of Piskowitz. The good-natured landlady brought us such a quantity of black pudding and liver sausage, that we were still eating it the day after; she gave us bread, she promised us breakfast and lunch for the next day, she also kept her promise, accepted only a very little money for everything and didn't take a single coupon from us. [ . . . ] We returned to our unpleasant quarters, Eva took the straw mattress out of the bed frame, put it on the floor for me, herself lay down on the bare wood—there were enough blankets for the two of us—we slept well. [ . . . ]

The next morning, Thursday, April 12, we left the closet, without looking for the Pulver people, went to the Klosterwirtin, and then over to the mayor. The police sergeant also appeared and soon after the commissar from the Reich Resettlement Office in Kühbach, a good-looking young man with an artificial right hand, not speaking in dialect, very polite, and with a certain air of authority. Result of lengthy deliberation: Inchenhofen was hopeless, at midday a military vehicle would take us back to Aichach with a letter from Commissar Klein to the county office there. Midday turned into three o'clock, but then the vehicle took fifteen minutes for what had taken us more than two hours to walk. Incidentally an uneasy pleasure, because there are always low-flying airplanes about, and are the few fir tree branches much use as camouflage?

[ . . . ]

In Aichach Eva once again negotiated at the office and returned with three addresses of requisitioned rooms, of which one might "perhaps" be suitable. (The commissar had already spoken on the telephone from Inchenhofen to the inspector in Aichach.) We fortified ourselves with coffee and set off on our search. The first room was a tiny space without bed or bedclothes, with a miniature sofa on which there was room only to sit, containing lots of luggage belonging to other refugees and all kinds of provisions; the housewife said she had to run her "lemonade factory" in here. (The sign "Lemonade Factory" is quite common in Aichach and, I think, also in Pfaffenhofen.) The second room, in a good house, was first— we were there twice—defended by an elderly lady, then by her giant of a son, a captain, with great politeness, but "fanatical tenacity." He, the captain, was returning to the front on Monday, but with respect to the room, the office had told an "untruth": It was not requisitioned as such, but requisitioned for the bombed-out and expected family of the captain. The third room was in a locked-up apartment; we could not be let in, because the tubercular occupant was in the hospital; her children had been taken away, the apartment was not yet "disinfected." Back to the county office: This third house really had been locked up by the police—open tuberculosis—and they didn't want to have a fight with the captain. We were given a letter for Unterbernbach, "only ten minutes" from the next station, Radersdorf; we would certainly find somewhere to stay there.

I was in a state of bitter despair; things would be no different in Unterbernbach than in Aichach and Pfaffenhofen; furthermore it was already late in the day, there was the prospect of a waiting-room night or worse. But we had no choice. So, to the station with our bags. There we fought and begged, until, giving an assurance that it was only to the next station, we were allowed to shove onto the platform of a carriage overcrowded with soldiers. Going in a northeasterly direction toward Ingolstadt, Radersdorf is the first station after Aichach (about 4½ miles). From there a pitiless country road winds in a NW direction to Unterbernbach, but it takes not ten, but a good thirty minutes. We arrived there dead tired, asked the way to the Ortsbauernführer; a young person said he would come soon, we should leave our bags in the hallway and meanwhile wait in the inn opposite. From this moment on things went well for us. At the inn we were given supper by a friendly landlady. Afterward, it was almost dark, we met the Ortsbauernführer, Flammenspeck, a gaunt, gray-haired man, who immediately took care of us with the most touching kindliness (a Quaker, says Eva). It was a matter of course for straw beds, pillows, and blankets to be laid down on the living room floor for us; we were to stay there until other quarters had been found for us in the village. We lay down to sleep relieved and happy (especially as the landlady at the inn had provided us with a feast, soup, jacket potatoes, bread, cheese, beer). And really the actual odyssey and the worst privation (even if far from all unpleasantness) was now behind us.

### April 20, Friday

We have now been properly resident here for a whole week and have settled down a little, I have been able to spend hours every day writing the above supplement, we have been able to go repeatedly into the lovely wood, strolling leisurely and without bags, collecting fir twigs for fuel, even reading aloud; sleeping in a bed has once again become something taken for granted by us. Certainly there is no lack of serious inadequacies; washing is half impossible and very messy, we are shoved around when it comes to food, we have to beg for it, as it were, drink is very difficult, we are always thirsty. But nevertheless we have a roof over our head, and the end seems really, this time really close. Today is the Führer's much-anticipated birthday. According to yesterday's military bulletin, the Ruhr, together with the army there and its Marshal Model, appears to be or is lost: "The battle is over," no more, not a single syllable more. The Russians are engaged in a major offensive, the others have Leipzig, Chemnitz, Plauen, are fighting to take Magdeburg. Where could a German counter-attack of any significance come from? And here in Bavaria Nürnberg has been captured.

But "Goebbel" (*sic*) spoke yesterday, and quite evidently he made an impression. "Wonderful!," we are to hear the repeat. We were holding our own, in the new Europe our cities would flourish again. Admittedly he did not say how victory could still be won—but the mood here is evidently bolder than before: Ingolstadt was a strong fortress, and Berlin could hold out for months!

The Flammenspeck family, on whose floor we slept for two nights (from Thursday to Friday and from Friday to Saturday; from the twelfth to the thirteenth and from the thirteenth to the fourteenth of April), is a model of friendliness. The man, deputy mayor and Ortsbauernführer (Sign on the house: "Reich Agricultural Estate. Blood and Soil." Underneath that: "Ortsbauernführer."), cannot do enough to help us, displaying all the while a good-natured dignity. His wife very ungrudging. Creased face, animated in her movements and speech, virtually incomprehensible dialect. A plump older daughter with a boy of about eight, her husband fallen. A younger daughter with a four-week-old bottle-fed child, around which everything happily and tenderly revolves. The child's father is a young wounded soldier with his arm in a sling. (The same one who told me his lieutenant was talking about a new offensive, he himself did not believe in it.) On the wall the picture of a son missing in Russia. The father says he is a National Socialist, but things cannot go on like *this*, peace has to be made, otherwise more blood will be shed in vain. He is not afraid of the enemy, *although* he is a Nazi, because he has oppressed no one. At the same time the teacher says of him that he was the first and most enthusiastic Nazi in the village.

### April 21, Saturday

On the first day we took in the village and its surroundings with some thoroughness. Unterbernbach is hardly any larger than Schweitenkirchen, but is divided into two quite separate parts by a large meadow. At the tip of the part now farthest away from us stands the church with its big tower rising in stages and bearing a gable consisting of two baroque scrolls. Around it a small churchyard. The village has no baker, no cobbler, nothing, only a little shop in which there is hardly anything to be had. But the village is evidently prosperous and kept very clean. The courtyards all swept very thoroughly, most quite expansive, the houses very nicely whitewashed, the window arches and their keystones in complementary colors, yellow with red keystone and blue with yellow. Everywhere there are plenty of cattle and pigs in big, solid barns and pigsties, a few sheep, a vast amount of poultry, hens, ducks, geese—I have never ever seen such a number of goslings together in one place. By the inn there stands a huge, ancient linden tree, which has been bound by metal hoops and burst them many times; nestling in the side of the tree is a massive dark cross with a golden bronze Christ and a golden Mary underneath. (Crucifixes by the roadside and in the corners of the peasants' rooms everywhere. But Catholicisme superficiel, ils n'ont pas de charité, says the prisonnier, the tailleur de Valenciennes.) Everywhere the prospect of the Upper Bavarian expanse as described before. To the west between wooded ridges the "gooseneck" of Inchenhofen, a couple of miles away. A wonderful piece of woodland, our favorite place, close to our present lodgings, in the part of the village without church or inn. The atmosphere of the hours in this wood must be recorded. Spring, tall, straight pine trees, not crowded together, plantation of various ages, clearings with field and meadow, bilberry bushes, broom, buttercups, blue skies above it all—and strips of tinfoil scattered everywhere, and always the humming of single airplanes, the deep hum of formations, from time to time the silvery glitter of squadrons or smaller groups as they become visible, then the bangs and the quaking caused by bombs falling not so very far away, again and again the dull thunder of the frontline artillery, indefinable individual explosions, impossible to say of what kind and how far away. We lie under cover beneath the trees, we hear the various warning sirens, we collect pine twigs for the fire, I read aloud . . . The route northwest to the villages of Halsbach and Hörzhausen passes through this wood. We walked it on our first day, from choice, later once again from necessity, because Hörzhausen has a cobbler. Even the smallest village has a church and an inn, but at the inn, if it is open at all, one is refused everything, there is no fire in the hearth—there is a lack of coal, but there is abundant wood, it is stacked up in the farmyards, it is collected as waste by *everyone*, natives and refugees alike—they don't have any coffee or a drop of milk—they do, of course, but on the whole they don't have much time for these strangers and locusts. And the country roads are treeless and dusty and threatened by low-flying aircraft. It is no pleasure walking along them. — The cobbler is not willing either. He has two journeymen, in the workshop and the hallway there are piles of boots waiting to be repaired. Out of charity and for twenty pfennigs he sews a seam of the shoes that Dressel gave me in Pirna, which are pinching dreadfully; he refuses to touch the completely torn neat leather shoes: the cobbler in Paar deals with jobs like that.

We live with the Gruber woman in the northern smaller part of Unterbernbach, and our favorite little wood and beyond that the villages of Halsbach and Hörzhausen lie to the north of us. Toward the south we know the villages and roads as far as Aichach, about 6 miles away. There is a straight road there, pretty much alongside the railway line by way of Radersdorf and Oberbernbach, and one that swings out in a curve to the east by way of Paar and the much larger Kühbach with its rambling palace, originally a Benedictine convent, behind a beautiful high iron railing, its big church and a flat cemetery laid out as regularly as if from a child's box of bricks and with a little modellike chapel. There are another couple of smaller villages along these roads. [ . . . ] The landscape, everywhere varying the same theme, is enlivened by a small river, the Paar, and here in Unterbernbach also by a stream, which we cross on a little stone bridge when we go from one part of the village to the other. The large amount of meadowland is often boggy. We have repeatedly walked and driven through the area at all times of the day. But we feel at ease only in "our" piece of woodland with its mixture of timber and plantation, its extensive meadow, field and boggy clearings and the distant prospects that open up. [ . . . ]

On our second day in Unterbernbach we traveled with the morning milk truck to Aichach by way of Paar and Kühbach. [ . . . ] In Aichach, in the first-aid room of the military hospital, an older nurse, who was changing the bandages of a number of soldiers, treated my thumb (it is still not healed). We bought bread, sausage, ink tablets (there is no ink any more), a steel pen; the kind-hearted landlady of Café Mayr gave Eva some thread, we ate at Ziegler's—then it was already time to go to the dairy, from which, after one o'clock, a truck was going in our direction as far as Kühbach. We walked back wearisomely from there. Then that evening, Saturday, April 14, we moved to our actual lodgings in the Gruber household.

I want to say something more about the Flammenspecks, with whom, as I said, we remain in constant close touch—the nice stewed dumplings at lunchtime today! They are always looking after someone or other. During our second night there, they put up in the barn and fed two Ukrainian workers who had been sent from Nürnberg for some "duty" somewhere. Meanwhile they have had plenty of soldiers billeted on them . . . Flammenspeck asked me once, whether the Russians were "really" so cruel, whether "American Jewry" really, etc., or whether it was partly propaganda. I explained very cautiously: The steel industry not in Jewish hands, and besides much better and more stable business was done in peacetime than in wartime. The youngest son-in-law, Asam, wounded five times, absolutely defeatist, living in the house of his mother, who "has not yet given it up," yesterday let us listen to the military bulletin with him "in the Asamhaus." The peasant living rooms are all very similar, also like those of the Wends: There is always a crucifix corner, there are always pictures taken during military service.

At the Gruber woman's we have an attic, very similar to the one at Agnes's. [ . . . ] The most interesting person in the house is the French prisoner of war, the tailor from Valenciennes, who lives with a group of prisoners next to the inn and who for two years has worked and been fed here. [ . . . ]

An even more interesting (and more fertile) acquaintanceship than the prisoner is provided by the teacher Fräulein Haberl and her married sister, Frau Steiner. There is no lending library in Aichach and the public library is open only in the evening, therefore inaccessible to us. So we called at the schoolhouse and I calmly introduced myself as who I am [i.e., as professor]. First we were received by young Frau Steiner. She showed us her books, I noticed several volumes by Vossler so there was an immediate point of contact. Herr Steiner, at present serving in Ingolstadt, had started a fine-art publishing house, had previously been in newspaper publishing, could no longer reconcile that with his convictions, they are devout Catholics. I found German translations of Georges Bernanos and Ernest Hello — Vossler had promised the publishing house something . . . was I "Pg"—a Party member? My heart grew lighter, and I replied diplomatically, I had already said that I was a student and admirer of Vossler, hence one could imagine my attitude to the regime. At about this moment her sister, also a teacher, appeared, and she provided the greatest surprise. Frau Steiner is gentle and dark-eyed, harmless-looking, so to speak; I would definitely have judged her sister, with her staring blue eyes, her overwhelming blondness, her tight short clothing and almost military posture, a super-Nazi, a fanatical BDM leader, a Nazi partisan. Her rough, brittle voice fitted with all of that. Les extrêmes se touchent: The girl is—I must say here—a fanatical opponent of the 3rd Reich, and an utterly incautious one. "If you are writing about the language of the 3rd Reich, don't forget Dachau. Thirteen thousand people have died there in the last three months, most of them of starvation, and now they're releasing the rest, because there's nothing left for them to eat. They've got to the letter H with the releases." Both women talked about Cossmann, the "hundred percent" nationalist, who had died in Theresienstadt. We pretended that we knew nothing about Theresienstadt, and were almost shaken to hear the name in a village in the middle of Upper Bavaria. We got reading matter—at the moment I am reading Bergengruen's magnificent *Grosstyrann* [The great tyrant] aloud—we got two eggs as a special present and were invited to come again. We went there at eight o'clock in the evening of the nineteenth and listened to the military bulletin. I said Goebbels would speak today. "He should be crushed underfoot!" responded the teacher. She was alone, her sister purchasing provisions. We want to go there again this evening; a number of air raids on Ingolstadt provide a good excuse to inquire after Herr Steiner. The two sisters are also of the opinion that it cannot go on much longer; I myself have meanwhile become doubtful again.

At Flammenspeck's I recently met an elderly south German Landesschütze. He explained the word: A kind of home-guard duty for those temporarily unfit for frontline duty, but who have been at the front and are returning to it. The man, aggressive in type and character, certainly no hypocrite, was completely convinced of the Hitler cause and of its final victory. *How* the turning point would come, he did not know, but he knew, that it would come. "Adolf Hitler" had always managed it, one had to "believe blindly" in him, one blindly believed in so much that had stood the test of time so much less than the Führer. Recently a bombed-out woman had said to him: "We owe that to the Führer!" He had shouted at her: "Without *him* you would not be bombed out, you would have been mincemeat long ago!" It could not be grasped with a "slide rule" and with "common sense," that was no use at all—one simply had to "believe in the Führer and in victory!" I was really rather depressed by these speeches. If this belief is widespread, and it almost appears as if it were . . . Then again the Haberl girl says the German army is disintegrating, and it's coming to an end. (In fact, today, April 21, Germany basically consists of no more than a generously defined Greater Berlin and a part of Bavaria.) But the Haberl girl also says: "Now I fear only the *German* soldiers."

[ . . . ]

Every day the sorrows and also joys (substantial joys "with cheese and eggs") of eating, every day and night the air-raid warnings, which here we can listen to in relative calm, the deep hum of the squadrons, which can often be seen in groups of six, or ten, or more, formation after formation flying in every direction, usually visible as silver fish thousands of feet high, this morning audaciously low, big and gray beneath gray clouds; day and night the distant banging of falling bombs, the very distant thunder of the front, the curious rattling and shaking of the windows, the chatter of a machine gun or an antiaircraft gun, the isolated indefinable explosion. And meanwhile we sit in the wood, feeling safe, and I read aloud. Today the flying went on incessantly all morning; afterward we heard that a low-flying aircraft had shot two girls and a team of oxen near Aichach. (All the peasants here are very much afraid of low-flying airplanes, the plowing is suffering badly because of it.) — During the night of April 17 we saw a "Christmas tree" over the railway line (the pattern of flares really does look like one).

Eva says: We're unlucky; going by the last report, Falkenstein must already be in American hands. And *we* are in Upper Bavaria — [ . . . ]

### April 22, Sunday morning

Toward evening yesterday there was a thunderstorm, but we got to the Flammensbeck (as it should be) house during a break in the rain [ . . . ] and over fried potatoes and a cup of warm milk I saw an excerpt from Goebbels's birthday speech [i.e., for Hitler] in the Aichach newspaper. The crucial sentence: Surely we shall not give in now, just when the "perverse coalition" of our enemies is about to fall apart. So they want to use *that* (and again and again reporting on the tensions of the San Francisco conference and of the Polish question) to keep the populace in line and still maintain a belief in victory. That it made young Asam angry goes without saying. But even Flammensbeck unbent. New weapon, offensive, turning point—he had believed it all, but "now he didn't believe in anything anymore." Peace must at last be made, the present government must go. Did I think it true that we would all be deported? I talked that out of him, said, they were whipping up resistance with demagogy. He agreed completely.

[ . . . ]

Frau Steiner and her sister had recently said: We are now afraid *only* of the *German* soldiers. Now they told us in alarm, that eight hundred SS men were expected here. (Which does yet appear certain: The billeting instructions change almost by the hour.) The reputation of the Steiner-Haberl sisters was well known in the village, and the SS would also be politically active. On the other hand, they also reported to their, and our, relief that the mood of the soldiers so far accommodated in the village and the schoolhouse was completely defeatist: "You should hear them complaining!" [ . . . ]

## After lunch

[ . . . ] At lunch today—Sunday lunch: frittata, soup, as much potato salad as we wanted, and real chicken! — I was able to be gently and forcefully enlightening. And I found the ground well prepared. Young Asam has been voicing it for a long time, and Flammensbeck senior has known it for a long time and is pleased to have me confirm it. "It," that's everything, the criminal murdering and propaganda, the whole catalog of sins of this government, which has to go. I am very calm, I avoid every accusation, I avoid all humanist and pious phrases. I constantly repeat only this: Our enemies do better business in peacetime than in war, they don't want to destroy us at all. They were surprised by the war, they want to get rid of our warlike government, etc., etc. And always: "But you know this conversation will cost us our heads, if . . ."

[ . . . ] While Eva sleeps and I wanted to write here, the Berliner sat chatting beside me for a long time. Utterly depressed, extreme opponent of the regime. How many more days could it last? His home is in Basdorf, 10 miles from Alexanderplatz, he is a master joiner, has a wife and child; runs a large business together with his father. Who and what of all that is still there? It is so long since he heard anything. This deceitful government, deceitful in everything! And so cruel: "I don't know if you know how they treated the Jews in Berlin. These poor people, they were truly excluded from the national community. Well, I wouldn't have cared if they had been excluded from public office! But from everything! They were not allowed into any theater, they were allowed to go shopping only at certain times, I saw children, ten-year-olds, completely segregated . . ." I said: "It was no doubt the same in every city, it weighs very heavily on me." He: And did I believe in the Russians' cruelty? I: On the whole, not at all, but there would be individual brutes everywhere . . . the hostility to the SS, etc. He: What the SS had on their conscience was common knowledge. He also talked about the collapse of the army. Many were deserting. In Heidelberg he had seen two hanged soldiers . . . And about the great quantity of stores distributed, squandered in Regensburg. There was again a cigarette and even a cigar left over for Eva; there will be a joyful awakening . . . I was most of all touched by his spontaneous speaking up for the Jews. He appeared to know more about the atrocities than he said. Apart from that: he was completely unpolitical, he wanted to live with his family and be able to work. The man wears the black jacket with the death's-head of the tank units; he is now a driver and talks about the serious dangers and losses because of the low-flying airplanes; he himself had already lost two vehicles.

### April 23, Monday morning

[ . . . ]

Yesterday evening outside Flammensbeck's house (where we ate), opposite the inn and on the square in between: Wallenstein's camp and Children's Crusade. A detachment of a Hitler Youth division had arrived from Ansbach together with refugees from the same place, other troops came and went. Terrible, this Hitler Youth gang. Lads of sixteen, fifteen, even younger ones and complete children among them, in uniform, a cape in brown sacking color or camouflage over their knapsack; they are supposed to fight with bazookas. Among them also, in civilian clothes, boys, children rather, who have been taken along from Ansbach. A few adults as leaders. In the taproom of the inn children's beds made up on benches.

[ . . . ]

### 2:00 P.M.

Today for the first time I saw the Flammensbeck family sitting down together to their meal: They were all eating, man, wife, both daughters, the little boy, each with his spoon, from a huge (wash) basin of thick gruel standing in the middle of the table. Aside from that, the room looked the same as the day before, soldiers and refugees on every bench and chair and settee, coming and going, two noisy baby carriages. We also sat on the bench and waited, until it was our turn for the nourishing feed. Meanwhile and afterward chatted and listened. Beside me a handsome young pilot with the Iron Cross, First Class. His wife in Magdeburg, which is in American hands, no news from her for weeks. "They've already crossed the Danube at Dillingen, we can't do anything about it. We've got enough aircraft, better than theirs, faster, better armed, we would bring them down—but we can't do anything anymore, we lack fuel, ammunition, everything." He shrugged his shoulders pityingly at the Hitler Youth. Perhaps there were individuals among them who were capable of something—but as a unit? Impossible. An Ansbach woman with a baby: her husband twice seriously wounded, now instructor with the Hitler Youth. Infanticide! One can only hope that it will be over, before these children are sent into action. [ . . . ]

## April 24, Tuesday afternoon

Yesterday afternoon old Tyroller turned up in a state of agitation, "they" had already reached Gabelinz, the airfield close to Augsburg, and at Dillingen they had crossed the Danube on an undamaged bridge. [ ... ]

In the newspaper we saw the "Führer's order of the day to the Eastern front." To the last the same features of language and thinking. Boundless abuse and vilification of the enemy. "The Jewish-Bolshevist mortal enemy" has begun his assault "for the last time." (Ambiguity of the "last time.") He wants to "exterminate" us. "While old men and children will be murdered, women and girls will be degraded to prostitutes. The rest will be marched off to Siberia." But we have foreseen everything and expanded "our army with *countless* new units." (Mendacious superlative.) But: "Bolshevism will this time experience the ancient fate of Asia, that is, it must and will bleed to death before the capital of the German Reich." Once again after that, the German nation hopes, that "thanks to your fanaticism . . . the Bolshevist onslaught will choke in a bloodbath." Again the pretense of a possibility of victory: "The *turning point* of the war will be decided at the very moment, that fate has taken *the greatest war criminal of all times* from this earth." — Rhetorically formulated: "Berlin remains German, Vienna will be German again, and *Europa* will never be Russian." *LTI.*

In the schoolhouse they don't believe that Hitler is in Berlin. He is too much of a "coward" for that. [ ... ]

## April 25, Wednesday morning

[ ... ]

Particularly shocking in Hitler's proclamation was the order not to obey any officer who called for retreat, but rather to arrest the man or shoot him. Fear of the Seydlitz and Paulus people or of an imitation of Paulus in the German ranks?

When there was talk of marching on, the instructor of the Hitler Youth boys here said: "What does it matter where the Americans catch us!" [ ... ]

I was back just before midday, and after lunch we went into the wood. But we did not manage much reading. From every side we heard the thunder of the front, bombs exploding, formations and fighter planes flying at a great height, fighter planes diving, the rattle of a machine gun . . . Suddenly two shots very close to us. "Here are the Americans!" said Eva, and we decamped hastily, repeatedly looking behind us, to see if the American tanks were rolling up. But they didn't come, presumably it had been only a couple of Hitler Youths up to mischief.

These Hitler Youths and their younger companions are accommodated in mass billets; mainly they are bursting out of a house and a shed on the square in front of the inn and the Ortsbauernführer. They are very diverse.

Since they are going around begging for food everywhere—they are said to be very badly or not at all supplied with rations; today we overheard one group: "When the Americans come, at least we'll get something proper to eat!"—we have been able to exchange a couple of words with a few of them. Two (particularly one here) appear to me to be from good homes and decent, innocent boys. I asked one of them, who was given a couple of potatoes here, how old he was: "Fifteen." — "Are you about to be sent to the front?" — "Only the volunteers." — "Are you a volunteer?" — Quite unheroic: "No." [ . . . ]

### April 26, Thursday morning

Two remarks by Frau Steiner: She did not like Wagner at all, the innkeeper, one of the wealthiest farmers here ( . . . ) I: But he was certainly not a Nazi. She: *"We shall soon see that a non-Nazi can also be very unpleasant!"* Truly a profound piece of wisdom. For me today all mankind divides into two parties: pro- and anti-Nazi, and all anti-Nazis appear to me as friends and allies. Tomorrow things will look different again.

On another occasion, although she had just declared her support for democracy, Frau Steiner said: "Don't you think, that Liberalism is to blame for everything bad?" [ . . . ] I must get her to talk about her opinions at greater length. I must explain to her: *A liberal is someone who stands by the sentence: In my father's house there are many rooms.* A scholar who does not agree with that sentence is no scholar.

### 5:00 P.M.

[ . . . ] At Frau Steiner's for a moment, who unfortunately had *no* business in Kühbach, so that the errand fell to me. We got to know her husband, the publisher, who is now a paymaster (after several years in the front line). Big, strong, well fed, blond, about forty. His opinion: The war will be over in two weeks. Fräulein Haberl complained angrily about the rough mischief, the destructiveness of the Hitler Youth quartered with her. Indeed the majority of them make a frightful impression. Street arabs and children, proletarian children in uniform, playing with guns. That's how I see them lying around the garden in groups, that's how I hear them banging away in the woods [ . . . ] that's how I saw a whole gang of them in front of the shed by the inn. During the solid Flammensbeck dinner, the beautiful woman from Ansbach (whose husband, after five years' frontline service, is a Hitler Youth trainer, who in peacetime had got as far as the first semesters of political economy, and who since then has got a wife and child and the rank of an NCO, and who now sees the future in the blackest terms—intensified repetition of the conditions of 1918!), the Ansbach woman, then, related under seal of silence: The Party was giving the war up for lost; the bulk of the Hitler Youths should try to get hold of civilian clothes and make their way home under their own steam; only a battalion

of volunteers who had already seen service at the front were to stay together. In an address, hopes for the future had been placed in them, because Russia and the USA would soon begin to quarrel, and then the
NSDAP will rise again! — [ . . . ]

### April 27, Friday, 2:00 P.M.

Yesterday toward evening, in the wood, shots from somewhere fired by
the brutalized Hitler Youth, a bullet smacked into a tree by the path. A soldier bellowed: "Stop it, you bloody stupid bastards!" but the shooting
went on. One could have died a hero's death for nation and Führer. General indignation in the village at this child soldiery.

[ . . . ]

Old Tyroller has already asked me twice, what will happen when Russians and Americans meet in Berlin? On both occasions there was the hope
in his voice, that Russians and Americans would immediately fall upon
one another and engage in bloody battle. That is the degree of confusion
that Goebbels has managed to create.

This morning in "our" wood close to our fallen tree trunk, great military activity, at once modern and *Landsknecht*-like. Motorized troops had
bivouacked in the open, since our village is crammed full. First a group of
heavy vehicles, between fifteen and twenty of them, pushed under the
trees, young firs along the sides and completely covering the canvas. The
men sitting and lying, cooking, eating, washing; kit bags, knapsacks, high
boots leaning against trees. After that horse-drawn wagons; the horses,
black, brown, white of varying size, by improvised troughs, mostly eating.
Such a strange collection of horses, which one hardly believed could exist
any more, between the trunks of the tall pine trees! The troops encamped
among them. Truly a painting from the Thirty Years' War! But twenty
paces away from them the trucks, and above it all the unceasing buzz of
the searching airplanes. And in addition the firing of the batteries, the rattle of machine guns. We talked to a few people, no one knew anything definite, everyone only rumors, everyone believed and hoped that the end of
the war was near. — [ . . . ]

### April 28, Saturday afternoon

[ . . . ]

Late yesterday afternoon we were sitting at the edge of the wood, a
thunderstorm was threatening—one never knew, is it thunder or artillery
rumbling, the two alternated—in addition Eva had a stomachache, so we
didn't go on, then first drops of rain and once again the irresponsible
banging away of the Hitler Youth drove us home early. Earlier, over coffee,
I had got to know a nice Hitler Youth leader, wounded parachutist, he had
volunteered three years earlier, now a sergeant major, from Hamburg, had
completed the upper fifth, very weary of the war and very reasonable. We

were just chatting, he had given me a cigar, when two SS men in leather jackets, arrogant mercenary types, presumably officers, came in with the thunderstruck Frau Gruber (to whom they were appallingly rude), curtly demanded quarters, threatened to throw out anyone who might oppose them. Outside in the kitchen the peasant woman and the young sergeant major afterward complained bitterly about the overbearing insolence of the SS. When we came back from the wood we saw a car with the hated SS symbol standing in the shed. [ ... ]

We ate in the kitchen in the light of a candle stuck in a beer bottle. Two SS members, as inoffensively decent as their comrades in the afternoon had been ill-mannered, radio operators, brought in their receiver, and so we could hear the military bulletin properly. Ingolstadt had fallen (and Siemensstadt in Berlin!), so we could expect the Americans to arrive here in the very near future. Also the Hitler Youth and several other units were to leave the village before the evening was out. (Also—it's unbelievable, but completely true!—the mayor has had the swastika, fastened above the coat of arms on the gable of the district office, removed!) — [ ... ]

**April 29, Sunday morning**

General te deum laudamus atmosphere. I slept in my clothes, it wasn't necessary. Only from a very great distance, closer to Munich than to Aichach, was there still the sound of artillery fire. Here the war is undoubtedly over.

[ ... ]

**2:00 P.M.**

[ ... ] Old Tyroller, only yesterday still fearfully retracting the Epp rumor and [saying]: "The SS is here!" today spits out his hatred of the Party and of the SS. In a village on the Danube a peasant had removed a bazooka from his house and thrown it into the river. Mayor and Ortsbauernführer had interceded for him. The SS had hanged all three for betraying the interests of the fatherland ... And how they had behaved toward religion! And the Hitler Youth ... They were against the Bolshevists and were Bolshevists themselves! ... Frau Wagner, the landlady at the inn, beaming ... The same mood at Steiner's, at the Flammensbeck's. Old Flammensbeck passionately: They had been "too radical," they had deviated from their program, they had not treated religion with consideration ... [ ... ]

**7:00 P.M., kitchen**

Between stormy gusts and downpours bright patches in a thundery dark sky; the entrance to Halsbach wood, a track under tall trunks leading to

the bright meadow, even more dramatic than usual. Here, in the late afternoon, a group of three young German soldiers comes hesitatingly, mistrustfully toward us; unarmed, all wearing camouflage capes. One has a
map, all three have good faces, undoubtedly from good families, perhaps
students. They just managed to escape from Ingolstadt, they want to make
their way toward Landsberg, they do not want to be taken prisoner. Were
"the Americans" in the village? No—but in Kühbach, probably also in
Aichach . . . They should see to it that they get hold of civilian clothes, the
war was almost over. "We have tried everywhere, but without success." —
"All we have left," says Eva, "is what we are wearing, we cannot help
you." We directed them to the Ortsbauernführer, but he will be afraid.

The three beaten and helpless soldiers were like an allegory of the lost
war. And as ardently as we have longed for the loss of the war and as necessary as this loss is for Germany (and truly for mankind)—we nevertheless felt sorry for the boys.

In the morning we had seen piles of cut firewood at the bivouac places
in the wood; we wanted to collect it now, but others had been there before
us, and we found only leftovers. [ . . . ] Here I have just met the tailleur; he
and his people are being taken away tomorrow. He comforted us: Aussi
pour vous la guerre sera bientôt finie. He says, there are a few American
soldiers and a lieutenant français in the village.

### April 30, Monday, 10:00 A.M.

The Frenchman took a warm leave of us yesterday evening. There was no
[electric] light, it was (and is) bitterly cold, we soon crawled into bed. Absolutely silent night, absolute silence also today; it appears as if Munich
has already fallen, because otherwise we would hear artillery from that direction. But we know nothing at all; since the recent thunderstorm there is
no electric current and hence not only no light, but also no radio. We have
not yet seen Americans face-to-face, neither tanks nor men nor decrees;
only the tailleur told us yesterday that one is not allowed on the street
after nine in the evening. I think we shall learn something at lunch in
Flammensbeck's house or afterward from the priest—I hope he will be
able to help me out with reading matter and a little writing paper.

We repeatedly experience a great feeling of relief and gratitude (gratitude to whom?) at now having really survived all this more-than-romantic
danger. It surges up in us again and again, but of course from hour to hour
it is increasingly overlaid by the unpleasantness—for those less badly affected it would be quite a misfortune, and even hardened cases like ourselves are not in the end simply hardened, but also exhausted and,
literally, worn-out—all the misery of our situation: the lack of space, the
primitiveness, the dirt, the raggedness of our clothes, our shoes, the lack
of each and every thing (like shoelaces, knives, bandages, disinfectant,
beverages . . . )

**May 1, Tuesday**

We are beneficiaries of the pig slaughters that take place out of fear of the enemy. First at Agnes's, then (for days now) at Flammensbeck's, and yesterday at the inn. It is not very elevated of me to mention every single meal, but my picture of the times would be untruthful if I did not do so. And as for Eva, I appreciate every calorie she gets. So now there is space at the Wagners'; we were able to spend an evening eating with them once again, and it proceeded in very friendly fashion in their heated little private room next to the big taproom. The landlord was talkative, related that for fifteen years he had been caretaker at the Stiegelbräu in Aichach, related proudly that he had never been in the Party, that he had been in a Catholic organization, and how he had been in fights with the SA and had made himself respected. To what extent are coats now being turned, to what extent can one trust? Now everyone here was *always* an enemy of the Party. But if they really *always* were . . . What appears to be genuine is the bottled-up hatred of the SS, also genuine no doubt is that they long ago had enough of tyranny and war . . . [ . . . ]

**May 2, Wednesday morning**

Terrible cold, snow on the fields and roofs, more snow falling. This and the constant absence of electric current make life more than uncomfortable. Nevertheless the feeling of having been saved is dominant.
[ . . . ]
After lunch, while Eva was sleeping, I walked to Kühbach to go shopping. [ . . . ] An American emergency or repair column was on the church square: A truck with a winch, one with tires, etc., smaller vehicles, jacked up high on one was a long, thin-necked machine gun with cartridge belt hanging down. A grinding machine or a lathe stood against the wall of a house; black, more precisely: brown Negro soldiers in indefinably gray-green, earth-colored jackets and trousers, all with steel helmets stuck on their heads, bustled and swarmed around—village children stood close by and among them. Later I also saw individual blond soldiers, in dark leather jackets, revolver strapped on, rifle (different from the German one, barrel without a wooden casing) slung over the shoulder. All the shops were shut, admittedly it was not quite three o'clock. I turned into a side street; a young blonde, certainly no peasant woman, presumably from Munich, answered my inquiries. I should wait until three o'clock, but they would probably not open. On the first day the occupation troops had taken everything out of the shops, but otherwise had been altogether decently behaved. "The blacks too?" She almost beamed with delight. "They're even friendlier than the others," there's nothing to be afraid of . . . Did she know anything about the situation? — Munich had already fallen yesterday evening (so on April 30).

I went back to the main square, asked two old ladies (more ladies than women) for information. Again, only more emphatically, the same response to the occupiers, exactly the same beam of delight because the Negroes were the especially good-natured enemies. (I thought of all the black children's nurses, policemen, and chauffeurs in our life.) And what had been said about the cruelty of these enemies, that all had been nothing but "slogans," that was only "rabble-rousing." How the populace is being enlightened! The two also knew in detail about Munich, in such detail, that today I still find it unbelievable. After all, there is no electric current in Aichach either and thus no radio, but the Americans had told people and shown it on the map: They had advanced on Munich from six sides [ . . . ]. But one could still hear artillery fire from there, I threw in. "That would probably go on for a while yet, because the SS was still defending itself in every little corner." — Was it true that there was fighting between army and SS? The information was unclear. [ . . . ]

The shops in the town were to remain closed for about a week, but I should try my luck around the back, "across the yard, past the dung heap, that's where you'll find Lechner." There I met a friendly woman, who immediately brought me a six-pound loaf. It cost 90 pfennigs. I handed her money and coupons, she refused the coupons, they were worthless. [ . . . ]

### May 3, Thursday morning

After coffee yesterday, the walk to the cobbler. To Haslangkreit as the day before yesterday, then we turned off onto a path across the fields to Paar. Thus far we had had thunderclouds behind us, now we were in driving rain and snow, which didn't stop, so that even today all our things are completely soaked. [ . . . ]

On the last part of the walk we were overtaken by Frau Steiner on her bicycle, her brown stockings dark to the knees with wetness. She was very depressed: Her husband had surrendered to the Americans as an officer the day before and not come back; she had now learned at the headquarters at Aichach that he had already been transported with other prisoners, presumably to France. I consoled her, it would not be for long. Whereupon she: *But yes*, perhaps it was really only starting now. In Aichach an American is supposed to have said, they would now go to war with Russia. I talked urgently to her, she should not let the lying Goebbels propaganda make a fool of her. Eva said: If we kept on hearing it for much longer, we would believe it ourselves. This morning the first words of the Gruber woman: "They say the Russians have declared war on the Americans!" — I trotted out my argument again: Our enemies were not so stupid, *first* they would secure their booty and afterward they would resolve their differences through horse-trading and not through an expensive war. But there was nevertheless a grain of truth to the "we'll end up believing it ourselves." [ . . . ]

**2:00 P.M.**

Eva has checked my diary and criticized me for not having sufficiently emphasized the actual climax on April 28. She means the moment when we were sitting reading in our attic in the morning. Suddenly the already familiar artillery fire turned into explosions very close by and the sharp reports of individual shots, Eva also heard the whistle of a bullet—evidently there was now fighting going on at the edge of our wood in front of our village, our corner. We hurried downstairs, the house was empty, they were already in the shelter, they had forgotten us. For quite a while we stood and sat pressed into a corner of the kitchen, which appeared safest to us. Gradually the shooting abated and our courage grew. We wanted to cross over to the Asam shelter—renewed shooting forced us to look for cover against the outside wall of the Asam shelter; not until some time had passed did we risk the final couple of steps. Admittedly these few steps along the passageway between the farm buildings led directly toward the enemy, because it faced toward the meadow and beyond it the edge of the wood from which the Americans had to come. After that we sat in the shelter, sometimes I stuck my head out, but without discovering anything; the farmer's wife fetched food for her people, *we* starved, and so at about two o'clock we ventured home again and made ourselves a coffee. The attack had rolled over our village, more exactly, it had rolled *around* it, only at the edge of "our" strip of woods had a last, small group of soldiers offered resistance for a couple of minutes before they, too, fled. The war lay behind us, even as we still thought it before us.

At the midday meal Asam told us, and afterward the gloomy Staringer, who lives opposite, who repaired Eva's shoe—but now mine is gaping, too!—repeated it with great certainty, Hitler was dead, it had been broadcast on the radio (by whom?) without any particulars. Asam, however, also added, he himself did not believe it, only yesterday officers had asserted with the greatest conviction, the "turning point" would come in two weeks, it would start from the Obersalzberg and would be brought about by "*the new weapon*." This faith appears ineradicable and finds ever new believers. The propaganda was simply too great and really was mass suggestion. [ . . . ]

### May 4, Friday morning, house 11, Tyroller-Gruber

Yesterday we had an argument with the Gruber woman, which continued today and will probably lead to a change of accommodations before the day is out. [ . . . ] We again had to take refuge with Flammensbeck. He looked around for new quarters for us, gave us an ample supper. [ . . . ]

At the Flammensbecks', who sadly, sadly do not have a room in which we could stay, we are not only fed on milk and honey and warmed in a well-heated room—today the ground was covered in frost again!—but it is also always the most interesting place. The sign "Ortsbauernführer" has disappeared, nevertheless people still turn up, and Flammensbeck feeds them and puts them up for the night in his barn. Everyone gets soup or a piece of meat or sausage, the round loaf and the knife lie on the table and everyone cuts as much from it as he wants. "It is as if," says Eva, "people smell his kindness." [ . . . ]

So yesterday evening Flammensbeck once again took in two soldiers, unarmed but in uniform, with whom we talked for a long time. Both in their early twenties, in the army for several years, before that one had been a commercial employee, the other—older, spectacles, more talkative, the dominant one, I took him to be a primary schoolteacher—a law student in his first semester, but since then a soldier for five years. Both Sudeten Germans, left their disbanded unit at Dillingen, trying to reach home by way of Ingolstadt, Regensburg. They had frequently passed Americans, finally some who were riding along the railway track on a trolley, so far unmolested. Yesterday they had listened to a radio, *everything*, including Berlin, had capitulated, and Hitler was dead. The student declared: "If anyone had told me that, even four weeks ago, I would have shot him down—but now I don't believe anything anymore . . ." They had wanted too much, they had overdone things, there had been atrocities, the way people had been treated in Poland and Russia, inhuman! "But the Führer probably knew nothing about it," the Führer was not to blame; they say that Himmler was in charge of the government. (Still the belief in Hitler, he undoubtedly had a religious effect.) Neither quite believed anymore in the "turning point" and the imminent war between the USA and Russia, but they did a little bit nevertheless. They were hostile to the SS, which was still fighting. "In the end they'll make a bolt for it in civilian clothes and get away." [ . . . ]

## May 5, Saturday morning, District Office

The District Office is right at the southern end of the village, as far away from our previous domicile as it is possible to be; through the upper window of the south-facing main door one can see the white strip of the road to Radersdorf, cutting between meadows, rising up the slope into emptiness, into an unlimited indefiniteness, far away on either side of the flat meadows and fields stands the forest. [ . . . ]

The swastika outside was just above our window—*was*—I, I, have slept on the wedge-shaped pillow of the SS, and the picture of Hitler burned in our stove; despite all momentary difficulties and inconveniences (to which the cold, the rain, and muddy roads contribute a great deal) it is a joy to be alive.

[ . . . ]

Our removal caused a stir in the village and showed us how many people here already knew us and sympathized with us: People repeatedly called out to us and asked questions. Among others, a young woman addressed us [ . . . ] in a rich Berlin accent, were we already departing. I said:

We should certainly like to, but we had not reached that point yet. With that we got into conversation.

The woman, from north Berlin, ended up here a week before us by way of Silesia; she told us, she had "heard from a sergeant that Fritzsche, as prisoner of the Russians, had announced on the radio": Hitler and Goebbels had shot themselves, the Russians were helping the Berliners to put out the fires, the war was completely over. (Father Moll even expects the railways to be running again in two weeks and that it will be possible for us to return home!) But it was impossible to find out anything reliable, we have been without electric current and therefore cut off since Saturday, April 28, that is, for one week. At supper young Asam had the most recent thing, a newspaper sheet with the title *Nachrichten* [News] dated April 28, thus also a week old. It is published in German by an American army in the territory it has occupied and had reached here from Aichach. The sheet reported on the "historic meeting" of American and Russian troops in Torgau—now the Reich was torn in two—on the handshake between American and Russian commanders. This *shakehands* was in stark contrast to the hopes of war originating with Goebbels, it was also, admittedly, reminiscent of the handshakes of German and Russian officers in Poland in 1939. [ . . . ]

The woman from Berlin became more important to me, not for the rumors she passed on but for this: She related that her brother had been in a concentration camp for ten years and she herself had been inside for eight weeks; she related it with *pride*. With the same pride and a degree of bitterness, Frau Steiner said—she was about to cycle for three hours to Neuburg, in terrible weather, to seek information about her husband, since her trip to Aichach had been in vain—she spoke proudly then, of how often her husband, who had been an editor on the *Gerade Weg* [Straight path], "under Gerlich, the fiercest opponent of the Nazis, whom they beat to death in Dachau" (find out: Who is Gerlich?!), how often he, how often they both had helped Jews, taken people in who had no papers, hidden them, passed them on—"and now *he* is to suffer, and in Aichach the worst Nazis are still running around free! The Americans have definitely been very much misinformed in many cases!" Under the same heading I should also like to record that Wagner, the landlord, recently boasted of his prowess against the SA, and the boundless cursing of an ordinary woman, who is quartered with him, and some open remarks on the part of young Asam, and some veiled ones on the part of Flammensbeck. And I myself: I told Frau Steiner perhaps I could be of assistance to her at some point, my name was respected, and the Nazis had forced me out of my post. I even said something similar to Flammensbeck, and he thereupon carefully noted my name.

So now everything comes triumphantly to light that until April 28 was fearfully hidden (note the peasant Tyroller's retraction, the rumors were false and the SS were in the village), but also no one who undoubtedly was a Nazi now wants to have been one. — What is the truth, how can it be established, even approximately?

And ever more puzzling, despite Versailles, unemployment, and deep-seated anti-Semitism, ever more puzzling to me, is how Hitlerism was able to prevail. Here, e.g., Flammensbeck, they sometimes talk as if Hitlerism had been essentially a Prussian, militaristic, un-Catholic, un-Bavarian cause. But Munich, after all, was its "Traditionsgau"—its oldest center. And how was this cause able to win over skeptical and Socialist Berlin and maintain itself there? (Flammensbeck says that the Party program respected religion, *insofar* as it did not encroach on politics, and at the beginning he had not grasped the perfidy of this perfidious word *insofar*, but Fräulein Haberl declares that Flammensbeck had been for a long time a "fanatical" National Socialist.)

To feed our stove, I delight in going berserk in the loft: Valuable picture frames have met their fate. If only we had an ax or a saw. I discover a heavy "Stürmer" display board. What pleasure it would give me to burn it!

[ ... ]

At the moment we are reveling in meat and fat and every kind of food surplus; only milk is missing, and that is an unpleasant reminder. Since the ration cards are out of circulation, a new order and authority has not yet established itself; we can very soon be in trouble. But there is no point in saving up; we must take every opportunity to build up our strength and take each day as it comes. Naturally we often discuss whether and when and how and where we should go from here. But everything is utterly uncertain. Except for two things: we no longer need fear any Gestapo or any bomb, and this "except" is nevertheless so much, that we should really become Catholics. —

### May 6, Sunday after lunch, one o'clock

Thus far unchallenged here. No mayor, no Americans—thus far. During the meal the Flammensbecks lent us an ax: so I can chop up bits of picture frames for the stove. Eva has made us a set of shelves out of two chairs—there are many fancy peasant chairs, wood with a little heart in the backrest and a depression in the seat—and two of the wicker children's stretchers. With a pleasant temperature now it's quite cozy up here. Only our cracked shoes and our socks refuse to dry out properly. The ground outside is still muddy, and with the continuing gale from the south, one needs to watch out for the showers of rain falling since this morning.

The latest rumor—someone is always "said" to have heard such a thing on some radio somewhere: Germany has capitulated to Eisenhower, but is continuing to fight against Russia; Goebbels has shot himself and his family, Hitler has disappeared.

[ ... ]

## May 8, Tuesday

[ . . . ]

This is now the eleventh day without light (presumably it did not, after all, fall victim to a thunderstorm on April 28, but to the fighting; the Steiner-Haberl sisters relate that on their cycle ride to Neuburg they saw wires down everywhere), without the radio, and without any news at all.

The greatest of our present anxieties and problems are related to that. Above all the question: When and how shall we be able to get away from here and get to Dresden? How on earth can we even get to Aichach, and what shall we find there? To obtain real help, I would have to reveal myself as a Jew. But I would want to do that only when I can definitely and immediately leave my present surroundings. The matter I am intimating here is one we are constantly considering from every angle; it is a difficult subject, with much to be said for and against. And it is impossible to solve as long as we have no news at all . . . One can still hear artillery fire from a great distance, formations and reconnaissance planes fly over us almost every hour, it is said—"it is said," rumor upon rumor—isolated groups are still fighting in the mountains. In the wood we again and again meet soldiers returning home, usually in civilian clothes, but always unmistakable with their kit. The Americans don't bother with them. The army is seeping away. I ask myself whether I can draw conclusions about the millions in the army from these individual returning soldiers. But how many ships sailed across the ocean in peacetime, and how few and how isolated were those we met on our long cruises. Germany is like the ocean . . . We talk to the returning soldiers; they all know nothing more than rumors. The war between the USA and Russia still plays a part in these. Yesterday I talked to two, who said: "The Americans are all right—but what will it be like with the Russians? Our homes are near Breslau." I: They won't do anything to the common soldier. Only the officers and the SS. Pause, then with an (uneasy?) smile: "We are not in the SS."

[ . . . ]

Eva's health continues to be very unsatisfactory, she is shockingly thin. A particular torture for her: the lack of tobacco. Now that the soldiers have gone, there are not even stubs on the streets.

My particular troubles: my thumb, which just will not heal, my completely cracked, damp, pinching shoes, carrying the heavy pails of water.

Now that the danger to our lives has gone, we have had more than enough of the minor, but cumulative misfortunes of our situation and no longer find any compensation in its romantic aspect. But the feeling of gratitude is nevertheless still constantly present, and many hours of the day are again and again enjoyable. Bucolic hours, so to speak. In addition also "close to the people" and therefore instructive.

[ . . . ]

**May 9, Wednesday morning**

[ ... ]

Electric light and with it the radio are expected hourly. Thus far in vain. Heckenstaller, the mill owner here, has his own electricity supply. Yesterday he gave out as reliable radio news: Total capitulation with the surrender of all submarines and "midget submarines" was signed yesterday, May 8, at 3:00 A.M., on the German side by Admiral Dönitz. "But the thing about the Russians wasn't true, it wasn't mentioned," added Asam. So he, too, had believed just a little bit in this war between the USA and Russia.

The many airplanes that passed over us yesterday in groups of three, very low and slow, are said to have been transports. Subjectively, from our point of view, the characteristic thing about them is that we no longer look for cover, are no longer afraid and yet with every airplane remember our past fear.

[ ... ]

**May 10, Thursday morning**

Today began with a lot of chopping wood. Flammensbeck lent us the ax, and there were many rafters lying around in the loft. There is also a huge, heavy display board, more precisely a display box of the "Stürmer"— "The Jews are our misfortune!" I should so much like to chop it to pieces [ ... ] but I fear I do not have the strength.

**May 11, Friday morning**

Yesterday essentially at home until 4:00 P.M. [ ... ] After that, a most unsuccessful errand to Kühbach. The evening then brought some consolation, i.e., a certain clarification or initial disentangling of the situation. 1) the milk truck began running again this morning, so that there is transport to Aichach at least. (But for the time being there is milk only for the children, and so we have to go on living from our tins of preserves.) 2) the electric light came on unexpectedly again, while we were drinking our late coffee at Wagner's. Light: That also means radio. (Why actually? I am always ashamed of my ignorance of science, every child knows more than I do. What is education?) So today we shall be able to hear the news in the schoolhouse. We now want some orientation and further clarification, in addition to waiting for Eva's condition to improve a little, and then travel to Aichach together perhaps on Monday.

The two most urgent misfortunes apart from Eva's tobacco things are now the condition of my shoes and the coffee running out.

The populace is absolutely without history, in every respect. In the evening a woman came to Flammensbeck to register her children's milk-ration card, young, not unintelligent. She appeared to be from Munich, had cycled to Munich one day recently. Evidently there has been unruliness on the part of the Slav prisoners, who here, too, appear as idle, troublesome, and overbearing, and evidently the American authorities restored order. The woman related with conviction, and Flammensbeck undoubtedly believed her, that America had issued an ultimatum to Russia to evacuate eastern Germany immediately. I asked the woman if she had heard anything about Hitler and the other Nazi bosses; *no,* she had had no time to ask about that, in other words: It no longer interested her. The 3rd Reich is already almost as good as forgotten, everyone was opposed to it, "always" opposed to it; and people have the most absurd ideas about the future. And patriotism? In front of the Petershof inn a couple of refugee women were complaining *they* had got less meat than the peasants. The landlady: "Let the peasants be," the peasants had worked, were the most important people, etc. The women: "*We* worked, in the armaments factories . . ." I nodded hypocritically to the landlady, but it was the women from the city who were right. The peasants were better off and are incomparably better off than the rest. I do not believe in the peculiar patriotism of the peasants, only in their peculiar egotism. [ . . . ]

### May 13, Sunday, 3:00 P.M.

When the light came on again the day before yesterday, the word was that we must still continue to black out. That was canceled yesterday, and yesterday, on May 12, 1945, therefore, we saw illuminated windows for the first time since September 1, 1939, almost six years ago. Only a few windows in the village, and yet the place immediately looked quite different. It made a great impression.

But what good is all awareness of the peril we have come through—you may put on the light, you may watch the never-ending flyby without a care, there is no Gestapo for you to fear, you once again have the same rights—no, probably more rights than those around you, what good is it all? Unpleasantnesses are more bothersome than the nearness of death, and the unpleasantnesses are piling up now, and our powers of resistance and patience are very much shaken. The terrible heat, the great plague of mosquitoes on top of that. The lack of anything to drink—now even the inn has run out of coffee. The lack of underwear, the unspeakable primitiveness of everything that has to do with eating: plate, bowl, cup, spoon, knife, partly (or mostly) *completely* absent, partly completely inadequate. In the long run (and in this heat) the distress caused by the inadequate way food is served at the Flammensbecks'—when the wife dishes up, we don't even get a plate each—the crudeness of preparation—today for the first time I could hardly stomach the warm, flabby, almost raw bacon, the tasteless bread soup has already been tormenting me for days. Eva, for her part, suffers agonizingly from the lack of tobacco, and unlike me she cannot drink water. I know it all sounds funny, one could also say: presumptuous, after everything we had to put up with before; these are no more than everyday calamities. But as such they simply do torment one very greatly. We are longing to get away from Unterbernbach.

[ ... ]

## May 15, Tuesday, about 2:00 P.M.

[ ... ]

Early today, when I was still fresh, I said to Eva I had more than "two horses" in my stable, all of them would give me pleasure, but I would like to be sitting comfortably in the saddle of one of them at least. I could: 1) take over a professorship, 2) a ministry of education, 3) the editorship of a newspaper desk, 4) the work on the Curriculum, 5) on the LTI, 6) on the 18ième, 7) a continuation of my modern French literature history and prose up to 1940. But I would really like to ride one of these seven horses for as long as my heart lets me. And in addition, garden and the possibility of making music for Eva and smoking and alcohol for both of us, and once again the pleasures of a car! When will these hopes be fulfilled? When one comes home hot, the knapsack and bag laden with noodles, and Eva complains about [the lack of] a cigarette and I about [the lack of] a drink—then all seven horses take on an illusory and phantasmal appearance. As yet no train is running, as yet there can be no thought of transport from here, as yet there is no coffee, no tobacco, no clothing, no possibility of movement, of newspapers, of getting or listening to news.

Tomorrow is our May 16. We shall be able to observe it with a lighter heart than in past years, but we cannot "celebrate" it materialistically, with wine and roast and real coffee and tobacco, we still cannot celebrate it.

The biggest impression of yesterday's trip to Aichach: On the main square, close to the old gate, waving on the flagpole, which is as tall as the Nazi ones were, as big and as extravagant in its use of cloth as the swastika banner, the white and red stripes and the stars on a blue insert of the banner of the USA. [ ... ]

There was a fairly large crowd outside the Strasser shop, mostly foreign workers who are being sent away first, for the time being to assembly centers, and among them German people. On the threshhold a civilian, like a Bavarian inn servant, with a white armband: "*Police.*" But he was a genuine Bavarian inn servant, and to my question whether there was an interpreter inside, he put a finger to his lips and replied, "There's not nothin'." [ ... ] There were yet more true Bavarian *policemen* around; I asked another one, and he said one could enter as one pleased and join the queue. Once inside I at first saw only a cloud of smoke beyond the head of the queue and the shop counter [ ... ]. A young woman with large, gray-blue eyes, not Jewish-looking, wearing very thick lipstick [ ... ] smoking cigarette after cigarette, talking animatedly in an Austrian accent, to the foreigners, to the Bavarians, to a male colleague, a female colleague, gesticulating vigorously, brief and definitive in dealing with those in front of her, but actually never discourteous. Only repeating continually there was no entry permit to Munich or anywhere else, and very often emphasizing: This and that would be solved by the civilian administration, but for the present the military government was here. [ . . . ] It grew emptier and the pressure on the Viennese woman was somewhat less. Then I told her in a low voice and in a few words, who I was, and pushed my Jewish identity card over to her. Immediately smiling courtesy, helpfulness, expression of respect. One "Herr Professor" after the other. Did I need financial help, did I have decent accommodation, clothing would be attended to, tomorrow she would have the mayor of Unterbernbach there, she would make a note of my name: "K-l-e-m-p-e-r-e-r," beaming: "I've heard of it"—she will no doubt have heard of Georg or Otto Klemperer, nevertheless it was to my advantage. — "I shall talk to the mayor, Herr Professor!" — "Madam, I really would not like people in the village to find out . . ." Vehemently: "Well, do you think you still have anything to fear? On the contrary: You will get *preferential* treatment!" Only I would still have to have patience with regard to departure. But I had nothing at all to fear. "Your house? But you will receive compensation . . . So, I trust, Professor, you may return to your post very soon!"

Then I was standing outside again fairly perplexed. Success or failure? For the time being there was no hope of departure and [ . . . ] God knows what she will say to the mayor and in what light I would then appear to the village. On the other hand I had undoubtedly established friendly relations with the Military Government. [ . . . ]

In the evening in the schoolhouse I said that I no longer wanted to keep my cards close to my chest, talked about myself, and showed my Jewish identity card. "We already suspected as much." [ . . . ] The two of them (Frau Steiner had also been a teacher before her marriage) then related their links with Jews—friendship, "in the family," sympathy, political tendency—[talked] about the Munich ghetto, of several cases where Jews had "died" and risen again with other documents and names and thus had survived the Third Reich. It turned into a long and intimate evening [ . . . ].

**May 16, Wednesday, 3:00 P.M.**

[ . . . ]

Among the people to whom I talked this morning was also the recently mentioned Berlin woman with the flat nose and the intelligent character. (Intelligent does not mean "educated": She talks in vivid Berlin dialect and really does say "*gorilla war*"—wonderful popular etymology.) She was put in a cell with fifteen others "because of things she said." With growing trust in me it is gradually becoming ever clearer, and with ever more details, how much her whole family, father, brother, husband, was attached to the Communist Party and suffered for the Communist Party. All of it in a fine Berlin accent, coarseness and feeling well mixed. [ . . . ]

We now repeatedly hear the same desire expressed by women refugees of every opinion and provenance: If we could only go home, if we had only some contact with the rest of our families! And again and again: My husband has been a soldier for five, six years now—are they going to send him to Russia? He wasn't in the SS, *only* in the army! [ . . . ]

## May 17, Thursday

My hand is trembling from the forced march in the heat to and from Aichach. From half past seven to half past ten to get there, fatiguing time in the office, Eva's fainting fit. Complete success, the march back took until now. End of the village episode, beginning of our return home: to Munich early tomorrow morning.

Yesterday afternoon a car with American soldiers, two of them Chinese. The mayor showed the people around the building, opened our door a little, said a few words to them, and that was all. The car drove on, two soldiers lay down on the grass until it returned, gave the children who came up to them candy or chocolate.

Then Fräulein Haberl appeared, brought bread and curd cheese from Aichach. Then the engaging Berlin woman with a packet of barley malt coffee and two cigarettes and we chatted with her for a long time. [ . . . ]

Then in the evening at the schoolhouse for a long time; we had to give an opinion of a petition for the release of Dr. Steiner (and moderate it); we talked about our past, our plans: we became friends. In a Swiss broadcast I was shaken and impressed by a sentence in an Allied declaration: Germany had "ceased to exist as a sovereign state," but the Allies could not encumber themselves with its administration, the Germans would have to work under Allied control. In addition I took in what the sisters told us from other radio reports: that in Aachen schools had already opened again, with pre-Nazi textbooks "retrieved from an American library"; that in Frankfurt 140 Jews had been found still alive and had immediately been employed in the reconstruction service. It was immediately clear to us both that I must right away attempt to play my part, register my claims and attainments. Thus today's forced march came about.

## Munich, St. Martin's Hostel

## (Catholic Home for old men and women)

## May 21, Whitmonday

υβρις! [Hubris] It has pursued me since Friday morning, when we fell from cheerful confidence into new misery, for a moment almost into despair. I had believed myself to be someone almost of importance again, and now sank back into a helplessness that was hardly less than that of the Hitler years. There were moments when I no longer made any particular distinction between the Gestapo and the Military Police, which blocked entry to the town hall with brute force. I have meanwhile come to see the tragicomical and provisional aspects of the relapse, regard things with greater patience and from the perspective of a new Curriculum chapter, supported in all of this by Eva's stoicism; but the emotionally significant words ὕβρις [hubris] and "Pierced by the knowledge of his nothingness," which emerge to stick in my mind again and again, are still dominant even now. —

[ . . . ]

On Thursday (May 17) we were already rather tired and flushed by the time we reached Aichach in the late afternoon. The office was crowded—just as it had been the first time I was there. Miss Lazar, incidentally wearing a wedding ring and this time more exhausted, serious, older than before, greeted me immediately as an admired acquaintance: Good afternoon, Professor, are things working out now? And then asked where I intended to go first: "The best thing for you is to go to Munich immediately, with your wife, with all your baggage—I shall supply the pass." I objected, that I had neither lodgings nor food, and furthermore it was uncertain, how I would get any farther. — But no, it was a matter of course, she assured me, etc., etc., I had only to report to the Military Government in Munich, and I—I! I was a VIP, after all—would of course be taken care of. There was an American soldier in the office who, by his appearance and gestures, I immediately recognized as a Jew. She whispered a few words to him, and he right away shook my hand and passed me two cigarettes. (*Do you speak German or French?* Shake of the head. I cannot say how much I regret my inability to speak English.) A very heavily made-up young woman then emerged, a colleague of Miss Lazar as I later discovered, Swiss-French—we then spoke French to one another. My J identity card was explained to her, I also heard something about "*many books* . . ."—the French woman, too, radiated affection. In between Eva got her fainting fit, had to lie down flat on the floor for a while. They wanted to take her to the army hospital, we said no: "merely overstrained, anemia." Sympathy for us now reached a high point. Our pass arrived. But how to get to Munich? An elderly gentleman, who had evidently already established friendly business relations with the *government:* He would gladly take us with him. He was the director of the Aichach Machine Mill Ltd., which makes deliveries to Munich every day. Departure quarter to seven—but how could we get to Aichach from Unterbernbach by 6:45 A.M.? — "You present the mayor with our order to have you conveyed here with baggage tomorrow morning—or the morning after—whichever suits you!" Good wishes and we were discharged; then the French woman whispered to me, we should wait outside, they had something for us, except "the *lieutenant* shouldn't see." Hardly were we outside, than the Jewish soldier came and silently dropped some provisions into my bag: Cheese with bacon and—evidently from German army supplies—Tilsit cheese in a tube. — How could I have expected, after all these expressions of sympathy, to encounter quite different treatment here in Munich? How could it not have gone hubrislike to my head that as a Jewish victim of the Nazis and as the very important person of *many books*, I was one of the Chosen?

We told ourselves that this was a great success, and we wanted to travel the next day without waiting, so as not to be caught up in the Whitsun office holidays. Perhaps already by midday on Friday we would be sitting in a car, even an airplane! and on Friday evening be in Berlin or Dresden. Berlin was Eva's idea, that was where the headquarters of the Allied administration must be. And I, too, was mightily tempted by Berlin. We ate a most meager lunch in the Bauerntanz; Café Mayr was shut, but the friendly landlady let us sit in the yard and made us a lemonade, for which afterward she did not accept payment. She was unable to offer us anything more, because everything had been looted by Polish and Russian workers and she had had to give up her crockery to the American officers' mess. We then walked back in great heat. Eva held up bravely; the feeling of the "great success," our hopes of the immediate future lifted our spirits mightily. Then from six o'clock onward in Unterbernbach we really were very important persons. Flammensbeck ordered a horse-drawn vehicle for five o'clock in the morning. According to American regulations one was not allowed to be on the street before 6:00 A.M. But I had a special mission and special documents. [ . . . ] After supper the Flammensbecks gave us, as additional provisions for the journey, a big block of bacon and ten eggs. We were truly departing from the fleshpots of Egypt. Then we went to the school. The sisters could not do us enough favors. We were given (just in case! if we had to stay in Munich for a little while after all) a letter of introduction for their apartment in Laim, they also gave us soap and a pair of stockings for Eva, and on Friday the Steiners' maid would fetch back the things we had borrowed from the priest and from the Steiners. The sisters undoubtedly envied us, they undoubtedly hoped for future favors from us.

[ . . . ]

On Friday, May 18, we woke up at three, rose at four, waited in vain for the vehicle at five, went to Flammensbeck at 5:20, who saw to it, cursing. At about a quarter to six the wagon was standing in front of our district office. An extremely unsprung farmers' wagon, we traveled as if on a gun carriage, but with two handsome horses in front; as fellow passengers two women we already knew, who wanted to shop in Aichach; beautiful fresh morning, blissful jolting journey, farewell views of the familiar landscape [ . . . ]. Reached our first goal at exactly quarter to seven. The Machine Mill, close to the entrance to the town, is a large complex of buildings around three sides of a vast square, which is both yard and garden. [ . . . ] Huge trucks rolled out of garages and moved into position. Ours had to load a hundred sacks, we had plenty of time. In the meantime the director talked to us. He had prevented the bridge from being blown up by having the detonators removed; the SS commander had wanted him hanged for that, he had almost lost his life, but had denied all knowledge. (The evening before, the sisters had related a nasty hanging case: A man "on leave" in Unterbernbach, that is, a deserter, a family man, had gone to Aichach to shop and had not returned. Then a belated letter, which he had written before being hanged, arrived, a last victim of the SS at the very last moment.) The truck ran on wood gas; we sat in the completely enclosed driver's cabin next to the driver and codriver. Despite the open window, it was stiflingly hot in the heated, confined space. The drive, which did not start until about eight o'clock, truly did not proceed much more swiftly than in the horse-drawn wagon: We took a good two and a half hours to cover a little more than 30 miles. Neither of us could say in detail what route we followed; we were soon on the autobahn, which ran monotonously and straight as an arrow through the landscape, usually past meadows, only occasionally through patches of woodland. We drove into Munich from the Nymphenburg side at about half past ten, but now, however, there were a number of stopping points at which flour had to be delivered. Only now did I get an idea of the strength of the American occupation. Vehicles of every kind were driving in all directions virtually without interruption. Huge transporters, which look like barges set on wheels, other giants in more familiar form, some packed with goods, some with crowds of soldiers, other giants with gasoline drums, long convoys of them, ever new convoys—and we wanted to fight that without any oil!—tractors pulling heavy guns. Constantly darting between them are small, not very pretty, but fast, open vehicles, often only seats on a chassis, but very often with tall metal fishing rods, which are radio antennae. Sitting in these ugly, gray worms are four or six, sometimes even only two soldiers. "Sitting" is not the right word. They sprawl, casually cheerful, one long leg is always hanging out sloppily somewhere, and to indicate driving straight ahead the left hand lies equally sloppily on the windshield (there is no indicator; when turning the driver stretches out his arm to right or left). Most of the vehicles, large and small, have been given names; on small ones I read women's names like Mary Ann, also Baby-Boy, on a truck: Chicago Gangster. There was deep water beneath a railway underpass (probably because of a burst pipe). Our truck had to wait there, because military convoys coming from both sides were plowing their way through the water. [ . . . ] Thanks to this holdup we had ample opportunity to observe the strength and the massive amount of this military traffic. We then drove farther into the city and to a bakery at the corner of Erzgiessereistrasse and Dachauer Strasse; it had been arranged that our luggage would remain here "only eight minutes' walk from the railway station," there was also supposed to be a tram going to the station. And it was here that the nightmare of the day began and our dreadful disappointment. There was no tram running in the whole of Munich. And we were not eight, but a good twenty minutes' distance from the railway station. Dust, shattered buildings, and American cars raising clouds of dust as they race through streets narrowed by rubble. Ever since then, that has been my hellish impression of Munich; I feel that I have been in this hell for an endless length of time, and yet today is only the fourth day.

At the railway station we had our second disappointment: The restaurants, which had still been open in April, were now all shut. Nowhere was it possible to get anything to eat or drink. Again and again: "Shut because of looting." [ . . . ] We have heard a lot about the looting, in Unterbernbach, in Aichach, and here. The foreign civilian workers and the prisoners of war evidently played terrible havoc; the Americans intervened only late and leniently, they presumably thought it natural that those who had long been held in poor conditions should now make up for it . . . We inquired about the American headquarters: at the town hall. Right behind it was the snack bar, in which we had eaten something in April. Now we got a cup of broth and a cup of undefinable "fruit jelly"—there was nothing else—which cost more money than a proper midday meal cost at Flammensbeck's. We went back to the town hall unrefreshed, and here I now had the most definitive and depressing disappointment. There were numerous Military Police guards there. A rope was stretched in front of them, and on this side of the rope there stood a large crowd of waiting people, largely foreigners. The sun was blazing hot. I attempted a couple of times to approach a guard, to make clear to him in broken English that I *had to* get into the town hall, that I had been sent by the Americans themselves, etc. Always in vain. I was grabbed by the arm and pushed back by a fellow as tall as a lamppost with a rubber truncheon, as well as by a less motion-picture-like soldier with a slung rifle.

### May 22, Tuesday, seven o'clock, refectory

A group of foreigners were called; they were permitted to climb over into another roped-off section—the whole square reminded me of a cattle market—and let into the town hall. The German group went on waiting. A young interpreter appeared beside the tall rubber-truncheon-motion-picture policeman: "All those who are here about bicycles, step over to the side!" A very large proportion stepped over the rope to the side. "You should apply to the German police." — Shouts: "We've already been there, they sent us here." — "We've got other things to do—you must go to the German police!" The people moved off resignedly. The interpreter then called out: "Travel permits will not be issued, travel permits will not be issued." The crowd shrank to a small group. Now the motion-picture boy waved over individuals, one after another slipped through the rope to the taboo inner space and exchanged a few words with the interpreter. Each one was dispatched at lightning speed, evidently negatively. It was my turn. I showed the young woman my papers, explained my business as briefly as possible. "You must go to Kaulbachstrasse 65, they will give you somewhere to live." — "But I don't want somewhere to live. You can see that my case is different, I have to continue my journey on the instruc-

tions of the military government itself! . . ." — "You must go to Kaulbachstrasse 65, there is also a housing office in Reisinger Strasse . . ." — "But I
don't want somewhere to live . . ." She did not understand, she was astonished, confused, the motion-picture boy became impatient. *He is university's professor, he says* . . . From on high: three times, four times, five
times, not roughly, but with motion-picture impassiveness: *No pass* (pess!)
*Kaulbachstreet 65, Kaulbachstreet 65.* I couldn't get anywhere against that;
another few seconds and he would have grabbed me by the arm again and
pushed me back. Ès chambres des dames we shall laugh about it, but at
midday on Friday in the blazing sun it was terrible.

Eva waited in a shady corner; so now we dragged ourselves to 65
Kaulbachstrasse, way out in the English Garden [ . . . ]. An imposing
building, hardly damaged. [ . . . ] I could not really make sense of the interior of the building. Later I heard that there had been a Gestapo department here. [ . . . ] At a little table in the corridor there was a young girl with
a list; one was then supposed to be dealt with in order of registration.
Which did not happen however. We sat there from two until four watching the activity. [ . . . ] Finally we had had enough, and simply went into
the room. At various tables, in various corners people were bargaining,
greeting one another and chatting. [ . . . ] I happened upon the gentleman
who was second in charge; he became exceptionally friendly when he
heard my story, immediately brought me over to Dr. Neuburger, chairs
were set down at his desk for us, and now there was a long and sympathetic (except inasmuch as it was interrupted by all the man's digressions)
consultation. The result, however, was not cheering. There could be no
thought of continuing the journey until the railways were running again.
And on top of that to Dresden in Russian territory! No one is allowed into
the town hall. He would write a letter to Dr. Maron, I should try to have
this letter sent up to Dr. Maron, perhaps Dr. Maron would then come
down to see me and be able to offer advice. But above all we must have
lodgings, the—I no longer remember which—school was nearer, St. Martin's Hostel was farther out, but a little less like a barracks; it would be better if he wrote us a pass for St. Martin's Hostel, but now we would really
have to hurry to reach the town hall, before they finished for the day, it
was already past four . . . "so, Herr Professor, the best of luck!" So we
dragged ourselves back to the town hall, where there were not so many
waiting as before. In dreadful English I asked a guard to send my letter up.
Later I heard another guard speaking French. I asked him, whether my letter had been forwarded. — Yes, and the gentleman was still upstairs. I
went on waiting. But no messenger came to take me up. Instead I saw officials leaving the town hall in little groups. Once Eva went up to a gentleman, whether he was Dr. Maron or whether he knew anything about him.
In vain of course . . . υβρις [hubris] "Pierced by the knowledge of his nothingness" . . . trapped beyond hope. We dragged ourselves, dragging is
truly no exaggeration, the endless distance to the East Cemetery, to which
St. Martin's Hostel is adjacent, by way of the Isar Gate. In all this time we

have experienced no more exhausting day of walking, hunger, heat, disappointment than on this Friday, May 20. We had truly been expelled from Paradise—the earthly one of Unterbernbach, the heavenly one of our hopes and our feeling of importance—to a new inferno. Because in its present state Munich, and again this is really no exaggeration, Munich is a more than Dantesque hell . . . When we arrived here at 7:00 P.M., Eva had no more strength left. She repeatedly felt so faint, that she had to lie down on the sofa at reception, on the bare floor in the refectory. The sisters of mercy—of which order?—with huge white coifs and collars—received us with great friendliness; we got a glass of wine, Eva got some lavender water in her washbowl, there was even a passable supper for us. But we were also told right away that the hostel was overcrowded and we were being taken in only temporarily. On a long corridor half a dozen old women, sick, in a row of beds one behind the other, then a folding screen, and then, isolated from the rest and close to an open window, likewise end to end, two further beds; they were meant for us. This is now where we live, God knows for how long.

The pattern of the next few days is determined by the house rules here and by our lengthy walks.

[ . . . ]

On Saturday we made a futile attempt to walk to Laim—it is too far out—on the way back we tried at least to get to Erzgiessereistrasse, by then it would not have meant a very great detour, but there was too little time even for that. Then on Sunday we went straight to Erzgiessereistrasse and brought the knapsack with the food and a few essentials here—but we forgot the shaving brush, and we left coats and warm clothes there, because it was terribly hot, and meanwhile the weather has broken, and today, Tuesday, we are sitting here shivering and trapped by downpours and know from experience that in Munich rain after thunderstorms goes on for days, three or four days. [ . . . ]

Has Munich's hellish state really become more hellish since April, or have I become only more sensitive? Presumably the air raids of the final month caused further destruction, and what has meanwhile been achieved in the way of cleaning up—the digger at the station is still in operation, without any noticeable diminution in the pile of rubble—only makes the destruction even more apparent. On all our walks of miles and miles through the city center and the suburbs, from the southeast to the southwest and northwest: the same picture everywhere in ever new variations, with ever new motion picture effects: piles of debris, houses that appear untouched and are no more than facades; houses, whose external walls and roof have been torn off, but the individual stories, the individual rooms with their variously colored wallpapers are still there; somewhere a washbasin is preserved, a table hangs in midair, there's a stove; houses that are burned out inside . . . [ . . . ] But I got the most terrible impression of all on Saturday afternoon on the far (west) side of the railway line, when we were making for Erzgiessereistrasse from the direction of

Laim. Along this stretch are (or were) situated big customs and railway administration buildings, etc. Here everything is destroyed, huge piles of rubble block the road, and the crumbling ruins and the suspended and fantastically hanging beams, blocks of concrete, tin roofs threaten to crash down with every gust of wind. Before us and across from us, to the north and the east, a blue-gray thundery sky contrasted with the gray-whiteness of the ruined city. It truly did almost make one think that a Last Judgment was imminent. And the cars of the Americans were continually racing through the dust, the ruins, the sound of the storm. It was these cars that made the picture of hell complete; they are the angels of judgment or the centaurs at the stream of blood or something of the kind; and they are the triumphant and cheerful victors and masters. They drive quickly and nonchalantly, and the Germans run along humbly on foot, the victors spit out the abundance of their cigarette stubs everywhere, and the Germans pick up the stubs. The Germans? *We*, the liberated, creep along on foot, *we* stoop down for the cigarette ends, *we*, who only yesterday were the oppressed, and who today are called the liberated, are ultimately likewise imprisoned and humiliated. Curious conflict within me: I rejoice in God's vengeance on the henchmen of the 3rd Reich—"today is the anniversary of Muschel's death" said Eva on the twentieth, and I: "Every hair on his thick little fur has been paid for by a German life"—and yet I find it dreadful now to see the victors and avengers racing through the city, which they have so hellishly wrecked.

Apart from that, the Americans make neither a vindictive nor an arrogant impression. They are not soldiers in the Prussian sense at all. They do not wear uniforms, but overalls or overall-like combinations of high trousers and blouse all in gray-green; they do not carry a bayonet, only a short rifle or a long revolver ready at hand; the steel helmet is worn as comfortably as a hat, pushed forward or back, as it suits them. Down by the Isar I saw one wearing a steel helmet and with an open umbrella and a camera in his hand—the umbrella appeared to be there for the camera. I have not seen even the smallest group marching: they all drive—as I have already described. Also the traffic policeman does not have the stiff posture and movements of the German. He smokes on duty, he moves his whole body, when he directs the vehicles with sweeping arm movements; he reminds me of film shots of boxers, or rather of referees circling around the fighters, separating them, counting them out . . . [ . . . ]

A small vehicle bore the words: "Alles kaputt." It probably expressed the same sentiment as the inscription chalked on the wall of a house: "Death to Hitler," where Hitler probably stands for the Hitler people. On the Feldherrnhalle, carefully painted in giant letters: "Buchenwald, Velden, Dachau—I am ashamed to be a German." It was followed by the name of the author, which I could not decipher. Very close by, on the entry to a building, smaller and only in chalk, not as large-scale and defined as the previous sentence: Au pays des crématoires. There are also French occupying forces here, I often see vehicles with the French flag and the word

"French" in big white letters, I have also seen the tricolor on buildings, evidently military quarters. [ . . . ]

The second new feature of this stay is St. Martin's Hostel. A huge, red complex of buildings by the East Cemetery, a rectangle open on one side, the side wings different in size and height, with a large, ugly block set back in the middle of the third side, incorporating a chapel, with a separate wash house and stalls for animals, with a large garden and very large kitchen garden. [ . . . ]

The hostel is a Catholic old people's home, it is said to have 500 inmates, men and women. At the moment it is overcrowded with refugees of every kind stuffed into every corner: Homecoming soldiers, Aryan refugees, Jews, people from Dachau concentration camp are all referred here. A proportion of these refugees—they come and go, I rarely know where from, still less where to, because no one can get out of Munich—are bedded down in the cellar air-raid shelter and eat in "our" refectory. [ . . . ] Our two beds are on a long corridor of the section for men and married couples. Several women are in the corridor day and night. The rooms leading off the corridor are full. Morning and evening old and very old men shuffle along to the toilet, chamber pot in hand. [ . . . ]

### May 23, Wednesday morning, half past six, refectory

The food here has become ever more inadequate and ever more frequently accompanied by the cries of woe of the sister without mercy, that everything is lacking, and how long is one going to stay. The climax came yesterday afternoon: From today, May 23, no more food will be provided, only "coffee with nothing else," we would have to see to it that we ate in town—the old people were complaining that the refugees were getting better treatment than they were! (But I myself see that a couple of the hostel employees are substantially better fed than the wicked refugees.)
[ . . . ]

### May 24, Thursday morning, seven o'clock, refectory

Yesterday another dies ater, even worse than the Black Friday of our arrival. On Wednesday afternoon we had had a similar experience in Kaulbachstrasse as on the first occasion, only this time I got through more quickly. Neuburger again gave me a couple of lines for Maron, who had looked for me on the town-hall square on Friday and either failed to see me or come too late. On Wednesday, therefore, I was supposed to be able to get to him without any problem. And I was successful in that I was let through, and upstairs in the endless Gothic passageways a sentry pointed to his room, no. 95. Dr. Maron, undoubtedly a lawyer, midfifties, attended to me with downright warmth. His office was crowded. I should wait outside as on "private" business—after a few minutes he was with me and was quickly put in the picture. [ . . . ] Maron deserted his office—"some-

thing must be done to help you!"—we went over to a building opposite
the town hall: "Transport Police for Deportees and Foreigners." [ . . . ] An
officer, young but very bald, fluent German, fluent English, fluent French.
I was very soon passed on to him, he led me into a separate room, was
quickly made aware of my case, relaxed, and became extremely courteous, indeed warm and personal. Evidently, certainly, he was himself a
south German Jew (by his accent), who had lost members of his family in
Germany. He hinted at it, he also said: "Our superiors like to talk about the
Nazi atrocities against the Jews and to express their shock, but unfortunately they do not do enough for the survivors." For all that he was at a
loss as to what to do about my case. He was, after all, in a subordinate position and strictly bound by certain orders. I was of course a Jew, but nevertheless a German citizen. And my wife was Christian and German. And
it was not permitted for a civilian to be conveyed in a military vehicle.
[ . . . ]
    I felt almost broken as I left and met Eva, who had meanwhile been
trying just as unsuccessfully to obtain food-ration cards in nearby
Sparkassenstrasse. We learned, that Reisingerstrasse [welfare office] was
near the Sendlinger Tor [Gate] and that located directly beside the
Sendlinger Tor was the Blumenschule, which had been offered to us right
at the beginning as a place where we could eat and stay. As on the first Friday we had only a cup of soup from the nearby snack bar in our stomachs.
We went to the Sendlinger Tor. Right next to the damaged gate itself, in the
midst of the most terrible destruction, this school is remarkably well preserved. But it is a dark, stinking building, more a neglected prison than a
dilapidated barracks. The dining room the darkest dive of a place with dubious tables and benches. There we were told: You must bring food cards
from Reisingerstrasse with you. I left Eva in the dive and went to the welfare office. Two secretaries and at a separate table, the lower part of her
body invisible, alarmingly doll-like, with little hands like those of a two-
year-old child, a dwarf, but without the wrinkles of other dwarf faces,
smooth, tiny, dark intelligent eyes, very elegantly dressed, speaking very
dignified and meticulous High German. Really only Kaulbachstrasse was
responsible, and without instruction from there I was not allowed . . . but
an exception could be made after all, and so I received 2 × 2 lunch chits. On
the strength of these we each got a deep plate of thick soup in which there
were even little bits of meat floating . . . On to Erzgiessereistrasse. We had
got only to the beginning of Dachauer Strasse when it began to spit with
rain; Eva was very lightly dressed, I left her in the entrance hall of a house
and walked the long distance to our baker alone. From there I took our
coats, a cardboard box, and a loaf with me. [ . . . ] I found the way back unspeakably difficult; after two minutes I realized that I would be unable to
carry the heavy box back to the hostel; my heart failed me, I had to set it
down every couple of steps. Finally I reached the hallway: Eva opened the
carton, made it lighter, took some things in her handbag, made a very

skillful bundle out of others. So, with the burden divided, I then managed the way back, but it was a great effort. [ . . . ]

At the hostel I went to see the mother superior and asked for clarification with respect to board. The conversation developed in such a way that I appeared as the protector of the refugees on the one hand and of the hostel itself on the other. I suggested to the mother superior a letter to "the appropriate authority," saying that it was absolutely necessary to allocate her food supplies for the refugees and only a limited number of refugees. I myself would attempt to reach the right person with this letter.

**8:00 P.M.**

This morning, Thursday, May 24, therefore, we resumed our accursed errands; I registered us at the police office at the corner of Direnhoferstrasse and Tegerner Landstrasse, in a cruelly devastated area—the office itself, in a partly destroyed house marked by a chalked sign, locatable only by those in the know: "lodgings" St. Martin's Hostel. (Here I saw the convoy of Poles returning home, a column of 60 to 70 trucks, decorated with flowers, garlands, white and red flags—one truck had a proper Polish coat of arms fixed to the front—black soldiers driving, the occupants, women with brightly colored head scarves, men in the most diverse clothing, the blue-and-white-striped linen trousers of the Dachau inmates among them, one Dachauer wore a top hat with his prison clothes.) Afterward to the town hall again and after that met Eva at the ration card issuing office. At the town hall the great turn for the better: I ran into Maron outside his room; he was not at all surprised at my lack of success and also said that 65 Kaulbachstrasse had already been instructed to organize further accommodation in the Simonschule. (He appeared to think the mother superior's letter irrelevant, but he would pass it on.) I said: Then we wanted to continue on foot, if that were possible. He immediately: If you want to take the chance! I: Was it possible? He: Why not, there was no risk attached, he could give me a permit allowing me to go more than 30 miles beyond the city, but hardly anyone was going to ask me for it, also one could make a detour around suspicious-looking guard posts. He talked as if the matter were easy and quite safe, he wished me the best of luck and shook my hand in relief. Eva and I were thereupon resolved "to take the chance." (But just now a young man here told me we would without fail be stopped somewhere and, if we did not have a permit, brought back. Now I am once again very doubtful.) We now ate at the Blumenschule again; a big crowd of German soldiers was drawn up on the square in front of it. They were discharged, whereupon 145 of them poured into the building to eat. But what we also saw were tramcars: The line from the East Cemetery as far as the Sendlinger Tor was running again, a wonderful relief for us. Now back again for a glass of slops at the Stachus and again to the good baker on Erzgiessereistrasse. There Eva packed the most important things in the gray bag, the rest we left for safekeeping until they could be forwarded; we bought a large amount of bread (which in many places is not to be had and would nowhere else be handed over on our expiring Aichach coupons), walked to the Sendlinger Tor, and rode triumphantly home on the tram. I reported to the mother superior giving the impression I had secured an easing of her burden through the Simonschule and forwarded her petition to a vital authority. I further told her, we would set out tomorrow or the day after, but could she have the hostel cobbler mend my shoes and could she keep a package for us for forwarding. She was agreeable to both, and as thanks for my "help" she gave us a bag of rolls and other baked things. [ . . . ]

### May 25, early Friday morning, before seven o'clock

This is the pleasant difference as compared to our situation on April 3 (departure from Falkenstein): One's life is no longer at risk. And this is the unpleasant one: Then we had no choice, we *had* to leave, whereas this time we have to choose. We are not risking our lives, but the most awkward situations, if we make the wrong choice: If we are "caught" on our journey, they can transport us back, perhaps put us in a camp for weeks. Then we are even worse off than here. If our ration coupons are not renewed, then we shall have to capitulate on account of hunger. On the other hand: If we stay, then, as was demonstrated yesterday, we shall also have coupon difficulties here. We are supposed to furnish "proof" and cannot, that we were properly deregistered at Aichach and directed to Munich; the American permit merely states: "For three days to see a doctor." So we could end up *without* coupons and completely dependent on the impossible catering of some Blumenschule place. That would be just as bad as some camp and perhaps worse . . .

Make further inquiries? The answer is either negative or wrong, is without doubt uncertain, because no one knows what instruction will be issued by the next department or in the next hour. [ . . . ]

We woke up at two o'clock in the morning, Eva came to the side of my bed and once again we thought things over backward and forward. Without result. Mariez-vous! Ne mariez pas! —

[ . . . ]

What I should have noted as fully as possible—but there was never the time—and what I am now only summarizing, is the La Bruyère of these days. In the refectory here, at 65 Kaulbachstrasse, in the dive that was the Blumenschule (in the canteen downstairs and upstairs in the clothes store), I have seen the greatest mix of people flocking together. Most conspicuous are the Dachau people in their white-and-blue-striped linen. Terribly embittered remarks. I heard the wildest utterances in the Blumenschule dining hall. There a soldier who had been discharged [ . . . ]—blond hair smoothly stuck down with grease, spectacles, scrubbed dumb-insolent face—asked what Dachau was all about and what the plans were of the former inmates. He more or less made himself an advo-cate of the 3rd Reich. Surely it had been "social," too. What did the two Dachau men think they were going to do now? Reply: They wanted to get home, they knew what they had to do, the camp was staying, now those who had wreaked such havoc on the KPD would be put inside. — But there was no KPD in Germany anymore, said the fool. — Wild, derisive laughter. At our table in their convict clothes: a boy, who had been inside from 16 until he was 20. Fragment: ". . . you had to get it up, the SS man was holding a gun to your hand. One guy really couldn't do it, no matter how hard he pulled. He got his fingers shot off. Others got their teeth knocked out . . ." (Now posters on the streets, "Dachau prisoners" should report for examination, if they have suffered injury.) The original comrade of this boy, with whom he is constantly playing cards, is a taciturn, tiny, al-most dwarflike man with a curiously pinched idiotic face, which is never-theless sly-looking at the same time. Also a Jew, it seems. Now a boy of at most fifteen has appeared, very soft features, big eyes, puffy, sickly pale cheeks, quietly cheerful, entirely in Dachau linen. Then two people in civilian clothes, probably in their late twenties. One of them, from Ham-burg, small, gleaming eyes, fanatical face. Once, when refugees were com-plaining about hunger, he burst out, without shouting, in a very low, dispassionate voice: The Allies were far too humane, 40 percent of the Ger-man population should be exterminated. [ . . . ] Then the ordinary civil-ians. A woman from Breslau with two small girls, very working class. She encourages the children (and even tells people so) literally to go begging. The children ask for food at middle-class homes, eat some of it on the spot, bring some of it back. The woman said: "What is 'Gestapo,' I've never heard the word. I've never been interested in politics, I don't know any-thing about the persecution of the Jews . . . ," etc. Is this true not-knowing or has it come into being only now? Of the Dachauers she always says only: "The convicts," she talks to them, yet nevertheless keeps a fearful distance. Her father, she says, was a Social Democrat, her husband—she does not know where he is—an "unpolitical" mechanic. What is the truth of this not-knowing? — The Apostel family from Oppeln presents me with similar riddles. The gray little husband is already quite senile, still talks about the "government of the Reich," doesn't seem to be all there any-more. His wife, on the other hand, is younger and very alert. Her boss, lawyer Steinitz, whom she admired so much, was such a good man after all, and "such harsh things" did occur. After that, however, she was in po-lice service as a clerk, "but doing responsible work," "with 190M net" . . . but quite unpolitical herself, and she had "not known a thing" about it all, and to her, too, the Dachauers are "convicts," and she is afraid of the Russians, and of Hitler she still says "the Führer." Since she knows my opinions and situation, she is of course very philo-Semitic and very cautious. — Also the nice nineteen-year-old at Kaulbachstrasse. Of mixed race from Mannheim, work on the Atlantic Wall, abducted by the SS, father in Buchenwald, dead or alive? mother in Mannheim—or where? Himself a senior, wanted so much to study medicine. [ . . . ]

### May 26, Saturday morning, half past six, refectory

Yesterday afternoon in città once again, after queuing a long time at a shop captured some cheese—validity, acceptance of our coupons as jellylike and uncertain as everything else: one man accepts, the next refuses [ . . . ], coffee at the Stachus hut, which does a tremendous trade with its slops at 20 pfennigs a glass. Returned very weary, even though we now have the tram, but for us the great weariness and utter exhaustion arises from Munich. This nightmare of destruction, dust, the Americans' speeding vehicles, of lack of everything and, above all, of absolute uncertainty, unreliability, vagueness—this terrible jelly, both literally and metaphorically, of debris, rubble, and dust.

We have notified the police of our departure: Moving from lodgings in Giesing old people's home to Falkenstein in the Vogtland, Hauptstrasse 5b. We *have to* go, I told the mother superior, that we are leaving today, I have presented myself as benefactor of the hostel, as a man of influence, in return we were secretly brought extra food (yesterday evening also we got bread and butter after our soup—*secretly* out on the corridor), in return she had my shoes from Pirna excellently and thoroughly repaired, in return she is keeping a cardboard box of things for us to be forwarded—disjecta membra: a part here, a part with the worthy baker [ . . . ].

Our escape attempt has much less chance of success than the one from Dresden. Except that then the price of failure was death, whereas now it is humiliation and exposure to considerable ridicule. If we do not get through, then I shall have to turn to Kaulbachstrasse for help and that will be very hard. But we have weighed up the pros and cons and the result was always the same: Flight will certainly be exhausting and have its disappointments, but so will remaining in Munich. We both came to the same conclusion: If we have to return because of lack of food, or the Americans send us back, then at least we have been out of Munich for a while.

Apart from that it is, of course, almost a crazy enterprise: to want to cover two hundred or two hundred fifty miles without proper hiking things, without any certainty about food-ration coupons, about lodgings. [ . . . ]

### Return Munich–Dresden

### May 26–June 10

After breakfast on Saturday, May 26, we took our leave of the mother superior of St. Martin's Hostel; to my embarrassment she thanked me, she was already feeling the beneficial effect of my intervention, because now no more refugees were coming to her. I acted as if I really were responsible for this.

We began our march through Munich at about ten o'clock; I liked the Isar promenade and the English Garden—some craters, but nevertheless very peaceful, undusty greenery—very much, just as on this occasion, for all its desolation, I placed Munich as a magnificent centuries-old city far above the dainty rococo casket of Dresden. [ . . . ]

A trolley car came, but got us only few a hundred yards farther. We walked on toward *Freimann,* following the route the bus had once taken. Nothing left of scattered village plots, rather houses and industrial buildings, much in ruins of course or at least damaged. Then the place came to an end, the main road curved out into the open country. Just at this point there was a large ash in the meadow close by the road. It began to rain a little, we rested in the shelter of the tree and began to unpack bread and eggs. A small group of travelers settled down a few yards away from us. At that moment a tractor with a rattling empty trailer came puffing up, the people beside us, returning soldiers, girls also with them, ran toward it, stopped it, and began to climb on. At that Eva snatched up our things, and then we, too, were sitting on the trailer. It went a little farther, then a checkpoint blocked the exit from Greater Munich. The first critical situation. *"Have you pass?"* — *"Yes, sir, a Jewish pass."* The sentry was satisfied by the identity card and my hope of success grew. The tractor took us about 3 miles farther, to *Garching.* There, squatting on the road, we made an exchange with the group of soldiers and girls, which made Eva happy: We got twenty Italian cigarettes for a piece of bread. (Though the collecting of cigarette butts has not stopped because of that.) We had taken no more than ten steps, when a farmer's cart came trotting slowly along, but still faster than we could walk. It took us about another 2¾ miles to *Dietersheim.* From then on, on this first day, we really did walk, apart from a very short stretch, where we rode on a harrow, and in the course of the following days the rides became much more infrequent. The country was completely flat, nothing but meadows and field, only far to the west was there a line of hills, and not until near Freising a few strips of lowland forest. One often saw the debris of battle, and that was true of the whole distance from Munich to Dresden: twisted, burned out, somehow wrecked cars and trucks, tanks, machine guns. The ashes of campfires, scattered ammunition, splintered trees, partly or completely destroyed farms, deep furrows in the road surface or the road broken away; the main roads everywhere, and that, too, is rather universal, are very busy. The Americans drive and drive, on what scale and with what prodigal indulgence will become entirely clear to me only in contrast with the Russian zone; in addition to their transport of men and matériel there are the trucks in which foreign workers and German soldiers are being removed. The German soldiers are presumably first taken to a camp or an assembly point, their identity cards have to be registered before they are really allowed to go home (and SS remain prisoners). In addition the never-ending crowd of those on foot. Most of the returning soldiers already have an American pass. Soldiers half and quarter in civilian clothes, with kit bags and knapsacks, with packages, with handcarts in which a whole group pushes its things along together, often there are women army auxiliaries with them. Apart from the soldiers, not always immediately distinguishable from them, those released from the concentration camps and prisons. Sometimes still dressed completely in blue-and-white-striped linen suits, sometimes with prison trousers or jackets, often in wild and patched-together civilian clothes. [ . . . ] On the harrow I sat next to an honest Bavarian tradesman in almost decent civilian clothes. He had come from Stadelheim prison in Munich, as a "political" prisoner released before the "criminals." "Listened to foreign broadcasts, the swine, but now!!" Every day "heads chopped off," later death from starvation, "intention of doing away with everyone . . . if the Americans had arrived only a little while later, then we would all be dead." I have heard such stories in many variations from various camps.

When we got down from the harrow, just outside the village inn of *Achering*, a heavy thunderstorm began and the tavern quickly filled. There was nothing but a ghastly peppermint tea, which everyone drank to the accompaniment of humorous and resigned remarks. We could not continue until half past six. The weather was now very fine, the landscape, the light also, the only threatening thing was the the 9:00 P.M. curfew. We reached the boundary sign "Town of Freising proper" in good time [ . . . ].

It was already half past eight by the time I found the German police station on the central Marienplatz and requested shelter for the night. Two easygoing civilians with armbands conferred, sent us with recommendations to two hotels, both refused us: both requisitioned by the Americans. At nine we were standing in the police station again: Let us stay here, otherwise the Americans will arrest us! At that one of the policemen came with us. He took us to a house close to the market square, led us up a stairway, we saw a great deal of bomb damage, into a large room, evidently quarters for a large number of soldiers, bunk beds on top of one another along the walls, washstand, table. Everything appeared to be in use: There was used water in the basin, scraps of food, two broken cigars, several knives, a spoon, a fork, a shaving brush with soap still clinging to it lay on the table; a gas mask and a haversack hung from the coatrack. The policeman said the people were gone, we should make ourselves comfortable, the tavern was downstairs, water and lavatory were on the corridor, with that he took his leave. The tavern downstairs was shut, not a soul to be seen. We stood helpless and thirsty in the courtyard, from which great devastation of neighboring buildings was visible. A young man opened a ground floor window, I took him to be the landlord. He said sympathetically that there would be nothing served in the inn before eight o'clock in the morning, but he would gladly help us out with a bottle of beer and a mug of water. We gratefully received them through the window, then returned to our lodging and had a very cheerful supper from our own supplies, wrapped ourselves in our coats, and slept splendidly on the used bedclothes of the top beds. This was our first day's tramping, Saturday, May 26, from Munich to Freising, 22½ miles.

On Sunday, in glorious sunshine, we awoke before six, fresh and confident. Throughout the first few days we were always in danger of being stopped and sent back; someone or other had put it into our heads: until you cross the Danube at Regensburg, you can expect to be sent back! and now, happily, we had put one of the dangerous days and the immediate environs of Munich behind us; also, instead of the daily pace of 12½ miles we had calculated, we had managed 22½ miles. We did not wash and were ready quickly, we took what we could use from the soldiers' legacy: a glass, the cutlery, a pocket knife (the things served us infinitely well), a haversack. [ . . . ] It was Eva's plan to bypass Landshut on the west, approach Regensburg in a more direct northerly direction; for one thing, to save a couple of miles, but also to get around any checkpoints and barriers more easily. [ . . . ]

In great heat the remainder of the day was very exhausting, in addition to knapsack and bag there was now the coat to be carried over the arm, and my very old and heavy and stiffly wrinkled army boots were ever more of a torment. About 3½ miles of country road, mercilessly lacking in charm and shade—the absence of trees along the highway is an unpleasant, widespread characteristic of Upper Bavaria, in some way related to the absence of balconies in Munich—had a very depressing effect. Something else occurs to me re the coat: the day before, when I was wearing it, the luminous button from last winter was still fixed to it. Two cyclists came toward us, and one called out laughing: "He's still wearing the Party badge!"

In the village of *Langenbach* we got, although we had to ask for it, a proper and adequate warm lunch, and that not only heartened us physically, but also spiritually, because we concluded, that we had left behind the real starvation zone around the capital. But the refreshment did not last long. The heat was too great. [ . . . ] The villages we passed were called *Inkofen, Kirchamper, Ambach.* Here we stood at 5:00 P.M., very thirsty, and here we each got a proper mug of beer—rare and almost a favor, much harder to obtain than milk.

Somewhere Eva had seen a detailed map from which it was apparent that we had to decide at the village of Thalbach, close to Moosburg, between Landshut and veering away in a northerly direction. We resolved to call on the village teacher there to ask for advice and to look at a map. The walking turned to marching, to silent expenditure of energy, gradually we began to march more with clenched teeth than with our feet.

The village of *Feldkirch,* then probably a small group of houses, and to the right, spreading out white and townlike, Moosburg, through which the road certainly led to Landshut—of Thalbach there was nothing to be seen, and a couple of passersby knew nothing of it. (It later turned out that we had already passed this little place.) Instead a road sign appeared, according to which Gammelsdorf was five miles farther north. Once we reached Gammelsdorf, we were definitely closer to our goal than if we turned off to Landshut. [ . . . ]

We walked doggedly on. [ . . . ] Finally a one-horse cart, two very young people, almost children, on it, brother and sister. They let us squeeze onto the tiny conveyance, they are going the same way but only for a mile, but after that it is not supposed to be far, and we can rest. But the benefit of the rest was short-lived, and it grew late, and the road stretched out endlessly, and went over yet another hill, and behind each rise we should "already be able to see" the church tower of Gammelsdorf and it is still out of sight. At last, at a quarter to nine, we are in *Gammelsdorf*, ask our way to the priest's house and ring in vain at the locked door. In despair to the nearby inn, a good-natured woman, but she has no room. She gives us beer to drink, promises, if need be, a place to sleep in the barn, but first I should inquire across the way at Wagner Schmid's. I go over, believe I am in the second inn of the village, am instead (the people laugh at my mistake) in the home of a peasant, who is at the same time Wagner—cartwright—by trade. At my short report that I had tried in vain at the priest's house, that as a professor I had to return home . . . presumably also because of my very exhausted appearance we were made wonderfully welcome. We got fried eggs for supper, we got coffee with milk, the radio reported the arrest of Streicher and the like, the master of the house and his family, of which I did not yet know who was who, talked interestedly and sympathetically about politics, in a Catholic anti-Nazi sense, of course. On such occasions I am always the probably Catholic, at any rate strongly religious senior educationist, who regularly wins hearts with the the the sentence: "Above all young people must once again learn the Ten Commandments." By saying that I really get to the heart of things and also express my own conviction (but at the same time nevertheless play hide-and-seek). [ . . . ]

So that was the second day of our journey, Sunday, May 27, from Freising to Gammelsdorf.

After these exertions we had set aside a half of Monday as a day of rest, and it passed in part well, in part badly. What was disappointing was that we neither found the priest nor were we able to make any purchases—we virtually never succeeded in this, because shopkeepers either demanded that our passage coupons be restamped or exchanged, or these coupons were not recognized at all, or a new regulation or a withdrawal from circulation had just been announced on the radio, or the shops were locked up, or we were simply laughed at, when we offered coupons—there was always something wrong, and either we just got our food for nothing or not at all. At the beginning it upset me greatly, later I became quite blunted to it: I became accustomed to periods of hunger and to begging, and starving to death was simply one possible death among the many possible deaths of recent months, and ultimately a very unlikely one, because after all for the time being we still happened upon ration depots for returning soldiers and refugees . . . As against the disappointment was the fact that I was able to wash and shave properly, that a second inn promised us lunch and a little bread, and above all, that the Schmid household treated us with uncommon friendliness. We got an ample breakfast (coffee with milk and bread) [ . . . ]. The still-young peasant, widower of a widow, dwelling with grown-up stepdaughters, proudly showed us his holding, the full barn, his hops [ . . . ], his workshop with several finished shafts and yokes, with several crooked pieces of untreated wood, chosen precisely for a cartwright's purposes. We wanted to pay the girl who kept house, she did not want to take anything, finally said, "so that you give me some peace," I could pay two marks for everything. I did so, and as we took our leave, she felt obliged to set a number of pancakes in front of us as well and to give us some bread for the journey. After that we still had to eat lunch at the inn as agreed, and here, too, we were given bread to take with us. Thus we had no more worries for a while . . .

At two, very full up and in very great heat, we set off again, walking slowly as far as the first strip of woodland, where we rested for almost an hour. It was no help, we were still tired, my feet were a torment; the pretty countryside [ . . . ] was of no avail against the heat and the abominable boots; a cup of buttermilk in *Obermünchen,* even a somewhat nervous rest on a heavily laden hay cart driven wildly by Hungarians did not help us over our depression. Nevertheless we managed a distance of 9½ miles, a good 7½ miles of it on foot. On the way, with my constant asking-what-time-is-it I for the first time (and not the last) came upon a Polish worker, who, being unable to speak German, held out his looted German ladies' watch. We reached *Pfeffenhausen,* a market town like Inchenhofen, with a great effort, but this time not so late at all.

Once again I called on the priest and this time happened upon him. An elderly man, pipe-smoking, to all appearance unspiritual, peasantlike [ . . . ]. His first response: Why hadn't I chosen a village, everything here in the market town was so full. But he immediately added, something could be done, left us standing and went, just as he was, across the road to a farm. After a very short time he came back, there was no need to worry, he would take us to some good people. On the way I told him of our intention of seeking out Dr. Ritter in Regensburg. Immediately: "Dr. Ritter at the hospital? He's had me on the operating table, too . . ." With that I knew *at once* that Dr. Ritter was alive, still held his old post, and was at home . . . The priest took his leave very hurriedly, we did not see him again. The peasant family and the peasant house to which we had been entrusted were dirty beyond imagining, fit for the stage [ . . . ], the wife fantastically ragged, the husband reminiscent of the poorhouse inmates who swept the streets in Landsberg an der Warthe, the infinitely garrulous daughter hardly any better dressed than her mother, all crowded together in a small and dirt-covered kitchen. But we were given a friendly welcome and reasonably fed, and the conversation was interesting insofar as they railed against the Third Reich (We fell for Hitler!), but nothing good was said about the Americans either, they looted too much, was the refrain. When we were led out of the stuffy and stinking kitchen to go to sleep, it turned out that the couple had given up their own bedroom, and that this bedroom was far more wealthily furnished than we could have suspected from the family's kitchen and clothing. Above the broad bed there was the Holy Family in relief, all kinds of children's toys were piled up, a wardrobe with a seaside picture, trinkets. There was also a proper night commode, a showpiece. But we were expected simply to go into the stall built up against the house.

For this day I must also add the feeling, later a frequently occurring one, of waiting for a motor vehicle. One distinguishes the sounds. The fast, loud American vehicles and convoys of vehicles are out of the question, as are the trucks provided by the Americans for returning soldiers. A tractor offers a better prospect, but sometimes it is pulling manure. Most reliable are horse-drawn vehicles—but suddenly, ten paces before they reach our resting place, they turn off into a field. There is also the disappointment of a horse without a cart, one which is merely being led. And then there are also oxcarts; these are not much slower than horse and cart, but they usually go only very short distances. I do not know why later on we did not manage to catch a lift with a vehicle as often as on the first day—perhaps because then we were more rarely walking along main roads? But the horse-drawn vehicle also prefers the side roads to the highways. (We regretted avoiding the main roads only because there were more cigarette ends to pick up on them—the wealthy Americans smoke like chimneys and often throw away half a cigarette. The Russians are not so rich, smoke tipped cigarettes and throw away only the tip.)

The achievement of this third day, Monday, May 28, was modest: Gammelsdorf to Pfeffenhausen.

For the following day we had been led to have hopes of motor transport; they were fulfilled, but very inadequately. The peasant's wife [ . . . ] took us to the dairy, where things were very much as in Aichach, except that here we had first of all to beseech the driver to take passengers. And then we had to wait at the ramp from eight until a quarter to nine in the ever hotter sun, until the loading and unloading was finished, and when we did drive off, we were set down again after less than four miles—it had hardly been worth it. The place was called—I think—Gisselsdorf. Here our walk began. In murderous heat we needed a whole seven hours for the roughly 9½ miles to Langquaid. Apart from the heat, we were this time tormented by hunger, all our efforts to obtain a decent meal at an inn or from peasants failed. Money seemed worthless. At one inn we were ill-humoredly given a plate of soup between the two of us and then payment was just as ill-humoredly refused; at another inn, they scraped together a tiny plate of potato salad for each of us; at peasant houses we managed to get a cup of milk for a few pfennigs or for the asking—it was horrid and depressing (yet only a prelude to our days of hunger in the Vogtland in Saxony). The landscape, always a variation on the same theme, this time displayed very many red and blue and yellow wildflowers, in addition a number of picturesque river views. Once, I see it in front of me, a group of Poles accompanied by women allow their horses to enter the water and drink, while the wagon waits ready to continue the journey. Once we come upon a very gypsylike traveling circus, their caravan has made a halt. I am carrying Eva's fire-eaten fur coat over my arm; a young woman with an impudent face, very gypsylike, grabs at the fur: What do you need it for, give it to me! I recoil involuntarily. The woman, offended, says contemptuously: I don't want it; I wouldn't have it, if you gave it to me. A minute earlier I had asked the people, whether we could come part of the way in their caravan, but they were going in another direction, toward Nürnberg. A third image from this part of the journey. Below us, near the village of Laaberberg an der Laaber, but quite isolated, on green grass, lies a big, gray teeming heap, like an inflated piece of rubber tubing, flat, at first indefinable. Then one distinguishes: an American army camp, vehicles parked between the tents [ . . . ]. For a long time cries float up to our high-lying road from the swarming mass below . . . [ . . . ]

At five we stop for a longer rest in *Langquaid,* a very large village [ . . . ]. At the inn, as everywhere in this district, there is a great deal of cursing of the Americans: They loot, they steal jewelry and watches, one had watches all the way up his arm . . . the commander, however, had replied to German complaints: "You're still living in paradise here, compared to what our allies in Russia and France had to bear from your soldiers." [ . . . ]

We are a little recovered, the sun is a little lower, so we soon put the remaining mile or so to the next village, *Schierling,* behind us—there is supposed to be a milk truck from there to Regensburg (20 miles) . . . [ . . . ]

We again found a good priest, I no longer recall what he looked like, I only know [ . . . ] that he immediately set off with great warmheartedness and attended to our request, while we drank a beer. [ . . . ] I know that we were very well fed and looked after, mattresses and bedding were put down on the floor of the upstairs front room, we were also given food the next morning and the people would not be persuaded to accept money. [ . . . ]

The fourth day therefore: Tuesday, May 29, from Pfeffenhausen to Markt Schierling, about 12½ miles.

The fifth day, Wednesday, began with a serious disappointment and yielded three dramatic climaxes. The milk truck man was a coarse blockhead and refused to take us with him. So we now began our hike crawling very wearily along to Eggmühl, 2½ miles distant. [ . . . ] Then later there was—well, what? here the catchwords have become mixed-up, and my memories too. There was a rest in a wood and the futile waiting for a cart, already described above; there was a camp for returnees with baby carriages and washing hanging up, there was Eva bare-legged in slippers, there was landscape like an "English garden" and in the far distance a line of hills that presumably marked the north bank of the Danube. There were two plates of soup, which we spooned up sitting on the step of the house of a charitable peasant, which reminded me of times in my parents' house. The beggar was given a plate of soup on the steps at the kitchen door, and x times the soup was afterward found untouched—the man had been after money for schnapps—he wasn't hungry, who in Germany before the Great War was hungry? Another rest in the early afternoon, and then the oxcart appears, which takes us a remarkably long distance at a respectable pace, and which already has two elderly women as passengers. The two, petites bourgeoises from Regensburg, returning home from an extended foraging trip, are drawn to us; one of them tells us with tremendously lively intonation, facial expression, and dramatic gestures about an incident in Regensburg. The Americans had issued an ultimatum to surrender the defenseless and already heavily damaged town, otherwise they would destroy it in a massive air attack. The SS refused, the women of the town demonstrated vehemently in the marketplace. At that point Dr. Maier, the cathedral preacher, got up and spoke—deep bow, arms spread wide, very emotional, soft, pleading voice ("This is just how he spoke!"): We demand nothing, we want no more than to ask that we be spared the worst! Then the SS came, pushed us back, drove us away . . . I screamed and wept and defended myself . . . and they tied Dr. Maier's wrists, and he managed to say "pray for me" . . . and the next morning his body was hanging in the marketplace, and he looked so beautiful and white, not like a hanged man at all!

After we had been kicked off the oxcart, we walked on with the women for quite a distance. Chatting helped keep weariness at bay, but gradually I fell behind nevertheless, I was limping all too painfully, also knapsack and other baggage were weighing me down. Suddenly, in a village, I think in *Köfering*, the women came toward us with a third party. Whether friend or relative did not become clear to me, at any rate Aunt Völkel lived here, and we were going to get a revivifying coffee from her, and now we had a piece of pancake stuffed into our mouths as a farewell present from the pair on the oxcart and a fatty (fatty! how marvelous) bag of pancakes pressed into our hands, and soon we were sitting in a clean and peaceful cottage garden, and Aunt Völkel, the widow of a teacher and the mother of a pretty little girl, really did give us coffee, and we regained our strength . . . It was our intention to make our way as close to Regensburg as possible, to spend the night in the last village and then to enter the town the next morning and seek out Ritter. It had become clear to us, that he must be a highly respected and very influential man . . . We had been warned: don't get too close to Regensburg, everything there was destroyed. But now that we had revived again, and since a horse and cart soon took us another mile, and the line of hills beyond the Danube—beyond! we knew that for certain now, and it drew us on, for it appeared to me that victory for our undertaking lay there—since, therefore, the line of hills was coming ever closer we marched on under a sky that threatened a thunderstorm, and all of a sudden we were in the last village before Regensburg, *Burgweinting,* and here suddenly in the midst of complete destruction (whereas thus far there had been little sign of damage, I think none at all). We asked our way to the priest: We were told he was in the church. He came out of the sacristy, a young man, a curate. He immediately and emphatically said it was impossible. Not a house was undamaged, not a corner empty, not a piece of bread to be found; we had to, simply had to overcome our tiredness and carry on for the last 3 miles to Regensburg; he would give us a recommendation to the Cäcilienschule, a church music school; we would certainly get accommodation there. I objected that it was already past 7:00 P.M. and I couldn't keep up a good pace anymore. Yes! we would manage it, we would enter the town not far from the Cäcilienschule, also the curfew in Regensburg had been moved forward to half past nine. Both pieces of information turned out to be wrong: It was lucky that we found out only afterward—we reached the school less than two minutes before the curfew time. The final spurt of the day really was no more than that, a supreme effort. Destroyed terrain at the edge of town, craters, ruins, the outer belt of a city, as we have repeatedly seen it. Then gradually there were streets and at last we had found the Cäcilienschule. [ . . . ] First my ringing brought a nun, then the mother superior to the door [ . . . ]. Finally we were assigned a clean, pretty room, but there was nothing to eat, nevertheless some resident of the house left coffee on the stairs for us. [ . . . ]

So on this fifth day of our journey, Wednesday, May 30, we had managed to get from Schierling to Regensburg and thus reached our first goal.

The sixth day was completely taken up with *Regensburg.* It began unpleasantly. It was a very long walk on an empty stomach, in the rain, the length of the city to the hospital district, Prüfeningstrasse. We found Ritter's private house, everyone knew it, and rang in vain. We went to one of the big hospitals, which was mentioned as his. Nurses and matron were very friendly, but Herr Doktor had just left for some meeting. His apartment was telephoned, there was no reply. Very weak and weary we went to the villa once again. This time we were in luck: A gentleman opened the door, from his appearance unmistakably a brother of Ritter. Younger, I thought, because he looked not unlike the Ritter of 1919. But he was an older brother, a bombed-out pediatrician from Cologne. We immediately got on with him. After a while a young girl, his eldest daughter, came and brought us tea. Then an hour later Ritter himself was there, giant of a man, fatter and older in the face, but the same warmth of feeling as in the old days. His wife and boy, he told us, were lodged in a nearby village. There was a moment of coldness, nevertheless, when his (still fairly young) wife turned up after all and at first appeared somewhat put out, but soon she, too, found the right note of friendship. A friend, who had been an engineer and businessman abroad, was also present and staying there.

Ritter arranged for us to have a room for the night in his hospital; we were his guests all day, were sumptuously feted at lunch and in the evening—merely sitting at a well-laid table was relaxation for us—I got

shoes (admittedly size 46 instead of 42) and socks and a little piece of soap
as presents; in short we were warmed both inside and out. Ritter had become a highly regarded, satisfied man, evidently one of the leading figures in Regensburg. He is in charge of two hospitals, one for men and one
for women, 700 beds altogether. [ . . . ] He was not very enthusiastic about
the Americans, they had looted, and they were not particularly wanting in
the brutality of the victor. Their attitude, too, was one of retribution. His
judgment of the Nazis was extremely harsh. I was surprised, in the light of
his pious views, when he declared of Himmler's suicide, cyanide acted in
a couple of seconds—that had been "too little" for this bloodhound. I also
mentioned the engineer (employed by AEG or Siemens). I found him interesting, because he thought the anti-Semitism of 1919 and after had a
commercial basis: On his return from India "they" had been in all the important business positions; I note this, not because I unhesitatingly believe
it, but because it suggests to me one of the many paths on which Hitlerism
could march.

[ . . . ]

We were most definitely assured, that from Regensburg, more precisely
from Walhalla station, goods trains were already running north. With our
hopes set on this and very much relieved we went to the hospital after we
had taken our leave of the family. Ritter himself took us there and saw to
us the next morning as well, but then he was already in his white coat and
with calls on him from all sides as head physician, leave-taking was somewhat abrupt. That was day six, Thursday, May 31, our day of rest in Regensburg.

The first and properly heroic part of our journey, in which we were almost exclusively dependent on our feet, very clearly ends in Regensburg.
[ . . . ] The degree of our hardships was subsequently hardly diminished, it
was only displaced. I walked less, but starved more. Or: I walked less, but
was also much more tired out than before.

[ . . . ]

On the morning of Friday, June 1, we walked through the not so heavily damaged city center itself and then crossed the river on a big pontoon
bridge, which was also used by vehicles. [ . . . ] After about 3 miles we
reached Walhalla station, without having seen the Walhalla itself. Disappointment: The train left from Regenstauf, 6 miles farther. So that day we
did nevertheless walk a total of about 12½ miles. [ . . . ]

*Regenstauf* itself, which we reached after 5:00 P.M., is a considerable village: In almost every house is an inn, and in not one of these could we get
even a mouthful of coffee. We had to walk through the village to the isolated linesman's cabin 7. Here beside the embankment and by the roadside and in the meadow an encampment grew up like the one we had seen
in Suchering. I could fill our jar of water at the cabin's box pump, so we ate
a meal on the grass and waited for the train, the first for us since the end
of the war. It came after six: a luggage van and two open freight cars. We
found places in one of the freight cars, it was bliss to be rolling sooo

quickly northward; the 19 miles to *Schwandorf* were covered in less than one and a half hours, we were in the Upper Palatinate, at the start of the industrial area. In the marketplace I received the information from the Americans—I naturally drew attention to my mission—that an American vehicle would take us on the next day, and the German police directed us to the municipal hall as the joint camp for refugees and returning soldiers. It was a chaotic and damaged building, the largest room in it a hall with a stage [ . . . ]; many soldiers, few civilians, very simple people with children were resting on mattresses; the mattresses had been distributed, but there was still straw and we cheerfully made up a bed for ourselves among the soldiers. There was also an ample soup eaten at greasy tables, and we were doubly cheerful. We explored the extensive bomb-damaged building. The floor of a side room was thickly covered with thousands of cardboard insoles (we took a few with us). In the courtyard stinking pieces of Russian uniforms and rags of every kind were smoldering in a bomb crater. Eva therefore concluded that there had been a cobbler's workshop or similar establishment with Russian prisoners of war here. Outside the hall there was also running water and washing facilities, where some soldiers were shaving. The windows of the hall were broken, so there was no lack of fresh air, and we slept well and romantically (on subsequent occasions only dirtily and primitively)—under our almost thirty-year-old coats.

Day seven, Friday, June 1, therefore: From Regensburg to Schwandorf, 31 miles.

On Saturday, June 2, awake before five and early to the marketplace, where soldiers were gathering in various groups according to destination. We joined the one making for Weiden. The day before, the Americans had assured us that we would also be taken. We then found one of the many inns open and prepared to let us have a coffee with our bread. American trucks began to draw up toward eight. We got places on the one bound for Weiden, however I was very much squeezed in and could not see much. [ . . . ] We had gone no more than 12 miles when the truck halted at the bottom of a hill near a high-lying place: *Nabburg an der Naab.* Everyone out, the truck is going back. Perhaps(!) another one will come along. The men stood grumbling at the roadside, "they" always did it like that. Many soldiers immediately continued on foot. I climbed up to the town, part of which we had already driven through, showed the civilian policeman an old (invalid) English language scrap of paper, which he could not read, was thus passed on to an interpreter; the man was from Cologne, knew the musician Otto Klemperer—and was immediately full of enthusiasm. I was given a recommendation to the person in charge of a neighboring refugee camp and a man [was detailed] to take Eva and myself to it. In the camp things did not look good, it contained civilians, women and children among them, who, poorly fed, had already been waiting long and impatiently for transport to travel on. Where had they come from? I don't know, in general in Bavaria civilian refugees were still being detained, in order to keep roads and transport free for the foreign workers and for soldiers returning home—and these civilians now saw us as illegitimate intruders. At first the camp superintendent, too, was overwrought and not very responsive. Only when I became forceful did he push me onto a truck that drew up and was stormed, even passed a loaf up to me. Once again Eva (as "frail") was accommodated beside the driver; once again I was very squashed, with unpleasant neighbors this time. It was still fairly early in the morning. Once again the drive did not last long: 4 miles outside *Weiden*, we were once more dumped in the middle of the road to the accompaniment of much cursing. We walked into the town, I again went to American headquarters; even with the help of the police, who let me have a mouthful of beer, there was nothing to eat or drink; after an hour the headquarters passed us on to a civilian policeman, who again brought us to a motor vehicle, which was surrounded by cursing people, and got us onto it. Tired and skeptical we drove off in the early afternoon through a pretty, mountainous region, and reached the little place of *Windisch-Eschenbach*. Once again imploring struggle at the American headquarters [ . . . ]. Nevertheless, once again it worked. For supper we got soup at a nearby inn, then we were yet again squeezed onto a vehicle packed with people, [driven] through always beautiful mountain country, finally coming to an avenue completely overarched by mighty trees that led to the village of Reuth. [ . . . ]

In the evening in *Reuth*, weak and weary, I go to the mayor, he gives me a billeting slip for bed and board and directs me to the inn, which belongs to a butcher; the landlord and butcher, bad tempered and very rude: "Do you think I'm going to get a parlor room ready for you? You can sleep on straw in the hall, if you want; you'll get nothing to eat or drink from me, we don't have anything left." — But it's an order from the mayor. — "The mayor can go and jump! He's a baker, he can give you bread himself." I left Eva at the inn, ran back to the mayor, found only his wife, helplessly beleaguered by other refugees. The village was overcrowded and eaten bare, her husband was out, trying to get everyone off the streets before the curfew—I think here it had been moved forward to 10:00 P.M. I paced around, until the mayor came back. He said he could not help me, the landlord really had nothing left. I returned at ten, we ate dry bread, which the mayor had given us, and drank water with it.

Eva had meanwhile discovered a garden pavilion, in which there were a great many pieces of baggage but only a very few people; we slept there in makeshift fashion, as in a waiting room.

That was day eight, Saturday, June 2, one of the most unpleasant and arduous despite having to walk very little. I don't know how many miles made up the much subdivided stretch from Schwandorf to Reuth.

Sunday, the ninth day of the journey, began with a wonderful walk, except that it was very exhausting on an empty stomach, of 7 miles to Wiesau station. We set out very early in the morning, well before six, so as to avoid the heat. We walked along proper hill paths, of the kind on which amenity societies put up signs (at useless points, never at necessary ones), with forest and meadow and good views. [ . . . ]

In *Wiesau* we thoroughly refreshed ourselves. Notes and clear memory resume again only on the goods train, which got us to *Marktredwitz* around midday. There we changed trains and first of all waited until four o'clock in the new open wagon for the journey to continue. Here there was a comic intermezzo. On the whole stretch from Wiesau to Hof only soldiers and soldiers alone were allowed to use the goods train (there were no passenger trains yet). For my part I had an identity document and a recommendation—but only of a dubious nature. At any rate if there had been an inspection I would have had to get involved in explanation, discussion, perhaps even a fight. And at Marktredwitz station an overzealous official really was carrying out an inspection. There were a number of civilians, including women, on board. They were hidden under pieces of baggage and clothing and helpful soldiers stood around them in such a way that the official did not notice them. The two of us also crouched down and camouflaged ourselves a little and were likewise unseen. Toward evening, at about six o'clock, the train reached *Oberkotzau,* 4 miles outside Hof, and there was a further train connection only from Feilitzsch, about 4 miles beyond Hof. So in great heat we walked to *Hof.* [ . . . ]

At the police station they could give no advice as to food, nor really as to accommodation either: A long, long way out of town there was supposed to be a refugee camp in a damaged and shut-down thread factory. [ . . . ] Thus we had no other choice except to drag ourselves all the way out to the factory in Leopoldstrasse, high above the town, although it was almost curfew time (here half past nine) and my strength really was exhausted. (My feet, the baggage.) For a moment I was tempted to spend the night in the bushes at the side of the road or in a freight car by a level crossing. Then we reached the factory at last. But the dormitory was so crowded and the air was so bad—always the poorest of people with babies and diapers, we smelled it with a shudder a hundred times over during these months—that we fled. The dormitory was up a couple of steps; down by the gate, off the courtyard (in which there was a lavatory), there was a corridor with a number of mattresses. An old factory watchman and several refugee women, who thought us in part arrogant, in part crazy, shook their heads as we bedded down there. Apart from that, the people had given us a jug of cold coffee from their own already prepared supplies. We slept as we were in sweaty clothes, it was the third night we spent in our clothes.

That was the ninth day, Sunday, June 3, from Reuth to Hof, with long marches at the beginning and the end of the day.

On the tenth day, Monday, June 4, we again started at 5:00 A.M.; beautiful early morning, beautiful mountain view—everything would have been beautiful but for the tiredness and the sum of everything else that weighed us down. Thus the summer joys of the tourist again very quickly turned into an arduous, hot, hungry, and weighed down progress, toiling up and down hill on a treeless and merciless road. At eight we were in *Feilitzsch*, the first village with a Saxon name [ . . . ]. From Feilitzsch there was supposed to be a train running to Plauen. [ . . . ] At the station I found out that no train came through here. Only a locomotive would pass through at 1:30 P.M., but since I was the Czar's courier after all (my dubious chits and papers worked wonders), I would be taken along. [ . . . ] We had an ample breakfast at the village inn (in this case ample means: We got black coffee and ate the rest of our bread with it), and then walked a mile to the village of *Trogen*, where there was a reception camp. It had been a youth labor camp of the Third Reich, very prettily laid out: big clean barrack huts around a large rectangular square, a lawn and all kinds of greenery, on the walls various Nazi moral homilies. Now the barracks had been emptied except for bundles of straw and a couple of tables without chairs, everything was desolate, without having quite lost its former prettiness. And in this camp, curiously, there was proper food, bread, soup, coffee. [ . . . ] We had a relaxed rest, sat down for a while by the edge of the road high above the camp, then walked slowly and confidently back to Feilitzsch station. A crowd of soldiers had meanwhile arrived there; I asked myself how a single locomotive was supposed to take us all. The telegraph announced it, everyone got ready. There appeared a locomotive pulling a high coal tender. Dozens of soldiers (coming from Hof) were sitting on the coal, standing in the locomotive; in a flash a couple of young fellows clambered onto the tender like monkeys, helped by their comrades; there was confusion and shouting; I roared at my official, who for his part was quite helpless, and the locomotive set off again, and those who had not managed to get on moved off in resignation. I raged at the official, but that didn't change anything, and so at about two o'clock we continued our journey on foot. [ . . . ]

We tramped 4½ miles along the motorway, then by the village of *Pirk*, about 10½ miles from Hof and already situated in Plauen prefecture, we came to a huge, half-finished motorway overpass, which looked like an antique viaduct, just as splendid and just as much a ruin—it seemed to me a symbol of Nazism's hubris. [ . . . ]

In the village of *Magwitz*, which is completely surrounded by forests, we were well accommodated on a wealthy and friendly farm: We were excellently fed, we slept in a big barn, could undress to a considerable extent and wash the next morning. [ . . . ]

On the tenth day, Monday, June 4, therefore, we got from Feilitzsch to Magwitz.

On the eleventh day, Tuesday, June 5, we set out late, not until eight o'clock, Eva with her hair washed, I shaved. [ . . . ] We came closer to Plauen than we had intended, we then found a road to *Oelsnitz*, and in this long and bleak place, a refugee camp in a school, which fed us bread and soup. Then from the early afternoon we walked along beautiful Erzgebirge mountain roads, which were now part of the district around Falken-stein, with places that in part we had heard mentioned, in part really did already know.

Once, the first time in a long while, we were given a lift by a horse and cart again, once in the *Tirpersdorf* inn, we found not only a big can of coffee, but also a south German news sheet, the *Hessische Post* of May 26. The actual final act of the war has, after all, remained obscure to us to this day. [ . . . ]

At half past eight we were in *Falkenstein*. The Scherners' private home heavily damaged, the pharmacy much less so. American shell fire, as we learned later. We called and clapped our hands outside the locked house. Trude Scherner opened the door, Scherner himself had gone to Leipzig with "his" Fräulein Uhlmann to buy stock, he returned at ten, just as we were about to retire, triumphant that he had been able to make purchases for 10,000M instead of the approved 200M; after the complete destruction of the other pharmacy, he now had a monopoly as it were. Great warmth, great hospitality, and it was not until eleven, the curfew hour in force here, that we were lying on our old resting places in the private office of the pharmacy. There the picture of Hitler had disappeared and been replaced by a landscape. Scherner related, how immediately before the Americans entered the town (it had been under fire for two weeks) the people from the Party had come to see him and forced him, in their presence, to burn all the Nazi books, which he had previously been forced to buy, and which he had promised to keep for me . . . So we now had the firm intention of resting here for a while [ . . . ]. This was the eleventh day of our journey, the last of the second phase (Regensburg to Falkenstein), from Magwitz to Falkenstein, Tuesday, June 5.

On Wednesday everything looked different. It was literally sheer hunger that drove us to leave Falkenstein as quickly as possible. On the evening we arrived, the Scherners had filled our stomachs with a meal of potatoes, which had already been cooked. But now they did not have another crumb. We would no doubt obtain coupons at the town hall, but there was nothing to be bought with them, bread sold out, no butter to be had for a long time, etc., etc. In the restaurant, for potato coupons, we got a plate of dry and tasteless turnip schnitzels—which we later repeatedly encountered as a typical dish of the impoverished Vogtland—and nothing else. Scherner took his crutch, leaned heavily on me with his other hand and went on a begging errand along the high street. He knew every passerby and talked to everyone, he knocked on the doors and display windows of closed shops and pushed his way in, he told our story everywhere, and thus a portion of meat was bought and a piece of bread given as a present. That was very touching and to some extent helped us over the immediate difficulty, but it was also very embarrassing and impossible to repeat. I immediately prepared to continue the journey. I went to American headquarters: A very young, impassive lieutenant and a very handsome, boyish, good-natured, slim half-Negro as interpreter. He offered me an easy chair at his lieutenant's desk, bent over me with a childlike smile, and asked in a soft voice: "Was willst du?" [What do you want?]. I explained myself, he explained it to the lieutenant, and the latter wrote in block letters, but without an official stamp, as he had understood it: "*This Professor Victor Israel Klemperer is a half-Jew and he would like to go to Dresden. He is one of Germany's famous professors in philosophy and languages. He is a good man and we would recommend everything possible to help him.*" I took this chit, which I would subsequently make a big show with, to the "motor pool." In vain. There were no vehicles at all going in the direction of Schönheide, where there was "supposed" to be a rail connection to Aue and on to Chemnitz, and from Chemnitz there was "supposed" to be a regular train to Dresden—so no vehicles at all going there from Falkenstein but perhaps from Auerbach. On Scherner's advice I also went to see a lawyer, Reichenbach, *a half-Jew* or a whole one, cousin at any rate—as it turned out—of our unfortunate Dresden Reichenbach, and in a senior administrative position since the changeover. He was very friendly and promised to take us to Auerbach the next morning, also to be of assistance to me there. Otherwise the day passed with various conversations. Scherner told us how badly Fräulein Uhlmann, who was morally intact, but had grown up believing completely in Nazism and the Führer, had suffered from the collapse and learning the truth. Without revealing my Jewishness, I nevertheless gave the girl all kinds of information—Eva thought I had treated her too roughly. Talking to the anti-Nazi Fräulein Dumpier was simpler. A few harmless words were exchanged with Norma Dettke. To my profound joy, her husband, the Baltic Nazi who believed in Hitler and victory, with whom the war agreed so well and for whom it had not lasted long enough at all, was evidently a prisoner of war of the Americans.

This the twelfth day, Wednesday, June 6, spent entirely in Falkenstein.

Thursday, June 7, depressed departure from Falkenstein, basically we were going into the unknown again. The lawyer and a companion arrived in a beautiful automobile and took us to Auerbach in a few minutes, but let us wait outside some office for a good hour. In the meantime Reichenbach came out once; there was a Russian officer inside, perhaps he would be able to help us continue our journey. But then, after an hour, we were told, unfortunately it was all in vain, the [American] headquarters were not allowing anyone into the adjacent no-man's-land and into the Russian zone; the most sensible thing was to return to Falkenstein with him, Reichenbach, immediately. When I indignantly objected, he said he admittedly knew of many who had crossed over secretly and on their own; he could also see whether I could get a pass at military headquarters. So we drove there. Many of the rooms were crowded but Reichenbach immediately knew the right one and the right interpreter. [ . . . ] The interpreter partly confused me with Otto Klemperer and made a "music professor" and owner of a farm near Dresden out of me. After some waiting I did then get my pass, which I did not use on a single occasion. I do not know where the notorious no-man's-land was, I do not know where the actual Russian zone began, I was not troubled in the least by soldiers or looters . . . We had the pass and were now supposed to be taken to Schönheide by a moving company. *Supposed.* But this company, which definitely went there and was very willing to take people with passes, did not go in that direction, and private cars, it was said, still avoided the uncertainties of the no-man's-land so, once again, we had to tramp the approximately 10½ miles to the "supposed" railway station. In Auerbach we got turnip schnitzels as a meal again, and that only with great difficulty and after a fight; shops were closed, we set off on foot in the noonday heat. A horse and cart helped us over the worst hour after lunch, thus we reached *Rodewisch.* [ . . . ] In Rodewisch we succeeded in buying bread, in *Rützengrün* a friendly grocer's family gave us a pot of coffee, which we drank on the steps, and here Eva also exchanged some sugar for tobacco, in *Schnarrtanne* I saw the last American sentry—he was letting children clamber all over him, as if he were a good-natured Saint Bernard.

This road to Schnarrtanne and then on to *Schönheide* was Baedekerworthy and lovely and a godsend for tourists [ . . . ]. But it rose and rose and rose and I was very much weakened by the constant heat. And then finally the long stretch from Schönheide to *Schönheidehammer.* But then we really had reached the rail connection. We spent the night in the Carlshof inn, without food, without any opportunity of getting out of our clothes. [ . . . ]

The thirteenth day therefore: Thursday, June 7, from Falkenstein to Schönheidehammer.

The fourteenth and penultimate day of the journey is characterized by dry bread and water. And by the fanaticism of the overwrought refugees, ordinary people, in the Carlshof. One woman, from Breslau, cursed Hitler fanatically, another, who had fled from the Russians, cursed the Russians equally fanatically and declared all German atrocities in Russia to be lies and propaganda—no German soldier had ever looted or done anything else bad . . . We kept out of the way and sat in the garden of the inn or by the railway line, until at last the train came, a proper passenger train, for which we should have bought second-class tickets. In three-quarters of an hour we were in *Aue,* which from the train appeared to be a larger town; in the waiting room I obtained the infamous turnip schnitzels—unfortunately they disagreed with Eva this time—at half past three we were in *Chemnitz* [ . . . ].

The fourteenth day of our journey, Friday, June 8, from Schönheidehammer to Chemnitz.

The city center of Chemnitz appeared completely destroyed, many buildings were certainly standing, but were uninhabited and uninhabitable, in between them ruins, heaps of debris, somewhere a large square with nothing but rubble and a huge, undamaged candelabra protruding from it—all in all the usual picture. [ . . . ] Then we saw a little group of people standing outside a half-destroyed building, it appears to be some kind of store; we ask whether one can get a cup of coffee here and are directed to the first floor. There a sight as if from a lost world, in a long room *the* elegant prewar music café. Tables with white tablecloths, all crowded—coats are left at the cloakroom outside!—a large quantity of tableware (no spoons, however), waiters in tails, coffee in pots, Brambacher mineral water, beer, coffee cups even seem to suggest real coffee, a jazz band, as negroid as can be, the beginnings of the elegance of painted demimondaines, the beginnings of inflation prices: It was the start of the goings-on of 1919, the mood of Hurrah-we're-still-alive and of black marketeering, but all of it incomparably more grisly and shocking and wretched than in those days, because the building was destroyed and the room patched up so badly, that one stumbled on the floor, and the city all around lies in ruins, and what is being offered at fraudulent prices, is ersatz and miserable and does not assuage hunger, only skims over it. Eva thought she could already discern a change to Russian hairstyles (Cléo de Mérode), I myself repeatedly had the impression that among the customers there were various members of the Russian civilian administration and no doubt also of the police—but that may have been autosuggestion. What I did conclude with certainty was that I found this coffeehouse life, the pleasure of my youth, really very boring, that I was a little ashamed to be sitting white-haired among all the young people and to observe sadly as ghastly variation or as sheer repetition what the young took up with delight (clapping their hands and showing off to women when they paid—I saw a—previously unknown to me—twenty-mark note of the Saxon State bank of April 1945, that, too, a beginning and a repetition). — For all that: I nevertheless had the momentary feeling of having emerged from the life of the vagabond and returned to the joys (even if for the time being the most mendacious ones) of civilization. — I was to be very disappointed, and again it was a double disappointment. I took up my load, we walked through the sultry heat for a while; some distance from the center we found a tram, which took us to Hilbersdorf station, there (where once again a crowd of refugees was encamped on the steps, etc.) we learned that the next train to Dresden would not leave until today, at "about" three o'clock. But "yesterday" it had not left until seven o'clock in the evening, and it was always overcrowded and irregular. What a calamity for us several times over! Here without ration coupons and support, and afterward, dumped in Dresden on Saturday night, equally helpless. But that is only the one side of my disappointment, the misfortune side. Weary and at the end of our tether we followed the streets leading out of the city and came across a simple inn. Inside there was great activity in the taproom and sitting room; German soldiers, civilians, and Russian soldiers all mixed up. I saw the Russians for the first time, gray-green and dressed in sporty light clothes like the Americans, but in tunics. Curiously the landlady immediately made us welcome; we should sleep in the back room, there were not many people there, she would also make coffee and potatoes for us (I gave her our potato and travel coupons). And truly, when she later brought us a bowl of jacket potatoes and a jug of coffee, after that even beer, we were as if delivered. A young man, a "loader" from Duisburg, separated from his family, sat down beside us. (Dölzschen, June 13) I got the same description of the Russians as was repeated to me before and afterward: in a sober state usually good-natured, in a drunken state quite wild, theft of watches and jewelry, frequent rapes. Soon after that someone from the landlord's family came up: The Russians wanted to know what kind of professor I was; one had asked quite agitatedly what kind of "character" that was. The fact that I stood out among ordinary soldiers and people in this humble hotel on the edge of town was hardly thanks to my distinguished face, but rather to the high white collar, which I had bought in Klotzsche on February 15 and always avoided wearing, and which I now had to wear, since *the* shirt with the soft, turndown collar was completely done for: in Eva's words this bourgeois stand-up collar and with it the threadbare clothing of the tramp and the several days' growth of white stubble—it looked like the bad disguise of a fleeing bourgeois and anti-Bolshevik. A huge fellow, a captain as I later discovered, came up to me and spoke in Russian. He came so close to me, sat on the edge of the table and settee in such a way that I was unable to move, and spoke in a not unfriendly tone, but very forcefully and insistently. I said: "Je ne comprends pas" and "Ja Gewree" (as Eisenmann had taught me), gave him my identity card, pointed out the "J"—he went on talking impatiently. Finally an elderly woman on a crutch appeared, a Baltic German, who understood Russian and acted as interpreter. The officer wanted to know, above all, when I "had come to Germany." It took a long time before I made clear to them, that my family had been living in Germany for 200 years, that until 1918 Landsberg a. W. had been part of the province of Brandenburg. After that I gave precise information as to my position before and after 1933, also said with some spirit, that three of our family had entries in the Brockhaus Encyclopedia and that my brother Georg had treated Lenin. At that the officer stood up, gave me a friendly and patronizing pat on the shoulder and left. I felt this business, together with everything I had by now heard about looting and rapes, to be all too unpleasant—after all it had not been so very far removed from the Gestapo arrest on the tram—"I want to frisk him!"

Next to the taproom was a back room with a stage and a bandroom, such as we had often seen before. It had evidently been fitted out as a kind of temporary barracks some time before: Apart from about twenty bunk beds in two rows one above the other, in which there were now only uncovered straw mattresses, the room contained only army lockers and a long table. At the moment there were very few soldiers sleeping there; still wearing our clothes we lay down under our coats and passed the night. There was no question of washing; there was no pump within reach, and the water was reputed a typhus risk.

On Saturday, June 9, I was awake very early, probably before five o'clock, and I sat down at a window table in the taproom to write these notes. After a while there was an imperious knocking at the window, a Russian soldier was standing outside, gesticulating vigorously and shouting, demanding entry. The front door was locked, no one awake, I could not open it, no one appeared. Finally I withdrew farther into the room, so that I could not be seen. A soldier who had woken up grumbled, how could I have been so incautious as to show myself at the window; the Russian could make trouble for all of us. After a while, when the Russki had given up making a racket, I bent low and carried coats and baggage into the sheltering darkness of a lower bunk bed and continued writing for a while at the table in the back room. I felt quite rotten. What I had experienced with the Russians so far did not look like personal freedom and safety.

On Saturday, June 9, I went to the barber in the morning and had my hair cut, then we waited—without having eaten, all attempts to obtain a lunch had failed—waited very skeptically in a huge crowd at the station. Had we not got transport, we would have continued on foot. [ . . . ] And so on the morning of the fifteenth day, on Sunday, June 10, we were in Dresden.

But really this Sunday is still part of our journey home, because this is when the fairy-tale turnabout came. The day began gloomily enough. Tired and hungry we walked to the Neustädter station—nada! We went to the police station opposite. Very friendly reception and one correct and one false piece of information. You must go to Dölzschen immediately! I objected, that it would take time, before I could move into my house there. The officer grinned: You've no idea, how quickly that can sometimes happen! And in that he proved to be right. Although I was helped by the fact that Berger had fled . . . But as far as our hunger was concerned, we were told, that we would be fed at the refugee camp on Glacisstrasse, but there the rooms were empty, with Russian sentries sleeping on the top floor. So the walk was entirely in vain. Now someone on the street told us there was a camp, I think on Marggrafenstrasse. There we found only an army hospital, but no food. Then, still hungry and after an impossible night, we walked right through all the destruction of the city center. In Theaterstrasse there was supposed to be an inquiry office with information about residents and people who had been bombed out. It was closed. Then we struggled—the word is no exaggeration!—along to the Swiss Quarter: Frau Ahrens's house, the Windes' house destroyed, no news about them to be had. Only an old man, who had lost his wife and whose dog had been stolen by a Russian soldier the day before, stated with certainty that the Ahrens family had been saved (but he did not know where they were). Finally we found the Glasers' building, it was a little damaged inside, but on the whole wonderfully preserved, with nothing but ruins all around. This was where the day turned into a fairy tale. Frau Glaser welcomed us with tears and kisses, she had thought us dead. Glaser himself was somewhat decrepit and listless. We were fed, we were able to rest. In the late afternoon we walked up to Dölzschen.

# NOTES

## 1942

**January 4** — The Neumanns in Kötzschenbroda: I.e., The Neumanns have heard on enemy broadcasts.

*I, Claudius:* Novel by Robert Graves, first published in 1934 (German translation, 1935).

**January 12** — Folder V. Hugo Poetry: The temporary hiding place for the most recent pages of the diary, before Eva Klemperer could take them to Annemarie Köhler in Pirna.

**January 18** — Forsechè sì, forsechè no (Italian): "Maybe yes, maybe no."

**February 5** — D'outre-tombe (French): "From beyond the grave."

Rommel: Field Marshal Erwin Rommel (1891–1944) was commander of the Axis forces in North Africa from February 1941 to March 1943. Later, he was placed in command of the French Channel coast before the Allied invasion. Aware of the plans to overthrow Hitler in July 1944, he committed suicide in October 1944. (Rommel was more or less instructed to do so by Hitler, who did not want to put a popular general on trial.)

**February 8** — the Pétain-Darlan government: the Vichy French government, subordinate to Germany. After the 1940 armistice, the Vichy French controlled southern France and most of the French colonies, including Tunis, and cooperated with the Germans in the northern occupied zone of France. In November 1942, the Germans also occupied southern France.

**February 12** — *Leipziger NN:* The *Leipziger Neueste Nachrichten*, a daily newspaper for which Klemperer wrote after the end of the First World War and before his appointment as professor in Dresden.

**February 26** — "Il faut que . . . pas parler!" (French): "Germany must lose the war." — "No talking!"

"Bon courage!" (French): "Chin up!"

**March 6** — Regnavi—sum sine regno (Latin): "I have ruled—I am without power."

**March 7** — when the earth shook in Naples: On January 14, 1915, the Klemperers experienced an earthquake in Naples. (Victor Klemperer had a junior post at the university there.)

**March 8** — Fetscher: Professor Rainer Fetscher (1895–1945). General practitioner and teacher at Dresden TU. Active participant in resistance to the Nazi regime. He was shot by the SS on May 8, 1945, on his way to a Red Army unit for discussions on the involvement of Dresden's anti-Fascists in normalization of life in the city.

**March 16** — a "privileged" Jew: After the introduction of the yellow star to identify Jews (September 19, 1941), several privileged categories were not required to wear it. This concerned, above all, Jews in "mixed marriages" with children who had been baptized as Christians. As becomes clear from Victor Klemperer's diary, such "privileges" were subject to arbitrary alteration, sometimes with fatal consequences.

Auschwitz: This is the first time that Victor Klemperer has heard the name Auschwitz. Auschwitz was one of six camps established by the Nazis in Poland to facilitate the "Final Solution," that is, to murder Jews. Originally a labor camp, it was in March 1942 that large numbers of Jews began to be deported there and either killed or worked and starved to death. Victor Klemperer, therefore, heard about this death camp very quickly, although he was not to find out for certain about the nature and scale of its operation until the closing months of the war.

Karl May: May (1842–1912) was an immensely popular German author of adventure stories, many set in the American "Wild West."

**March 17** — Arthur Rosenberg: Rosenberg (1889–1943), not to be confused with namesake Alfred Rosenberg, the Nazi ideologist and leader, was a radical politician and historian who wrote some of the most acute contemporary studies of the failure of Weimar democracy. He went into exile in 1933.

**March 19** — *Sir Basil Zaharoff:* Zaharoff (1849–1936) was an international arms dealer. He became a notorious figure, indeed the symbol of ruthless and unprincipled trading in armaments. The phrase "merchant of death" was coined originally to describe him.

**April 2** — Houston Stewart Chamberlain: Chamberlain (1855–1927) was an English-born race theorist and philosopher of history who had a strong influence on the Nazis' racial ideology. Marriage to Richard Wagner's daughter, Eva, put him at the center of right-wing *völkisch* circles.

*Friedemann Bach:* a novel by Albert Emil Brachvogel (1824–1878).

**April 5** — in judaeos (Latin): "Against Jews."

**April 28** — Arthur Eloesser: Eloesser (1870–1937) was a famous theater and literary critic in Berlin.

**May 11** — *Tohuwabohu:* Satirical novel by the German Zionist author Sammy Gronemann; see note, May 15, 1941, Vol. 1.

**May 14** — *Wilhelm Meister's Years of Travel:* The second part of Goethe's novel *Wilhelm Meister.*

**May 19** — semper idem (Latin): "Always the same thing."

**May 23** — d'altra parte (Italian): "On the other hand."

**May 29** — Je n'en ai qu'un très faible espoir (French): "I have only a faint hope of that."

**May 30** — Eva Chamberlain-Wagner: Daughter of Richard Wagner, wife of Houston Stewart Chamberlain (see note, April 2).

**May 31** — that I was also in mortal danger in 1915: i.e., during his period of service on the western front.

**June 2** — *The Myth of the Twentieth Century:* The principal work of Alfred Rosenberg, the Nazi ideologist and leader.

**June 4** — the Vorwärts bookshop: i.e., a bookshop of the Social Democratic Party.

**June 6** — c'est à dire (French): "That is to say."

**June 8** — It was declared to be "Jewish arson": On May 18, 1942, members of the Herbert Baum group (a Jewish Communist resistance group) caused a fire at the National Socialist propaganda exhibition, *The Soviet Paradise,* in Berlin. In a revenge operation carried out between May 27 and 29, 154 Berlin Jews and 96 Jews imprisoned in Sachsenhausen concentration camp, near Berlin, were shot. Many of their relatives—the figures given vary—were deported to Theresienstadt, Auschwitz, and Sachsenhausen concentration camps. More than twenty members of the resistance group were executed.

the attempt on Heydrich: Reinhard Heydrich (1904–1942) was the central executive official of the "Final Solution." He was in charge of the mass killings of Jews following the German attack on the Soviet Union and chaired the Wannsee Conference in January 1942. He replaced Neurath as governor of the Czech lands in September 1941 and inaugurated a reign of terror. Following Heydrich's death in Prague on June 4, 1942, there were further atrocities, including the razing of the village of Lidice and the killing of its male inhabitants. (The assassins supposedly had sheltered in the village.) The killing of Heydrich also meant the disappearance of the last vestiges of Czech autonomy.

Dubnow memoirs: Semjon Dubnow (1860–1941) was a Jewish historian, perhaps the most distinguished modern historian of Jewry. He left Russia for Germany after the Bolshevik Revolution; after Hitler's seizure of power, Dubnow emigrated to Riga, where he was murdered with the other Jews of the city after German troops entered it in summer 1941. The German translation of his memoirs was published in 1937.

**June 13** — Professor Gaehde: Victor Klemperer was very harsh in his condemnation of Christian (Professor) Gaehde and his wife, Stephanie. From the diaries it is evident that in the months and years after the suicide of Julia Pick, he became less severe in his judgment of Frau Gaehde, though not of her husband.

However, in a letter (September 29, 1996) to the German publisher of the Klemperer diaries, Joachim Gaehde, surviving son of Christian and Stephanie Gaehde, describes Victor Klemperer's response to his father as unjust. He argues that the former underestimates the pressure the family was under at the time and the very real dangers his mother faced. Her father, Carl Pick, had committed suicide on March 15, 1942; her aunt Else, on January 27, 1942. (These were Julia Pick's brother and sister-in-law.) In January 1942, Joachim Gaehde's brother had died in mysterious circumstances in Bucharest. Stephanie Gaehde had been present during several house searches of the Jews' House in which her father had been forced to reside. At the same time she was being threatened day and night by anonymous phone calls and had been summoned by the Gestapo.

Joachim Gaehde writes, "What Victor Klemperer saw outside the Jews' House on Caspar David Friedrich Strasse was no display of ingratitude and cowardice — real cowards would not have come at all — but the consequence of a difficult and painful choice between two human duties: one she owed her aunt . . . the other she owed her own family, her husband, her surviving son, and most particularly an eight-year-old grandson, whose parents had been detained in the Far East because of the war."

**June 22** — Povera e nuda vai (Italian): Abbreviation of "Povera e nuda vai, o filosofia" — You go poor and naked, O philosophy.

**July 1** — *Glückel von Hameln:* Glückel (1646–1724) was the author a book of memoirs that provided an insight into the family, cultural, and economic life of German Jews around 1700.

**July 4** — Cras mihi (Latin): "Tomorrow me" or "tomorrow my turn."

**July 7** — Oldenburg-Januschau: Klemperer was reading the memoirs of Elard von Oldenburg-Januschau (1855–1937), an extreme conservative politician who represented the interests of big landowners; anti-Republican after 1918 and an intimate friend of Marshal Hindenburg, who was German president from 1925 to 1934.

**July 10** — Werner von Siemens: Siemens (1816–1892) was an inventor and founder of the Siemens electrical engineering company.

**July 24** — Lord Lansdowne: Lansdowne (1845–1927), British politician, first Liberal, then Conservative. Variously war and foreign secretary, governor-general of Canada, and viceroy of India.

**July 26** — Schönerer: Georg, Ritter von Schönerer (1842–1921), Austrian politician. Became one of the leaders of the German nationalists in Austria; anti-Semitic, anti-Catholic, and an advocate of unification with the German Empire. Influenced Karl Lueger and, not least, Hitler.

Lueger: Karl Lueger (1844–1910), Austrian Christian-Social politician. Populist anti-Semite and anti-Socialist. From 1897 mayor of Vienna, where he promoted progressive municipal policies; unlike Schönerer he was an advocate of accommodation with the other nationalities of the Austrian Empire.

Eyselsberg: Probably Anton, Freiherr von Eiselberg (1860–1939), prominent Viennese surgeon and university teacher.

Schnitzler: Arthur Schnitzler (1862–1931), playwright and prose writer, one of the most influential of modern dramatists; his treatment of sexual themes was considered scandalous at the turn of the century (and after).

**July 31** — y en a tant (French): "There are so many of them."

**August 6** — J'en doute (French): "I doubt it."

**August 7** — Sedan: Decisive battle (1870) of the Franco-Prussian War — surrender of the main French army together with Emperor Napoleon III. Sedan Tag (Sedan Day) subsequently became a holiday in the German Empire. (In nationalist terms, Germany had at last avenged the humiliations of previous centuries.)

in semiticis (Latin): I.e., on the Jewish question.

**August 10** — *j'accuse* (French): Literally "I accuse," a reference to Émile Zola's famous 1898 open letter that opened with the words "J'accuse." In it, he condemned the injustice inflicted on the Jewish officer Dreyfus, falsely accused of spying for Germany.

comme une vieille édentée (French): "Like a toothless old woman."

**August 16** — Harald Kreutzberg: Kreutzberg (1902–1968) was a dancer and choreographer. He trained at the Dresden Ballet School, but became a leading exponent of modern dance.

Eppure (Italian): "Nevertheless."

**August 17** — "Les extrêmes se touchent" (French): "The extremes"—extreme points of view or positions—"meet."

**August 19** — Les faits nouveaux (French): "The latest news."

**August 22** — Georg Hermann: Hermann (1871–1943) was a very successful Jewish novelist of Berlin themes, perhaps undeservedly neglected today. Emigrated to the Netherlands, but was deported during the German occupation and died in a concentration camp.

**August 25** — la maison juive morte (French): "The Jews' House is dying."

**September 1** — *Schlachtfest* (German): Party following the butchering of a pig for domestic use (sausage making, etc.).

**September 4** — the Marienburg: The Marienburg (Castle of Our Lady), today Malbork in Poland, is a great brick Gothic castle and cathedral on the banks of an arm of the Vistula in West Prussia. It was for a while the chief seat of the German Knights. Formerly, it was seen as one of the representative architectural works of German culture.

Albrecht Palaces: Mid-nineteenth-century princely residences on the north bank of the Elbe.

**September 6** — Ravensberg: I.e., Ravensbrück, a concentration camp, whose inmates were mainly women.

**September 7** — So I shall probably seen Marckwald for the last time: In German: So werde ich wohl Marckwald wohl zum letztenmal gesehen. According to Walter Nowojski, the German editor of the diaries, the slippage in this sentence is one of the rare occasions where Victor Klemperer's emotions disrupt his self-imposed role as observer, recorder. On September 8, 1942, fifty Dresden Jews were sent to Theresienstadt on Transport V/6. Thirty-nine died in Theresienstadt, Fritz Marckwald as early as September 14. Those who did not die in Theresienstadt were transported to Auschwitz and died there.

**September 8** — tout nu (French): "Completely naked."

**September 11** — the Milke couple: An Aryan couple living in the same house.

Ralph von Klemperer: A Dresden businessman, no relation, who had emigrated to South Africa.

Piazza di Spagna: Square in Rome, with the famous Spanish Steps on one side.

**September 24** — Arnold Zweig: Zweig (1887–1968), not to be confused with his namesake Stefan Zweig, was one of the most successful German authors before 1933. A left-wing radical (and pacifist) and Jewish, he emigrated to Palestine. Disillusioned with Zionism, he returned to (East) Berlin in 1948.

**October 30** — comme si de rien n'était (French): "As if nothing had happened."

**November 2** — "rachmoness (Yiddish) position": Position or post granted out of charity.

**November 6** — Maximilian Harden: See note, July 12, 1938, Vol. 1.

**November 15** — Ne hibsh (Yiddish): "Not nice."

**November 19** — y compris (French): "Included."

**November 21** — summo jure (Latin): "With the greatest justification."

**November 24** — "Jews' Camp Hellerberg": See preface.

**November 26** — Darlan . . . the "traitorous admiral": François Darlan (1881–1942), 1939–40 commander in chief of the French navy; from 1940 a member of the collaborationist Vichy French government; 1942, commander in chief of the French armed forces. When Allied forces landed in French North Africa in November 1942, he concluded an armistice and surrendered, but was killed by an anti-Vichy assassin shortly afterward.

**December 11** — menu peuple (French): "Humble people" or "classes."

Solamen miserum, miserrimum (Latin): "Poor comfort in the worst comfort."

Schmidt: Henry Schmidt (born 1912), SS Obersturmführer, was, from April 1942 until February 1945, the Gestapo officer in charge of the "Final Solution of the Jewish Question" in Dresden and environs, and in this capacity organized the extermination of 985 Jews. After the war, Schmidt lived in East Germany under an assumed name, but was arrested in April 1986 and sentenced to life imprisonment on September 28, 1987, by the Dresden district court.

**December 20** — "prise de pouvoir" (French): "Seizure of power."

**December 29** — The city . . . rid of Jews: In the Nazi plans, the cleansing of Vienna of Jews was the model for actions elsewhere in the Reich.

## 1943

**January 3** — Kaddish (originally Aramaic): In this context, the Jewish prayer for the dead.

**January 18** — Hebel's: Johann Peter Hebel (1760–1826). Popular poet, teller of stories and anecdotes. Still admired today.

Herbert Norkus: Hitler Youth killed during political disturbances in Berlin on January 24, 1932. Turned into a martyr by the Nazis.

**January 27** — It has been admitted . . . have been lost at Stalingrad: The German Sixth Army and various allied forces had been cut off from the main German forces on November 22, 1942. The actual capitulation of the southern pocket did not in fact take place until February 2, 1943, and the capitulation of the northern pocket, under Field Marshal Paulus, not until January 31, 1943.

**January 28** — Armin Wegner: Wegner (1886–1978) was a prominent German writer of the interwar period. In 1933, after the first call to boycott Jewish businesses, he protested against the Nazi anti-Jewish policies. He was arrested, and passed through a number of prisons and concentration camps until his release in 1936, when he left Germany. Klemperer was reading a travel book on Palestine by Wegner, published in 1930.

Boileau's *Art poétique:* Nicolas Boileau-Despréaux (1636–1710), French poet and critic. In his *Art poétique,* he summed up the rules of literature as they had developed in France during the seventeenth century, based on Aristotle and his commentators.

faculté maîtresse (French): "Outstanding talent."

**January 30** — Signum coeli (Latin): "Sign from heaven."

oraison funèbre (French): "Funeral oration."

**February 14** — the Zentrum: Before 1933 the Catholic political party in Germany.

**February 28** — evacuation was imminent: At the end of February 1943, Commissar Schmidt (see note, December 11, 1942) received an order from Adolf Eichmann in person to liquidate the Hellerberg camp. During the night of March 2–3, the inmates were taken to Dresden-Neustadt goods station, loaded into cattle trucks, and deported to Auschwitz. The transport, which eventually consisted of thirty trucks containing several thousand people, arrived at Auschwitz–Birkenau on the evening of March 3. The majority were "selected" on arrival and had to make their way directly from the ramp to the gas chambers.

**March 17** — "Paper soldiers": A phrase, drawn from a childhood game, which Klemperer had already used in *Curriculum Vitae,* the autobiographical account of his life from 1881 to 1918, to describe plans and projects that had not been or might not be realized.

**April 5** — di nuovo (Italian): "Once again."

**April 16** — voce populi (Latin): "Through the voice of the people."

peu à peu (French): "Little by little."

**April 25** — le leurre éternel du printemps (French): "The eternal lure of spring."

**April 26** — Dwinger: Edwin Erich Dwinger (1898–1981), nationalist German writer, propagandist for the Nazi state.

**April 29** — young . . . Aris: Helmut Aris (1908–1987) was one of the hundred Dresden Jews who received deportation summonses on the morning of February 13, 1945, the day of the bombing of Dresden. Like Victor Klemperer, he survived. Later he was, until his death, president of the Association of Jewish Communities in the GDR (East Germany).

**May 1** — conspiracy trial in Berlin: Precise reference is unclear, but during 1942 and 1943 the Gestapo broke up a number of resistance groups whose members were tried in batches, the majority being executed.

The man in Wehlen: i.e., the address, which Richter had arranged, where Klemperer could go into hiding if need arose.

**May 3** — Perez: Jichak Lejb Perez (1851–1915), Yiddish writer.

Rastelli: Enrico Rastelli (1896–1931) was considered the greatest juggler of all time.

**May 5** — Katyn: At the end of February 1943, German soldiers discovered the bodies of more than 4,000 Polish officers in mass graves in Katyn forest, about twelve miles west of Smolensk. The officers had been taken prisoner by Soviet forces in September 1939, when Nazi Germany and Soviet Russia partitioned Poland. There is no longer any doubt that they were killed on Stalin's orders in May 1940.

**May 11** — tant mieux (French): "So much the better."

**May 20** — Africa lost: The "Army Group Africa" surrendered on May 13, 1943. Two-hundred-fifty-two thousand German and Italian troops became prisoners of war.

**May 21** — the river dam business: The "Dambusters" raid on dams south of the Ruhr took place on the night of May 17–18.

**May 29** — Matthias Erzberger: Erzberger (1875–1921), leader of the left wing of the Zentrum (Catholic Party); key role in organizing the Reichstag (parliament) peace resolution of 1917, which advocated peace through negotiation and without territorial gains. Erzberger was one of the signatories of the armistice of November 11, 1918, was subsequently vice chancellor and foreign minister. Favored acceptance of the Versailles Treaty conditions. A hate figure of the Right, he was assassinated by members of a nationalist organization on August 26, 1921.

**June 1** — a bloodbath in Warsaw: Presumably a reference to the second phase of the Warsaw Ghetto Uprising—resistance to deportations from the ghetto—between April 19 and May 16.

**June 5** — dissolution of the Comintern: On May 15, 1943, as a conciliatory gesture to the alliance with the Western powers, Stalin dissolved the Comintern—the Communist International—the institution whose task was seen as furthering world revolution.

**June 12** — Kahlenberg and the Hirschels would be evacuated "tomorrow": The Kahlenbergs and the Hirschel family are recorded as arriving in Theresienstadt on June 21, 1943. On November 28, the Hirschel family with their two sons, and Kahlenberg and his mother, were taken to Auschwitz on a so-called family transport and apparently gassed immediately.

a part in my opus: Klemperer kept his promise. He drew a portrait of Frau Hirschel in the chapter "Die Sprache der Sieger" (The Language of the Victors) of his book *LTI.*

The National Association of Jews in Germany has been dissolved: That is to say, the association, a Nazi creation, had served its function in the prosecution of the "Final Solution" in cleansing Germany of virtually all its Jews. Its property was confiscated. Nevertheless, organizations to represent the remaining Jews were revived within a few months. See diary entry for September 21, 1943.

**June 14** — Que faire? (French): "What is to be done?"

**July 11** — Kursk: In summer 1943, the Germans attempted to regain the initiative on the Eastern front; however, the offensive that began on July 5 had ground to a halt within a few days, and the Russians counterattacked. Russian victory was announced on August 5. Kursk is often referred to as the greatest tank battle in history.

Allied landing in Sicily: On July 10, 1943, British and American forces landed in Sicily. They soon occupied the whole island, and on September 8 Allied forces landed on the mainland of Italy.

**July 13** — the strip he has occupied: I.e., in Sicily.

**July 26** — Mussolini's resignation: At the request of the Fascist Grand Council, King Victor Emanuel III assumed supreme command. Mussolini was dismissed and arrested on July 25, and the Fascist Party was dissolved on July 28.

**July 27** — Marshal Badoglio: Pietro Badoglio (1871–1956), Italian chief of staff, resigned 1940. He was appointed prime minister after Mussolini's arrest; on September 3, 1943, he concluded an armistice with the Allies.

the Quirinal: Roman residence of the Italian king.

Camicie nere (Italian): "Blackshirts."

**August 2** — proprio (Latin): "Indeed; actually."

**August 26** — χατ' εξοχήν (kat'exochen—Greek): "Plain and simple."

**September 9** — the Italians have capitulated: Despite assurances of loyalty to Germany, the Italians had been conducting secret negotiations with the Allies since March 3, 1943. An armistice was signed on September 3 and announced by Eisenhower, the Allied commander in chief, on September 8.

**September 13** — Pacelli!: Klemperer places an exclamation mark behind the Pope's name, because there is a certain irony in the fact that the pontiff, who had been papal nuncio in Germany and was suspected of Axis sympathies, would now be a virtual prisoner of the Germans in the Vatican enclave.

**September 14** — the student of Lamprecht: Karl Lamprecht (1856–1915), historian; his work helped make social and cultural history acceptable to scholars.

**September 15** — the freeing of the Duce: On September 12, 1943, German special forces freed Mussolini from imprisonment and took him to northern Italy, where he became the head of a new Fascist countergovernment.

**September 21** — On verra (French): "We shall see."

**September 24** — tempi passati (Latin): "Past times" or "bygone days."

**October 7** — Stahl: Friedrich Julius Stahl (1802–1861), a baptized Jew, was Hegel's successor as professor of philosophy at the University of Berlin. More importantly in this context, he was both a political theorist and a prominent parliamentarian. During the 1850s, he became leader of the Conservatives in the Prussian parliament.

**December 11** — e bene (Italian): "Well," good, okay.

**December 17** — Felix: Klemperer's brother Felix (1866–1931).

**December 22** — La Bruyère: Jean de La Bruyère (1645–1696), French writer famous for his *Characters*, containing something like four hundred character studies.

## 1944

**January 4** — ou petite guillotine (French): "Or little guillotine."

**January 5** — DAF: Deutsche Arbeits Front (German Labor Front), the official Nazi labor organization set up after the dissolution of the trade unions in spring 1933.

**January 15** — communis opinio (Latin): "General" or "popular opinion."

the Italian treason trial: Trials in Verona of those members of the Fascist Grand Council who had not supported Mussolini on July 25, 1943.

Paulus: Field Marshal Friedrich Paulus (1890–1957), commander of the German Sixth Army, who surrendered to Soviet forces at Stalingrad. In captivity, he joined the Nationalkomitee Freies Deutschland (National Committee for a Free Germany), a kind of popular front of captured officers who had declared themselves against Hitler.

Seydlitz: Colonel-General Walther von Seydlitz-Kurzbach (1888–1976), commander of the LI army corps at Stalingrad. In favor of a breakout from the pocket in November 1942, then of capitulation (in defiance of Hitler's order to fight to the end). In captivity one of the founders of the Nationalkomitee Freies Deutschland.

**January 23** — omein (Hebrew): "Amen."

**February 10** — Hauptmann's *Emanuel Quint*: Gerhart Hauptmann's novel *Der Narr in Christo, Emanuel Quint* (The Fool in Christ, Emanuel Quint).

**February 15** — Ma come? (Italian): "But how?"

**February 21** — Tumler: Franz Tumler (1912–1998), Austrian writer, German army officer in the Second World War. His post-1945 work is in part governed by an effort to come to terms with his attraction to Nazism as a young man.

Jean Giraudoux: The French dramatist and novelist died in Paris on January 31, 1944.

Siegfried: I.e., the novel *Siegfried et le Limousin*, which addresses the relationship of France and Germany before and during the First World War.

Russian Vendéeans: After the French Revolution, the rural, conservative, and very Catholic region of La Vendée in the west of France was the scene of a popular uprising against the revolution. It was brutally suppressed. Russian Vendéeans, then, are Russian counterrevolutionaries.

**March 4** — sub specie tertii imperii (Latin): "With respect to the Third Reich."

**March 12** — Hauptmann's weavers at the dog roast: Allusion to an incident in Weber's Naturalist play *The Weavers*, about a textile workers' revolt in Silesia during the "Hungry Forties."

**April 2** — Ludwig Finckh: Finckh (1876–1964), popular regional (southwest German) writer; anti-Semitic.

**April 4** — A. J. Cronin: Cronin (1896–1981) wrote popular novels with a touch of social criticism, often drawing on his experiences as a general practitioner in mining districts. He is today best known for the British TV series *Dr. Finlay's Casebook*, which was based on a number of his novels.

**April 13** — Hinc sympathia (Latin): "Hence the sympathy."

**April 14** — the Emperor and the King: That is, the German emperor and the Saxon king.

**April 30** — the Reichsbanner: In the years before the Nazi seizure of power, the paramilitary organization of the democratic parties and the trade unions.

**May 2** — ma vue baisse (French): "My eyes are failing."

**May 24** — *maquis* (French): Shrubby vegetation of southern France and Corsica made up of small evergreen trees and bushes. It was a name taken by resistance groups in France because the "maquis" provided cover, a hiding place.

MOI (Mouvement d'ouvriers immigrés): "Movement of immigrant workers."

Marcel Déat: Déat (1894–1955), French politician. After resignation from the Socialist Party in 1934, he became an advocate of understanding with Germany. Condemned to death in absentia in 1945.

normalien (French): A graduate of the elite École normale supérieure.

*Munichois* (French): I.e., a supporter of the Munich agreement, which appeased Hitler by giving in to his demands with respect to Czechoslovakia.

Vichysoiss: I.e., supporters of the pro-German Vichy government.

Laval: Pierre Laval (1883–1945), former Socialist, prominent politician since 1914; deputy prime minister in Pétain's government in 1940 and again from 1942. Subsequently prime minister. Sentenced to death in 1945.

Darnand: Joseph Darnand (1897–1945) was chief of the *milice*, a militarized police force raised by the Vichy government, which collaborated with the Germans in fighting the resistance. Executed in 1945.

Action Française: Extreme right-wing monarchist and anti-Semitic political movement in France, founded at the end of the nineteenth century.

Maurras: Charles Maurras (1868–1952), French writer and politician, cofounder of Action Française, sentenced to life imprisonment in 1945, but pardoned in 1952.

Henriot: Philippe Henriot (1889–1944), French politician of the extreme Right, assassinated in 1944.

Johst . . . Johsts: The reference is to novels by Hanns Johst, a right-wing German writer.

the Nettuno front: On January 22, 1944, Anglo-American forces had landed at Anzio and Nettuno, south of Rome and behind the German lines. The Germans, however, contained the bridgehead until May, when they were forced to retreat.

**May 26** — *The Last Laugh:* Murnau's film of 1924 in which Emil Jannings took the lead role.

**May 29** — tant bien que mal (French): "After a fashion."

the *Fischmanns:* Novel by Henry William Katz (1906–1992), published in 1938 in Amsterdam.

**June 6** — that the invasion had begun: I.e., the Normandy landings of June 6, 1944.

**June 10** — moire (Yiddish): "Fear."

**June 17** — new types of weapons: A first reference to the V-1 (Vergeltung 1 or Retribution 1). The V-1 was a pilotless aircraft with a range of 150 miles. Between June 13, 1944, and March 29, 1945, more than 16,000 were launched against London and other targets in southern England and in Belgium. The V-2, a ballistic missile with a slightly greater range, was first launched, against Paris, on September 6, 1944.

**June 24** — nada (Spanish): "Nothing."

**July 1** — Ilse Frischmann . . . "fetched": Ilse Frischmann, then 22, was sent to Auschwitz. She survived the camp and returned to Dresden after the war.

**July 7** — Wilna and Dünaburg: Today, Vilnius in Lithuania, and Daugavpils in Latvia.

Franzos's *Der Pojaz:* Karl Emil Franzos (1848–1904), born in Galicia, became a prominent German editor and writer. *Der Pojaz,* his best-known work, is an autobiographical account of growing up in Jewish eastern Europe.

**July 8** — Propter pecuniam nigram (Latin): "For black money" (i.e., to get money that they were not supposed to have).

**July 11** — Dietl: Eduard Dietl (1890–1944), colonel-general, early member of the Nazi Party, took part in the abortive Munich putsch of 1923, later, in 1940, in charge of the invasion of Norway. He was killed in an air crash on June 23, 1944.

Field Marshal Rundstedt: Gerd von Rundstedt (1875–1953), supreme military commander in the West from 1940, removed from command in July 1944, reinstated in September, finally dismissed in March 1945.

**July 12** — Fritzsche: Hans Fritzsche (1900–1953), in charge of the broadcasting section of the Propaganda Ministry. One of the leading Nazi commentators.

**July 17** — Reading Rosenzweig: Franz Rosenzweig (1886–1929) was a philosopher, theologian, and educational reformer. Described as a religious existentialist, he is one of the most influential modern Jewish thinkers. He published his magnum opus *Der Stern der Erlösung* (The Star of Redemption) in 1921. In collaboration with Martin Buber, he also began a new translation of the Hebrew Bible into German.

**July 21** — the attempt on Hitler's life: Often referred to as the officers' plot, although not only military personnel were involved. On July 20, a bomb intended to kill the Führer was planted at Hitler's headquarters. The assassination was supposed to be the signal for a coup d'état. Hitler, however, was only wounded, and in the subsequent confusion, the anti-Nazi officers failed to seize power. This failure was followed by a wave of suicides, arrests, and executions.

Bürgerbräu affair: An earlier attempt on Hitler's life (see note, November 12, 1939, Vol. 1).

**August 2** — thirty years ago: On August 1, 1914, Germany declared war on Russia and issued the order for general mobilization.

**August 4** — Goerdeler: Carl Goerdeler (1884–1945), mayor of Leipzig from 1930, came into conflict with the Nazi Party from 1935, resigned 1937. Goerdeler became a central figure in conservative circles hostile to the Nazi regime. Went underground after July 20, 1944; was denounced, tried, and executed in February 1945.

**August 7** — Knut Hamsun: Hamsun (1859–1952), great Norwegian writer of realist novels inflected by neo-Romanticism, and one of the most influential writers of the early twentieth century. Won the Nobel Prize for literature in 1920. Became a supporter of German National Socialism during the Second World War. In 1948, a Norwegian court sentenced him as a traitor.

**August 8** — among those shot . . . Nebe: The rumor that Schacht and Neurath had been executed was false. If both had become increasingly critical of Hitler's war policies, they were not involved in the circles that prepared the July 20 plot. Arthur Nebe, an SS officer and police general, the senior commander of the criminal police, went underground on July 24, 1944, was arrested on January 16, 1945; tried and executed in March 1945.

**August 16** — landing in southern France: Early on August 15, American forces landed in southern France on a wide front between Toulon and Cannes. This was followed by a rapid withdrawal of German forces northward.

**August 19** — guerre totalissime (French and Latin): "Most total war" or "totalest war."

**August 20** — notes on Stresemann: Klemperer had read two volumes of speeches and writing by Stresemann. Gustav Stresemann (1878–1929) was a right-liberal German politician. Briefly German chancellor in 1923 and subsequently German foreign minister until his death, Stresemann became a proponent of peaceful revision of the Versailles Treaty.

**August 25** — the defection of Romania: An armed insurrection led to the fall of the pro-German Antonescu regime on April 23, 1944, and to Romania changing sides and joining the anti-Hitler coalition.

**August 26** — *broche* (Hebrew): "Blessing"; *mitzvah* (Hebrew): "Blessing or commandment."

**September 1** — mezuzah (Hebrew): Small parchment with religious texts, which is rolled into a case and fixed to the doorpost of each door in a Jewish home.

**September 5** — Finland has capitulated: After the Finnish army had been decisively defeated by Soviet troops in July 1944, the country capitulated on September 19, 1944, and drove German units out of northern Finland.

**September 6** — Prien, Mölders, Dietl: For Prien see note May 24, 1944, Vol. 1; Werner Mölders (1913–1941), fighter-pilot ace, killed in a flying accident; for Dietl see note July 11, 1944.

**September 11** — Kluge: Field Marshal Günther von Kluge (1882–1944) took over as supreme commander in western Europe in July 1944, but was removed from command on July 20. Suspected of complicity in the July plot to assassinate Hitler (he was not in fact involved) and fearing arrest, Kluge committed suicide near Metz on August 18, 1944.

**September 19** — Thälmann and Breitscheid are among the dead: Rudolf Breitscheid, a leading Social Democratic politician of the period before 1933, was indeed killed in an air raid on Weimar and the Buchenwald concentration camp nearby on August 24, 1944. Ernst Thälmann, however, leader of the Communist Party when the Nazis took power in 1933, was murdered in Buchenwald on August 18, 1944, after eleven years' solitary confinement. Victor Klemperer's suspicions were thus retrospectively confirmed.

**September 21** — "Lebensborn": (Fountain of Life). Homes that were part of Himmler's Lebensborn program to create a superrace through selective breeding. Carefully chosen young German women were encouraged to become pregnant by racially and politically desirable SS men, then sent to one of the twelve Lebensborn homes, where they got special maternity care. Another aspect of the Lebensborn program was the kidnapping of racially acceptable children from occupied countries.

the sig runes: The SS identifying flashes.

**September 23** — the annihilation . . . at Arnhem: British airborne troops had attempted to secure bridges across the Rhine at Arnhem in advance of the Allied forces, but the operation failed.

**September 27** — Yom Kippur (Hebrew): The Day of Atonement, central religious festival of the Jewish year; a time of fasting and penitence.

**October 5** — Hic et ubique (Latin): "Here and everywhere."

**October 8** — my Göring notes: Klemperer had been reading a biography of the Nazi leader Hermann Göring.

*Tonio Kröger:* Thomas Mann's early novella.

**October 10** — Organization Todt: A semimilitary works organization set up in 1938, whose main purpose was the construction of military installations and infrastructure.

**October 12** — Wilhelm II book: A biography of the last German emperor, who abdicated in 1918.

**October 24** — the Landsturm of 1813: The general conscription of all men between seventeen and fifty who were not already in the army or the militia (Landwehr).

**November 14** — Lamprecht's *1809, 1813, 1815:* Karl Lamprecht's book on the Prussian-German war of liberation from the French.

**November 30** — notes on Paul Ernst: I.e., notes on *Tagebuch eines Dichters* (Diary of a Poet) by Paul Ernst (1866–1933), a minor author, prominent in the early years of the century, who attempted to use classical forms to renew German literature.

leaving Dostoyevsky aside: Klemperer had been reading a biography of the writer.

and Stefan Zweig: And also Zweig's novella *Amok*.

**December 11** — Berthold's birthday: Berthold, Victor Klemperer's brother (1871–1931).

**December 19** — A major offensive started unexpectedly: The last major German offensive of the Second World War, it usually goes under the name of the Battle of the Bulge. On December 16, 1944, German forces attacked in the Ardennes, but after initial successes were pushed back once again.

## 1945

**January 14** — Talmud and Shulhan Arukh (Hebrew): The Talmud is the comprehensive term for the cumulative compilation of discussions in the rabbinic schools of Palestine and Babylon and of later commentaries on them. Shulhan Arukh is the standard guide to Jewish law and practice, compiled in the sixteenth century.

**January 27** — "Better a terrible end!": I.e., better a terrible end than no end at all.

Walter Lippmann: Lippmann (1889–1974) was perhaps the most influential political commentator of his day in the United States. His columns were printed in more than two hundred fifty newspapers.

**January 29** — had found the books: A reference, in fact, to Thomas Mann's broadcast of January 14, 1945. In it Mann stated: "Between April 15, 1942, and April 15, 1944, in these two German establishments [the concentration camps of Auschwitz and Birkenau] alone, 1,715,000 Jews were murdered."

**February 5** — a feared Xanthippe: I.e., an ill-tempered woman (after Socrates' wife).

**February 12** — tu parles! (French): "You don't say!"

a couple of times: Roland Freisler (1893–1945), president of the People's Court, the judge entrusted with the show trials of those implicated in the attempted coup against Hitler on July 20, 1944. He was killed in an air raid on Berlin at the beginning of February 1945.

**February 22–24** — For discussion of the bombing of Dresden, see preface.

burning in the prison: In fact, a large number of prisoners, including political ones, did escape.

the Albertinum: A building containing art collections and museums.

**February 15–17** — a little too populusque (Latin): I.e., a little too much of the people, too plebeian.

**February 21** — Philip Bouhler: Bouhler (1899–1945) was a senior Nazi, holder of various important positions. He was, among other things, in charge of Hitler's office.

**March 7** — passed Dux and Brüx: The train was taking a route to Falkenstein, southwest of Dresden, by way of northern Bohemia, now in the Czech Republic. Dux is today known as Duchcov and Brüx as Most.

Komotau: Today known as Chomutov.

**March 10** — and strong anti-Nazism: After 1918, Falkenstein had been a well-known center of working-class radicalism.

**March 23** — Wassermann's *Maurizius*: *Der Fall Maurizius* (*The Maurizius Case*), 1928 novel by Jakob Wassermann.

**March 24** — Ludendorff: Erich Ludendorff (1865–1937). General; during the First World War he was Hindenburg's chief of staff and the brains behind the latter's military victories. Fled to Sweden in 1918, returned to Germany, and became a leading figure in extreme nationalist and racialist movements. Participated in the Kapp Putsch of 1920 against the democratically elected government and in Hitler's putsch attempt of 1923. From 1924 to 1928 he represented the Nazi Party in parliament.

Bebel: August Bebel (1840–1913), cofounder of the German Social Democratic Party in 1869 and leader of the party for many years until his death. He was one of the great leaders of European parliamentary Socialism.

the shooting of Karl Liebknecht: Liebknecht (1871–1919) was a radical politician and the first active opponent of wartime government during the First World War. Expelled from the SPD, he founded the antiwar Spartacus League. At the end of the war, he was cofounder and leader of the new Communist Party (KPD) together with Rosa Luxemburg. He and Luxemburg were murdered by Freikorps (irregular) officers after a misconceived left-wing revolt in Berlin in January 1919.

**April 2** — Bergengruen: Victor Klemperer was reading the historical novel *Am Himmel wie auf Erden* (In Heaven as on Earth) by Werner Bergengruen, published in 1940.

**April 15** — *Eger:* Today Cheb in the Czech Republic.

Messina: Before the First World War, the Klemperers had visited Messina in southern Italy shortly after the great earthquake that almost completely destroyed the city in 1908.

Maximilianeum: Built in the mid–nineteenth century, in a mixture of neo-Gothic and neo-Classical styles, as a gallery of historical painting.

the Pinakotheks and the Glyptothek: The Old and the New Pinakothek are galleries of pre-nineteenth-century art and nineteenth-century art respectively; the Glyptothek is a sculpture gallery.

gendarmerie: The name, taken from the French, given to the police in rural areas of Germany before 1945.

**April 20** — Marshal Model: Walther Model (1891–1945), enthusiastic supporter of Hitler, appointed commander in chief in western Europe after the dismissal of Field Marshal von Kluge. The remains of his forces were surrounded in the Ruhr and surrendered in mid-April 1945. On April 21, Model committed suicide rather than face capture.

**April 21** — Catholicisme superficiel . . . tailleur de Valenciennes (French): "Superficial Catholicism, they are without charity, says the prisoner [of war], the tailor from Valenciennes."

**April 22** — the tensions of the San Francisco conference and of the Polish question: The San Francisco conference of April and June 1945 established the United Nations; there were differences between the Western Allies and the Soviet Union regarding the constitution of the Polish government.

**April 23** — Wallenstein's camp: I.e., like a scene from the Thirty Years' War.

**April 24** — *the greatest war criminal of all times:* U.S. President Franklin Roosevelt, who had died on April 12, 1944.

**April 29** — te deum laudamus (Latin): "Lord, we praise thee."

the Epp rumor: Tyroller had declared that there had been a broadcast announcement that Franz Xaver Ritter von Epp (1868–1947), conservative general, influential early supporter of the Nazi Party, gauleiter of Bavaria, was negotiating with the Americans. Epp was indeed involved in a failed revolt by the anti-Nazi Freiheitsaktion Bayern (Action for freedom of Bavaria) in April 1945.

Aussi pour vous la guerre sera bientôt finie (French): "For you, too, the war will soon be over."

**May 3** — Hitler was dead: Hitler had committed suicide in the chancellery bunker in Berlin on April 30.

**May 5** — Gerlich: Fritz Gerlich (1883–1934) was an uncompromisingly anti-Nazi Catholic newspaper owner. The editorial offices were stormed by the SA on March 9, 1933, and Gerlich was taken to Dachau concentration camp.

**May 9** — Admiral Dönitz: Karl Dönitz (1891–1980) was appointed supreme commander of the German navy in 1943; briefly Hitler's successor, he signed the armistice with the Allies. He was arrested on May 23, 1945. Sentenced to ten years' imprisonment at the Nürnberg war crimes trials.

**May 21** — "Pierced by the knowledge of his nothingness": Quotation from Friedrich Schiller's *Don Carlos* (act 2, scene 1).

Miss Lazar: Klemperer thought he detected a likeness to Auguste Wieghardt-Lazar's sister, Maria, and hence had given the Viennese woman the name Miss Lazar.

**May 22** — Ès chambre des dames (French): "The ladies' room."

Au pays des crématoires (French): "In the land of crematoriums."

**May 25** — Mariez-vous! Ne mariez pas (French): "Marry! Don't marry!" — a quote from Rabelais's *Gargantua and Pantagruel*, book 3, chapter 9.

the La Bruyère of these days: I.e., the study of character types; see note, December 18, 1943.

**May 26** — disjecta membra (Latin): "Scattered limbs."

**May 26–June 10** — Gisselsdorf: In fact, Gisselthausen.

Himmler's suicide: Himmler was arrested by British troops and committed suicide on May 23, 1945.

the Walhalla itself: Imitation Greek temple, built 1830–42 on a hillside overlooking the Danube, to contain the busts of famous Germans. A "hall of fame," in other words.

the Czar's courier: An allusion to Jules Verne's novel *The Courier of the Czar*, usually known in English as *Michel Strogoff*.

to American headquarters: Falkenstein, in Saxony, was, of course, well inside the territory allocated to the Soviet zone of occupation that would become the future GDR—East Germany. At this point, however, American forces had not yet evacuated those areas that they had captured in the closing stages of the war.

the adjacent no-man's-land: Between the American and Soviet forces in Saxony there was for some weeks after the German surrender an unoccupied area. A German anti-Fascist committee established the rudiments of administration. It remains unclear why "The Republic of Schwarzenberg" was allowed to exist, even if only for a short time. The episode has been the subject of at least one film and one novel.

Dölzschen, June 13: Klemperer had interrupted his diary and resumed it only after the return to Dölzschen.

# CHRONOLOGY

**1881** — Victor Klemperer born in Landsberg an der Warthe (today Gorzow Wielkopolski in Poland) on October 9. Father: Rabbi Dr. Wilhelm Klemperer; mother: Henriette Klemperer (née Franke).

**1884** — The family moves to Bromberg (today Bydgoszcz in Poland).

**1890** — The family moves to Berlin to 20 Albrechtstrasse, in the old center of the city. His father becomes second preacher of the Berlin Reform Congregation.

**1893** — Attends the French Grammar School in Berlin.

**1896** — Attends the Friedrich-Werdersche Grammar School. The family moves to 26 Winterfeldstrasse in the Schöneberg district of Berlin.

**1897** — Begins a commercial apprenticeship in the haberdashery and fancy-goods export company of Löwenstein & Hecht at 2 Alexandrinnenstrasse.

**1900–1902** — Attends the Royal Grammar School in Landsberg an der Warthe, and takes the final examination.

**1902–1905** — Studies philosophy, and Romance and German philology in Munich, Geneva, Paris, and Berlin.

**1905–1912** — Works as a journalist and writer in Berlin.

**1906** — Marries Eva Schlemmer, a pianist and musicologist.

**1912** — Takes up his studies again in Munich.

**1913** — Takes his doctorate with Franz Muncker. Embarks on his second stay in Paris. Studies Montesquieu for an habilitation thesis (qualification as university teacher).

**1914** — Completes his habilitation under Karl Vossler.

**1914–1915** — Becomes an assistant at the University of Naples as a private, unsalaried lecturer of the University of Munich.

Publishes two-volume work, *Montesquieu.*

**1915** — Serves at the front as a volunteer from November 1915 until March 1916.

**1916–1918** — Works as a censor in the Book Examination Office of the Press Section of the Military Government of Lithuania, first in Kovno then in Leipzig.

**1919** — Named an associate professor at the University of Munich.

**1920–1935** — Appointed a professor at the Technical University, Dresden.

**1923** — Publishes *Moderne Französische Prosa* (Modern French Prose).

**1925–1931** — Authors *Die französische Literatur von Napoleon bis zur Gegenwart* (French literature from Napoleon to the present) in four volumes (new edition issued in 1956 under the title *Geschichte der französischen Literatur im 19. und 20. Jahrhundert* [History of French literature in the 19th and 20th centuries]).

**1926** — Publishes *Romanische Sonderart. Geistesgeschichtliche Studien* (Romance particularity. Studies in intellectual history).

**1929** — Publishes *Idealistische Literaturgeschichte. Grundsätzliche und anwendende Studien* (Idealist literary history. Basic and applied studies) and *Moderne Französische Lyrik* (The modern French lyric).

**1933** — *Pierre Corneille* is published.

**1935** — "Retired from his duties" in accordance with the Law to Re-establish a Professional Civil Service.

**1945–1947** — Reappointed a professor at the Technical University Dresden.

**1947** — Publishes *LTI—Notizbuch eines Philologen* (LTI—Notebook of a Philologist).

**1947–1948** — Professor at the University of Greifswald.

**1948–1960** — Takes on a professorship at the University of Halle.

**1951** — Eva Klemperer dies on July 8.

**1951–1954** — Professor at the University of Berlin.

**1951** — Receives honorary doctorate from the Technical University Dresden.

**1952** — Marries Hadwig Kirchner.

**1953** — Becomes a member of the German Academy of Sciences in Berlin.

**1954** — *Geschichte der französischen Literatur im 18. Jahrhundert, Bd. I: Das Jahrhundert Voltaires* (History of French literature in the 18th century, vol. I: The century of Voltaire) is published.

**1956** — Publishes *Vor 33/Nach 45. Gesammelte Aufsätze* (Before 33/After 45. Collected essays).

**1960** — Victor Klemperer dies in Dresden on February 11.

**1966** — *Geschichte der französischen Literatur im 18. Jahrhundert, Bd. II: Das Jahrhundert Rousseaus* (History of French literature in the 18th century, vol. II: The century of Rousseau).

**1989** — *Curriculum vitae. Erinnerungen eines Philologen 1881–1918* (Curriculum vitae. Memoirs of a philologist) is published.

**1995** — *Ich will Zeugnis ablegen bis zum letzten. Tagebücher 1933–1945* (I will bear witness unto the last. Diaries 1933–1945) is published.

**1996** — *Und so ist alles schwankend. Tagebücher Juni bis Dezember 1945* (And so everything is in the balance. Diaries June–December 1945) and *Leben sammeln, nicht fragen wozu und warum. Tagebücher 1918–1932* (Collecting life, not asking what for and why. Diaries 1918–1932) are published.

# INDEX

# Discussion Guide

1. In his diary entries from as early as January 1933, Victor Klemperer foresaw the coming horrors of the Third Reich more distinctly than did most Germans. Why do you think this is? Why do you think he had the prescience to document Hitler's rise?

2. Historians can write about war from many points of view, from that of general, statesman, soldier, or citizen. How do the diaries document World War II in Germany differently than do most histories? What, in your opinion, are Klemperer's most important insights into life in Germany during the Third Reich?

3. Victor Klemperer was a diarist in the tradition of Samuel Pepys in that he was a relatively ordinary citizen who proved brilliant at recording the quotidian details of life during an extraordinary period in history. Why do you think Klemperer's diaries succeed as well as they do? What makes the diaries so compelling to read?

4. About the diaries, *The New York Times* wrote, "This is history raw." What do you think is meant by this?

5. Because Klemperer's wife, Eva, was a Christian, he escaped the death camps, but just barely. What other roles did Eva play in Klemperer's long struggle to survive the Nazi years? Had she kept diaries, how do you think they would have differed from her husband's?

6. On February 13, 1945, Victor Klemperer opened his diary entry, "Odysseus in Polyphemus's cave." Later that night the Allied destruction of Dresden commenced. What in Klemperer's subsequent description of the firebombing reminds you of a great odyssey? What about in the diaries as a whole?

7. Many people have compared Klemperer's diaries to Anne Frank's. How would you compare them?

8. After reading the diaries, would you agree with historian Daniel Goldhagen's argument that ordinary Germans were, to use his catchphrase, "Hitler's willing executioners"?

9. Ultimately, Victor Klemperer's diaries—through their amassing of detail about life in Dresden—take on the scope of world history. The *Los Angeles Times* calls them "one of the great testimonies of our century." What in the diaries makes this assessment accurate?

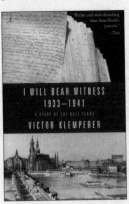